Selected works of Jawaharlal Nehru

Enquiries regarding copyright
to be addressed to the publishers

PUBLISHED BY
Jawaharlal Nehru Memorial Fund
Teen Murti House, New Delhi 110 011

ISBN 019 568123 1
ISBN 978-019568123-9

DISTRIBUTED BY
Oxford University Press
YMCA Library Building, Jai Singh Road, New Delhi 110 001
Mumbai Kolkata Chennai
Oxford New York Toronto
Melbourne Tokyo Hong Kong

TYPESET BY
Digigrafics
D-69, Gulmohar Park
New Delhi 110 049

PRINTED AT
Lordson Publishers Pvt Ltd
C 5/19, Rana Pratap Bagh
Delhi 110 007

Editor

Mushirul Hasan

Jawaharlal Nehru is one of the key figures of the twentieth century. He symbolised some of the major forces which have transformed our age.

When Jawaharlal Nehru was young, history was still the privilege of the West; the rest of the world lay in deliberate darkness. The impression given was that the vast continents of Asia and Africa existed merely to sustain their masters in Europe and North America. Jawaharlal Nehru's own education in Britain could be interpreted, in a sense, as an attempt to secure for him a place within the pale. His letters of the time are evidence of his sensitivity, his interest in science and international affairs as well as of his pride in India and Asia. But his personality was veiled by his shyness and a facade of nonchalance, and perhaps outwardly there was not much to distinguish him from the ordinary run of men. Gradually there emerged the warm and universal being who became intensely involved with the problems of the poor and the oppressed in all lands. In doing so, Jawaharlal Nehru gave articulation and leadership to millions of people in his own country and in Asia and Africa.

That imperialism was a curse which should be lifted from the brows of men, that poverty was incompatible with civilisation, that nationalism should be poised on a sense of international community and that it was not sufficient to brood on these things when action was urgent and compelling—these were the principles which inspired and gave vitality to Jawaharlal Nehru's activities in the years of India's struggle for freedom and made him not only an intense nationalist but one of the leaders of humanism.

No particular ideological doctrine could claim Jawaharlal Nehru for its own. Long days in jail were spent in reading widely. He drew much from the thought of the East and West and from the philosophies of the past and the present. Never religious in the formal sense, yet he had a deep love for the culture and tradition of his own land. Never a rigid Marxist, yet he was deeply influenced by that theory and was particularly impressed by what he saw in the Soviet Union on his first visit in 1927. However, he realised that the world was too complex, and man had too many facets, to be encompassed by any single or total explanation. He himself was a socialist with an abhorrence of regimentation and a democrat who was anxious to reconcile his faith in civil liberty with the necessity of mitigating economic and social wretchedness. His struggles, both within himself and with the outside world, to adjust such seeming contradictions are what make his life and work significant and fascinating.

As a leader of free India, Jawaharlal Nehru recognised that his country could neither stay out of the world nor divest itself of its own interests in world affairs. But to the extent that it was possible, Jawaharlal Nehru sought to speak objectively and to be a voice of sanity in the shrill phases of the 'cold war'. Whether his influence helped on certain occasions to maintain peace is for the future historian to assess. What we do know is that for a long stretch of time he commanded an international audience reaching far beyond governments, that he spoke for ordinary, sensitive, thinking men and women around the globe and that his was a constituency which extended far beyond India.

So the story of Jawaharlal Nehru is that of a man who evolved, who grew in storm and stress till he became the representative of much that was noble in his time. It is the story of a generous and gracious human being who summed up in himself the resurgence of the 'third world' as well as the humanism which transcends dogmas and is adapted to the contemporary context. His achievement, by its very nature and setting, was much greater than that of a Prime Minister. And it is with the conviction that the life of this man is of importance not only to scholars but to all, in India and elsewhere, who are interested in the valour and compassion of the human spirit that the Jawaharlal Nehru Memorial Fund has decided to publish a series of volumes consisting of all that is significant in what Jawaharlal Nehru spoke and wrote. There is, as is to be expected in the speeches and writings of a man so engrossed in affairs and gifted with expression, much that is ephemeral; this will be omitted. The official letters and memoranda will also not find place here. But it is planned to include everything else and the whole corpus should help to remind us of the quality and endeavour of one who was not only a leader of men and a lover of mankind, but a completely integrated human being.

New Delhi
18 January 1972

Chairman
Jawaharlal Nehru Memorial Fund

EDITORIAL NOTE

Jawaharlal Nehru once commented that his "popularity is connected with our pre-independence movement, not any actions since." The fact is that, by the end of 1956, the record of nine years in office spoke for itself. The political integration of the country had been completed except for a small part of the territory on the western coast—Goa. The states were reorganized and a new map of India took shape on 1 November 1956. Important changes in industry and agriculture were underway. These were impressive gains achieved under the stewardship of Jawaharlal Nehru. He therefore, wanted the Congress party to fight the general elections of 1957 "aggressively". He told the Congress Parliamentary Party on 29 December 1956: "I am not prepared to say that the soul of the Congress is bright and shining at the present moment. I don't think so. Nevertheless, we still possess a bit of it and that gives us some strength."

This volume covers the short period from 1 December 1956 to 21 February 1957. As in previous volumes, we begin with 'General Perspectives' and conclude with miscellaneous papers. The final section begins with the Prime Minister's statement in the Lok Sabha on the death of B.R. Ambedkar, one of the architects of the Constitution. "The main thing was that he rebelled", he stated on 6 December 1956, "against something against which all ought to rebel and we have, in fact, rebelled in various degrees."

Even though domestic issues figure, the bulk of this volume is devoted to 'External Affairs'. This is not surprising. Apart from the Prime Minister's travels overseas during this period, he entertained several special visitors: Shukri el-Kuwatli, the President of Syria, Norodom Sihanouk of Cambodia, Chou En-lai, the Chinese Premier, the Dalai Lama and the Panchen Lama.

We reproduce in full the record of Jawaharlal Nehru's talks with Chou En-lai. They clear the air on several controversial issues that figure in scholarly treatises on India-China relations.

The Prime Minister's main attention was focused on the Anglo-French action in Egypt and on the reactions to the Soviet invasion of Hungary. "It is important", he told the Chief Ministers on 8 December, "that we should have a clear idea of these happenings because the burden of shaping our own country's policy rests on us." The cables to V. K. Krishna Menon, leader of the Indian delegation to the UN (1952-62) and Minister without Portfolio (1956-57), are particularly instructive and document India's stand on Hungary and the Suez crisis. So are Jawaharlal Nehru's long statements in the Rajya Sabha on 3-4 December 1956. They also illuminate the key aspects of India's foreign policy.

Jawaharlal Nehru visited the United States, Canada, Great Britain and West Germany in December 1956. His talks with President Dwight D. Eisenhower, extending over twelve hours, were quite useful. G.L. Mehta, India's Ambassador to the US, informed Nehru that "the duration of talks held by the President with the Prime Minister is the longest since he assumed office over four years ago", and added that the "press coverage was larger than I have seen in the case of anyone not excluding Churchill." In sum, the visit augured well for relations between the two countries.

The future of Kashmir remained a contested issue, especially after the UN Security Council passed a resolution on 24 January 1957 which reiterated its commitment to hold a plebiscite and asserted that no decision of the Constituent Assembly of Jammu and Kashmir could determine the future of the state. The Security Council rejected India's stand, and spoke of the subject as a dispute and not a question. Starting with a cable to Krishna Menon on 29 December 1956, this volume reveals how the Prime Minister and his aides tackled the Kashmir imbroglio globally.

Soon after returning to India, the Prime Minister devoted his time energizing the Congress party for the second general elections that were going to elect, from nearly one million booths, 3,700 candidates to both the Parliament and the State Legislatures. The first general elections had taken place in the beginning of 1952. Every adult man and woman in a population of nearly 360 million was entitled to vote and a very large number of them did so. "In two or three days", he wrote to the Chief Ministers, "we celebrate Republic Day and then we plunge into the elections, probably forgetting this ferment and turmoil of the world and our own major difficulties. But we cannot escape them and we shall have to keep in mind always that these elections will mean little if we weaken." The Congress Election Manifesto sums it all:

> Whether in the field of international affairs or of our national and domestic problems, India's star has grown brighter and her achievements have been notable. Keeping faith with the old, we have sought to build up a new India, a modern state which would remove the burdens of those who suffer and give opportunity for progress to all.

It is a great privilege to inherit the mantle of editing the works of Jawaharlal Nehru from the late Professor Sarvepalli Gopal and Professor Ravinder Kumar, two of the foremost historians of modern India. I thank Dr Karan Singh for the confidence he has reposed in me. I gratefully acknowledge the debt of my two senior associates, Shri H.Y. Sharada Prasad and Shri A.K. Damodaran, for their guidance and encouragement in recent years.

We thank various individuals and institutions for their help in publishing this volume. Shrimati Sonia Gandhi granted us permission to consult and publish the papers in her possession. They are referred to as the JN Collection. We have also had access to important collections at the Nehru Memorial Museum & Library, the Secretariat of the Prime Minister, the Ministries of External Affairs and Home Affairs, Planning Commission, National Archives of India, and the Press Information Bureau. The All India Radio allowed us to use the tapes of Jawaharlal Nehru's speeches. Two speeches published in *Jawaharlal Nehru's Speeches*, Vol. 3, and one letter from *Letters from Gandhi, Nehru and Vinoba* by Shriman Narayan have also been included in the volume.

For their scholarly and secretarial assistance, we are grateful to Dr Bhashyam Kasturi, Shri Shyamal Roy, Shri Amrit Tandon, Dr Etee Bahadur, Smt. Saroja Anantha Krishnan, Smt. Malini Rajani, Smt. Kulwant Kaur and Shri Anuj Srivastava.

November 2005   MUSHIRUL HASAN

CONTENTS

1. General Perspectives

2. National Progress

I. The Economy

3. Issues of Governance

I. Administrative Matters

II. States

III. NEFA

4. Congress and the Elections

5. Kashmir

6. Defence

7. Portuguese Possessions

8. External Affairs

I. General

II. Visit to the USA and Canada

III. Suez Crisis

ILLUSTRATIONS

GENERAL PERSPECTIVES

1. March of the Nation[1]

I have been here a week. I came here on the 2nd and am going back to Delhi tomorrow. In these six days, we had the meeting of the Congress Working Committee and then the Subjects Committee meeting and finally, on the last two days, the open session of the Congress. Many of you would have attended it. The work of the Congress came to an end last night. There was no particular reason for me to stay on here except to address your meeting this evening.

I have had a holiday today and visited Mandu for a few hours. I have been there before. But I like to revisit ancient historic sites for they conjure up pictures of the olden days. When I go to Ujjain, it takes me back to the days of Vikramaditya and Kalidasa and others. I went to Mandu to refresh myself mentally and physically, and to cast a backward glance at our past, away from the problems of the present. I do not like to look back too often because we have to live in the present, understand the problems of this age and find a solution for them. But if we are tied to the present, with no sense of the past or the future, there will be no continuity. We have to build on the foundations of the past for the future that is to come. In this way the link between the past, present and the future remains unbroken.

People come and go, great men and ordinary men live and work and then pass on. But the life of a nation goes on, particularly a country like ours which has a history dating back to thousands of years. Indian philosophy, thought, culture, arts and religion have spread far and wide. Streams of culture and thought have poured into this country and been absorbed. Peoples and races have come and mingled and have merged into the melting pot of India. There has been constant interaction between them.

Absorbed in the day-to-day problems of the present, I feel a keen desire to pull myself away from them and to take a look at the past because our roots lie in the past. I like to think of the future too though nobody can say what it will be like. The astrologers who pretend to do so deceive themselves and others. What we are doing today is for the sake of the future. So we have to draw a picture in our minds of the kind of future we wish to build. If we are not interested in the future, we will not feel any enthusiasm for the present either. When we feel that

---

1. Speech at a public meeting, Indore, 7 January 1957. AIR tapes, NMML. Original in Hindi.

we are building something and moulding the future, it gives us enthusiasm for our work just as a creative artist feels about his work.

The people of India are faced with a great creative task of building a new India, to change and build our society anew. It is true that our country, our society is rooted in thousands of years of history. It has been moulded by thousands of years of events and experiences, ups and downs, and accumulated good as well as bad on its long journey down the centuries. If the accretions of the past had all been good, we would not find ourselves in such great difficulties today. We would not have become so backward while other nations had advanced. It is because of the evils that we have accumulated that we became weak and forgot the noble principles and ideals, which we once stood for. We became bogged down by petty squabbles and so we fell.

We have now come out of that mire. We have become independent and once again acquired the right to determine which direction we wish to take. This is the new goal that is before us now. We had met here in the Congress to discuss where the path that we have chosen is leading us. We did not meet merely to discuss who should get tickets for the elections to the Parliament or the State Legislatures. Those are minor matters which may become necessary for a short time. But the important thing was to discuss whither we are bound. You may wonder what I mean. I do not mean only the people of this state, or the Congress. I am referring to India's thirty-six crores of people, men, women and children, and where they are bound. Please remember that we have embarked on this long and arduous journey as a nation.

Now there are bound to be difficulties when we set out on such a big task. For one thing, no two people are alike and when millions of people are involved, there are innumerable difficulties in the way. Some are quick, others slow. Does that mean that those who can run should be held back because of those who drag their feet? That would be criminal. At the same time, we have to take into consideration the fact that if a few quick ones outstrip the rest, they may benefit. But those who are left behind have to be coaxed along too. Therefore a way has to be found whereby, as far as possible, everyone can march in step. I mean at least the majority of the people must move on. Those who are enthusiastic and move fast must give the others a helping hand.

India is like a huge caravan. We met here to discuss where this caravan is bound. Until we are clear in our minds about our destination, how can we get there? Once we decide what our goal is then we have to choose the right path to reach that goal. If we leave it to individuals to do as they like, there will be no unity of purpose or sense of direction. Therefore it is very essential to meet and discuss these matters and then arrive at a consensus. Even then we may occasionally lose our way or be led astray. So we have to be constantly vigilant and guard against such mishaps. This is how, with constant care and thought and mutual consultations, a nation can grow and progress.

We have just had the sixty-second session of the AICC here.[2] As far as I remember, there have been sixty-one sessions before this. But then the Congress is seventy-two years old. How does this discrepancy arise? This is the sixty-second session. We could not hold the sessions in five years at the height of our struggle against British imperialism. Our confrontations with the British were often in the field or in jails. If there was an attempt to hold a session, the delegates would be dispersed by lathi charges or firing and resolutions could not be passed. So there were no sessions in five years.

The Congress is a very old organization. Of the seventy-two years, sixty have gone in our tussle with British. There have been many great leaders in the party during these years. When Gandhiji came on the scene he organized the Congress into a strong and peaceful national force with martial discipline. He gave us great ideals and taught us to be fearless because we were on the right path. He taught us that even if we had to face lathi charges or bullets, we should carry on because once there is determined will power, fear is automatically removed.

I remember when he first talked about starting a great movement here nearly thirty-eight years ago,[3] those of us who were very young would often fail to understand all that he said. But we had great confidence in him. Our elders understood him even less because his ideas were novel. But I remember, on one occasion, when a large number of leaders were assembled, he said he was not in favour of long speeches or passing resolutions and shouting slogans.[4] "I do not prevent you from going to the Viceroy to bargain for small concessions. You must set forth your minimum demands in polite language and say that you hope they will be conceded peacefully. If they are not, we regret that we will have to fight. We shall fight but by peaceful methods." He used to tell us not to make long demands which would not be conceded, nor abuse or shout slogans. Whatever we set out to do, it must be with the firm determination to succeed. If you could not, then you must be equally determined to fight to the very end, unmindful of the consequences and sacrifices it may entail. There must be no bitterness or hatred in our hearts. This was one of the things that he taught us.

Secondly, he told us that we were engaged in fighting a battle though it was by peaceful means. So we became an army but one without weapons. We had to

2. From 2 to 6 January 1957. No session of the Congress was held in the following years—1930, 1935, 1941-45, 1947, 1949 and 1952.
3. Satyagraha against the Rowlatt Bills in April 1919.
4. Nehru in his *Autobiography* wrote that Gandhi made these remarks to a Khilafat delegation at Delhi in January 1920.

acquire military discipline and habit of cooperation and follow the leader implicitly. He said that he understood the concept of satyagraha better than the others. "If you choose me as your leader, I shall accept and you will have the right to kick me out whenever you like. But so long as I am your leader, you will have to obey me implicitly." This is war and we will have to imbibe a martial spirit of discipline and obedience. He had a very soft, sweet voice and never would he utter a bitter word. But whoever heard his voice felt its impact. There was steel behind the softness. In this way, Gandhiji trained and educated the nation.

It was difficult for a weak people like us to follow the path shown by him immediately. Sometimes we felt angry when we wanted to do more than what he said and then he would stop us. At the height of the civil disobedience movement, Gandhiji called a halt to the whole thing because in a little village in Uttar Pradesh, some poor, ignorant peasants had killed a few policemen and set fire to the police station.[5] We agreed that it was a terrible thing. But we could not understand why the whole of India had to pay for the sins of a few villagers of Gorakhpur district. We were in jail at that time—my father and I—we felt very bad.

When we were released, we went to him with our grievance. Then he explained his point of view to us. What was done was done. But gradually we began to realize that what he had in mind was to discipline the thirty-six crores of people in India. We had taken on a great task of challenging the armed might of British imperialism. We had the task of freeing India from the yoke of foreign rule. The challenge we had taken on was unique in the history of the world. We had no weapons except emotional strength and determination, discipline and unity. But these things can add up to a great source of strength. Without discipline, we could have done nothing. Therefore, Gandhiji had the task of unifying the people of India, particularly the poor, downtrodden peasants, and of teaching them to follow his lead. He had to infuse a new spirit of fearlessness and cooperation among the masses. The moment anyone made a mistake, he would call a halt.

Anyhow, those days are gone. Now we have another kind of work to do. The Congress spearheaded India's struggle for freedom in the first sixty years of its life. After that, new responsibilities of running the government have devolved on our shoulders. We had become experts in satyagraha and civil disobedience.

---

5. On 4 February 1922 an angry mob set fire to a police station at Chauri Chaura, a village in the Gorakhpur district of UP. This led Mahatma Gandhi to call off the non-cooperation movement.

But now the new tasks before us require new techniques of working. We have achieved the political goal of independence. Now we have to eradicate poverty from the country. We had got into the habit of opposing foreign rule. Now whom are we to oppose when it is our own government?

Now that the British have gone, on whom can we vent our anger and frustration? Immediately after India became free, many people were under the impression that they could relax after the long years of prison-going and hardships. But there was no time for rest or relaxation, for independence brought fresh difficulties and responsibilities, of shouldering greater burdens.

The moment India became free, we were faced with the problem of partition. Pakistan came into being with our consent. We gave our consent because otherwise our problems would be never-ending and independence would have receded further. Even if we had got freedom under such conditions, it would have been a crippled affair. So we accepted the partition of India with grief in our hearts. We had hoped that partition would heal the bitterness and we would be able to live in friendship and cooperation. We felt that at least in independent India we would be able to work with greater freedom without too many obstacles in our path. In short we accepted partition and Pakistan came into being.

You may remember that almost at the very hour of the dawn of freedom another storm cloud burst upon us. The whole of North India and Pakistan were rocked by violent communal riots and those who lived through those days can never erase the memory of the horror. We had to bow down our heads in shame that we who had talked so righteously about freedom and non-violence should stoop to such bestiality. It was a terrible nightmare and the bloodshed on both sides, was unbelievable. You can imagine what Gandhiji must have felt, a man who had led us to freedom, when he saw the inhuman barbarity perpetrated on both sides.

To fight in the name of religion was to malign religion and India's fair name. It could lead to our downfall and soon freedom would have slipped away too. Hindus and Muslims were killing one another in the name of religion. We had to put a stop to it. Hinduism had not flourished for more than 5,000 years by such bestiality but by its high principles which had survived all the ups and downs of history. Gradually things were brought under control. Later, as you may remember, Gandhiji was assassinated by a Hindu youth. Perhaps his assassination was a good thing because it opened our eyes to the cancer hiding within us. If it was allowed to exist, it would surely destroy the nation.

I am reminding you of the bygone days because public memory is short. The youth of today have not had first-hand experience of those days. For us, those memories are imprinted in our minds for the events of the last thirty to forty years are unforgettable. There are a thousand memories and pictures of joy and sorrow and we have been moulded by them. But for you all that is in the past.

The women of India were in the forefront of the struggle in those days. Women who had never before stepped out of their houses jumped into the fray and gave a good account of themselves. When news of their brave deeds reached us in our barracks in jail we were deeply moved. We were thrilled to hear about our sisters facing the might of British imperialism boldly. I think that was the greatest aspect of the freedom struggle. You can judge the degree of awareness in a country by its women. The state of a civilization can be gauged best by the position of women, laws pertaining to them, etc. At about the time that women came into the arena, I remember my father was with me in Naini prison. He died a few days later.[6] He was grieved that his own daughters and daughters-in-law were suffering such hardships. But at the same time, he was extremely proud too that Indian women had come to the forefront. He said on that occasion that he used to wonder sometimes when India would finally become free. But now he was left in no doubt. Seeing the women of India taking the place of their menfolk who were in jail had reassured him. He said he had only a few days left to him—as a matter of fact he died a few months later—but he would be able to die happy because he had seen the vision of independent India.

So these pictures come to my mind. We have difficult tasks ahead which require hard work and effort. They do not supply the excitement that challenging the enemy does. We have to be constantly vigilant, not get carried away and maintain unity and cooperation. We do not have to face bullets and jails any more. But the country demands different kind of sacrifices. There is a price to be paid for everything. We do not value what we get free. Independence is dear to our hearts because we have paid the price for generations. A hundred years have gone by since the first war of independence was fought in 1857. We are celebrating its centenary this year.

If we want progress it cannot be achieved without paying the price in terms of hard work and effort. Only then will our progress be enduring, and we can gradually improve the economic condition of the country and remove poverty. These are the tasks before us. We have completed one Five Year Plan and embarked on the Second which will also be over in a few months time. Then will come the Third and the Fourth Plans because a country's progress does not come to a halt. It will go on whether we are there or not. We will pass on and others will take our place. After all, India has existed for thousands of years and has never known to have faltered in times of stress and challenge.

6. Motilal Nehru died on 6 February 1931.

We have taken up these great challenges at a time when the world is in a revolutionary ferment and the nuclear age has dawned. We cannot compete with nuclear weapons for that is the road to ruin. We cannot fight a nuclear war with guns and tanks. So we have to forge a new kind of weapon as we did under Gandhiji, to challenge the British rule, to take on the world. If we had tried to fight the British with arms, they could have crushed us effortlessly. But we found a new method to challenge them and in the process rendered the might of arms somewhat useless.

Similarly in this age of nuclear weapons, we have to resort, not to more atom bombs or guns and swords, but to a method more or less similar to what Gandhiji taught us. This is a lesson which the whole world has to learn because it is now faced with a choice between destruction and a better life for humanity.

The West has advanced so much because they use electricity for agriculture as well as industries. If electricity is made available in every village, our progress will gather momentum. Atomic energy is an even greater source of energy. It can be used for good as well as evil purposes. If it is unwisely used, it can destroy the whole world. Otherwise it can benefit humanity enormously. The world now faces the dilemma of choosing between these two things. It is obvious that any sensible world will choose to utilize this great source of power for the good of humanity. Yet nations keep preparing for war, out of fear and hatred and suspicion of one another.

You know what our policy is in this regard. We want to keep away from the armed camps of the world and serve the cause of peace. But how can we talk of peace in the world if we are unable to maintain peace and unity in our own country? Therefore, if India is to make an impact upon the world, we must foster unity, peace and cooperation in the country. Irrespective of our religion, caste, province or language, all of us are in one boat and if that capsizes, all of us will sink too. If India progresses, we too will progress. Secondly, we must work very, very hard to make India strong in order that her voice is heard in world forums.

Have you ever thought why India is respected in the world today? Wherever an individual with an Indian passport goes he is respected. Firstly, it is because he hails from the land of Mahatma Gandhi. Secondly, we got independence by peaceful and civilized methods. So they feel that India is a very cultured nation. We have had no grievance against the British after independence. We have friendly relations with them which amazes the world. But above all, the world is impressed with the great strides India has taken during the last ten years and solved insurmountable problems which would have crushed weaker people. India is on the march and is growing stronger day by day. If we continue at this pace, within the next fifteen to twenty years, India will become an extremely powerful nation. So the world respects us.

Respect for India depends on our strength and civilized behaviour. We must remember that we cannot go very far by making a noise or abusing others. That is a sign of weakness. We must do nothing which betrays weakness on our part. Therefore the only path before us is that of peace, unity, mutual cooperation and hard work if we want to build a new India. The Five Year Plans are a blueprint for our nation-building activities. Every individual can contribute his mite. But the Five Year Plans give an overall picture of our development.

We have opened three huge steel plants[7] because steel is fundamental for a nation's progress. Production of steel leads to industrialization and greater production of wealth, reduction in unemployment and poverty, etc. We need to generate more power for industries. So we have built dams on the larger rivers to supply water for irrigation as well as for power generation. These are fundamental to our progress.

The other revolutionary steps that we have taken are the community projects and national extension service schemes for the development of the rural areas. They have spread to 1,25,000 villages and within the next five years, all the five lakh villages would have been covered. I cannot think of a greater revolution than this anywhere in the world. These schemes will transform the rural areas, generate new employment and wealth and instil self-confidence among the villagers. I want to draw your attention to them because India can progress only when the villages change and progress. Calcutta, Bombay, Madras, Delhi and Indore are all good cities. But India's progress does not depend on them. It is only when 80 per cent of the population which lives in the rural areas progresses that India can progress.

As I said I had gone to Mandu today where groups of tribals came to meet me. I am very fond of tribals. They are strong, simple, good people. You are deceiving yourselves if you think they are inferior. I do not know who is inferior or superior. Men like Rabindranath Tagore and Mahatma Gandhi were very great and all of us are of small stature before them. That is a different matter. But I am not prepared to accept if anybody claims superiority by birth. If a community is suppressed for thousands of years and is not allowed to come up and then they are called low castes, how can anyone accept that? It is like the British saying that Indians were not ready for independence when we had not had the chance to prove ourselves. That is absolutely wrong. It is why when downtrodden sections of society like the tribals and others progress that India

---

7. These were at Rourkela (Orissa), Bhilai (Madhya Pradesh) and Durgapur (West Bengal).

can hope to go ahead. You cannot judge the state of a city like Indore by its palaces but by its slums. That is the test of a city. Similarly the progress of a country has to be judged by the condition of the weaker sections of society. That does not mean that the others should be dragged down. But everyone must get equal opportunities for progress.

These are the tasks before us. They are all part of the Five Year Plans. You can read the small pamphlets which have been printed in all the languages. It is the blueprint for India's future. We want democratic socialism in India so that individual freedom is not jeopardized. Now these great tasks cannot be accomplished by passing a law or a government fiat. They require an awareness among the people and their willing help and cooperation. The women in particular have a greater responsibility in the matter because for one thing they are half the population of the country and secondly, if the mother is illiterate, her children are bound to grow up as good for nothing. Children learn more from their mothers than their fathers. The first four to five years are crucial in a child's life because his character is moulded during that period. He may learn a great deal later in school and college. But the fundamental character is formed during the first few years. *Jai Hind.*

Please say *Jai Hind* with me thrice.

2. The Hirakud Dam—Fulfilment of a Dream[1]

Please be quiet. Today's agenda includes a speech by me. At the end of my speech, I shall press a button and put on the switch and the waters of the Mahanadi will flow over the dam. It has been arranged that the electric light will play upon the water. But I think it would be better if I were to press the button first and then make a speech because I want to see the play of light upon the falling waters. But first I would like to see the dam working by daylight too. So I shall press the button before sunset and hope that it works. After that I shall say whatever I have to you. Now please do not stand up when I press the button. You will be able to see better if you keep sitting. If one and then another stands up,

---

1. Speech at the inauguration of the Hirakud dam, Cuttack, Orissa, 13 January 1957. AIR tapes, NMML. Original in Hindi.

nobody will be able to see anything. Anyhow, you live here and can see it often. I want to see it properly. I shall now go and press the button.

Please be quiet for a few minutes. This is not right. You are standing on top of one another's shoulders. You are not building a dam here. This is a public meeting. The dam is over there. You have made a human dam here by standing upon one another.

The water is flowing from both sides. It looks beautiful from a distance because you can see the spray. Soon it will be dark and the water will sparkle even more under the electric light. Exactly eight years and nine months ago, I had come here to lay the foundation stone for this dam.[2] I have come in between too, to see how the work was going on. It was a huge construction, with gigantic machines and innumerable workers doing the work. All kinds of strange thoughts come to my mind when I see this Hirakud dam completed. Pictures flash across my mind of thousands of workers engaged in constructing this dam like so many beavers.

Visitors to this place will find this dam beautiful. They will realize that it is a huge project. But they may not be able to picture what it was like when the work had first started; of thousands of people at work. Under the mounds of earth, cement and concrete of which this dam is built is concealed the sweat and hard labour of thousands of people for years. This is not merely earth or cement but something that represents the labour of thousands of human beings. Out of their labour, they have created something which will last, I hope, for hundreds of years. People may come and go, but this dam will continue to benefit the future generations. Perhaps they may sometimes pause to consider how much labour has gone into building this. Engineers, mechanics, overseers and workers from all over the country came here and worked together for years to build the dam. The cement which holds it together is made up of our hopes and dreams and sweat and toil. It took nine years to complete this. Now our dreams have come true. It is given to very few people to dream a big dream, full of hopes, and then live to realize it. I congratulate all of you, particularly those who by their skill and labour have helped to build this dam. Special thanks are due to them. I agree that momentous decisions are taken in the offices in Delhi and Cuttack. But we must always think of the people who actually implement those decisions.

So first of all let us pay homage to the memory of all those who by their mental and physical skills, have helped to build this dam in the last nine years and whose labour has been captured in this mammoth construction. I hope that the organizers

2. See *Selected Works* (second series), Vol. 6, pp. 313-314, for Nehru's speech at the Hirakud dam on 12 April 1948.

will think of putting up a special plaque as a tribute to their memory. Nobody's name need be mentioned. It should be a nameless tribute to those who laboured to build this dam. Both men and women have toiled here. So nobody will be mentioned individually by name. It will represent each one of the people, men and women, who played a role here, and particularly those who lost their lives in accidents or suffered a loss of some kind in the course of work.

We are standing at a very beautiful spot atop this hill, with the huge big lake on one side and on the other, the waters of the Mahanadi. I hope some gardens and trees will come up in the space in between. As I said earlier, this conjures up old memories and the picture of thousands of human beings working under the earth, huge machines at work, and trains puffing here and there. This is one picture. There is the other picture, of the havoc that the Mahanadi has caused to the people whenever it was in floods, practically every year. Now we have made friends with the Mahanadi because man has to befriend nature, not be in constant conflict. Only by befriending nature can it be brought under control. Now I cannot promise that there will be no more floods. There are bound to be floods for we have a great deal more to do in connection with this river valley project, though the Hirakud dam is complete. It will take years for the work to be completed. But this is a big step towards controlling the floods. It will provide irrigation for miles around when canals are built and it will help to generate power.

Electricity is the symbol of progress in the modern times. It is essential in every sphere of life, whether it is in the rural areas or for industries. We want every single village in India to get electricity for wherever it goes, it will bring progress and prosperity. It is not merely useful for providing light but also opens up new avenues of employment. It will automatically raise the standard of living of the people and help to generate new wealth in the country.

Do you know the most urgent task that we have confronted for the last 10 years? Before that, our only goal was to throw off the yoke of British rule. True, our war was a peaceful and non-violent one. Gandhiji taught us to walk that path. We in our weakness often behaved foolishly. But some of his greatness rubbed off on us. Our struggle for independence came to an end ten years ago and India became free. A great pilgrimage was over at last. But our problems were by no means over. There was great poverty and unemployment in the country which did not disappear automatically with the coming of freedom. Freedom only provided us with the power to do what we wanted to and to choose a path for ourselves. In a sense the barrier which had obstructed our path, the barrier of foreign rule was broken down. But then immediately the question arose as to what we should do next. Even during the years of the freedom struggle, the need to alleviate the people's hardship and suffering was constantly in our minds,

13

to remove poverty and unemployment from the country, and to improve the standard of the millions who lived in India. We were aware of the need to increase the national wealth and ensure its equitable distribution.

Once the struggle for freedom was over, we had to embark immediately on yet another long and arduous journey. There was no time to sit back and relax though some people thought that now that India was free, they could relax. The goal that we set before us was to remove the poverty of the people which was possible only by producing more wealth in the country. After all wealth does not come from somewhere else. So we had to gird ourselves up for a fresh effort. By 'we', I do not mean only myself or a handful of others, but everyone of you who lives in India. We had to declare a war immediately. You may wonder that a peace loving country like ours should talk about waging a war. But our war was not with another country or even among ourselves, which is worse. Our war was against poverty, disease, hunger, illiteracy and the thousand ills that crushed the people. We wanted progress, a better standard of living and opportunity for education for everyone and our main enemy was poverty. So we had to brace ourselves for a new kind of war against our own weaknesses.

Now how were we to fight this war? It could not be done by my giving a lecture or speech. If our engineers here had been content to make speeches, the Hirakud dam could not have been built. I am saying this because people in India are very fond of making speeches and soon the fever will mount rapidly. As you know, in another six weeks, there are going to be general elections in India.[3] At election time, the floodgates of speech-making and haranguing will open up.

Anyhow, when we declared war against poverty, the question was how we should go about it. You must understand that this was a far more difficult task than the battle for freedom. The battle for freedom was to remove foreign rule whereas here we were facing the gigantic task of uplifting an entire nation which had fallen into a mire of poverty, ignorance and weakness for centuries. It was not a question of a handful of people but of thirty-six crores of men, women and children. It was an extremely difficult task. There was no magic formula for it. If there had been one, our task would have been easy. Ultimately people can progress only on their own strength. We cannot lead the people by the hand or provide crutches. If we do not have the strength to stand on our own feet, we cannot go very far leaving others behind. So it was an extremely complex situation. We could not get rid of our poverty by passing a law in Delhi. We would have done it long ago, if that had been possible. The question was how to

3. From 25 February to 12 March 1957.

improve the condition of millions of people in India. They would have to do it themselves.

We gave it a great deal of thought, and then, the First Five Year Plan was drawn up. We did not have much experience of planning at that time. It is extremely difficult to plan for the future of an entire nation. We did not have the full statistics about our resources, manpower, their capability and intelligence and skill, etc. It comes gradually with experience. Well, the First Plan was drawn up. The river valley projects like Hirakud, Bhakra-Nangal, the Damodar Valley were all part of that plan which came to an end six months ago. The work of a nation cannot of course be put in compartments of five years. We had to start on the Second Five Year Plan immediately and we are in the midst of it at the moment.

We managed to achieve most of the targets that we set before ourselves and in some cases even exceeded them. This has given us a new confidence in ourselves for we can complete what we take up. The engineers who have helped to build the Hirakud dam during the last seven to eight years have gained greater self-confidence. So apart from the direct benefits of completing such large projects, the bigger benefit to the country is that thousands of people have gained new skills. Now that our engineers and others have gained experience and self-confidence by working on these projects, we will be able to go ahead with greater assurance.

What is the wealth of a nation? It is not gold or silver which are useless things. The real wealth of a nation consists of the goods that are produced and more than that, the number of trained and skilled human beings available in the country. A country which has a large number of trained human beings is rich because it can produce great amount of wealth. Without such people, a country remains backward. As you know, this is the age of science, technology and machines. The country where there are a large number of people who understand these things is advanced. Otherwise it remains backward as we have been so far. So we are trying to train large numbers of engineers and doctors and other technical personnel. They will, in future be ready to undertake tasks of great responsibility.

Even in Hirakud, all the work has been done by our own engineers. There has been hardly any outside help. At Bhakra, we had to ask for help from other countries for which we are grateful to them. But now our people are ready to do it themselves. We have taken a step forward in the Damodar Valley too. But now the time is coming when with all this experience, our engineers can take on the biggest jobs without guidance or advice from outside which is a very good thing. I do not mean that it is a bad thing to take advice from outsiders. We will certainly do so whenever necessary. The important thing is to get the job done well. We do not want second-rate work to be done in India particularly when we

15

are doing something for posterity. If there is any mistake or shoddy work, it will be a bad thing. We must not try to stint on the cost of expert advice for that will ruin everything. So, we must certainly learn from other countries and take their help. But gradually we too become experienced and will be able to undertake the work ourselves.

Well, an auspicious task has been performed today and a dream has come true. As you know, the state of Orissa is full of famous temples like that of Lord Jagannath in Puri, and other temples at Bhubaneshwar and Konarak. People come in large numbers, many of them to worship in the temples, other to admire the beautiful architecture of these ancient monuments. Konarak, for instance, or the temples of Bhubaneshwar are of extraordinary beauty. So, in Orissa, there has been a great tradition of building temples and worshipping in them. Now that tradition needs to be linked to the modern temples and a new form of worship. Places like Hirakud are the modern centres of pilgrimage for us. Many more will come up in Orissa and we should now concentrate our energies on worshipping productive labour in order to build dams and other such projects. All this is for the people of India. Our biggest temple today is India. The whole country is open to us for work and our goal ought to be service to the people of India, by means of unity, cooperation and hard work. All these new places of pilgrimage are coming up all over the country where the people of India are performing a new kind of *yagnya*. The people of India are greater than the gods in the skies and we should serve them. Those are the goals that we have set before ourselves.

As I told you, the First Five Year Plan has come to a successful end. We have begun the Second Plan which is more ambitious because our hopes and resources and self-confidence have grown. The Second Plan is twice as large as the First. We had to invest enormous sums of money in the First Plan.

Now we want to turn our attention towards industrialization in India. I talk about heavy industries. But please remember that no matter how many industries come up in India our most important concern will be agricultural production. No industry can take the place of land or displace the farmer. Therefore our chief concern will always remain the condition of the farmer and the rate of agricultural production. That is the basis for our industries. We cannot build in the air without the basic foundations. We must bear this in mind.

Let me tell you that it is a very good thing that the Hirakud will help you to generate power and aluminum plants and other industries will come up. It will provide jobs for the people of Orissa. We want this to happen. But I feel that the benefit to the people by building canals for irrigation will far exceed anything what an industry can do. This is my view. There is no comparison. We want Orissa to benefit in both ways. On the one hand, the canal waters will provide irrigation for miles around and farmers will not have to live in constant fear of a failure of monsoons. There will always be water for irrigation which will help Orissa to grow more food. That will benefit not only the people of Orissa but the whole country as well. The constant threat of food shortage is now over. In the past we had to often go running to the United States or some other country for foodgrains. It will not happen any more. On the other hand, generation of power will enable us to set up new industries. A decision has already been taken to do so. So, in this way, the people of Orissa will benefit on all sides. I am particularly happy about it. I want the whole of India to progress. But I particularly want Orissa, which is poorer than the rest of the country, to progress quickly and catch up with the rest. We do not want uneven, lopsided development in India, with some states advancing very far and others remaining backward. We want the entire population of India to be equal shareholders in the country's progress and prosperity.

It is regrettable that Orissa is very backward. There is great poverty here. Therefore it is essential to help this state to progress faster. The poor people of Orissa who work so hard should now be able to enjoy the fruits of their labour. I am particularly interested in the success of the Plan in Orissa because I can see the future of the state lies in that. As I said I have memories of the past, of floods and havoc, of thousands of people at work building this dam. Then I look to the future, to a few years hence when the waters of the Mahanadi will be supplied by canals far and wide. It will benefit the farmers and the other people of Orissa and the whole country. On the other hand, industries, big and small, will come up which will produce goods. Village and cottage industries will help the people of Orissa. I do not agree that their welfare lies in one large industry coming up in an area though it is a good thing. In the Second Plan, we have rightly paid attention to food production and at the same time to building industries too. That is the only way the problem of unemployment can be solved.

Many things are necessary for building industries. But two things are most essential; one is steel. In the modern world, you can do nothing without steel. The second thing is electricity or power of any kind. Progress of a nation is linked to the production of steel and power. You can tell how advanced a country is by looking at the amount of steel and electricity it produces. It is not necessary to read books. All you need to ask is how much steel and electricity a country produces to say how far it has advanced.

We are trying to increase generation of power in India. There are power plants here in Hirakud, in Bhakra and in various other places. In the beginning, some people thought strangely enough that the power generated in Hirakud and other places in Orissa will not be fully utilized. I remember that the scheme for generating power from the Mahanadi was postponed because it was felt that

Orissa did not need so much electricity. Now we suddenly find the need for power going up and there are shortages. You must understand that no matter how much electricity we may produce in India, it will fall short of our needs. The question of not being able to use the power simply does not arise. Even if one produced hundred times as much as we do now, it will not be enough. You can see from this how essential electricity is. Now we are trying to generate more power. You must have heard about the three huge steel plants which are coming up. As you know, there are two or three old ones, including the one at Jamshedpur. The three new plants will be in the public sector and one of them is coming up in Orissa.[4] That is another thing which will benefit the state greatly. We have laid the foundations for heavy industries and now I hope they will spread.

I have talked to you about the Second Five Year Plan and outlined all the big tasks that are going to be taken up in the next five years. But it requires hard work and effort. We cannot expect to sit idle and hope that the work will get done. So we are determined that all of us must work hard and make whatever sacrifices that may be necessary. We must be prepared to shoulder greater burdens, only then can we hope to get returns. What we do today is for the future, for our children. We naturally want that the people should benefit in the present too. But the real fruits of our labour will be reaped by our children. This is how nations are made.

There is great tumult and upheaval in the world. A great arms race is on and bitterness and enmity are spreading. We want to follow the path of peace so that we may get all the time we need for our developmental work, for the welfare of our people. At the same time, we want to work for the cause of world peace. We do what we can at present too. Projects like Hirakud are tasks of peace and welfare. What we do for the welfare of the country today will benefit the future as well. Therefore they are auspicious tasks and those who participate in them honestly and sincerely earn great merit. As I told you, these are our new temples and the people of India our new gods whom we must serve.

The list of people who have participated in this project for the last nine years is a very long one. There are engineers who have been here from the beginning and others who came later on. I remember in the beginning, there was Khoslaji.[5] Then Kanwar Sainji[6] came and after him, Tirumale Iyengar[7] who is here at present.

---

4. At Rourkela.
5. A.N. Khosla, Chairman, Central Water and Power Commission, 1945-53.
6. Kanwar Sain, Chief Engineer, Hirakud Dam Project, 1951-53.
7. Took over as Chief Engineer from Kanwar Sain.

Thousands of other engineers and overseers have worked with them. Responsibility depends on the merit and training and experience of the individual. But the man who works wholeheartedly in a high post or low, has equal rights. What I mean is that all such individuals earn equal merit. I congratulate all those who have worked here for the past nine years. I would like to tell you that people may or may not remember your names individually. But ultimately a man is remembered by the work that he does. This work of yours will stand here for centuries to come to remind people of the engineers who were responsible for constructing this dam. So this will serve as the best memorial to all of you.

I remember that when I had come here nine years ago in this connection, I was brought by Hare Krushna Mahtabji.[8] He was full of enthusiasm about this project and I think his heart would be full of joy today to see his hopes come true. I want to congratulate him and also my colleague, Gulzarilal Nandaji.[9] I do not know how far you are aware of his role in this project. But I know how hard he worked in this connection.

Some years ago, there was an uproar here in Orissa and in our Parliament.[10] I remember it started with an agitation in Orissa against the Hirakud project saying that it was wrong and bad, and the poor farmers were being deprived of their land. I can understand the perturbation of the farmers. But there were people who invited them and among them were some whom I had thought were wise people. The problem is that it takes much more time to explain what is sensible but easier to incite people over foolish things. Somehow people here have got into the habit of shouting slogans and slogans are loud enough to be heard, whether they are wise or foolish. I remember that agitation very well. We received memoranda signed by engineers saying that the Hirakud dam could not be built. I would like to ask those engineers whether what they are seeing today is a dream.

Whenever we take up a big task, some people are bound to suffer some losses. The poor farmers in this region were displaced. They have all been resettled elsewhere but it is not a nice thing to be evicted out of your house. I understand that. Then there was another uproar in Parliament that a great deal of money had been embezzled.[11] An inquiry was held. I cannot say definitely that a certain amount of dishonesty was not there. It is possible that some funds were embezzled. But we must make an effort to see to it that there is constant

8. Chief Minister of Orissa.
9. Union Minister of Planning, and Irrigation and Power.
10. In 1951.
11. In 1955.

supervision and no loopholes exist for these are public funds. It is extremely wrong to allow anyone to misuse public funds. Misappropriation of public funds is of course a sin. But even extravagant expenditure of public funds is wrong, because after all, the money comes from the pockets of hard working people. They earn their living by the sweat of their brow and pay taxes which we spend. We invest hundreds of crores of rupees in various projects hoping it would benefit the people. We tighten our belts for the sake of future. But this hard-earned money belongs to the people of the nation and we must always take care not to waste it on useless expenditure. Every government official must constantly bear this in mind.

Well, an inquiry was held and since then, Gulzarilal Nandaji has worked hard. There had been such an uproar that if Nandaji had not worked so hard, I do not know what the outcome would have been. The entire project would have earned a bad name because of the mistakes of a few individuals. Anyhow, these were the difficulties which arose on the way, and as Nandaji said, we have learnt something from them. We may make mistakes. But we must have the ability to learn from our experiences and mistakes.

When I pressed this button, there was still light so you could not see the play of light on the water. Now it has grown dark, I shall finish my speech in a short while. Then you can see the picture it presents at night. You can see it again in the morning. I congratulate all of you in Orissa once again. Please say *Jai Hind* with me thrice. *Jai Hind, Jai Hind, Jai Hind.*

3. Science, Tolerance and Compassion[1]

It has almost become a custom for the Science Congress to do me the honour of inviting me year after year to inaugurate its sessions. I believe, I have been doing this for ten years or so. I consider this a great privilege and honour for a variety of reasons, although I sometimes fear that repetition of a practice makes it rather stale.

---

1. Inaugural address at the forty-fourth session of the Indian Science Congress, Kolkata, 14 January 1957. AIR tapes, NMML.

I come here every year in a dual capacity. As the head of the Government, I come to convey the greetings of the Government to the delegates, both those who come from abroad, and those from our own country, to tell them of the Government's keen desire to help and encourage the pursuit of science and the applications of science. I come also in my personal capacity because I am deeply interested in the work that has been done in India and abroad in the various fields of scientific activity. Those fields become ever wider and wider, and are impinging today on realms which might almost be considered to be unknown and which threaten the future of the human race. Every sensitive person, therefore, must necessarily be interested in what science and scientists do.

I am coming here today from Hirakud where yesterday I performed or helped in the opening ceremony[2] of a very magnificent piece of work of Indian engineers, the great Hirakud Dam which, I am told, is the longest in the world. A day before, that is, day before yesterday, I participated in a completely different function at Nalanda, a great university centre 1,500 years old ago in Magadha, which is now Bihar.[3] At this great university centre, where the ruins of this University of Nalanda still exist, my mind went back to the old days, when the Buddha flourished and went to Nalanda or Rajgir and when his message had powerfully affected the Indian people. And so, I wondered at the close association of this ceremony at Nalanda and the memories of the Buddha coming to me and of subsequent events of that University, and the next day at a product of modern science—this Hirakud dam—and today, I am here before you at this Science Congress. And the centuries seem to come together before me, and again I thought, how India is a bundle of centuries, where you can find almost every century represented here from the remote past to the modern age. Somehow we jog along with the past and the present, and even work for the future together, and the cow and the tractor march together in this country. I do not know what the future will hold. It does not seem terribly incongruous that the cow and the tractor are side by side.

So, my mind wandered, again going back to Nalanda. I thought of the message of the Buddha which was, apart from its religious significance, a message of tolerance, a message against superstition and ritual and against dogma. It was a message essentially in the scientific spirit. He asked no man to believe anything except what he could prove by experiment and trial. All he asked was the people to experiment and trial and thus to seek the truth and not to accept anything by the word of another even though he might be the Buddha. That seems to me the

2. See the preceding item.
3. See *post*, pp. 185-188.

essence of the Buddha's message and it struck me that the message, far from being out of date had a peculiar significance even today.

Then I found greater rigidity coming into people's thinking, in whatever plane they may function. The spirit of dogma which had badly affected the religious quest and made minds rigid and their practices conform to ritual which have no significance. I find that the rigidity of this dogma which had applied itself chiefly to religion was apparently projecting itself in the realm of politics and economy. The idea that you are in possession of the truth, the whole truth, and every bit of the truth—that kind of rigidity, with certain forms of religious approach—had narrowed men's minds, perhaps to some extent even in the scientific region. The tolerant and objective approach not only looked into the heavens without fear, but also looked down into the pit of hell without fear. All this becomes narrower because of this dogmatic and rigid approach to life's problems, the feeling that you have got the key to them and the other person who does not accept your thesis, is your enemy and has to be combated. And so apparently the key to life's problem is combat, violence and destruction of the person who does not hold your own opinion.

It seems to me that somehow people in the Buddha period were more advanced in tolerance, not in technology, not in the development of science, but in some other phases, not only in compassion but in the tolerant approach. It struck me that quite apart from the religious issue, there might be something worthwhile in the pagan view of life; not from the religious point of view, because the pagan view of life is a tolerant view of life. While it may hold to one opinion, it respects the opinion of others, and thinks, there may be truth in the other opinion too. It takes the universe and the mysteries of the universe, tries to fathom them no doubt, in a spirit of humility and it thinks that truth is too big to be grasped suddenly, and whatever one may know, there is much else to be known, and others may possess a part of that truth. So, while it worshipped its gods, it also honoured the unknown gods whom it did not know.

I venture to say all this because during the last two days, physically and mentally, I have wandered between various centuries; 2,500 years ago when the Buddha was here, 1,500 years ago when that great University of Nalanda was flourishing and attracting students from distant countries. I was there this time to celebrate that occasion when a great traveller from China became a student of the Nalanda University and spent seven years there and has written about his experience during that period. [4] And then the next day this great engineering feat, the Hirakud Dam, and the other advances in engineering or other

4. Huen Tsang was at Nalanda from 637-642 AD.

22

departments of science and technology that are taking place in India. And then my mind travelled to the problems we have to face in India and the world. The overwhelming problem of course is this: whether we or any other country or people will continue to function in peace, serving at the altar of science and using them for the good of humanity, or whether we shall distort the power that science gives us and use it for evil purposes.

The scientist is supposed to be an objective seeker after truth, and science has grown because, in a large measure, the great scientists have sought truth in that way. But no man, I suppose today, not even a scientist, can live in a world of his own, in some kind of an ivory tower, cut off from what is happening, cut off from the effects of his own work, which are so powerfully affecting the destiny of humanity. And therefore science today has perhaps begun to overlap the borders of morals and ethics. If it divorces itself completely from the realm of morality and ethics, then the power it possesses may be used for evil purposes. But above all, if it ties itself up to the gospel of hatred and violence, then undoubtedly I feel it has taken the wrong direction and that will bring much peril to the world. I plead with scientists here and elsewhere to adhere to the temper of science, to remember that this temper is essentially one of tolerance, one of humility, to the great truths which they are seeking to discover and which they are unveiling from day to day, realizing that much remains still for them to discover in future, but always remembering that somebody else also may have a bit of the truth. They do not have the monopoly; nobody has a monopoly, no country, no people, no book. Truth is too vast to be contained in the minds of human beings, or in books, however sacred they might be.

I remember that once a deputation went to Cromwell, the English dictator, some hundreds of years ago, and insisted on his following a certain line—rather hard line. Cromwell's reply became rather well known; he said, "I beseech you gentleman in the bowels of Christ, to consider whether it is possible that you may be in the wrong."[5] But we all think ourselves in the right. That would not matter so much if we did not want to impose our right on the other persons, forcibly if necessary, and that creates conflict; and when you have a great power, the conflict is all the greater, and the consequence and the disaster are all the greater.

Let us be a little humble; and let us think that the truth may not perhaps be entirely with us; others may possess it too. Let us cooperate with the others; let us even, when we do not understand what the others say, respect their views and

5. Oliver Cromwell, English soldier, politician and General. He made these remarks in a letter to the General Assembly of the Kirk of Scotland on 3 August 1650.

their ways of life, etc. Emperor Asoka has left memorials to himself and his thinking all over this great land—memorials which you can see today, great pillars of stone carved with his message, or on the rock or elsewhere. Among the many messages that he gave, the one which I think we should all remember not only in this country, but elsewhere is this one. Remember the period when he spoke; 2,300 years ago. People in those days spoke more in terms of religion than other matters. But what he said had a wider application. Addressing his own people, he told them, "If you reverence your faith, while you reverence your faith, you should reverence the faith of the other who differs from you. In reverencing the faith of others, you will exalt your own faith and will get own faith honoured by the others." I do not quote the exact words but this is the sense of it. Now apply that message of toleration not only to the field of religion but to the other activities of human life today, politics, economics and science, and you will find that it puts things in a different context. It is a context which is not very much in evidence today in the world, where opinions that differ are not liked, where ways of life that differ are not liked, where the tendency is to suppress the view, or the opinion or way of life that one does not approve of, where ultimately science itself becomes vitiated by this narrow outlook. That would have been bad enough at any time but when we have these new weapons forged by the work of scientists hovering above us and the possibility of their being used, then it becomes far more important and vital as to how people think today, how people react to other people's thinking, whether their minds are full of hatred and violence and intolerance, or whether they grow more in tolerance and in appreciation of others. Then it becomes much more important today than in Buddha's time or any other time, because a mistake today carries you very far, may carry you very far.

And so the burden falls a great deal on scientists, men and women of science, who have given to humanity many good things, and will no doubt give more of the good things of life, but who have also given great power, which may be used for good or evil. It is not good enough for the scientist to say that I have done my job by unveiling truth or releasing sources of power, let others use them. He may not control it of course but he has to go on with his quest for truth whether it leads the world to destruction or not, because it is absurd for our scientists to stop research for truth, simply because humanity may use his discoveries for evil. That cannot be done. The world marches on, and so we have got caught in these inner conflicts today, at the national and individual level. Many countries cannot keep pace, or many individuals cannot keep pace with the changes that are taking place. We adapt ourselves outwardly to the changes, but mentally we do not keep pace with them.

The rhythm of history goes on developing and each individual country sometimes does not fall in line with that rhythm. Or it lives in some old rhythm of its own, and thus conflicts arise; while chiefly because of the work of the scientists, development in communications and all that, there has to be fundamentally one basic rhythm for the world today, or else it is conflict.

I have ventured to place before you some thoughts that have been coursing through my mind and more specially during the last two to three days, as I have wandered from 500 B.C. to today, and seen these various centuries at work in India, and to some extent in the distant world. But here we are in the middle of the twentieth century. After all, the past is there only for us to learn from, both from its successes and failures. We have to live in the present and we have to build the future; and here in India as, no doubt, elsewhere people are engaged in building this future, and we seek your sympathy, your cooperation, your earnest and passionate attention to this great work of building up not only our country, but building up a world of peace and tolerance and compassion.

4. India and the World[1]

You must have heard that this huge meeting has been organized in connection with the general elections. You will perhaps expect that I will speak mostly about the forthcoming elections. I will say a few words about that. But I want to share with you my thoughts about conditions in India and the world in general.

What should I say about this election? As you know, I have been working for the Congress for the last 40 years, I have had a very close relationship with the Congress and so I have deep affection for it. In my view, the Congress has played a historic role in India. The history of India during the last few decades has been largely moulded by the Congress. That does not mean that there are no defects or shortcomings in the Congress. All institutions suffer from them to some degree. An effort has to be made to remove them. But you have to take everything into account and then decide what is in the national interest.

1. Speech at a public meeting, Kolkata, 16 January 1957. AIR tapes, NMML. Original in Hindi.

There has been a great deal of noise about the elections during the past few days and speculation about who will get the Congress ticket. But I am not really interested in that. I want, as I am sure you do, that good people with ability should stand so that they can serve the country and in particular their constituencies well. I agree that an effort must be made to select the best candidates. But it is an extremely difficult and complex task. If someone is left out, it does not mean that there is something wrong with him. Often good people are left out. After all, we have to select one out of four or five candidates. It is wrong to think that those who are not selected are not worthy. Everyone cannot be elected to the legislative assemblies or the parliament. There are other jobs to be done in the country. After all everyone sitting here is not aspiring to become MLAs and MPs. Only a few people are elected. We have decided to inject some new blood into the organization. One third of the candidates who are given tickets will be new. We must of course have the old and experienced hands. At the same time we need new blood too. How can we do that if we close the doors to new entrants? We have also decided to have more candidates from among the minorities and women because we want as wide a representation as possible of all sections of society.

The selection of candidates is a very difficult task and to tell you the truth, I keep myself aloof from it. Those who take a keen interest in it work at it. I do want good people to be selected to represent the Congress. As far as I know, strenuous efforts are being made to select the best candidates. There are various committees and vigorous process of screening has to be gone through. The antecedents of the applicants are thoroughly investigated and nominations are made by the PCC. Then the final selection is made by the High Command. So a great effort is made to select good people. But it cannot be helped if mistakes are made in spite of this. I cannot tell you who have been given tickets from here. But I would like to tell you why, in the context of the situation in the country, it is absolutely essential that you should vote the Congress to power in the state assemblies and the parliament for the sake of prosperity and in the interest of the nation.

All of you know the history of Congress. I do not know if you have read the election manifesto issued by the Congress. If you have not, you should, because it gives a brief history of all that we have done in the last ten years and what we intend to do in the future. The Congress was born more than seventy years ago. A long time has gone by. Almost sixty years of that have been spent in the struggle for freedom. The Congress threw up great leaders all over the country, in Bengal, Maharashtra, Punjab, Uttar Pradesh, Madras, and soon it became a huge national party. Then Gandhiji came on the scene and under his leadership, the Congress led the country in a peaceful struggle for freedom which is unique in the world. Ultimately we won and India became free.

Ten years have gone by since then and Congress has been in power at the centre and in the states as well. So the Congress has had experience of two kinds, one of leading a movement and two, of running the country by being at the helm of affairs. The achievements of the Congress are there before you to weigh in the balance and judge for yourselves. This is a good thing for the Congress but in one way a bad thing too. It is bad because other parties and organizations have never had to shoulder responsibilities and so they can make tall claims and talk in the air knowing well that they will never be called upon to fulfil them. There is no need for them to consider anything carefully. The Congress, on the other hand has to be careful in what it says because it has to fulfil its promises. Otherwise if we talk big without doing anything people will have no confidence in the party. Right from the beginning and particularly since Gandhiji's time, the Congress has tried to fulfil the promises it makes and not to make tall claims, which cannot be put into practice.

Well, the Congress has held the reins of this country for the last ten years and everything that has happened during this time is before you. It is up to you to judge what we have done. It is obvious that all our hardships have not been removed during this time. India has a long, long way to go yet. But I think it would be true to say that India has made amazing progress both within the country and outside too during this time.

What was India's position in the world ten years ago? It did not occupy a position of respect in the world. India was under British rule then. Mahatma Gandhi's name was famous. But India was not held in respect for it was in bondage. Today, though India is a poor country and does not have a large army or powerful weapons, it is held in great respect throughout the world. India's voice is heard with respect. Even in dissent, there is respect for our country. This is not a small achievement for a country within ten years of its getting independence.

Serious problems beset the country from within. As you know, we drew up the First Five Year Plan and succeeded in achieving the targets that we have set out for ourselves and in fact exceeded them. About eight months ago, the Second Plan was started. We have been a little more ambitious this time because our confidence in ourselves has grown. We hope to go very far with this Plan. If we succeed in doing what we have set out to do, as I am sure we will, India will have progressed very far. I will go into that later. First I would like to tell you that I do not wish to criticize the other parties in connection with the elections. Recently, in the AICC session at Indore, a resolution was passed to the effect that we must do high-class work and not indulge in abuse or criticism of other parties.[2] India's prestige would go up in the eyes of the world if we conduct the elections with dignity. There should of course be public debates on national issues so that the people may understand their pros and cons and then come to a decision. It is not becoming to abuse one another. I do not want the Congress workers to indulge in such behaviour, nor do I wish to criticize anyone. India has earned a reputation in the world for not maligning other countries. We try to maintain friendly ties even with the countries whose policies we may not be in agreement with. All this has contributed to India's stature so I want these elections to be conducted peacefully, in a civilized manner, no matter what the results are ultimately.

We must not criticize or abuse others. But it is our duty to evaluate the platforms and policies of the different parties objectively. Which is the party most likely to lead us in the right direction? Who will solve the problems of this vast country? These are some of the things which we must take into account. Ultimately the decision will be made by the people of India, I want you to remember that nowhere else in the world are elections held on such a large-scale. I think there are nearly twenty crores of voters in the country which is a much larger number than any other country's voting population. In some countries like China, the population is larger than India's. But elections are not held in China, they have adopted a different method. They have every right to do so. We do not wish to interfere in their affairs. But democratic elections on such a large scale are not held anywhere else in the world. It makes one pause and think.

Five years ago, when the first general elections were held,[3] people in other countries thought that we would not be able to manage because of the vastness of the country and the complexity of the problem. They thought that there would be riots. But the arrangements were so good that people voted peacefully for whichever party they liked, and then the parliament and the state assemblies were constituted. So this is the first thing to remember. We must conduct these elections also peacefully in a civilized manner because that is the sign of our greatness and strength. India is not a newcomer to the game of politics and public affairs. We are mature enough to conduct ourselves with dignity. I am saying this because sometimes people tend to forget this and some of the parties seem to think that politics consists of hooliganism and chaos. That is not quite proper. There can be no democracy in such politics, which is reduced to the level of might being right. The question is whether we want such hooliganism or peaceful democracy in which everyone has the right to vote as they like.

2. See *post*, p. 279 for Nehru's draft resolution.
3. From October 1951 to May 1952.

If the people of India vote against me or my party, I shall not make a noise. I will accept the verdict of the people, whether it is in my favour or not. I shall reserve the right to express my point of view before the public, before and after the elections too.

There are two major questions before us. There are innumerable problems of course. Once I was asked by a newspaperman in England what India's problems were. I had replied that there were thirty-six crores of problems in India. Every man and woman in the country constitutes a problem. All of them have to be looked after. But at the moment, there are two kinds of problems before us. One is the internal problem and the other, external. It is no doubt our duty to set our house in order first and improve the condition of the masses. Why should we be concerned about what happens elsewhere? Why should we burden ourselves with the problems and responsibilities of the world when our own burden is so heavy? That is quite true. We can hope to count for something in the world only if we set our own house in order and ensure peace and stability in the country. Only then will our voice be heard in the world. Who will respect us if the country is disunited and the people fight among themselves?

Therefore, whether you take the internal problems or the external it becomes necessary first of all to strengthen India and ensure progress and prosperity. We must get rid of the crippling poverty and open new avenues of employment. This is the issue which has first priority. But, at the same time the world has become so close-knit that we cannot shut our eyes to what is happening in the rest of the world. If a war breaks out anywhere in the world even if we do not join in, we cannot escape the consequences. Modern warfare has become a terrible thing with the invention of nuclear weapons. The radioactive particles of the fallout can scatter over thousands of miles and kill and maim. Therefore even if we do not enter the war it is bound to affect us when the whole of mankind faces the threat of extinction. Therefore we have to take an interest in the big international issues. The world has shrunk today in the sense that travel has become extremely fast. You can reach London from here within twenty-four hours, the United States in forty-eight, and in seventy-six hours, you can go all around the world once. When you switch on the radio, you can hear London, Moscow or Washington instantly. Then there are other things about which you may not even have heard. There are radars and all kinds of things, which have knit the world together. Today all nations are in a sense neighbours. Earlier, the foreign policy of a nation meant that country's relations with its neighbouring countries. Nobody bothered about distant countries. Now the whole world has become close-knit. There is no such thing as a distant land. You can go from one country to another in a matter of hours. Therefore we cannot shut our eyes to the problems of the world because they affect us too. So it has become necessary for us to take an interest in international affairs.

29

There have been two new developments in the world today. You may have read in the newspapers. One is in Egypt and the second in Hungary. The British and French forces launched a surprise attack on Egypt and tried to capture some of its territory. At the same time, Israel also attacked Egypt.[4] Our sympathies are with Egypt in any case. We have friendly ties with Egypt. Secondly it was very wrong of some powers to force Egypt to do something by the threat of force. It smacked of the days of colonialism when the European powers had gained a foothold in Asia and Africa and built their empires by force. So the whole thing was wrong on principle as well. We raised our voice against it because India has friendly ties with Egypt and made all efforts to bring the fighting to a close and to rectify the injustice against Egypt. Other countries also joined in and the fighting stopped. But the incident is by no means closed. The Suez Canal is being cleared. This is the development in Egypt.

The development in Hungary is of a different kind. There was an internal revolt against the presence of foreign forces on their soil. The foreign forces were mostly Russian. Hungary declared that it is an independent country and must be allowed a free hand in its internal affairs. Now on principle it is absolutely right. If we cannot accept foreign forces in Egypt, how can we do so in Hungary? We said right from the beginning that it was not proper for foreign forces to be in Hungary and the people of Hungary should decide the issue. There was fighting in Hungary and nobody knows how many people were killed. It is said that twenty or thirty thousand people were killed. The capital of Hungary, Budapest, was completely ruined.[5] It is really very sad.

The issue, which arose both in Hungary and Egypt, was the same in the sense that a foreign power tried to interfere in the internal affairs of another and by means of military force to get a decision in its favour. This is not proper. As you know, we have talked a great deal about Panchsheel. The first principle of Panchsheel is the sovereignty and integrity of a nation. Two, non-aggression. The third principle is non-interference in the affairs of another country. Four, mutual respect for one another. Finally, even in case of a difference of opinion every nation is entitled to follow its own path. There is no need for war. There must be peaceful coexistence among the countries of the world.

4. On 29 October 1956, the Israeli army launched an attack on Egyptian positions in the Sinai peninsula. The following day the British and French governments sent a 12-hour ultimatum to Israel and Egypt to stop the fighting. As a result of Egypt's refusal to comply with this request, British and French forces launched an offensive on 31 October against Egyptian airfields and other military installations.
5. See *Selected Works* (second series), Vol. 35, p. 452.

Now, in my opinion, though the developments in Egypt and Hungary concerned two separate issues, they violate the principles of Panchsheel. I have given you a broad outline. There are various complications. But the broad fact is that they do not abide by the principles of Panchsheel. So we raised our voice. At the same time, we made all efforts to see to it that the matters are settled peacefully. The greatest worry is that if the war escalates, ruin will stare us in the face. The problems which have arisen in Egypt and Hungary will not be solved by a war and both the countries will be ruined. Therefore our primary consideration was that the war must not escalate. We did not want to take any step which might lead to a world war for nobody can control it then. So we tried to speak out with great restraint. There was no point in making fiery speeches against other countries or abusing them in an irresponsible way.

How can India keep aloof from such major international problems? We cannot plead that we are engrossed in our own affairs and will have nothing to do with the rest of the world. When the world is drawn towards the vortex of war, we have to take steps. As far as international affairs are concerned, I feel that the world at large knows how India has served the cause of world peace. India is held in great respect for this reason. It has often posed a great dilemma for us. There are complex problems within the country. As I said, they are thirty-six crores in number. How are we to uplift thirty-six crores of human beings? I cannot go into the details. It is a very complex problem which cannot be solved by shouting slogans or by a magic formula. It requires hard work and effort. A nation cannot progress by a government fiat or law. If it did, the matter would be very simple. Ultimately, people progress by learning to stand on their own feet and working hard. How is this to be done?

We have adopted planning in this context so that we can have an idea of our priorities. We have limited resources and very few trained personnel. If we fritter them away in wrong channels, or at least in things which are not essential, then the essential tasks will not get done. The Five Year Plan lays down a list of priorities so that we can get the maximum benefit out of our limited resources. We want to do a great deal. If we make a list of what we would like to do, it will be a very long list. But it is not enough to make a list. People often come to me with demands for jobs, industries and this and that. I am sure their demands are justified. But it is beyond our control to do everything at once. We do not possess vast resources for that.

Recently, I said in Indore that I was ashamed of the fact that teachers in village schools are so poorly paid.[6] Unless we give them the respect due to a

6. On 4 January 1957, while speaking at the Subjects Committee meeting on the Congress Election Manifesto.

teacher and pay them well, how can our educational system function well. This is my opinion and I am sure you will agree. But if you make a demand that the salaries of all teachers should immediately be doubled, that would be beyond my control. I do not have the resources. I want to do it and hope that we can do so by and by. But at the moment, it means a choice between closing down a steel plant or two in order to pay the teachers better. Now that creates a dilemma. We are setting up the steel plants so that India's national wealth and the resources for further development may increase. Two things are absolutely fundamental to a nation's progress, steel and power. Both are essential for India's progress.

We are setting up three huge steel plants in India. There are some old ones, at Tata Nagar and elsewhere and the total output of steel per year is about fifteen lakh tonnes. Now we are setting up three new ones and expanding the one at Tata Nagar so that within five years we will be able to produce sixty lakh tonnes a year. We will continue to increase the production. We are trying to increase the production of power. These are all basic things. With a combination of these two items, we can set up thousands of industries and undertake other tasks of development. Our resources are limited. So if we take up one thing, we have to tighten our belts on another front.

So we must make an effort to gradually increase the wealth of the nation. Wealth means production of goods so that wages and salaries and trade may go up and everyone will get employment. But basic essentials are steel and power. That is why we are caught up in a dilemma today. We cannot take up even necessary projects because we do not have the resources. We hope that the position will improve in five years and the masses will have a better standard of living. You must bear in mind that it is not a question of a few thousand people getting better wages. The real problem is to raise thirty-six crores of human beings in India. We cannot go about it selectively. The condition of the masses will improve only if we help the farmers to progress. Nearly 80 per cent of the population depends on land in India and there can be no progress until the condition of the farmers improve. It is not enough for the cities to grow and advance. It is only when the farmers of Bengal and other provinces become better off that there will be progress.

We have to ensure two things. One, we should increase production from land. Two, we must try to open up other avenues of employment for large numbers of people who are dependent on land now. There are far too many people who depend on land for their livelihood. I have no doubt about it that production from land can be increased by adopting small improvements. It is already being done. At the moment the average yield per acre in other countries is more than double of what it is in India. Why is this so? Our farmers are extremely hard working. Why is the production so low? We must find ways and means of increasing agricultural production.

Secondly, we must try to set up more industries in the country, big, medium and small industries, cottage industries, so that the purchasing power of the people increases and so will the nation's wealth. Broadly speaking, this is what we are trying to do through the Five Year Plans. We have laid great stress on improving agriculture which has led to an increase in food production. You must have heard about the great river valley schemes like the Damodar Valley, Hirakud, Bhakra-Nangal and Tungabhadra. These river valley schemes will help in providing water for irrigation on the one hand and on the other, to generate power. Apart from that we are laying stress on setting up more industries. We want to lay the foundations of industrialization by producing steel and set up machine building industries. At the moment we have to import machines from outside, from Europe or the United States. There can be no progress if we continue like that. So we must produce machines in India and in our own factories.

Once the foundations are laid, we can progress much faster. New industries will come up, more avenues of employment will be opened up and wages will increase. It would be absurd for us to promise more wages to the people at the moment. After all, a nation's expenditure is limited by its income. It cannot exceed it. Otherwise we will go bankrupt. We must increase the earning capacity of the country in every possible way, from land and industries. We have to keep the larger national perspective in mind. As you can imagine, it is a pretty complex thing. It means taking into account the work of millions of people in society. We cannot allow development to be lopsided. If we pay attention only to agriculture and neglect the industries, the development will be uneven. So we have to pay equal attention to all these things.

I talked to you about Hungary. Poland and Hungary adopted planning. But they neglected agriculture and laid stress on industrialization. As a result they faced food shortages while huge industries came up. They are in deep trouble today. Therefore planning has to maintain a balance. We have said quite categorically that our Five Year Plans are not rigid documents. We will bring in changes as and when we feel necessary.

We have adopted a broad framework of socialism. What is the meaning of socialism? People define it in various ways. You have innumerable institutions in Calcutta calling themselves by different names which profess to practise socialism. What I am trying to say is that everyone has his own definition of socialism. The communists refuse to budge from the definition of socialism which was popular a century ago in another country with totally different conditions from ours. I cannot quite understand this. A society is a living, changing thing. Everything is different in the nuclear age. I cannot understand

33

how we can apply the same yardstick which was used in Europe to gauge its condition a hundred years ago to conditions prevailing in India today.

Let me tell you that it is by making the mistake of following an extremely rigid line that the economic difficulties in Hungary and Poland have become so acute. We do not wish to make the same mistake here. First of all, as I said in Hungary there was great resentment against foreign forces being stationed on their soil. Secondly, there was a conflict of opinion about planning. They have every right to do what they like. But we have seen that their method of planning has plunged them into great difficulties. You will be amazed to know that a famous Polish economist[7] said in a lecture a few months ago that they were following a wrong policy in economic affairs and that they must learn from India's Second Five Year Plan. He has gone so far as to say that more attention needs to be paid to cottage industries and handicrafts in Poland. So you can see from this that we can go terribly wrong by continuing to repeat old lessons by rote. There are many people in India who keep doing just that without realizing that the world has changed. We must remain vigilant and keep our eyes and ears open. We must make changes in our plans whenever we think it is necessary, always keeping the broad national perspective in mind.

I do not wish to criticize any party. But I would like to say a few words about the election manifestos issued by the various parties and their method of functioning. The Communist Party of India has been feeling slightly lost from its moorings during the past few months. There have been certain strange developments in the world which have left them feeling confused and perturbed. For years, they had been used to repeating lessons learnt by rote. In their opinion, a revolution meant violence and chaos. Their idea is to break up the existing system in order to build from a clean slate. Their concept of a revolution is moulded by the French and the Russian Revolutions and the attendant violence and chaos.

The Russian Revolution occurred at a time when the entire government machinery had broken down and ruin stared the country in the face. There were innumerable factors responsible for the Russian Revolution which are not present in India today. Are we then to go to war and bring ruin upon the country so that the communists can build a new India? Is it some kind of a joke? We must use our common sense after all. The problem is that though our communists are full of enthusiasm, they lack common sense. Their minds have fallen into such a rut that they think of nothing better to do than to go around waving a red flag and

7. Oskar Lange.

shouting slogans. They do not achieve anything by all this except confuse and mislead others.

The country is facing grave problems today. I do not say that everything that the Congress does is right. It has made mistakes. But the strength of the Congress lies in the fact that we learn from our mistakes and change with the times. Otherwise do you think the Congress could have lasted this long? It is over seventy years old and still going strong. That is because in spite of our innumerable faults and weaknesses, our finger is always on the pulse of the nation. We consult thousands of people instead of sitting in a conclave of a handful of men to produce a long thesis, as our communist comrades or even to some extent, the socialists do. In the conditions which prevail in the world and India today, every step that we take has to be carefully considered. It is obvious that we cannot solve our problems by shouting slogans or waving a flag about. Enthusiasm is a good thing. I feel sad that though there are excellent people in the Communist Party and the Praja Socialist Party, some of them old colleagues of ours, they are so wrong in their thinking and approach. I have no quarrel with anyone. But I wonder why they have gone wrong, particularly the Communist Party.

For one thing, in my opinion, the communists make one big mistake in placing their faith in violence and chaos. I think any sensible individual will realise that if any party in India seeks to achieve its ends by such methods, it will fail. On the contrary, it can only lead to a civil war in the country. A nation cannot progress in this way. It would be far better to make a mistake in good faith for it can be rectified. But once we move towards violence, our strength will be dissipated by internal squabbles.

There are some things, which must be borne in mind. One is national unity without which the entire fabric of the country will be torn asunder. India is a vast country with various provinces, languages, religions and castes. Casteism has been the bane of the Hindu society. All these forces create barriers in the country. Unless we get rid of these fissiparous tendencies and ensure harmony in the country, there can be no progress.

What led to India's downfall in the past? It was because we lacked the spirit of nationalism. We tended to put our own street, village and province before the country. In a sense, it is the Congress, which has gradually fostered a spirit of nationalism. It was a party in which people of every province, religion and caste speaking different languages were welcome. So the Congress became a vast nationalist party and fostered the spirit of nationalism. There are still many weaknesses in the country. You may have seen the picture that India presented when the question of states reorganization came up. But even if we protest about something, it should be done in a civilized manner. Otherwise we will fall.

I do not wish to compete with other countries or criticize them. But in most countries of Asia you will find that there is a lack of stability. So they are not able to progress. Internal dissensions and uncivilized modes of behaviour are obstacles to progress. So it is absolutely fundamental to our interests to maintain unity and peace in the country and behave as a civilized nation. The moment we resort to hooliganism and are led astray, progress and planning will come to a halt and I feel that our communist comrades have either failed to realize this or deliberately forgotten it.

The communist leaders jumped into the fray when trouble broke out over the question of states reorganization.[8] What is the connection between communism and the boundaries of two states? After all, there is no question of ideology involved. But you will find that many of our socialists and communists had jumped into the fray. Why? I think the only reason was that they thought they could gather some votes in the coming general elections by doing so. That is not right. You must do what is right. But the prospect of elections has turned many people's heads and we have seen the result in the last one year.

As I was saying, the communists in India are somewhat perturbed because the picture they had had of the world has changed. The developments in Hungary in particular have hurt them badly. They are in a bit of dilemma. In the beginning they expressed their grief over what happened in Hungary. But then they found that it upset all their preconceived ideas and left them without any moorings. So they did a volte face and declared that the developments in Hungary were entirely justified including the fact that foreign forces marched in and the subsequent firing and what not. I hope you remember that whenever by some misfortune there is police firing in any major city of India in a clash with the people, it is severely criticized in newspapers and public meetings. Nearly 35,000 human beings have been killed in Budapest and they do not condemn it. What does it mean? It means that it is entirely justified if the communists kill but not if someone else does.

I have no quarrel with the economic principles of communism. I am not entirely in agreement with them. But that is a different matter. I have no objection to communism provided the members of the party go about their work peacefully. Let the parties put forth their own programmes for the people to decide. The mistakes will be rectified by the people themselves. But when their activities are accompanied by violence and unrest, it is bad for any country and specially for India. The fact of the matter is that even today the barriers dividing the people are numerous and if we adopt the path of violence even once it will ruin all that we have been trying to do in the past few years.

8. See *Selected Works* (second series), Vol. 35, p. 583.

We have friendly ties with our comrades in the Praja Socialist Party. But it does not necessarily follow that we should like their policies. They have not found their moorings yet. They keep repeating worn-out cliches like "socialism means to expropriate foreign ownership of industries without giving compensation." They seem to think that that would solve all the problems. It is absolutely childish.

Anyhow, it is against the principles of our Constitution to take away anything without paying adequate compensation. So the communists would have to first change the Constitution. But apart from that, when our most urgent priority is to produce more wealth in the country, it does not help very much to take away the wealth from a few pockets. It may give you some satisfaction to take away the excess wealth from some rich men. But our job is to make the machinery of production work at greater speed. We cannot achieve very much by mere moneylending tactics or transferring wealth from one pocket to another. India will progress faster if we increase production in the country. We will only earn a bad name for ourselves in the world if we snatch away the property of others. We may be able to get a few crores out of it. But how can we sacrifice the reputation and honour of the country for a sum like that?

We are prepared to sacrifice anything for the honour of our country. But apart that, we have to see what is in our national interest. If we nationalize the few industries which are in the private sector today, we will not have anything new to show for it. We want to invest our money in new industries in the public sector which will mean more jobs for people and production will go up in the country. The existing ones will continue to function and the new ones will be an additional investment. It is a waste of money trying to take over the old industries. So we do not accept that principle. You will find that the public sector is expanding day by day with huge plants and industries coming up all over the country. There is no doubt about it that the public sector will continue to expand which will have a great impact on the country's economy. At the same time, we want to encourage the private sector too because everything that adds to the production of national wealth is good. We can levy taxes on them as we think proper. In short, we want to increase production in the country by every possible means, in the public sector and the private sector, through heavy industries as well as small, medium and cottage industries. The wealthier India becomes, the faster we will move and the burden on the people will become lighter. So this is our thinking.

You can get the entire picture in the Plan document. But as I said, we are not prepared to accept it as a rigid document. We will do what we think is right at any given time. Nor do we wish to keep repeating lessons by rote meant for conditions and circumstances of some other country in another century. It is really strange. I cannot understand how any thinking individual can have this kind of outlook.

I gave the example of the Soviet Union. A great revolution took place there and there is no doubt about it that they have made great progress in the last forty years. But it was not done in a day. They have had to work extremely hard. There is nc magic formula. You can compare the progress made in any country in a period of ten years with what has happened in India. I am prepared to accept that. It would be a fair comparison. I feel no anger against the opposition parties. They are my friends and comrades. I want to take them along and enlist their cooperation in national tasks. But I am unable to understand the manner of functioning of parties like the Communist Party or the Praja Socialist Party and the Socialist Party. How can there be any progress by following the course being charted by them? If by any chance, they get hold of the reins of power all progress will come to a halt and there will be disunity in the country with each faction pulling in a different direction. This is the first thing that will happen. I do not know what will happen twenty-five years later. It was in a way a good thing that when grave troubles descended upon the country immediately after independence and thousands of refugees fled from one side to the other in the wake of partition, there was a strong party at the helm of affairs. Otherwise, we would have been in the same boat as some of our neighbouring countries where upheavals are common place and their entire energy is spent in making a noise.

There is one other kind of party, completely communal in outlook, like the Jana Sangh, Hindu Mahasabha and others whose names I cannot recall. They talk of a Hindu nation and what not but have nothing to say about an economic policy or foreign relations. If we do what they propose India will be dragged back at least a couple of thousand years. Well, anyhow, nobody can put the clock back to that extent. But I feel sorry to see such backward thinking, which fails to understand the world of today.

Apart from the fact that people are misled by these parties, communalism in itself is a terrible thing. Partition was a direct consequence of such feelings. It is the communalist outlook of the Muslim League which led to the creation of Pakistan. Now the Hindu Mahasabha wants to follow in its footsteps and spread the same poison which can break up India. What does a Hindu nation mean? It means that those who are not Hindus are not full-fledged citizens of India. It cannot mean anything else. Do they want to start off a civil war in the country among the Hindus, Muslims, Christians, Buddhists, Parsees and other communities? Even a little child will understand that no country can behave like this in the modern world. It can only lead to terrible ruin. We have seen from India's past history the consequences of disunity and fissiparous tendencies which have led to India's downfall again and again. Communalism is irrelevant in the context of modern history and conditions in the world and India. These communalist organizations have nothing to do with the present times.

You must think carefully about what the alternative for India is. Is there any other party apart from the Congress which can hold this country together? The Congress may make mistakes. A strange question which seems to be agitating the people is what the Congress will do when Jawaharlal has gone. I shall counter that by asking what will India do if the Congress is no more. You can conjure up all kinds of problems. I can tell you what will happen if the Congress were not at the helm of affairs. That does not mean that there are no intelligent men in other parties. I do not say that they are all fools. But even intelligent men pulling in different directions remain backward. The question is to progress in unity and strength. We have embarked on a journey in which we have to take the thirty-six crores of human beings in India with us.

I am often told that we have not spelt out clearly what we mean by socialism. Everyone knows that we have laid down the broad principles like equality and equal opportunity for everyone in the country as our goal. We want to ensure the equitable distribution of the wealth produced in the country so that a handful of men do not grab all of it. But what it all boils down to is that the path which these small, narrow communalist parties follow in politics is completely unconcerned about whether the rest of the country is with them or not. They think that they can coerce the rest to follow them. It is simply not possible. We must take the whole country with us.

The Congress is a very large nationalist party. I agree that there are various strands of opinion in the Congress. The good thing is that we are able to take them all with us. Similarly we are able to take the different sections of society with their differing viewpoints along with us instead of looking at things as merely black or white or imposing a rigid thinking on the others. The problem is not of a handful of people going ahead but of taking thirty-six crores of human beings on a chosen path. Sometimes we have to move slowly in order to allow everyone to catch up. If a section of society gets ahead leaving others far behind, India as a whole cannot benefit. That is why I lay stress constantly on unity and the need to follow peaceful methods. That leaves one with no alternative but to persuade the people by explaining what we are trying to do. If we want democracy in India, there is no choice but to take the people along with their consent.

I can say with authority that neither the Communist Party nor the Praja Socialist Party can take the country as far on the road to socialism as the Congress has done. You can say that the socialism practised by those parties is superior to what the Congress believes in. That may be so on paper. But who has had an impact on the hearts and minds of the nation? My job is to take India's millions with me, not just my own family. I cannot shut myself up in a room and come out with a learned thesis. One of the greatest lessons that we have learnt from Gandhiji is to take the people with us, to explain things to them patiently, and never to lose sight of the fact that the millions in India must march together. We cannot go very far by forming a small party and passing resolutions or shouting slogans. The problem is to take thirty-six crores of human beings in a particular direction and to take our clue from them about the best way of ensuring cooperation. So in a sense politics, particularly during election time, consists of educating the people and evolving a consensus. It is not a question of asking for votes. What is the value of a vote. Our task at the moment is to take the people with us by explaining what we are doing. The nation's progress depends ultimately on how much the people grasp what we are doing and are prepared to cooperate. I do not want anyone to vote for me merely because they like me. They should vote for a party because they like the path that it is following. For a long time now, the Congress has considered it a duty to take people of different strands of opinion with it.

I agree that opinions are bound to vary among different kinds of people. The person who wants to achieve something through violence and chaos has no place in the Congress. Communalism has no place in the Congress, but there is plenty of room for people of different strands of opinions. We take them deliberately because they represent people of similar views in the rest of the country. We want to explain our goal of a socialistic society to them and take them with us. We have been able to convince large sections of the population which were opposed to socialism that it is in the national interest.

So you will find that a large mass of public opinion has emerged in favour of socialism. It could not have been done by coercion and threats. The method followed by the two parties, the Congress and the Communist party are quite different. One believes in peaceful methods and the other in violence. I agree that the Praja Socialist Party also believes in non-violent, peaceful methods of functioning. But whenever it presents its manifesto, its thinking invariably appears to be that of a petty narrow-minded party, unconcerned about larger national issues.

There is no doubt about it that the people by and large accept the foreign policy of the Congress and the present government. We have seen where the Communist Party would take us in foreign affairs from the manner in which they have changed their views about Hungary again and again. The Praja Socialist Party is also very shaky about foreign affairs. There can be no room for slackness in the world of today when there is grave fear of war. It is not a question of making long-winded speeches. We have to think carefully about safeguarding national interests and maintaining peace in the world.

As I am speaking to you, the Kashmir issue is coming up before the Security Council in New York.[9] I do not wish to say very much about it. But I would like to draw your attention to a couple of matters. One is regarding the attitude of Pakistan whenever this issue comes up. I am amazed when I read the kind of things that are being written about in the Pakistani newspapers by their leaders and others. They use all kinds of threats. It is amazing that they have absolutely no control over their pen or speech.

The last decade or so since the end of the war has been marked by a cold war in the world. A new trend in this atmosphere of cold war is the unrestrained use of threats and abuses by leaders and statesmen of various countries. But I do not think the cold war has reached such degrading depths except as in Pakistan vis-a-vis India. I am amazed at the things that they say. They have every right to present their arguments and points of view. But there ought to be a limit to the lies and abuses they indulge in.

The Kashmir issue is nine years old now. We try not to rake it up as far as possible. It has been our effort to maintain friendly relations with Pakistan. But that does not mean that we should give up all our rights on a platter to them. We have repeatedly said that we have no designs on even an inch of territory outside India. We want to maintain friendly ties with Pakistan and seek their cooperation. We have no desire to see Pakistan weakened or breaking up. But their leaders keep saying that India's policy is to break up Pakistan. It is really strange. Even if they do not believe us, they must at least have the sense to see that we are not so stupid as to try to break up Pakistan. Do we want to break up our own country? Let me tell you quite clearly that, that is what parties like the Hindu Mahasabha want. I do not want Pakistan to be merged with India, not because it was I who had agreed to partition earlier but because such a step would lead to India's ruin. We want cooperation and harmony with Pakistan. We want to establish trade relations with Pakistan. What we do not wish for is a constant state of confrontation with Pakistan. We are not trying to placate them. But Pakistan goes about saying that India has designs on Pakistan.

Let us leave aside Kashmir. All of us know that refugees are daily pouring into West Bengal from East Pakistan. Forty lakhs have come in the last one year. On top of it, they accuse India of trying to dismember Pakistan and rake up the Kashmir issue. They go about spreading a tissue of lies about the Kashmir issue

9. The UN Security Council met on 16 January 1957 at New York to consider Pakistan's request for a discussion of the Kashmir question, in view of the entry into force of the new constitution of the state of Jammu and Kashmir on 26 January 1957.

and say India was the aggressor. We will have to first settle which side is telling the truth before we can reach an agreement. What will be the attitude of the statesmen in the Security Council if such lies are spread?

We have to make it quite clear that there are certain things which will not be tolerated by India. We are not prepared to sacrifice Kashmir. We will not tolerate the use of threats and chaos as a means of settling this dispute. Kashmir is progressing fast. But you can go and see for yourselves the conditions which prevail in what is known as "Azad Kashmir." There is a tremendous difference. Does Pakistan want ruin to descend upon Kashmir and destroy the ancient arts of this province? It is bound to happen if unfortunately Kashmir falls into the hands of Pakistan.

Well, anyhow, that is upto the people of Kashmir to decide. We feel that they have shown by their behaviour that they want to be with India. Otherwise we could not have stayed on in Kashmir against the wishes of the people. Now, if you compare the issues of Kashmir and East Pakistan which are divided by a thousand miles, you will find that Pakistan is not able to prevent people from fleeing its territory in thousands.

Pakistan has been given massive arms aid by the United States using the threat of the Soviet Union as a pretext. I do not know if anyone has heard of an impending attack on Pakistan by the Soviet Union. There is no doubt about it that Pakistan is adopting a belligerent attitude because they have got massive arms aid from the United States. The Pakistani leaders have said quite openly to the Soviet and Chinese leaders that those arms are intended for use not against them but against India. But they sing a different tune to the American leaders. We have no desire to interfere in the internal affairs of Pakistan or what they say to their allies. But it is pretty obvious that if the arms aid continues, the danger to the subcontinent will be considerably enhanced. I am deeply grieved that they should be creating a real danger in trying to ward off an imaginary one.

As you know, I had gone to the United States recently and met their President. He is a great man and I was deeply impressed by him. I feel that he is a peace-loving human being. The United States is a great and powerful country with untold wealth and arms. They could do a great deal of good in the world. What I feel sad about is that they should wish to solve the problems of the world by an arms race and military methods. They have recently sent a proposal[10] which is

10. The Eisenhower Doctrine, placed before the US Congress on 5 January 1957 and passed on 7 March, authorized the US president to extend economic and military aid to any West Asian country requesting assistance "against armed aggression from any country controlled by international communism."

good in many ways and yet its main emphasis is on military power. That implies giving arms aid to the Asian countries, to Pakistan and other countries in West Asia. This is not the way to solve the problems that we face today. As far as Pakistan is concerned, it only complicates matters even further.

As you will notice, we are facing extremely complex and grave problems today. It is very essential that we should be calm. We must not fritter away our energy like Pakistan in futile squabbles. We have not been moaning about Kashmir though Pakistan attacked us first. We have behaved in a civilized manner though Pakistan is sitting on one-third of Kashmir. Yet they accuse us of all kinds of things. We have made innumerable efforts during the last nine years to come to an agreement about Kashmir. We have sent a number of proposals which we would not have normally done if we had been rigid in our attitude. But the attitude of Pakistan is to grab more and more. So we come round once again to the root of the problem. It must be decided who is at fault. In our opinion, the attitude of the people of Kashmir is ample evidence.

Anyhow, let us see what happens. But the Kashmir problem is a case in point to demonstrate the need for unity in India in tackling the problems before us. At the same time, peace-loving does not mean weakness. We have to behave in a civilized but firm manner. I do not know what the future holds in store for us and we must be prepared for all eventualities. We have had to face tremendous problems in the last ten years and successfully overcome them. We must not give in to the panic but always bear in mind that we are passing through a crucial stage of our history. Unity is of the essence at a time like this. Fissiparous tendencies are always harmful but particularly so just now. We must help in every possible way to maintain stability and unity in India.

We are going to have general elections. I am not bothered about it. But I am concerned that we must not allow the divisive forces to come to the fore. The country can break up unless we maintain a strong united front in our dealings with the world. At the moment India speaks with one voice and is heard with respect. But if we are disunited and in disarray nobody will listen to us. You must think about the repercussions on our Five Year Plans. Some people want to put an end to planning, while others want to reverse the trend completely.

The opposition parties have got into the habit of negative thinking and making a great deal of noise. But nations need hard work to progress as you can see from the example of China, Japan, the Soviet Union and Germany. They have reached their present position through hard work. Every ideology has to be backed by hard work. I want all of you, the citizens of this great city of Calcutta and Bengal to think about all these things and come to the right decision so that we can face the crucial days ahead successfully and overcome our difficulties. *Jai Hind*. Please say *Jai Hind* with me thrice. *Jai Hind, Jai Hind, Jai Hind*.

5. A Hundred Years of the Madras University [1]

I feel somewhat overwhelmed on this occasion, not merely by the present but rather by the past that this great University has represented, and a past in which it has played such an important part. A hundred years is a fairly considerable period in the life of a university, in the life even of a nation. And the last one hundred years in India have seen very great changes, tremendous happenings, and ten years ago a new leaf was turned when India became independent. During these ninety years before independence, how much has this University done, the alumni of this University going out and taking part in national activities; how much did they further the causes which India had at heart? You know what an important part they played in every field of activity including the great adventure, in which we engaged when we struggled for India's freedom. So when I come here or when I go to these other sister universities, which were founded about the same time, Calcutta and Bombay, I feel this rush of history coming upon me, a hundred years of India. Out of the one hundred years, about forty years or more have been connected with us, some of us more intimately, because we also have been some kind of actors on the mighty scene. On this occasion, the past and the present rather mingle in my mind. Of course, both of them impinge upon the future, the future which is so much in our minds, the future for which we work and live and devote all our energy.

First of all, I should like in all earnestness to express my deep gratitude for the honour done to me by the University in giving me this degree, honoris causa. [2] It is not the degree so much that counts but the fact of this association with the University of Madras, that you have made me an alumnus of this great University which I honour.

India is a country of great variety and I am always astonished at discovering new facets of India, which show me something different from what I had known. All my life I have spent in trying to discover what India is, and all the energy that I might possess has been spent in trying to fashion out the India that we hope to have. And so it is a little difficult and perhaps rather invidious to compare different parts of India with each other. They are different and yet they are so alike, and taken together they have woven this magnificent pattern which is

---

1. Speech on the occasion of the laying of the foundation stone of the centenary buildings of University of Madras, Chennai, 31 January 1957. AIR tapes, NMML. Extracts.
2. Nehru received an Honorary Degree of the Doctor of Laws.

India. We cannot detach any part of it, because if you take away any part of it, it ceases to be the India that we know of. Each part of India has participated in weaving this beautiful pattern. Each part also participated in the struggle for freedom and now that we have launched in the great endeavour of building up India, each part has to play its own big part in it. But perhaps, without any invidious comparisons, I might say that the south of India has been rather noted for its intellectual quality. Intelligence is always good, always necessary, though perhaps sometimes intelligence by itself might lead people astray. Some other restraining or balancing factors are necessary. I do not mean to say that the intelligence that has been displayed in the past in the south of India, did not have those balancing factors, because indeed in two other fields, the south has played a rather dominant part in India's history — in the cultural field and to some extent in the spiritual field. These three together—intelligence, culture and a measure of spirituality—have produced a mixture, which is of great value to India. Other parts of India have also given a great deal to this rich pattern. Anyhow, in the present context of events in the country we require many things. We require above all, calm thinking and vigorous action, both together. Action without thinking may lead nowhere, thought without action may well be an abortion, leading to nothing.

Whatever picture you may have in your minds about the future of India, inevitably the universities of India and the other institutes of higher learning must play a vital part. You have finished a hundred years of this University. And every end of a period is the beginning of a new period. You are celebrating the end of a hundred years. But I would prefer to call it the celebration of the beginning of the second hundred years, because then you look forward to the future which you are going to build. The men and women who come here are trained, and get to know each other, and get to converse and discuss, and thus train themselves for the great and honourable burden which they will have to carry later, in working for India.

Yesterday, I believe a very eminent scholar, Prof. Raman[3] addressed you. I read about it in the newspapers and he laid great stress on science. You know that during the past ten years we have laid very considerable stress on science, and built-up these great national laboratories all over the country. We have built them because they are essential if we are to progress and understand the modern world. But even more so, they seem to be necessary for us to develop the temper

3. C.V. Raman, founder-director of the Raman Research Institute at Bangalore, inaugurated a symposium on science subjects on 30 January as part of the centenary celebrations of the Madras University.

of science. The real temper of science, which I take it, is a temper for the search for truth, regardless of what it may bring out. Sometimes truth is unpleasant, but it does not cease to be truth by being unpleasant. And so science has to be encouraged and technology has to be encouraged. There is no other way for us to go forward without science and technology and yet science and technology, by themselves, may lead to a somewhat lopsided development of our people, and of the country, unless both of them are balanced by something else, something that pertains to the character, to the mind, to the restraining and widening influences of culture. So the university comes in and supplies that important element which may lead to some part of wisdom coming into our minds and hearts.

The more I look at the future of India, the more I realise the utmost importance of the work that a university is supposed to do. It may not always do it. To some extent it does. Sometimes some universities may do a little better than others. Then I see this difficulty which faces us in India today, when the very demand and the understandable demand for wider and wider opportunities for higher education tends to swamp us, tends to bring down the quality. We cannot deny people education. We must give opportunities to all who are capable of profiting by them. But in doing so there occurs a danger of quantity pushing out quality. And surely we do not want quality to suffer in our country.

You and I are proud of our country. What are we proud of? Some kind of a vague picture in our minds of India, if you analyse it, what does it lead to? What does it mean? Probably everyone of you has a somewhat different picture. But surely if we are proud of India, it is not because of her length and the breadth, or her mountains and rivers and forests, or her cities or villages, but something of the quality of India which has come to us through the ages, something of the quality of her people. When I say her people, I am not merely referring to the great ones who have distinguished themselves, but the quality of the peasant of India, the simple, suffering individual who has borne the weight of India on his shoulders and on his back for ages past and yet has had an element of wisdom in him which is always astonishing. I cannot tell you how much I admire the peasant of India. I admire, of course, the great people of India. Many of these great men are produced by this University. But there is something of the quality of India which has permeated to her common people, if I may call them the common people. It is that, that we admire. But I do not wish to idealise anybody. I know very well that the so-called common people, or the so-called uncommon people have many failings. We have failings. Our long history of many thousands of years has given us a great heritage. It has also given us many burdens, unwelcome burdens of mind and habit, which come in our way. We have to take the good and the bad, to preserve the good and to throw out the bad. But in doing so, we must not act in a narrow, sectarian way, of considering ourselves better than the rest, but remember that in this long journey that we are taking, our fellow-travellers are the thirty-six crores people of India. It is not an individual who seeks betterment or salvation, but it is the thirty-six crores people, whom we always have to keep in mind. I have sometimes been asked in foreign countries, 'What are your problems in India? How many problems do you have?' And I have told them that we have thirty-six crores problems. And I want you always to think of them, because only then will you get any kind of true perspective of the nature of our problems. Naturally, the thirty-six crores people are not going through universities. All of them are not going to be very eminent in the arts or sciences. But out of them, if you give them the opportunity, some will be great geniuses, great mathematicians, great scientists and great engineers.

In this University a reference has been made on this occasion to Ramanujam[4], who by sheer chance got an opportunity. Otherwise, he was a humble clerk in an office. He proved to be the century's greatest mathematician. He died young. There are others. So when we give the opportunity to millions of our people, I have no doubt that we shall find many who will distinguish themselves and distinguish their country. But above all we shall have given all of them the chance, at least, to live the good life. I take it that our people should be enabled to lead a good and creative life. Now it is for the University to give the lead to our thinking, to prepare the ground, as the Vice-Chancellor[5] said, to irrigate the minds of our people, so that they may go out and take part in the adventure in which we are engaged in India.

I want you, to some extent, to realize what this adventure is. You can read about it in our books, in our Second Five Year Plan, in our community schemes, in our great river valley projects, in scientific laboratories and the like. But there is something more about it than all these great buildings and great dams that are being put up. I want you to understand and feel that something, which I cannot easily describe, which I feel. I felt that something forty years ago or more, when a great change came over many of us through the impact of Gandhiji, when not the educated few but the millions of this country suddenly felt lifted up out of their misery and poverty and could stand straight and raise their heads and look you in the eyes. During the years that followed, we lived, to some extent, in a dream world because we dreamt of a free India. We worked for a

4. Srinivas Ramanujam; mathematician at Trinity College, Cambridge; known for his researches on the theory of numbers and fractions; died at the age of 33 in 1920.
5. A.J. John, Governor of Madras, 1956-57.

new India and sometimes we even forgot our immediate surroundings in the glamour of that vision. We lived, what I call a very full life. Sometimes people with whom we spent ten years in prison, came with misery on their faces to us, not realising all these years were the fullest of their lives. Because our thinking and our actions were coordinated, we thought and acted as if there was no discord between them. The real difficulty comes when there is a discord between our thinking and action. And so we functioned in a more or less integrated way. Whether we functioned, ultimately, rightly or wrongly is another matter. But we had the sensation of functioning well, and that is a big thing for an individual to have that integrated feeling of functioning. So we became partners in a mighty undertaking. We were small folks, small fry compared to the bigness of the task, but because we were associated with this mighty task, we also grew a little in stature, all of us, even the peasant in the field. He grew in stature to the extent that he was associated with something much bigger than his daily round and something a little beyond his own individual life. So he became bigger. Now I think of that and I see that although the nature of our work has changed, something even bigger calls all of us, the building up of this new India, in physical terms of course. I do not think that any real spiritual life can flourish if a nation starves and is miserable. That is the basis, the physical basis. But always with the physical basis, there has to be a mental and moral accompaniment and I pray that we may not forget that in our search merely for the physical basis, although I attach the greatest importance to that physical basis, without it I do not think we can build this temple of new India.

My days, as everyone's days, are numbered. And we come to the afternoon or evening of our lives, with a little more strength left for work and adventure. But to you who are young, this great vista opens out, this tremendous vista of being partners in this great undertaking, working for it, and what is more, seeing the fruit of our work before our eyes just as we saw it when independence came. Having laboured and dreamt for it for years and years; we saw the fruit of that labour. It is not often given to people to see the fruition of their dreams. We saw it. And now we dream afresh, other dreams, of bigger dreams and we shall work, of course, to the utmost of our capacity and energy but ultimately the privilege of working will come to the younger generation, to the generations that follow my generation. You are fortunate to have that privilege and that opportunity. But I want you to have that feeling, of being a partner in a tremendous undertaking, in a great adventure, that glow and enthusiasm and exhilaration of working for great causes. If you have that then you will feel you have lived a full life and all the little squabbles and troubles will count for little.

Today is a kind of staging post after a hundred years for this University. But the world also appears to be on the threshold of big and strange happenings. All kinds of things happen which trouble us and this talk of war and preparation for war and threats and violence and all that, and yet on the other hand tremendous vistas open out. The men of science tell us strange things and science itself has moved into a realm which is perhaps difficult to describe as purely a physical realm. They are in other realms. What the future can be, or will be, I do not know, except that we all dream of a better future. We have ideas about it, we should have ideas and work for their realization. But whatever the future may be it will depend on the quality of human beings, not merely even on their technical training, important as it is, but on their inner quality. Philosophers have often told us that in spite of all the advance of humanity in the scientific and technical field that it is the quality of the human being that counts.

Prof. Raman said yesterday that Einstein was the greatest scientist of the century. Well, of course. Those who met Einstein, as I had the privilege of doing,[6] were rather overwhelmed by his genius. But what struck me even more was his extraordinary simplicity and modesty. Then I felt how truly in every respect Einstein was a great man. He was the greatest scientist of the age, but he was simple, modest and gentle. His heart went out to suffering or misery wherever it occurred. That showed the real nature of the man. I hope that in our pursuit of the Second Five Year Plan, or whatever other objectives we may have, we shall always remember this quality of the human being, the gentleness, the modesty of the human being.

We have been sometimes referred to in terms of contempt as "mild Indians", or "the Hindus". I am proud of my people being mild. I do not want them to be brutal. There is enough of brutality and violence in the world. It is a good thing to be gentle, to be compassionate. It is not a good thing to be weak. It is not good to be afraid. Neither gentleness nor compassion is the companion of fear or weakness, and therefore Gandhiji told us to be strong and fearless. And it is said, in our ancient books that the greatest thing that could be given to our people is the quality of fearlessness: *abhaya*. If we have that quality, even in a small measure, it is well with us. Unfortunately today, the world, as you know is pervaded by fear. The more powerful you are the more afraid you become; just as the richer you are, the greater your fear of guarding your riches. And so, fear pervades the world and when fear comes it brings with it other undesirable companions. It brings hatred with it, it brings violence with it, and then whatever your other accomplishments might be, the hatred and the fear somehow crush them and your life ceases to be happy, or even very creative.

6. On 5 November 1949.

Gandhiji tried, and in a large measure succeeded, in teaching us the lesson of fearlessness and at the same time of non-violence as a measure of peaceful action. I do not pretend to say that we are better human beings than others. We are all much the same, with some failings, and perhaps, some virtues. But anyhow, we had this great training. We went to this countrywide university of Gandhi. That training was good for us and good for the country. We may not live up to his expectations, but anyhow we could not forget all that we learnt, and sometimes even when we forget, it comes back to us in a rush and shakes us up and we try to pull ourselves together. I should like you to remember that lesson. Be not afraid of anything. Gandhiji, the prophet of peace and non-violence, said: "rather than be afraid, take a sword and use it." He did not want peaceful action and non-violence to be tagged onto fear. He himself was a man truly fearless. So do not think that fearlessness means inaction and do not think that peaceful action means submission to evil. You have to be strong in order to be peaceful. You have to be strong and gentle. Only the strong can be truly gentle. And you have, in so far as you have inherited some of these traits, to nourish them, and to develop them, and at the same time develop the qualities of strength which the West exhibits so much and which is good, provided it is restrained, provided it is balanced with gentleness and compassion.

We live in this very difficult age where from day-to-day problems confront us, which are not easily solved. It depends upon what you are. You may be optimistic or you may not be. Of course, if you are not optimistic about the future and if you have no particular function, then you will have an unhappy time. Perhaps it is not good to indulge in fiery optimism, as it is not good to indulge in fiery anything. But apart from this it is good to be optimistic, but keeping your feet on the ground and having faith in yourself and your people in the world and in the destiny of man. For man has survived tremendous disasters. Probably at the time of each big disaster and upheaval, the people in the world thought that the end of the world was coming. Yet man survived and went ahead. So in these days of hydrogen bombs and atomic energy, people are frightened of what might happen if these tremendous forces are let loose on mankind for evil purposes. Well, we do not want them to be used for that. We want to stop that being done. We work for that. Nobody in the world really wants that to happen. We should work for that but if that does happen, well, you and I will not be there to worry about it. So, why worry now? But I do believe, and I can offer no logical argument for it—that man is not going to be annihilated even by the hydrogen bomb, and that humanity is going to go ahead. And going ahead involves not merely technological progress and scientific progress, important as that is, but something deeper. Some moral standards too come in, some

50

kind of a spiritual basis. I am not talking in terms of religion but something wider and deeper than that. You cannot really control a hydrogen bomb by another bomb. Everybody knows it. You can only control it by some force on another plane entirely which affects people's minds. Perhaps you know that the constitution of the UNESCO begins by saying that: 'It is in the minds of men that wars begin,' which is perfectly true. So we come back to the training of minds of men, and so we come back to the tremendous function of the universities which trains individuals, and which trains the leaders of the country.

I hope, and believe, that this University will not only continue its great work which it has done in the past and sending out men—outstanding men and women—but will particularly devote itself to training the leaders of the country and of the nation, so that they may be capable of facing these problems and of solving them; so that they may have something of the spirit of a crusader who crusades for the right causes and to take part in this tremendous adventure of India that faces us today.

6. A Survey of Domestic and International Affairs[1]

I came to Madras city to attend the centenary celebrations of the University here. It is a great event in the life of a University to complete a hundred years. But since I have come here, I am glad of this opportunity to meet you again and address you.

I believe this meeting is called an election meeting and I am supposed to talk about the elections. Frankly, I have not got much to say about the elections. I would rather talk to you about the problems in India and the world so that we may understand them. We have to deal with them from day-to-day and they are difficult problems and it is important that you should understand them. After all it is you, the people of India who have to act, and decide what policy we should pursue in the country and outside. That becomes important even from the point of view of the elections because you have to choose people who will carry out the policy you want pursued. Elections are not prize-giving competitions, that

1. Speech at a public meeting, Island Grounds, Chennai, 31 January 1957. AIR tapes, NMML. Extracts.

you give prizes to the most beautiful or to others whom you may like. Elections ultimately are tests of the policy which a country should pursue and if that test is to be applied correctly, then you should consider that policy, and understand it.

I am not very much concerned with individuals who go to the parliament or to the assembly. I am concerned much more with broad policies. I am concerned much more with this country, working to its utmost capacity to build India, a new India, to fulfil the Second Five Year Plan, to work for peace in the world and to do many other things. Naturally I want good men to be returned to the parliament and to the assemblies. How does one make sure that good men and women are returned? This is the most difficult thing in democracy. We in India have some experience, but not too much, of these big elections. If you look at the world, there are not many countries which have a system of parliamentary democracy. They are very few, and even those few countries have got adult suffrage only in recent years. Wide electorates and adult suffrage are a relatively new thing in the world, not only in India, and they have brought new problems. We had our first big election five years ago and it was a very successful election, competently done. Now we have our second election, which I am sure, will also be a successful one—the biggest election in the world history.

Now, how do you choose people? Some people may tell you: "Choose good men or women". How does one decide as to who is good and who is not so good? Not an easy matter. Suppose I have to build a bridge, I have to choose a good engineer. How do I choose the engineer? For different kinds of work different types of people are chosen. Naturally, we want above all men of integrity, men of competence, men of enthusiasm. Another fact you should remember. Suppose we got in our parliament a large number of men of integrity, all thinking differently. Suppose we even got a number of high-class philosophers in our parliament, all philosophizing in their own way. They will all be excellent people, most interesting people to talk to, but the parliament will not function. This system of parliamentary democracy, therefore, requires good people of course, but also a certain discipline from top to bottom. Otherwise you can get nothing done. It is because of that requirement of discipline that the system of parties has arisen. If every one of the five hundred Members of Parliament did what he liked exactly, there will be so much confusion that really the result would be almost nil. Therefore, it becomes necessary to have the party system where each person, of course, has his say, but ultimately some decision is arrived at, which is acted upon in the parliament and ultimately in the country, when the parliament passes it. I want you to remember this because people talk vaguely and loosely about "Oh! Elect good people". Of course, you want to elect good people. How to choose them? During the last two or three months, our Pradesh Congress Committees and our Central Election Committee have been engaged in choosing candidates. I am sorry to say that I took little part in this, partly because I was very much engaged otherwise, partly because I am just not enough interested in this business. But I can tell you, that the amount of time that our Committees have spent on this, is something amazing. They had to choose 3,600 candidates all over India. Naturally they did not know all of them or most of them. I have no doubt that in spite of every care they look, mistakes have been made. I have no doubt that in many cases deserving people have been left out, maybe some undeserving people have got in. Because it is impossible to be perfect in these matters and one has to balance many factors. But I can tell you this, that the amount of care that has been given to this, by the Congress President[2] and his colleagues in the Central Election Committee, has been very great indeed. I do not think any party in India or for that matter, outside, has given that care to the choice of its candidates. If even so mistakes are made, well one cannot help it, in a big business like this. But very great care was taken to choose the right people. And in choosing the right people, one has to consider not only their competence and goodness, not only their service but their acceptability to the area, their chances of election and so on. This is not naming somebody by a royal decree of nomination, because after all those people have to be elected by the people. So this great care was taken more than ever before. Still mistakes have been made. One cannot, in a big business like this, stop the functioning of a great machine because some odd mistake has been made, or somebody does not like this decision or that. The whole machinery of the country would stop running that way.

What I want you to remember is this that having come to that decision, then it becomes essential for all members of that organization, to abide by that decision. I can tell you privately, between you and me, that I do not like many of the choices made by our Central Election Committee. But I accept them. I am a soldier of the Congress. I do not raise the flag of rebellion and shout: "I do not like this." I accept them. My boss in the Congress is the Congress President and the Congress Central Election Committee having thoroughly considered every matter, comes to a decision. I have not given that consideration to it. Who am I to challenge the decision of persons who have spent so much time and energy over it? So whether I like it or not, I accept the final decision. It was open to me and sometimes I did put forward my viewpoints before the Committee. If it was accepted, well and good; if it was not accepted, also well and good. That is the only way for an organization to function. Therefore whether we like some decision or not, we have to function in discipline, not merely to win an election, although

2. U.N. Dhebar.

one fights an election to win it, but because if we are to do anything effective or worthwhile in India, we must be a disciplined nation. Among the great services that Gandhiji rendered India, one of the greatest I think, was this discipline that he instilled in our people and in the Congress organization. I was in the Congress before Gandhiji came. It was a body of very eminent people, great leaders and others, but it was not a body of action. It was not a disciplined body. Big people met and talked and went away after talking. Nothing happened. Gandhiji brought this element of discipline. Of course, we were fighting a great battle against the British, and although that battle was a peaceful one, a non-violent one, nevertheless, it was a great struggle. You cannot fight any struggle, you cannot do anything big without discipline. Small countries with discipline have performed great deeds. Big countries without discipline have gone to pieces. Therefore, in this election, as in other matters, we must inculcate a sense of discipline, more especially in Congressmen. It is wrong for them to start complaining after a decision is taken, that injustice has been done to them. It may have been done. One tries to be just, one makes a mistake. But what is the business of our hankering so much after a seat in the parliament or the legislature? You cannot cure an injustice by going out in the open and shout, that you hanker after a seat. That itself is a bad exhibition. So I submit to you that decisions, having been taken, we must abide by them, because the work we have to do in India, is a tremendous one. It staggers the mind, when one thinks of it, whether you think of the national sphere, the domestic one or the international one. In the international sphere, you see these tremendous conflicts and power blocs, and all kinds of things happening, which may bring the world to war. And if you had taken only a few philosophers sitting in the assembly, well, they will philosophize when the war came. You have to take effective, united and disciplined action when these emergencies arise.

Nationally, we have undertaken the Second Five Year Plan which, no doubt will be followed by the third and the fourth, because we are out to change the face of India, we are out to revolutionise India, we are out to create, after our political revolution, an economic and a social revolution. This will take a mighty long time. I hope that every few years, every five years, we shall see big advances, but the work of building new India is not going to be finished in five or ten years. We talk about socialism. And we have made some strides towards that aim, and we shall make further strides. But socialism, in its essence, in its fullness, cannot come by some resolution. We have to go step by step to it, in the economic plane, in the social plane and in the minds of men and in their social behaviour, their social relationship and adjustments and all that. It takes many years. It is a tremendous work. Are we going to do it by functioning as a debating society, talking, each person talking in his own way?

I am not a warlike individual, but when you have to do these big things, think in terms of a war; not in military terms, but in terms of a great crisis which a nation has to face, when it sends all its resources to the successful prosecution of the war. Can you imagine, an army sitting down, debating what to do and what not to do? The army will never function. Some great English writer[3] said, many bad generals have won battles, but history does not give an example of a debating society ever having won a battle. That is true. Now, people may say: 'What is all this military phraseology and metaphor? We are not in war. We are in peace.' It is true we are in peace, but it is a very precarious peace, whether it is internationally considered or nationally, and we have to make good quickly or else we go under. It is a hard world we live in, a callous world and it does not care very much for your philosophising, and we have to strengthen ourselves in the economic plane and the other planes, but above all strength comes from discipline and from unity. And, therefore, I ask for the unity of the whole nation. But, so far as the Congress organisation and the sympathisers of the Congress are concerned, if they cannot show that unity and discipline, what example will they set to the nation?

I read yesterday that my friend, and old colleague, Jayaprakash Narayan, has said recently appealing to me that I should help, I forget his words, in establishing or in strengthening a strong opposition to the Congress.[4] Now, this is a very strange request to make. I believe completely in any government having stout critics, having an opposition to face, because without criticism, people become complacent, governments become complacent. The whole parliamentary system of government is based on this criticism. The free press is based on this criticism and other things. If the press was not free to criticise, if people were not allowed to speak and criticise government fully, in the open, it would be a bad thing. That would not be parliamentary government, that would not be proper democracy. That is all right. And I welcome criticism in parliament. In fact we welcome criticism from our own party members, the amount of rules we have in our own party for criticism of government's policies, is great, subject always to important policies, having been decided upon, to be acted upon. It is all right. We want all this. But when Jayaprakashji says that I should build up an opposition, does he want me to build up some bogus things to oppose the Congress? What value has that, what virtue has that? He gives an example, I think, of the great

---

3. T.B. Macaulay.
4. On 28 January 1957, the Praja Socialist Party leader, speaking at an election meeting at Begusarai, said that Nehru should help in the growth of a strong opposition party.

Turkish leader, Kemal Ataturk.[5] With all respect to Jayaprakashji the example is not a good one. There was no democracy in Turkey, real or if I may say so, even unreal. In Kemal Ataturk's days, it was a dictatorship. Does he want that kind of thing to happen in India? Surely not. And Kemal Ataturk did certainly put up a very artificial party to oppose him when he wanted to be opposed. The strings were in his hands. Really that artificial thing is, surely not an example for us to follow. The point is, that the opposition should have the freest opportunity of expressing its opinion, of fighting elections, or in the press, in the platform. That is the point. I cannot choose candidates for the PSP or the Communist Party. It is absurd on the face of it. What does it mean? And I think that they have the fairest opportunity. The Election Commission is independent of government. It is open to any of you to vote as you like. You know that. Whether it is in favour of the government or against it. There is no question of pressure or there is question of coercion. That is what a country wants and I do submit that we in India have that freedom in elections and outside elections, more than almost any country in the world. There may be a few countries which have about the same freedom as we have. But a far greater number of countries in the world have no such freedom. We have it and I am proud of it and I hope and I am sure it will continue. I want every type of opposition to come and try its chance with the people. But if the people will not have him, what am I to do? Am I going to coerce the people to vote for him?

Jayaprakashji says it would be good for the Congress to be defeated. I might perhaps agree with him that it may be good for the Congress to be defeated, but surely the question of whether it is good for the Congress or not is not for him, but for the Congress to decide. At least, at any rate, it is not something for Jayaprakash to bother about. The question before us is, what is good for the country, not what is good for the Congress or for anybody else. And my difficulty is, that our friends like Jayaprakashji have got so entangled in their dislike of the Congress that they have forgotten that there is such a thing as India, the good of India, and things to be done for India.

It is my belief that if by any mischance the Congress was defeated, it would be very very bad for India for a variety of reasons, and one or two I shall mention to you. I do not say that Congressmen are better people than others, that they are great patriots and others are not. I don't say that. There are good men in other organisations and there are our friends in other organisations also. It is not a

5. Mustafa Kemal (1881-1938); Turkish army officer, politician and President of Turkey from 1923 to 1938; after a nationalist rebellion in 1923, became a virtual dictator; in 1935, assumed the surname Ataturk, meaning father of the Turks.

question of personal friendship, it is a question of getting something done. Suppose in the parliament, we had instead of the strong Congress Party, a dozen groups, twenty groups, small groups with nobody having a majority. What would happen? No stable government, intrigue, one little group intriguing with another, and offers being made "all right if you join us, we will give you a ministry, if you join us, we will give you this," that is bound to happen. I do not say that to criticise any group, but that inevitably happens, when you get this kind of opposition—all kinds of odd parties, none having a majority, each pulling in its own direction, no work is done, no effective work is done. At any time that is bad. And I can give you instances in other countries, where countries are failing because of the failure of any stable government. But at a time like this, when we talk about the Second Five Year Plan, when we talk that all energy of the nation should be put into this, when we have an international situation, when we have Pakistan shouting itself hoarse about jehad and war, are we to experiment then with numerous odd groups? It is a strange idea.

It surprises me and it amazes me that a person of good sense should suggest something which totally ignores the facts of life in India today. What are the facts of life in India today? The Congress may be in a big majority in parliament or in your Madras Assembly. But the facts of life are these, that we have to fight a tremendous opposition in India, not a party, but our own failings. These include, our disruptive tendencies of communalism, provincialism, casteism, and the tendency to break out in violence. We who pride ourselves in ahimsa and all that, break out in violence. Our history shows that we are very prone to disruption, and fissiparous tendencies. There is no good hiding our faults, our failings and this tendency to disruption, has been inherent in the Indian people for a long time. And if British rule in India did one good thing, if you like, it forced on us a unity to fight the British. But really the first effective mass-scale attempt to build-up this unity of India, was by Gandhiji. And it brought results—and yet you see how soon we go to pieces. Take the states reorganization issue. Whether the decision was right or wrong, is it not fantastic for people to commit arson and murder, because of that? Does it not show an inherent weakness in us? Maybe, this was done for political reasons, because elections were coming. I put it to Jayaprakashji because his own party, the PSP, took a considerable part in this agitation. I am not, for a moment, criticising having their views on the matter or their taking part in that agitation about this boundary or that. But I do submit that by doing that, in the way they did and are still doing in some places, they encourage the most dangerous thing in India, that is this tendency to disruption. They encourage the tendency to violence, violence of one group against another, one linguistic group against another, just as in the old days, the Muslim League and others encouraged the violence of one religious group against another. These are the dangerous things. We, you and all of us, have constantly to combat the biggest opposition in India, that is the fact of Indian life today. Do you imagine that we have an easy time because we can vote something in parliament? It is this that we have to fight and all the world knows that, the weaknesses of India. They are not hidden from anybody. The fact that we have a majority or not, does not take away from the real facts of Indian life. And every party should recognise that. And when the PSP or the Communist Party oppose us, I do not mind. But I do think that it is wrong of any party to take any step which encourages those disruptive tendencies, to violence, to bring one group into conflict with another. The Communist Party, wherever there was a linguistic agitation, there they jumped into the fray. Why? Not that they were terribly interested in that particular problem, but they simply imagined that they can only flourish in an atmosphere of toil and trouble. This is an extraordinary thing. So, let no man imagine that the opposition is not strong. Take the communal parties, Jana Sangh, Hindu Mahasabha and others in the north. Here no doubt there are communal parties, some of which are even more peculiar in their make-up than the parties in the north. What are these? Are they parties? Have they any logic, have they any programme? They are out of date, something out of the Middle Ages, of some archaic time. It is a throwback from the modern age to some past age. You see they have no real programme, you will find that because they have no real programme, every one talks of socialism. What does socialism consist of for the Jana Sangh? It has nothing to do with socialism, it consists of some demands which are purely communal or it may consist of some demands against Pakistan.

I believe one of the major demands of your communal parties here is to kick out the Brahmans or to become an independent *Dravida Desh* or Tamilnad, independent of the rest of India. Of course, all this has a certain comic aspect, in spite of its tragedy. It is comic that any intelligent person should say these things foolishly and it has a tragic aspect because many people are led away by these foolish cries, led away sometimes into paths of violence. Now one thing is dead certain. Not even if the heavens fall, can any part of India be taken away from it. Nothing will disunite India, no power in India or outside can disunite India. Let this be understood quite clearly. We have had one Pakistan. No more, whatever happens....

There is plenty of opposition in India and quite apart from all that I have said, there is another opposition, that of the inertia of a big country which we want to move forward and move forward rapidly. It is a tremendous factor, this inertia. On the other hand, we see the PSP and the communists, I am leaving out these communal parties because they are primitive. One can't reason with primitive people. But the PSP and the communists are not primitive in that sense, they consist of many people who were with us in the Congress, good people, friends of ours. But they encourage, and do strange things in their desire to win an election. I have been appealing and the Congress Manifesto has appealed that this election should be conducted without malice, without ill will, in a decent way.[6] I want you to remember that. Now the Secretary of the Communist Party, Mr Ajoy Ghosh said the other day: "Oh, Jawaharlal Nehru talks about decent elections but attacks viciously the Communist Party."[7] I do not understand what he is talking about. I have criticised the Communist Party and its deeds as he has a right to criticise the Congress. I have not criticised any individual personally. Am I not to criticise the policy of the Communist Party which I consider absolutely wrong and completely out of place today in India? I welcome criticism of Congress policy from the PSP, from the Socialist Party, from the Communist Party, or from anybody. It shakes us up. And I propose to criticise the Communist Party and the PSP and others also vigorously but always decently I hope. There is no question of malice in it.

Take the Communist Party. I put questions to them. I know that during the last year or more specially in the last six months, they have had many shocks, and no doubt some of them have been powerfully affected by these shocks, I do not know how far they have been as a party, because I find recently, they are falling into line again in spite of the shocks. Hungary was a shock and must be a shock to every sensitive person. After first rather allowing people to think that they had been shocked by what happened in Hungary, now they justify everything. I am not talking about Hungary now, but I do say that the Communist Party, I repeat, is not in a position, mentally it is not in a position to lay down any policy. It has to tow the line. Individuals may not like it, they have a strong sense of discipline. But apart from that, what is the whole theory behind that policy? It is not a theory. I should like them to tell me, is it a theory of encouraging parliamentary democracy? Obviously it is not. It is a theory of the "dictatorship of the proletariat". It is a theory of many other things, in which violence comes in. I know that they do not intend doing violence. I don't say that, but I say so far as violence is concerned, it is an opportunistic theory. I consider this idea of "dictatorship of the proletariat" completely out of date. I do not say it is wrong always. I say it might have been right in the middle of the 19th century in Europe, but we are in the middle of the 20th century in India. Remember, when these theories were started, there was no democracy in any country. Even in so-called

---

6. See *post*, pp. 260-273. For Nehru's draft resolution a code of conduct for the elections, see *post*, p. 279.
7. Ghosh made this remark on 21 January at an election meeting at Guwahati. He referred to the Congress resolution passed at the Indore session on the code of conduct for the elections.

democratic countries, the voters were a very small proportion of the population, landholders and the like. So one could conceive of these theories of rebellion and war and violence. But when in our country there is parliamentary democracy and adult suffrage, it becomes completely illogical to my thinking, to talk about dictatorships and all that. Anyhow the Communist Party's theories can only be carried out by upsetting our present Constitution, as far as I can understand them. It is up to them to clear it. And if they did, then they are not communists, they are something else or communists have taken a new turn.

So far as the PSP is concerned, who as I said, are, in a sense, the nearest to us. My mind reels really at the various combinations that come and go in the PSP. Here in Malabar they go through some kind of a arrangement with the communalists—some kind of arrangement with the Malabar Muslim League Party. In other places, for a long time, there was talk of their coming to some electoral arrangements with the communists, whom they disapprove of thoroughly. What is wrong with the PSP? I say so with all respect that they have ceased to have a really solid programme of their own. Some of the socialists, mind you, hobnob with organisations talking about free enterprise which is the opposite of socialism. In Bombay they are very closely aligned with organisations which talk about free enterprise. I have no objection to this. It is open to them. But in their extreme desire to get aligned, to win elections, they are losing the platform completely. I am sorry for that. I do wish them success. Let them stick to a certain socialist programme, teach the electorate, win the electorate if they can, teach us—I am willing to learn from them instead of shifting about on these political sands.

What is all this due to? People shout and criticise the Congress. The Communist Party, the PSP, the SP and others, are angry with the Congress and when they fail in elections, they do not learn wisdom from it. Surely there is something wrong with their thinking or with their action. Either their thinking is some kind of bookish thinking, relating to some past events in Europe or America, or in any event they are out of touch with the facts of life in India. Obviously if you are a socialist, if you are a Marxist, the first thing you must learn is, to be in touch with the facts of life and not grumble and be frustrated because people will not listen to you and follow you and vote for you. I remember Lenin said, or wrote somewhere talking about communists of Russia: "Stop prattling politically. Stop talking too much about reason. Look closer into the facts of life and through the people." There is too much political prattling about forgetting the facts of life in India. The Congress is successful in spite of its many failings. We have failings of course, and if we have failings, it is easier to understand because we are a vast organisation. A select organisation like the PSP and others should have less chances of having failings because they are more select and more sectarian like. But the Congress, in spite of its many failings, has by and large remained close to the facts of life in India. That is why the Congress has succeeded and will succeed. That is why the Congress can pay dividends in the shape of progress in India.

What is the socialist programme? What is the communist programme? Expropriate all foreign capital in India, seize hold of the tea gardens, nationalise this and that. They seem to think by doing so, vast hoardes of money would come to us and then India becomes socialist. This is very immature and childish thinking, quite apart from its being opposed to many things in our Constitution. By getting a few crores of rupees, by expropriating others, you will pay very heavily. You pay with the honour of India. And the honour of India is worth many, many billions and more. I am not going to tamper with the honour and good name of India just to get a few crores of rupees. We have full authority to control the industrial undertakings so that they may fit in with the Plan. Our public sector is growing and becoming more and more important. We have a private sector, we want to encourage it within its domain, to grow. We want to encourage everything that will produce results. We are going to produce by the method of trial and error, not by any doctrinaire method, not by anything written down in a book, one hundred or fifty years ago, not by any book merely written in Washington or Moscow or Paris or London. Although we shall learn from them, we have to deal with conditions in India, the mentality of the Indian people. And I think we have shown already that the only way to progress is to develop our own way of thinking and action, no doubt, learning from others. All the parties have my goodwill, but what am I to do if they will function in such odd and doctrinaire way, a primitive way, a lopsided way. Am I going to risk the future of India on this kind of immature thinking and immature action. It is a very serious matter for us to consider. That is why I come inevitably and almost reluctantly to the conclusion that there is no help for it in India, if India is to progress, but for us to have the strongest possible Congress organisation, strong Congress Party in the legislatures, working unitedly to build a new India through the Five Year Plans....

I have talked about the domestic scene. Look at the international scene. What is the policy of the Communist Party, or the PSP or others? Continuously criticising and sometimes running down our international policy, from opposite directions. The PSP generally thinks that we should line up with one bloc. The Communist Party generally thinks that we should line up with the other bloc. Both of them do not like our independent policy of non-alignment. Now it is for you and for the people of India to decide in this election, whether this policy of non-alignment that we have followed, is the correct policy or not. And remember this, if by any chance the communists or the socialists have the chance to decide our foreign policy, it means that the present policy will not remain. Other policies will come, this way or that way. I do not say they will change everything in our policy because after all foreign policies have a certain coherence, a certain continuity which cannot be changed suddenly. That is true, but the result would be that the whole of this structure that we have built up internationally would begin to crack, would not remain as it is—the strong firm structure of friendship with all nations and non-alignment with any military bloc or military pact. What am I to do—ask people to support an opposition which will upset the foreign policy on which so much depends for India? I cannot do it obviously, much as I want an opposition to come. But I should like these opposition parties themselves to be clear about this matter. When some resounding success comes to our policy, then there is certain quietening down. When something happens which appears to be a failure of our policy, then there is a big outcry. "See our policy has failed", as if we can carry the world on our shoulders and as if we get the approval of the whole world for our policy which necessarily cannot please everybody.

So in this election I want the nation to decide clearly and effectively, on our policy, not only domestic, but also international. The domestic policy means not only the Second Five Year Plan with all that it contains, but it means also the social legislation that we have promoted and that we shall go on promoting, because we want an economic revolution and a social revolution. I am proud of the social legislation chiefly in regard to women, the Hindu women, that has been passed by our parliament. It is of the utmost importance that the women in India should have fair play, and a fair chance to progress. India will not go ahead till the women in India have their chance. I am proud of that and I want you to vote on that, because there again we come up against all the bigotry, all the narrow thinking of ages. We have to face that in a friendly way and convince the conservative people. I do not care losing an election, but I am not going to give up the principles for which we stand.

So this election means this: that in the domestic sphere, all this economic thinking, and ideals, not of doctrinaire socialism, but socialism which we are evolving by trial and experience in this country. Then the Five Year Plan, the Community Projects, and the social changes and all that. I want you to think and if you are agreeable to that, vote for it. I want the people of India to vote, and I want them to vote for the international policy that we have pursued. That is particularly important in the present context because it is true, completely true that we have to face difficult problems in India, apart from world problems. We faced them in regard to this question of Kashmir. We face them in other matters too, whether it is Egypt or other places. It is necessary that the world should know what India thinks. I do not expect every individual to think alike, but broadly speaking the world must know. A challenge has come to us from the world about our foreign policy. I want the people of India to answer that challenge. Are we going to answer it by electing some critics here and some critics there, and producing confusion in the minds of India and in the minds of the world about what our foreign policy is? The Communist Party and the PSP, quite regardless of other things, have by their attitude towards our foreign policy made themselves not well suited for election. I am quite convinced that they do not represent the Indian viewpoint, because the Indian viewpoint, which our national and international policies represent, is a viewpoint which is in direct continuation of our thinking during these last twenty or thirty years. I would go further. I would say it is in line with Indian thinking for ages past applied to modern conditions.

I want to say a few words about a question which must be in many of your minds. That is the Kashmir issue. First of all, I find that some of our people tend to get rather excited about it. Excitement is not good in considering serious problems. There is no need to get excited although we realise that this is a serious problem. Some people have suggested to me—some Members of Parliament— to summon a session of Lok Sabha immediately because of this.[8] I do not see any need for that. Some have even suggested: "postpone the elections because of this, amend the Constitution so as to carry on for another year or two." I entirely disagree. These elections are going to be held, whatever happens. We are a mature enough people to carry on with our Constitution and our democratic working and face serious problems at the same time. We are not going to run away from elections or from anything because something happens in some other country or because danger threatens us. In fact, I think because of this situation, it has become all the more necessary for us to have elections, so that the country may give its verdict on this policy or that, which we can pursue with single-hearted vigour afterwards. Therefore, forget getting excited and getting cold feet. We have no cold feet, we have stout arms and I hope, calm and stout heads. Nevertheless it is true that some recent developments in Kashmir have caused us concern and some distress also. Distress because it seemed to us that this serious problem, which has existed for nearly nine years now, was dealt with very casually recently in the Security Council. It is a problem which has roused up people emotionally, certainly in Pakistan, certainly in India and most of all, of course, in Kashmir itself. There is a great deal of sentiment behind it. But we cannot solve problems by sentiment. Where there is a strong emotional background to it, where there is this nine years' history involving all kinds of problems—legal problems, practical problems, problems of consequences of any action that might be taken—then, it seems to me that wisdom requires something more than a casual consideration and a casual decision.

8. See *post*, p. 351.

You know that our case was presented there by my colleague Krishna Menon, and I want to say to you that he did this work brilliantly and most effectively. And the line he took there represented completely our views on this subject. I say this although, it is not necessary for me to say so, because a representative of ours, a colleague of ours in government, naturally says what we feel, jointly feel. Nevertheless, I want to say it because there are some people in this country and some people in other countries, whose job in life appears to be to try to run down Krishna Menon. Because he is far cleverer than they are, because his record of services for Indian freedom is far longer than theirs, because he has worn himself out in this service of India. It is not necessary for them or for me or for you to agree with Krishna Menon or anybody. I do not agree with Krishna Menon in everything, although he is a close colleague. We do not all agree about everything. But we do agree in our broad approach to problems, we do agree about our belief in each other's bona fides and integrity. Otherwise we cannot cooperate. But repeated attempts to undermine our policy by casting blame on a colleague, seems to me not very desirable or proper.[9] Krishna Menon is a member of the Rajya Sabha.[10] It was not necessary for him to seek election. But we have agreed to his seeking election in the city of Bombay deliberately, because Bombay is a cosmopolitan city and we want our foreign policy to be voted upon in Bombay. It is for them to say whether they agree with our foreign policy or not. Let them not raise any other questions. We do not run away from criticism and it is a challenge to those who disagree with our policy.

Coming back to the Kashmir question. It is a complicated thing and it is not quite proper for me to say much, when the Security Council is considering it. Nevertheless, I wish to say something. What is the basic issue in Kashmir? There are many issues, but the basic issue about Kashmir is the good of the people of Kashmir. Nothing else counts. Of course, other things count and I, as the Prime Minister of India necessarily have to take into consideration the interests of India. I have no business to relinquish or throw away the interests of India because of some sentiment. Nevertheless, the major consideration for me and for my Government has been the good of the people of Kashmir. Some people chiefly in foreign countries, sometimes even in India, talk about our

9. On 29 December 1956, Nehru expressed his distress at reports appearing in *The Hindustan Times* and *The Times of India* about Krishna Menon. These reports, according to Nehru, criticized in "very unbecoming language" the part played by Menon during the debate on Kashmir in the United Nations. He felt that the criticisms were "entirely unjustified" and added that "they gave a handle to many of our opponents in foreign countries."
10. From May 1953 to March 1957.

moral standards and say that: "Nehru, who pretends to be such a high moral figure, doling out moral advice to everybody in the world, forgets his own morality when he deals with Kashmir; that he has a double standard." Well, it is very difficult for me to know my own failings, naturally. But I am not personally conscious of any double, or separate standard. If I judged the Kashmir issue by any different standard, then indeed I would stand condemned not only before other countries, but also before my own people and even more so before myself, my mind and my heart. I have thought that if moral issues come in, India stands rather well over this Kashmir matter.

Look at the history. Invasion through Pakistan, later by Pakistan; destruction, arson, loot, rapine, murder by people coming through or from Pakistan. This is the beginning of the story of Kashmir, a story that goes back over nine years. It is also known that afterwards Kashmir acceded to India. I am not going into legal matters. But according to our thinking and according to the thinking of many, it became our right and duty to protect Kashmir. Quite apart from this, if we had not done it at that time, Kashmir would have been a smoking ruin and there would have been a large-scale war between India and Pakistan.

I know how troubled I was at that time. All our background had been one of non-violence and peace. Were we, immediately after independence, to be dragged into a war? It was a terrible thing and yet there was Kashmir being looted, people being murdered and frantic appeals coming to us from the people of Kashmir, apart from the ruler. It was a very, very difficult decision to make. Fortunately at the time, we had Gandhiji with us. I am not taking Gandhiji's name to entangle him in this matter, but merely to tell you, that as usual I ran to him for some advice. I believe he spoke publicly to us about this matter. Then he told us it was our duty to go to the help of the Kashmir people.[11] He, a man of peace, told us to do so. We went and we found that the invasion was not by mere raiders only, but the Pakistan Army had entered Kashmir. It became a big job. The normal consequence of this would have been war with Pakistan. They had come, they had committed aggression. Whatever argument you may have about the accession to India, about India's right to have troops in Kashmir, there is absolutely no argument, even a flimsy one, to justify Pakistan sending troops there. There is no doubt from any point of view that it was aggression by Pakistan and we were entitled in law and fact to attack Pakistan all over. We were much stronger than Pakistan at that time, militarily. We did not do it. We went, in order to avoid war with Pakistan, to the Security Council.[12] Even then we put ourselves mildly. We said please ask Pakistan not to encourage aggression over India. We

11. On 29 October 1947 in New Delhi.
12. On 1 January 1948.

65

have never in these nine years had an answer to that question. The Security Council and their Commissions indirectly, once or twice, have said that Pakistan has in a sense committed aggression. They admitted the right of India and the Jammu and Kashmir Government to have sovereignty over the whole territory including the territory which Pakistan is occupying. But the Security Council said: "Why should we condemn anybody? Let us come to some arrangement." We agreed, we said: "Pakistan has done us grievous wrong, but we do not want to condemn Pakistan, because we want to live in peace with Pakistan, we want to be friends with her and we are neighbours." So time and again, we moderated our policy. We did not put forward with all the vigour, that we could have done, the principal facts, the original facts of this dispute. And we talked about many other matters, and we agreed to a plebiscite on certain conditions, in a certain context of events. The very first condition was, the withdrawal of the Pakistan Army from the territories of Jammu and Kashmir State. There were many other conditions, but that was the first because the aggression had to be purged before we could take any other step. That was the principal thing stated in the UN resolution[13] which dealt ultimately with the plebiscite. First of all there was to be a ceasefire, then a truce, then other things, then a plebiscite. But immediately after the ceasefire or as part of the truce, the Pakistan Army had to withdraw from the territory they had invaded. They have not done that to this day.

I am told that India comes in the way of a plebiscite, that we do not fulfil or honour our international commitments. If Pakistan says so, I can understand it, because Pakistan is in the habit of making entirely irresponsible and often untrue statements and they are a party. But when others say so, it surprises me and pains me. What international commitments have we not honoured? If I am convinced that, I have not honoured any international commitment, well, either I shall honour them or I shall resign my prime ministership of India. Let others run India. During all this period of nine years or more, we discussed these matters with Pakistan. Sometimes, they made suggestions, we made offers and they made offers and this question of plebiscite was discussed, and this question of conditions, all this has been in the nature of discussing how to solve the problem. Once or twice some steps were agreed to, but the steps were not taken by Pakistan. Now, any such offer is a conditioned offer, first of all, it is strictly conditioned. Secondly, it cannot last for ever and ever. Things happen, things change, and in these nine years the situation has changed tremendously. For three years we waited and then we said: "We are not like Pakistan, carrying on without Constitution, carrying on without elections. Carrying on all this." The Jammu

13. Of 13 August 1948.

and Kashmir Government had a Constituent Assembly to frame a Constitution and they had elections for that.[14] In these five or six years, they had been framing the Constitution, and finally they have framed it.[15] The question of accession of Kashmir to India was really decided in 1947. So far as the Constitution is concerned, it declared it again,[16] it confirmed if you like, that too some months ago. Nothing was going to happen on the 26th January and yet there was a tremendous noise that on 26th January something was going to happen, and this resolution was pushed through, hustled through Security Council, without even trying to understand what the position was, and that nothing was going to happen on the 26th January. Indeed as you well know, the resolution, which the Council passed, was drafted, was in existence even before they have taken the trouble to hear our representative. That is what I call, a casual way of dealing with an important question.

So they had to draft a Constitution of Jammu and Kashmir. The Constituent Assembly is now over. Just as we are holding elections, they are going to hold elections in Jammu and Kashmir.[17] In a sense you will see that we have gone pretty far, not in the old plebiscite sense, but in getting through elections and getting people to elect their representatives. There is going to be new elections in a month or two months time. I think, I believe they are going to be fair and impartial elections. The Prime Minister of Jammu and Kashmir[18] Government has invited pressmen and foreign journalists to come and see, anybody can go and see. There were 70,000 tourists in Kashmir last year. There is no iron curtain or any other curtain there. You can go there also, any of you, and see. We have done all this. What has happened on the other side? Well the area of Kashmir, which is occupied by Pakistan, has of course, had no election, far from that. But look at Pakistan itself. For nine years, ever since they were formed they have had no true elections. Think of that. They talk about plebiscite and other things, and yet in their own great country, they have not been able to have real and true elections, in all these nine years. After enormous effort, they made a Constitution, I think a few months back or a year back, but no elections, even under that. And as for the area which they call "Azad Kashmir", that poor area, has of course,

---

14. Elections to the Constituent Assembly of Jammu and Kashmir were held in September-October 1951.
15. The Constitution of Jammu and Kashmir was adopted on 17 November 1956 and came into force on 26 January 1957.
16. Section 3 of the Constitution of Jammu and Kashmir 1956, states: "The State of Jammu and Kashmir is and shall be an integral part of India."
17. Elections to the Jammu and Kashmir Assembly were held in March 1957.
18. Bakhshi Ghulam Mohammad.

had no chance of elections and it has been incorporated into Pakistan. Another interesting thing for you to remember. There has been this great fuss made about Jammu and Kashmir Government framing its Constitution, in which it reiterates a fact that has been done, that is, its accession to India. But so far as I remember, the Pakistan Constitution has incorporated that part of Jammu and Kashmir State which is in their possession into Pakistan.[19] Nobody shouted then. The Security Council did not move. This fact was mentioned before the Security Council now. But apparently, it did not create any great impression because all that I can say is, they did not listen to what was being said. They have not applied their minds to it. It is extraordinary for people to say that we came in the way of a plebiscite. We could not have had a plebiscite, because no conditions were fulfilled. Plebiscite was to be on both sides. We got stuck up on the preliminary thing of withdrawal of forces. What was said was Pakistan forces must go, root and branch before anything else could be done. Meanwhile, something else happened, and that was the supply of arms to Pakistan in considerable quantities from the United States of America.[20]

The United States has every right to supply arms to Pakistan and Pakistan I suppose has every right to take them. They are independent countries. Who am I to object? But that supply of arms made a great difference to the military situation in regard to India. It made a great difference to the situation even in Kashmir. We told the Pakistan Government that and we also told the other governments that. But we were told—I quite believe their word—by the American Government that these arms are not to be used against you, against India, these are only to be used against aggression. True, I accept it. But how can even the great United States Government stop their use! Everyday or every other day I read in Pakistan newspapers, statements to the effect: "Let us have war, now that we are strong. We are building up our strength." They have got heavy armour, they have got plenty of the latest types of aeroplanes and they live on a fear of hatred and violence. Naturally this causes us concern. I do not want you to reply with hatred and violence. I do not want our students to do what their students in Pakistan did or are doing. I don't want that. But as a responsible government, we have to take all these factors into consideration. They have built airfields in

19. On 29 February 1956 a new Constitution of Pakistan was adopted. This contained a clause stating that territories of states "in accession with or may accede to Pakistan" were a part of that country. Pakistan incorporated Chitral, a part of the state of Jammu and Kashmir, which they said acceded to it in November 1947, by this clause.
20. On 19 May 1954, the Defence Assistance Agreement was signed between Pakistan and the USA for the supply of arms. See *Selected Works* (second series), Vol. 25, pp. 333-335.

Gilgit, Muzaffarabad and other places, which I think, is completely against the ceasefire arrangement or the resolution of the UN Security Council. Gilgit is in the heart of Central Asia in the mountains. It is a serious matter for us that all these big airfields have been built, apart from anything else. Nobody talks about these things because we took up as accommodating an attitude as possible. And now, all our virtue in accommodation is forgotten. We are bound down to it. "Do not go into the past, do not go into aggression. Only talk about the plebiscite, which you agreed to." And even the conditions governing the plebiscite are forgotten. It is a most extraordinary state of affairs. This is a matter of human beings of Kashmir and I do not want any final decision which is against the interests of the people of Kashmir. I do not want to ask for a decision on a legal issue. But when I am charged with dishonourable practices by Pakistan and to some extent by other countries, that I have abrogated my commitments, I have the right to state, what the legal position is and to abide by it. I demand a decision by those people who dare to challenge our bona fides, on this basic issue of aggression because it can occur at any time again.

But leave out the legal aspect, the real thing is the practical aspect, the factual aspect. Let us consider that. Krishna Menon talked about them for nine hours.[21] But there was no reference in subsequent speeches to the points that Krishna Menon had raised. They merely went on and passed a resolution as if nothing had been said on our behalf.[22] It is strange. But look at another aspect. What concerns me and what should concern the Security Council and the world, is that nothing should be done in Jammu and Kashmir State, which instead of solving a problem, creates greater problems. Nothing should be done, which upsets everything. Nothing should be done, which might bring before us the horrors of August and September and October 1947 again. That has been a governing consideration in our minds, and in whatever step we have taken, we have thought of that. Take even this question of plebiscite. From the very first day we said to the UN Commission and Pakistan: "If the conditions we lay down are satisfied and there is complete peace and order, we are prepared to have a plebiscite." I have no doubt in my mind that under fair and peaceful conditions, in conditions where religious fanaticism is not allowed to play, the great number of the people of Kashmir in a plebiscite would decide for India. But apart from the other conditions, we laid stress always that the elections or

21. On 23/24 January 1957.
22. On 24 January 1957, the Security Council passed a resolution stating that the new Constitution of Jammu and Kashmir did not constitute a disposition of the State in accordance with a "free and impartial plebiscite" sought by the UN.

the plebiscite must be held on political and economic issues. We do not want communal riots there and a raging, tearing campaign based on religious bigotry, rousing people's passions. And the Commission agreed. So that this question of Kashmir became, apart from the good of Kashmir, a question of deep significance. Because if a wrong step was taken, it would upset many things in the whole of India, in the whole of Pakistan. We have never accepted and we do not propose to accept the two-nation theory on which Pakistan was founded. In the days before partition when the Muslim League in India flaunted this theory, the Muslims of Kashmir refused to accept it, rejected it, because Kashmir throughout history has been a place of very little communal tension. The Hindus, Muslims, and Buddhists of Kashmir have lived together in amity, whether the rulers have been Muslim or Hindu. Their customs are similar, their religions might be different. They live together, meet together. When India was at the height of communal frenzy, even in August 1947, Kashmir was calm. I do not want Kashmir, in the name of plebiscite, to be made the scene of a fratricidal war and for this to spread to the rest of India and upset the delicate balance that has been established here. It is a matter, therefore, of the most serious concern and consequence to us, that no step is taken in Kashmir, which has these tremendous reactions, whatever may happen then, refugees streaming into Pakistan, refugees streaming into India and all kinds of things happening. And ultimately this is not a solution of the Indo-Pakistan problem, but a worsening of it, and may ultimately lead to war to prevent that happening. So, judging simply from the point of view of consequences, no responsible person or authority can think of a step, which creates these grave upsets in the life of India and of Pakistan and which possibly ruin Kashmir. That is the position.

We talk about the plebiscite and the elections in Kashmir. It would have been more becoming for Pakistan to have their own elections before they talk about it in other places. Many countries are called in, and the Baghdad Pact and the like are referred to. We do not approve of these military alliances. We think they have been the cause not of bringing security but of bringing trouble. And it is quite possible that it is due to all these military alliances that these strange resolutions are passed in regard to Kashmir. But I would venture to say with all respect, that some at least of the countries of the Baghdad Pact, indeed many, were supposed to belong to the 'Free World.' How much freedom do they have? Do they have elections? Do they have a free press? Do they have a free right of assembling? This is the 'Free World' which calls us to have elections and plebiscite in Kashmir, when these countries themselves have no elections and have authoritarian systems of government which everybody knows, do not represent the public mind there. And they censure us! It is a strange world, my friends.

What pains me is that countries which are friends of ours, because we are friendly with all countries, should have considered this difficult question in this casual way. I hope that they will give more thought to it in the future. What pains me is that in Pakistan, all this hatred and passion are raised. It is not good for us, of course, but it is much worse for Pakistan. All our minds are concentrated, on building up our country and our Second Five Year Plan, etc. We do not want it diverted to other matters. If I could help it, I would not take part in any foreign affairs or international issue, but I cannot help it, when issues concerning us come up there. But unfortunately Pakistan's mind is sought to be tied up in this way with violence and hatred against India. I hope they will get over it, because we are not going to reply in kind. We will continue to be friendly with them. Only the other day while all these things were happening, we signed a trade pact[23] in which we went as far as we could to oblige Pakistan. We shall continue this policy because we consider this basically the right policy.

Well, I told you at the beginning that we need not get cold feet and get excited about these matters. That does not help us at any time. Nevertheless, it is a serious situation. We have to keep our minds right and alert. The best way, of course, is for us to work, strengthen our country through the Five Year Plan, etc., and when the elections come, to answer this challenge in the proper way that I have suggested to you. Thank you. *Jai Hind*.

23. See *post*, p. 643.

7. The Challenges Ahead[1]

I returned from the South three hours ago and am here before you now. As you heard just now the excuse for this meeting is elections and sitting behind me are the candidates. Only five are here I am told, because it is not possible to accommodate everyone on the dais. I am bothered about other things besides the elections. There are more complex problems before us. I want to share with you my thoughts about the situation in the country and the world. It is not enough to make an ordinary election speech before you. It is obvious that as a member of the Congress of forty-five years standing, my entire life is linked with the Congress. I have become a part of it and whatever I have done or become, it is through the Congress. I have grown a little through the Congress. So it is obvious that I love this grand and strong party which has made history in India in the past decades and will undoubtedly do so in the future.

Many weaknesses and evils have crept into the Congress as is inevitable in a large organization of this kind because if it represents the people of India, then their weaknesses as well as excellence gets reflected in the party. We make efforts to get rid of these evils and sometimes we succeed and sometimes we do not. But the question that we come round to again and again, is the fundamental path that we have to follow and the institution through which we can achieve our goals. Individuals can function separately and do good work. But national tasks can be done only through institutions. I do not mean only in politics but whatever the task may be, only organized effort can show results. We cannot implement the Five Year Plans by allowing individuals, however good they may be, to do as they like. That would not yield any result. But if there is a united effort in a particular direction, it will be fruitful.

Take, for instance, the problem of war. We recruit an army. The basis of a good army is discipline and the capacity to work together. Once a decision is taken, everyone follows it. It is better that even if the decision is second-rate, everybody falls in line rather than take a great decision in which nobody cooperates. So discipline and organized effort is absolutely essential in all big tasks including governmental work.

Two or three things are very important. One, if there is real democracy in India, we have to involve the maximum number of people in the task of decision-

1. Speech at a public meeting to inaugurate the election campaign of the Delhi Pradesh Congress Committee, Ramlila grounds, Delhi, 3 February 1957. AIR tapes, NMML. Original in Hindi.

making and implementation. The maximum number of people must shoulder the responsibilities. When the king rules, the responsibility is solely his and perhaps that of his ministers. But the ministers are also appointed by the king. We do not want that. A good king may do a great deal for the country. But the entire system is wrong. The masses do not grow in stature under that system. They can grow only by shouldering responsibilities. The modern nations in particular cannot grow unless the responsibility is delegated to the people. Power should not be concentrated in the hands of a few. We have elections every five years or so. It is not a very satisfactory method. Elections are all right but some arrangement should be made whereby the responsibilities of the nation are delegated among the people and remain so. Only then can a nation become really strong. But these things take time. It cannot be done by passing laws. On the one hand people must have complete freedom to express their opinions and thrash out issues. But once a decision is taken, the people must have the ability to implement it together. Democracy is not a matter of passing laws, it has to take roots among the people.

There are not many countries in the world today where there is democracy. Even those which are called democratic lack the essential qualifications of a democracy. Take, for instance, the right to vote. In India, everyone above the age of twenty-one has the right to vote. Some other countries have this system. But I think just thirty or forty years ago, it was not the practice in any country. There are many countries even today which call themselves democracies but do not have adult franchise. In some European countries, women even today do not have the right to vote. What is democracy? There should be adult franchise and the people's right to choose their own government. These are by no means enough. There should be other things as well. But the important thing is to have some system of checks and balances and a control over the government so that it does not ride roughshod over the people's will.

So, as I said, adult franchise is a new development in the world. Other countries have had it for the last thirty, forty years and India for about ten years. It has not been put to a long test yet. We had general elections five years ago which were conducted on a grand scale. It was completely open and fair, people had freedom to express their opinions and the final decision had to be accepted by everyone. There is no other method for the alternative can only be to rule by force where a handful of people can suppress others. These are the only two alternatives. If you look around you, you will find that there are very few countries where democracy in the real sense has been established. I am talking about political democracy.

Then comes economic democracy. The fact is that by giving a vote to every adult, we cannot ensure equality. It is obvious that we are not doing a starving individual a favour by giving him the right to vote. But by giving him a vote, we are giving him the right to demand food. So it is a good step. Democracy is a pretty complex thing and it is very essential that people should understand it well. You can have a democracy only by shouldering responsibilities and gaining experience. It is very essential in a democracy for the masses to understand the problems which the country faces. After all, ultimately it is they who will have to find a solution. So it is not a question merely of casting a vote but of understanding the issues and shouldering responsibilities, to learn to carry the burdens as well as enjoy the benefits of the system. Democracy does not mean merely presenting your demands. You have to discharge your responsibilities to society and the country too. Rights involve responsibilities. If you have the right to get something out of society, you have a responsibility towards it too, to help society in any way you can. We are all parts of a society which involves the entire population of the country. Democracy cannot function if, as some people seem to imagine, it is regarded as merely the right to make demands upon the society. The scale has to be equally balanced. You can get out of society only as much as you give to it. You cannot get more than that. Otherwise you and the society will go bankrupt.

Everyone lays stress on rights but hardly anyone on duties. It is essential to conform to some discipline even in small things. For instance, there are rules regulating traffic which everyone has to conform to. Otherwise there would be chaos. As a society grows more complex, traditions and rules governing the people's way of life start evolving. If you choose to live in a jungle, cut off from society, you can do what you like. You will not do anyone harm but neither will anybody benefit. You live for yourself. When millions of people live together in a society, then duties multiply. As a nation advances and production and trade increase, the life of the society becomes more and more complex.

How is the life of a society to be regulated so that everyone can benefit? If every individual follows the law of the jungle and looks only to his own interest, there will be chaos. In a democracy, everyone has to understand their rights and duties. It is obvious that there are great difficulties in that. If you have a crowd of ten thousand people, we cannot say with any degree of certainty that they will always follow the right path or understand the issues involved. They can always go astray and do wrong things or behave in an uncivilized manner. It is not right to say that the opinion of a crowd is always correct. But there is no alternative. If the people follow the wrong path for too long, democracy will fail.

We have often seen this happening in countries where there was democracy once. I am talking about Western countries. In Asia, it has not taken roots at all. There are very few countries in the world today where there is democracy. Democracy can be of many kinds. The Soviet Union calls itself a democratic republic and it is, in a sense. But on the other hand, it is not truly democratic in that there is no freedom of expression. They too have elections but not like we do in India. A list of names is published which has to be accepted. There are no other candidates to choose from. The people have to vote for the official candidates only. I am not criticizing anyone. I am merely pointing out the various systems which prevail in the world.

You are to some extent familiar with the system that we have adopted. Its basis is freedom of thought and expression, whether it is in newspapers, books or speeches, provided there is no abuse or slander involved. Politically, there is complete freedom. People have the right to criticize the government and to point out its mistakes. In all this free discussion, mistakes are often rectified. The only problem is that if there is too much of discussions and debates, it becomes difficult to stick to something for very long. It can be pointed out that in the Soviet Union and China, there is only one line to follow and everybody has to toe the line. The people are not free to criticize it. That has certain advantages in that everyone follows a single line and the work gets done quicker. On the other hand, human beings cannot develop fully under such a system for the lack of freedom of expression is stultifying.

We have chosen the path of parliamentary democracy. We have a parliament to which members are elected by the people. For instance, in the coming general elections, if I or my colleagues or the Congress party loses, we cannot protest against it. We will have to accept the decision of the people. I would have the right to criticize the people who are elected but I would have to accept them whether I like it or not. This is what democracy means. It does not give you the right to reject those who are not to your liking. The real test of a democracy lies in accepting something which is opposed to your own views provided there has been an opportunity for everyone to express their opinion and for fair and free elections before that. After that, the verdict of the masses has to be accepted. Even if it means a slight slowing down of the pace of progress it ensures that the strength of the entire country is behind the ultimate decision.

I am trying to put before you some very ordinary facts which even a school child must know about. Children must be taught in schools about our Constitution, democracy and the responsibilities it entails, etc., because all of you have to shoulder them. People often tend to forget the ordinary things. So I thought I should remind the people about them particularly in view of the coming elections. There are some fundamental things which will make India strong. There must be a fundamental unity, strength and understanding among the people. I do not mean that everybody should become "yes men". Unity means that everyone must have the opportunity to express his views and be heard. Then it is up to the people to make up their minds. But there must be a basic tolerance of other points of view, tolerance for other religions and castes and provinces and languages. All of us belong to one large family.

There is great diversity in India and yet we are one. Therefore we must live in mutual harmony and cooperation. It is in that that our unity lies. It is by showing a united front that we got independence. Casteism is an ancient malady which has divided India into innumerable compartments. There was no unity in the country. The various kings and rulers used to fight among themselves. This is a very old weakness of ours. So the first lesson that we had to learn in order to get independence was of unity. We had to forget our differences and remember that we are all Indians.

Many factors were responsible for spreading this idea. But there is no doubt that it was the Congress, which did the most in this direction. Its doors were open to everyone, to people of all religions, provinces and to anyone who considered himself an Indian. It unified the people under one banner. One of the greatest services that the Congress has done to the nation was to take up the cause of the poor, downtrodden untouchables and work for their uplift.

Secondly, under the leadership of Mahatma Gandhi, we learnt to work in mutual harmony and cooperation, to make sacrifices and to achieve our goals through the path of non-violence. This was great training. Gandhiji was the greatest apostle of peace and non-violence. We learnt a little from him. But apart from the fact that they are good principles, can you imagine what would have happened if we had not fought for freedom by peaceful methods? The result would have been that the country would have broken up. Everyone would have been at one another's throats and warring groups would have sprung up everywhere. India would have broken up into fragments. So, even apart from the morality of these principles, if you look at it from the practical point of view, you will reach the same conclusion.

As far as democracy is concerned, it means peaceful method of working. Every issue must be open to free discussion and the majority opinion should be accepted. That does not mean that the majority should suppress other viewpoints. The minorities, religious or otherwise, must have their say. They must enjoy equal rights and ought to be protected. On the other hand, the majority opinion must prevail. Only then can there be a balance.

Well, these are some of the aspects that we should bear in mind. The fact is that the Congress has done the most during the last seventy-two years to spread these ideas in the country. Others outside the Congress have also done a great deal. I do not say that there are people outside the Congress are no good. There are extremely intelligent and able people with a spirit of sacrifice. But at the moment, we are not judging individuals though that must be done too. When we have to take on great tasks, we have to see which organization can enable us to achieve our goals. Looked at from that point of view, it is obvious that the Congress is the only party which fits the bill.

There are various other parties in the country. But among the prominent ones, there are three or four communal parties. I have said repeatedly that they have no place in the modern world. It is our stupidity that we still have them in India. I say this because they have no understanding of the problems of our age. They keep repeating lessons learnt by rote which have no relevance to the present. They incite people in the name of religion, but they have no concrete economic programme. The moment you adopt the path of communalism you weaken India's unity which has been created with great difficulty. There can be no nationalism if the people of different religions stand under separate banners. Everyone is welcome to his own religion. But the moment you mix religion with politics, it destroys the spirit of nationalism.

Nationalism implies that people of different religions and provinces, speaking different languages live under a single banner in harmony. Therefore these communal parties have no relevance in the present times. It is precisely this kind of attitude and thinking which led to India's downfall in the past. We must stay far away from them. Then there are other parties like the Socialist Party, the Praja Socialist Party and the Communist Party, etc. I do not want to say very much about them because I do not wish to criticize other parties. There are old friends and colleagues in all of them. The question is what each party has to offer as a concrete programme and whether it is capable of delivering the goods. Anyone can sit down and draw up a list of things that we want to do. But they will not get done by putting our wishes down on paper. It is an extremely difficult task to uplift millions of human beings and to eradicate poverty from the country.

How is this to be done? It is obvious that we cannot expect other countries to give us money. We will take whatever is given with grateful thanks. But ultimately India can progress only by the effort and hard work of the people. Whatever the people produce from land and factories, etc., constitutes wealth. The harder we work, the more wealthy India will become and the standard of living of the people will improve. We must of course, ensure that the wealth which is produced does not remain in a few pockets. That is why we have adopted socialism as our goal so that there is greater equality among the people.

I do not know what the thinking of the Communist Party is. I am saying this because it is fundamentally opposed to democratic methods of functioning. Their method is different. I do not wish to criticize anyone. So the question that arises is whether upheaval and turmoil can benefit the country. The communists believe in violence. I do not say that that is their intention here. But they believe in turning everything upside down and making a complete break. There is no freedom of expression or thought in communist countries. So the question is whom you should vote for. Are you in favour of democracy and constitutional government? Do you believe that India will progress by following this method? Or do you like the communist method of creating chaos and then building afresh? I cannot understand why anyone must break something which exists. Why must we face the difficulties and problems which followed in the wake of revolutions in other countries? So this basic question must be resolved.

The communists talk of a joint front which is good thing. But a joint front can function successfully only when there is a consensus of opinion. Otherwise it will be a joint front only in name to mislead the people. The Praja Socialist Party is not very different in its principles from the Congress though there are other differences. But I am sorry to say that I cannot see any other party in the country with the strength to carry India's burdens. There is no cohesion in any of them. Efforts are made to form alliances with parties which are completely opposed to them in principles and ideals.

Taking all this into account, I think that at this juncture in our history, we cannot allow ourselves to become weak. If small splinter groups come to power, even if they are good men, they will lack the strength to shoulder the responsibilities of the country. That will be extremely harmful to the country. I am always in favour of a strong opposition with complete freedom of expression, and the liberty to criticize the government and point out its mistakes. Healthy debate can help to rectify mistakes and educate the people. But the conclusion that can be drawn at the moment is that only the Congress can take on the big responsibilities of the nation. I am referring to the biggest responsibility of all, the effort to create emotional integration among the people.

India is no doubt one on the map. But did you see the kind of storm that was raised over the question of states reorganization? I agree that this is an issue over which people can have strong views. But ultimately, whether you live in Madras, Delhi, Uttar Pradesh, Bombay or anywhere else, your basic status is that of a citizen of India. That is the only thing that counts. Your progress depends on the progress of India.

In spite of all this, there was such a storm in some parts of India that I was aghast. There were firings and hooliganism. This shows a fundamental weakness in us. It was wholly opposed to the principles of democracy. Everyone has the right to express his views, to hold meetings and debates. But to beat up people and indulge in looting and arson, etc., is not the way to force an issue. Take for instance, the provinces of Uttar Pradesh and Bihar. There is no quarrel between them. I am merely giving you an example. Suppose there is a district or two on the borders of both the states, there should not be any problem in deciding the issue one way or the other. I for one am not interested if a district or two or a few villages go to Bengal, Bihar or Uttar Pradesh. It is all the same to me. All I want is that matters should be settled to the satisfaction of everyone as far as possible. Uttar Pradesh and Bihar cannot go to war with one another over this issue. If they do, we will reach a stage when India will be divided into hundreds of fragments, all at one another's throats.

Therefore such matters should be considered peacefully and the decision acceptable to the majority must be arrived at. Even if it is not to the liking of a few, it does not matter much because after all there is no decision which is binding for all times. It can be changed if necessary. It is not proper that we should squabble over petty issues like this. I have seen that the smaller parties are only too keen to jump into the fray when such disputes arise. I personally feel that the big uproar which was created last year over this issue was, at least in part, due to the fact that elections were round the corner. The path was being paved for that. It was not so much a question of states reorganisation as an attempt to incite the people before the elections.

I am giving you an example to show how we can be led astray. It is not a sign of strength but of weakness. It is not a sign of democracy but just the opposite. If it spreads, a few hundred hooligans with lathis will try to bully the people into falling in with their viewpoint. This is not democracy. Therefore the most important task before us even today is the emotional integration among the people. Political integration has taken place. But we must not deceive ourselves into thinking that that is enough. It is the Congress which brought about political integration and can do a great deal more for the country.

The second great task before us is the economic betterment of the people and the Five Year Plans are symbols of our effort to achieve that goal. It is an extremely complex problem. How can the people become better off? There are no reserves from where money and goods can be distributed. The people can acquire a better standard of living only by their own effort. We have to make arrangements to see to it that production increases. The Five Year Plans are aimed at this. We want to step up agricultural production to the level which obtains in other countries. We want to industrialize the country and set up cottage industries which will reduce the level of unemployment and add to the national wealth.

How is all this to be ensured? We cannot leave it to individuals to do as they like. Planning is extremely important. I do not mean that the Plan document is something rigid which cannot be improved upon. We have done what we felt was right. We will try to rectify the mistakes that we may have made. We will learn from our mistakes and experience. That is why we have adopted socialism as our goal. But even there we are not in favour of a rigid dogma but have adopted the fundamental principles of socialism. It has to be suited to the needs of the country and a pattern will emerge gradually with time and experience.

You must have read about the painful events which have occurred in Europe recently, particularly in Hungary. But I want to draw your attention to the fact that their economic condition had deteriorated because they were insisting on following a rigid line. They opted for industrialization on a very large-scale which made the development in these countries lopsided. There were food shortages and unemployment which have led to great hardships among the people. The political upheavals were as a result of the economic problems, they were facing.

So these matters can neither be left to the people nor be put in a rigid framework imposing a great burden upon the people. That is why we have adopted the broad principles of socialism. The pattern that will ultimately emerge depends on our own experience. We have to see to it that agriculture and industrialization are equally balanced. If it is weighed down one way or the other, it will be harmful. Then, as I said, industrialization can be at various levels. There are heavy industries like the steel plants. Then there are medium industries which produce basic consumer goods. Thirdly, cottage and village industries are also extremely important because there is great unemployment in the country. All these things have to be finely balanced. This is where planning comes in.

Moreover people have to be trained to man all these industries and projects. We have taken up huge river valley schemes for which we need thousands of engineers and overseers. We are trying to spread the Community Projects and the National Extension Service to the rural areas. I consider these to be revolutionary schemes because 80 per cent of India's population lives in the rural areas and is largely dependent on land. Until that segment of the population progresses, India cannot develop. The rural areas have been stagnant for centuries. The cities of Delhi, Bombay, Calcutta and Madras have grown at the expense of the poor farmer for more than a century. Well, we mean no harm to the cities. We want them to progress. But ultimately India's progress depends upon the 80 per cent of the population which lives in the rural areas. I feel that the development projects are revolutionary because they are transforming the rural areas. They help the people to step up agricultural production, open schools, build roads and help in a hundred other ways. If everyone contributes a little the result would be staggering. The Government cannot do it by itself. These block development schemes were started about four years and five months ago,[2] which is not a long period. It has already spread to a lakh and thirty thousand villages. Our aim is to cover thirty to forty thousand villages every year. The impact has not been uniform. But taking everything into consideration, it has transformed

2. On 2 October 1952.

the face of the villages which have these schemes. That is why I say that it is a revolutionary step.

There has to be careful thinking about all these matters. Even as far as the plans are concerned we have declared that there will be an annual assessment and whatever changes are necessary will be made. Now we are facing another great problem in the form of inflation. I am not talking about the price rise in India because we can take steps to curb it. But we have to import machines from abroad and great inflation has taken place in the United States and Germany. We are having to pay more for everything which has upset our previous calculations. As it is, the burden was heavy and the inflation has increased it further. On the one hand, we do not wish to slow down our rate of progress. On the other hand, it makes our burden heavier. This is the complication which you must understand. After all, ultimately the burden has to be borne by all of us. If we want to accelerate the pace of progress, we will have to reconcile ourselves to carrying heavier burdens. It is up to us to decide how fast we wish to go. If the pace is too slow, we cannot get rid of our poverty quickly. If we increase the pace, we will have to carry a heavier burden. All these things have to be taken into consideration. The Five Year Plan is a big task. I do not say that only the congressmen should do the work of planning. People of all parties are welcome to join in. The problem is that some people are averse to doing so. The communists and the socialists are not very keen and feel that given the opportunity, they would change the whole thing drastically. We will only waste our time in making all these changes and there will be no concrete results. Taking all this into account, I arrive at the conclusion that it has become more than ever essential to have a strong government capable of shouldering these burdens. Everyone is welcome to join in these national tasks.

There is another aspect of the problem. That is the situation in the world. It is often said particularly about me and the Government too that Jawaharlal spends all his time in thinking about international affairs and less about the domestic problems. This is absolutely wrong. Left to myself, I would concentrate all our energies on national tasks. I do not wish to interfere in the affairs of any other country. Our first task is to set our own affairs in order. We can make an impact on world affairs only when we become strong. Otherwise it is futile to make statements in the air. So I want to put all our energies into solving our domestic problems.

However, this is not a matter of my choosing. The world has shrunk and we cannot remain aloof, particularly an independent country like India. We come into contact with the outside world in innumerable ways, for trade and other purposes. Indians are spread out all over the world. We have to send our students abroad for training in engineering, science, etc. We need trained personnel. We are a member of the United Nations. No nation in the world today can afford to remain aloof. Yes, in one sense, we have remained aloof and that is from the military agreements and pacts which exist between the great powers. As you know, we have not come to a military agreement with any country. We have always said that we wish to maintain friendly relations with every nation and not get into military pacts against one or the other. This has been our fundamental policy. It has angered some nations in the past. But we have stood firm and I think benefitted by it. We could not have chosen any other path because our thinking has been conditioned by the tradition of thousands of years. We cut ourselves off from our moorings if we give up this path. So in that sense, we have remained aloof. But we have contacts with the outside world. We cannot remain aloof. We have to express our views on various issues, in the United Nations and elsewhere.

The problem is that as a nation becomes more important and gains in stature, its contacts with the outside world grows in proportion. We did not have much to do with the outside world when we were under British rule. The British Government conducted India's foreign policy so much so that we were not consulted when India was to be involved in the Second World War. But since independence, our contacts have grown. So you may be rest assured that I am fully convinced that our most important task is to set our own house in order and find a solution for our problems. Above all, we would like to keep away from the disputes in the world. But no independent nation of any stature in the world today has any hope of keeping aloof from other countries. Contacts have to be maintained for various purposes.

We do not wish to go to war with anyone. But if there is a war anywhere in the world it is bound to have an impact upon us. As you know, modern warfare has become extremely dangerous with lethal weapons like the atom bomb which can lead to total destruction. So we have to make an effort as far as our strength permits to mediate and throw our weight in the cause of peace. So we are drawn willy-nilly into world affairs. It is not that we are particularly enamoured of playing a great role on the world stage. Those who think so are mistaken. India's voice will be heard in world affairs only if we are strong as a nation. Our problem is that though we lack military and economic strength there is great respect for India in the world. Our strength does not match our stature in any way. This is a fact. We do not wish to deceive anyone. It is simply not possible. India's stature in the world has grown immeasurably.

India is in great demand in world affairs. We were asked to mediate in the Korean war. We were called in in Indo-China. We have had to send in our troops to both places in the cause of peace, not to fight. India is often chosen to mediate between two warring sides because we have no enmity with any country. So we are involved even though we try to refuse to do so. Moreover, how can we refuse when it is in a good cause? The main thing is that the world has become so tightly knit that no nation can afford to cut itself off.

I have been talking at random. But I am sure the question of Kashmir must be uppermost in your mind. First of all, I would like to say that when I reached here and saw the newspapers today, I found that our students had taken out a procession to the Pakistan High Commissioner's house to demonstrate and made a great deal of noise and threw stones and what not.[3] I was extremely unhappy to read about this not merely because I think that what they did was wrong but also because it has come in our way. The Kashmir issue is an extremely complex and difficult one. As you can understand, we cannot solve this problem by demonstrations and shouting slogans. It will have the opposite effect on world opinion. It is most improper that our students should try to copy the behaviour of Pakistan. Such things have happened in Pakistan. There were demonstrations in front of our High Commissioner's house and effigies were burnt.[4] All this is absolutely wrong and does not solve any problem. I do not have any control over the actions of the people of Pakistan. But we must not imitate them in a fit of anger. I request you, particularly our students, not to indulge in such activities because they will harm us now and will continue to do so. It is easy to hold demonstrations. But against whom? Against Pakistan. Two wrongs do not make one right. You will only complicate things more.

Everyone is free to express their views, hold meetings, etc. Even then I would say that you should not behave in an uncivilized manner or abuse the Pakistani leaders and statesmen. You are welcome to express your views on issues. But the more patiently you express yourselves, the more conviction you will carry. Hooliganism does not solve anything. Such elements are there in both the countries. Therefore I shall humbly but forcefully point out to all of you and particularly our students that we are facing difficult problems and such activities do not help us in any way. So please be patient. This is a testing time for all of us. You must prepare yourselves mentally and physically for the problems that the future may bring. A nation in panic cannot think or act clearly. We need stout hearts and calm minds at the moment.

This is one thing. The second thing is that no matter what the problems are, my request to you is not to get carried away. We must abide by the decision

3. On 2 February, anti-Pakistan demonstrations took place in Delhi. The police used tear-gas to disperse students demonstrating outside the Pakistan High Commissioner's residence.
4. On 26 January, anti-India demonstrations occurred in Karachi, Lahore, Hyderabad (Sind) and Dhaka in protest against the adoption of a new constitution for Kashmir. In Karachi, demonstrators attacked the Indian High Commissioner's office and burnt Nehru's effigy. In Lahore, the Deputy High Commissioner's office was attacked and his residence stoned.

taken on behalf of our country. This is very essential. This is the real symbol of a strong nation. Other things are childish which often cause harm. As you know, the Kashmir dispute is nine years old and there have been great many ups and downs. You may remember how the whole thing started. There was an attack on Kashmir by Pakistan. The war went on and the United Nations appointed a commission. I will not go into those things. It is true that right from the beginning, we have been so keen to settle the matter peacefully that we tried everything. We did not lay as much stress on what was rightfully ours as we should have. We have said all along that if some minimum conditions were fulfilled, we would accept a plebiscite in Jammu and Kashmir. This was one thing.

However, you must remember that various issues are linked to this. It cannot be considered in isolation. First of all plebiscite can be held only when the Pakistani forces are withdrawn from the soil of Kashmir. There are various other things. Once they are settled peacefully, a plebiscite can be held. I am repeating this here to show that we have not forgotten our promises. The complaint is often made particularly about me and to some extent about India that we break our promises made to the world community. I do not care about myself but it grieves me to hear such things being said about India. I think that India is a great nation and her greatness lies in abiding by her commitments. We must be firm in our intentions whether they are to do with domestic policy or international affairs.

In short, we must keep our promises. Speaking in Madras two or three days ago,[5] I had said that I would like to be shown in what way we have reneged on our promises. If it is true then there are only two courses open to me. Either I fulfil that promise or if I cannot, I should quit my post as Prime Minister. I did not say that I was quitting. I said that if I cannot keep my promises, I do not want India's reputation to be soiled. India's honour is sacred to me and having grown up under Gandhiji's shadow, it would be wrong on my part to do anything to sully that.

I would like to point out humbly that for anyone to say that we have broken our promise is totally wrong. I would like to ask the foreign countries and their newspapers what is the promise that we have broken. They say that we had promised to hold a plebiscite there which we have not done. My answer to that is that they should see what our conditions for doing so were. There is no secret about it. It is clearly laid down. Our first condition was that the Pakistani forces must be withdrawn. We would have been within our rights to demand that the United Nations should rule that Pakistan had committed aggression. But Pakistan

5. See the preceding item.

is after all our neighbour. We did not want to humiliate them unnecessarily. But that does not mean that we should give up our rights. So we have tried our best to arrive at some peaceful solution so that our relations with Pakistan remain good as is proper between two neighbours. The people of India and Pakistan have lived as one nation for centuries.

So we presented various proposals. What I am trying to point out to you and others is that I am quite clear in my mind that we have not gone back on our word in any way. Anyone who can prove to the contrary is welcome to do so. As far as a plebiscite is concerned you have to see whether Pakistan has fulfilled our conditions. Promises cannot be kept unilaterally. The fault lies with Pakistan. The strange thing is that India is made out to be the culprit before the United Nations whereas it was we who took the dispute there.

Now what can I say? I cannot understand why people do not understand something which is crystal clear. It is unfortunate that some of the powers are annoyed with India for various reasons. Then there are some countries which are linked together in military pacts and alliances and so they have to help one another. The Kashmir issue is not considered on its merits by them and their judgement is swayed by other considerations.

I mentioned the Baghdad Pact. Every nation has the right to enter into agreements and pacts with other countries. Who are we to object? But when the Baghdad Pact was signed, we had raised our voice against it because it would vitiate the already tense atmosphere and would not help the cause of peace. That is exactly what did happen. It created a rift among the Arab nations and the atmosphere has become very tense. I do not think anybody can claim that the Baghdad Pact has helped in any way to maintain peace.

You may remember that two or three years ago, the question of American aid to Pakistan came up. The United States is a great power and has every right to give aid to whomever it likes. Pakistan is an independent country and is free to take aid. Who am I to interfere? American statesmen had said even then that if India wanted military aid, they were prepared to give it to us. We thanked them and said that it was not our policy to accept military aid from anyone.[6] We buy what we need. But we saw that American military aid to Pakistan would be bad for the region though we could not object to a free country taking aid if it wished to. Our fears were realized. One of the reasons for the complexity of the Kashmir problem is that Pakistan has got a large volume of military aid from outside. It is true that the American Government assured us that the aid was not directed against India. On the contrary, the United States had warned Pakistan particularly

6. See *Selected Works* (second series), Vol. 25, pp. 335-343.

against misusing the aid in this way. I am sure the United States must have instructed Pakistan. But you can also imagine that once arms are acquired, it is difficult to say when and against whom they are likely to be used. This is the complication in this matter.

However, it is obvious that the issue is so complex that I hesitate to say very much about it in public meetings. Our representative[7] will discuss the matter and put forward the government's point of view. I do not want to go into the complexities of the affair in a public meeting. But I would like to place some broad facts before you. First of all, we have not gone back on any kind of international commitment and nor will we do so. I want to make that quite clear. All I can say is that those who say such things in the Security Council or in foreign newspapers do not know the facts. Secondly, as we have said right from the beginning, we do not wish to solve the Kashmir issue or anything else by military methods. If there is an attack on India, it is obvious that we will have to use our armed forces. But right from the beginning we have been in favour of a peaceful solution to these disputes.

Thirdly, in the last eight to nine years, this affair has taken many turns. Volumes of papers have accumulated on the subject, ten or twelve of them. There have been a great many ups and downs. The reason is that eight years ago, when the question of plebiscite first arose, we had accepted it with certain provisos, one of which was that the sovereignty of Kashmir was linked with India's. The Commission had accepted it at that time.[8] Why has it not been fulfilled in all these years? It gives one food for thought, doesn't it? There have been obstacles. Let us leave aside the question of who is to blame. The United Nations has sent down various teams which tried to find a way out. In our opinion, the blame lies at Pakistan's door. But even leaving that aside, the fact remains that no solution has been found. The Pakistani forces have not been withdrawn. But the world does not stand still because plebiscite had not been held in Kashmir. Elections were held in Kashmir, that is, in the areas which were not under Pakistani occupation. An Assembly was duly elected which is more than one can say about the territory under Pakistani occupation. We did things our way and laws were passed. This has been going on for years. The entire face of Kashmir has been transformed in the last six to seven years. Circumstances have changed. Now it is absurd to make accusations as if nothing had happened all these years as though the world had been standing still. All aspects of the problem must be taken into account before deciding why we have had to do what we have done.

7. V.K. Krishna Menon, leader of the Indian delegation to the UN.
8. See *Selected Works* (second series), Vol. 7, p. 303.

The problem is that the Security Council Resolution[9] does not go into all this. They have accepted without proper inquiry that something dramatic is going to happen on the 26th of January and that perhaps Kashmir will be merged with India. This is wrong. Whatever could be done legally was done nine years ago and it has been incorporated in the Constitution of Kashmir in last November. Nothing was going to happen on the 26th of January except that the Constituent Assembly of Kashmir was going to be dissolved. The whole thing was blown up as if we were doing something. The Government of India had done nothing. The Kashmir Constituent Assembly had started its work, three or four years ago, of drawing up a constitution which was completed in November. The Constitution reiterated what had been accepted earlier, that Kashmir would remain with India. Nothing new was about to take place in the 26th of January. But a resolution was quickly passed in the Security Council saying that we were breaking our word. There is no truth in this. The newspapers have been playing it up.

I said that I hoped the Security Council would bear in mind what was in the interest of Kashmir. It is obvious that there are many other considerations before us like the question of India's rights and national interest. I am responsible for that but I would not for a moment think of doing something which will be against the interests of Kashmir. It is obvious that India does not want to hold on to Kashmir by force, nor can it do so. Ultimately, we can maintain this relationship only with the consent of the people of Kashmir.

However, as I said the foremost consideration in my mind has always been the interest of Kashmir. Anyone can see for themselves what has been happening there in the last few years and compare it to conditions in "Azad Kashmir". But apart from looking at the superficial advantages it is crucial to consider the consequences of any step that we may take. If the step that we take is bad for the people of Kashmir and instead of bringing about peace it leads to war, then that step is bad.

How can I go into all the details in one single speech? But I would like to tell you that it is a complex matter. First of all, I want to see where the interests of the people of Kashmir lie. Secondly we do not want to take any step which will lead to so much upheaval that all that we have done in the past will be undone. The consequences of such a step would be far-reaching. Moreover it is always my desire that relations between India and Pakistan should improve because two neighbouring countries cannot live in a state of tension and under threat of war. Any upheaval at the moment would cause a setback to that too. Therefore

9. Of 24 January 1957.

87

we have to tread very carefully. That is why we have to request the Security Council humbly to take all these things into account and not get carried away by other considerations. But it is difficult. As I said, so far at least, there has been hardly any examination of these facts.

There is some talk in the resolution introduced by the Pakistani representative[10] to the United Nations that both Indian and Pakistani troops must be withdrawn from Kashmir and the UN forces sent there. Even eight years ago, when the UN Commission was going into this issue, this was never suggested. On the contrary it was decided that Pakistan should withdraw their forces completely. On our side, it was accepted that we had the right to maintain our troops there since there had been one attack already. It is true that it was agreed upon that when Pakistan withdrew its forces, we would reduce our own troops to the minimum. The exact words were to the effect that we would remove the bulk of our forces.[11] But Kashmir's security was our responsibility and it would have been a breach of promise to withdraw the troops completely. This was made clear even at that time. I am amazed that anyone should come up with something diametrically opposite now.

I do not want to go into more details, but I have also said in another context that we would not tolerate foreign troops on even an inch of Indian territory. We have tolerated Pakistani troops only for the sake of peace. Unfortunately they are still there in our part of Kashmir. I have not broken any promise. They cite the example of our forces which have been sent to Egypt. But there is no comparison. Our forces have gone there with the consent of the Government of Egypt.[12]

You will find that the foreign newspapers are very annoyed with me personally. They are gloating over the fact that Jawaharlal has been humiliated. Well, they are welcome to do. My stature depends on my own countrymen. Outsiders can do nothing. But I do feel upset to see India being maligned. Individuals come and go. But it grieves me to hear such one-sided views about my beloved country. We are not a great military power. But we have tried to follow the right path, to strive for peace and to be friendly towards all countries. If in spite of our efforts we do not succeed and other countries have an adverse opinion about us, I agree that it must be my fault. I must have taken some wrong step. I do not know. I keep looking for that. But my request to you is that you must not allow yourselves

10. Feroz Khan Noon, the Foreign Minister of Pakistan proposed this to the Security Council on 16 January.
11. Under the terms of the Truce Agreement of the UNCIP Resolution of 13 August 1948.
12. See *Selected Works* (second series), Vol. 35, p. 438.

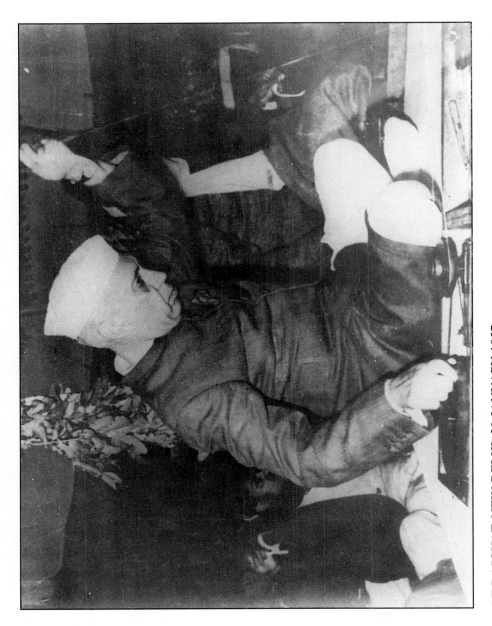

AT RAJGHAT, NEW DELHI, 30 JANUARY 1957

COLLECTING RUNS

February 17, 1957

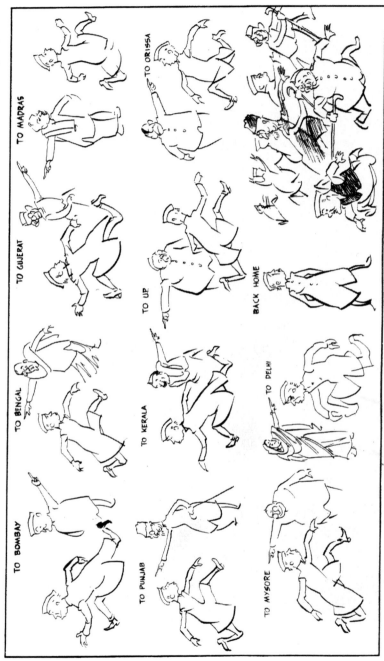

Nehru's presence to bolster the Congress election campaign is demanded in every state

(Top row) S.K. Patil, Roy, Morarji Desai and Kamaraj Nadar (middle row) Maulana Azad, Dhebar, Govind Ballabh Pant and Hare Krushna Mehtab

FROM: "*DON'T SPARE ME SHANKAR: JAWAHARLAL NEHRU*"

to be carried away over this Kashmir issue. You must keep yourselves under control. We must be calm and try to find a peaceful solution. *Jai Hind*. Please say *Jai Hind* with me thrice: *Jai Hind, Jai Hind, Jai Hind*.

8. Congress and India's Emotional Integration[1]

In what capacity have I presented myself today, as a candidate for election or something else? I function in many different capacities. If I had been merely a candidate for election, I would not have come here for I would have been ashamed to do so. It seems somehow wrong to me that I should mention to you that I am standing from this constituency and ask you to vote for me. Ours is an old relationship and we ought to know one another well. My asking for votes makes no difference. But I feel it is my duty to visit my constituency at least once. Allahabad is no doubt my city, my district. But now all the cities and districts of India have equal claims upon me. It is true that I have great fondness for this city, this district because I have worked for years in the beginning in this area and other districts of Uttar Pradesh.

I have been offered many places in different parts of the country to contest the elections from. I would stand from any constituency because whatever my good points or weaknesses may be, I consider myself a soldier who should do the job which is entrusted to him. Let me tell you a secret. Those who decided that I should stand from this particular constituency[2] in Allahabad did not consult me about it. They decided and I accepted without any question.

I contested from Allahabad district in the last elections also. The difference is that last time my constituency had nothing to do with the city of Allahabad and now one ward of the city, Rasulpur, has been included in it. Well, I prefer to contest from my own city or its neighbouring areas.

You may remember that last time my old friend and comrade, Shri Tandon,[3] had contested from Allahabad. I think politically we are the oldest associates in

1. Speech at a public meeting, Allahabad, 6 February 1957. AIR tapes, NMML. Original in Hindi. Extracts. Nehru arrived on a election tour of Uttar Pradesh on 6 February 1957.
2. Phulpur constituency.
3. Purushottam Das Tandon, Congress member from Allahabad and a former Congress President.

Allahabad and Uttar Pradesh. I have had a great fondness for him since childhood. He is a brave comrade. Sometimes we had differences of opinion. But that made no difference to an old and trusted relationship. I would have liked it if he had stood this time also from Allahabad. But he did not agree on grounds of health and so we had to accept it. I hope that even now he will agree to come into the Rajya Sabha so that we can have the benefit of his advice.

Another old and trusted colleague, Shri Lal Bahadur Shastri,[4] is now contesting from Allahabad in place of Tandon. I think there is no other individual in India or in the district of Allahabad whom I would have preferred as a candidate from Allahabad to Lal Bahadurji. I am very happy that we are together.

General elections are a complex business and pose great difficulties for those who are responsible for conducting them. In general I am not scared of responsibilities. But to tell you quite frankly I am not terribly interested in the complex business of selecting candidates. I have not really done my duty even this time. For one thing, there is great pressure of work. So lack of time and inclination were responsible for the fact that though I am a member of the Central Election Committee of the Congress I have attended very few of its innumerable meetings. So I have not done my duty in this respect. I do not mean that if I had taken a more active interest I would have worked miracles. I am merely stating a fact. I was sure that the matter was in good hands, of people with a great deal of experience and integrity who would see to it that the best people were chosen as candidates.

It is a pretty complicated job because there are many aspirants and the seats to be contested are few. Sometimes good people are left out. Then there are other complications which have to be given due consideration. After all, the Central Election Committee does not start with a clean slate. Recommendations come from the district committees. So the whole thing is extremely complex. To a very large extent, we are new to this game of general elections on such a large scale. This is only the second and people are not experienced enough, the common man and the district administration, in conducting elections. The preliminary elections should be held at the district or local level by the experienced members of the organization. There should certainly be supervision from above too because very often there are local pressure groups and internal pulling and pushing which create problems.

Very often, specially in democratic elections in any country there are caucuses which want to bring in their own men. All these difficulties are inextricably linked to democracy. Democracy is not free of all shortcomings. But its good

4. Shastri contested from Allahabad District (West) in the 1957 General Elections.

points outweigh the bad, which is why we prefer it. After all nothing in this world is free of shortcomings. We have had problems in connection with these elections.

I am not referring only to Uttar Pradesh but to the whole country. I find that very often people whom I would have liked to have been selected, have been left out. Others were considered more suitable. So I do not say that no mistakes have been made or that the candidates who have not been selected are not good. The best people have been left out. There are other jobs to be done. After all, joining the parliament or the assemblies is not the only job. I do not want those who have not been selected to think that they have been slighted or discredited in any way. It is obvious that when there are four applicants for one post only one can be selected.

I am concerned that the minority communities in the country must be fully reassured. In a sense, the minorities should have trust in the majority which has the strength of numbers. Therefore the majority must always strive to ensure that the minority enjoys its rights fully. It should not feel oppressed in any way. In India, the minorities are religious groups like Muslims and Christians. It is our misfortune that we are backward enough to think along these lines. Political minorities are all right. I hope we will gradually get out of the habit of thinking along religious divisions. At the moment it is our duty to reassure the minorities fully by making sure that they take their rightful place in the national tasks.

Let me give you an example. The number of Christians in North India is not very large unlike in South India. There are large numbers of Christians in Travancore and Cochin. I do not know if you are aware that Christianity had come to the Indian shores 1900 years ago, even before it went to Europe. Christians have lived and flourished in South India for nearly 2000 years with no allegiance to any other country. It was only during British rule that it acquired a political hue. There are Christians in North India too, good people who participated in the freedom struggle. I would have liked it if their representation in the parliament and the assemblies had been increased. Sometimes they feel a sense of panic and frustration. Therefore they must be given full opportunity. But they are so spread out that they do not get the opportunity.

I am fully aware that the Central Election Committee people have worked very hard and faced great responsibilities. I was not involved most of the time. They decided after taking everything into account and careful scrutiny. That does not mean that all the decisions are absolutely right. Mistakes are made. Right from the beginning, I used to convey to the Congress President if I felt that a candidate was suitable and then left it to the committee which decided after taking everything into account. Sometimes I could not quite understand or like some of their decisions. But I have some soldierly discipline and so I accepted their decisions for two reasons. One, those who were responsible for scrutinizing the cases ought to know better than me. I may like or not like someone, the opinion of those who had gone into the matter carefully should be trustworthy. Secondly, when we have adopted a procedure for selection, the decisions should be accepted even if we do not like it fully. Otherwise, matters will get out of control. This is how things are done, not only in elections but in other matters too. When we talk about democracy, two things are fundamental to it. One, all shades of opinion must be given full opportunity to be heard. Every aspect of a matter must be taken into account before a decision is taken. It is obvious that the majority decision is final and binding.

Though the majority decision is binding, the views of the minorities must be taken into account whether it is religious minorities or political minorities. For instance, today the Congress has more than 350 seats out of 500 in Parliament which is a huge majority. But they must always give due respect to the views of the minority. The majority must not try to steamroll everyone else. That is not democracy. Democracy means giving due respect to the views of others. Decisions must be arrived at by giving due weight to others' points of view.

Anyhow once the selection is done, the chapter is closed. I have accepted the decision of the Committee like a soldier and I hope that others in the Congress will also do so even if some people are hurt in the process. We are helpless. Someone or the other is bound to be hurt in such matters.

I do not wish to say very much about the various candidates who are standing in these elections. But I would like to point out that looking to the conditions within the country and outside I am firmly of the opinion that the Congress must come back to power with a large majority, both in the Lok Sabha and the Assemblies. I may be partial to the Congress because I have belonged to it for nearly forty-fives years. I joined the Congress formally in 1912[5] and have been deeply involved in various tasks. I have attended Congress sessions since my childhood days. In a sense, my life became so closely linked with the work of the Congress that for years I did not give much thought to my personal life. This was true not only of myself but millions of my countrymen. When Mahatma Gandhi came into the field new avenues opened up, a new wave of hope and enthusiasm pervaded the whole country. We were young then with the turbulence of youth and we became completely obsessed with the Congress. It is obvious that after years of such close association, I am naturally partial to the Congress.

5. The first Congress session Nehru attended was at Bankipore in 1912. He became a member of the AICC in 1918.

How can I dissociate myself from something which has been an integral part of my entire life and emotions and thinking? You can say that I am a part of it.

It is obvious that in any such party or organization there are bound to be shortcomings as well as good points. That is true of a nation or an individual too. Specially when there is an organization consisting of innumerable people, it is impossible that everything about it should be good. People are of different kinds and pull in various directions. So an individual has to choose whether to work through a party or on his own. If he chooses to work through a party he has to decide which one. I do not say that in politics individuals can have no impact. But if there are too many people working on their own, it does not make much of impact for their energies are scattered. For instance, no matter how brave individuals may be, there is no sense in saying that they can fight a war on their own. You need an army with strict discipline and a commander, with everyone obeying orders without question. A long time ago the English writer, Macaulay,[6] wrote that many wars have been won by bad generals but no war has ever been won by a debating society. That is pretty obvious.

I have given you an example. Any great task assumes the significance of a war requiring organization and united effort. Individual efforts cannot help very much. Individuals may make good sanyasis who can work for the good of others and give them good advice. But it is obvious that in politics such things cannot work. So it follows that the responsibility devolves upon political parties in modern times. I do not know what will happen if the people become very advanced, perhaps they may not require a government at all. But that is a long, long way off, if ever it comes.

We have to understand quite clearly that no party can be 100 per cent to our liking. It is not possible because there are hundreds of thousands of people in it. Either we force them to submit to our views in which case it will not remain a party. It will become an authoritarian government with a personality cult at the top with one individual issuing orders to which everybody else is forced to submit. We do not accept this.

In any democratic institution, there are bound to be divergent views. Yes, there is a broad link between them. But within that parameter, views do differ. Decisions may be taken which some of the members may not like. It happens all the time. As I told you, I have been in the Congress for the last forty-five years and have held positions of some importance. In the beginning, I was the secretary and president of the district Congress and then of the state. For years I was the

---

6. Thomas Babington Macaulay (1800-1859); English Whig politician, essayist, poet and historian best known for his *History of England* in five volumes.

secretary and then president of the All India Congress Committee.[7] So I have
enjoyed great influence in the Congress. But very often the Congress has taken
decisions which I did not like. There were occasions when the decisions that I
was in favour of were not liked by my colleagues. But we accepted them after
due consideration and debate and followed them to the letter. This is the only
way a party can flourish. There is no alternative. There are people who are
easily upset and get frustrated if something goes against their wishes. But that
cannot be helped. You have to understand the ways of the world and adjust
ourselves to them. We must of course constantly strive to improve as we go
along. But who knows what the future holds for us? A nuclear war can lead to
total disaster. Anyhow, we have to accept the majority decision and try to rectify
our mistakes in future.

One other trend has emerged this time. In a sense I feel perturbed by elections
and on the other hand I like them too. In any case, in a democracy there is no
alternative. I dislike elections because people get carried away in the heat and
passion of electioneering and do and say wrong things. This is so all over the
world. It is believed everywhere that political standards fall during elections.
Even here, as you may have noticed, elections whether they are for municipalities
or something else, are not very beautiful to behold. The best of human beings
often come down a peg or two in electioneering. This is a weakness of human
nature. But we cannot say that we will not hold elections. That would be most
improper so we must try as far as possible to conduct ourselves in a civilized
manner.

So in a sense, I welcome elections because they shake the country up and
compel the people to think and formulate their views one way or the other.
Election time is a time for education. It is also the time for various evils and
hooliganism to come to the fore. But it is a time for political education too in
which different viewpoints clash and people are forced to listen, to think, discuss
and debate issues and to reach some conclusions. Elections are a university for
political training. At least, they ought to be if they are conducted properly, which
they are to a large extent. So we should make an effort to throw our weight
towards educating the people on national issues, to behave in a civilized way
and not indulge in abuse or vulgarity.

7. Nehru was President of the Allahabad Town Congress Committee and Secretary of the
United Provinces Provincial Congress Committee in the early 1920s. On 4 June 1923, he
resigned from the latter post. Nehru was AICC General Secretary from 1923 to 1925 and
again from 1927 to 1929. He presided over the Lahore session of the Congress in 1929.
Nehru was also President in the years 1936, 1937, 1946 and from 1951 to 1954.

Recently the AICC passed a resolution[8] at Indore laying special stress on a code of conduct during electioneering. We are determined to stick by it in the Congress. Winning and losing is part of the game. The important thing is to educate the people because ultimately we have to educate millions of people in India on political issues.

You live in Allahabad and it is obvious that you take an interest in political issues. The students in particular discuss and debate among themselves. So you have a high standard. But it is the millions of farmers and workers, good, hard-working people of India who must understand these complex issues. Once they do so, their views will be sensible. So we must think of these elections as a great university for education which is available every five years or so.

The Congress has issued a brief manifesto[9] running into six or seven pages which I would like all of you to read because it gives a glimpse of what the Congress wants. I want you and others to read it. The problem is that it is easy to put down on paper what we wish to do. You can also make a list of what you want. But we cannot achieve anything by that. So we have to weigh carefully what we can do before we put it down in the manifesto. We cannot talk vaguely in the air about things which we know cannot be done. That would be deceiving ourselves and others.

Now I am not complaining. But the fact is that on the one hand, you have before you what the Congress has done in the last ten years. You can judge for yourselves whether the achievements have been satisfactory or not. There are other parties which have not been given this opportunity. So they have not been put to the test in any way.

Secondly, there is a widely held belief, rightly so in my view, that the Congress will have to accept the mantle of responsibility of governing the country for some time to come. So the Congress cannot make promises in the air because if we cannot fulfil them, the Congress will get a bad name and be weakened. That would be bad for its image. Other parties can say what they want because for one thing, they are not in the habit of exercising restraint in speech. Two, they have no fear that they will ever be called upon to fulfil their promises. So they are grandiloquent about what they will do. Apart from that, their chief preoccupation is to criticise and abuse the Congress and the government, and say that the Congress has ruined the country. It is obvious that in a sense the government is responsible in every way. But it is not very wise to criticize someone else instead of thinking of what one can do.

8. See *post*, p. 279 for Nehru's draft resolution.
9. See *post*, pp. 260-273.

So I hope that the elections will be conducted peacefully, in a civilized manner, in the city and district of Allahabad. No party or individual must be criticized personally. All discussions must be about principles. In this connection I appeal to the press also to help by not reporting wrong things or exaggerating them out of proportion. This creates misunderstandings. Let me give you an example. I read a brief report of Indiraji's speech.[10] It said that in the speech, Indiraji had said that the Praja Socialist Party and perhaps the Communist Party too, receives money from other countries. It is a different matter whether they do or not. But personally I do not like the idea of anyone and specially Indiraji saying such a thing about any party. When I came here today, before I could ask her about it, she told me that such a report had appeared when she had not said anything of the kind. She had not seen the report earlier because she was on an election tour. In fact, she has issued a statement[11] denying that she had said such a thing. It will come out in the papers tomorrow. She had said something else in a different context and the reporter linked up the two things. In short, a wrong report appeared in the newspapers which has made a wrong impression upon the people's minds. Whatever the facts are, we must not drag in these issues at any time and Indiraji certainly had no such intention. She has denied it. But those who read it must have been hurt by it. They will make other accusations and we may counter them. But the whole thing is wrong. Therefore I request the press to be a little more careful in this matter.

Looking to the conditions in India and abroad, it has become more than ever necessary that the Congress must continue to hold the reins of power. It is essential for India's progress as well as to face the complex international problems before us. I cannot think of an alternative at all except that power may pass into the hands of splinter groups and pulling in different directions. That would not be in the interest of the country.

Look at the countries which do not have strong governments. No party is strong enough to ensure stability. So there is constant pull and push, changes in government and it is not possible to follow any principles. This is wrong. We find this happening in some of the Indian states too. No work is being done because there is no stable government. A stable government is always necessary but particularly so in the times that we live in. For one thing, we are implementing the Five Year Plans and other projects. Then there is the international situation. It is not the Kashmir issue alone though it is uppermost in our minds. It could have far-reaching consequences. But the situation in the rest of the world is also not very good.

10. At Allahabad in the last week of January 1957.
11. Indira Gandhi's statement appeared in the newspapers on 7 February 1957.

A year ago if you had asked me about the world situation, I would have said that there was progress and we were on the right track. There was a lessening of cold war tensions and the preparations for war had abated somewhat.

Today the situation has been reversed. The world is again in the grip of cold war and fear, tension, bitterness and enmity holding sway. There is nothing worse than the vicious circle of fear and hatred. It warps man's judgement. People do and say wrong things in a fit. So things escalate and the situation becomes worse.

On the one hand, nations and governments have begun to realize that it is impossible to fight a nuclear war because nothing is to be gained by it. There will be no victor or vanquished in a nuclear war for it will destroy our entire civilization. But on the other hand, the world is in the grip of such tremendous fear that neither side is prepared to relent. They keep amassing great nuclear arsenals.

It is a strange situation. Yet I feel that the new trend that is emerging will probably help to resolve this matter and reduce cold war tensions. The great thing is that people are realizing that war is bad. It is possible that some steps towards disarmament may be taken, if not immediately, then in the near future. But on the whole, the atmosphere is bad and at such a crucial juncture, India cannot afford to slacken in any way or get bogged down in petty internal squabbles and disputes.

For all these various reasons I feel it is essential that there should be a strong government in India which enjoys the confidence of the people. It should represent India and speak for the country in world forums. In my opinion there is no other party in India at the moment which can form a strong government except the Congress. I do not wish to criticize other parties. I shall refer to their programme. But that is a different matter. As Lal Bahadur mentioned just now, Jayaprakash Narayanji feels that there should be a strong opposition in the country. I accept that because it would be dangerous for the Congress to hold complete sway in the Lok Sabha or the State Legislatures. It is not a question of numbers. In the last five years, the Congress had a majority of 350 while all the other parties put together had 150 seats. But the opposition was vociferous and the debates were extremely effective. It is not a question of numbers, it is a matter of ability. There were a number of able speakers in the opposition who could argue their point of view forcefully. So there was an effective control over the ruling party.

I would like to draw your attention to another aspect. When we talk about the opposition, its role is not limited to the Lok Sabha alone. If you look about you, you find that India has become independent after centuries of foreign domination and is facing tremendous problems, political, social and economic problems.

We are at a crucial stage of our history when on the one hand, the rising expectations lead to greater demands for progress and better standards of living, opportunity for employment, etc. It is an extremely complex matter to turn an underdeveloped country into an advanced country. It cannot be done by shouting slogans. We are trying to progress at a time when the world is in a great turmoil and the threat of nuclear war hangs over our heads.

In this situation, let us take the role of the opposition. The Praja Socialist Party and the other opposition parties are good in their own way. But their opposition is superficial. The real opposition to our progress comes from our weaknesses and outmoded habits and customs which have a stranglehold upon us. On the one hand, we are facing the economic problems inherent to an underdeveloped country. We do not have the capital necessary for development. Just like a poor individual, a nation which is always half-starved does not have a surplus to invest in development tasks. It is only when the income exceeds expenditure that an individual or a nation can progress. This principle is constant whether a country follows capitalism, communism or socialism. It is only when there is a surplus, that there can be progress.

The most urgent problem before us today is to cross the abyss of poverty and take a leap forward from being a underdeveloped country to become a developed country. No matter which ideology a country follows, it cannot progress without undergoing some privations. There was a great revolution in the Soviet Union forty years ago and there is no doubt about it that there has been great progress since then. But in the interim they have had to undergo great suffering and privations. I am not criticizing them. I am trying to show you how they made up their minds to go ahead and forced the people to follow. The first ten to fifteen years were terrible for them. Once they overcame the initial difficulties, their progress gathered momentum.

This is something all the countries in Asia have to do. Except for Japan, all other countries face the same problems. India is slightly ahead of the others economically and we have laid the foundations for future progress to some extent. But we are not yet over the abyss. We are still in midstream. But others have not reached anywhere near that stage. It is not a question of putting up some industries here and there. The true yardstick to judge a nation's progress is by the direction in which the general economy is headed for. We are at a crucial stage which is a good thing because it means that we will progress faster after this. But it also means that we have to shoulder greater burdens.

I am amazed at the irresponsibility shown by the Communist Party and the PSP in the manifestos that they put up. They repeat old lessons learnt by rote even if the world changes. When I mentioned this a few days ago, the members of the Communist Party were upset with me saying that I was abusing their party while talking of not indulging in abuse during election time. Is it an abuse to say that they do not see the light? I am merely examining their principles, not criticizing anybody personally or their party.

There is one more thing. I do not wish to say anything against the communist countries because each country is free to choose its own path. But I wish to point out that the Communist Party is putting up candidates for elections even though it does not, as a fundamental principle accept parliamentary government. The basic tenet of communism is a belief in the party capturing power through violence, followed by a dictatorship of the proletariat.

This concept may have been relevant a hundred years ago. I do not know. All I can say is that in India particularly in these times, it is absolutely meaningless. It has no connection with reality. Anyhow, I want to know if they have given up the fundamental principles of communism or choose to sit on the fence, acting as the occasion demands. That would be extremely opportunistic. My argument is that the fundamental tenets of communism are irrelevant to conditions in India and they can do nothing but harm, create chaos and disunity. There is a danger that instead of making any progress, the country will remain backward.

The Praja Socialist Party, unlike the Communist Party, does not advocate violence and accepts parliamentary form of government. In that sense they are closer to the Congress. But I regret to say that they have strayed so far and become so irresponsible that it does not give the impression of being able to act in a responsible manner if called upon to do so. You cannot build a strong base for a party if you are constantly wavering. At the moment, it has allied itself with the Communist Party and in the south with the Muslim League. I have no right to stop them. But I do have the right to say that they cannot form a strong political base by such acts. There is no fundamental difference between the Congress and the Praja Socialist Party. They are old comrades of ours. I would like the Praja Socialist Party to become a strong party. It should pull up the Congress if it makes mistakes. But instead of that, they are constantly wavering. So they are unable to form a strong base. I do not deny that there are good people in the Praja Socialist Party. They have done good work in the Lok Sabha and often pointed out our errors. That is a good thing. All I am saying is that as a party it has failed to serve a strong base.

The Praja Socialist Party in Allahabad in particular occupies a very special place. It has absolutely nothing to do with the mind. I have wandered all over India but my experience in Allahabad with the PSP is unique. Whenever I visit Allahabad, the PSP takes out a procession to welcome me and holds a demonstration in front of my house. They shout slogans by the hour. Anyhow, one has to put up with these things. The slogans are about nothing in particular but an expression of anger and a reminder that they too are on the scene. I am really amazed. After all, they must have some consideration for the dignity of the party. It is true that there are no great leaders of stature in the party. But there is not a vestige of dignity in their behaviour which is extremely painful. I feel very sad. I would like the Praja Socialist Party in Allahabad to become a well-knit party with which we can have a proper dialogue. How can there be a dialogue when there is no attempt at a mental approach to any problem. After all Allahabad is regarded as a city of the educated intelligentsia. The Allahabad University is an old and famous one. The citizens of Allahabad have played a prominent role in the freedom struggle. Allahabad has produced great leaders not only in the Congress Party but in other parties too. At one time Allahabad was known as a nursery of leaders and we were proud of the fact. Now the behaviour of the Praja Socialist Party makes one feel ashamed for Allahabad. I do not know if they will ever learn that political parties should work with a sense of responsibility. I am not bothered about their shouting in front of my house. After all, one can only get a headache listening to their shouting. What upsets me and makes me sad is the fact that Allahabad which was so politically-minded should have fallen so much in stature that any party can dare to behave in this way.

Anyhow, I was telling you about the opposition. It is not a question of numbers. There have always been great stalwarts in the opposition. Opposition is in our very blood, in India's history, our habits and weaknesses. We have to fight against some of these tendencies. It has always been our habit for hundreds of years or more to be disunited, forming factions, and displaying fissiparousness. India's history shows you how India was weakened by internal dissensions among the rulers and the ruled fighting in the name of religion and caste. It has become an occupation with us. The biggest service that the Congress has done is to knit the country together. It was actually Gandhiji who taught us the lesson of unity. Under his leadership, there was an integration in the country, not only political integration brought about by Sardar Patel, but an emotional integration too. This is what we need most urgently today. There must be no thought of majority and minority. Everybody has equal rights....

I have great respect for India's culture and traditions which have made the country great. But I do not respect everything merely because they have come down for thousands of years. The world changes, nations change. Progress would have no meaning if we remained just the same as always. We have amassed a great heritage as well as a great deal of debris during the 5,000 odd years of our history. We have to rid ourselves of the accretions. Is there anyone among you who would think of going by bullock-cart to Bombay today? No, you will not. But you are perfectly ready to allow your thinking and outlook to belong to that age. We have to fit into the modern world and adapt ourselves to the changing conditions. We must imbibe and strengthen the tradition and customs which have made India great in the past.

One is amazed to learn how great was the quality of the people who lived in India in ancient times. We must adopt those values once more. India's culture is the very foundation of our life. But to carry the accretions of thousands of years on our backs would be stupid. A society is a living, growing organism. We are living in the industrial age today. We read of the great French, Russian and Chinese Revolutions. But the greatest revolution of them all has been the Industrial Revolution and the discovery of steam power. We read in mythological tales of the mighty weapons wielded by Bheema and Arjun. I do not know about that. But mankind holds far greater power today in the form of atomic energy and nuclear weapons than dreamt of ever before.

The world changes all the time. We must be in tune with the changing times. Take travel for instance. For thousands of years the fastest mode of travel all over the world was on horseback or chariots. There was nothing faster than that as far back as 2,000 years ago or just 200 years back. The world remained unchanged for thousands of years. Then 150 years ago came the discovery of steam. It was nothing new and yet man grasped its potential for the first time and there was a revolution in locomotion. Railways, motor cars and then aeroplanes made their appearance.

The same thing happened in communications. Messages used to be sent on horseback, whereas now instant communications can be established by telephone, telegram, radio, etc. So you can imagine the revolutionary changes that have occurred during the last 150 years or so. The entire way of life has been turned topsy-turvy. We take the day-to-day things like radio, telephone, telegraph, etc., for granted. In Europe and the western world, there has been a total revolution in lifestyles and habits. The same thing is happening in India. So we cannot continue to be in a mental rut. The society changes and we too must change with it.

In the beginning, India and Hinduism in particular had a great capacity for change and adaptability. It shrank only later with the growing rigidity of the caste system and other factors which led to stagnation. Foreign travel became taboo and all kinds of rituals and shibboleths got a stranglehold. Until we reverse this trend we cannot progress. We will lag behind as we did in the past and fall prey to foreign invaders. Therefore our first priority is to uphold the honour and dignity of the country and utilise science and technology for the country's progress.

We have set up huge national science laboratories all over the country. Mere BA and MA degrees are of no use now. We must not copy others but undertake original research in India. The most urgent task is to cultivate a scientific temperament which brooks no mental shackles of any kind.

Last year we celebrated the 2500th anniversary of the birth of the Buddha. Buddha was the greatest son of India. His teachings come to mind more and more often in this day and age. He said repeatedly that we should not accept anything blindly but question and put everything to the test. He said he could only show the path but it was upto every individual to learn the truth by a method of trial and error. All his teachings were 100 per cent scientific. It is through his extremely scientific temper and approach that a great religion like Buddhism was born. That is why I repeatedly tell people that if we do not wish Indian society to remain stagnant, we must separate the fundamental principles and ideals of society from the harmful accretions of centuries.

Two years ago an agitation was launched against my re-election from this constituency. There were two kinds of agitations, neither of them specifically to do with politics. One of them concerned the Hindu Code Bill, which gave women more rights. The other was to do with cow-slaughter. It was said that I was against protection of cows. First of all to raise these issues meant diverting the attention of the people from the larger national issues. Well, I countered those attacks. I am happy to say that the Hindu Code Bill[12] has been passed and the status of women has improved. It was a very big step towards social progress and has opened the doors of new opportunities for women. I firmly believe that a nation cannot progress until its women progress. I can tell you what a country is all about by looking at the condition of women.

There is no doubt about it that there have been great women in India. But by and large, they have been shackled by social customs and taboos. Gandhiji did many great things. But one of the most important achievements of his was to draw the women out of their purdah and shackles. It was a revolutionary step. I would say that the women's role brought us to freedom more quickly than the work of the men.

No nation today can progress until women come forward. I do not mean that they should become aggressive, or militant. But they must take part in national tasks and do what they can by shouldering responsibilities. We have tried to bring as many of them as possible into parliament. We are happy that our new laws have improved women's status.

Two, about cow-slaughter. I would like to clarify my ideas on this. I am fond of all animals, horses, cows and tigers. I like keeping pets and am always grieved to see one of them getting hurt. But I am not prepared to worship them whether it is a cow or some other animal. I know that cows are very important particularly

12. The Bill was passed by Parliament in May 1955.

in an agricultural country. They must be protected and looked after. But there is a method to do all this. It is strange that in India where the cow is worshipped it is so badly looked after. If you go to England, America, France, Switzerland, Germany or the Soviet Union, you will find that the cows are extremely well looked after and yield a great deal of milk. So what it means is that worshipping something is the surest way to ruin it because it closes one's mind. You can pass laws to ban cow-slaughter. I am not in favour of such a law. I do not like the slaughter of cows. But the result of this ban is that the condition of the cows is becoming even more pathetic. Innumerable cows have been chased away into the jungles to become wild, particularly in Uttar Pradesh. Now they are ruining the crops.

So this is not the way. I agree that cows are very essential and useful and ought to be looked after, protected and well fed. But to blindly worship them and ban their slaughter is to condemn them to starvation and death. Is that wise? I am quite clear in my mind and I hope the Congress shares that concern with me. Gandhiji's views were also more or less similar in this matter.

Well, I have been talking at random. There are grave challenges before us. The Second Five Year Plan is going on and everything depends on how far we succeed in it. One important step that we are taking is the Community Projects and the National Extension Schemes. They are extraordinary schemes which have drawn the attention of the world to them. They were started four years and five months ago and a year went by in experimenting. So in fact, we have had only three and a half years and even in this short time, they have made a revolutionary difference in the rural areas.

The Community Projects are the most revolutionary schemes in India today. They are bringing about a rapid change in the rural area where 80 per cent of the population in India lives. India cannot progress unless the rural areas change and progress. So far the schemes have spread to 2,20,000 villages in India out of the five lakh—all within a period of four years. I do not think there is any parallel to this anywhere in the world. Secondly, about thirteen or fourteen crores of the population have been covered. The total rural population of India is estimated at thirty crores which means that nearly 44 per cent of the population has been covered. Now it is our intention to see to it that all the remaining villages are covered by the end of five years and I think we will succeed. It is not a question of covering all the villages on paper or putting a clerk in charge. What it really means is to change the atmosphere and create conditions for greater autonomy at the village level so that the people may learn to stand on their feet. Nobody else can help them unless they learn to help themselves.

The most urgent task is to increase food production, to double the agricultural produce in the country. It is very low compared to other countries. Two, village industries must be promoted; three, roads must be built. Four, arrangements must be made to set up proper schools in all the villages. Five, health care facilities, small hospitals must be available. Six, proper houses must be constructed. In a sense, what we are aiming at is to transform the entire rural way of life through the people's own efforts. These are revolutionary changes and I want to remind you that gradually the attention of the whole world is drawn towards the gradual transformation which is taking place in the rural areas. People come from far and wide to study them. Soon a team will come here to Allahabad also.

Anyhow, we are taking these big strides. Heavy industries are coming up on the one hand and light industries, village industries and national extension schemes, on the other. All these things are interlinked. This is what planning is all about. Our communist comrades feel that we are going about it in the wrong way and the entire thing should be changed.

These are some of the developments which are taking place in India. As far as I can see, taking the good and the bad and the ups and downs, the overall picture is that of a dream slowly coming true and it fills one with a new hope. Once upon a time we dreamt of freedom and saw the dream come true. Now we must build the India of our dreams....

I want to say a few words about foreign affairs, particularly about the Kashmir issue which is uppermost in your minds. It has become extremely complex and so it is necessary that you should understand its significance. But at the same time you must not get carried away in any way or do something wrong, hold demonstrations, etc. It is not dignified. Our case is with the Security Council. I do not like the complaint which is often made that we have broken our word. I feel that in spite of innumerable mistakes that we have made, we will always keep our word. What is the meaning of accusing us of breaking our word about holding a plebiscite and going back on it?

First of all, the Kashmir issue has to be considered in its entirety. It is not just to take something out of context in an eight year long story. A great deal of injustice has been done to us because the fundamental issue has been lost sight of and our complaint has not been even considered yet. It is true that the Government of India had said that we will hold a plebiscite if certain conditions were fulfilled. None of those stipulations have been met. It is also true that when the matter came up in the Constituent Assembly in Kashmir and the Security Council took it up, we had made it quite clear that we would abide by any decision that the Constituent Assembly took. We said we would not go back on our word. But we have to look to the circumstances. For one thing though nine years have passed, Pakistan has not fulfilled even one condition. Let us leave aside for the moment the fact that the question of Pakistan's aggression upon

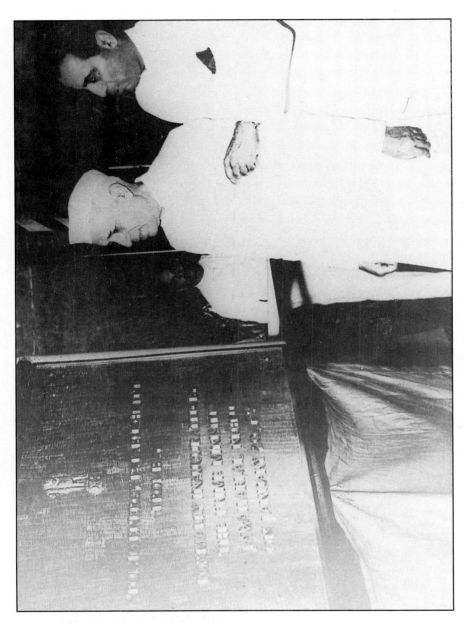

INAUGURATING THE ATOMIC REACTOR APSARA AT TROMBAY, NEAR MUMBAI,
20 JANUARY 1957
Homi J. Bhabha is also seen

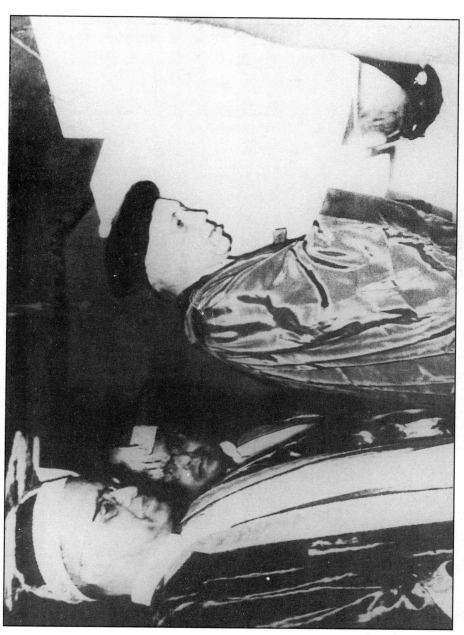

LAYING THE FOUNDATION STONE OF THE CENTENARY BUILDING, UNIVERSITY OF MADRAS, CHENNAI, 31 JANUARY 1957

India has not even been taken up yet. Years have passed and none of the condition were met. What could Kashmir do? The Constituent Assembly met and a Constitution has been drawn up. There has been an uproar in New York over this. The first step in implementing the Constitution was to throw out the Maharaja.[13] We too had to take some steps legally in the parliament here. After all, the world does not come to a standstill.

I do not wish to go into the legal aspects of the case though that is also equally important. The fundamental issue is that no step must be taken which would lead to upheavals and chaos, whether by the Security Council or anyone else. After all, it is the job of the United Nations to maintain peace in the world, not to sow seeds of discord. As I was coming here somebody shouted "Kashmir is ours." I want to tell you that Kashmir is not ours, it belongs to the people of Kashmir. They are our comrades. Kashmir is not our property. We do not wish to do anything which would harm the people of Kashmir. Anybody can see how they have benefitted by voluntarily joining hands with India. There is no coercion in all this. We would not have gone in if they had not invited us. So it is wrong to think of Kashmir as our property. As you know in about a month or so elections are going to be held in India and in Kashmir. There have been no elections in Pakistan, let alone in Pakistan occupied Kashmir.

Ideas keep crowding into my mind and I want to share them with you. I need your cooperation in full. You can vote as you think best. But elections come and go. The work of the country goes on. I want you to understand what is happening in the country. You are living in epoch-making, and revolutionary times. You must forget your petty quarrels, slogan mongering, etc., and prepare yourselves to shoulder great responsibilities in the future. The burden of running India will fall upon the shoulders of our youth. My time is almost up. *Jai Hind*, *Jai Hind*, *Jai Hind*.

---

13. Maharaja Hari Singh.

9. The Caravan of India[1]

The whole of India is in the grip of election fever. The people cannot see anything except the elections. It is obvious that I too am interested in the outcome of the elections. But I do not get carried away by it. The obsession that gripped me long years ago leaves no room for anything else. I am constantly concerned about the direction in which this huge caravan of India, with its millions of people, is going, the goals that we have set before us and where our duty lies.

So these are the questions which are constantly in my mind. It is concerned in some ways with elections. But above all, I think the elections force political leaders to explain to the people about their plans and aspirations, goals and policies. This is a more important aspect of the elections than merely voting. Therefore in the Congress resolution[2] passed at Indore last month, attention was drawn particularly to one or two important matters. One was that there should be no hooliganism or misbehaviour in the course of the elections. Such things are wrong at all times but particularly so at a time when we have taken up important tasks. The eyes of the world are constantly upon us and particularly now when we are about to have elections. Nearly twenty crores of voters will go to the polls. So everybody is interested in seeing how we conduct ourselves and whether elections are held peacefully, in accordance with the procedures laid down. Elections on such a massive scale are not held anywhere else in the world. Every adult, male or female, in India has the right to vote.

Secondly, everyone is interested in the outcome of the elections because on that depends the path that India is likely to follow. It will also show whether India is united or not. The eyes of the world are upon us, not because the world loves India but because of India's stature and size which makes an impact on the whole of Asia and the world. I do not mean to exaggerate India's importance. In spite of our size and population, we are among the weaker, more backward nations of the world. So we can not boast about our achievements. We must understand our position and make promises which we can fulfil. You can shout slogans which may make you happy. But you must not deceive yourselves.

---

1. Speech at an election meeting, Aminuddaula Park, Lucknow, 7 February 1957. AIR tapes, NMML. Extracts. Original in Hindi. Nehru toured Lucknow and Bara Banki from 7 to 9 February 1957.
2. See *post*, p. 279.

India is not a strong nation. We are neither militarily nor economically strong enough to do something big. This is a fact. At the same time, it is also true that India has been stagnant for centuries, constantly engaged in internecine feuds and dissensions. We had lost our vitality and spirit and were vulnerable to external attacks. All that is in the past now and millions of human beings are now on the march towards progress. India has made tremendous progress during the last decade or so and the world has watched with amazement a people working hard with strength and determination towards our goals. This has made an impact upon the world not because of what we are today but because of the potential they see in us for the future. Provided we continue to follow the right path, maintain unity in the country and work hard without slackness we will go far. The world has seen that India has come out of the old ruts and is progressing rapidly, in unity and in harmony. All this has impressed the world and the transformation which has occurred in a few short years in India has drawn the attention of countries far and wide.

So both these things are there. On the one hand, we must not talk big or make empty claims. We must take on big tasks and complete them. Work is the most important thing and will tell the world what we are. Slogans and noise will not be of any use. Those are signs of a weak nation which is incapable of anything better. A nation which takes up big tasks and goes forward boldly has no time to indulge in such useless activities and does not fritter away its energies uselessly.

The greatest problem which we face today and will continue to in the years to come is of progress in India. India's progress implies the progress of thirty-six crores of human beings, not of a few cities alone. You must not forget that there are thirty-six crores of men, women and children abroad the caravan of India. So their progress is of utmost significance.

At the same time other problems arise, some of which are constant and others assume importance now and then. The world is rife with tensions. On the one hand, there is talk of peace and everyone knows how destructive a nuclear war is likely to be. People are afraid of another war. No country wants it, neither the people nor the government. Yet preparations for war are going on simultaneously out of mutual fear and suspicion. Each side is armed to the teeth with lethal nuclear weapons. Nobody knows when a spark may ignite a great conflagration which will engulf the world.

If you had asked me a few months or even a year ago about the situation in the world I would have said with some confidence that we were going towards peace and that there was a reduction in tensions. The world is dominated today by the two superpowers, the United States and the Soviet Union, and militarily, they are far stronger than all other countries. No other country can reach anywhere near these two. Most of the others are ranged on one side or the other. There is

107

constant tension and tussle between the superpowers. Their superiority in arms and technology breed great fear and suspicion of each other. They are constantly worried about what the other side will do. It is like the very rich living in constant fear of thieves and robbers. There is no peace of mind.

It is not a question of wealth but fear that the other side may steal a march over them in military superiority. So the competition grew. This was the situation for years. Then a year and a half ago, the world took a slightly different turn and gradually it looked as if we were going in the direction of peace and towards solving the major issues affecting the world. It seemed as if the talks on disarmament would progress. I am telling you about the situation which existed seven to eight months ago. But then there were various developments which led to greater tension and renewed fear and suspicion. We are back to the days of the cold war once more.

All of you are aware of the developments in Egypt and the attack by Israel, the stand taken by England and France, and the consequences that followed. Hungary was shaken by stormy events which led to great turmoil. It was evident that some of the countries of Europe were going through a period of turmoil and internal upheavals....

Take the consequences of the Suez Canal affair. It has had a tremendous impact on our plans. Prices have shot up especially of the machines that we are importing. Moreover there have been delays in supplies. At a time when we are going ahead at great speed, even a few weeks' delay causes problems. I do not know if you are aware but India is progressing at a great pace. You should go to Bhakra-Nangal and see the work that is going on there. It is an incomparable feat of engineering work. Huge cranes lift cement and stones five or six hundred feet in the air, day and night. Any delay in supplies causes great loss. We need enormous quantities of steel in building the dam. Without steel, there is a danger of the dam not being strong. The daily expenditure in Bhakra-Nangal is eight lakhs. You can imagine the loss that we would incur if there is a delay of even ten days. Therefore there is no scope for slackness. The work must be done on time and there has to be constant vigilance....

To come back to the Suez Canal affair and our interest in it, we were annoyed about the attack on Egypt. We raised our voice in protest. Whether we were involved in it or not, we were affected by the consequences. It had an impact on our plans. If the conflict had escalated you can imagine what the impact would have been. We do not wish to get involved in wars. We are a peace-loving nation and want to promote the cause of peace in the world. All that is no doubt true. But even our national self-interest demands that there should be no upheavals in the world which would stand in the way of our progress. We want peace and above all, we need fifteen, twenty years in which to build the edifice of a new

India. We want to raise the standard of living of the people and build a strong nation, capable of withstanding any challenge or crisis. We want to use that strength in serving the country and the world. All this is in our self-interest. There is no scope for slackness because if we slow down our momentum, we will be engulfed on all sides by problems and difficulties.

It is a strange situation. We are living in revolutionary times. I have said repeatedly that a real revolution does not imply violence and chaos, throwing bombs, or breaking up things. That is absurd. This is a truly revolutionary age when the world is balanced, in a sense, on the razor's edge. It is possible that this age may produce new sources of energy like atomic energy which will enable the world to take a big leap forward. War among nations may become a thing of the past. On the other hand, it is equally possible that we may fall into a bottomless pit of destruction and ruin. What can be more revolutionary than all this?

Look at it from another angle. The advance made in the field of science has generated new sources of energy which, whether we understand them or not, are capable of transforming the world, for good or evil. There was a time about 150 years ago when science and technology began to change the face of the world. Railways, steamships, aeroplanes, electricity, wireless, telephone, radar and innumerable other inventions and discoveries were made—India remained backward and ignorant of all these developments. Even now, India lags behind in these things. These new forces transformed the world without waiting for anyone's permission. If we are intelligent, we will learn to bring these forces under control.

Therefore it is essential that we should get out of our old mental ruts and try to understand what is happening in the world, the dangers that surround us and how we can protect ourselves. It is of the greatest importance to guard the country against external threats and at the same time to lead the country towards progress. Unless we are safe from external threats, how can we progress? That is why we are interested in world affairs. Left to myself, I would not waste my energies or of the country in playing a role in world affairs. I want that all our energy should be concentrated in making India strong and prosperous. Once we have advanced, there will be time enough to take part in world affairs. But the problem is that we have no choice in the matter. We cannot isolate ourselves from the world. No independent nation can afford to do so, particularly a vast country like India. We have trade relations with other countries, we need to import machines from outside. We have to send our people to be trained in new techniques of working because we do not have arrangements for training. I agree that we are trying to make arrangements in India. But that will take time. So it is essential to keep up contacts with the outside world.

Moreover, how can we keep away from the United Nations where all nations are represented? In my opinion, though we may not always like the decisions of the UN, it is absolutely essential to the world. Without the United Nations, nobody knows what troubles might have descended on the world during the last ten to twelve years.

Therefore, whether we want it or not, we have to maintain relations with the outside world, with every nation in the world. Otherwise we will become backward. So we have to play an active role in world affairs, participate in them, and express our opinion. Sometimes we are forced to participate in some developments as we had to in Korea. We sent our troops to Korea,[3] not to fight but in the cause of peace. Our forces are still stationed in Indo-China.[4] We have sent some troops to Palestine too for peace-keeping. We get drawn into these things because we are a responsible nation and cannot behave in an irresponsible manner. I want you to understand this. We are regarded as one of the responsible nations of the world for we express our view after mature consideration and do not make a noise unnecessarily. That would be a sign of weakness. There are many countries which lack strength but make a great deal of noise. We do not want India to be among them. So we are regarded as a responsible nation because we follow our policies with honesty and integrity and do not bow down to external pressures. Moreover we have dedicated ourselves to progress in India.

At present, the problem of Kashmir is bothering all of us. I cannot go into all the details. Our case has been very ably represented in the United Nations by our representative, Krishna Menon. You may have read the details. The matter is becoming more serious day by day. Our effort has always been to uphold the honour of the United Nations because without a common meeting ground for the ambassadors of various nations, the danger of war escalates. So we acquiesced. But sometimes their decisions create problems. How can we take a step knowing fully well that it will go against not only our rights but our responsibilities too, and that such a step would lead to great violence and chaos? Instead of solving anything, it will create fresh problems. It has been pointed out quite clearly, but it does not seem that the matter has been seriously considered. It is not merely a question of our honour, a whim of Jawaharlal's because my family comes from Kashmir. It is true that my family came from there about 245 years ago[5] and I have ties of affection with Kashmir. But this is

---

3. In 1953-54, with the NNRC and then the Custodian Force.
4. From 1954 to 1970. As part of the International Commission for Supervision and Control.
5. Pandit Raj Kaul, the great-grandfather of Motilal Nehru's grandfather, who was a Sanskrit and Persian scholar attracted the attention of the Mughal Emperor Farrukhsiyar, when the latter visited Kashmir. The family then migrated to Delhi in 1716.

not a personal issue. It is a national issue and in the ultimate analysis, a matter of life and death for the people of Kashmir.

These are some points to be borne in mind. If our rights in Kashmir are questioned, I am prepared to argue. But who can justify that Pakistan had the right to send troops into Kashmir and keep them there? The question does not arise. Who can deny that Pakistan has committed aggression on territory that had legally become a part of India. These two issues are important legally. Pakistan says that we had promised to hold a plebiscite in Kashmir. That is true and India is not in the habit of making empty promises. But you must see the conditions that were laid down for doing so. Has Pakistan fulfilled any of the conditions? The first condition was that Pakistan would withdraw its forces. Far from doing that, they have increased the number of troops. There is a well-trained armed force stationed in the area known as "Azad Kashmir." Pakistan has no dearth of arms. The United States gives them arms aid.

As I said, Pakistan has not fulfilled our condition that they should withdraw their forces from Kashmir. That was a fundamental issue. Instead of that, they are taking more arms aid which puts a different complexion on the matter. Why does Pakistan bring up the Kashmir issue so shrilly now? It is clear that they are proud of their armaments. At a time like this Pakistan should not talk vaguely in the air and demand that we should keep our word when our conditions have not been fulfilled. In the meanwhile, their military presence in that area has grown. How can we keep harping on old matters when so many new developments have changed the complexion of the matter entirely? Ultimately any step that we take will be to ensure that the problem is solved by peaceful methods. When it is obvious that one wrong step could lead to ruin in Kashmir which will have far-reaching consequences for India and Pakistan, one has to think carefully. The matter is not so simple as the members of the Baghdad Pact being annoyed with India because we are opposed to the Pact. The matter is far more complicated.

Pakistan says that when the Constituent Assembly was formed in Kashmir, India had promised that it would not take any final decisions which would militate against India's promises to the United Nations. All this is in the past. First of all, it is not true that we had said we would not take any decisions no matter what the Constituent Assembly does. We have always laid stress on some conditions which have not been fulfilled. Pakistan is increasing its troops and arming them. That is no small matter. It has changed the complexion of the matter completely. Why should we be expected to keep our word when the other side has deviated so much?

There was a great uproar that the Constituent Assembly was going to decide finally to accede to India on the 26th of January. The fact is that the Constituent

Assembly was formed in Kashmir about four and a half years ago to draw up a Constitution. It made changes right from the beginning. As far as I remember, its first act was to remove the ruler and elect in his place a Sadr-i-Riyasat. It was the ex-ruler's son who was elected but not because of his birth.[6] He is a very able young man and so he was elected by the people of Kashmir. In short, the Constitution began to be amended right from then. The Constituent Assembly changed the existing land laws. Other changes took place. After all, a nation cannot remain stagnant forever. Ultimately, the work of the Constituent Assembly came to an end about four months ago.[7] I cannot understand the bother which has been created about the 26th of January in the Security Council.

The matter is once again up before the Security Council. But ultimately the problem will have to be solved after taking into account various factors. It is obvious that we cannot break our word. I would like to point out very humbly that we have not done so, nor do we have any intention of doing so. But on the other hand, in a complex issue like this which is likely to have far-reaching consequences, it is not proper to pass a superficial resolution. The matter should be gone into in depth and examined fully. Thirdly, it has to be constantly borne in mind as to what the consequences of a step are likely to be. Does it lead to war or peace? It would be foolish to take a step in the name of peace which leads to war.

I have been talking about Kashmir. I would like to say that it is possible we may have to face dangers and problems. How are we going to face them? It is obvious that threats and abuses cannot work. Large national issues cannot be solved by making a noise or staging demonstrations. It is extremely important to keep one's self-control and not give in to panic. We must do our duty in mutual harmony and cooperation. It is important to bear in mind the principles upon which our Constitution has been founded.

India is not a country of one religion or caste. In this vast land of ours, there are different kinds of people, religions, castes, provinces and languages. All of them belong to India and those who go against it weaken the country as some of our communalist organizations are doing. We have seen enough of the harm that a communal party like the Muslim League can do. The Muslim League no longer exists in India except in a corner of Malabar. But the Hindu Mahasabha, Jana Sangh, Ram Rajya Parishad and others with equally beautiful names are trying to copy the Muslim League and you only have to look behind the curtain

6. Karan Singh, son of the former ruler Maharaja Hari Singh.
7. The Constitution of Jammu and Kashmir was adopted on 17 November 1956. It came into force on 26 January 1957.

to see their real face. They are all extremely communal in outlook and narrow-minded. They talk of a *Hindu Rashtra* and *Akhanda Bharat*, of merging Pakistan back into India and what not. If you think about it carefully you will realise that such things are meaningless. It would be obvious to the meanest intelligence that such things are meaningless. Can nations be run by such foolishness or behaviour more fitting to the *pandas* of Allahabad?

Consider what the communalists want. One is *Akhand Bharat* and the other is *Hindu Rashtra*. What do the two things add up to? Pakistan was created with our consent though we did not like the idea of dividing India. Circumstances were such that we had to accede to it. Since then there has never been any question of reversing the decision, not only because it was a pledge but for various other reasons too. It would be extremely harmful for India and Pakistan to think along these lines, more especially for us. How can we give up all that we are doing towards progress and get involved in such futile squabbles and old quarrrels which we had rid ourselves of? What can be more harmful than that? You cannot reverse the trends of history. What has happened is done with and was accepted willingly by us. I do want that relations between India and Pakistan should remain cordial. We are neighbours and you cannot change geography. We have made efforts in the last ten years to establish friendly relations. We have to choose between establishing trade relations and friendship and constant tensions. It is obvious that a wise nation will not choose the latter. Tensions are harmful to both sides. You must bear in mind that gone are the days when kings and emperors used to go in for territorial conquests for personal glory. That was the old feudal way of thinking. Unfortunately the communal parties are still of that mentality. They seem to think that territorial expansion constitutes strength. A nation's strength does not depend on its size. On the contrary, it can lead to internal dissensions and weakness. It is wrong to think that by annexing another country we can improve our stature.

The students tend to lean towards violence which is very wrong. I am not afraid of a little violence. But in India, a spark could easily ignite a conflagration and ruin everything that we have tried to do. Such developments could weaken the country which is in its formative stages at the moment. Our weaknesses are our real opposition parties and we must challenge and overcome them.

You can imagine what the consequences might have been if instead of a majority party like the Congress, six or seven splinter groups had been in power. There would have pulled in different directions. Even now, there is constant barter and haggling between the various opposition parties and alliances are formed between the most unlikely of them. There is no question of principles or programmes. What can anyone say to an alliance between the communists and the Jana Sangh except that it has nothing to do with principles or ideologies?

The only principle that seems to be operating is that they should somehow win the elections. How can we progress at this rate?

The Congress has been trying to combat the fundamental weakness of disunity and fissiparous tendencies for a long time now. The Congress was formed to allow people of all religions, castes, communities and provinces to join in. It was not a narrow, sectarian party by any means. Gradually it grew and became a great organized party of the masses. It led the country towards freedom. It is obvious that the Congress did so with the help of great leaders like Mahatma Gandhi. But its main task has always been to combat the fundamental weaknesses of India. The other parties, no matter what their intentions are, indulge in activities which break up the basic unity of the country. When there was an agitation over Gujarat and Maharashtra the communists jumped into the fray.[8] How is any principle of communism concerned in any way with Gujarat being a separate state or not? Their sole intention seems to be to create chaos and break up India into fragments. They have no hope of ever coming to power in a united India and so they want to break up the country so that they may rule over the fragments. Is this a farsighted point of view to take? I am not trying to blame anyone. But the various opposition parties are bent upon weakening India's unity.

There are good people in the Praja Socialist Party many of whom have been our comrades in the past. I can only say that they have been led astray. None of them have their feet firmly planted in the ground. They are suspended in midair. The Praja Socialist Party has already got divided into two.[9] I shall not say anything about that. You can judge for yourselves what most of the opposition parties are doing these days.

There are great problems waiting to be tackled in India. But the opposition parties only indulge in gimmickry like undertaking satyagraha or taking out a procession of a hundred people. I have no objection to anyone undertaking satyagraha or going on hunger strike. They are welcome to do so. But you will forgive me if I carry on with my work. I cannot understand what our politics is coming to these days. People seem to think that the great problems which beset the world today can be solved by shouting slogans, going on hunger strikes or taking out processions. We cannot hope to build a new India by such tactics. I do not say that you should accept everything that I say. Everyone is welcome to his own views. But there must at least be an attempt to behave like normal human beings.

8. Soon after violence broke out in Ahmedabad on 8 August 1956 over the Government's decision to have a bilingual state of Bombay, A.K. Gopalan and Parvati Krishnan of the Communist Party of India, along with some others went to the city. Gopalan was arrested on 17 August for addressing a meeting at Sarangpur.
9. The PSP split in July 1955, and Ram Manohar Lohia formed a new Socialist party.

I want to say a couple of things more. The Congress has adopted the goal of socialism and adopted, planning. We are accused of bandying the name of socialism to deceive the public as though socialism is the sole prerogative of others. I want to point out first of all that the fundamental weakness of our Communist and Socialist or Praja Socialist Party comrades is that they think they have the copyright and patent on socialism. They have made a religion of socialism. Well, that is nothing unusual in India. In Calcutta, you will find twenty or twenty-five Marxist parties each with a handful of members. The communists, socialists and praja socialists want to add to the already existing religions and ideological groups in the country.

As I said right in the beginning, we have to march to our goal with thirty-six crores of people. It is not enough for a handful of people to go ahead. Therefore I agree that the pace gets slowed down somewhat. If it had been a question of a few, we could have raced to our goal. But we have to take the whole country with us. I do not say that everyone in India is slow. But the pace is slow because we want everyone to march hand in hand and attain our goals by peaceful methods. If we tried to follow any other path, everything will turn topsy-turvy and progress may come to a standstill. You will be completely mistaken if you think like the communists that the existing system should be completely broken up and the field cleared in order to progress fast. That is absolutely wrong. If something breaks up on its own, it cannot be helped. But nobody breaks up a precious heritage deliberately. The other parties have got completely carried away and complain that we should not talk of socialism. I would like to make it quite clear that we have not adopted the rigid dogma of socialism. We have deliberately not done so because we want to have room for alterations and changes according to the country's needs. We will learn from experience and practice. But whatever we do, it has to be in the light of our problems and needs. Only then can we progress steadily and firmly.

I want you to remember the events that have rocked Europe in the past few months. For eleven years, a nation was fighting against communism. I will not go into the details but it shows how strong the spirit of nationalism is in Europe. Wherever communism has succeeded, it has been the country's own particular nationalist brand of communism. This was so in the Soviet Union as well as in China. Wherever communism has parted company with nationalism it has failed to put down roots as we are seeing, in Eastern Europe.

Therefore, we have adopted a socialist pattern of society as our goal, keeping the conditions of India in mind. I do not agree with the praja socialists who say that everything should be nationalized immediately. We have no objection to nationalization. But it is not a question of doing something vaguely in the air as a gimmick. Our goal is to increase production in India and then ensure the proper distribution of the new wealth. If nationalization will help us to gain momentum, we shall certainly resort to it. Every step that we take has to be carefully considered. We want production to increase in every possible way in the public sector, as well as the private sector. We will certainly help the private sector wherever we feel the need. But we will at the same time ensure that it does not grow so powerful that it can affect our economic policies. So we have other means of control. The communists want that we should freeze all foreign capital and throw out their businesses. Apart from the fact that this is against our Constitution as well as our policies, you can imagine what it implies. Firstly, it would destroy the trust and respect of a very large part of the world in India. That would be a big loss. It is not a good thing to deliberately destroy the trust and respect of other countries.

Apart from that, even if you look at it from a narrow point of view, of short term profits, it means that many running concerns will come to a halt. It will be difficult to restart them. Even now we are facing great shortages of trained and skilled human beings. We are trying to train people as fast as we can. On the one hand, there is unemployment, and on the other, shortage of trained human beings. If we try to turn everything topsy-turvy, it will take us a long time to gain our equilibrium. We would waste years of precious time. But the communists want us to take these steps because they know that this is what the Russians did after the Revolution. They seem to forget the circumstances in which the Russian Revolution occurred. The First World War had brought ruin and havoc in its train, the Government had fled and the entire economic system had broken up. So the communists took over. There was a civil war in the country and chaos reigned everywhere. Since our communist comrades are constantly looking to the Soviet Union for inspiration, they undoubtedly feel that there should be a civil war in India so that they can jump into the fray. Can a country's policies be formulated in such a manner?

Take the Second Five Year Plan. It is not a rigid document. But it shows what our thinking is. We are trying to bring about all-round development. We want to progress fast and that is not possible until we have a base of heavy industries. Its ancillary, the light industries will automatically come up. Let me put it this way; India cannot progress without industrialization and the base for that is heavy industries. There is no point in putting up textile mills in Kanpur and Lucknow. We need heavy industries like the fertilizer plant in Sindri or the steel plants in Jamshedpur and elsewhere. The offshoots come up as ancillary industries. We are producing steel because we cannot go ahead without it. We are setting up three huge steel plants at an enormous investment of four and a half or five hundred crores of rupees. It is a very difficult thing for a poor country to invest such large sums. But we are tightening our belts in order to do so because we cannot move a step without steel.

There are our big river valley schemes which too require hundreds of crores of rupees. But we are taking them up so that the generations to come might benefit. Canals will supply water for irrigation and electricity can be produced. So we are taking up big tasks. Heavy industries are very essential and so we will go in for them. But no industry can come up if our arrangements for agricultural production are not adequate. There must be progress in this field. It is absolutely essential that the condition of the farmer should improve and production increases.

At the moment, the average yield per acre in India is less than what it is in Europe, United States or even Egypt. Why can we not produce more? We must double and treble production. It can undoubtedly be done as we have proved wherever we tried. It is only a question of applying that experience to the whole country. There is no need for despair. If we work hard, we are bound to succeed. We must go in for more intensive cultivation and increase the average yield per acre. At the same time we must spread industrialization too. There is no alternative way to increase the national wealth and employment, except by industrialization.

Heavy industries will not produce daily necessities or consumer goods like cloth, shoes, etc. So we must go in for light industries, cottage industries and handicraft, etc. The scales should be even in planning between agriculture and industry. In India, the scales are tipped on the side of agriculture. People are totally dependent on land. We must open up new avenues of employment which will lead to production of wealth also.

We have to keep in mind the relation between agriculture and industry, and in that context study the relation between heavy industries and light industries, cottage industries, etc. We cannot keep these things in compartments. There has to be a constant effort at keeping a balance particularly in India where the problem of unemployment is acute. I think that industrialization is the only solution. We cannot compete with the advanced countries of the world with outdated techniques. At the same time, it is essential to make arrangements to tackle the problem of unemployment. The unemployed cannot wait for years for jobs. Therefore, cottage and village industries will continue to be extremely important. There is no competition between cottage industries and heavy industries. Both have their own place in our system. The only thing is that even in cottage industries we must try to introduce the latest techniques as far as possible. This is the balancing act that we are engaged upon. We also want the public sector to spread more and more.

This is one thing. Secondly, we want to establish socialism in a democratic framework. We want to maintain the personal freedom of the individual unlike in other countries. I do not wish to advise anyone. Every country has the right to choose the path that it thinks right. But we want both socialism and democracy in India. This rules out communism because it does not accept personal freedom of the individual. Even in planning, we have to be constantly careful about the freedom of the individual even if it sometimes means slowing down our tempo.

I would like to draw your attention to another thing. The community development schemes are spreading all over the country without any fuss or fanfare. There is nothing spectacular about them, like the Bhakra-Nangal dam. But they are something which will change India in a fundamental way. It is changing the farmer and the peasants and the 80 per cent of the population which lives in India. It is exactly four years, five months and five days since we took up the scheme. That is not a very long period. But it has already spread to 2,20,000 villages in India out of a total of five lakh. They have covered nearly thirteen crores of the rural population. All this is not merely on paper but something which has been undertaken by the people themselves. We have sent in trained officers and *gram sevaks* to the villages. The *gram sevaks* have been given training for nine months or a year. Then there are engineers, teachers, doctors, agricultural experts, etc., one each for a block of hundred villages. The hierarchy goes from the top organizers to the village-level worker.

Under the community development schemes the real responsibility rests with the people. The Government merely helps and trains workers. These schemes are transforming the rural areas. The work has spread so fast that we are having difficulties in bearing the burden. There are not sufficient numbers of trained workers though we are training nearly 30,000 of them at a time. You will be surprised to know that we have opened nearly 200 training centres to train workers for the community development schemes. Each centre trains thousands of boys and girls. You can imagine what a large-scale operation this entire thing is. *Gram sevaks*, organizers, nurses, etc., are all given training.

So this is a revolutionary development taking place in India. It is not publicized because we do not want any fanfare. But the attention of the world has been drawn more to these schemes than to our bigger schemes. People come from far and wide in deputations to see what we are doing. We intend opening a big institute to train our workers as well as people who come from other countries. Why have the community development schemes succeeded so well? I do not mean that they have succeeded in all the 2,20,000 villages equally well. There are degrees. But the overall success has been really astounding. In this connection I would like to mention that I want greater stress to be laid on these schemes in Uttar Pradesh.

There are various reasons for our success in this task. Ultimately it has been the responsibility of the states, not of the centre. The states do the actual task of administering the schemes. We provide some funds and technical advisers. The real success has come in blocks where there are good workers and organizers full of enthusiasm, self-confidence and dedication. This is not a task which involves paper work alone. I am glad to see that there are a number of dedicated workers in the field.

Another reason for our success has been that we have not tried to copy anyone. We have learnt from the experience of others. But we have evolved the development schemes to suit the condition of the rural areas. That is why they have fitted in so well and are relevant to the lives of the people. The imagination of the people has been fairly well caught. But ultimately everything depends on the workers. It has been proved that the farmers and others in the rural areas are fully prepared and receptive to the schemes. We do not have sufficient number of trained people though we are doing our best to increase the number. Those who say that the Indian farmer or the common man is wary of change does not know anything about them. Once you explain something to him and demonstrate how it works he is very quick to grasp it. Those of you city-dwellers who have had something to do with the villages will know this. I am merely drawing your attention to it.

The fact of the matter is that India is on the move. I go back to my old example of a caravan on the move. It is obvious that some people may drop by the wayside or move more slowly than others. But the caravan is moving very swiftly and so there is respect for India in the world. They can see how we are progressing and reaching out to our new goals. The other countries are convinced that India will go far and will have a strong influence on the world.

Well, I have talked of many things. You can connect any of this to the elections. I can only advise you that looking to the situation in the country and the world, India has to move with a firm step and adhere to our domestic and foreign policies. Our domestic policy is to have a secular state and ensure justice and equality of opportunity for people of every community, religion, caste and province. If you approve of these policies, it is obvious that you will choose to vote for the Congress candidate. The elections will soon be over. But the problems before us will not be solved so easily. We are trying to lay the foundations for the future which cannot be done by narrow-mindedness. We have to grow in stature, physically and mentally. We must not allow India to lapse into mediocrity. It is strange that India has always attained pinnacles of glory or been in a deep mire of degradation. There is no middle path for us. So since we cannot allow ourselves to fall, we must build a great nation. A nation's honour and strength depends not on military might but on its prosperity, civilization, culture and the manner in which it conducts itself towards the world. India has a myriad forms. There is a great diversity and amidst it lies an invisible bond of unity.

There are various languages in India. We want all of them to grow. In this context, I would like to mention here in Lucknow that it is our duty to help Urdu in every way without thinking of it as a competitor to Hindi. Hindi is the national language. But Urdu is the special heritage of North India and particularly of the city of Lucknow.

So in this way, you will find that we look upon the world as a free nation. There should be no narrow-mindedness. We have been rigidly bound for centuries by the caste system and shut the doors and windows of our minds. We must get out of all these ruts. There was a time when India had scaled great heights of glory. The people of India travelled far and wide with our arts and culture. They were not bound by narrow-minded caste distinctions or fear of foreign travel. India could never have attained such fame as she did if it had been otherwise. The time has now come once more to grow as a nation. I may not be alive to see the result. But those of you who are young are to be congratulated for not only will you see India become a great nation but will participate in the task of making her one. You will live to see a dream coming true. Say *Jai Hind* with me. *Jai Hind, Jai Hind, Jai Hind.*

10. The Role of Women[1]

I thank you for the *Abhinandan Patra*. You pointed out many things in it, one of which was the role played by the women of Orissa in the freedom movement under Mahatma Gandhi's leadership. Two, you have mentioned that the women of Orissa are backward compared to the women in other parts of India. Well, I do not know where women are more backward. But there is a strange condition in India. On the one hand, throughout history and in the modern times as well, there have been women who have earned a name for themselves by their work and spirit of service. There is no doubt about it that in the last three decades women have played a major role in our freedom struggle. When Gandhiji's call came, women came out in large numbers to participate in national tasks. They were called out at a time when we were engaged in a head-on collision with the British Empire. It was a very difficult time and thousands of people were in jail.

---

1. Speech at a gathering of students of Shailabala Women's College, Cuttack, Orissa, 13 February 1957. AIR tapes, NMML. Original in Hindi. Nehru unveiled a statue of Madhusudan Das, the grand old man of Orissa, at the college.

It was at such a time that he asked the women to join in and women who had never set foot out of their homes, came out in large numbers to join the freedom struggle. I have no doubt about it that women's participation gave a renewed strength to the movement. It enhanced the stature of our struggle in India and in the eyes of the world too.

But once the movement was over, the women somehow slipped back, by and large, into their old, traditional roles. However, even now you will find that women are leading in many fields in India. There is great respect abroad for the quality of our women's work. There are many women in the forefront of national tasks and at the same time, it is equally true that the majority of our women are backward and suppressed.

We have tried to see to it that women in large numbers should stand for elections. I hope more and more of them will come forward. It is not so much a question of numbers. But it is our belief that their coming forward will open up new avenues of work and also have an impact on Indian women as a whole. It is happening slowly. We want the pace to grow because we want India to progress and that is possible in a real sense only when Indian women progress.

There are many factors which create obstacles in their path and suppress them. Your *manpatra* mentions superstition and bad customs and traditions. We must hold on to the good cultural traditions of our country, there is no doubt about that. But India is a very ancient country. The older a country grows, many good as well as bad accretions cling on and the bad things shackle growth. Harmful customs tie down a society. India has had a wealth of high principles and ideals and a rich cultural heritage. But there are outmoded customs too which have shackled Indian society and weakened it. This weakness led to India's downfall and we fell to foreign invaders.

Now that we are free once more it is our duty to cut down those shackles. The yoke of foreign rule which shackled us has been cut. Now other shackles remain and we must rid ourselves of some of our evil customs and habits and outmoded traditions. As a matter of fact, the worst shackle of all is poverty. We must get rid of it.

There are many goals before us. We must see to it that every man, woman or child in India gets the opportunity for living a good life. Every citizen of India has the right to have a good lifestyle and standard of living. Everyone must get enough to eat, clothes to wear, houses to live in, facilities for education and health care, and the means of earning a livelihood. Once these basic necessities of life are assured, each individual can go as far as he can. Everyone is not exactly alike in physical or mental ability. But everyone must have the opportunity to go ahead. Above all there must be no unemployment. It is a great burden on society.

It is a gigantic task to make arrangements for thirty-six crores of human beings. Who will do it? It will have to be done by the people themselves. They must produce food, clothes and other basic necessities through their own effort and hard work.

I find that our children are not being looked after in villages, as well as cities, but particularly in the rural areas. There is no arrangement for their education. They are not adequately clothed and perhaps they do not get enough to eat either. It grieves one to see this because I feel that the welfare of India's children is a national responsibility. We cannot absolve ourselves of this responsibility by saying that we do not have the resources or strength. That is wrong. I agree that it may take time because there is no magic formula. It may take time. But we have to ensure that there is no child in the country who is not looked after properly. Every single child must get enough to eat, proper clothes to wear, facilities of education and health care, so that they can grow up to become good citizens and serve the country well.

You hear of the Five Year Plans and great projects which are under way all over the country. They are not aimed at building a bridge here or something else there. Those things are a part of it. But their real aim is to raise the standard of living of the people and make them well off. But it is only the people themselves who can ensure all this by their hard work. Who can uplift thirty-six crores of people? They have to do it themselves.

There are community development schemes for rural uplift. It is not possible for the central or state governments to do these things unless the people in the villages themselves do them. They can get help but it is the people in the villages who must strive to improve their condition by building roads, schools, hospitals— and by increasing agricultural production. It is only through cooperation that India can progress. Women must be a part of that otherwise the country will go down further. Therefore it has become very essential that women must be educated so that they can participate in national tasks in whichever way they can and benefit themselves as well as the nation.

There are many outdated customs and traditions in India. We have passed some laws in parliament last year pertaining to the status of women.[2] Some people are opposed to these reforms saying that they were against our ancient traditions. They were wrong and the laws have been passed. They have helped

2. The Lok Sabha passed on 8 May 1956 the Hindu Succession Bill, which for the first time provided for a share of the father's property to a daughter and granted women absolute right to self-acquired property.

to improve the condition of women in India somewhat. I feel that they will help women to progress.

We must try to understand these things well. The days of blind superstition are over. The superstitious cannot progress. We must certainly respect and cherish our ancient ideals and values. But to believe blindly in something is not really giving it due respect. You must have heard about the 2,500[th] anniversary of the *Mahanirvana* of a great human being, Gautama Buddha.[3] He was a great son of India. The teachings of Mahatma Buddha are relevant even today, 2,500 years later. He had laid special stress on giving up of blind faith. He taught us that we must try to understand with our intellect and only then believe if we are ready to accept the truth of something. He also laid stress on improving one's character.

We must live together in harmony as one nation irrespective of our religion and caste. We are all part of one large family and our interest lies in harmony and cooperation. The women have a special role to play in all this.

I thank you for inviting me to participate in this function and giving me a *manpatra. Jai Hind.*

3. The 2,500[th] Buddha Jayanti celebrations were held in India from 26 to 30 November 1956.

11. Congress, Rajasthan and the Nation[1]

As you know, we are going to have elections in a few days. I have undertaken this tour in that connection. But I may not have done so if it was not connected with other things as well. I have no special interest in the winning or losing of individuals. But I am greatly interested in India's verdict at a moment like this.

1. Speech at an election meeting, Jaipur, 18 February 1957. AIR tapes, NMML. Original in Hindi. Extracts.

What does India represent in the world? At the same time, the direction that we wish to take within the country must also become clear. This is very important. The winning or losing of individuals may be of some significance. But the thing that really counts is what I have just pointed out to you. Ever since India has become free, we have been suddenly catapulted onto the world stage. Moreover, we were inundated with problems, both from within and outside. So long as a nation is not free, it faces only one problem and that is to acquire independence. There may be other problems too. But broadly speaking, that is the only important issue. The formulation of other policies, domestic and foreign, is not in the hands of the people.

So the moment a country becomes free, the reins of its destiny come into its own hands. For instance, we were thrust willy-nilly into the last war without being consulted. The Viceroy and the British Government declared that India too was at war with Germany. In this way, all important decisions concerning us were taken elsewhere, whether we liked it or not. That was changed when we got freedom and the responsibility of making decisions descended upon us. It is obvious that independence means the right to take our own decisions. That is why people want freedom. But it also means greater responsibilities. Once a nation is free, it cannot be irresponsible or childish about things. Freedom involves greater responsibilities, whether a nation behaves in a responsible manner or not is a different matter. But the responsibilities devolve upon it and if they are discharged properly, it benefits the nation. Otherwise it would prove itself unworthy of freedom. Freedom does not mean, simply the removal of foreign yoke or the creation of a vacuum. If the dominant power is removed and there is nothing else to take its place, freedom itself is weakened. What should take its place? It must be something responsible, experienced and it is obvious that no man is born with wisdom. That comes with experience. Nations learn by facing difficulties.

We have learnt a great deal during the course of our freedom struggle. Have you ever paused to consider the real meaning of the movement spearheaded by the Congress under Gandhiji's leadership? You may think that it was aimed at the removal of the British from India. In my opinion, that was not the real meaning at all. It was a result, a necessary consequence. Gandhiji was faced with the need to make India a strong nation and infuse vitality, spirit and forge unity among the people of India. In short his goal was to uplift the downtrodden people of India and to teach them to hold their heads high. This was his chief consideration in all that he undertook. He knew that British rule would come to an end automatically once India became strong as a nation. His aim was, therefore, not so much on getting rid of the British as on strengthening the moral fibre of the nation. He knew that if, by some chance, we were able to get freedom by creating chaos or due to some external factor, when we were not ready for it, that freedom would be worthless. It would soon be snatched away or we might ourselves destroy it by our foolishness. We have innumerable examples in our history, when we have lost our freedom through our own folly and disunity.

What is the history of India? There is no doubt about it that there are some glorious episodes in it. Every child in India has heard about the deeds of valour of the brave warriors of Rajputana. But at the same time, there are innumerable instances of disunity and internal dissensions leading to a weakening of the country. In a sense we did not have a picture of India as a whole in our minds. Politically, the country was divided into various kingdoms and their rulers were constantly fighting with one another. The masses did not have much to do with that. But I would say that the picture of India's unity did not have a place in the minds of the people. There was a bond of cultural unity which held the people together. But politically, India was not one nation except on occasions when the whole country was unified under the rule of a great emperor. That was short-lived. The British rule unified us politically by subjugating us which was not desirable. Unity is a good thing but not in slavery.

Then India was faced with the problem of converting the unity of bondage into the unity of freedom. Only then could India progress once again. It was inconceivable that India should again break up into fragments. There could be no freedom under such circumstances. Keeping all this in mind, our elders started a movement nearly eighty years ago which resulted in the founding of the Indian National Congress in 1885, which is a momentous date in our history. It was backed by the thinking of the entire nation. Earlier there had been institutions and organizations which came up in various provinces and cities, belonging to different castes and religions. They were all good in themselves. But none of them were concerned with the whole of India. They were fragments which did not contribute in any way to Indian unity. On the contrary, they kept people in different compartments. The worst of these institutions was the caste system which had broken up India into innumerable little compartments. It is impossible for India to become strong and progress if the caste system continues. I have no doubt about that. I am glad that it is breaking up. In a sense, there can be no democracy in India under the caste system. I would go to the extent of saying that all our talk of socialism can also have no meaning if we allow the caste system to continue. Only one of them can exist.

The caste system has for thousands of years, prevented the unity of India. Then there are various provinces and religions in India, though we have not heard of wars being fought in the name of religion in our country, as in Europe. It was only under the British that divisions in the name of religion were created which came in the way of Indian unity.

Right from its inception seventy-two years ago the Congress faced this problem. In the beginning the Congress was not a revolutionary body but a simple, mild organization. You will be surprised at the mildness of the speeches which were made from the Congress platform. But you have to understand the times in which the Congress was established. In those mild beginnings lay the seeds of a great revolution. It had very few members in the beginning. But they were all men of great vision. First of all they stopped thinking about any one part of India or religion or caste. They laid the foundations of an organization whose doors were open to everyone in India, from Kanyakumari to the Himalayas, irrespective of their religion, caste, language or sex. Everyone could join the Congress. This was the first time that such a thing had happened in India.

So, in this way, the seeds of Indian Independence were sown and the process of preparing and training the people began. Our young men today seem to think that they can achieve great things by making a noise. That is obviously childish. Great tasks require great effort and preparation. If, for instance, you want to build a bridge, you have to learn to do it. You cannot build a bridge by making a noise. You need engineers to do it. So in the case of nation-building what we need is not ordinary engineering skills but something extraordinary for we have to work not with bricks, mortar and cement but with millions of human beings, each one of them different from one another.

We are in the process of nation-building. It is the people who make up the nation. So we have to train human beings which is a very difficult task and takes a great deal of time. Let me give you a small example. We are setting up huge steel plants in the country. Even when the work is progressing very fast, it is likely to take five or six years. But it will take ten to twelve years to train a first-class engineer, qualified to run the steel plant. It takes time to train human beings. All great tasks are complicated. We are interested in building a new India. So it is not enough to shout slogans or do superficial things. We have to lay the foundations from the roots in which men, women and children may slowly get moulded.

Look at the work that Gandhiji undertook in the country. He was constantly aware of the need to mould millions of human beings and to infuse strength in them. He had the millions of the poor and downtrodden in mind, not a few educated urban middle class individuals. His goal was to ignite a spark in the tired hearts and minds of the people and bring a new sparkle into their eyes. He wanted them to walk with heads held high and straight backs once more. As you know, he had tried out this method in South Africa. Then he came here. The leaders in India invited him to join the Congress and take part in politics. But he preferred to work in a small corner of his own and promised to help when he could. Just imagine, an individual who had succeeded so well in the great task that he took up in South Africa and became famous in the world and specially in India, hesitated because he felt he was not ready. He wanted time to learn and think and understand. We, on the other hand feel no hesitation whatsoever and are ready to air our opinion on every subject under the sun whether we understand it or not. This is particularly true of our youth. There is no harm in that because such opinions do not change the world. I am merely trying to show you how Gandhiji trained the country.

Gandhiji did not believe in shouting slogans. He taught us to go ahead step by step, examining and questioning at each step, and to stop when a wrong step was taken. I shall never forget the incident at Chauri Chaura in 1922 in the Gorakhpur district in Uttar Pradesh. That was at the height of the satyagraha movement in India and we were full of exhilaration. In the small village of Chauri Chaura, a mob of angry peasants burnt up the police station, killing six or seven policemen. It was an extremely unfortunate incident. But we were amazed when we heard that instead of condemning the incident, Gandhiji called off the satyagraha movement, saying the country was not prepared for it. At a time when the country was filled with hope, enthusiasm and anger, our Commander-in-Chief called off the whole movement because of one mistake. That was his way of telling us to atone for our mistake. I do not know if a war has ever been fought along these lines anywhere in the world. But we in jail were deeply perturbed and angry that so much effort was going to waste. After all, how could we guarantee the good behaviour of everyone in the country?

Well, anyhow, we could not understand him at that time. But gradually we realized that Gandhiji was trying to train the people and instil discipline and that the removal of the British Raj would take second priority. He saw that if he allowed the attention of the nation to wander, the atmosphere would be vitiated and the people would have learnt nothing. So he meted out punishments again and again by calling off movements. His soft voice and implacable views were censure enough. In the course of twenty or thirty years, he gradually moulded India's millions, rooted out fear from their hearts and infused courage into them. He taught them to face bullets and jail going boldly and without fear. He taught us to do all this without showing anger or bitterness towards the British. He always maintained that we had no quarrel with the English people but only with British imperialism. Therefore at a time when firings and lathi charges were common occurrences in the cities and there was deep anger in the hearts of the people, an Englishman could walk alone through a crowd unharmed. I would like to point out that there is no parallel anywhere in the world to the lessons taught by Gandhiji to the people of India. It gave greater strength to the nation because we learnt to control our passion. Thousands of people went to jail. They were no angels but men of ordinary stature like all of us. But we came out of our shells and in working under the shadow of a great man and by taking on a great national task which was above our narrow personal interests, we grew in stature. We were engaged in a great task, were part of a great organization, the Congress and in that way too we grew in stature.

I am repeating all this because I want you to understand that our job is not merely to win elections and stay in power. The task before us is to uplift and mould thirty-six crores of people and give them a better standard of living by removing poverty from the country. These are the historic tasks which are waiting to be done. We completed a historic task by wresting freedom for India from a great imperial power and did it peacefully without violence and chaos. Then we also demonstrated to the world that we could be friendly with our erstwhile enemies. You will not find many examples of this.

However, we have a more difficult task before us now, the task of nation-building. We do not have to go to war with our enemies though there are some who are inimical. Now we do not have to fight external forces, but we have to fight our own weaknesses. Whenever India has fallen, it has been because of her own weakness.

What are the factors which were responsible for India's downfall in the past? First, as I pointed out in the beginning we never understood the concept of national unity. Even now, there are various divisive forces. People fight in the name of religion, caste, language and province. As you saw, last year, there were riots over the question of language. It is really strange. This shows how uneducated we are in politics and prone to fits of anger. Until we learn to control ourselves, we cannot go far. We have to fight on one front with our weaknesses and on another, compete with the world. This is the age of atom bombs. Economically, the world has advanced very far with the help of science and atomic energy and other new sources of power which we do not fully understand. Going to college and getting degrees of BSc and MSc is merely the first step. It does not make you very highly qualified. I want that you should learn to do original research. We must not copy others. That is why one of the first things that we took up, nearly nine years ago, was to open new national laboratories because science is the basis of modern life. I do not say that our progress depends on science alone. Other things are also necessary. But until we advance in the field of science, we will remain backward and weak, economically and militarily. Science has led to the invention of new and lethal weapons which we do not have. We cannot keep importing them from the Soviet Union and the United States. If we do, we will be at their mercy. I do not want India to be armed to the teeth or go to war with anyone. But that is an altogether different matter. Not that I want to keep India weak. When someone tells me that he likes peace I wonder whether he says it out of fear or courage. I do not want the peace of cowards. I want the peace of the brave and the courageous.

Gandhiji was a great apostle of peace and non-violence. But even he said that he did not want cowards. It would be far better for them to go armed. Gandhiji's non-violence was a philosophy of courage and daring. I do not want India to go to war with anyone. But India must have the ability and strength to fight back in case of external aggression. India's voice will carry weight if we speak from a position of strength.

Leave aside the question of war. We must advance in the field of science and not be overawed by it. We must benefit fully from science and then follow the path that we have chosen. As you know, whichever way you look at it, this is the age of science. We are surrounded on all sides by scientific inventions and discoveries, whether we are travelling by train, car or plane, send telegrams, speak on the telephone or use the microphone, as I am doing just now. I have pointed out some of the day-to-day things. A very hopeful sign is that at the moment, nearly six or seven thousand young men and women are engaged in work in our science laboratories. They are doing excellent work without any fanfare. Some of them are absolutely first-class and I am sure that they will earn a great name for themselves and India in the field of science. They are doing work of fundamental importance—forgive my plain speaking—unlike the gentlemen who sit in the Lok Sabha and Legislative Assemblies making speeches. I agree that in a democracy, the parliament and assemblies have to function too. But if you imagine that India moves because of them, you are wrong. They may give a sense of direction and purpose to the country. That is true. But India's progress and advancement depends on the millions of educated, trained and skilled human beings who excel in their own fields whether they are —farmers, scientists, engineers or doctors. They are the people whose efforts lead to progress. So the question is, apart from other things which need to be done, of moulding people's thinking and training them to do useful, productive work and acquire special skills. I agree that one of the essential tasks is to run the Lok Sabha and the Legislative Assemblies. But let nobody be misled into thinking that that is the only important thing. Above all, we must learn a fundamental lesson from Indian history, that we should not allow religion, language or anything else to come in the way of our unity. Hinduism, Islam, Christianity and all other religions have an equal place in India. We must accord respect to all of them. Everyone in the country has the freedom to follow the religion of his choice. There must be no interference with one another. This is not new. This has been part of India's ancient culture.

You may have read about Emperor Asoka who has had the message of religion toleration engraved on rock edicts in various parts of the country. They are standing to this day 2,300 years later. He believed that respect for other religions begets respect for one's own. These are some of our noble ideals which we tend

129

to forget. The communalist parties bring religion into politics, thereby demeaning both. They talk glibly of Indian culture. But I say that they do not understand what Indian culture and civilization is all about. They stand for things which are wholly opposed to Indian culture and civilization. India could not attain greatness in the past because of the fissiparous tendencies among the people. India's greatness lies in the fact that there was something intangible, a unique bond which gave her strength and kept the country together for thousands of years. We have lost battles and seen a great many ups and downs, and yet there is a vitality in us which has enabled us to pick ourselves up and go on. How could India have lasted amidst the fissiparous tendencies and communalism and casteism but for that invisible bond?

So whatever the situation was in the past, if we fail to understand the importance of unity, India will remain weak and cannot hope to progress. Parts of India cannot progress while the rest remain backward or vice versa. At the same time, you must also remember that we can go ahead only by peaceful methods. We do not want to go to war with anyone. The principles of peace and non-violence are good in both our foreign and domestic policies.

Last year when we reorganized the states on a linguistic basis there were riots, looting and burning; people were killed all for the sake of a few districts. Even if their arguments had been sound, they proved by their actions that they have not been able to grasp the idea of a nation yet. They are steeped in narrow-mindedness, bothered only about their village and area. They are not bothered about India. Moreover they are prepared to fight and kill, to burn and loot for their narrow self-interest. We have had to bow down our heads in shame. Why do our young men behave like this? These things weaken the country. We are progressing and at the same time, being a large country, some parts get carried away very easily too. Therefore we must make an effort to foster unity and peace in the country. It is only on such strong foundations that the edifice of a new India can be built. I do not want you to agree with me in everything. There must be complete freedom of expression. But everything must be done in a civilized manner. Nothing is gained by hooliganism and uncivilized behaviour. This is of fundamental importance because I see such things all around me. The historic task of the Congress is still to be completed. One goal was reached when India became free. The credit goes to the people but the organized strength of the Congress was behind it. If we allow it to weaken in any way, we will not be able to do very much even with the best of intentions. We need an organized force. The government is also of the people and constitutes a major source of strength. But that is not enough. There has to be an organized political force to run the country properly.

There are various political parties and groups in the country. I accept that there should be opposition parties. But when I look at these parties, I feel disappointed. I can tell you quite honestly that I would welcome a good party in opposition. If it won, I would congratulate it. This is how a democracy grows. But I feel extremely dispirited when I see the various parties which exist in the country. I do not count the communal parties at all because they do not belong in these times at all. They belong to some distant past and are now trying to bring religion into politics though in my opinion, they know nothing about religion or culture or about the modern age. If we followed their path, there is no doubt about it that India would be fragmented. So I want to keep away from them.

There are other parties like the Praja Socialist Party, the Communist Party, etc. There are good people in them, believing in good principles. But they have all been led astray somehow. I have a number of complaints against the Communist Party, chiefly that it believes so completely in violence. Whenever there are disturbances they jump into the fray. There was no connection between the riots over the linguistic provinces and communism and yet the members of the Communist Party had jumped into the fray. It is indeed strange....

Please remember that the Congress is a true political party. It has two aspects. One is its political form. In another way, it represents Indian nationalism. People from all walks of life are in the Congress. It is not a narrow, dogmatic party following a rigid line. Practically anyone in India can join the Congress provided they accept the broad principles of the party. So it is understandable that people from various strands of society are in the Congress. The Congress has a long history and is a large organisation. We do not wish to close our doors to anyone. But the communist and socialist parties believe in certain rigid principles and ideology. Therefore what they are doing now is wrong. The PSP in particular is not true to its principles—and yet it is a socialist party. It complains that the Congress talks about socialism almost as though socialism is their hereditary right. On the other hand, I know a number of socialists who take a keen interest in free enterprise which is wholly opposed to socialism. Not that I have any objection. I am merely showing you how these parties are shaping up. Many of their members are old comrades of ours. But I cannot imagine what they will do if they come to power in the assemblies and the Lok Sabha...

Such developments will be magnified far more if small splinter groups were to come to power. There can be no strong government then. Barter will be the order of the day. Once that happens, there is no room for a firm commitment to principles and policies. Therefore when I see how India is progressing under the Five Year Plans or again the dangerous situation which exists in the world, I reach the conclusion that it is extremely important to have a strong party in power. India must speak out in a strong voice which will be heard in the world. For that it is essential to have the support of a well organized party. Internally, it will enable us to work with determination towards the goals we have set before ourselves. We cannot do any of these things if we are constantly engaged in arguments and debates.

Among all the tasks that we are taking up in India, the most important is the Five Year Plans. Perhaps China is the only other country where work of such magnitude is going on. But we have undertaken something far more difficult than China which is to ameliorate the condition of thirty-six crores of human beings within the framework of democracy and personal freedom. There has never before been a combination of these two things in the history of the world. On the one hand the democratic countries like the United States have advanced but they have taken a couple of centuries to do so. On the other hand, there has been tremendous economic progress in the Soviet Union in a very short period, but at the cost of personal freedom. We want to have both rapid economic progress as well as freedom for the people. Why do we want freedom? We feel that a nation's progress ultimately depends on the quality of every one of its individuals. We want every one to have complete freedom—to flower and bloom. In this way, the real quality and calibre of a nation can get a chance to emerge. Not everyone in India gets opportunity for education now. Once there is equal opportunity for education and training as it should be, innumerable people of very high quality will come up.

I want to create conditions in India whereby everybody can get equal opportunity. I do not say that all human beings are equal. People may excel in different fields. Some are good artists, doctors, scientists, engineers, carpenters or blacksmiths. Others may be extremely stupid. How can anyone make them intelligent? But I want to give equal opportunity to every single man, woman and child in the country. Then each individual can go as far as he can.

We have taken up the Five Year Plans. I do not say that there is no scope for improvement in it. It is obvious that nothing is perfect. We keep consulting others and making alterations wherever necessary. This is not an exclusive prerogative of the Congress, though I agree that it is the Congress government which has adopted planning. But we have consulted people from every walk of life and experts from China, Japan, United States, Soviet Union, Germany, Canada, France, etc.. There is no groupism in planning. We have consulted people from various parties and right down to the panchayats. Then, finally, about nine months ago, the Second Plan was drawn up. But it is by no means a rigid document. We will keep making changes as we gain more experience. The Plan shows the broad outline on which we wish to proceed. We can succeed only by working very, very hard. It is a great burden.

Progress itself means bearing great burdens. It cannot come by making a noise. The progress of the country will be proportionate to the amount of burden the people are willing to bear. That is a broad fact. Anyhow, there are various aspects to planning. It includes agriculture, industry, social service and all kinds of other development activities. There has to be all-round development for a country to progress. We cannot allow uneven development with progress in some areas and backwardness in others. That is why planning becomes essential.

It is extremely important that agricultural production in India should increase. Our average yield per acre is very low, perhaps lower than in any country in the world. It is not surprising that we are so poor. We must double and treble production. All we need is to use better implements and improved techniques of agriculture, good seeds and fertilizers, etc. There is no doubt about it that production can be doubled or even trebled. It will immediately increase our resources for further development and to invest in industries. We want to become self-sufficient in all the basic consumer goods so that we do not have to import from outside. Then people need jobs. Therefore all these aspects have to be carefully balanced. We have to constantly guard against mistakes....

I want to draw your attention to one particular aspect of the Five Year Plan, that is to the community development projects in the rural areas. I have said it elsewhere and will do so again that it is the most revolutionary development in the country. It is changing the face of the five and a half lakh villages of India which is a big thing. You must not think that revolutions can come about only through violence and chaos. That is not so. Nor is this project going to set up huge, big palaces. But it is going to transform India's villages. Ever since it was started four and a half years ago it has reached 2,20,000 villages, so you can gauge the speed at which we are progressing. We want that within the next five years every single village in India should be covered. I am sure we will achieve our target. It does not mean appointing some officials from the top. It means that the villagers themselves are prepared to take on the burden, with the help of the Government, no doubt. What we are aiming at is to infuse a new vitality into the rural areas, a new way of thinking and cooperation. The nation cannot progress unless the people themselves work hard. The Government cannot do it alone by passing laws. People must become aware of their duties and cooperate with one another. If every village makes a firm determination to do certain things, you will find that five lakh villages will be transformed. It is not a question of passing laws. Anyhow, it is happening gradually.

There is yet another difficulty which we have to face. That is the problem of inflation and the rising prices of foodgrains, in particular. There is no doubt about it that there has been some rise in price and it is very essential to curb it. We will do all we can to keep prices from rising further. But why are they rising

133

in the first place? Several factors are responsible. For one thing, it is a worldwide phenomenon. Prices are spiralling everywhere, in the United States as well as other countries. That has an impact upon us. We have to pay more for the machines and other goods that we have to import.

Secondly, we are taking up huge development projects all over the country which provides employment for millions. So it is a good thing. There is a greater circulation of money. But when the production of goods does not keep up with the demand, there are inflationary trends. We will make all efforts to bring the matter under control. We must not panic. But there has to be constant vigilance and every step must be carefully considered. The Government cannot function if its members pull in different directions. In the elections, candidates are standing from various parties like the PSP, Jana Sangh, Ram Rajya Parishad, etc., in alliance. If, by some misfortune, they come to power, what will be the consequences? They will all pull in different directions. You cannot manage a country's affairs in this way.

In Rajasthan, I have heard that many *jagirdars* are standing in opposition to the Congress. There are *jagirdars* in the Congress too. They have accepted the Congress principles and programmes and so we have welcomed them because the doors of the Congres are open to everyone. We take anyone who accepts the broad principles of the Congress. For instance, one of our goals is a socialist pattern of society. An individual who is opposed to the principles of the Congress cannot enter the Congress. There is no place for him. But he does have the right to say what form of socialism we should have and the steps that we should take.

Anyhow, some *jagirdars* are standing against the Congress. They have every right to do so. My sympathies are with the *jagirdars* here because it is obvious that in the last few years they have undergone a traumatic experience. The entire system suffered. That was inevitable. History demanded that the system should be abolished. Soon after independence, it was clear that the princely states all over India could not be allowed to continue. India would be in fragments if they continued. So they were merged peacefully and by mutual consent in order to ensure a smooth transition. The Central Government was extremely liberal in the pensions that were to be given to the ex-rulers and princes. You will find very few examples in the world where problems of such magnitude as the merger of four or five hundred princely states have been solved within a couple of months. There is no parallel in history for this. As you know, all of us were responsible in a way. But the biggest role was played by Sardar Patel. People forget the splendid job that he did when they complain about the large privy purses which are being given. I agree that we are giving too much. It bothers me sometimes because it sets a bad example. I am not bothered about the money.

But such examples are harmful to our goal of socialism. But you must remember that it was a small price to pay in order to solve the problem peacefully. Otherwise nobody knows how long the matter would have dragged on and there would have been civil war and chaos.

Well, soon afterwards we took up the question of *talukedari*, zamindari and *jagirdari*. These systems may have been relevant once upon a time. But they had become anomalous in the present. That does not mean that *jagirdari* or zamindari systems were fundamentally bad. Perhaps a few centuries ago it may have fitted in. But as times changed, so did society, and a time came when they began to obstruct the growth of society, by binding it rigidly. It was impossible to uplift the peasantry or increase agricultural production under these systems. Therefore they had to be removed.

However, we had no quarrel with the *jagirdars* because this was not a personal matter. I have many good friends among them whom I respect just as I have friends among the ex-rulers. It was the system which had become anomalous. I have several English friends. But that does not mean that I should tolerate British rule in India. Similarly there are some good people among the *jagirdars* and others who are bad. We put an end to the system because it was bad. In fact, it took a little time to do it and should have been removed earlier.

It was essential to abolish the zamindari and *jagirdari* systems. Not that we wanted to harm them personally or because we were their enemies. We want them to participate in national affairs. But we had seen that the system had become anomalous and harmful to the whole country. When a drastic step like this is taken, it is bound to hurt some people temporarily. There is no doubt about it that many of my zamindar friends in Uttar Pradesh had to suffer great hardships when zamindari was abolished. But we were helpless. When there are social changes, there are bound to be some ups and downs. Our aim was to achieve our goal with the minimum amount of damage. But the others had to realize that fundamental social change was inevitable. Their cooperation ensured a smoother transition and in most cases we did get it, I accept that willingly. I hope that the others will also cooperate in the future.

I have told you all this to clear up the misunderstanding that we are opposed to the *jagirdars*. Why should we be? They are our friends and comrades. We need their help in shouldering the nation's burdens which are so large that we do not wish to leave out anyone. The only breed of people that we are opposed to are those who sit idle and live off the labour of others. That is not good either for the country or the individual. There was a time when the entire thinking in the country was wrong. Manual labour was looked down upon. Scholars and intellectuals were respected. But the highest regard was reserved for those who did nothing, the idle rich. This is absolutely wrong. We must respect labour,

135

particularly manual labour. It is obvious that intellectual labour must also be respected. But it is wrong to look down upon manual labour. We must not encourage the thinking that idleness is to be respected. Idleness is neither good for the mental health of the individual nor for the society.

We are living in revolutionary times. I cannot think of any other country where such exciting things are happening as in India. Innumerable new avenues are opening up. There is no doubt about it that it is not an easy task. There are problems and difficulties. It is obvious that there are bound to be difficulties when we try to cross jungles and barren land. That is the sign of progress. The greater the difficulties the more we progress. It is only those who do not stir at all who face no problems. So we must not be afraid of difficulties. I want you to grasp the fact that we are engaged in tasks of great national importance. The world has already grasped the fact that India has taken a new turn and is progressing steadily even if it takes ten or fifteen years. It is clear that India is bound to become a strong and advanced nation. So the eyes of the world are upon us. People come from all over the world to see our development projects and other activities.

By a strange chance—even though we were not interested—we have been drawn into international problems. I want to put all our strength into the task of national reconstruction. But since India is an independent country, we cannot remain aloof, particularly because we are bound to be affected by anything that happens in the world. If there is a war, we are bound to suffer. So we have accepted our role on the world stage. Anyhow, I want you to grasp what is happening in the country. We must get out of our narrow ruts and look at issues from a broader perspective. It is obvious that you who live in Jaipur, in Rajasthan, are bound to have its interests at heart. I do not say that that should not be so. But that should be kept in a larger national perspective. You must try to understand the revolutionary steps which are being taken in the country. After all, they are being taken by the people of India, every man and woman, by their own talent and ability.

I talked about external affairs. The problem of Kashmir is agitating our minds. It has taken a disquieting turn. I think there is a debate in New York today about it, probably at this very moment. As you are aware, the debates that have so far taken place in the Security Council have not been very reassuring. I will not go into the details but merely warn you about the ruthless world that we live in. We can come to grief if we slacken a little or make mistakes. Therefore it is even more essential to be vigilant and strong and organized, and not allow ourselves to be fragmented. We must not indulge in too many arguments. All these factors lend a special significance to the coming elections.

Why do I exert myself going from place to place for these elections? As I said right at the beginning I have no personal interest in them. But I am interested that the outcome of the elections must be such as to make India strong, that India may be able to speak with a determined voice which will be heard in the world. I want our neighbours to know that India cannot be fragmented. I want them to see that we are capable of hard work, in unity and harmony. The best way of doing this is to vote the Congress which is our largest national party to power.

I have been talking to you at random about various thoughts that come to my mind. I want you to think about them and understand the changing picture that India presents. You must try to understand your responsibility to the nation. It is obvious that people like Jainarainji Vyas[2] and myself belong to a generation that is passing. I have worked with Jainarainji for years. We will carry on as long as we can. But the burden will ultimately fall on others. It is obvious that our young men in schools and colleges will have to shoulder these burdens. It will be well for the nation if they are prepared. If they are not, the best of policies will not prevent the country from becoming weak.

So I want you to realize your responsibility. The responsibility of the country will always rest with you because the nation cannot be run from the top. People in government will come and go. But the real burden will fall upon you. Anyone who is born in this revolutionary world must be prepared to brave dangers which are a part and parcel of daring ventures. There are dangers as well as great advantages in engaging in great tasks. Human beings grow in stature. The doors of opportunity are open to everyone in India. There is no dearth of jobs for those who have ability.

Please think about what I have said and prepare yourselves for the future. The elections will be held in a month or perhaps less. If you like my advice you can act upon it. But the other things that I talked to you about are relevant in the long-term too.

There is a beautiful view of all of you sitting before me. I have attended many public meetings here. I shall long remember the sight which presents itself from my position here on the terrace of this museum. *Jai Hind, Jai Hind, Jai Hind.*

---

2. President, Rajasthan Pradesh Congress Committee, 1956-57.

12. Disunity in India[1]

I was slightly delayed in reaching here. Please forgive me. Crowds of people thronged the roads. As Lal Bahadurji told you, I have been touring the villages of Allahabad district since this morning. I went first to the Ganga and have now come here. Tomorrow morning I shall go to Nagpur and then to Hyderabad. So it will go on till I reach Rameshwaram in the South.

We are going to have general elections in India. It is true that I am standing from a constituency in Allahabad district. But there are other candidates standing from other places in the country. I am not interested in the victory or defeat of individual candidates either in the South or the North. After all, I do not stand to gain or lose personally in any way from all this. What concerns me is that the Congress which has served India for so long and organized the people into a strong and united force and ultimately led the people to freedom must go from strength to strength. It is only through the Congress that the people of India can progress.

There are great tasks to be done and it is possible only if the people are organized under one banner. As you know, we won freedom by being united under the banner of the Congress. If there are different parties they tend to pull in different directions and the impact is not very great. Before independence our task was to get rid of the yoke of British imperialism. We could not do it until we became a strong and united force. In the beginning, people believed that we could win freedom by passing resolutions. Then Mahatma Gandhi came on the scene and taught us two things. One was to organize the people into a strong and disciplined force. The Congress was formed seventy-two years ago, even before I was born. But Mahatma Gandhi gave it a new garb and organized the country under its banner. The peasantry joined the Congress in full force. Secondly, he taught us a unique lesson, to fight for freedom by peaceful methods. As you know, generally wars are fought neither peacefully nor with love. He taught us to challenge the might of British imperialism by peaceful methods. Our quarrel was not with the British but with the imperial system.

Later on, as you know, the Congress raised its voice against the zamindari and *jagirdari* system. We had no personal enmity with the zamindars. There may be good as well as bad zamindars. So there was no personal quarrel. But we considered the zamindari system to be bad and anomalous. A system which

---

1. Speech at an election meeting in Karchana, Allahabad district, 20 February 1957. AIR tapes, NMML. Original in Hindi. Extracts.

may be good in one age may not be so in another. Times change and so does a society. Unless we change with them, we will become backward. As you know, India had become backward in spite of the great souls who were born here. The West, on the other hand, advanced and became extremely wealthy and militarily powerful. They made rapid strides in science and technology while we lagged behind. A backward nation becomes weak and its freedom slips away. This is what happened in India.

For one thing, there has always been great disunity among us. Secondly, we were content to repeat lessons learnt by rote and refused to learn anything new. It is only the minds constantly in search of new truths which advance. The people in Europe and the United States advanced rapidly because they learnt new things and consequently grew strong and powerful while we were weak. They came and conquered us. England, which is a small country, could easily establish an empire in India because it was powerful. Strength does not come from size but from unity and quality of the people. A crowd of ten to fifteen thousand has no strength because everyone pulls in a different direction and holds different views. Even a small platoon of a hundred soldiers has more strength because there is discipline and unity and it is used to working under the command of a single officer. So it is unity and discipline which make a nation strong. Gandhiji taught us many things but the two most important were, one, to work as a united organised force and two, to follow the path of peace and friendship. We gained enormously in strength from these and ultimately won freedom.

What do I mean when I talk about national unity? India is a vast country stretching from the Himalayas to Kanyakumari in the South, with innumerable provinces. Our province is Uttar Pradesh and as our neighbours we have Madhya Pradesh, and Bihar. Then there is Bengal, Bombay, Madras, Punjab, Assam, Orissa, Andhra, Mysore and many more. All of them put together make up this country of ours. India is not merely Karchana or the district of Allahabad. This vast country of ours belongs to every one of us. Karchana does not belong to you alone but to the people who live in Bombay too.

Secondly, there are many religions being followed in India like Hinduism, Islam, Christianity, Sikhism, Buddhism, Zoroastrianism, and Jainism. We must allow everyone to follow the religion they want and not interfere with anyone. There should be no disputes in the name of religion. Fissiparous tendencies led to our downfall in the past. Thirdly, the caste system has divided society into innumerable compartments which has further weakened national unity. Many sections of the society were downtrodden. Mahatma Gandhi gave them the name of Harijans and laid stress on their uplift. After all freedom is for everyone in the country. So long as some sections of society were downtrodden, how could we challenge British imperialism. We had to fight for the freedom of the whole country. We must root out casteism completely and provide equal opportunity for everyone to go as far as they can.

You must bear in mind that unity is fundamental to all these things. We were able to get freedom by organising ourselves into a strong and united force under Mahatma Gandhi's leadership. But immediately after freedom we had to decide what our next course of action would be because freedom did not solve all our problems. It merely removed an obstacle from our path by bringing to an end British rule in India. The reins of government have passed into the hands of the people. Gone are the days of kings and emperors. Power has been taken away from their hands and they have been pensioned off respectfully.

However, the question then arose as to how we should go about solving our problems. We cannot achieve anything by allowing everyone to do what they like. As you know, a country needs a body of advisers and officials and administrators. We did not want to have officials as in the days of British rule who considered themselves as the masters. We need capable administrators with training and experience. So we decided on a parliamentary form of government, and a panchayati raj for the whole country. People elect representatives to the parliament and assemblies. They are not imposed from above. The coming elections are for the whole country to elect representatives to the Lok Sabha and the assemblies in the states. They are elected by the people from all over the country. We are going to have elections in five days and men and women over the age of 21, irrespective of their caste and religion will have the right to vote. Some names may be left out by mistake from the electoral rolls. But everyone has the right to vote. We want everyone to enjoy equal rights irrespective of their caste, religion, and whether they are rich or poor.

The elections do not mean a general distribution of rewards and offices. The elections are held to decide who should govern the country and the path that we should follow. Therefore you must vote not for the candidates as individuals but the party that they represent and the programme that they have to offer. Here, I think, two or three parties have put up candidates. One is the Congress Party, which has been in existence for seventy-two years and many among you may belong to it. Then there are candidates from the Praja Socialist Party. I enquired about the other parties which have put up candidates. I know that Lal Bahadur Shastri is standing on the Congress ticket for the Lok Sabha seat. All of you know him. He is an old colleague of ours and is held in great respect by everyone. He has done excellent work and has been a member of the Central Government. I think the Praja Socialist Party and the Jana Sangh have put up candidates in opposition to him.

For the Legislative Assembly in Lucknow the Congress candidate is Shrimati Kamal Goindiji.[2] If you are in favour of Congress principles and organization, you will have to vote for Lal Bahadurji and Shrimati Kamal Goindji. I advise you to do so because they are both soldiers of the Congress and belong to a strong organization which is capable of handling great national tasks. Splinter groups and independent candidates cannot be expected to take on these tasks. Therefore I feel that it is extremely important to back the Congress and strengthen its hands. The Congress has held the reins of power for ten years, a difficult ten years since independence. But we faced those difficulties squarely and I think we have brought stability to the country and laid the foundations of progress. If small splinter groups or independent candidates come to power, they will fight among themselves. That is why wherever I go, in the north or south, though I am not acquainted with individual candidates I help the Congress candidates because they are standing from a great platform. I hope you will also help them....

It would be wrong and harmful for people to vote on the basis of caste. There can be no unity in the country if we allow the caste system to continue. The whole idea of contesting on grounds of caste is wrong. You should vote for the best candidate. But at the same time you must bear in mind the party platform which he represents. Independent candidates cannot do much. Can one individual carry the burden of an entire nation?

Now take the Jana Sangh. It is a new party which has been in existence for the last five to six years. It is a communalist party which brings religion into politics. Communalism does great harm to a nation. The communal parties like the Jana Sangh, Hindu Mahasabha, Ram Rajya Parishad, etc., may sound very good but as a matter of fact they foment disunity among the people. Therefore, I would advise you not to be misled by communal parties like the Jana Sangh.

The Praja Socialist Party has put up candidates for both the Lok Sabha and Legislative Assembly seats. The PSP has been behaving very peculiarly, forming alliances with others and in general does not adhere to any concrete programme or policies. It is a weak party. I regret to say that their method of working in our district has not been very good. Many of its members are old colleagues of ours. They were in the Congress but were led astray. Now their programme consists of nothing else except to criticize the Congress.

I would like to point out to you that none of these parties are capable of delivering the goods. They cannot carry the burdens of a vast country like ours and the need of the hour is of a party which can be strong. I have heard people saying that some votes should be given to the Congress as well as the other

2. Kamal Kumari Goindi (b. 1922); MLA from the Karchana Constituency in Allahabad.

parties. What is the meaning of this? When we need a strong army, how can we function with a divided house. We have to strengthen our forces. Then there are others who object to women candidates. I would say that such people are ignorant and foolish. Can India progress by keeping the women in the background? We have deliberately put up women as our candidates wherever it was possible. After all, if our aim is that the thirty-six crores of people in India should progress, half of them happen to be women. How can we leave out half the population? Therefore I would like to point out that not only in these elections but in all our national tasks it is extremely important that women should participate in large numbers. I am not asking all of them to go to Delhi. They must work in their own villages and homes. It is extremely important for women to be educated because they are responsible for the upbringing of the children. They may be able to give love and affection. But that is not enough. They must have education and a grasp of the modern world. Only then can they bring up their children well. We want to build a great nation and so it is essential that women should get full opportunities for progress. In my opinion, you should vote for the Congress candidates to the Lok Sabha and Legislative Assembly in large numbers. Please remember that the Congress symbol is a pair of bullocks. If all of you had been educated there would have been no need for symbols. The problem is that everyone is not literate. I hope it will soon be rectified. I want that children as well as adults should be educated.

A great many things are happening in the country like the community development schemes, river valley projects, improvement of agriculture, spread of industries, small industries, big industries and cottage industries, etc.. All these things will open up new avenues of work and add to the national wealth. Gold and silver are not wealth. A country can become rich only by increasing production of consumer goods. The more we produce from land and industries, the richer the country will become. It has become imperative to increase production because we want to pull India out of the mire of poverty. At the moment what we produce from land is very little. Production in other countries is far higher. The average production per acre of land is not even one-fourth of what it is in other countries. We have taken up community development schemes and are setting up fertilizer plants, building dams to provide water for irrigation and providing good seeds. These are small improvements which all of you can adopt if you pay attention to them. It is to make you understand and adopt these improvements that we have started the community development projects.

We started the community development scheme four and a half years ago and now it has spread to 2,20,000 villages in the country, that is to half the villages in India. I do not think work of such magnitude has been done so quickly anywhere in the world. We want that the rest of the villages should be covered in the next five years. It will transform the rural areas and increase the production of goods, help to improve agriculture and set up small industries which will raise the standard of living of the people. But all this is possible only if all of you understand and participate in these tasks. I do not want you to agree blindly to what I say but understand what we are trying to do. Above all, you must bear in mind, the importance of national unity and the need to get rid of casteism. We must work hard and increase production on every front. The government will of course do everything it can to remove the disparity between the rich and the poor and to give equal opportunities for everyone. This is the path that we have adopted and the harder we work, the faster our progress will be.

At the moment, elections are to be held. You must vote for the Congress and back them with all your might. After that, you must participate in the Five Year Plans and other national tasks. *Jai Hind.*

Oh yes, there is one more thing. I am told that the opposition parties are going about saying that the Congress candidate, Kamal Goindi, does not belong to this *tehsil* at all. She does belong to another *tehsil* but she is not an outsider. She belongs to this district. Such distinctions are not proper. As I said, these are mere excuses. The fact of the matter is that the opposition parties have no other concrete arguments to advance and so they say such meaningless things. You must not be misled by them. Please say *Jai Hind* with me thrice. *Jai Hind.*

13. What the Congress Stands for[1]

I have been in a dilemma as to what I should speak to you about at this meeting. There are many things to talk about both in internal as well as international politics. I have come here in connection with the forthcoming general elections. As you know, my association with the Congress goes back forty-five years. I became a full-fledged member of the Congress forty-five years ago, I have seen a great many ups and downs during the time and my life has been inextricably tied up with that of the Congress. Whatever I am today and if I am worthy of the love and confidence that you have in me, I owe it to this great party the Congress. I have been moulded by it and have grown in its shadow. So it is obvious that I

---

1. Speech at an election meeting, Nagpur, 21 February 1957. AIR tapes, NMML. Original in Hindi.

have had a very close association with the Congress and I think that it has served the country very well.

What is the Congress? It is not some select band of people but an organized strength of the masses. It is not something apart from the people. It belongs to all of you whether you are a subscription paying member or not. The masses have been helping the Congress for years.

The Congress was born seventy-two years ago and has grown gradually over these decades. Please bear in mind that in the beginning it was a very small organization and even then it was far-sighted. Whenever it raised its voice, it was on behalf of the entire country for people of all religions, provinces, castes and languages. From the beginning it has been a national party and its doors have always been open to every man and woman in India. So it grew and threw up great leaders. As you know, it has taken many new turns during the last seventy-two years.

It was the great Congress leader, Dadabhai Naoroji, a Parsee gentleman, who first coined the word *swarajya* fifty years ago.[2] Then Lokmanya Tilak came on the scene and infused a new life into the Congress. Under his influence, the Congress grew and spread among the masses. Then Mahatma Gandhi came and helped it to spread to every village in India. Mahatma Gandhi was deeply concerned about India's villages above everything else. Secondly, he transformed the Congress from a body, which believed in endless debates, into an army without guns or weapons to fight for India's freedom. He trained and prepared the people into a great organized force. The world witnessed a unique phenomenon of an unarmed people engaged in a peaceful struggle against a mighty imperialist power. In the beginning, people in other countries would laugh at our efforts. In fact, in our own country there were people who could not grasp what Gandhiji was trying to do or how we could succeed in a struggle without weapons. But history is witness to what happened. Time and again it seemed as if the Congress had been suppressed and the Indian people crushed. Thousands of people went to jail, received blows from lathis and even faced bullets. But the Congress bounced back, again and again with renewed vigour.

Mahatma Gandhi taught us many things. But the most important lesson of all was never to accept defeat and to pick oneself up and go on even in the face of adversity. When people of a country grasp this fully, they become invincible. We may stumble and fall but we will pick ourselves up and go on. This has happened again and again in India during the last forty to fifty years and many were the times when we became depressed. But Gandhiji was there to infuse new life into us, to impart some of his strength to us. He was a man of tremendous

2. At the twenty-second session of the Congress held at Kolkata in December 1906.

144

inner strength which was drawn from India's millions. He became a symbol of India's innate strength, the spiritual resources of an unarmed people which can achieve the impossible once they are organized.

So Gandhiji taught and trained us. How do people learn? Not by going to schools and colleges though that education is also good, but from their own experience, their happiness and sorrow. He taught us difficult lessons lovingly but he was a strict taskmaster and did not allow slackness. Those who wanted to work with him had to work extremely hard. He was not prepared to overlook even small mistakes but expressed his opinion clearly. You may remember how he called off a great movement at its peak because a mistake made by some people. I do not think that a leader like him has ever been born in history.

My mind goes back to those days gone by. There was one occasion in particular when I was extremely upset. I was in the Lucknow jail thirty-five years ago when the satyagraha movement had been launched for the first time. The whole country had awakened and British rule seemed in danger of collapsing. In a small little village in the Gorakhpur district in UP some poor, misguided peasants attacked the police station and burnt it, killing, seven or eight policemen. I agree it was a bad thing. But Gandhiji called off the movement all over the country the moment he heard about the incident.[3] Those of us who were in jail were amazed and angry that the whole country should be punished for the foolishness of a handful of people. Anyhow, we could not do anything then. When we came out of jail we began to realise that he had done the right thing. It is not that the movement had weakened but its character was changing. It was going out of control. The moment we resorted to violence it would have been easy for the British forces to put the movement down ruthlessly. We would not have stood a chance against the might of arms.

So apart from adhering to the principle of non-violence in order to succeed in our struggle we had to maintain unity among ourselves. If we slackened even a little we would have been weakened and the British would have got an opportunity to crush us completely. I have given you one example of how Gandhiji worked. The goal before him was not only to push out the British from India but to train and mould the people of India to be a strong, organized, fearless force, capable of working unitedly. You may say that he opened a vast school, a great university in which he taught millions of people how to infuse new hope into hearts crushed by hopelessness, to rebuild a downtrodden country. He taught a nation of millions which had been crushed and stunned for a couple of centuries to hold its head

---

3. Mahatma Gandhi called off the non-cooperation movement on 12 February 1922. The incident at Chauri Chaura took place on 4 February.

high once again. The poor peasants with backs bent and lacklustre eyes learnt to stand erect once again.

This was a great task which could not be accomplished by mere book-learning. Every step that he took during the freedom struggle aimed at training the people because he knew fully well that once they learnt the lesson of unity, British rule would disappear. On the other hand, if by some chance we succeeded in getting rid of British rule without the country being fully prepared for it, lacking in unity and strength, freedom will be short-lived and anyone can snatch it away from us. The British established their empire in India in the first place because we were weak and backward, disunited and with a great tendency to fight among ourselves. If we wanted to get rid of the yoke of foreign rule and consolidate our freedom, we had to learn a lesson from our past. We quarrel among ourselves very easily and must overcome that habit. We had to become fearless and united and hard working if we wished to get rid of British rule from India. Gandhiji trained us in this manner for nearly three decades.

You may remember that he started his movement in South Africa for the first time.[4] I remember that Gopal Krishna Gokhale had gone to South Africa at that time.[5] I was very young then. He wrote that Mohandas Karamchand Gandhi was an extraordinary human being who could transform figures of straw into brave men. It was true. He instilled great courage in the weak, downtrodden people, constantly at one another's throats and transformed them into brave warriors in the cause of freedom. I am repeating this because our youth may not have heard all this. Our struggle for freedom was no easy achievement. It went on for a long, long time and we learnt a great deal in the course of it. Those who are under the mistaken notion that big goals can be achieved by making a noise must learn that what we need is hard work, sacrifice and discipline. Take a capitalist country or communist country, the United States, the Soviet Union, Germany, China or Japan which are considered advanced countries. You will find that their progress has been due in every case to discipline and hard work. No great tasks can be done without that. A great revolution took place in the Soviet Union forty years ago and it has progressed enormously in that time. But people tend to forget the hard work put in by the people of the Soviet Union, the price that they paid in sweat and tears for that progress. The United States, following a different ideology has also progressed by working very, very hard.

With the coming of independence, the old bonds have been severed and we have once more got the opportunity to progress. The question uppermost in our

4. The first passive resistance movement took place in 1908.
5. Gokhale visited South Africa in October-November 1912.

146

minds has been, how to go about achieving this and what our goals ought to be. It is up to us how far we can go and how. Some people seem to think that now that India is free we can sit back and relax or even indulge in acrimonious debates and quarrels as of old. That is wrong. Our real work starts now. Before independence, our major task was to challenge British rule in India. But with the coming of independence, we are facing innumerable problems both within the country and in the world. The entire responsibility rests on our shoulders now which makes it more difficult. Independent countries have to shoulder a very heavy burden. That is the price that we have to pay for freedom. If India is capable of shouldering her responsibilities, we will go far. Otherwise at the slightest complacency or slackness freedom itself may slip away.

Many countries have gained independence in Asia and elsewhere almost at the same time as India did. Look at those countries today. We have friendly ties with all of them. But you will find that they have been facing great problems since independence and are even now bogged down in trouble. There is no stable democracy in those countries and nor is their economic condition very good. They are pulling along by being dependent on the West for economic aid. Compare that with what India is today. I do not say that we have worked some magic here. But at least India is better off than most of them. We stand on our own feet and speak with an independent voice in the world. We follow a foreign policy of our own, of friendship towards everyone, based on our cultural and historical traditions as well as what we have learnt from other countries. Peace has always been part of our ancient tradition which we have incorporated into our foreign policy.

I do not say that we have performed a miracle. But I think perhaps there is no other country which can boast of so many achievements in so short a period. We have laid the firm foundations of future progress. It can be done only by improving our economic condition and the social structure. These are far more difficult goals to achieve than fighting for political freedom. In the war for political freedom, we had to fight British imperialism. Now in our battle against social and economic ills we have to fight against our own weaknesses, against poverty which is far more difficult. It cannot be done by some magic formula. It is obvious that we cannot turn India from a poor country into a rich one by chanting mantras or consulting astrologers. That is for the weak hearted. The strong and the hard working have faith in themselves, in their country's strength.

Now we have the task of eradicating poverty. How is it to be done? We will not get wealth from outside. We may get some aid which we will accept with gratitude. Where is the wealth in India? I agree that the princes and ex-rulers have some wealth. There are a handful of rich men. It is true that there should not be too much disparity in the country between the haves and the have-nots.

147

The gap must be closed as far as possible. It is with this in mind that we have formed our taxation laws. I accept all that. But you must bear two things in mind. One, there are in fact so few real wealthy men in India that even if we took away all their personal wealth it would not make much difference. Two, if we try to snatch away personal property in this manner it will harm us in the long run. For one thing, our Constitution does not permit such arbitrary action. Secondly, real wealth does not consist of gold and silver or currency notes but of the goods produced in the country every year from land, and from industry. In a sense, a house or other property is also wealth. But the real wealth of a nation is what we produce. We do not produce new wealth by transferring it from one pocket to another. If we want India to become affluent we must produce large quantities of goods by various means, from our agricultural land, and from our factories. The United States of America and the European countries are affluent because their production from various sources every year is enormous.

Take land for instance. India is predominantly an agricultural country with 80 per cent of our population living in the villages. But our average yield per acre of land is one-fourth of what it is in other countries. Why can we also not produce more? It can be done. We have good fertile soil. But we have become backward in these areas. For one thing our social traditions are such and moreover we tend to hold on to outdated methods. For one thing, the average farmer has very small landholdings which do not permit improvements.

It is obvious that our first and foremost task is to increase agricultural production. It is equally obvious that we can do it because we have seen that whenever the effort has been made, we have succeeded. It is difficult to spread it over the entire country. But it has to be done. There is no alternative. We want to set up huge industries too. But that cannot be done until we solve the land reform issue. We abolished the system of zamindari, *jagirdari* and *talukedari*, not because the people are bad but because the system had become anomalous for our times. It was a great obstacle to progress. You must bear in mind that the same system which is considered good in one age becomes an anomaly in another. We merged the princely states too. The princes and rulers were not bad people. But the world changes, society changes and if we continue in our old ways, we will become backward.

We became backward because we remained ignorant of what was happening in the rest of the world. Science was making rapid strides and new machines and weapons were being invented. The West became powerful and wealthy. We remained untouched by it. Secondly, our social structure became stagnant and outmoded. Casteism weakened the country by dividing it into compartments. There can be no democracy so long as casteism persists. There can be no socialism too for that matter because the caste system divides the people into superior and inferior. The moment you accept that principle, there can be no democracy or socialism. The caste system also creates inequality of opportunity. Some sections of society get the opportunity to progress and enjoy the benefits of democracy while others are deprived of them.

The caste system weakened India while other countries went ahead. That is why I want to point out that we have to bring about a revolution in India. We completed a political revolution by freeing the country of British rule. Now we have to bring another kind of revolution, a socio-economic revolution, in order to make India a strong and stable nation and break off the old shackles which tie us still. We want to do all these things within the framework of democracy. I do not wish to criticise other countries. But the path followed by the Soviet Union, for example, is not a democratic path. There is tremendous coercion and severe punishments are meted out to those who dare to raise a voice. We want to maintain the personal freedom of individuals in India. Everyone should have the right to do what they like without any question of coercion. At the same time we want to progress quickly. These two things have not been done at the same time anywhere in the world. The United States and Europe have progressed over 200 years gradually. Even the Soviet Union where a great revolution occurred forty years ago has not been able to progress very quickly. Moreover their progress has been at the cost of personal freedom and democracy. We want to progress without sacrificing either. This is a problem which no other country has ever tried to solve.

History will record later how far we succeed in this venture. I hope that we will achieve our goal. Ultimately it is because I have complete faith in the Indian people. I feel that they have the strength and ability to do this. However the most important requirement at the moment is that the people of India must understand what they are. We do not belong to our cities and provinces alone. It is the stamp of Indianness which is important. If you go abroad, you will not be asked which province or city you come from. Your passport carries the stamp of the Republic of India and it is as a citizen of India that you will be respected. This is the picture that you must carry in your heart. Unfortunately people do not understand this fully even now. We must not try to hide our weaknesses. Indian unity is not yet stable except on paper. Fissiparous tendencies show up at the slightest provocation.

Last year we saw the furore that was created over the issue of states reorganization. What grieved me most was not that there were riots though that is bad but the fact that emotionally we do not consider ourselves as one nation even now. Until that happens, the ancient malady of disunity will persist and the country can break up into fragments. Casteism, communalism and provincialism create barriers among the people. How can we become one nation until there is

149

emotional integration among the people? It is not enough to be one country on the map. The Congress has served the country well for the last sixty to seventy years. And the greatest service it has rendered India is to teach the people the lesson of unity and organize them into a strong homogenous force. People from all provinces belonging to different religions and castes are in the Congress. The doors are always open to everyone in India. This is the greatest service that Congress has done for India, to foster a feeling of oneness, and of unity among the people to the extent that we organized ourselves. We succeeded in getting independence for India. But it has not been fully consolidated yet.

For one thing, in the very hour of freedom we underwent a traumatic experience. India was divided into two and Pakistan came into being. It is true that we accepted partition. The fact of the matter is that in a sense that was the price we paid for our freedom. We had reached a point of saturation and were fed up with the internal dissensions. We wanted somehow to get the chance to run our country by rooting out the very cause of disunity. We did not wish to inherit a country with the seeds of dissension in it which would make progress impossible. Communalism was at the root of discord and dissension in India. Pakistan came into being as a result of that. We do not wish to reverse the process. Nobody can turn the clock back. Secondly, we are not in favour of repudiating partition. The Hindu Mahasabha and other communalist parties are wrong to mislead the people with their talk of *Akhand Bharat*. It is harmful and simply cannot be done. I want you to understand this.

The problem is that the communalist parties in India like the Hindu Mahasabha, Jana Sangh, Ram Rajya Parishad, Rashtriya Swayamsevak Sangh, etc., live mentally in an age which bears no resemblance to the present day realities. They are completely divorced from it. It is that outlook which has been responsible for India's downfall in the past. India became divided and fell into the hands of foreign invaders. Now that India is once again free, the communalists want to start all over again. If you look at their election manifestos, though they pay lip service to progress, there is very little mention of the social and economic evils which afflict India. Instead there is great stress on an undivided India, a Hindu nation and what not. What they say is absurd and self-contradictory. A Hindu nation and an *Akhand Bharat* are completely opposed to one another. That just shows how their minds work. Not only is their thinking completely outdated, it is feudal too. They seem to think that by acquiring a piece of territory, India can become powerful. Gone are the days when rulers and zamindars became powerful by extending the territory under their control. A nation's strength is its inner quality of unity and integrity and depends on how far a people have a goal before themselves and whether they regard themselves as part of a large family.

150

To boast that we have thirty-six crores of people in India does not add to our strength in any way. A nation's stature depends on the quality of the people, not on their numbers. A human being is judged by his quality and strength. Small countries have succeeded in building vast empires on the strength of their courage, ability and unity. A big country always stands in danger of secession. Therefore, I come round again and again to the need for emotional integration in India. The communalist parties which try to incite people in the name of religion earn a bad name for their religion and do incalculable harm to the country. Communalism has been the cause of India's downfall many times in the past.

Communalists often pose as the champions of Indian culture. I am not a great authority on the subject. But I feel that if anyone is completely ignorant of what Indian culture is all about, it is parties like the Hindu Mahasabha, the Jana Sangh and the Rashtriya Swayamsevak Sangh. India enjoyed great fame in her thousands of years of history because of her innate greatness of mind and heart, her noble ideals and the greatness of spirit. We have just celebrated the 2500th anniversary of Gautama Buddha's enlightenment. He was a product of the Indian soil. A few centuries later Emperor Asoka was born. The story of Asoka is unparalleled in the history of any kingdom in the world. I would like to draw your attention to the rock and pillar edicts which Emperor Asoka had erected all over the country with the message of unity and religious tolerance for his people. His message was that respect for another religion begets respect for one's own. This happened 2,300 years ago. This is India's voice. This is the ideal which pervades the entire culture of India and we have translated it into our foreign policy known as Panchsheel.

I feel that I simply cannot understand anything that the communal parties stand for or that I can have any link with them. I am reminded of what happened when we first raised the issue of Goa with the Portuguese Government a few years ago.[6] Pat came the reply that we had no right to Goa because five hundred years ago, the Pope in Rome had gifted half the world including Goa to the Portuguese. This was the argument that they could think of 500 years later. This is exactly the mental outlook of our Rashtriya Swayamsevak Sangh and the Hindu Mahasabha.

I have strayed away from the subject of India's problems. The most urgent problem before us is to increase agricultural production. But that is not enough. We have to open up new avenues of production and employment. We must have a grasp of modern science and technology and establish industries, small, medium and big. This is the other aspect of development.

6. On 27 February 1950. See *Selected Works* (second series), Vol. 14, Part I, p. 403.

When I talk about industrialization I mean big, medium and small industries. But in everything including cottage industries we must take advantage of scientific knowhow and machines. There is no sense in clinging to outdated methods when new and improved techniques are available. We must make use of small machines appropriate for cottage industries. Heavy industries are also necessary and I have no objection to them. But there has to be the development of heavy industries as well as small industries in order to keep the balance right. There is no conflict in our minds about this.

Industries need a proper foundation in agricultural production. We must pay attention to irrigation and build canals wherever possible. We are building huge river valley projects for purposes of irrigation and power generation. Power is extremely important for no nation can progress without power or steel. Then we must select good seeds, ploughs and fertilizers. We are making arrangements for all this. We are putting up huge fertilizer plants in Sindri and elsewhere.

However, there is one more step that needs to be taken. As I was coming here by plane I noticed that the land was criss-crossed into small holdings. I agree that the farmers work very hard. But if fifty or a hundred farmers got together and formed a cooperative, their income will go up. Their title to the land will remain intact and the profits can be divided equally. Cooperation can help the farmers to buy small machines and adopt improved techniques. Production will double and treble. In this way, the farmers as well as the country stands to gain. I do not think that we can make much headway until we adopt the cooperative method of farming. In fact I want cooperation in industries and other areas of life as well.

In this connection I would like to say a few words about our community projects which have earned great fame in the world. We started them four and a half years ago on Gandhiji's birthday, in October 1952. In this short time, community projects have spread to 2, 20,000 villages. There are five lakh villages in India and half of them have already been covered with a population of thirteen crores. I do not think any scheme has ever been implemented at such speed anywhere in the world. This is not something superficial but aims at organizing the people in the rural areas to learn to stand on their own feet. We will give them whatever help they need. This is the most revolutionary development taking place in India or the world for that matter today. It is transforming the rural areas and infusing a new life into the stagnant economy of the villages. The people in the rural areas had become impoverished and downtrodden during the days of British rule. It is difficult for a people to make any progress when they are bogged down in a mire of stagnation. The community development schemes are aimed at uplift of the rural population because India can progress only when there is progress in the villages. It is a revolutionary programme.

We want heavy industries in India. But we do not want more textile mills though they are all right in their own way. A country benefits most by machine-building industries. We have to import heavy machinery now from England, Germany and the United States of America. So long as we continue to do that we cannot accelerate the pace of industrialization. We must have machine-building industries if we want a proliferation of other industries. So the problem before us is not merely of setting up new industries but of producing the machines that we require for them. Then ancillary industries will come up in their thousands.

We need steel to set up industries. We can do nothing without steel. As I said steel and power are two basic necessities for industrialization. You can judge the progress of a nation by the amount of steel and power that is produced there. We produce steel in Jamshedpur and in other steel plants. But it is not enough for a developing country. We produce only fifteen lakh tonnes of steel per year. Now we are setting up three new steel plants each with a capacity to produce fifteen lakh tonnes a year. We want to be able to produce sixty lakh tonnes of steel by the end of this Five Year Plan. Each steel plant requires an enormous investment of a hundred to hundred and fifty crores of rupees every year. It is a vast sum for a poor country like India. But we have to invest it in order to reap the benefits a few years hence. India will be truly set on the path of progress if we achieve this target.

So as I was telling you, we are laying the foundations of progress in India. I agree that there has been no startling improvement in the living conditions of the people. There has been some improvement in the condition of the farmers. But the overall improvement is not as much as we want. There is great unemployment. But that problem cannot be tackled by some superficial steps taken from above. We have to strike at the root of the malaise. It is with this in mind that we have taken up the river valley projects, community development schemes, building of steel and machine-making industries all over the country. Once we have laid the firm foundations, progress will be rapid in the area of industrialization, agriculture and new avenues of employment will open up. That means waiting for a little while to reap the benefits of development. We are laying the foundations on which the edifice of a new India is going to be built. The foundations are not visible to the naked eye. But no edifice can be built without proper foundations. This is what we have been doing in the last ten years.

Then there is one more thing. The modern world is a product of science and technology. India has lagged behind in these areas while the other countries have advanced into the atomic age. We have to catch up with the others. The first thing we did ten years ago was to establish huge national science laboratories in which thousands of our young men and women are working. They are doing excellent work. I am trying to show you the various ways in which the foundations are being laid. It is true that we cannot get the benefits immediately. Anyhow, we are now going ahead with the Second Plan. Even there we will look at it periodically and make changes wherever necessary.

Our goal is socialism. I do not say that we can achieve that goal within this plan period or even in the next ten years. It takes time. Socialism does not mean opening up a few industries. It means a complete change in the social structure in the relations between its various classes, a complete change in outlook. All these are difficult problems which can be overcome only gradually. We are going in that direction. But I would like to point out once again that behind all this the need for unity and emotional integration of the people is of the utmost importance. We must rid ourselves of the habit of quarrelling over petty issues and wasting all our energy in futile squabbles. We cannot progress until we consolidate India's unity.

As I mentioned just now, we celebrated Buddha's 2500th anniversary last year. It was proper that we should do so for it brought before us an ancient chapter of India's history.

Nineteen hundred and fifty seven is a strange year. Two hundred years ago the British won the battle of Plassey in Bengal which is supposed to mark the beginning of the British empire in India. If you have read Indian history you will be aware that they did not win because of their superior strength but due to the treachery of an Indian who sold his country to the English. India has fallen again and again due to our own weaknesses. Then a hundred years ago, in 1857, a great war of independence broke out with the armed forces in open rebellion against the British. The rebellion was crushed. It took another twenty-eight years before the Congress was established which ultimately led India to freedom. We will be celebrating the tenth anniversary of Indian independence in August. So 1957 is a very special year.

On the other hand, the world situation is not very good. If you had asked me a year ago I would have said that war could not break out in the prevalent atmosphere for there was a gradual lessening of mutual fear and tensions. But today my answer would be different. The situation has taken a turn for the worse and once again, relations between the great powers are fraught with tensions and fear. Preparations are once again afoot for war. We are facing tremendous problems in our struggle to build a new edifice of India. As you know, the prices of foodgrains have shot up. We will not allow them to go up too much. We have enough buffer stocks. But inflation is not a good thing and we are worried about it. I would like to point out to the traders that they must behave circumspectly and not harm the country. Well, we will overcome all these problems. But they pose an obstacle in the way of our Five Year Plans.

Now yet another problem has cropped up, the Kashmir issue, which is uppermost in all our minds. We must be vigilant and prepared to face the dangers inherent in the situation. At the same time, unlike what happens in Pakistan, I do not want you to panic and make a noise or give vent to your anger by shouting abuses and indulge in uncivilized behaviour. That is not the tradition in this country. We must show our strength but in a controlled manner.

Last night a resolution was presented at the Security Council in New York by some countries.[7] It was not very fair to us and we have said quite clearly that it is not acceptable to us. Yet it has been presented. Not that it will be decisive in any way. But it has been given a slant which harms India's interest and attacks the principles for which we stand. I am sorry that this resolution should have been presented by the United States and England in spite of the fact that they know what our views are.

I do not wish to say any more about this except that the matter is extremely difficult. It is a severe test which we must face with equanimity and calm minds. There is no point in giving in to panic.

Some of the opposition parties are highly critical of our entire foreign policy because of this setback. Well, they have every right to criticize, for foreign policy is not a party issue but concerns the whole country. However, I am not prepared to accept what the opposition parties say. What is our foreign policy? It is based on friendship towards all nations without tying ourselves up in any military alliances. The world today is divided into two armed camps with the protagonists of the two superpowers, the United States of America and the Soviet Union, ranged against one another. There is constant preparation for war. We try to maintain friendly relations with both sides but do not join either of the camps. This is our policy and I feel that any nation which does not follow this policy cannot be truly independent. The moment you tie yourself up with the great powers, you are to some extent under their influence and pressure. If war breaks out, the allies on either side will be drawn in willy-nilly. We do not want India to be embroiled in a war and I am sure none of you would want it either. I do not want India to come under the pressure of any other power. We listen to all points

7. A four-Power resolution sponsored by UK, USA, Australia and Cuba was introduced in the UN Security Council on 20 February 1957. This resolution proposed the visit of Gunnar Jarring of Sweden to India and Pakistan in order to examine proposals for a solution to the Kashmir issue. Among other things, the resolution asked Jarring to specifically discuss the question of demilitarization of Kashmir and suggested an examination of the Pakistani proposal of sending a temporary UN force to Kashmir. The resolution was vetoed by the Soviet Union.

of view and give our balanced opinion. We do not want India to get involved in the cold war at any cost.

This is our policy. You may say that it has not been liked by some countries and consequently they are giving Pakistan economic aid and weapons on a large scale. Pakistan is free to accept. But I cannot accept that we should be pressurised into giving up our policy because of this. Is it for this that we have won freedom after such great effort and sacrifice that we are not free to follow a path of our own choice or be cowed down by threats from others? I cannot be a party to this. If this is what the country wants, let somebody else hold the reins of power. Why don't the critics of our foreign policy come out and say clearly what we should do? Perhaps the socialists want in their hearts that we should join the Soviet camp while others wish that we should join the other side and get more aid. Whichever way we go, it will mean that we will become a satellite of one or the other of the superpowers.

This is not my idea of India's freedom or her future. I am fully aware that India is facing great odds and difficulties. To take up the Five Year Plans is a difficult task in itself and particularly so in this world of ours which is obsessed by the madness of war. It is difficult for the voice of sanity to be heard when war drums are reverberating constantly. But I am convinced that if we are on the right track, people will realize the fact someday. Even now, a change is visible. So I cannot understand how we stand to gain by adopting the wrong course at the instigation of others.

I have said very little about the coming elections because my mind is full of larger national and international issues. I want you to grasp them fully because it is you who will decide, through these elections, the path that India is to follow. The party that you vote to power will govern this country. So it is up to you to decide whether we should go ahead with the Five Year Plans and continue our foreign policy or not. In a sense, unless you have a grasp of these issues, you cannot come to the right decision. You are not required to express your views about individuals but on larger national issues. The entire burden is upon you. That is what democracy really means. I am here to ask you to vote for the Congress candidates because the Congress policy is the only one which can work today. I hope that you will return the Congress to power in great strength and thereby show the world our determination to continue on the path that we have chosen. I want in particular that the world should see that India is strongly united on the broad aspects of national policy. We do not want to present a spectacle of small splinter groups each pulling in different directions.

Please think what the consequences would be if by some misfortune the Congress is not elected in a strong majority and a coalition government is elected to power. For one thing, there would be no strong government and secondly

India will present a picture of a weak country to the world, with different parties pulling in different directions. The Praja Socialist Party, the Jana Sangh, the Communists and the independents will all sing different tunes. How can such a government run this country? It is no joke at the best of times. In this revolutionary age of the atom bomb, it would be disastrous not to have a strong government. Small, small splinter groups at the helm of affairs will be so busy bargaining for positions and personal advantages that national issues will be forgotten.

Only this morning I read in the newspapers that Jayaprakash Narayanji has said in Nagpur, I think, that Indian democracy will be defeated if the Congress comes back to power. Therefore, the Congress must be defeated at any cost. Now I have great respect for my friend. But it is becoming increasingly difficult to maintain silence in view of what he says. I cannot understand what he is trying to say. What does it all mean except that he is so annoyed with the Congress that no matter what the consequences, he wants the Congress to lose? Since he has decided this I cannot say anything. One can counter arguments in a debate. I cannot say much because Jayaprakashji is involved in the Bhoodan movement and doing excellent work. But he jumps into the political arena now and then, abuses the Congress and then goes away. I cannot understand this. I would like it if Jayaprakashji were to come into politics fully, and take on the responsibility so that we can have a proper debate on all issues. The Congress and the people and Jayaprakashji would benefit. That is the act of a responsible individual. But to say something now and then, with no thought to what has gone on before or after is irresponsible and improper.

There is one more thing which bothers me. To give up the work of *Bhoodan* in order to oppose the Congress is not proper for the movement. The Congress is bound to win, but *Bhoodan* will suffer, which I do not want. It is entirely separate from politics and rightly so. The Congress governments in all the states have helped in this task. Congressmen are also involved personally. Others are also doing good work. But if the *Bhoodan* workers—I am not referring to Acharya Vinoba Bhave for he is a great soul—made it their duty to oppose the Congress, it will not auger well for the work of Bhoodan.

I find it strange that Jayaprakashji should say such things when he knows quite well what is happening in the rest of the world and Asia. It is only because India has had a strong party, the Congress in power, with close links with the people, enjoying their full confidence, that we have been able to follow a broad framework of domestic and foreign policy. We have completed one plan and started on another. I do not say that what we have done is perfect. It is possible that Jayaprakashji can chalk out a better path. But it is not enough to draw up a plan or write a thesis. The government in power must have the strength to implement it with the help of the people. Even the best of plans cannot be

157

implemented by splinter groups. They will remain on paper while everyone argues his head off. This is an ancient habit of ours.

For the first time in the history of India, there is a government at the helm of affairs which enjoys the confidence of the people and can deliver the goods. The people have confidence in the Congress because they have seen it at work for the last seventy-two years and are familiar with the workers. I am not praising myself but merely pointing out a historical fact. The Congress has been moulded by its seventy-two years of history and has an inner strength, has close links with the masses and enjoys their confidence. This was a fortunate circumstance for India. If at the time when terrible troubles descended upon the country in the wake of freedom and partition, there had been divergent opinions and we were busy arguing, India could not have been where it is today. We are facing problems even today. We have solved many problems too. You can compare India's achievements with any country in Asia, old and new. China is undoubtedly doing very well and comparisons would not be right. China is a communist country and it has every right to follow any path that it chooses. It is possible that China has succeeded better than us. But I have no doubt about it that Jayaprakashji could not seriously want India to follow China's example.

It is my heartfelt desire that democracy should become strong and stable in the initial years so that we can move with a sure step towards a socio-economic revolution. I want that the right atmosphere should be created to lay the firm foundation of democracy. The panchayats should be strengthened. The question as to, who after Jawaharlal seems to agitate people. At the same time, the same people say that it would be a good thing if Jawaharlal or the Congress were to be ousted right now. I cannot quite understand this. Jawaharlal will quit the moment you want him to. He will serve the nation in other ways. But I cannot run away in panic. It is absurd that some people should feel upset because decisions on national issues do not conform to their views. I can not go around advising everybody.

I want you to understand these things because we are at a crucial juncture in history. We are laying the foundations of a new India and the sights that meet my eyes wherever I go gladden my heart. There was a time when we used to dream of freedom. Then we saw that dream come true. It is given to very few to see their dreams come true in their own lifetime. Anyhow, we had other dreams, that India should become a great democracy upholding the freedom of the individual and equality of opportunity for everyone. We dreamt of a land free from disparity between the haves and the have-nots. It gladdens my heart to see that that dream has come true partly. It gives one fresh strength and confidence in the people of India.

I have great faith in India. For one thing, the history of India down the ages shows a great capacity for survival through ups and downs. We have fallen again and again, and yet emerged victorious. But more than that, I believe in a bright future for India because I have great faith in the people of India. I do not say that we are superior to everyone else. But we have the spirit and ability acquired through 5,000 years of history and what we have learnt during the last 30-40 years under Gandhiji.

So I am confident that we will rise to the occasion and fulfil the demands of the times. We must have unity and strength and determination for if we do, there is no power on earth which can shake us. We will be ready for any eventuality.

I have talked to you about various things. It is upto you to decide. In my opinion, for what it is worth, it is extremely important that you should vote for the Congress candidates to the Lok Sabha and the State Legislatures and strengthen our hands. You must show to the world that the country is solidly behind the Congress and that the Congress represents India and speaks with India's voice. You must demonstrate that we are capable of facing any danger and adversity. Please say *Jai Hind* with me thrice. *Jai Hind*.

2
NATIONAL PROGRESS

I. THE ECONOMY

1. The Foreign Exchange Situation[1]

I should like you to send to all the Ministries and Departments of Government the following note under confidential cover:

Note

The Finance Minister has drawn my attention to the serious foreign exchange situation.[2] This has deteriorated still further during the last month or so. It is clear at we cannot go on at this rate and that we must take urgent and effective steps to stop this drain.

The Planning Commission has constituted a Committee of senior officials to scrutinise the various Ministries' projects with a view to phasing their progress. We are asking this Committee to start this work immediately and to submit its proposal as quickly as possible to the Planning Commission. Doubtful cases of foreign exchange expenditure will be examined by the External Finance Division of the Finance Ministry. It is no longer possible to sanction foreign exchange for all the schemes which have been included in the Plan. This also means that fresh schemes are not undertaken so as to avoid having to stop them halfway for want of foreign exchange. In regard to schemes which have already been started, it will have to be considered to what extent the foreign exchange expenditure involved can be re-phased without serious difficulty.

I trust that every Ministry and Department of Central Government will appreciate this serious situation that has arisen in regard to foreign exchange and give its wholehearted cooperation to the steps being taken to save foreign exchange.

1. Note to Y.N. Sukthankar, Cabinet Secretary, 3 December 1956. File No. 37(35)/56-59-PMS.
2. T.T. Krishnamachari, the Finance Minister, informed Nehru on 3 December that the foreign exchange reserves at the time stood at Rs 544 crores. He also pointed out that allowing for the statutory minimum of Rs 400 crores by way of currency reserve and a minimum working balance of Rs 40 crores, there would remain about Rs 100 crores, and suggested immediate action "to stem the present trend of withdrawals and to strengthen our reserves at least to tide over the coming six months."

2. Balanced Planning[1]

I should like to send my greetings and good wishes to the 39th session of the Indian Economic Conference and the 17th session of the All-India Agricultural Economics Conference which are going to be held at Cuttack towards the end of this year.[2] India is firmly committed to planned progress and has taken some substantial steps to that end. But the further we go the more our problems increase and demand thought to be given to different aspects of planning.

In this work of planning it is desirable that there should be as wide an area of consultation and discussion as possible. In particular, our economists must necessarily play an important part in this great work. We have seen that lack of planning does not lead anywhere. But planning unless carefully balanced may well lead to undesirable consequences.

I hope that the economists who gather together at the conferences in Cuttack will consider these problems not only from the theoretical but also from the practical point of view and help us, more especially, in our approach to long-term and perspective planning.

1. Message to the thirty-ninth session of the Indian Economic Conference and the seventeenth session of the All-India Agricultural Economics Conference, 6 December 1956. File No. 9/2/56-PMS. The message was released to the press on 26 December 1956.
2. The two conferences were held on 26 and 28 December 1956.

3. The Importance of Agricultural Production[1]

In his opening remarks, the Chairman[2] referred to the fact that the present meeting was the first meeting of the National Development Council since the reorganisation of the states[3] and extended a cordial welcome to the new members of the Council. He said that as the developmental activities increased, the movement got its own impetus apart from the push that they might give it. As the tempo of activities get geared up and the movement developed speed, new problems were brought out. The Council had to be alert and wide awake all the time and it might be necessary to have more frequent meetings than before.

2. Apart from the development programmes and activities, certain other happenings made it necessary for them to be more alert and wide awake. The international situation continued to be a highly explosive one. The Chairman expressed the hope that there might not be war but the fact remained that the international situation produced new problems which had to be faced. Any improvement in the international situation would be a slow process. The blocking of the Suez Canal made a considerable difference in the imports and exports. There was a tendency all over the world for inflationary effects to be produced and machinery, goods, etc., had become more expensive.

3. The Chairman observed that the foreign exchange resources had been rapidly depleted and a stage had been reached when brakes had to be applied even at the cost of certain activities. On the other hand, because of external and internal causes, the figures embodied in the Plan had to be revised upwards. Because of the rise in prices and of certain very important additional items, the size of the Second Plan might go up by Rs 400 or Rs 500 crores from the figure of Rs 4,800 crores mentioned in the Second Five Year Plan. Even when the figure of Rs 4,800 crores was discussed, the difficulties in raising the resources and implementing a Plan of this magnitude were realised. It was going to be a far more difficult job now that the figures went up by Rs 400 or 500 crores. At the same time, to the extent possible the major activities contemplated under the Plan had to go through.

1. Remarks at the eighth meeting of the National Development Council, New Delhi, 8 December 1956. Summary record of the meeting, File No. PC/CDN/29/4/57, Coordination Branch, Planning Commission. Extracts.
2. Jawaharlal Nehru.
3. The new states came into being on 1 November 1956.

4. All these factors had raised very important problems for consideration, namely, the question of resources, the question of meeting dangers of inflation, the international dangers, etc. A time had come when every item had to be carefully considered and a view taken as to whether it was absolutely necessary or not and whether it involved the slightest degree of waste and whether it could be postponed or not, keeping in view the fact that the main features of the Plan must go through.

5. The Chairman observed that the question of inflation obviously revolved round the production capacity of the country. The foreign exchange situation could be remedied only by more exports. Some welcome external help might come but the basic way was to increase exports and limit imports. Even necessary imports would have to be limited because more necessary things had to be done. Even though production had to be increased in all sections, in the final analysis, it was agricultural production that was going to be of crucial importance. The people had to work with their sweat and blood to increase agricultural production and if they did not do it, they could not get on with the Plan. This was a patent fact. The choice was to get on with the Plan by increasing the agricultural production or to get on with the Plan at all. There was no other way out.

6. One had to be careful that in the enthusiasm to get things done and to go faster, the entire economy was not overstrained. At the back of the political conflicts in Eastern Europe, there had been tremendous strains on their economy resulting from each country trying to do too much in some directions and could not do it and therefore had to suffer greatly in other directions. By and large, it was the lessening of agricultural production that has affected Poland and Hungary. They were anxious and eager to promote industrial growth and they did it. Ultimately, this would be of advantage. But the main incentive for building up heavy industry was the cold war. Because of the possibility of war coming, they tried to build up all industries connected with war even at the cost of agriculture and many other fields of development. War fortunately did not come but their economy suffered very greatly and more particularly agricultural economy suffered. In some cases they did not have manpower for agriculture due to rapid changes. The Chairman emphasised that they all should learn from the experience of these countries. He drew attention particularly to the fact that almost in any country agriculture was the pivot; in India, it was infinitely more the pivot of what was intended to be done and the slightest slackening on the agricultural production front was likely to be fatal to planning.

7. The Chairman added that the questions for consideration by the National Development Council were grave and serious. The members of the Council met in some respects as custodians of the interests of the States; but even more in the other capacity as the members of the National Development Council of

India, looking at the picture of India as a whole and realising that the health of India was absolutely important for any part to be healthy. The stress was to be on the progressive health of the country....

4. Technical Manpower and Training[1]

...The Chairman observed that the question of man was most important. A competent observer who visited India sometime ago said that the problems in India might be put under four heads: man, land, water and cows.

17. The Chairman observed that there should be an undertaking by people who were sent for training and were given scholarships that they would devote 3 or 4 years to the job for which they had been trained so that there was no wastage. The Chairman also referred to the importance of providing training facilities through the existing factories, plants, etc.

18. The Chairman observed that it was strange that while there was lack of technical personnel, quite competent and healthy people were pushed out because they attained the age of 55. Nowhere else in the world was a scientific or medical man or a trained person pushed out simply because, he was 55. He suggested that the age limit should be completely removed subject, of course to the competence and good health of the persons concerned. If necessary at the age of 55 the officer could be examined to find out whether he was fit and proper. It was a very difficult process to produce highly trained officers and it would be ridiculous not to utilise them for national good simply because there was some service rules which required that they should go and somebody else should be promoted. In any case the question did not arise when the need was for more and more people....

26. The Chairman said that technical people should not stick to administrative jobs. They should go backwards and forwards....

28. The Chairman observed that the following might be recorded as the view of the National Development Council on the question of age limit: In the course

1. Remarks at the eighth meeting of the National Development Council, New Delhi, 9 December 1956. Summary record of the meeting, File No. PC/CDN/29/4/57, Coordination Branch, Planning Commission. Extracts.

of its review of manpower problems, the National Development Council was of opinion that in view of the growing demand for trained personnel, especially scientific and technical personnel, it is desirable to continue the service of trained scientific and technical personnel after the specified age limit, subject to efficiency, fitness and satisfactory health. This question should be examined more fully....

30. The Chairman suggested that the Planning Commission might consider the case of students belonging to States which did not have training facilities of their own. Dr J.C. Ghosh[2] observed that seats were reserved in various institutions for Kashmiri students.[3] The Chairman suggested that the matter might be considered afresh. He referred also to the large number of students from Africa, Fiji, Mauritius and other areas who preferred to come to India rather than go to European countries or to America....

34. The Chairman then referred to the National Cadet Corps and the Auxiliary Cadet Corps and observed that these corps had produced good results. Some States had made ample provision for the development of the corps but in others, the provision was inadequate. He suggested that the Chief Ministers should encourage the development of these corps which were important from the point of view of discipline.

35. The Chairman referred also to the National Discipline Scheme which was started by the Ministry of Rehabilitation for children in schools of refugees from the Punjab. The scheme was started in Delhi[4] but it is now spread to Bengal and elsewhere. The Deputy Minister of Rehabilitation (Shri Bhonsle)[5] was in charge of it. The Chairman said that extraordinary results have been achieved and it was most impressive to watch 3,000 children, boys and girls display such fine discipline. The display given by them recently[6] impressed Mr Chou-En lai, Prime Minister of China, very much. The Chairman observed that Shri Bhonsle had done remarkably well and every encouragement should be given to the scheme in the schools....

2. Member, Planning Commission, 1955-59.
3. Bakhshi Ghulam Mohammad, Prime Minister of Jammu and Kashmir who attended the meeting observed that owing of the absence of technical and medical colleges, the state government had to send their students to other states. The other states naturally tried to show preference to its own personnel. He also suggested that the deficiency in technical personnel should be covered in the same way as the deficiency in resources.
4. In 1954.
5. Jagannath Rao Bhonsle.
6. On 29 November 1956.

37. The Chairman then made a few observations on the importance of sports. Every country attached importance to sports; the importance was due not merely to the aspect of physical fitness but to the mental outlook which sports developed. The material available in India was good and would prove successful if suitable opportunity was given. In the Olympic games, even in the Asian Olympic games, India was far behind other countries except in respect of hockey. One reason for the deficiency was that the top people never got the chance to practice or to function together as was done in other Commonwealth countries. The aim should be to achieve higher standards and better coaching. It might be necessary even to obtain coaches from abroad....

40. In his concluding remarks, the Chairman observed that he attached great importance to the National Development Council not only because of the work that was done but because of the fact that it enabled all of them to develop an integrated outlook in considering the problems facing them. In the Central Government, they were thinking of India in a rarified atmosphere and it was necessary that they should be brought to ground by the more practical knowledge and experience of the Chief Ministers. On the other hand the Chief Ministers might tend to think of their States rather than the whole of India. The Chairman said that the National Development Council might gradually begin to deal with a growing number of subjects. The Chairman also referred to the world situation and in particular to the happenings in Egypt and Middle East in general and to the situation in Hungary. He concluded by saying that in these difficult times they had to take difficult decisions and adhere to what was considered to be the right course.

5. To V.T. Krishnamachari[1]

New Delhi,
December 30, 1956

My dear V.T.,[2]

I presume you have seen the first report of the Committee of Secretaries for the fixation of priorities in relation to our foreign exchange position. The Finance Minister has forwarded to me a copy of this report.

The report reveals an unsatisfactory position. Indeed, it shows that unless some rather drastic measures are taken, we might get ourselves tied up in a number of knots. One of our first difficulties is that, while there is no cushion at all for additional defence expenditure, our Defence Ministry attach the greatest importance to this and want to give it a high priority. I do not myself see how we can avoid that, in view of the risks that face us.

In this report, reference is made to an urgent review of the Second Five Year Plan so as to re-arrange it in a way that its overall foreign exchange content from year to year is not greater than our resources assessed on a most optimistic basis. It is clear that this will have to be done. Otherwise, the whole Plan may be upset by some part of it not functioning at all. The report indicates that this review should be completed by April next.

I hope that the Planning Commission is taking this matter in hand. There should, of course, be the closest coordination with the Finance Ministry in this matter.

Yours sincerely,
Jawaharlal Nehru

1. File No. 37(35)/56-59-PMS.
2. Deputy Chairman, Planning Commission.

6. Yojana[1]

There are many magazines and periodicals published in India. I think, however, that the proposal to issue *Yojana* is to be welcomed. Its very name tells us what its function is going to be.

We have framed and published the Second Five Year Plan and many resolutions have been passed in regard to it and yet I feel that adequate publicity has not been given to it. This Plan is not meant merely for the few at the top. It is definitely a people's Plan requiring the understanding and the willing cooperation of our people all over India. It is necessary, therefore, that the message of the Plan should reach our masses and more particularly to those living in our villages. *Yojana,* I understand, is intended to be a journal for mass circulation which will go to all our Community Projects and National Extension Blocks, to cooperatives and Panchayats and to voluntary organisations and our workers in different fields of national life. Much of this field is yet untouched and, therefore, *Yojana* will be doing pioneer work of great importance. I hope that it will be written and produced in simple language so as to be understood by the villager. I hope also that its printing in the Indian languages will be such as can easily be read by those who are not too much used to reading.

I welcome this journal and wish it all success in the great task to which it will be devoted.

1. Message for *Yojana,* a journal published by the Planning Commission, Indore, 3 January 1957. File No. 43(98)/57-70-PMS. The first issue of the journal appeared on 23 January 1957.

7. New Commitments on Foreign Exchange[1]

Your Ministry will be receiving from the Ministry of Finance a series of memoranda designed to limit the expenditure of foreign exchange on projects for which you are responsible. In essence, the scheme propounded in these memoranda is that each Ministry is given an allocation of foreign exchange for the next six months beyond which it may not enter into fresh commitments. The ceilings, you will have observed, are so low that their effect is really to place an embargo on practically all fresh commitments involving foreign exchange. This will undoubtedly have the effect of slowing down the tempo of your work but in the circumstances that have arisen, this has unfortunately become inevitable.

You will recall that in the Second Five Year Plan it was estimated that over the next five years we would draw down our sterling balances to the extent of no more than Rs 200 crores. In fact, during the last nine months the reduction in these balances has amounted to Rs 218 crores giving an average of about Rs 6 crores per week. These balances now stand at Rs 530 crores. The minimum legal reserve required for the backing of the currency is Rs 400 crores. You will, therefore, observe that we have now only Rs 130 crores left before the minimum figure is reached.

There are a number of reasons for this rapid decrease in our foreign exchange reserves, one of which is that a large number of projects have been started both in the public and the private sectors, all at the same time. This has resulted in very large commitments having been made against which payments will fall due in the near future and our resources have to be conserved to meet these commitments. If we take on any additional commitments now, we shall not have the funds to meet them. As it is essential that our past commitments should be honoured, the Ministry of Finance has, with my concurrence felt it necessary to place a virtual embargo on the taking on the fresh commitments. The position will be reviewed in June and if it is improved, the drastic restrictions now imposed will be reduced.

The purpose of my writing this letter to you is to request your cooperation in making the ceiling allocated to your Ministry fully effective. It would be appropriate for your Ministry itself to review all the proposals that it might have for entering into foreign exchange commitments and to present to the Ministry of Finance only those which it finds to be of the highest priority within the

1. Note to Cabinet Ministers, 9 January 1957. File No. 37(35)/56-59-PMS.

ceiling allocated. Priority will, of course, have to be given to expenditure on maintenance or inescapable replacement and then to schemes on which a substantial foreign exchange expenditure, say 90 per cent has already been incurred. Other schemes, I fear, will have to wait till the situation improves.

8. To Chief Ministers [1]

New Delhi,
9 January, 1957

My dear Chief Minister,
I enclose for your information a copy of a note [2] on the foreign exchange situation which I have written to all Cabinet Ministers of the Government of India. You will also receive from the Ministry of Finance a communication on the same subject.

The foreign exchange situation is difficult and the utmost effort has to be made to conserve our foreign resources. I would therefore request your cooperation in ensuring that your Government does not send up to the Ministry of Finance proposals for foreign exchange not covered by the criteria mentioned by them.

The virtual embargo that is being placed on fresh foreign exchange commitments may seriously affect some of your projects. I trust, however, that you will appreciate that in present circumstances such a temporary embargo is inevitable and such inconvenience as it may cause has necessarily to be borne.

Yours sincerely,
Jawaharlal Nehru

1. JN Collection.
2. See the preceding item.

II. INDUSTRY

1. To Swaran Singh[1]

New Delhi,
December 4, 1956

My dear Swaran Singh,[2]

You told us at the Cabinet meeting that the petrol position was fairly satisfactory. This was comforting, but nevertheless, I am a little anxious about future developments and I want this situation watched very closely. We cannot wholly rely on assurances from the oil companies. No one quite knows what developments may take place and we should also give a hint to the public to check consumption as far as possible.

You will remember that I suggested doing some such thing as has been done in some other countries including Ceylon. One way of checking consumption might well be increasing the rate of excise duty somewhat.[3] We should at least examine this question. Perhaps you could have this examination made and so could the Finance Ministry. We could then have facts before us to enable us to come to a decision.

I am writing to T.T. Krishnamachari also on this subject. You might have a talk with him.

Yours sincerely,
Jawaharlal Nehru

1. File No. 17(205)/56-66-PMS.
2. Minister of Works, Housing and Supply.
3. T.T. Krishnamachari wrote to Nehru on 4 December that he was not satisfied with the assurance given by Swaran Singh on the petroleum and aviation gas position. He thought the Ministry of Works, Housing and Supply was "apt to be guided by the complacent attitude adopted by the oil companies." Krishnamachari suggested that one way of checking consumption of petrol was to increase the rate per gallon by 50 per cent.

2. To V.T. Krishnamachari[1]

New Delhi,
January 29, 1957

My dear V.T.,

The Ministry of Production have sent me a letter which they received from R.S. Krishnaswamy,[2] Managing Director of the National Coal Development Corporation.[3] This letter gives some account of the coal position which they expect to be. Apparently, the main difficulty that has arisen relates to foreign exchange. That difficulty faces all of us.

Although you must be fully acquainted with this problem, I am sending you a copy of this letter. It is, of course, true that coal is of basic importance and the Planning Commission now want the target raised from 60 to 65 million tons.[4] The question always is what is relatively more important.

Yours sincerely,
Jawaharlal Nehru

1. File No. 17(225)/57-PMS.
2. (b. 1906); joined the ICS, 1930, posted to Bengal; Secretary, works and buildings, irrigation and waterways department, 1947; special officer, anti-corruption; secretary, civil supplies, West Bengal, 1948; Director General (Food), Government of India, 1950; held additional charge as Vice President, Indian Council for Agricultural Research, May 1953-October 1953; appointed as Vice President, ICAR, January 1955; transferred to Ministry of Production, Commerce and Industry, November 1955.
3. In his report of 22 January, Krishnaswamy remarked that the increase of coal production in the public sector seemed to have started somewhat inauspiciously. Regarding his discussions in Delhi about reducing the foreign exchange requirements, he noted: "The problem ... is not only of ensuring adequate foreign exchange ... for the plans in hand but also knowing to what extent foreign exchange later on will be available. As opening coal mines is an operation particularly projected in terms of long-term planning, ad hoc arrangements and frequent chopping and changing will make the position extremely incoherent."
4. Krishnaswamy wanted the extra 5 million tons to be produced in the public sector beyond its target of 12 million tons.

3. To T.T. Krishnamachari [1]

New Delhi,
January 29, 1957

My dear T.T.,

The Soviet Ambassador[2] came to see me today and brought with him the Soviet engineer Babich,[3] who presented me with the report on the construction of the Heavy Machine Building Plant in India. He also gave me a big volume of photographs of mining and metallurgical equipment.

I have glanced through this report. There is no point in my keeping it here as it would be much more useful to you or to the Ministry of Heavy Industries. I presume you have got or are getting a separate copy; so also the Heavy Industries Ministry. Nevertheless, I am sending these books to you.

As I was looking through this report, Homi Bhabha[4] saw me and I mentioned this to him. He said he would very much like to see it. I am therefore giving it to him for a few days. He will return it. You will, no doubt, have your own copy. The book of photographs is being sent to you straightaway.

Babich told me that this Heavy Machine Building Plant could manufacture all types of heavy equipment including those necessary for atomic reactor. I see that the report recommends some place near Ranchi for this plant.[5]

You may be interested to know that we have received information from our atomic geologist to the effect that the area round about Ranchi is very rich in atomic minerals. Indeed it is probably richer than Travancore, etc., in Thorium, Uranium, etc. This is a big find.

Yours sincerely,
Jawaharlal Nehru

1. File No. 17(226)/57-61-PMS.
2. Mikhail Menshikov.
3. Deputy Minister for Heavy Machine Building, USSR.
4. Chairman, Atomic Energy Commission, and Secretary, Department of Atomic Energy, Government of India.
5. An agreement based on this report was signed in November 1957 between India and the Soviet Union. Construction of the plant began in 1961 and was completed in 1964.

4. To Swaran Singh[1]

New Delhi,
February 12, 1957

My dear Swaran Singh,

Two or three days ago, I went to the Ashoka Hotel. I took Lady Mountbatten to see it. I had a talk with the Swiss Manager. The general impression I get on this Manager is that he is efficient and knows his job.

He did not complain to me about anything, but in the course of the talk, two or three points came up. His chief difficulty appeared to be the large staff which had been engaged in a hurry and which had not been properly trained. In fact, there was no time for training them. Apart from the lack of training, there were large numbers of people who were not at present required. It is always difficult to push out people once engaged.

In this connection he said that if he had had a few trained assistants with him he could tackle this work of training much more easily and satisfactorily. He had apparently suggested that he should be allowed to engage some—I forget the number, but probably it was three or four—assistants from Switzerland for a year. This would help him very greatly and facilitate the task of putting the Ashoka Hotel on an efficient basis. I gather that the Hotel Directors had not thus far agreed to this, chiefly on the ground of foreign exchange.

I cannot give any particular opinion, and of course, we must save foreign exchange. But it seemed to me that it might not be wise to carry on in an inefficient way. That is not good economy. Also that the Ashoka Hotel should not be allowed to drift on for long without pulling it up and giving it a satisfactory and efficient basis.

I am writing to you merely to give you my impressions of my visit. The Ashoka Hotel is a big institution which will make money or lose money in a big way. Everything depends on the efficient management and the service. If it gets a bad reputation about either, then it will suffer in the long run.

Yours sincerely,
Jawaharlal Nehru

---

1. JN Collection.

III. EDUCATION AND CULTURE

1. The National Discipline Scheme[1]

The enclosed letter[2] from twenty-five Members of Parliament may interest you. This refers to the school children of Kasturba Niketan trained by Shri Bhonsle[3] and the National Discipline Scheme.

I might add that Premier Chou En-lai was also much impressed by what he saw of them. Indeed he is reported to have said in Bombay that two of the most impressive things he has seen in India are this display of discipline by the school boys and girls in Delhi and the National Physical Laboratory.

I think this national discipline scheme deserves encouragement and spreading.

---

1. Note to Abul Kalam Azad, Union the Minister of Education, 5 December 1956. File No. 40 (44)/56-63-PMS.
2. Not available.
3. Deputy Minister for Rehabilitation.

2. Discipline Among Youth[1]

I have come here today laying aside all my routine work and, as you know, I am going away from India tomorrow morning.[2] But I thought it proper to come here even though it meant setting aside my other tasks. Why did I do this? My normal, routine work is quite different from this. When Acharyaji[3] told me about this movement a few months ago, I liked the idea. So though normally my path is different, sometimes various paths do meet and strengthen one another. The world is full of people doing all sorts of tasks for everyone cannot do the same task. The world needs carpenters, ironsmiths, other artisans and all kinds of workers. It is not necessary that everyone should do the same kind of work. But it has to be remembered that no matter what the profession or task is, there are some fundamental principles which apply to everyone, to human beings or the society or the country and if they are forgotten, weakness creeps into other spheres also.

History tells us of great empires, great powers and ups and downs of nations. And yet again and again, men who had been considered great in their own times were forgotten by the world. They were mentioned in the pages of history. Others who had not been so well known began to have more influence and the fame of their memory and words began to spread in the world. So there must have been something which had nothing to do with time or rather, something which conquered time itself. So times keep changing but some things remain.

As you know, my work lies in politics and the general belief is that politicians are often unprincipled. People think that there is a separate yardstick for politicians, for individuals and another for the society or the nation. When Mahatma Gandhi came into politics, he said he did not believe in this differentiation. We must use the same yardstick to measure the character of our lives as well as social and political life of a nation. This is true and others have said this before Gandhiji. He did not merely say it but followed it himself and tried to teach the whole country to do so. Now, there are all kinds of people in a

1. Speech at the inauguration of the Anuvrat week, New Delhi, 13 December 1956. AIR tapes, NMML. Original in Hindi. Anuvrat was a programme for moral awakening and national character building.
2. Nehru left on a tour of the United States and Canada on 14 December 1956.
3. Acharya Tulsi (1877-1957); the ninth acharya of Terepanth order of Jainism; started the Anuvrat movement in 1946 to quell communal passions at the time of partition.

country, some weak or greedy, some strong and what not. After all, the people of India are not superior to the people of other countries. The people of every country think that they are superior, which is a false notion.

But Mahatma Gandhi tried to implement his ideas of a moral code of conduct among the masses during the freedom movement. It cannot be said that every individual in India could follow that path unswervingly for, after all, human beings are weak. But his teachings made a strange impact upon the country and in a sense, our politics was uplifted to a higher plane than the usual rung of politics.

Another thing happened. He showed during this movement, which was a non-violent one, that it was not a philosophy born out of weakness but of strength. The country grew in strength, so much so that in the end, we were victorious. Generally, conflict of any kind normally leaves a trail of bitterness and a desire for revenge, etc., which goes on and on. If you look at the history of the nations of the world, you will find that neighbouring countries often have a long history of conflict, and victory goes sometimes to one and at other times the other. The vanquished nurses a grievance and broods about retaliation and strikes when he is stronger. That is, there is no end to the conflict.

In today's world, no conflict can remain isolated. The modern weapons of war have become so lethal that they can destroy the whole world. So, what had earlier been a principle, began to be adopted in practice in day-to-day life. People began to realize that the path of violence is dangerous for it does harm to everyone. There have been wars earlier too but their effect was not so widespread. Now the people have begun to realize the havoc which a war can wreak. But when we talk about non-violence, it does not mean that there should be no wars or guns and swords and atom bombs be eschewed, all the while nursing bitterness and hatred. That is no peace. Peace means not only eschewing of arms but is an attitude of the mind.

Recently a large conference of the UNESCO was held.[4] I do not know if you are aware of it but the Constitution of the UNESCO starts with the preamble that wars first start in the minds of human beings.[5] So what is the point in stopping actual fighting if the minds of the people are filled with thoughts of

4. The 1956 UNESCO General Conference was held at New Delhi from 5 November to 5 December 1956.
5. "Since wars begin in the minds of men, it is in the minds of men that the defences of peace must be constructed."

war? Why, once Gandhiji had said that if there is a sword in your heart all the time, it is better to take it out and use it, instead of shredding your heart with it.[6]

What is a country or society, after all? It is a conglomeration of human beings. A society or a nation is what its people make of it. What will India be? She will be what her people are—she can neither be higher nor lower than what they are.

So, there are two ways for a human being or society to progress. If an individual or society grows in status, it has an effect on the neighbours and they too grow a little. Another method is to create an atmosphere, a social atmosphere which influences people to become better. Both these ways have an impact.

Anyhow, this is a long story. There are many great tasks before the country, and we can succeed in only one way. We can successfully uplift the people and make them better-off, but not by passing laws. The government cannot change the country by law, though laws help to pave the way and make things easier. But the character of a human being cannot be changed by law. So we come around once again, whether it is a question of international or national tasks or that of an individual, to what the character of the people is like. Are they good or bad, clean or unclean, strong or weak? That is how the country will be ultimately for after all, nobody can be fooled forever. That is quite clear. Neither an individual nor a country can be fooled forever.

When there are such complex problems before the world and India, it is essential to think about the fundamental principles on which we should mould the character of the new India that we are building. If we build on sands, it will collapse soon, even if it looks imposing in the beginning. That is not right. The foundations should be deeper and that ultimately depends upon the character of the nation and its people, of every single individual who lives in the country. This applies to everyone but especially so to the boys and girls of today for after all, they are the future of India. We belong to a generation that is old and our days are numbered. The future of India lies in the hands of the youth of today for whom we are toiling and it is upon their shoulders that the burden of national and international tasks will fall. In such a situation, it is essential that their character is moulded properly.

I talked of moulding. We, the people of my generation, have been moulded for over forty years in a pattern which Gandhiji put before the country. It had a profound impact on millions of people, some more, some less, but to some extent on everyone. We are what we are today because we were moulded by him. Now the question is how the new generation is going to be moulded because

---

6. Mahatma Gandhi referred to this in his article 'The Doctrine of the Sword', *Young India*, 11 August 1920.

the tasks before us are extremely complex and cannot be handled by weak-hearted and narrow-minded people. We need stout hearts, broad minds and strong character and self-control. Otherwise, our energy will be wasted in futile ways. We have to learn many things but the most fundamental thing is the character of the people.

Therefore when I heard about this movement, I felt that the more impetus that is given to it, the better it will be. So I gladly accepted the invitation to come here. I hope that the movement will have great success.

3. To Jagjivan Ram[1]

The Residency,
Indore,
7 January, 1957

My dear Jagjivan Ram,[2]

I presume that as Railways and Transport Minister you are in charge of the tourist section.

I went to Mandu which is about sixty-five miles from Indore. This was my second visit. For the first time I went over four years ago.[3] Both from a historical and romantic point of view, the place is of great interest. But in addition to this it has some remarkable archaelogical remains dating back chiefly to about five hundred years ago. Some go further back. These buildings represent the Pathan period in Indian architecture and in the opinion of some experts are extraordinarily important.

Mandu used to be known as the city of joy. It has an equable climate, the altitude being over two thousand feet. When it was heavily populated it had apparently a population of about six or seven lakhs spreading out in the neighbourhood. From the natural scenery point of view it is very attractive and in the rains it is beautiful. Altogether it is probably one of our top ranking places

1. JN Collection.
2. Minister of Railways and Transport.
3. Nehru addressed a meeting of the Bhils at Mandu, the ertswhile capital of the Malwa Sultans on 15 September 1952.

suitable for tourists and others to go to. I find that in the course of the last four years, since I went there last, the fame of Mandu has spread more and a considerable number of tourists go there. I was told today that more than twenty thousand people visited it this year. Most of these go there for a day from Indore and come back. A few stay for the night.

There is some kind of a rest house there which is really not very suited for this purpose. In an old building some rooms have been converted for such use.

I think it is very necessary that a proper rest house should be built there. This need not be pretentious at all but just a few comfortable rooms and a common dining room. I would suggest six bed rooms and a dining room. To this should be attached some kind of a restaurant for casual visitors. All this should not cost much and it would be a great convenience to numerous visitors who go there. I should like your tourist department to consider this matter.

The approach to Mandu is by rather a long road, but I suppose that cannot be helped. Electric lighting will be an advantage but that too, I think, is not such an urgent matter. Perhaps when the Chambal gives power this may be feasible.

Yours sincerely,
Jawaharlal Nehru

4. To Rajendra Prasad[1]

New Delhi,
January 8, 1957

My dear Rajendra Babu,[2]
Thank you for your letter of the 8th January.[3]
The 1857 Centenary Committee has, I believe, already decided that some

1. JN Collection.
2. President of India.
3. Rajendra Prasad wanted a memorial to be erected at Delhi and a museum to be established to preserve the writings of all those political sufferers who had worked for the freedom of the country. The President felt that such a museum should not be confined only to those who participated in the 1857 movement.

kind of a Central memorial should be erected in Delhi for all those who have suffered in the cause of India's freedom. There will be no names and this will not be confined to the movement of 1857.

I am forwarding your letter to the Committee as regards the other proposals contained in it, such as a museum and a rally. So far as the rally is concerned, it may be difficult to select people for it.[4]

Yours sincerely,
Jawaharlal Nehru

4. This related to Rajendra Prasad's second proposal that there should be a rally of political sufferers in several states and also in Delhi in connection with the centenary celebrations of 1857.

5. Transplanting the Ruins at Nagarjunakonda[1]

I have seen these papers. I do not think that the question of expense need trouble. The money will be found for this most important project of excavation, removal and reconstruction.[2]

As for the monuments to be transplanted, we should endeavour to get as many of them as possible to be removed. It is for the archaeologists to advise us. The point is that we should not merely remove odd monuments and put them elsewhere, but rather to recreate, as far as possible, the old city.

The old amphitheatre is unique and I would certainly like it to be removed and reconstructed. But I was told that this might not be possible as it was crumbling away. This matter might be examined afresh—even if it cannot be transplanted, a replica of it should be constructed.

1. Note to K.G. Saiyidain, Education Secretary, 8 January 1957. File No. 40(21)/56-63-PMS.
2. The construction of a masonary dam on the river Krishna in Andhra Pradesh threatened to submerge Nagarjunakonda, the seat of the Ikshavaku kings of Andhra in the second century AD. The government therefore decided to excavate and relocate the ruins to a safer place. See *Selected Works* (second series), Vol. 32, pp. 95-96.

6. The Relics of Huen Tsang[1]

I went to Nalanda today with the Dalai Lama,[2] Panchen Lama[3] and the Chinese Ambassador.[4] The Governor of Bihar[5] and some Ministers were also present at the ceremony of the handing over of the relics of Huen Tsang.[6] This took place at a largely attended meeting held in Nalanda.[7]

(Huen Tsang's name is spelt variously. A fairly common way of spelling is Yuan Chuang. I am, however, using the spelling in this note which is better known to me).

2. At the meeting the following articles were given to me by the Dalai Lama on behalf of the Chinese Government :-

   (i) Relics of Huen Tsang (apparently a small part of the skull). This was placed in a large gold-covered casket or vase.

   (ii) Two books in Chinese characters. One of these is a biography of Huen Tsang and the other Huen Tsang's book *Records of the Western Land* in Chinese. There was also a long list in Chinese of books translated by Huen Tsang from Sanskrit texts into Chinese.

   (iii) A cheque from the Chinese Embassy in Delhi for Rs 574,713/-.

   (iv) A plan of a building in Chinese style to be erected in Nalanda in memory of Huen Tsang; the casket containing the relics to be kept in this building.

3. The first thing to be done is for a formal letter of thanks to be sent by the External Affairs Ministry, preferably by the Secretary General,[8] to the Chinese Ambassador in Delhi. In this letter our gratitude should be expressed for the gift of the relics of Huen Tsang which we value greatly and which we shall preserve carefully, not only because of the intrinsic worth but also as a symbol of the old

---

1. Note to the Union Minister of Education, Camp: Rajgir, Bihar, 12 January 1957. JN Collection.
2. Tenzin Gyatso, the Fourteenth Dalai Lama.
3. Chokyi Gyaltsan, the Tenth Panchen Lama.
4. Pan Tzu-li.
5. R.R. Diwakar.
6. (602-664 AD); Chinese Buddhist scholar and traveller, who spent fourteen years in India from 630-644 AD.
7. Nehru received the relics of Huen Tsang from the Dalai Lama in the premises of Nava Nalanda Mahavihara, situated in the valley of Rajgir Hills, a mile from the remains of the Nalanda university.
8. N.R. Pillai, Secretary General, Ministry of External Affairs.

friendship and cultural relations between India and China. Thanks should also be given for the books in Chinese which have been given to us and finally for the generous donation of Rs 574,713/- for the erection of a building to house these relics in Nalanda. SG should request that the thanks of the Government of India be conveyed to the Chinese Government. He should state that the plan of the building which we have received will be carefully examined by our architects and any suggestions they make about it will be forwarded to the Chinese Government. A site for the building will also have to be chosen.

4. The two Chinese books have been handed over to the Bihar Government's representatives to be kept in the Institute at Nalanda. The list of books translated by Huen Tsang from Sanskrit into Chinese is itself in Chinese. I have given this to Prof Tan Yun Shan[9] of Santiniketan and requested him to get it translated in English and to send one copy of this to the Education Ministry and a second copy to the Governor of Bihar.

5. The Chinese plan for a building has, I think, been taken by Shri A. Ghosh,[10] the Director-General of Archaeology. He said that he would have copies made of this and one copy will be sent to the Bihar Government. This plan will first be examined by the architects of the Archaeological Department who should send their comments to the External Affairs Ministry. They should also recommend a suitable site in Nalanda for the building. A rough estimate of the building should also be made. The building should necessarily have some kind of a garden roundabout it.

6. I presume that the actual sum of money given by the Chinese Government for this building will be adequate for the purpose. If, by any chance, this is not ultimately considered sufficient, then we shall have to give the balance ourselves. We cannot ask the Chinese Government for more money for this purpose.

7. The casket containing the relics has, for the present, been deposited in the little museum at Nalanda. This, however, is not a suitable place for it. It is a valuable casket and requires to be placed where its security is guaranteed. Temporary arrangements have been made at Nalanda for this purpose and it may even have to be kept in a safe. Obviously this is not satisfactory. Till a new permanent building is made to house this casket and the relics, some other arrangement has to be made. I suggest that these relics and the casket should be kept in the Patna Museum where it can be looked after properly. When the new building is ready, the relics will be transferred there.

9. (1898-1983); Chinese Buddhist scholar; founder, Sino-Indian Cultural Society, Nanking, 1933; founder-director, Cheena Bhavan, Visva-Bharati, 1937; China's cultural ambassador to India, 1939; retired from Visva-Bharati in 1967,

10. Director-General, Archaeological Survey of India, 1953-68.

8. I have suggested above that SG should write to the Chinese Ambassador thanking the Chinese Government for these gifts. I think he should also write to the Dalai Lama through whom we received these gifts.

9. The question will arise ultimately, though not now, as to what permanent use we can make of the new building that will be put up. According to the Chinese plan, this consists of a big hall which will be the central memorial of Huen Tsang. On either side of it there are two smaller structures. It has been suggested that one of these should be a memorial to Fa-hien and the other to I-tsing, two famous Chinese travellers to India who preceded Huen Tsang.[11] Presumably some constructive work should be done in these buildings.

10. The buildings can, of course, have a library primarily consisting of Huen Tsang's works and secondly of other Chinese works on India and Chinese translations from Indian classics. One of the important activities connected with this institute might well be to further translations into English or Indian languages from Chinese works dealing with India. It is said that above five thousand Indian manuscripts were translated from Sanskrit into Chinese in the early days. In regard to many of these there is no original Sanskrit version available. Therefore, the only way to get at them is through Chinese or translations from them. This work of translation will be a big one and will no doubt take many years. While this work may be done at Nalanda through competent scholars, the Cheena Bhavan at Santiniketan should be associated with it. There is also a Pali Institute at present in Nalanda. That should also be associated.

11. The Honorary Director of the Pali Institute is Bhikku Kashyap.[12] It was, I believe, largely at his instance that this gift of Huen Tsang's relics etc. has been made to us. He went to China last summer and saw some of the leading personalities there and made this suggestion which was approved of.

12. The Education Ministry will naturally be in charge of this matter, i.e. both the preliminary steps to be taken now in regarding to the building, etc. and, later, permanent arrangements for the use of this building as well as the work of translations etc. External Affairs Ministry must be kept in intimate touch with

11. Fa-hein came to India in 400-411 AD. On the other hand I-tsing came to India in 671-695 AD.
12. Jagdish Narayan Kashyap (1908-1976); Principal of Sanskrit Vidyapeeth at Baidyanathdham in Bihar 1931-33; ordained into the Sangha and became a *Bhikku*, in 1934; taught Pali at the Banaras Hindu University, Varanasi, 1940-49; director, Nava Nalanda Mahavihara, 1951-59, 1965-1973; founder-president of the Magahi Cultural Association, 1954; first Professor and Head of Department of Pali and Buddhism, Banaras Hindu University, 1959-65; became Mahanayaka of the Indian Bhikku Sangha, 1974; published the 1st volume of *Tripitakas* in Devanagari on the occasion of Buddha Jayanti in 1956. The whole set of 41 volumes of *Tripitakas* was published by 1961.

this and all communications to the Chinese Government or to the Chinese Ambassador should go through the External Affairs Ministry. The Bihar Government should also be kept fully informed and their advice taken whenever necessary. Their cooperation is essential.

13. This note is addressed to the Minister of Education and copies are being sent to Secretary General, External Affairs, the Governor of Bihar and the Chief Minister of Bihar.

14. The cheque for Rs 574,713/- is being sent to the Secretary General. He should deal with it in accordance with our practice in such matters.

7. To Sri Krishna Sinha[1]

Circuit House,
Hirakud (Orissa),
January 13, 1957

My dear Sri Babu,[2]

I shall be grateful if you will kindly enquire and let me know what has happened to the Saraikela troops of mass dancers.[3] Their dances are unique in India and worth encouraging. I was much struck by them when I saw them first and on subsequent occasions also they seemed to me to be remarkable. Most of the dancers consisted of members of the princely family of Saraikela.

I am anxious to encourage them and I shall gladly send you some money for this purpose.[4] I shall, however, await your reply in which I hope you will be able to give me some information about their present position and what they are doing.

Yours sincerely,
Jawaharlal Nehru

1. JN Collection.
2. Chief Minister of Bihar.
3. The *Chhau* dance is a form of folk dance of the Seraikella-Kharsawan region, the word *Chhau* signifying a mask. The dancer's identity and sex are concealed on account of the mask worn while performing.
4. Nehru, on the same day wrote to Harekrushna Mahtab the Chief Minister of Orissa, that he would send Rs 10,000 for the encouragement of Mayurbhanj *Chhau* dancers.

8. Aims and Ideals of Visva-Bharati [1]

It is a great happiness to me to be present here on this occasion and to imbibe again something of the spirit of this institution and of the memories that cling to this soil and these buildings and the gardens that we have around us. My only regret, if any, is that we are holding this convocation in this manner and not in the mango grove where we used to hold it. I suppose this is the inevitable price we have to pay for progress. I do wish that we could go back to the mango grove lest this one innovation should lead to others which will take us farther and farther away from the mango grove and all that it stands for. I have previously listened to the proceedings of your convocations, but whenever I listen to them, the repetition of the old Vedic hymns, of the aims and ideals of Visva-Bharati [2] and of some of your songs, have a significance for me which does not become stale. There is a freshness about them because there is an essential truth and vitality in them. I feel that if those who teach and those who study in this institution will only remember and act up to these precepts, even to a small extent, it will do credit to this institution. And if by any chance the rest of India can do that, it will be a good thing indeed. For in this time of trouble and problems in the world, when people feel terribly frustrated and are in doubt about what to do and what not to do, and when it is not often easy to come to a decision, it becomes essential to hold on to something by which we can measure problems and questions, some anchor not only for our personal life but for our national life. I think that the ideals which Gurudev [3] laid down and which you have enshrined in your Visva-Bharati's aims and objectives, give us that anchor. If we adhere to them, we shall never go wrong really though we may make many a mistake. Small mistakes do not matter; it is the basic mistakes that matter. One can recover from the small mistakes but it is much more difficult to recover from any basic error in our approach. This is how I feel whenever I come here. I do not know whether I am helpful to you in any way or not, but I can tell you

---

1. Address at Visva-Bharati, Santiniketan, 15 January 1957. *Jawaharlal Nehru's Speeches,* Volume 3, March 1953-August 1957, Publications Division, Ministry of Information and Broadcasting, pp. 435-439.
2. Visva-Bharati was formally inaugurated in 1921. It seeks to realize the meeting of the East and the West and thus to ultimately strengthen the fundamental conditions of world peace through the establishment of free communication of ideas between the two hemispheres.
3. Rabindranath Tagore.

in all honesty that you and this institution and the memory of Gurudev are of enormous help to me in the problems that I have to face from day to day. And often when doubts and difficulties arise, that memory inspires me, and if it does not solve the problem, at any rate it puts me in a better frame of mind to tackle it.

The more I think of the wisdom of Gurudev the more astonished I am, even though I ought not to be. Long ago when many things that he said had not become current coin in this country, his analysis of the disease, if I may call it a disease, that was enervating India, and his way of seeking to cure it, stood out as remarkable prophecies of the shape of things to come. Three months before his death he wrote his famous essay 'Crisis in Civilization'[4] from which a brief extract has been quoted by Professor Mahalanobis.[5] I remember reading it when I was in some prison or the other, and I remember how powerfully I was affected. And I then wondered—as I do again listening to it now—how very intimately and precisely what Gurudev wrote in that essay is applicable today, perhaps even more so than when he wrote it. Because he was a seer he could see ahead things yet unborn. Here we are facing this crisis of civilization and people talk and act more and more in terms of might and the insolence of power; and others, afraid of power, line up behind that power. And the good things of life suffer. The very basis of a decent approach to life—call it religious, call it spiritual, call it scientific—they are submerged in this deluge of hatred and violence and fear. Fear and hatred and violence are the worst companions that an individual or a nation can have. And yet today these probably are the dominating urges in many countries and many people. I do not know what an individual or even a nation can do to fight this menace or to face it. In the final analysis one has to rely on some kind of a basic faith in the future of man, to which again Gurudev made such frequent reference. Without that basic faith in something in man, it would be difficult enough to see or save a world which is drifting apparently towards an almost irretrievable disaster. And yet that basic faith gives one the strength to survive. Looking back on the long perspective and panorama of

4. Written on the occasion of the poet's eightieth birthday in May 1941.
5. The extract from Tagore's essay quoted by P.C. Mahalanobis while delivering the convocation address is as follows: "As I look around I see the crumbling ruins of a proud civilization strawn like a vast heap of futility. And yet I shall not commit the grievous sin of losing faith in man. I would rather look forward to the opening of a new chapter in his history after the cataclysm is over and the atmosphere is rendered clean with the spirit of service and sacrifice. Perhaps that dawn will come from this horizon, from the East where the sun rises. A day will come when unvanquished man will retrace his path of conquest despite all barriers, to win back his lost human heritage."

history, one sees periods when great crises faced the world, and people living then thought that their time was the worst of all times, the most critical, the most dangerous. And yet the world survived, and not only survived but went ahead and made good in some other directions. Likewise, perhaps, we who live in these times may be attaching too great an importance to certain evil and unhappy aspects of these times, not realizing that under this crust, good things may be happening which will break out and take humanity further. It is good to have that faith and it is good to have some anchorage which will prevent us from drifting too much. Here in Visva-Bharati we have something which is not easy to reproduce elsewhere. We can build up a great university, great in the sense of big buildings and equipment and all that, but it is very difficult to build up traditions, to build up an atmosphere which surrounds a place, and to build up memories which are so powerful in guiding and in affecting our minds and hearts. You have that inestimable advantage here, which you cannot have merely by the reading of books, though books should no doubt be read. And I hope you will take full advantage of this inestimable heritage, because I feel that in many ways that is needed in India more than almost anything else.

We have in India a large number of universities which are producing good people. But we sometimes complain of their behaviour, though I am not worried about it. What I am rather worried about is whether these people have the depth that they should have, because that is more important than the passing of examinations. Creativeness, productiveness, a certain sincerity of purpose, a certain depth, are the very things on which here at Santiniketan and in Visva-Bharati, Gurudev laid stress all the time. He emphasized those things to which enough attention is not paid in other institutions of learning. He wanted to provide the widest possible cultural background so that the narrowness of spirit and mind would be removed. It is not easy to do so, even if a great teacher tells us. But it helps if we are constantly reminded of that wider vision. This institution was meant to be a kind of symbol of that spirit—the international, universal spirit.

You started under good auspices. You have had difficulties here, but these should not trouble you very much. It is always a very difficult thing to follow a great founder, a great teacher, a great man. If you had the privilege of having as your founder one of the greatest sons that India has ever produced, well, you have to suffer for it. You cannot have these great men age after age. You can have them only in your memory and in the vivid and vital traditions that they leave in their words and in their works. Apart from the crises in the world, here in India we face many difficult problems. You too, no doubt, will be thinking about them. Don't be worried. Don't be frustrated by the immensity of the problems. The problems are immense, no doubt, but so is our will and our determination and so is the will of the innumerable people in India who will work for the solution of those problems. It is not you and I alone that will do it. One has to put one's individual life in some relation to the national life that is developing, and the national life in some relation to the international life. Thus you spread yourselves out and though your feet may be and should be certainly on the firm ground, your head should occasionally touch the clouds.

I wish you well and I wish this institution well. But it is not my wishing you well that will matter much, but to what extent you remember the message of Gurudev and the ideals enshrined in this Visva-Bharati.

Our Upacharya[6] referred to the necessity of developing science in this institution. If you want to develop science more, you could not have done better than have as your Upacharya one of the most eminent men of science not only in India but in the world. I certainly agree with him that it would be the right thing for Visva-Bharati to stress science more, so that the kind of training that is given here is more balanced and more suitable for what is happening in India, and for the calls the country might make upon you and everyone of us. We are being called constantly to greater endeavour in many fields of activity, not one only. We have to train ourselves for them because only those people who are trained in mind and body can really do effective work. Mere goodwill is not enough. It is good to have goodwill, it is good to have enthusiasm, but it is essential to have training. No handicraft or other work can be done merely by enthusiasm. You have to learn the art, and we want to train men today and to develop institutions which give the basis of that training. We want trained men in technical fields. In the world today technology has made such great progress that people tend to forget other things, and culture in the real sense decays. A kind of technological culture of course progresses, which is good in so far as it goes, provided it is balanced by other forms of culture. It will not profit a man very much if he is clever with his hands, or even with his tongue or brain, but has no foundations of character or wider vision. Such a society will ultimately perish. So this drift to technology which is inevitable today in the world and in India has to be balanced by the other aspects of culture, which, fortunately, Visva-Bharati has laid stress on. It is necessary that the development in scientific teaching should also take place, otherwise you may find some difficulty later in even understanding what is happening in India or in participating in the developments in the full way that you really ought to.

I should like to express again my great happiness at being here today. I wish all of you in this great institution prosperity in the future.

6. S.N. Bose, Vice Chancellor of Visva-Bharati.

9. To K.G. Saiyidain[1]

New Delhi,
February 5, 1957

My dear Saiyidain,[2]

When I was in Madras the other day,[3] I learnt that it was proposed to take away a large area of land, about five hundred or six hundred acres, from the Guindy Estate for the new technical institute that is to be established in Madras. I gathered that the Madras Government has even agreed to this, although not very happily. Many people came to me to complain of this cutting up of the Guindy Estate, which is used as a public park by the people of Madras.

2. I myself feel that it will be unfortunate to deprive Madras city of the one big park that they have got. I have been thinking for some time past that this large area, consisting I believe of about one thousand two hundred acres or so, should be converted into a real public park and separated from Raj Bhavan. Raj Bhavan may be given fifty acres or even a hundred. If the technical institute takes six hundred acres, the proposed park would be very much reduced in size. Madras has really no parks, and this is the only place which can be made into a good park. The city is growing, and it is very difficult to produce parks when too many buildings have been put up all over the place. We must, therefore, think of the future. The park can contain a botanical garden, possibly also a zoo, a children's park and so on. Every city should have this and especially a big city like Madras.

3. I do not understand why the technical institute should acquire five hundred or six hundred acres. I am quite sure that in England or America or other places, such large tracts of land are not available for any institute, and they have to do with a much smaller area. We spread out too much because it is a little easier to get large areas. I realise that an institute requires a fairly extensive piece of land for accommodating its officers, hostels, etc., apart from the actual institute buildings. Nevertheless, I would have thought that about two hundred acres is ample and more. In case you require more land, surely it would be better to acquire land other than the Guindy land. I understand that such land is available roundabout.

1. File No. 40(114)/57-PMS.
2. Secretary, Ministry of Education.
3. Nehru was in Chennai on 31 January 1957.

4. I would, therefore, suggest to your Ministry to reconsider this matter and not to cut up this poor Guindy Estate. At the most, take one hundred acres out of it, or say even two hundred, but not more. The public park should contain at least one thousand acres. It would also be a great pity to cut up the fine trees that have grown there.

Yours sincerely,
Jawaharlal Nehru

10. Film on the Buddha[1]

Two or three days ago I saw the Buddha Jayanti film again.[2] This is the film in which the story of Buddha is told through sculptures. I think it is a very fine film and we should send copies of it to at least some of our principal Missions abroad and also especially to Burma and Ceylon.

I do not quite know what the arrangements were to make this film. It appears that it was a private venture supported by Government. Is this so? There is one thing about the film which I should like to point out. After the Buddha's story in sculpture is over, we are shown pictures of some famous temples, pagodas, etc., in some Buddhist countries. Then pictures of Chaitanya,[3] Guru Govind Singh,[4] etc., and lastly of Gandhiji. I do not think these additions are at all suitable. Artistically they do not fit in. I think the film should end with the death of the Buddha, possibly the last picture should be one of the good Buddha statues.

---

1. Note to B.M. Lad, Secretary, Ministry of Information and Broadcasting, 11 February 1957. JN Collection.
2. The Buddha's teaching were packed into a ten-reel film titled *Gotma the Buddha*. It was produced for the Films Division by Bimal Roy Productions and the script was written by Raj Bans Khanna.
3. Chaitanya Mahaprabhu (1486-1533); religious saint and protagonist of neo-Vaisnavism; an intiator of a movement through a novel method of mass *Samkirtana*; an upholder of the cult of Radha and Krishna.
4. Guru Govind Singh (1666-1708); the tenth and the last guru of the Sikhs.

Also the film is just a bit too long. I think it lasts about an hour and a half. Perhaps the taking out of the last parts would reduce it by ten or fifteen minutes. As far as possible, it should be for about an hour only.

11. To Abul Kalam Azad[1]

New Delhi,
12 February 1957

My dear Maulana,

When I was in London,[2] I saw a large number of portraits and sketches which were made in Tipu Sultan's time by some Englishman who visited his court. We obtained these from the Duke of Wellington.[3] I arranged to have them sent to the Victoria and Albert Museum[4] to get them properly conditioned. They will be sent to India later.

We obtained these in exchange for the portrait of the Duke of Wellington[5] which was in Raj Bhavan in Madras.[6]

At the back of one of the portraits of Tipu Sultan there was a hand-written inscription.[7] This was evidently written by an Englishman at that time. This was

---

1. File No. 40(89)/56-58-PMS.
2. In July 1956.
3. Gerald Wellesley, the Seventh Duke of Wellington.
4. The Victoria and Albert Museum in South Kensington, London opened in 1857 as South Kensington Museum. It has been housed in its present building since 1909.
5. Arthur Wellesley, the first Duke of Wellington.
6. For an earlier reference to this, see *Selected Work* (second series), Vol. 34, p. 83.
7. The inscription said that during the third battle of Srirangapatnam in 1799 it was common amongst the British to call Tipu Sultan "The Tyrant". But Lord Cornwallis in his public dispatches stated that Tipu's country was "a garden from one end to the other; and had not a deserter from him" during the war. The inscription also recorded an eyewitness as saying that Mysore under Hyder Ali was really patriarchal. Hyder Ali's code of laws was "simple and concise in theory, summary in practice, breathing the pure spirit of justice and mercy." The unnamed eyewitness concludes after having analysed Hyder's reign by saying: "What splendid proofs of tyranny!"

a very interesting inscription and I copied it out. I give you separately a copy of this inscription at the back of Tipu Sultan's picture.[8]

Yours affectionately,
Jawaharlal

8. Nehru also sent a copy of the inscription to Sri Prakasa, Governor of Bombay.

12. To K.G. Saiyidain[1]

Jaipur,
February 18, 1957

My dear Saiyidain,

Thank you for your letter of February 16th.[2]

I am all in favour of the technical institute being situated in the south. I also agree that round about Madras would be a suitable location. If your committee thinks that five hundred acres of land will be required for the development of this institute, I have nothing further to say.[3]

The only question is about the location and the site. I think that you might discuss this matter with the Madras State Government. I was told that land was

1. File No. 40(114)/57-PMS.
2. Saiyidain in his letter stated that the Southern Region Committee of the All India Council for Technical Education had recommended that the Southern Higher Technological Institute should be located at Chennai. The state government had offered to make available 500 acres of land from the Raj Bhavan estate for this purpose. Saiyidain further stated that as an area of about 500 acres would not be adequate for expansion and development of the institute, a further examination in consultation with the state government regarding the location of the institute at some suitable alternative site should be made.
3. The Indian Institute of Technology, Chennai, was inaugurated at the Guindy Estate on 31 July 1959, by Humayun Kabir, the Minister for Scientific Research and Cultural Affairs. The institute was developed on a 600 acre site in Guindy.

available near the Guindy Estate. Perhaps you could take a small part of the Guindy Estate, say 100 acres or so and add to it further adjoining or nearby land which may be available. All I am anxious about is that the Guindy Estate should not be broken up and that at least a thousand acres of it should remain to be converted into a public park.

Yours sincerely,
Jawaharlal Nehru

IV. ATOMIC ENERGY

1. Apsara [1]

Both the Governor[2] and Dr Bhabha have expressed their thanks to the representatives of various countries and their atomic energy establishments who have come here from long distances. I should like to convey to them my own feelings of gratitude. Some of them will no doubt find this a 'small fry' affair because they are used to things much bigger. But I have no doubt they will appreciate that in the conditions which exist in India, and in Asia, the work that has been done here has some significance.

We are told, and I am prepared to believe it on Dr Bhabha's word, that this is the first atomic energy reactor[3] in Asia except, possibly, the Soviet areas. In that sense, this represents a certain historic moment in India and in Asia. Though today's is only a formal inauguration ceremony of something which really has been working for some time, it is also a recognition of what is likely to take place in the future.

1. Speech at the inauguration of India's first atomic reactor at Trombay, near Mumbai, 20 January 1957. *Jawaharlal Nehru's Speeches*, Vol. 3, March 1953-August 1957, Publications Division, Ministry of Information and Broadcasting, pp. 504-508.
2. Sri Prakasa, Governor of Bombay.
3. A swimming pool type reactor of 1,000 kW capacity, designed and built by Indian scientists and engineers, went into operation at Trombay on 4 August 1956. It made available atomic energy for experimental purposes.

We in India and, in a greater or lesser degree, in other countries in Asia, are involved in raising the standard of living of our people. Some people may think that the development of atomic energy is not directly related to the question of economic improvement. But we must remember that few things that we do produce results immediately. Dr Bhabha has given you some figures showing how important it is for India to develop atomic energy.[4] Just as the Industrial Revolution went ahead whether people liked it or not, so this atomic revolution has something inevitable about it. Either you go ahead with it, or others go ahead and you fall behind and drag yourself in their trail.

As I stand here, I have this Swimming Pool Reactor behind me, and the island of Elephanta in front of me, not far away. For 1,300 years now, Elephanta has continued to present a great aspect of our history. People go to see it, even the distinguished scientists who have come here for this function, because Elephanta presumably represents something of lasting value and significance. Thirteen hundred years lie between the sculpture in the island of Elephanta and this Swimming Pool Reactor which represents the middle of the twentieth century. Both, I take it, have their place, and any person who ignores either of them misses an important element of life. I don't suppose humanity can live on reactors alone. Certainly it cannot live on Elephanta alone. In a sense, it is the combination of Elephanta and the Swimming Pool Reactor—odd as it may seem—that might produce a proper balance in life.

In the old days men of religion talked about the mysteries. In Greece, the high priests who reputedly knew about these mysteries exercised a great amount of influence on the common people who did not understand them. That was so in every country. We now have these mysteries which the high priests of science flourish before us, not only flourish but threaten us with. They make us feel full of wonder and full of fear. These new mysteries of science, and of higher mathematics, unveil various aspects of the physical world to us. No one knows where this will lead us. Some of us may feel frightened, but in the ultimate, we should never be frightened of the truth. We cannot suppress truth; we cannot suppress the desire of man to unravel, to discover, to progress, even though it may land him in dangerous situations. If the human mind by chance takes the wrong turn, well, it suffers the consequences. Therefore, it is no good trying to stop this quest. It cannot be stopped. But it can be and has to be organized in such a way as to bring good to the world instead of evil. I believe people in every country of the world, and more especially those countries which are

---

4. Homi Bhabha stressed the need to develop atomic energy as a source of power, and to promote its use in agriculture, biology, industry and medicine.

advanced in atomic energy development, realize this. Even though they possess this fearsome power, which is ever growing, they also realize the dangers of using it in the wrong way. I imagine that everybody now realizes that with things as they are today, a global war in which strategic use of atomic weapons is made is out of question. Some people dally with the idea of what is called tactical use of these weapons, as distinct from strategic use. With the little I know about these matters, it seems to me dangerous to play about with atomic weapons in this way. Any use of it must be forbidden because it will bring disaster to everybody. Hence the importance of the talks that go on from time to time for controlling the use of nuclear weapons. When you think of controlling the use of this power, you have to think in terms of disarmament. This is not the occasion for me to talk about this complicated subject. But I believe that in spite of apparent and real difficulties, people's minds and the minds of those who control the destinies of nations, are beginning more and more to take what I may venture to call a realistic view of the situation. Let us hope that they will arrive at some decision which will put an end to the terrible fear that these weapons might be used. Indeed, this itself will be helpful in controlling the use of any weapons of large-scale destruction.

So far as India's development of atomic energy is concerned, we are at the beginning of the journey, although, I believe, we have done rather well in the last few years. I should like to congratulate those responsible, Dr Bhabha, Dr Krishnan[5] and all the young men and women of the Atomic Energy Department, who are doing such good work. It is really when I talk to them and see their trained minds and informed enthusiasm that I realize what very good material we have. The future becomes much more assured not because of these cement-and-steel buildings we put up, but because of the human material we have. I should therefore like specially to congratulate these people on the work they have done. What you see here is the result of their work.

We are not reluctant in the slightest degree to take advice and help from other countries. We are grateful to them for the help which they have given—and which we hope to get in future—because of their longer experience. But it is to be remembered that this Swimming Pool Reactor in front of you is the work, almost entirely, of our young Indian scientists and builders. Having said that I should like, as Dr Bhabha has done, to express my gratitude to the countries which have been generously helping us. We have received help from many of them. Presently you will see what is called the Canada-India Reactor which is

5. K.S. Krishnan, Director, National Physical Laboratory, and member, Atomic Energy Commission, Government of India.

being built with the generous help of the Canadian Government.[6] You have learnt of the continuous help we have had from the atomic energy establishments of the United Kingdom and the United States, and of the cooperation we have had from France. There has been cooperation with the Soviet Union also in this matter, and it will no doubt develop in future.

We have built these atomic energy establishments here not only to help ourselves, but as a centre where we can share such knowledge and experience as we possess, and as these establishments might offer, with people of other countries of Asia or Africa. I believe some of them have expressed their willingness to take advantage of them. I should like to repeat that we shall gladly welcome the association in these training facilities, of people from countries which do not possess them, more especially in Asia and parts of Africa.

I am happy today, but with that happiness it is impossible not to think of the likelihood of this development taking a malevolent turn. No man can prophesy the future. But I should like to say on behalf of my Government—and I think I can say with some assurance on behalf of any future Government of India—that whatever might happen, whatever the circumstances, we shall never use this atomic energy for evil purposes. There is no condition attached to this assurance, because once a condition is attached, the value of such an assurance does not go very far.

As I formally declare open this atomic energy establishment, I wish to say one thing more. It has been suggested that we should give a suitable name to the Swimming Pool Reactor. In the course of the afternoon, while we were having tea, this subject was discussed. Dr Krishnan, from the fund of his Sanskrit lore, suggested various names. Dr Bhabha pondered over them, and the Governor, who is a Sanskrit scholar, was consulted, and we thought of a name for this Swimming Pool Reactor. It may be that when you hear the name that we are suggesting, you will be somewhat surprised. But on further thought you will see how very appropriate it is. The name we suggest for it is Apsara which, you all know, means a celestial damsel or water nymph. This is a Swimming Pool Reactor and an *apsara* is specially associated with water. The name is therefore appropriate. So, with your approval, I name this Swimming Pool Reactor Apsara.

6. The Canada-India Reactor US (CIRUS) was a 40 Megawatt reactor that Canada offered to build for India under the Colombo Plan in 1955. It went critical in July 1960.

V. HEALTH

1. To Satya Narayan Sinha[1]

New Delhi,
December 3, 1956

My dear Satya Narayan,[2]

As you know, we are anxious to get the All India Medical Council Bill through Parliament during this session. Fortunately, an agreement has been arrived at about the changes to be made in it. There will be quite a number of amendments. I hope you will arrange to have this Bill considered by the Lok Sabha soon. It will then have to go back to the Rajya Sabha.

Please find out from the Health Ministry if they are quite ready with it.

Yours sincerely,
Jawaharlal Nehru

1. File No. 28(32)/56-PMS.
2. Union Minister of Parliamentary Affairs.

201

2. World Cooperation in Medicine[1]

The President of our Republic has already accorded you a warm welcome here, to our city of Delhi. There is little that I can add to it. But I should also like, nevertheless, to express to you my happiness that all of you have come here and done us the honour of being our guests and that you are engaged in a task of vital importance. That goes without saying. Whether we ourselves have escaped from the scourge of tuberculosis or not there is probably hardly a family which has not had to do something with this dreaded disease and so everybody is interested in the great work that you are doing. We shall cooperate with you in this country to the best of our ability. But I can say very little which would be of any value in the domain of your work. I shall, therefore say a few words, perhaps of some wider significance.

You are engaged, delegates coming from a large number of countries, in a common task. You cooperate in that task forgetting national boundaries, national prejudices, national fears and deal with a common enemy, that is, this disease. As you are doing in this particular activity so also do others—other organisations dealing with other subjects of world importance, whether in the domain of disease or other matters—meet together as they did in this hall some time ago in the UNESCO Conference or in specialised conferences. They work together in this constructive activity of the world, forgetting to a large extent their national differences. And so in a way we develop more and more what may be called the world mind, the world approach to world problems. Some problems fortunately are easily capable of that cooperative world approach, others unfortunately come up against particular interests or rivalries or passions of different nations and we are all, wherever we may come from, to a greater or lesser extent, affected by these particular interests of our countries and particular prejudices that come from them. Now it seems to me that it is to the extent that we develop this world mind or world approach to our problems that we solve them. Presumably, you will feel that it is not much good approaching this campaign against tuberculosis in a narrow way in some areas here and there, but the right approach is to confer together and to profit by each others experience and then to combat it wherever you can all over the world. It may be more at some places because the

---

1. Speech at an international conference on tuberculosis, Vigyan Bhavan, New Delhi, 10 January 1957. JN Papers, NMML.

opportunities and facilities are greater and resources are greater and a little less in other places. But, nevertheless your approach is a world approach. So also, as I said, in some other matters there is beginning to develop this world approach to various problems. On the other hand we find that in certain matters chiefly connected with the political field, maybe sometimes the economic field also, this world approach, though admitted comes up against a number of obstructions and difficulties and yet it seems quite inevitable that unless we develop more and more of that world approach, we shall not be able to solve problems which affect and afflict the world. Various developments, possibly, most of all the tremendous development of communications, has brought the world so near and made it so compact that every country is neighbour to the other country. We become neighbours of one another; we do not live distinctly or separated from each other. Therefore these developments have made this world one-world, although our thinking and our national boundaries and national interests and national prejudices still maintain those tremendous barriers—the barriers are not so much geographical, not so much physical but much more are they barriers in our minds.

Just as it is said in the UNESCO Constitution that 'wars begin in the minds of men' so also these barriers exist in the minds of men which come in the way of this united and cooperative approach to our problems. We have great organizations struggling to bring about this cooperative approach, organizations like the United Nations and we wish them all success, but the problem is after all how to overcome the narrow outlook, the parochial outlook, even the national outlook and try to look at these problems from this larger world point of view—in fact to develop the world as one-world. I have no easy way to suggest to you to do this. We are all struggling against circumstances, against difficulties and I do believe that the tendency to develop this world mind and world cooperation is so strong and so powerful that it is bound to succeed in the end.

I have ventured just to express some thoughts which often come to my mind and they must also perhaps trouble you sometimes. Those thoughts occurred to me specially because you here represent a particular activity, no doubt, but nevertheless you represent, many countries of the world, for that activity. And the more activities we undertake for discussion in this international fashion the more perhaps this habit of thinking in terms of the world would grow and it might even ultimately affect people of my profession, that is, politics—they are the hardest people to be affected, I believe—and when their minds begin to think in this way then I suppose victory will not be far off.

You represent an important branch of science and science, if it is anything at all, is international, medicine is international. It would now be rather absurd to talk of national science or national medicine. So this idea or this concept of international thinking and cooperative working, in spite of differences of course, must inevitably grow. We cannot solve problems, any major international problem, by a purely nationalised approach because then you come into conflict with each other. So not only of course do I wish you success in the great work you are doing, but I should like you to somehow bring the spirit of that work throughout in every field of human activity so that you might progressively help in making the world think cooperatively and attempt to solve the world's problems after removing those prejudices and narrow barriers that usually limit our thinking and our action.

I should like to welcome you again most cordially and I should like you, now that many of you have come from foreign countries here, if you have the time, to see some parts of our country and to find out what is moving us in this country. You will see what we are doing. We are a curious mixture in this country of the old and the new. Many thousands of years cling to us with all their good and bad. However, there is much good. We have been conditioned by this long past but this long past also brings many burdens which are not only unnecessary these days but come in the way of progress. So while we adhere to much of the past and take inspiration from it too we have a great deal to do of the present and even more so of the future. And so in India you will find almost every century represented in the past and in the present and those who work for the future. It is this strange combination of past, present and future which occurs everywhere to some extent but it is perhaps more evident here which is sometime perhaps a little irritating but often very exciting because after all there are two, if I may say so, basic forces at work among human beings, the forces leading to change and the continuity. Even though they happen to be opposite to each other, they both function. If we break the chain of continuity we become rootless. If there is no continuity and no change, we become stagnant. How to balance the two? To go ahead and yet have roots. It is the problem more especially for an ancient country like ours. Anyhow we are trying to address ourselves to these problems with our hearts and minds, and we want your sympathy, your goodwill and your affection for it. Thank you.

3. The Importance of Medical Research[1]

Doctors cannot get into grooves and claim that they alone possess the key to the riddle of life. In such a case, doctors are doomed and their minds will stop functioning. It is by trials, errors and experiments that one can get results that could be accepted. I fail to understand what the controversy is about among the different systems of medicine, namely, allopathy, ayurveda, homoeopathy and unani. Surely the way of science is to examine things and find out what is the right way to pursue and not to begin with axioms, which are ultimately turned into incontrovertible truths, tying you down and not allowing you to deviate. And you must accept change, whenever you find something acceptable. In the matter of science, one has got to keep one's eyes and mind open and try to adopt something if it is good or useful.

In ancient times the Indian systems of medicine were so advanced for those days that even the Caliph of Baghdad, Haroun Al Raschid, called in an Indian doctor from Taxila to treat him. The point, however, is not what you do, but how you do it and the state of mind you adopt.

I do not doubt that ayurveda is equipped with helpful knowledge, but if its practioners get into a group and talked without looking out of it, it becomes a difficult thing to accept.

Medical education and research has always to balance the activities between two forms of research. Firstly, pure scientific research, unrelated to the common man's needs and, secondly, definite research, with a particular aim in mind. One cannot live in a kind of isolation doing some amount of work which has no relation apparently to world problems. As it is, most discoveries have emerged from related research, but both the forms are required for the benefit of humanity.

It is important for the country to provide qualified medical men to look after the needs of the health of the rural areas of India. We lack them greatly and till we have proper provision for our remote villages, we have not really done our job. We have, however, to meet those needs. I hope that the medical research facilities will be expanded in India as these are insufficient now.

1. Speech while inaugurating the Institute of Postgraduate Medical Education and Research at the Seth Sukhlal Karnani Memorial Hospital, Kolkata, 16 January 1957. From *The Hindu*, 17 January 1957, and *National Herald*, 17 January 1957.

3

ISSUES OF GOVERNANCE

I. ADMINISTRATIVE MATTERS

1. To Lal Bahadur Shastri[1]

New Delhi,
5th December, 1956

My dear Lal Bahadur,[2]

I have already announced in Parliament about your resignation and this fact has been broadcasted to the world and is well known.[3] I have not, however, thus far formally asked the President to accept it, even though I have kept him informed throughout. I am now requesting him to accept your resignation.

I am asking Jagjivan Ram to take charge of the Ministries of Transport and Railways. He will, of course, relinquish his present charge of the Ministry of Communications.

Probably the Presidential notification accepting your resignation will be issued tomorrow.

I have already expressed in public my feelings about your resignation and about you.[4] I need not repeat them in this letter. I think that you are quite right in offering that resignation. Nevertheless, it was no easy matter for me to accept it. But I was heartened, however by the fact that your resignation was not only the right thing from the public point of view but would also redound to your

---

1. JN Collection.
2. Union Minister for Railways and Transport.
3. Nehru announced in the Lok Sabha on 26 November that Shastri had tendered his resignation following the railway accident at Ariyalur on the Southern Railway on 23 November. In his letter of resignation sent to the Prime Minister on 25 November, Shastri felt "that it would be good for me and for the Government as a whole if I quietly quit the office I hold. It will to a great extent ease the people's mind and also mollify the critics of the Government."
4. Nehru told members of the Congress Parliamentary Party on 27 November that acceptance of Shastri's resignation would be "a healthy democratic convention". He added that this was in the interest of the party, the government, the country and Shastri himself. Nehru noted that it was sad to see him go "although it is for the time being" and added that Shastri himself "felt strongly on the point."

credit and not come in the way of the responsible public work that you have been doing and will do in the future. Indeed, it will rather be an encouragement to all of us to entrust you with responsibilities.

Even so as we are parting in Government I feel sorry. The parting is only superficial because we shall be together in many activities in future, and you will always have my affectionate regard and good wishes.

There is no hurry for you to leave your present house or, in any way, to upset your arrangements. I understand that Swaran Singh can place at your disposal a suitable house not far from the AICC Office. When you and I have a little leisure and before I leave for the United States, I should like to have a talk with you.

Yours affectionately,
Jawaharlal

2. Retirement Age for Scientific Personnel[1]

As it is stated above that Professor Sharma is only agreeable to serve for another period of three years and not on a year to year basis, I do not see how the proposal of the Minister for NR & SR can be fitted in with this. To give effect to that proposal means that Professor Sharma be allowed to leave us.

2. I am not personally acquainted with Professor Sharma and can express no opinion about him. But it always seems to me extraordinary that competent scientists should be governed by our present age limit for superannuation. Much of the biggest scientific work in the world has been done after that age. We are very short of scientists as is obvious from the fact that the UPSC cannot often find persons required. We are drawing up plans for the production of scientists and technicians in large numbers. At the same time we are not prepared to utilize the existing scientists because they happen to be above a certain age, although they are otherwise presumed to be fit and competent. This seems to me a wrong policy.

1. Note to the Home Ministry, 6 December 1956. File No. 35(9)/56-66-PMS.

210

3. Cabinet has repeatedly stated that this age limit should have no particular application to scientists, engineers, technicians, etc., except in so far as the matter might be considered in regard to fitness.[2]

4. Also, it is not usually fair or desirable to ask a person employed in a university or an institute in teaching to continue on a year to year basis. He does not take enough interest in his work and he is constantly thinking of finding some other work. In fact, because of the demand for scientists, etc., usually they do get other work. Some of our very good persons who retired because of age have been employed by the agencies of the United Nations. We then go to the United Nations asking them to give us trained people. This seems rather odd.

5. I think that in the circumstances stated, Professor Sharma should be given a three year extension. This presumes his fitness for the work.

2. Regarding the question of extension of the service of R. Viswanathan, Deputy Director General of Health Services, Nehru wrote to Amrit Kaur, Minister for Health, on 5 December: "I agree with you that there is or should be no question of our letting competent medical men or experts go away simply because they attain a certain age, when we are so short of them. I would have no hesitation in giving a three-year extension to Dr Viswanathan."

3. To G.B. Pant[1]

New Delhi,
December 9, 1956

My dear Pantji,[2]

Lal Bahadur has forwarded to me a letter he has received from the Chairman[3] of the Railway Board, in which he states that he and his colleagues have been profoundly shocked by the resignation of the Railway Minister. As they feel that this resignation implies the existence of a serious shortcoming in the Railway Ministry as a whole, they say that they are prepared to submit their resignations. They add that they do not wish to embarrass Government in any way.

I am writing to Lal Bahadur to inform them that I do not propose to ask them for their resignations.

Yours affectionately,
Jawaharlal

1. JN Collection.
2. Union Home Minister.
3. G. Pande.

4. To B. Rama Rau[1]

New Delhi,
12th December, 1956

My dear Rama Rau,[2]

The Finance Ministry have sent me your letter dated 10th December addressed to H.M. Patel[3] with which you have sent a memorandum issued by you on the 10th December to the Central Board of the Reserve Bank. In this memorandum you have examined the implications of certain provisions of the Finance Bill, 1956.[4]

I have read this memorandum with great surprise. Apart from the contents of the memorandum, the whole approach appears to me to be improper. It is, if I may use the words, an agitational approach against the Central Government. To address your Directors in this way seems to me extraordinary.

Further, it has also surprised me that you should refer in a memorandum of this kind to a private talk with the Finance Minister. I am told that the report of that talk is not accurate. But whether it is accurate or not, this kind of reference to a private talk in a memorandum of this kind appears to me to be against all conventions and practice.[5]

---

1. JN Collection.
2. Governor, Reserve Bank of India.
3. Secretary, Ministry of Finance, Government of India.
4. B. Rama Rau criticized the provision in the Finance Bill to substantially increase the stamp duty on usance bills against which any licensed bank could borrow money from the Reserve Bank under the Bill Market Scheme. He stated that the increase amounted to an increase in the bank rate by ½ per cent. He added: "This increase was decided upon without any prior consultation with the Governor or the Board of the Reserve Bank, on whom rests the statutory responsibility for altering the bank rate." Arguing that the decision of the Government and the procedure adopted raised important issues, Rama Rau wrote to the members of the Board that "we should explain to the Government the full implications of this proposal and request them to reconsider it." Announcing a series of taxation measures in the Lok Sabha on 30 November, Finance Minister T.T. Krishnamachari proposed to increase the stamp duties on the bills of exchange from the existing flat rate of two annas per Rs 1,000 to Rs 10 per Rs 1,000.
5. Rama Rau wrote that a few days after the introduction of the Finance Bill, he attempted to discuss with the Finance Minister the implications of the measure to increase the stamp duty. But the Finance Minister told him that "he took full responsibility for the Government decision, that the Bank was a 'Section' of the Finance Ministry of the Government of India and that we would have to accept the decision whether we liked it or not."

When you talked to me,[6] I pointed out to you that it was for the Central Government to lay down policies and the Reserve Bank could not obviously have policies contrary to those of the Central Government. You agreed with this. And yet I find in your memorandum a different viewpoint expressed.

The Central Government, as you know, is directing its policy to attain certain objectives laid down in the Five Year Plan. It would be completely absurd if the Reserve Bank followed a different policy because it did not agree with those objectives or with the methods of achieving them.

You have laid stress on the autonomy of the Reserve Bank. Certainly it is autonomous, but it is also subject to the Central Government's directions. The question of fixing the bank rate is a matter for the Reserve Bank to consider. The stamp duty proposed by the Central Government is not the same thing as varying the bank rate, although it has certain effects upon it. That decision in regard to stamp duty was taken by the Cabinet after full consideration and I cannot accept any plea that Cabinet should not do so till the Reserve Bank approved. It is certainly desirable that the Reserve Bank's views on such matters should be obtained for us to consider. In fact, even according to your letter, this matter was mentioned to you six days before the Bill was introduced in Parliament and you were asked to advise as to what the rate should be.[7]

Monetary policies must necessarily depend upon the larger policies which a government pursues. It is in the ambit of those larger policies that the Reserve Bank can advise. It cannot challenge the main objectives and policies of Government.

There are apparently some sections of the business community who disapprove our basic policies and who have in fact criticised them.[8] They have every right to do so. But it is surprising that the Reserve Bank should encourage this criticism and indirectly participate in it itself.

Yours sincerely,
Jawaharlal Nehru

6. On 6 December.
7. Rama Rau wrote: "The decision of the Government was announced to the Governor and senior officers of the Bank six days before the introduction of the Bill, but it was made quite clear that it was a definite decision of Government on which the views of the Bank were not invited. The Bank's opinion was asked for only on the question whether the immediate increase be Rs 5 per Rs 1,000 or Rs 10 per Rs 1,000."
8. Rama Rau told the Board that the Indian Banks Association had stated that the "unprecedented increase in stamp duty will prove of great harm to the functioning of banks and increase the cost of credit facilities for business and industry."

5. To B. Rama Rau[1]

New Delhi,
January 1, 1957

My dear Rama Rau,

I have received your letter of the 29th December.[2] I wrote[3] to you on December 12 on the basis of the note you had circulated to the members of your Board. That note appeared to me to be improperly worded and did convey an impression to me of, what I called, "an agitational approach". I did not say anything about underhand tactics, nor did I refer to any previous incident or complaint. So far as I am concerned, I had no reason to complain previously of your not working in coordination with the Government. I have not of course been in intimate touch with these matters.

2. My letter was, therefore, confined to this particular instance and I thought that I should let you know what my own reactions were to the memorandum circulated to the Board. I still think that that was not a proper memorandum.

3. You refer to the Finance Minister using the expressions "a Department" and "a Section", in regard to the Reserve Bank. I think that these expressions can only be understood in a larger context. Obviously the Reserve Bank is a part of the various activities of the Government. Obviously also it has a high status and responsibility. It has to advise Government, but it has also to keep in line with Government.

4. You have quoted some sentences from my letter and say that you take strong exceptions to those statements. Those statements lay down a policy which I think the Reserve Bank and the Government of India should follow. I think the tone of the memorandum you issued was not in keeping with these broad policies.

5. I agree with you that it is not desirable to carry on such controversies in public.

6. When you spoke to me about your resignation on the previous occasion, I asked you not to resign. I did not think that any need for such a resignation had

1. JN Collection.
2. Not available.
3. See the preceding item.

arisen.[4] But since you feel now that it is absolutely impossible for you to continue in office, I do not know what further advice I can give you. If you so wish, you can submit your formal resignation to the Finance Ministry.

Yours sincerely,
Jawaharlal Nehru

4. After talking with Rama Rau on 6 December, Nehru wrote to T.T. Krishnamachari: "I told him that I would not advise him to resign. I considered these matters from an impersonal point of view and his resignation at this moment did not appear to me at all desirable. After some talk, he said that he would not like to go against my wishes in this matter." Nehru added: "I think it is definitely desirable not to have this resignation now. By itself, it may not mean much, but every little thing counts and adds an element of worry. I am glad, therefore, that he has agreed not to resign."

6. To Vaikunth L. Mehta[1]

Camp: Indore,
3rd January, 1957

My dear Vaikunthbhai,[2]

I have this evening received your letter of the 30th December.[3] I remember your telling me about H.V.R. Iyengar.[4] The fact that you recommended his appointment to the State Bank helped us greatly in coming to a decision. I might tell you that so far as I know his work there has been good. The Finance Minister, T.T. Krishnamachari, has also spoken well of it to me.

You have referred to some statements made by the Finance Minister during the last week or two. I have not myself seen these statements, but I heard

1. JN Collection.
2. Vice-Chairman, State Bank of India.
3. Not available.
4. Chairman, State Bank of India.

216

something about them. I do not think he could have criticised H.V.R. Iyengar because, as a matter of fact, he has spoken highly of him to me. Probably, he was referring in general terms to the past policies of these banks.[5]

So far as the Reserve Bank is concerned, we had some difficulty with it before I went to Europe. This was in regard to certain proposals which had been approved by our Cabinet and which were subsequently passed by Parliament. Rama Rau took exception to one of these as being an infringement on his powers as Governor of the Reserve Bank. He said that no decision should have been arrived at before he had been consulted. As a matter of fact, he was told about these proposals before the matter was put before Parliament. But it is true he was told that the Cabinet had so decided. In the matter of consultation I agreed with him that such consultation should always take place with the Reserve Bank in matters which might affect it. But I made it clear to him that decisions on such matters must remain with Government.

Subsequently he circulated a memorandum to the members of the Board of the Reserve Bank which, I thought, was improperly worded. It was practically an indictment of Government's policy in that regard. It also related (not very correctly) a private conversation he had with the Finance Minister. I wrote to Rama Rau and said that I did not think that his memorandum was a proper one.[6]

It was probably, I think, as a reaction to this memorandum[7] that the Finance Minister made some remarks of a general nature.

I do not see why you should think of resignation at all. So far as the State Bank and H.V.R. Iengar are concerned, there has been no controversy and indeed Iengar's work has been appreciated.

Yours sincerely,
Jawaharlal Nehru

5. Speaking in Chennai on 24 December 1956, the Finance Minister said that the government was examining the possibilities of providing credit facilities for short and medium term needs of industry. For this purpose, it was necessary to expand the base of the RBI and SBI. T.T. Krishnamachari made these remarks while addressing the South India Chamber of Commerce.
6. See *ante*, pp. 213-214.
7. In his memorandum to the Central Board of the Reserve Bank, Rama Rau wrote: "[In] a letter dated December 3rd, the Chairman of the State Bank,... after consulting his experts, stated that 'with the stamp duty enhanced as proposed by the new Finance Bill the cost will, of course, be increased substantially and the Bank could no longer make use of the Bill Market Scheme without loss to themselves'."

7. To Keshava Deva Malaviya[1]

The Residency,
Indore,
6th January, 1957

My dear Keshava,[2]

Your letter of the 4th January in which you suggest that the Fuel Research Institute, the Ceramic Research Institute and the National Metallurgical Laboratory should have a more direct relation to the Ministry of Natural Resources.[3] The Ministry should, of course, have this direct and close relation with the work of these laboratories. But I think it is important that the system we have thus far followed should be broadly kept up. All these and other Research Institutes and laboratories function apart from Ministries as such and under the CSIR. This keeps them out of the Government routine work and scientists have a sense of greater freedom than they would have if they were tied up with departmental routines. I have often found all kinds of conflicts arising between our scientists and our Ministries and departments. They function in different planes of thought and action.

It was for this reason, among others, that these laboratories were kept outside the direct scope of the Ministries. We must not change that. But the close relationship that you have suggested is certainly desirable. You might, on this basis, have a talk with Professor Thacker.[4] The point is that these laboratories and institutes should in no sense be put under the officials of the Ministry.

Yours affectionately,
Jawaharlal

1. K.D. Malaviya Papers, NMML.
2. Union Minister of Natural Resources.
3. Malaviya pointed out that since the three laboratories functioned under the Council of Scientific and Industrial Research, all the problems that arose in connection with fuel chemistry and mineral physics in the Ministry of Natural Resources or the Indian Bureau of Mines or in the private sector had to be routed through the Council. But most of the problems remained unsolved for they did not practically reach the laboratories. Malaviya argued that the existing system of working, based on the UK pattern, did not suit the Indian conditions anymore and suggested that there should be direct relationship between his ministry and the laboratories, a practice followed in the USA, Canada and the USSR.
4. M.S. Thacker, Director, Council of Scientific and Industrial Research.

8. Police Arrangements during Prime Minister's Tours[1]

I am sorry to trouble you again with a matter about which I have spoken to you on previous occasions.

2. It seems to me that the police arrangements in Calcutta and elsewhere in West Bengal, on the occasion of my visits here, are excessive. They create a very bad impression on me as well as, I imagine, on others. Yesterday at Bolpur it was astonishing to see hundreds of policemen all over the place, lining the roads as well as standing in bunches in various places. Apart from the bad impression caused on account of this, the expense is considerable and is waste of public funds. I have always agreed to adequate security arrangements, but I am quite sure that it does not help at all even from the security point of view to have these large numbers of police everywhere and, more especially, lining the roads.

3. When I mentioned this matter to your Chief Secretary,[2] he told me, much to my surprise, that the Home Ministry in Delhi had sent a circular recently pointing out that the West Bengal Government was apparently not following the instructions sent by the Home Ministry in regard to my visits. The Chief Secretary understood this to mean that adequate precautions were not taken. As a matter of fact, the purpose of the Home Ministry's circular was, I understand, the opposite of this. That circular was sent when I complained of excessive police arrangements and it was meant to point out that these excessive arrangements were not in accordance with the instructions issued.

4. I shall be grateful if steps are taken to make this clear to your police officers so that these vast displays of the police force might not take place.

---

1. Note to B.C. Roy, Chief Minister, West Bengal. Camp: Kolkota, 16 January 1957. JN Collection.
2. S.N. Ray.

9. Helping C.V. Raman[1]

Dr C.V. Raman of the Indian Institute of Science, Bangalore, came to see me today. He is rather worried about the delay in extending his appointment as University Professor or whatever he is called.[2] When this appointment was originally made, the period fixed was for two years on the understanding that this would be extended. It has, I believe, been extended since then on more than one occasion. The present period expires early in February. As he was not informed of the extension, I think he wrote to your Ministry. Thus far, apparently no action has been taken.

I think that we should certainly continue to help Professor Raman. He is our most eminent scientist. In Europe, leading scientists like him are almost always appointed for life. Even when they retire from a University, they are supposed to do research work and continue to get paid by the University or the Government. Professor Raman is doing important work still at his Institute and will continue to do so. We should therefore extend his appointment. Our normal rules do not apply in such cases. This is a special case to be treated specially.

As a matter of fact, the proper way to appoint him is not for a period but indefinitely during the pleasure of the Government. This means that the appointment goes on till such time as we indicate that it is ended.

Will you please look into this matter have necessary orders passed as early as possible?

1. Note to the Minister of Natural Resources, 23 January 1957. File No. 17(221)/57-59-PMS.
2. Raman was appointed National Professor at the Indian Institute of Science, Bangalore, in 1948.

10. Republic Day Festivities[1]

I should like to congratulate the Defence Ministry and all those in charge of the arrangements for the Republic Day Parade and especially the Parade itself. There are some points, however, to which I should like to draw attention.

2. The parade is becoming an increasingly bigger function and attracting very large crowds of people. Many people come from abroad just to see that parade and other functions connected with Republic Day. I think, therefore, that some further thought should be given to the seating and like arrangements for visitors and others.

3. The two pylon like erections put up at the Great Place[2] end of Raj Path, with flags at the top, were completely out of place and did not fit in at all. I hope that this idea will be given up in the future. The view should be kept open from the Secretariat right down Raj Path to India Gate.

4. There were a large number of policemen on either side of Raj Path. Probably they were necessary to prevent people pushing in front. If the seating arrangements are better organised, it might not be necessary to keep so many policemen there though, no doubt, a fair number will be necessary. The main thing, therefore, is the seating arrangements.

5. I think that we should have proper stands made to be placed on either side of Raj Path along the entire route from Great Place to India Gate. These stands should be moveable stands. I suppose this is possible, so that they can be used year after year. This will no doubt cost some considerable sums of money, but this will be a great improvement. As for the expense, it can easily be realised and more than realised by the issue of priced tickets.

6. These stands should be placed, as indeed they were placed this time wherever they existed, some distance away from the Raj Path and children allowed to sit in front on *durries*. This appears to be a good arrangement. This will really mean that ticketholders can bring their children free and these children will be allowed to sit in front. I should like children anyhow not to be charged.

7. In foreign countries where such demonstrations take place, I believe that huge stands are put up by private agencies and they make a lot of money out of them. We shall have to do this ourselves. We need not price the tickets too high. They may vary perhaps from Rs 5/- to Re 1/-. People will gladly pay this sum for a relatively better seat from which a view can be obtained. At present, people

1. Note to M.K. Vellodi, Defence Secretary, 28 January 1957. JN Collection.
2. Now known as Vijay Chowk.

at the back can hardly see. The stands can indeed be even bigger and higher than the ones put up recently.

8. It might be a good thing for even Ministers and the like to pay something for their seats. That will set a good example. Only invited guests from abroad might be given free seats.

9. These are some odd suggestions which I am sending for the consideration of the Committee in charge of this Day's arrangements. Others will no doubt occur.

One or two other matters have struck me since I wrote this note.

1. The industrial and other workers who joined the Republic Day procession, were badly arranged and were not at all impressive. A large bunch of them walked together without the least sign of life. I do not know how they are chosen. I think that they should be separated according to trade unions, each carrying its trade union banner. It would also be desirable for them to carry some slogans which, of course, should be decided upon beforehand. This would give some colour and life to them.

2. The second thing is about the folk dances. The second day's performance was much better than the first day's.[3] I think it should be arranged that when each item ends, the dancers should go down the slope dancing and not as they usually do it now. This would add very much to the effectiveness of the show. This need not take any more time because, meanwhile, the others will be walking up towards the stage.

3. The singing of *Jana Gana Mana* at the Stadium at the end of the show was again unsatisfactory today. It would be desirable to train some persons specially to sing it on that as well as other occasions. I imagine it will be better to have some men trained, say from the Army. Girls can join in. Better loudspeaker arrangements should be made for the song to be heard all over the place. The people singing should be told to sing in a good voice. Other small groups might be, perhaps, placed in the audience. They may consist of our Army men also who would be told to join. In this way, one would induce the crowd to join in.

4. Now that we have got a first class hall at the Vigyan Bhavan, with a big stage, it would be a good thing to have a performance of the folk dances next year in the Vigyan Bhavan, with tickets, of course. This might well be in addition to the two at the Stadium. The Vigyan Bhavan show should be limited to the ticketholders, except for a few special guests.

---

3. The folk dancing on 26 January was part of the Republic Day Parade. The next day a separate Folk Dance Festival was organized at the National Stadium as part of the Republic Day festivities.

11. To Mehr Chand Khanna[1]

New Delhi,
February 12, 1957

My dear Mehr Chand,[2]

I have been reading more carefully the note you sent me recently on the rehabilitation of displaced persons from East Pakistan. I think I wrote to you about this matter that we might consider this informally before it is put up before the Rehabilitation Committee of the Cabinet. As a matter of fact, there will be no harm in the Committee itself discussing it straightaway. We might, therefore, fix a meeting of the Committee somewhat later, but it is no easy matter to get all the Ministers together now.

Meanwhile, I hope you have sent this communication to the Planning Commission and the Ministry of Finance for their consideration and comments.

In regard to the suggestions you have made in paragraph 17, it is clear that we cannot have a conference of the Chief Ministers in the near future. Indeed, it will not be possible to have such a conference till at least two months after the elections are over, that is to say, some time in June. I rather doubt if this conference will yield any substantial results. We have discussed this matter repeatedly on various occasions with Chief Ministers, and they have tried to help. Probably the best course would be for us to have a conference of the new Chief Ministers for various purposes. Among the questions discussed should be this question also. But it is not likely to be very helpful to go on pressing them in the old way. We have to take a bigger initiative ourselves and then ask the States to help.

You have referred to these displaced persons from East Pakistan being rehabilitated in the community development schemes. I am not clear how far this is possible. Of course, in West Bengal itself this should be done, but the intrusion of an outside element in development blocks in other parts of the country may well prevent those blocks settling down and making any progress. New problems will arise which will interfere with the development of the psychology of cooperation and partnership which a block must have. However, this may be considered. I suggest that you should discuss this matter with S.K. Dey[3] and ask him to indicate how far this procedure can be followed.

---

1. JN Collection.
2. Minister for Rehabilitation.
3. Administrator, Community Projects Administration.

About the big public projects, something might be done. Presumably you refer to more or less untrained labour. Trained persons would be more easy to absorb. Normally speaking, it is expensive to import untrained labour in a big project, as special arrangements have to be made for it. But there is this also to be kept in mind, that anyhow we have to keep these people from East Pakistan going. Therefore, in the balance, it might be financially profitable for us to use them and make arrangements for them in the new projects. It would not be fair, I think, to ask the new projects to bear the burden of these new arrangements. Therefore, the approach should be that the Rehabilitation Ministry shares that burden somewhat, though to a lesser extent than it would otherwise do. Of course, the persons so taken must be able to do the work properly. We cannot allow a project to suffer by mixing it up with humanitarian reasons.

All these matters referred to in your note really require careful discussion with the Ministries concerned. These discussions should be undertaken from now onwards, so that we may have some data to consider when we meet. It is not much good our meeting together and passing some general resolutions and appeals. Your Ministry, therefore, has plenty of work to do, and I hope they will pursue these matters with the Ministries concerned in some detail.

In particular, the Planning Commission should be kept in close touch.

Yours sincerely,
Jawaharlal Nehru

12. Coordinating Oil Affairs[1]

About a month ago, I received a letter from the Deputy Chairman,[2] Planning Commission.

In this letter, reference was made to a recommendation by the Adviser on Oil Affairs that there should be a single unit, either a separate Ministry or a high powered Commission, dealing with all problems of the oil industry as a whole. The Deputy Chairman informed me that the Planning Commission had considered this matter in consultation with the three Ministries concerned mainly with oil, namely, the Ministries of NR & SR, Production, and Works, Housing & Supply. The concensus of opinion at the meeting was that all matters relating to oil should be under the administrative control of one Ministry. This recommendation of the Planning Commission was forwarded to me.

2. In the forwarding letter it was stated that the Ministries of NR & SR and WH & S fully supported the recommendations, but the Ministry of Production considered that the refining and processing of crude oil should be in a separate Ministry.

3. It is clear to me that the present arrangement in regard to matters connected with oil is not satisfactory and is out of date. Oil, in its various aspects, is becoming not only a very important, but an ever-growing, subject for us. Some kind of greater coordination is, therefore, essential. This broad approach should, therefore, be accepted, though there might be some minor variations to it.

4. It is not possible to take this up, or to consider any reorganisation of Ministries, during this period of general elections and for some time after. It will have to be considered when the new Government is formed after the elections. This means probably in April or May.

5. Meanwhile, it would be helpful if the Planning Commission could give some further thought to this subject and make more precise recommendations in consultation with the Ministries concerned. This will be helpful to us in the future when we come to grips with this subject. I shall be grateful, therefore, if the Planning Commission does so and if the Ministries concerned, that is, the Ministries of NR & SR, Production and WH & S, also accept this broad proposition suggested above and confer with the Planning Commission to work it out in some greater detail.

6. Copies of this note are being sent to the Deputy Chairman, Planning Commission, the Minister of NR & SR, the Minister of Production, the Minister of WH & S, the Minister of Finance and the Minister of Home Affairs.

1. Note, 12 February 1957. JN Collection.
2. V.T. Krishnamachari.

13. To G.B. Pant[1]

New Delhi,
12th February, 1957

My dear Pantji,

When I was in Bombay recently, Sri Prakasa spoke to me about the various allowances to the Bombay Governor for the running of the Raj Bhavan, etc. He was somewhat worried about this matter and said that some recent proposals emanating from the Home Ministry would make it difficult for him to keep up normal standards at Raj Bhavan. I asked him then to send me a note on this subject. He said that he would send me a copy of the note he proposed to send to you.

I have now received a copy of his letter to you dated February 11th and I have read through it. It is rather difficult for me to express any opinion about the numerous items in this list. But, broadly speaking, some facts stand out. Also, that Sri Prakasa is a very careful person in money matters. While he takes care to maintain adequate standards, he is also economical.

The first thing is that Bombay is undoubtedly the heaviest charge for a Governor in India. The only possible comparison is Calcutta from the point of view of the numerous and important guests and VIPs that go there. Both Bombay and Calcutta have far more VIPs and foreign guests than any other Raj Bhavan in India. While in this matter Bombay and Calcutta are more or less on a level, Bombay is a much bigger charge than Calcutta. The Bombay State is huge while West Bengal is relatively small. There is and should be a great deal of travelling in the Bombay State and there is the necessity of maintaining additional residences as well as staff. I think therefore that both Bombay and Calcutta should be considered as special cases from the point of view of important guests. In addition, Bombay should be considered as a special case because of its size and the need for a great deal of travelling, etc. I would, therefore, pay particular attention to what Sri Prakasa has written, keeping in view, of course, the need for economy.

So far as important guests are concerned, we have sometimes followed the practice of the External Affairs Ministry contributing to expenses on special occasions. This may be done in future also but only on very special occasions as

---

1. JN Collection.

when somebody with a huge retinue like the King of Saudi Arabia or the Dalai and Panchen Lamas come. But, generally speaking, the entertainment allowance should be adequate to meet these special requirements which are inevitable in a place like Bombay. Standards in Bombay for entertainment, etc., are also higher than elsewhere. Much depends upon the Governor. But I think it is right that relatively high standards should be kept up and in this matter I would trust the judgment of Sri Prakasa.

I think that the Government House in Nagpur should be maintained for some time at least. Nagpur has suffered and has a sense of frustration. To take away the Government House completely would be a further shock. In any event, the Governor should spend sometime there. Therefore, I think we should provide for the maintenance of this Government House. It may not be necessary to have a separate Government House in Saurashtra, though the Governor should visit the Gujarat area pretty frequently.

I thus think that the sumptuary allowance and the entertainment allowance should be increased. The establishment charges might also have to be increased.

I do not know why the medical establishment is sought to be ended. A large staff is kept there and there should be provision for their proper medical treatment.

So far as the contract allowance is concerned, it is difficult for me to make any suggestion. But it does seem odd that it is greater in Madras than in Bombay.

Tour expenses in Bombay State are bound to be heavier than elsewhere and touring by the Governor should be encouraged. Sri Prakasa suggests that the Governor should have a small plane. I think that it is desirable and worthwhile for the Governor to have a plane. In fact, I imagine this will be cheaper than going about in a train with a long retinue. Nevertheless, I think that it would not be a good thing to provide a plane for the Governor at this stage. This would become a precedent for other places. The right thing would be for the Bombay Government to keep its own plane or planes which the Governor can occasionally use.

I am not considering the other items in the list because I do not know much about them. But, broadly speaking, I think that we should give favourable consideration to what Sri Prakasa says. In some matters his suggestions may be cut down. But I do hope that the special interests of the case will be borne in mind.

Yours affectionately,
Jawaharlal

14. Unnecessary Security Restrictions[1]

Yesterday I paid a visit to the Horse Show which was being held in front of the Red Fort in Delhi. Both going there and coming, I formed part of an imposing procession. Traffic had been stopped in Faiz Bazar and right up to the Red Fort and people were lined up on both sides of the road. My car was accompanied by four motorcycle outriders. There was the usual police car behind as well as a car in front. I gathered that somewhat ahead of us a warning car had gone in order to stop the traffic and clear the roads.

Normally I have one outrider and a police car behind me in Delhi. Later an addition was made to it when I passed through any part of Old Delhi. This addition was one more motorcycle outrider. On this occasion, however, further additions have been made as stated above and traffic has been stopped during a busy hour of the afternoon. A day earlier I went to the University and the same procedure was adopted. In fact, because traffic was stopped on account of my going there, important guests of the Delhi University were delayed.

I cannot understand why I should be made to travel about Delhi in this ceremonial procession. This has nothing to do with security. In fact it rather lessens security if previous notice is given all around that I am coming. I had expected an additional motorcycle outrider when I went to Old Delhi. But four motorcycle outriders are not only a great nuisance, but they create a feeling of humiliation in me. In any event, it is completely wrong to stop traffic even though the stoppage might take place a little before I pass through. As I have repeatedly stated, this is not done in any country that I know of. It is only done on ceremonial occasions when big processions pass. It is not done for security reasons. In particular, it is a great burden on me to have to put up with this kind of thing in Delhi itself.

1. Note to the Home Ministry, Camp: Jaipur, 18 February 1957. JN Collection.

15. The Future of Raj Bhavan, Nagpur[1]

As I am spending a night here, the question of the future of Raj Bhavan, Nagpur, and the grounds attached to it came to my mind. There is some proposal to use it for offices or some institute.[2] There is also a suggestion that it should continue as the official residence of the Governor of Bombay during his visits to Nagpur.

2. It seems to me that the Governor of Bombay should have an official residence in Nagpur and should come here from time to time. Nagpur has been the capital of a State for many years and it has felt rather hurt at being deprived of that position.[3] It is a great and growing city. I think that the Governor should certainly visit it and spend some days here from time to time. If he does so, it is obvious that he should stay at Raj Bhavan and not at the Circuit House.

3. There is also some proposal that this Raj Bhavan should be converted into some kind of an enlarged Circuit House. I dislike this idea. There is already a Circuit House in Nagpur, and it would be a pity to use Raj Bhavan as a glorified Dak Bungalow, as unhappily the old Allahabad Government House is used with all its very fine grounds.

4. Raj Bhavan, Nagpur, has about 112 acres and land attached to it. Of this, about 30 acres are cultivated garden. The rest are left in their uncared for condition. The house is situated at the top of a little hill and the grounds are all round that hill. It is a good position.

5. I think that part of Raj Bhavan should be reserved for the Governor and for such important guests as would normally stop at Raj Bhavan. The other part may be used for other purposes, which should not conflict with the house being Raj Bhavan. Even Rashtrapati Bhavan in Delhi has a number of offices, such as the Planning Commission. I would suggest that the lands attached to Raj Bhavan

---

1. Note to the Home Ministry, Camp: Nagpur, 21 February 1957. JN Collection.
2. Morarji Desai, Chief Minister of Bombay, wrote to G.B. Pant on 19 February that the Raj Bhavan could perhaps be better utilised if the IAS Training College is located there. As the capital of the Bombay state was moved to Mumbai from Nagpur, Desai felt it necessssary to consider utilising the accommodation and "to maintain its importance". He noted that tentative plans were worked out for the IAS and IPS training colleges to be located at Nagpur.
3. Morarji Desai said the people of Nagpur and Vidharbha were "anxiously waiting" to know about the decisions taken on locating government offices there. He added that "there will obviously be a very keen sense of disappointment" if some important institutions were not located in Nagpur.

except for about ten acres or so, should be converted into a park of about a hundred acres. I think we should encourage parks in our great cities. Very often they lack them. This park should have a particular section of it devoted to children, say about 20 or 25 acres. This park may develop gradually.

6. It might be worthwhile considering that the part of Raj Bhavan not used by the Governor might be converted into a Bal Bhavan or a children's museum, rest house, etc. I attach great importance to these Bal Bhavans in our cities. We should encourage such institutions where children can play and learn in good surroundings. Naturally it should be open to all children and not to a few well-to-do ones. If this idea is approved of, this Bal Bhavan would easily fit in with the children's park.

II. STATES

1. School for Tibetan Studies in Ladakh[1]

Shri Kushak Bakula gave me a paper today,[2] a copy of which I enclose. I think that it would be desirable for us to help in the establishment of this Tibetan School.[3] I suggested to Kushak Bakula that the local monastries should subscribe to some extent for the establishment of the school. He said he would try. He also said that in any event, the local monastries would put up hostels for their students and feed them.

2. If a school is established,[4] it should have some other subjects also.

---

1. Note to the Minister for Home Affairs, 10 January 1957. File No. 2(21)-K/56, MHA.
2. Kushak Bakula, Deputy Minister for Ladakh Affairs in the Jammu and Kashmir Government sought financial help from the Central Government to set up an institution in Leh for teaching the Tibetan language and philosophy to Lama boys. According to Bakula these boys would otherwise have to go to Lhasa for this purpose.
3. The Home Ministry, while considering Bakula's proposal of 8 December 1956, noted that this was of a different nature from his earlier initiative on which Nehru recorded a minute on 8 January 1955 that it was not proper to set up an institution for imparting religious education. The Home Ministry opined that Bakula had this time around made a good case for giving consideration to the proposal "on merit".
4. A college for Buddhist philosophy was started in Leh in 1959.

2. To Mehr Chand Khanna[1]

New Delhi,
January 10, 1957

My dear Mehr Chand,

You know how pained and shocked I was and am by the construction of Lajpat Rai Market in front of the Red Fort. I am now surprised to learn that a second storey is going to be put up on them.[2] Surely some consideration should be paid to the Prime Minister's wishes in this matter.

Yours sincerely,
Jawaharlal Nehru

1. JN Collection.
2. Nehru noted to his Principal Private Secretary the next day that he had received a letter from the President of Delhi Municipality that the Central Public Works Department was adding a second storey. The Prime Minister recorded that in response to his objections, the Minister for Rehabilitation had said they intended to build only "some bits here and there", so as to make the buildings fit in with the environment.

3. To B.A. Mandloi[1]

New Delhi,
January 10, 1957

My dear Mandloi,[2]
I have your letter of the 8th January.[3]

As I told you when you and your colleagues came to see me in Indore, it was not particularly easy for me to relieve Dr Kailas Nath Katju from his membership of the Central Cabinet and as Union Defence Minister. But, in view of the request made to me by all the leading members of the Council of Ministers of Madhya Pradesh and also because I realised the difficulties facing this great State of ours at its very inception, I agreed to accept your proposal, provided Dr Katju himself was willing. I understood later that Dr Katju had given his consent.

I am glad that he has been unanimously elected by a meeting of the State Congress Assembly Party.

I am afraid it is not possible for me to ask Dr Katju to leave within the next few days. I think he should stay here till about the end of this month. I cannot indicate a date just now, as this will depend on various arrangements that we have to make here as well as the convenience of Dr Katju.

With all good wishes,

Yours sincerely,
Jawaharlal Nehru

---

1. JN Collection.
2. Bhagwantrao Annabhau Mandloi (b. 1892); Lawyer and politician; member, Legislative Assembly of the Central Provinces and Berar, 1935-37 and of Madhya Pradesh from 1937; imprisoned for political activities, 1940 and 1942; member, Constituent Assembly and Parliament; Chief Whip, Madhya Pradesh Assembly; member, Congress Parliamentary Party Board, 1951-52; minister, Madhya Pradesh Government, 1952-61; acting Chief Minister of Madhya Pradesh, January 1957; Chief Minister, 1962-August 1963; President, MPCC from November 1963.
3. Mandloi said that Kailas Nath Katju had been formally elected as the leader of the Madhya Pradesh Congress Party in the State Assembly. He therefore requested Nehru to relieve Katju as defence minister to enable him to take up his new position before the current session of the Assembly ended on 17 January.

4. To C.P.N. Singh[1]

New Delhi,
February 4, 1957

My dear CPN,[2]

This is a brief note about Slocum's[3] talk with me.

He laid great importance on the next seventeen months, i.e., till the monsoon of 1958. This was a critical time for Bhakra. He was not getting the support he wanted. The gates from Germany and Austria must reach in time, so that they could go ahead with them after the next monsoon.

After the next twenty-four months, the critical period will be over. Nothing can stop further progress of the work then.

He said something about the full use of power from the right power house being available after the monsoon of 1962,[4] provided supplies come. So far as the left power house was concerned, it should function in 1960.[5]

He said that he was only very rarely invited to the meetings of the Central Bhakra Board. He hinted that the members of the Board get irritated at what he says. He had no authority to hire or fire or promote.

He repeated the extreme importance of the next twenty-four months and that certain things had to be done by a certain time. The gates must be ready. The whole work had to be done in proper sequence. If something does not come in time, the whole sequence goes wrong....

Yours sincerely,
Jawaharlal Nehru

1. File No. 17(50)/57-59-PMS. Extracts.
2. Governor of Punjab.
3. Harvey Slocum headed a team of American engineers as an advisory body for the construction of the Bhakra-Nangal dam.
4. The right bank power house comprising 5 units of 1,20,000 kW each was commissioned on 17 April 1969.
5. The left power house with 5 units each of 90,000 kW was commissioned on 10 December 1961.

5. To C. Rajagopalachari[1]

New Delhi,
February 4, 1957

My dear Rajaji,

Thank you for your letter of the 3rd January.[2]

I have no doubt that the telegram you have received has come from Shaikh Abdullah. I have received a similar but longer telegram from him.[3] He is spending a large sum of money on sending telegrams to all manner of people.

I am sorry that Shaikh Abdullah is in detention, partly because it does not fit in with any approach to such questions and secondly because it has had a bad effect on our Kashmir case in the outside world. But, unfortunately, there is little doubt that Abdullah, if he came out, would create a great deal of trouble. Just before he was interned,[4] he appeared to me to have lost all balance of mind. He talked of blood and thunder and setting fire to the Kashmir Valley and so on.

Although he is in detention, which of course no person concerned can like, the fact is that he is living in very great comfort with all kinds of facilities. There are several good houses at his disposal and that of a few others with him. His wife and children visit him from time to time and spend some days with him. No doubt they carry messages also. He gets an allowance of Rs. 2000/- a month, apart from many other expenses being paid.

I think you are quite right not to send a reply to him.

Yours affectionately,
Jawaharlal

1. JN Collection.
2. Not available
3. Abdullah, in his communication of 2 February, referred to Nehru's remarks on Kashmir at a public meeting at Chennai and submitted: "Nobody can claim that there is freedom or that the coming elections (in Kashmir) would be free and impartial." Abdullah claimed that this was because of the "monstrous laws", "crippling restrictions" and "strangling control" in force in Kashmir. He added that Nehru had on innumerable occasions guaranteed India's pledge to hold a plebiscite in Kashmir. See *ante*, pp. 63-71 for Nehru's remarks on Kashmir on 31 January in Chennai.
4. Shaikh Abdullah is reported to have spoken of a possible dissolution of Jammu and Kashmir's accession to India, a day before his arrest on 9 August 1953. Some press reports quoted Abdullah as saying that an independent Kashmir was the best option.

6. School for Tibetan Studies[1]

I imagine that any school for Tibetan study in Kalimpong would stand on a completely different footing from anything that was started in Ladakh. I entirely agree with you[2] that for a proper school of Tibetan studies, Leh is hardly suited, although Ladakh is the only place in India which is a Buddhist area intimately connected with Tibet.

2. Shri Kushak Bakula's scheme was to provide something which Ladakh needs and lacks. For the want of this, Ladakhis have to go all the way to Lhasa for training, and this is a troublesome business. Such a school cannot be a proper school for Tibetan studies as is envisaged in Kalimpong.

3. I discussed this matter with the Prime Minister of Jammu & Kashmir State[3] and he said that he entirely approved of it.[4] This, of course, does not mean the details of the scheme. So far as these details are concerned, the principal sum involved is for building. If this is taken out, the amount is not considerable. Then there is a Tibetan press which I imagine would be very helpful in Ladakh. It is not expensive. I suggest that perhaps the Education Ministry might correspond with the Jammu & Kashmir Government about this proposal.

4. As for sending a cultural delegation to Tibet,[5] this can only be sent after previous reference is made to the Chinese Government and their permission taken. This will have to be done through the External Affairs Ministry and details will have to be given about it.

1. Note to the Union Minister for Education, Camp: Patna, 15 February 1957. File No. 40(110)/57–PMS.
2. Maulana Azad in his note of 6 February agreed with Nehru that Tibetan studies should be promoted, but added "that the proper place for developing Tibetan studies should be in or near Kalimpong." Azad was not impressed by Bakula's scheme being restricted to Ladakh. And also because no details were supplied "to justify the scheme." Azad said: "I fear this scheme is not his own but has been given to him by someone else". He therefore sought Nehru's permission for the Education Ministry to prepare a separate comprehensive scheme.
3. Bakhshi Ghulam Mohammad.
4. Azad had wanted to know if the Jammu and Kashmir state government had examined the scheme.
5. Azad noted that he thought of sending a cultural delegation to Tibet in the summer of 1957.

III. NEFA

1. To G.B. Pant[1]

New Delhi,
December 13, 1956

My dear Pantji,

A young Naga Christian[2] who has recently returned from America and who has been recommended to me by an American friend of Vijayalakshmi's, came to see me a few days ago. He has sent me a letter, a copy of which I enclose.

Some of his suggestions[3] do not seem to me feasible at all. But I have been thinking about this matter for a long time and I feel that we must not allow this question to rest where it is. From the point of view of any major military resistance, we have succeeded in breaking it. But small-scale guerilla warfare and occasional raids may continue indefinitely. As you will have noticed, there have been a number of raids in the villages in the plains from the Sema area. I think the Intelligence reports also say that the position is not satisfactory. General Thimayya[4] also feels that from a military point of view he can do little except to protect convoys and hold the Nagas in check.

We must, therefore, give fresh thought to this matter and I think we must do it certainly before the elections. What exactly we should do, is not quite clear to me. But, as a first step, I think we should decide to put the Naga Hills district and the NEFA area together under the Central administration. This may involve a change in the Constitution. We need not do that immediately. But we might get the Assam Government to agree to this and make an announcement to that effect.

This will not be enough of course, but the rest can follow.

I should like you to give thought to this.

Yours affectionately,
Jawaharlal

1. JN Collection.
2. I. Ben Wati.
3. See the next item.
4. General Officer Commanding-in-Chief, Eastern Command.

236

2. To I.B. Wati[1]

New Delhi,
December 13, 1956

Dear Wati,[2]

Thank you for your letter[3] of December 11th which I read with much interest.

As I have told you, we have no desire to punish or harass the Nagas. They can have as much freedom as anybody in India, and more in a sense, that in the shape of local autonomy. This trouble in the Naga Hills was none of our making. I am not referring to mistakes of some civil officers previously, but to the violent methods that Phizo[4] and his supporters have adopted. No government in the world can submit to this kind of thing. I doubt if any government anywhere would have dealt with the situation in the way we have done.

So far as Phizo is concerned, he has repeatedly broken his firm promise to us and has brought this misery on his people.

We have offered amnesty to the Nagas who give up fighting.[5] It would be rather extraordinary to pardon people who go on shooting our men and who have killed any number of Nagas.

Yours sincerely,
Jawaharlal Nehru

---

1. JN Collection.
2. A Naga Christian and an admirer of Nehru. He met Nehru on 11 December.
3. Wati suggested the following steps to solve the Naga problem: (i) the Nagas imprisoned in connection with the political movement be unconditionally released on Christmas eve; (ii) the rebel leaders Phizo and Imkongmeren and their subordinates be given a general pardon, leaving the doors open for a reasonable settlement; and (iii) the majority of the Nagas being Christians, the National Christian Council Relief Committee be invited to do relief work among the Nagas to restore their confidence.
4. A.Z. Phizo, President, Naga National Council.
5. Raj Kumar Kochhar, General Officer Commanding, Assam, issued a declaration in May 1956 assuring full protection to those Nagas who surrendered their arms, unless they were involved in murder or heinous crimes. See also *Selected Works* (second series), Vol. 33, p. 185, p. 187 and p. 189.

3. To S. Fazl Ali[1]

New Delhi,
1st January, 1957

My dear Fazl Ali,[2]

Your letter of December 26th, 1956, about Rathee,[3] Financial Adviser for the NEFA. I am surprised to learn of his frequent visits to Delhi and his subsequent behaviour in this respect. I am asking our Secretary General to inquire into this matter. I am quite clear in my mind that the Financial Adviser for the NEFA[4] should function there and not visit Delhi so frequently. Also, that his behaviour in this respect does not appear to be satisfactory.

Rathee in his note says something about his visits being undertaken at the request of the Ministry of External Affairs. I am inquiring into this matter. But I am quite clear that he had no business to try to bypass you in the manner he has done.

As regards the development programme in the NEFA, I am beginning to have serious doubts about one matter and I spoke about this to our Foreign Secretary[5] soon after my return from Assam some weeks ago.[6] I mentioned this matter also, I think, in Shillong itself when I was addressing some of your chief officers. We are anxious to improve conditions in the NEFA, but there is considerable danger, in my opinion, in our trying to push things too fast in an area which is still very primitive. This may well produce bad reactions. In particular, I do not want too many people from outside to be sent there in subordinate capacities. They do not fit in there. There is friction between them and the local people and sometimes, I am told, there are entanglements with the local women which leads

1. JN Collection.
2. Governor of Assam.
3. K.L. Rathee was Financial Adviser for the NEFA since April 1955.
4. In view of the large-scale development projects and the urgent need of establishing and extending administration in the North East Frontier Agency, the Government of India appointed a Financial Adviser, with effect from 24 June 1954, for assisting the Agency in effecting economy, expediting financial sanction and avoiding delay. The Financial Adviser, an ex-officio Deputy Secretary in Finance Ministry, had the power to grant financial concurrence on the spot within certain limits.
5. Subimal Dutt.
6. Nehru visited Assam from 17 to 20 October 1956.

to dissatisfaction and possibly greater trouble. I am therefore beginning to think that we should go more slowly in regard to these so-called developments. Probably, the most important development is roads.

Some of our enthusiastic people even think of transplanting some of the Indian institutions to the NEFA such as boy scouts and the like. I think this is rather absurd.

I am going away tomorrow to Indore. Our Secretary General, N.R. Pillai, will be dealing with this matter.

A happy New Year to you. `

Yours sincerely,
Jawaharlal Nehru

4. Functioning of the Financial Adviser[1]

I enclose a letter from the Governor of Assam and my reply[2] to him. I should like you to enquire into this matter. Prima facie, Rathee's behaviour has been undesirable and I get the impression that he is not too much interested in the work there and has some other objective in his seeking to come to Delhi frequently. If this is so, this is not the kind of man who is suited for the NEFA. He must be clearly made to understand that he is functioning there under the Governor and he must not bypass him in any way and should carry out the Governor's directions.

2. His long absences from the NEFA are really extraordinary. On one occasion he was away for 44 days in July and August. In April for 22 days. In May and June for 25 days. It passes my comprehension how he can possibly be required in Delhi for these long periods.

3. One would almost think that his post is a surplus one.

4. You will notice that in my letter to the Governor I have referred to my

1. Note to N.R. Pillai, Secretary General, MEA, 1 January 1957. JN Collection.
2. See the preceding item.

anxiety about our development programmes not being pushed too fast. I do not want to upset the life of the NEFA too rapidly and I am particularly anxious that too many people from outside should not go there. We have had enough trouble with the tribal people and it would not be right to uproot the NEFA tribals suddenly. I spoke to the Foreign Secretary on this subject sometime ago.

5. To S. Fazl Ali[1]

Camp: Indore,
January 3, 1957

My dear Fazl Ali,

You sent me a copy of your letter to the Home Minister dated 26th December. Pantji has now sent me a copy of your letter again as well as the other papers you sent him and I have read through them a second time at some leisure.

In the circumstances mentioned by you, it seems clear that we have to carry on operations against the hostile Nagas. The methods adopted might vary and will have to be decided upon by our military advisers. We cannot, for the present, think of any long-term solution. Nevertheless, I think we should give thought to this and I hope you will do so. I do not think that constitutional difficulties need ultimately come in the way of what we wish to do.

I was much interested to read your note in which you refer to having visited Nowgong jail and met a number of persons, chiefly relatives of Phizo. I am inclined to think that we should err on the side of leniency with such persons. If you feel that any of these people are in a proper frame of mind, why should we not release them. There may be a risk but there may also be a definite advantage.

It is perfectly true that women have considerable influence among the Nagas, especially some educated women. Ranu,[2] I think, was quite an important member of the independence movement. I have an idea she once came to Delhi though I did not meet her. If by any chance she wants to see me, and you think she might be released, she can be told that she can see me in Delhi.

1. JN Collection.
2. Ranu Iralu, a niece of Phizo's.

I entirely agree with you that we should show kindness to these people and help them with money wherever this is considered necessary for their education or other purposes. I shall gladly send you some more money when you write to me for it.

You refer in your letter to the location of the oil refinery. Presumably you want the decision about the location postponed because you think that the decision is likely to be adverse to Assam. Suppose the decision is in favour of Assam, would you still want it postponed? I have myself no idea of what the decision is going to be. Personally, I am in favour of Assam but this view is not based on any detailed consideration of the problem. I have not even seen the report of the committee appointed for this purpose.

Yours sincerely,
Jawaharlal Nehru

6. To S. Fazl Ali [1]

New Delhi,
January 22, 1957

My dear Fazl Ali,

Your letter of January 14 from Dhubri. I have read this as well as its enclosures with interest and care. I am glad that you are applying your mind to various aspects of the Naga problem. It seems to me that many of us have got into some grooves of thought and cannot easily get out of them. To some extent you have brought a fresh mind to this problem and can, therefore, perhaps see more light.

To begin with, it is clear that no important step can be taken in regard to the Naga Hills or Assam till the elections are over. We shall then consult together and assess the situation and decide on any new line of action. But the thinking part must go on and before we meet for the purpose of a decision, our own minds should be fairly clear.

1. JN Collection.

241

You refer to the question of the refinery. I agree with you and see your point now which I had missed previously. It is desirable to defer the decision about the refinery till after the elections. It may be helpful to have a decision then about the same time as we deal with some aspects of the Naga problem.

I might mention, however, that our present thinking about the refinery is on somewhat different lines from that of the Special Committee's report. We are now thinking that instead of having a pipeline for 400 miles through Assam and another 400 miles then to Calcutta the crude oil should be moved by river in specially made barges. This would save a great deal of capital expenditure on the pipeline. Also it could be taken in hand much more quickly. The special barges would have to be built. This method of transportation by river is not considered efficient from the American point of view, but in our circumstances it seems to me far better.

In any event, a pipeline would have to be constructed from the Brahmaputra to Calcutta. That would be a subsequent development. So far as the refineries are concerned, it is possible that we might have more than one refinery. One of these could be situated in Assam and another perhaps somewhere in Bihar and so on.

I am merely mentioning this to you not because anything has been decided but this is the general approach that is being considered.

About the Nagas, I am much worried. This worry is not due so much to the military or other situations but rather to a feeling of psychological defeat. Why should we not be able to win them over? I do not like being pushed into repressive measures anywhere in India. I can understand that action has to be taken and the action must be effective, when necessity arises. But this long drawn out business has a bad effect, both internationally and nationally and, if I may say so, personally on me. I am, therefore, prepared to consider any reasonable approach to this problem which promises a settlement.

We rule out independence. I do not know what Chummini means by saying something "short of complete independence." I cannot conceive of anything just short of complete independence being feasible. I can conceive of local autonomy. But my mind is not clear yet how far all this is feasible in these present circumstances. Much as I regret, I do feel that the Nagas must realise that they cannot indulge in this kind of violence and warfare and that we shall not submit to it.

About an amnesty I have no difficulty. I would be prepared to extend the principles of amnesty as far as possible though I think it would be dangerous to include Phizo in it. But even this declaration of an amnesty has to be a part of a settlement and not in the air, although we can make some general approach to it even earlier.

The more I think of it, the more convinced I am that the first step that we should take is to take away the Naga District from the jurisdiction of the Assam Government and to put it together with Tuensang Division under the Central Government. This would be a temporary provision to enable us to deal with them separately, if necessary. I know that this will not be to the liking of the Assam Government or the people but they will have to swallow it some time or other. This can only be taken up after the elections and we may make it clear then perhaps that this is a temporary provision, the whole problem being considered step by step a little later.

We shall, of course, have to meet and discuss these matters. I think it is desirable for you to come to Delhi some time after the elections are over. We can fix this later.

As for my interviewing some of the Nagas, I should leave this entirely to your judgment as to when and whom I should see.

I am sending your letter with its enclosures to Pantji, as desired by you.

As you know, Dr Katju is leaving the Defence Ministry and is taking over as Chief Minister of Madhya Pradesh.[2] It is my intention to take over the Defence Ministry myself. This will add to my work but, in some ways, it will have some advantages also. This is for your private ear only at present.

Yours sincerely,
Jawaharlal Nehru

2. Katju was sworn in as the Chief Minister on 31 January 1957.

7. To S. Fazl Ali [1]

New Delhi,
February 4, 1957

My dear Fazl Ali,

Thank you for your letter of January 28th. I have read the letter as well as the note attached, with much interest. I do not think it is ever wrong to meet people in the normal way. But I am more than ever sure that we cannot do anything which looks like a surrender to these people.

Thimayya saw me the other day. He told me that the hostile Nagas were suffering greatly because of lack of supplies, etc. In fact, he was surprised that they were so tough that they were still holding out.

I am very sorry to learn about further raids on our villages.[2]

Yours sincerely,
Jawaharlal Nehru

1. JN Collection.
2. Hostile Naga gangs were reported to have attacked villages in the southern tracts of Sibsagar district adjacent to the Naga Hills.

8. To M.K. Vellodi [1]

New Delhi,
February 5, 1957

My dear Vellodi,[2]

I am going away tomorrow morning to Allahabad and Lucknow, returning on the 8th February morning. I shall be frequently touring during this month. I am asking my office to send you my tour programme for this month. If necessity arises, you can telephone to me or send me a message. The most feasible way of doing so is to leave a message with Mathai,[3] who can telephone it to me. It will be taken down at the other end by my PA. I shall be moving about most of the time.

As you perhaps know, there is a threat of a Post and Telegraph strike in Assam.[4] Perhaps, it may not come off. But there is a fair chance that it will take place, and that too fairly soon. If our efforts fail to prevent the strike, we shall naturally have to make some arrangements for carrying on important work in the P & T Department in Assam. It is obvious that this strike is aimed at giving us trouble just when the elections come, in order to coerce Government. Assam is a particularly difficult place because of the Naga trouble also. Anyhow, if necessity arises, we shall have to give all the help we possibly can from our Army or the NCC. I realise the difficulties, but there is no help for it. I hope you will keep this in mind and keep in touch with the P & T Department about it, so that some preliminary steps may be thought out.

I am rather worried about these repeated border raids by the hostile Nagas.[5] I sent you a frantic telegram which I had received yesterday. Apart from creating

1. JN Collection.
2. Defence Secretary.
3. A close member of Nehru's personal staff.
4. The Post and Telegraph employees stationed in Assam threatened to strike if their demand for the Assam compensatory allowance was not conceded.
5. A large number of Naga hostiles infiltrated, in small batches into the forest reserves on both sides of the railway tract which passed through southern Sibsagar. They were reported to have committed raids and dacoities in the railway section between Diphu in Mikir hills and Furkating in Golaghat sub-division since 31 January. The hostiles burnt down three villages adjacent to Dhansiri station on the night of 31 January and set fire to a sawmill near Dhansiri the next day. They attacked Barbari on 1 February and committed a dacoity in Barjabasti on 2 February.

a good deal of panic in these border areas, this also becomes a means of supply to the hostile Nagas, who are otherwise, I understand, in great difficulties in the hill areas. We must try to do something to stop them.

Shrinagesh[6] has just been there. I understand that he has had a talk with the Governor. He seemed to be rather reluctant to take any step without consulting Thimayya. Thimayya, of course, should be consulted in any event. Shrinagesh will be coming back, I suppose, soon to Delhi. Please discuss this matter with him and get in touch with Thimayya also. Something has to be done as soon as possible. Something indeed has been done I believe, but this might be followed up by some further action. Otherwise, even the hostile Nagas revive a little and the effect of our pressure on them will be minimised considerably.

Yours sincerely,
Jawaharlal Nehru

6. Chief of the Army Staff.

9. To B.P. Chaliha[1]

New Delhi,
February 8, 1957

My dear Chaliha,[2]

I am writing to you about the threat by the P & T Employees in Assam to strike. Whatever the grievances of these employees might be, I think that any such threat at the time of elections and when there is the Naga trouble, etc., in Assam, is highly improper. I understand that even the P & T Federation is opposed to the strike, although they sympathise with the demands. I am sorry to find that some Congress people, presumably because of the elections, are encouraging these people.

1. File No. 26(26)/57-PMS.
2. President, Assam Pradesh Congress Committee.

We are perfectly prepared to consider any demands at the proper time, but no Government can submit to such threats on the eve of an election. If these employees adopt a proper attitude, they can come and see our Minister[3] here, but in no event are we going to give in to the threat at this time, whatever the consequences.

Yours sincerely,
Jawaharlal Nehru

3. Raj Bahadur, Union Minister for Communications.

10. Situation in the Naga Foothills[1]

....PM mentioned that the additional force required for meeting the new situation in the Naga foothills area can be found:
- (i) either by strengthening our Armed forces in the area by sending units from other parts of India, e.g. Rajasthan;
- or (ii) by thinning out the Assam Rifle battalions in the Tuensang Frontier Division.

2. PM was of the view that to rely entirely on the latter alternative will be undesirable because though the activity of hostiles in Tuensang Frontier Division was not at present intense, the possibility of a fresh flare-up cannot be ruled out, judging by reports. He also thought that while administration in Tuensang and other parts of NEFA need not be extended further at this juncture, there was at the same time no good reason why a situation should be created in which the administration actually had to be withdrawn. The solution therefore was to send at least one more Army battalion into the area from elsewhere in India....

1. Note recorded by B.K. Acharya, Joint Secretary, MEA, on Nehru's meeting with the Defence Secretary, General Shrinagesh and Secretary General MEA at New Delhi about the Assam Chief Minister's request for further military assistance, 8 February 1957. File No. 15/5/57-T, MHA. Extracts.

11. To S. Fazl Ali[1]

New Delhi,
9th February, 1957

My dear Fazl Ali,

I have just read your long letter to the President dated February 5th. I am glad you undertook this tour in the NEFA. I hope, however, that you will not overdo this touring at the expense of your health.

Broadly speaking, my own approach to the NEFA problem is that we should be rather cautious in making too many innovations in these areas. We tend to do that, in all goodwill of course. But suddenly to change the whole background of living of primitive tribes involves considerable dangers and upsets. There has been a tendency in the past for us to go too far. I have already written to you about this.

I am particularly anxious that too many outsiders should not go to these areas. Some have to go for administrative and other purposes. But the number should be limited.

About the Naga situation generally, I entirely agree with you and the Chief Minister[2] that we must deal with these border raids effectively. Yesterday, on my return to Delhi, I held a conference with the military people and the Home Ministry.[3] The night before I had had a long talk with Thimayya in Lucknow.

You know the position, but I shall state it briefly. In a military sense we have succeeded in pushing the hostile Nagas further and further away and in making it more and more difficult for them to function. Considerable areas in the Naga Hills District are slowly returning to something like normality. In fact, the Nagas have little hope of doing anything effective in the Naga Hills District and hence they have broken out in the plain areas.

While we must deal with the raids on the plains, it would be a very bad policy to loosen our grip on the hill areas. That would mean undoing all the work we have done. Therefore, we must continue in the hill areas and we cannot afford to take away any forces from there for the plains.

On the whole, we cannot afford to take away any substantial number of forces from the Tuensang area. We may be able to thin out a little there but not much.

---

1. JN Collection.
2. Bisnuram Medhi.
3. See the preceding item.

The question is therefore of sending additional forces. We have decided to send almost immediately an army battalion as well as armed police. The army battalion will be sent probably from Calcutta so as to reach there soon. It would be replaced in Calcutta by forces moved from Western India.[4]

I hope that this will produce an immediate effect.

In your letter to the President there is some talk of amnesty. We have never been opposed to amnesty and we shall gladly give it to almost anybody. This may not only be kept in mind, but privately mentioned. But making a public announcement of complete amnesty perhaps would not yield much result at this stage.

Yours sincerely,
Jawaharlal Nehru

4. Nehru stated in a note to the Foreign Secretary on 10 February: "I have discussed this matter with General Thimayya and the Army Headquarters here. There is no question of the Army being withdrawn from the Naga Hills. In fact, General Thimayya told me that he could not spare any troops from the Hills for any operations in the plains. The Army had at last come to grips with the Naga hostiles in the Hills and had made life for them very difficult. The conditions in a large area were becoming a little more normal. In fact, it was because of this that the Naga hostiles had taken to the plains. Any relaxation in the Hills would be harmful." Nehru further wrote: "At the same [time] it is quite clear that we cannot allow these Nagas to function in the plains." He added that the government had decided to send an Army battalion from Kolkata to the plains as well as some armed police, and a fresh battalion of the Assam Rifles was also being trained.

12. Telegram to Bisnuram Medhi[1]

I have seen your telegram to Pantji and Raj Bahadur about the threatened Posts and Telegraphs strike in Assam.[2] Also perhaps Railways in Assam. We fully realise the difficulties of the situation in Assam and are prepared to discuss these matters. But I want to make it perfectly clear that I consider these threats of strikes on the eve of general elections highly improper and we shall surrender to no threat, whatever the consequences. The Communications and Railways Ministries have repeatedly expressed their willingness to discuss these matters, and the Federation of P & T Unions has expressed itself against the strike at this stage. The local P & T Unions however have taken up a most objectionable attitude. If, in spite of our efforts, they strike, we shall deal with the situation. It is impossible for any Government to be carried on if some people want to take advantage of a difficult situation.

I am sorry to note that some encouragement has been given to these local P & T Unions by Congressmen.

We are taking necessary steps in the event of a strike occurring.

---

1. New Delhi, 10 February 1957. File No. 26(26)/57-PMS.
2. Medhi informed G.B. Pant and Raj Bahadur, the Union Minister for Communications, on 7 February that all Post and Telegraph employees and a large number of Railway employees in Assam proposed to strike from 11 and 14 February and suggested that they should immediately impress the concerned employees' federations not to do so pending a sympathetic consideration of their demand for the Assam compensatory allowance. He also requested the government to "take immediately all possible action as any strike now will seriously disturb [the] law and order position and impede elections and handling of [the] Naga Hills situation."

13. Respect for Tribal People in NEFA[1]

Some four or five months ago, Dr Verrier Elwin[2] sent me a typescript of this small book and suggested that I might write a foreword to it. It was easy enough to write a few lines, but I did not wish to do so before I had read the typescript. I would have been in any event interested in reading it as the challenge to us from the North-East Frontier Agency fascinates me. I was fully occupied with various activities at the time, and so I put this typescript aside for a leisure hour or two. That leisure did not come. A few days ago there was a gentle reminder from Verrier Elwin and I felt a little ashamed at having kept him waiting for all this time. And so, in spite of numerous other activities and engagements, including election work, I have read through this very interesting little book.

Verrier Elwin has done me the honour of saying that he is a missionary of my views on tribal affairs. As a matter of fact, I have learnt much from him, for he is both an expert on this subject with great experience and a friend of the tribal folk. I have little experience of tribal life and my own views, vague as they were, have developed under the impact of certain circumstances and of Verrier Elwin's own writings. It would, therefore, be more correct to say that I have learnt from him rather than that I have influenced him in any way.

I came across the tribal people first, rather distantly, in various parts of India other than the North-East Frontier. These tribes were the Gonds, the Santals and the Bhils. I was attracted to them and liked them and I had a feeling that we should help them to grow in their own way.

Later, I came in touch with the tribal people of the North-East Frontier of India, more especially of the Hill Districts of Assam. My liking for them grew and with it came respect. I had no sensation of superiority over them. My ideas were not clear at all, but I felt that we should avoid two extreme courses: one was to treat them as anthropological specimens for study and the other was to allow them to be engulfed by the masses of Indian humanity. These reactions were instinctive and not based on any knowledge or experience. Later, in considering various aspects of these problems and in discussing them with those who knew much more than I did, and more especially with Verrier Elwin, more

---

1. Foreword, written on 16 February 1957, to the book *A Philosophy for NEFA* by Verrier Elwin. The book was first published in 1957.
2. English anthropologist who worked amongst the tribals in Central and North-East India and became an Indian citizen in 1954; Adviser for Tribal Affairs, NEFA, since 1954.

definite idea took shape in my mind and I began to doubt how far the normal idea of progress was beneficial for these people and, indeed, whether this was progress at all in any real sense of the word. It was true that they could not be left cut off from the world as they were. Political and economic forces impinged upon them and it was not possible or desirable to isolate them. Equally undesirable, it seemed to me, was to allow these forces to function freely and upset their whole life and culture, which had so much of good in them.

The reading of this book has clarified my mind and helped me to have more definite views on the subject. I agree not only with the broad philosophy and approach of Verrier Elwin, but with his specific proposals as to how we should deal with these fellow-countrymen of ours. I hope that our officers and others who have to work with the tribals of NEFA will read carefully what Dr Elwin has written and absorb this philosophy so that they may act in accordance with it. Indeed, I hope that this broad approach will be applied outside the NEFA also to other tribals in India.

I hope the reading of this book will not be confined to our officers, but that it will have a wider audience. Our people all over India should know more about this problem and should develop affection and respect for these fine people. Above all, I hope there will be no attempt made to impose other ways of life on them in a hurry. Let the changes come gradually and be worked out by the tribals themselves.

It is true that the isolated life that our officers live in some of these tribal areas is a strain on them. But they must remember that the problems they deal with are a challenge to us and that they are privileged to be engaged in this great adventure.

4

CONGRESS AND THE ELECTIONS

1. To U.N. Dhebar[1]

New Delhi,
6th December, 1956

My dear Dhebarbhai,[2]

It might interest you to know of a report that I have received. It is presumably true though obviously I cannot guarantee it.

It appears that the Democratic Research Service group in Bombay and the Forum for Free Enterprise[3] have come to an arrangement with Jaipal Singh,[4] MP according to which Jaipal Singh will support some Parliamentary candidates in the Jharkhand area of Bihar. The candidates mentioned in this connection are:

1. M.R. Masani[5]
2. H.P. Mody[6]
3. A.D. Shroff[7]
4. Leslie Sawhney[8] (he is brother-in-law of J.R.D. Tata).

Obviously Jaipal Singh is going to receive considerable sums of money for this. It is stated that this is three and a half lakhs of which he has already received fifty thousand.

1. JN Collection.
2. Congress President.
3. The Forum was founded in Mumbai in May 1956. Its manifesto published on 18 July stated: "Democracy is an essential element in the Indian way of life. Free enterprise is an integral part of it and as such it should be permitted to play its legitimate role in our national life."
4. Member of the Lok Sabha from Ranchi representing the Jharkhand Party.
5. Founder of the Bombay-based Democratic Research Service, Masani fought the 1957 elections as an independent candidate from Ranchi and was sponsored by Jaipal Singh. After winning the election he resigned from the Tatas after 16 years of service.
6. Industrialist from Bombay and president of the Employers' Federation of India. Mody stood for the elections to the Lok Sabha from Bhilwara in Rajasthan.
7. (1899-1965); Director, Tata Sons, 1939-61; founder, Forum for Free Enterprise.
8. (1915-1967); industrialist; served in the British Indian Army during the Second World War; after independence, served as Deputy Commandant, Defence Services Staff College, Wellington; joined the Tata Group of companies as executive assistant to the Chairman, J.R.D. Tata; appointed, Director, Tata Industries, 1961, and made Vice-Chairman of Tata Chemicals.

255

Tulsidas Kilachand[9], MP, is apparently also associated with this matter.

These groups are also said to be negotiating with N.C. Chatterjee[10] for support to Parliamentary candidates set up by the Hindu Mahasabha and the Jana Sangh. It might be that these candidates stand as Independents.

It is also stated that money is likely to come from foreign sources also, chiefly from the funds of the American Secret Service.

Yours sincerely,
Jawaharlal Nehru

9. Independent member of the Lok Sabha from Bombay.
10. Member of the Lok Sabha of the Hindu Mahasabha from Hooghly, West Bengal.

2. The Peaceful Revolution[1]

Seventy-one years ago, the Indian National Congress was born. Its early beginnings were small but significant and this infant organisation was to grow into a mighty organ of the Indian people representing their wishes and urges for freedom. Year by year it grew in scope and outlook and great men and women, famous in India's story, took part in moulding it so that it might play its destined part to bring independence to this country. Lokamanya Tilak broadened its base and gave it strength and drive; Mahatma Gandhi made it the representative of the vast masses of India and endowed it with faith and self-reliance. Under his leadership it chalked out a new path of peaceful revolutionary action based on the high principles for which he stood. Hundreds of thousands of our countrymen followed that path willingly and sacrificed everything that they had in the pursuit of freedom for their beloved country. Gradually also the Congress developed a social content for that freedom and stood ever more for the advancement of the

1. Draft preamble of the Congress Election Manifesto, New Delhi, 10 December 1956. JN Collection. This was read to members of the Congress Working Committee at a meeting on 11 December 1956. Nehru then agreed to complete the draft of the manifesto and place it before the CWC on 12 December.

dispossessed and the unprivileged and those who had to suffer political, economic and social disabilities.

2. Decade after decade this peaceful and revolutionary struggle continued in India, often convulsing the life of the country and drawing into its fold millions of our people. At last on the 15th August 1947, freedom came and the pledge that millions in India had taken year after year for independence was redeemed and largely fulfilled. At that solemn and historic moment when India stepped out from servitude to freedom, we took another pledge of dedication to the service of India and her people and to the still larger cause of humanity.

3. Immediately the sun of freedom was darkened by conflict and disaster and, soon after, the Master who had led us from darkness to light, passed away making the ultimate sacrifice for the cause he held dear. Sorrow overwhelmed us, but his voice rang in our ears and his message gave us strength. We laboured to face this challenge to our new-won freedom and the people of India defeated the forces of darkness and reaction.

4. The new Constitution of India took shape after much labour and in 1950, on the 26th of January, a date hallowed in our long struggle for freedom,[2] the Republic of India came into existence. Thus the old pledge was fully redeemed and a new chapter began in India's long story.

5. The Congress had fulfilled its old pledge for independence, but the other pledge to fight poverty and ignorance and disease and inequality of opportunity remained, and the Congress set itself to this tremendous task. Nearly seven years have passed since then and the story of these seven years of work and achievement is before our people and the world. Whether in the field of international affairs or of our national and domestic problems, India's star has grown brighter and her achievements have been notable. Keeping faith with the old, we have sought to build up a new India, a modern state which would remove the burdens of those who suffer and give opportunity for progress to all. The great adventure on which we embarked involves a long and arduous journey and we can only progress step by step along that path. We have far to go before we reach the end of this journey. But we have made good progress and laid the foundations of the new India of our dreams.

6. The Congress, throughout the struggle for India's freedom, had always stood for the betterment of the masses and the underprivileged. A precise direction was given to this objective by the famous Avadi Resolution of the Congress laying down as its objective a socialist pattern of society for the

---

2. On 26 January 1930, the Lahore session of the Congress pledged itself to the goal of complete independence.

country.[3] While we aimed at socialism, we also adhered to a democratic structure of society and we proclaimed afresh that our means would be peaceful. Thus the Congress stood for democracy and socialism and for peaceful and legitimate methods. These are the basic policies of the Congress on which we have laboured to build the noble edifice of new India.

7. A planned approach to the problems of India was made and, as a first effort, the Five Year Plan took shape. Most of the targets laid down in this Plan were fulfilled, and some of the achievements exceeded the expectations laid down in the targets. The zamindari and *jagirdari* systems were largely abolished. Production in food and other articles was considerably increased. Science, the basis of modern life, was nurtured, and great laboratories and institutes grew up all over the country. Vast river valley schemes made substantial progress, leading to the spread of irrigation and the production of electric power. Many industrial plants came into existence, more particularly, the great fertiliser factory at Sindri and the Chittaranjan Locomotive Factory. A beginning was made in the scheme of community development in rural areas, which was of revolutionary significance and which was to spread far into the villages of India. Above all, self-reliance and a new confidence were created in the people of India, who became planning conscious.

8. At the conclusion of the First Five Year Plan, the Second Plan came into being. In this Plan, emphasis was laid on a more rapid development of industry and, at the same time, the importance of greater production in agriculture was pointed out. In order to facilitate the rapid industrialisation of India, the production of steel was given first importance, and three large new iron and steel plants are being erected, in addition to the expansion of the old plants. Machine-making industry also finds an important place in the Plan. Ship-building is being increased, and aircraft production is being organised. Transport and railways form an essential part of the Plan. An integral coach factory of the latest type was established in Madras. The rural community schemes, it is hoped, will cover the whole of rural India by the end of the Second Plan period. It is not possible to enumerate all that is being done and that is envisaged to be done during the Second Five Year Plan in this manifesto. The Plan itself is before the public and lays down in detail the innumerable activities that have to be undertaken in the country.

3. For Nehru's draft of the resolution on a socialist pattern of society passed at Avadi in January 1955 and his speech on the resolution, see *Selected Works* (second series), Vol. 27, p. 255 and pp. 279-283.

9. These numerous activities are not confined to the economic sphere, but include also social progress and cultural activities. Legislation has been passed for the reform of the Hindu Law in regard to marriage and divorce and the inheritance by women.[4] Thus, out of date customs which bore down upon our womenfolk have been ended, and in this and other ways a larger freedom has been ensured to the women of India.

10. A significant development has been the growth in the cultural field, in literature, art and music, song and dance, which indicate the new life and creative urges that are pulsing through the nation.

11. The political revolution was largely completed on the establishment of the Republic of India. But, full achievement can come when there is a real emotional integration of the people of India. To that end, efforts will continue to be directed, so that the feeling of separateness, whether communal or provincial or due to caste distinctions, is ended. We realise fully the dangers of communalism and have struggled against them throughout Congress history. The recent past has demonstrated that the feeling of provincial separation is still strong and has to be combatted. Caste is an evil which has weakened our society, introduced innumerable fissiparous tendencies and resulted in the suppression and humiliation of large numbers of people. The Congress is entirely opposed to this system, as it is opposed to everything that creates divisions and inequality.

12. The revolution in India will only be completed when the political revolution is followed by an economic as well as a social revolution. These two latter are gradually taking shape in India. But, according to India's own genius and method, they take place peacefully. Great progress has been made and changes will continue to take place, so that ultimately we can establish a full socialist order of society giving freedom, welfare and equality of opportunity to all.

13. The basic objectives, it must be repeated, have to be democracy, socialism and peaceful methods. We have to adhere to peaceful methods not only because they are in tune with India's thinking and genius, but because only thus can we maintain the unity and integrity of India and not waste our substance in internecine conflict. Only thus can we achieve socialism through the democratic method, which we value as ensuring the freedom of the individual.

14. The task before the country is a tremendous one, for it involves the raising of nearly four hundred millions to freedom and prosperity and equality. This task means establishing a progressive economy in an underdeveloped country and taking out these millions from the morass of poverty. It is essential to add to

4. The Hindu Marriage Act was passed by the Lok Sabha on 5 May 1955.

the productive wealth of the country and this can only be done by industrialisation on a large-scale and by improved methods of agriculture. The process of industrialisation involves saving and investment for future progress, which means an avoidance of waste and a measure of austerity. We have to work hard today to ensure our tomorrows.

3. The Election Manifesto[1]

Seventy-one years ago, the Indian National Congress was born. Its early beginnings were small but significant and this infant organisation was to grow into a mighty organ of the Indian people representing their wishes and urges for freedom. Year by year it grew in scope and outlook and great men and women, famous in India's story, took part in moulding it so that it might play its destined part to bring independence to this country. Dadabhai Naoroji first enunciated the goal of *swaraj*; Lokmanya Tilak broadened its base and gave it strength and drive; Mahatma Gandhi made it the representative of the vast masses of India and endowed it with faith and self-reliance. Under his leadership it chalked out a new path of peaceful revolutionary action based on the high principles for which he stood. Hundreds of thousands of our countrymen followed that path willingly and sacrificed everything that they had in the pursuit of freedom for their beloved country. Gradually also the Congress developed a social content for that freedom and stood ever more for the advancement of the dispossessed and the unprivileged and those who had to suffer political, economic and social disabilities.

Decade after decade this peaceful and revolutionary struggle continued in India, often convulsing the life of the country and drawing into its fold millions of our people. At the end of 1929, the Lahore Congress defined *swaraj* as full independence, and on January 26, 1930, people all over the country took this

---

1. New Delhi, 12 December 1956. File No. G-21/1956, AICC Papers, NMML. At its meeting held on 12 December 1956, the Congress Working Committee considered the draft of the election manifesto prepared by Nehru (see the preceding item). The CWC members considered the draft paragraph-wise and put forth their suggestions. Then Nehru incorporated the suggestions in the draft. This version was placed before the Congress at its Indore session.

pledge. At last on the 15th August 1947, freedom came and the pledge that millions in India had taken year after year for independence was redeemed and largely fulfilled. At that solemn and historic moment when India stepped out from servitude to freedom, we took another pledge of dedication to the service of India and her people and to the still larger cause of humanity.

Immediately the sun of freedom was darkened by conflict and disaster and, soon after, the Master who had led us from darkness to light, passed away making the ultimate sacrifice for the cause he held dear. Sorrow overwhelmed us, but his voice rang in our ears and his message gave us strength. We laboured to face this challenge to our new-won freedom and the people of India defeated the forces of darkness and reaction.

The partition of India resulted in the uprooting of millions of people. Vast migrations took place, and the problem of rehabilitation assumed colossal proportions. This problem was also faced with determination and millions of displaced persons were rehabilitated and given new hope for the future. The success attending these efforts has been one of the most remarkable features of the past nine years. Although the problem of dispossessed persons from Western Pakistan was largely solved, unfortunately, the migrations continued from East Pakistan and still take place in large numbers affecting the whole of India and, more especially, the state of West Bengal. Every effort has been made, and will continue to be made, to help these people, who have had to leave home and hearth and have to begin a new life.

The numerous princely states of India were absorbed and integrated into the union of India. This remarkable achievement within a short period of time did credit to the Government of India and to the rulers of the states concerned. Similar problems in other countries had led to violent struggles and major conflicts. Here, in India, according to our way, we solved it peacefully and cooperatively, thus laying the foundations of an integrated India.

The new Constitution of India took shape after much labour and in 1950, on the 26th of January, a date hallowed in our long struggle for freedom, the Republic of India came into existence. Thus the old pledge was fully redeemed and a new chapter began in India's long story.

The Congress had fulfilled its old pledge for independence, but the other pledge to fight poverty and ignorance and disease and inequality of opportunity, remained, and the Congress set itself to this tremendous task. Seven years have passed since then and the story of these seven years of work and achievement is before our people and the world. Whether in the field of international affairs or of our national and domestic problems, India's star has grown brighter and her achievements have been notable. Keeping faith with the old, we have sought to build up a new India, a modern state which would remove the burdens of those who suffer and give opportunity for progress to all. The great adventure on which we embarked involves a long and arduous journey and we can only progress step by step along that path. We have far to go before we reach the end of this journey. But we have made good progress and laid the foundations of the new India of our dreams.

The Congress, throughout the struggle for India's freedom, had always stood for the betterment of the masses and the underprivileged. A precise direction was given to this objective by the famous Avadi Resolution of the Congress laying down as its objective a socialist pattern of society for the country. While we aimed at socialism, we also adhered to a democratic structure of society and we proclaimed afresh that our means would be peaceful. Thus the Congress stood for democracy and socialism and for peaceful and legitimate methods. These are the basic policies of the Congress on which we have laboured to build the noble edifice of new India.

A planned approach to the problem of India was made and, as a first effort, the Five Year Plan took shape. Most of the targets laid down in this Plan were fulfilled, and some of the achievements exceeded the expectations laid down in the targets. The zamindari and *jagirdari* systems were largely abolished. Production in food and other articles was considerably increased. Science, the basis of modern life, was nurtured, and great laboratories and institutes grew up all over the country. Vast river valley schemes—Bhakra-Nangal, Damodar Valley, Hirakud, Tungabhadra and others—made substantial progress, leading to the spread of irrigation and the production of electric power. Many industrial plants came into existence, more particularly, the great fertiliser factory at Sindri and the Chittaranjan Locomotive Factory. A beginning was made in the scheme of community development in rural areas, which was of revolutionary significance and which was to spread far into the villages of India. Above all, self-reliance and a new confidence were created in the people of India.

In 1951-52, the first general elections under the new Constitution took place all over the country. Never before anywhere in the world had democratic elections taken place on such a vast scale. Every adult man and woman in a population of thirty-six crores was entitled to vote and a very large number of them participated in the elections. Every group and party and individual, whatever his political or economic programme of ideology, had the right to participate in the elections. These free and impartial elections resulted in a great victory for the Congress. At the same time, other parties were also represented in Parliament and in the new legislatures that came into existence in the states. Through these elections the people of the country proclaimed afresh their faith in the Congress and gave it strength. The country gained stability and confidence to plan for the future.

At the conclusion of the First Five Year Plan, the Second Plan came into being. In this Plan, emphasis was laid on a more rapid development of industry and, at the same time, the importance of greater production in agriculture was pointed out. In order to facilitate the rapid industrialisation of India, the production of steel was given first importance, and three large new iron and steel plants are being erected, in addition to the expansion of the old plants. Machine-making industry also finds an important place in the Plan. Organized attempts are being made to exploit the mineral resources of the country, especially oil and coal. The chemical industry is being developed and considerable progress has been made in atomic energy research for the production of atomic power for industrial development. Ship-building is being increased, and aircraft production is being organised. Transport and railways form an essential part of the Plan. An integral coach factory of the latest type has been established in Madras. The rural community development schemes, it is hoped, will cover the whole of rural India by the end of the Second Plan period. It is not possible to enumerate all that is being done and that is envisaged to be done during the Second Five Year Plan in this manifesto. The Plan itself is before the public and lays down in detail the innumerable activities that have to be undertaken in the country.

These numerous activities are not confined to the economic sphere, but include also social progress and cultural activities. Legislation has been passed for the reform of the Hindu Law in regard to marriage and divorce and the inheritance by women. Thus, out of date customs which bore down upon our womenfolk have been ended, and in this and other ways a larger freedom has been ensured to the women of India.

No subject was dearer to Gandhiji than the removal of untouchability and the uplift of those classes who had been suppressed by social custom and practice. The Congress made this cause of the Harijans its own and laboured for them throughout the period of our national struggle. By our Constitution and the legislation passed thereafter the practice of untouchability was made an offence and a great and essential reform affecting millions of our countrymen took place.

India is a country of great variety not only in climate and physical features, but in the ways of living of her people. It is the manifold aspects, linked together by a basic unity, which give beauty and richness to her culture. The tribal people of India are an essential and important part of the country. They vary greatly among themselves. But all of them are noted for their vigorous life, their artistry and their folk songs and dances. The Constitution has made special provision for them,[2] so that they may progress according to their own genius and ways of

2. Under the Sixth Schedule.

life. It has been a misfortune that some people living in the Naga Hills have taken to violence. The Nagas are a brave people, who are a credit to India. They have every right to preserve their own customs and ways of life in their own way and to enjoy a measure of autonomy for this purpose. It is hoped that the misunderstanding and apprehensions that have misled them will be removed, and they will become free and contented members of the large family of India.

A significant development has been the growth in the cultural field, in literature, art and music, song and dance, which indicate the new life and creative urges that are pulsating through the nation.

During the past year or more, the question of the reorganization of the states gave rise to much controversy and even conflicts. Such questions, involving languages and a new distribution of provincial areas, have often roused strong passions in other countries also. But, after full discussions and consultation, the states were reorganized and a new map of India took shape.[3] In spite of the strong feelings which these changes had aroused, the people of India showed their basic resilience and vitality and their capacity for peaceful adjustment, even when they disagreed. It is this capacity which gives strength to our people and the hope that, however much there might be occasional disagreements unity prevails and good sense reasserts itself.

Recent amendments to the Constitution have ensured the protection of every language, even where it is the language of a minority community. Minorities in India, whether religious or linguistic or other, must have the assurance and the feeling of playing their full part in the varied activities of the country. The Constitution is a secular one, but it respects all religions prevalent in India and gives full scope for their functioning. Every attempt must be made to ensure that these assurances are carried out and no minority is made to suffer because it is either a religious or linguistic minority. Secularism does not mean lack of faith but protection of all faiths and the encouragement of spiritual and moral values.

The political revolution was largely completed on the establishment of the Republic of India. But, full achievement can only come when there is a real emotional integration of the people of India. To that end, efforts will continue to be directed, so that the feeling of separateness, whether communal or provincial or due to caste distinctions, is ended. We realise fully the dangers of communalism and have struggled against them throughout Congress history. The recent past has demonstrated that the feeling of provincial separation is still strong and has to be combatted. Caste is an evil which has weakened our society, introduced

3. The new states came into being on 1 November 1956.

AT THE CONGRESS SESSION, INDORE, 4 JANUARY 1957

AT THE CONGRESS SESSION, INDORE, 4 JANUARY 1957

innumerable fissiparous tendencies and resulted in the suppression and humiliation of large numbers of people. The Congress is entirely opposed to this system, as it is opposed to everything that creates divisions and inequality.

The revolution in India can only be completed when the political revolution is followed by an economic as well as a social revolution. These two latter are gradually taking shape in India. But, according to India's own genius and method, they take place peacefully and cooperatively. Considerable progress has been made and changes will continue to take place, so that ultimately we can establish a full socialist order of society giving freedom, welfare and equality of opportunity to all.

The basic objectives of the Congress, it must be repeated, are democracy, socialism and methods have to be peaceful. We have to adhere to peaceful methods not only because they are in tune with India's thinking from the time of our ancient sages and Asoka to Gandhi, but because only thus can we maintain the unity and integrity of India and not waste our substance in internecine conflict. Only thus can we achieve socialism through the democratic method, which we value as ensuring the freedom of the individual.

The Congress, throughout its long history, has represented political, economic and social advance. It has represented something more, which is vital to our growth. Gandhiji impressed upon the Congress and our people, the importance of moral values and of the maintenance of high standards in public as well as in private life. It is of the utmost importance that these standards and values should be maintained, more especially during a period of transition in India and the world, when values change and many old standards appear to have less significance. The story of man from his early beginnings at the dawn of history, is not merely a story of economic and technological advance, but is essentially an advance on the moral, ethical and cultural plane. Without that foundation, advance in other fields may lead, and has indeed often led, to conflict and disaster. Scientific and technological growth, bringing in its train the atomic and the hydrogen bomb and astonishing growth in means of communications, has made the moral and ethical approach of vital significance today, if human life is to survive in any civilized form.

Socialism does not merely signify changes in the economic relations of human beings. It involves fundamental changes in the social structure, in ways of thinking and in ways of living. Caste and class have no place in the socialist order that is envisaged by the Congress. It is important, therefore, that these new ways of thinking and of living should be encouraged, and old ideas about privilege on the basis of birth or caste or class or money or the hierarchy of office, should be discarded. Men should be judged by their labour, their productive and creative efforts and their services to society and community.

265

The dignity of labour should be recognized, as well as the dignity of the individual in every grade of life. The socialist order is a way of life based on the people and not merely on the efforts of Government. It is in the measure that the people develop their strength, their discipline, their capacity to work and their cooperative activities that socialism comes into being. Governments derive power from the people and reflect that power as well as the other urges of the people.

In economic relations there should be no exploitation and no monopolies, and disparities in income should be progressively lessened. A national minimum in the general standard of living should be aimed at, so that everyone has the necessaries of life and the opportunity for education, for maintaining his health and for productive work.

Even as there are disparities among people, there are disparities in the development of different parts of the country and some areas are more developed than others. It is necessary that these backward areas and regions should be particularly helped to develop themselves, so that there is balanced growth of the country as a whole.

Many years ago, the Congress stated its objective in Article I of its constitution, and declared it to be the well-being and advancement of the people of India and the establishment in India by peaceful and legitimate means of a cooperative commonwealth based on equality of opportunity and of political, economic and social rights and aiming at world peace and fellowship. Since then, the Congress has stated that it aims at a socialist pattern of society and, thus, the object becomes the establishment of a "socialist cooperative commonwealth". Cooperation is the law of life in human communities, and it is in the measure that there is lack of cooperation that troubles and conflicts arise. Therefore, the cooperative element should enter into every aspect of life and, more particularly, in industry and agriculture. In industry, the cooperative principles should lead to industrial democracy and the progressive participation of workers in industry; in rural areas the community should be based on cooperative management of villages.

The task is a tremendous one, for it involves the raising of nearly thirty-six crores to freedom and prosperity and equality. It can only be accomplished by a mighty cooperative effort of the people all over the country. In an underdeveloped country the task of taking the people out of the morass of poverty and establishing a progressive economy is peculiarly different. It requires a combined and persistent effort for a considerable period and a measure of austerity and avoidance of all waste so that the maximum use can be made of the nation's resources in productive channels. False standards of living and display have to be given up and those who lead the people in various parts of the country have to set an example. The process of building up a new India involves industrialisation on a large scale and improved methods of agriculture. It involves saving and investment for future progress. We have to work hard today to ensure our tomorrows.

The Second Five Year Plan was prepared after full consultation and discussion. It represents, therefore, the combined wisdom of the country and it has to be given effect to by the joint effort of all our people. This plan represents broadly the approach to the problems of India in the various fields of national activity. It is a flexible plan. It will have to be adjusted from time to time as circumstances demand and as the resources of the country permit. Already, certain important changes are being made in regard to resources and the target for food production as well as other matters. The experience of other countries has shown how difficult it is to keep proper balance between industry and agriculture and between heavy, light and small-scale industries. We have to profit by this experience and aim at a balanced and at the same time, rapid growth. The growth of heavy industry is essential if we are to industrialise our country and not be dependent on others. But this has to be balanced by small-scale and cottage industries. A large measure of centralization has become inevitable in modern life. But we have also at the same time to decentralize in so far as this is possible.

The major problem of India is to fight poverty and unemployment and to raise the standards of our people. All planning has this for its objective. This necessitates greatly increased production and equitable distribution. Production in the world has grown rapidly ever since higher techniques were employed. Such higher techniques must, therefore, be encouraged in industry and agriculture, as without them production will continue to be at a low level. In introducing higher techniques, however, the human element, the utilization of India's abundant manpower and the question of employment must always be kept in view, so that any changeover in methods of production does not lead to unemployment and unhappiness.

The pace of progress depends upon the resources that are available or that can be raised. While help from any friendly source must be welcomed, the principal burden of finding resources must inevitably fall on the people of the country. This burden has to be borne. But it should be spread out in such a way as to fall chiefly on those who are in a better position to shoulder it. The structure of taxation is being reconstructed with this object in view. This process will also help in reducing disparities in income and wealth.

The Congress welcomes the nationalization of the State Bank[4] as well as of life insurance.[5] This is another step towards a socialist pattern and it gives a

4. In July 1955, the Imperial Bank was nationalized and renamed as State Bank of India.
5. Life Insurance was nationalized by an Act of Parliament in May 1956. The LIC Act came into force on 1 July 1956.

267

greater measure of strategic control for planning and other purposes of the state. The resolution on industrial policy of the government of India defines the areas reserved for the public and private sectors. It is not intended to nationalize the existing private industries, except where such is considered necessary in terms of planning or where they occupy a strategic position in the economy of the country. Private industry will be encouraged, but always in the context of the Plan.

It is of the highest importance to keep prices at reasonable levels and to prevent inflation. To some extent inflation is almost inevitable in a developing economy, but this should be kept fully in check and all necessary steps should be taken to that end.

In order to add to the resources of the country and also to check inflation, saving is of great importance. The Congress, therefore, commends to the people that every effort should be made to save and to invest in the various savings schemes or in productive enterprises.

On the land, all intermediaries must be progressively removed, so that land is owned by the cultivator himself. The principle of ceilings on land has been accepted and should be progressively introduced, so as to bring about a better distribution of land. Mechanized agriculture may be useful in some areas, but in view of the manpower available and often not fully used, it is desirable to encourage intensified methods of cultivation on a cooperative basis. It is of the highest importance from every point of view that production should increase. This is the surest way of adding to the country's resources and of combating inflation. The recent World Bank mission has stated that:

"Proper application of known techniques in conjunction with the possible expansion of irrigation and the cultivated area, could increase India's agricultural output four or five fold. By the time that has been achieved, new techniques will have been evolved and the way will be open for further progress. Results of the crop competitions organized for the grow-more-food campaign show yields about seven times higher than the local average. India's yields are at present among the lowest in the world. With the labour force available, they could be among the highest. There is thus a great deal of scope for progress that is technically easy but is retarded by poverty and ignorance."

The Planning Commission has increased the target of additional food production during the Plan period to between 35 and 40 per cent. In view of the remarks of the World Bank mission, this is a modest estimate. It is essential that this target should be achieved.

For this purpose, various steps have already been taken to add to our irrigation by a large number of minor works, by the construction of field embankments and contour bunds, by soil conservation, and by the introduction of dry farming methods in the semi-arid regions of Bombay, Madras, Hyderabad and UP. But the greatest need of all is to have comprehensive village planning and the organisation of the cooperative movement for agricultural production. The panchayats have an important role to play in this planning. Agricultural cooperatives should have a popular basis at the village level. Cooperation is essentially a voluntary effort and without the active participation of the people, no amount of governmental direction will yield adequate results. There may be larger cooperatives where necessary, but normally the size of a primary cooperative society should not be so large that its members do not have the sense of mutual obligation. Cooperation, therefore, has to be developed as a popular movement with the help and guidance of the state. This is not only necessary for the purposes of higher production, but also in order to develop that way of life which is based on individual freedom as well as cooperative effort.

The community projects and the national extension service are bringing about a revolutionary change in the countryside and developing a spirit of self-reliance and joint endeavour in our village people. The old static Indian village is changing and yielding place to a more dynamic conception. These community schemes must always keep in view the necessity of bringing this psychological change among the people. Their primary objective must now be greater food production and the growth of small-scale and village industries.

With the advance in agriculture and the growth of small-scale and village industries, the disparity that exists today between village and town should be progressively lessened. Local initiative in the villages should be encouraged, local resources utilized and higher techniques introduced.

Unemployment is not only bad for the individual concerned but is a disorder injurious to social health. Planning has, therefore, to aim at the progressive lessening of unemployment and its final elimination. This will chiefly take place by the growth of industry and, more especially, small-scale and village industries. Higher techniques appear to increase unemployment, but ultimately lead to far greater employment. Unemployment is partly due to the wrong type of training given to our youth. They should be trained especially from the point of view of fitting into the scheme of the Plan and being utilized for greater production in land and small and cottage industries. With a view to introducing higher techniques in agriculture and to help production, trained cadres for agricultural work should be organised.

Every kind of progress in industry, agriculture or any other activity requires training and education. In spite of the existing unemployment, the question of the lack of trained manpower is already coming in the way of advance and is likely to prove a great hindrance in the future unless adequate steps are taken from now onwards. It is therefore necessary for training and education to be organized systematically so as to help in fulfilling the purposes of the Plan. Education must help in introducing new social values. The system of Basic Education is especially suited to give a new direction to primary and secondary education. It would be desirable if some kind of labour was made an essential feature of education. More particularly, there should be some labour contribution before degrees or diplomas are given.

At present, there are large numbers of unemployed among those who have received some education. This unemployment is partly due to their not having received the proper type of education which would fit them into the nation's activities today. Apart from absorbing them in such vocations as may be suitable, an attempt should be made to give them some additional technical or specialized training so as to enable them to find suitable work more easily. The Second Five Year Plan has made provision for a number of schemes for reducing unemployment among the educated classes. Among these is the establishment of industrial estates.

Special attention to public health is necessary in order to raise the standard of the people. This requires not only governmental action but also changes in some of the habits of the people. A cooperative approach to this problem will prove more effective both for the individual and the community.

The administrative machinery should be adapted to suit the purposes of the Plan. Cumbrous procedures and red tape should be avoided and it should be so organized that rapid decisions are taken and given effect to. In particular, it should not isolate itself from the people but function in cooperation with them. The administration of justice should be simplified and made less expensive.

Prohibition has long been the Congress policy and has been introduced in some parts of the country. Progressive steps should be taken to introduce it in other parts.

All these activities in industry and agriculture or in the special services require combined effort in peaceful conditions. If the attention of the people is diverted into wasteful channels or conflict, then the nation suffers and the rate of our progress is slowed down. It is necessary, therefore, to have industrial peace as well as peace in our educational establishments which are training people to shoulder the burdens of the nation. Strikes and lockouts are peculiarly harmful when the main purpose is to add to production. Where any problems or controversies arise, they should be solved by peaceful and cooperative methods without stopping or slowing down the great machine of production which is so essential to the march of the nation to the next great stage in its journey to a socialist commonwealth.

The political integration of India has been completed except for a very small part of territory on the western coast – Goa. The other enclaves of foreign territory, which were governed by France, have been incorporated into India by a friendly settlement. But Goa still remains a symbol of the worst type of colonial rule and degradation, and the Portuguese Government have resisted all attempts at a peaceful settlement of this problem. Hundreds of Indian patriots and many thousands of Goans have suffered and are suffering in Goa because they laboured for freedom and for integration with India. It is impossible for India to tolerate a colonial enclave in any part of her territory and the continuation of it is an affront to the people of India. Nevertheless, attempts to solve this problem have been peaceful and will continue to be peaceful. These attempts must and will succeed.

India has no claim on any territory and desires no expansion. She wishes to live at peace with her neighbour as with other countries. It was with regret and under the compulsion of circumstances that partition was agreed to and it brought much distress and suffering to the people of India and Pakistan. India has fully accepted that partition and the independent state of Pakistan and has no wish to interfere with it in any way. Even though Pakistan committed aggression on Indian territory in Kashmir, India has pursued peaceful methods and will continue to adhere to them. She has offered a no-war declaration[6] to the Government of Pakistan, so that in no event should these two neighbour countries, which were one not so long ago, go to war. It is essential for the good of both that they live at peace with each other as good neighbours bound together by many links of common tradition and interest. Unfortunately, several problems have arisen between India and Pakistan and, in spite of India's efforts, they have not been solved. India will continue to seek peaceful solutions.

During the last few years, the State of Jammu and Kashmir has made considerable progress and the burdens of its people have been greatly reduced. The Congress welcomes the new constitution of the State.

In the Union of South Africa, racialism in its most acute and offensive form has continued. The problem of the people of Indian origin in South Africa, who are citizens of that country, has merged into the larger problem of all those who are not considered to be of the white race. These are denied the rights of citizenship and are segregated. Recently, 140 persons, coloured, African and Asian, were arrested by the Government of South Africa in a general round-up.[7]

6. India offered Pakistan a no-war pact through diplomatic channels in December 1949.
7. On 5 December 1956 at Cape Town.

271

Thus, a white minority suppresses the people of the country and others who are supposed to belong to an inferior race. Nowhere in the world is racialism so rampant and authoritarianism so evident. India has sought to solve this problem by peaceful and cooperative methods. But the Union Government of South Africa have refused even to discuss it. They have even ignored the resolution and directions of the United Nations, and sown the seeds of a terrible racial conflict. The conduct of the Government of the Union of South Africa is a challenge to the conscience of mankind and to the United Nations.

In international affairs, India has consistently pursued the path of peace and friendship with all nations. In a world full of the spirit of conflict and hatred and violence, she has endeavoured to free herself from these passions and avoided military pacts and alliances. She has sought and obtained friendship and cooperation from nations which are often hostile to each other, and has been of some service to the cause of peace in Korea and Indo-China.

India's relations with the countries of Asia and Africa have been particularly close and the Bandung Conference was a historic example of the coming together of all these nations. India and China first enunciated the Five Principles for the governance of international relations, which have subsequently become famous as the Panchsheel. It is on the basis of these principles alone that world peace can be assured.

The years following the Second World War have witnessed great changes and have seen many colonial territories in Asia and Africa attain freedom. The old balances have thus been upset and the domination of European countries over parts of Asia and Africa has been greatly lessened. It is essential that these changes should be understood fully all over the world and no attempt should be made to deal with the countries of Asia and Africa in the old colonial way. We have seen recently that such attempts are doomed to failure, just as we have seen that any imposition of foreign authority or ideology cannot succeed.

During these years China has established a people's republic and has developed into a strong nation, which is advancing at a rapid pace. China is a great neighbour of India and the two countries have neighbourly and friendly relations, in spite of differences in their political and economic structure. India has sought the admission of China into the United Nations year after year, but unfortunately this has been opposed by some countries. The United Nations cannot be a fully representative world organization if it does not include this great country which has nearly one-quarter of the world's population. Nor can the problems of East Asia or South-East Asia be solved without the cooperation of China.

India's foreign policy has had as its objectives the avoidance of war and the maintenance of friendly relations with all countries. India is opposed to cold war which keeps up the mentality of war and promotes race in armaments. As the UNESCO constitution states that 'since wars begin in the minds of men, it is in the minds of men that the defence of peace must be constructed.' A cold war is a negation of this approach, for it fills the minds of men with fears and thoughts of war.

In the year that is just ended, India and many other countries have celebrated the 2500th year of the passing away of the Buddha. The message of this great son of India has again resounded in our ears. In a world torn by hatred and violence, his gentle voice carrying the message of compassion has come to us through the ages. That message was repeated in our own day by Gandhiji. That is the message of India throughout these thousands of years of her history. Whatever activities we may indulge in, whether they are political or economic or social, we have to keep that message ever before us, if we are to remain true to the spirit of our country and to the service of humanity.

For three generations, it has been the privilege of the Congress to serve and identify itself with the people of India. For over sixty years it was the standard bearer in India's struggle for freedom and, under the inspired leadership of Mahatma Gandhi, it achieved success and opened a new chapter in India's long history. For ten years it has been responsible for the governance of this great country. In the years of struggle, as in the years of fulfilment, it has derived its strength and its capacity to work from the faith and confidence that the people of India have placed in it. Because of the people's confidence it became a strong and well-knit organization, capable of preserving the unity and integrity of India and undertaking the great tasks necessary for her advancement and the well-being of the people. The work it has done in government or among the people during these ten years is before the country for the people to judge. The great adventure still beckons every person in India and to the success of that adventure the Congress has dedicated itself. It seeks again, therefore, a renewal from the people of India of that faith and confidence which they have given it in such abundant measure in the past. With renewed strength firmly based on the goodwill of the people, it is determined to labour for the advancement of the Indian people and for world peace.

4. To U.N. Dhebar[1]

New Delhi,
December 13, 1956

My dear Dhebar Bhai,

I wanted to mention a matter to you today, but forget about it or rather had no opportunity for it.

This relates chiefly to the Uttar Pradesh, but it might to other States also. You will remember that we discussed in the Working Committee about accepting candidates who had opposed Congress during the last elections. We agreed that we must not accept anyone who had taken the Congress pledge and subsequently broken it. But, as far as I remember, we had no objection in principle to nominating a person who had opposed the Congress during the last General Election, but without asking us for a ticket and without taking the pledge. A number of old Congressmen did so, chiefly because of conflicts inside the State. This applies to the UP especially and some good men were thus pushed out of the Congress by circumstances. Even on larger grounds, I think we should take them back as individuals of course, if they are eager to come back. I remember one case was mentioned at the Working committee meeting. This was that of Govind Sahai.[2] He has been somewhat erratic in the past, but there is no doubt about his competence and earnestness. He left the Congress of his own accord before the elections and stood as an independent for the UP Assembly.

I hope you will make it clear as to what our position is in the matter as there appears to be some doubt.

1. JN Collection.
2. (b. 1907); participated in the freedom struggle; Home and Revenue Minister, United Provinces, 1937; elected to the Uttar Pradesh Assembly, 1947; appointed parliamentary secretary to Rafi Ahmed Kidwai and later to UP Chief Minister G.B. Pant; left the Congress in 1952 and elected to the UP Legislative Council as an independent candidate; rejoined the Congress in 1957 and elected to the UP State Assembly; Minister of State for Relief and Rehabilitation, UP, 1961-63.

There is just one thing which I should like to mention also, although it is, I am sure, not necessary. I do not think we should accept Kumbharam[3] as a candidate in Rajasthan. His record has been very bad.

Yours sincerely,
Jawaharlal Nehru

3. Kumbha Ram Arya (b. 1914); associated with the Congress after independence; Minister of Revenue, Bikaner State, 1948; Minister of Health, Police, and Minerals and Industry, Rajasthan, 1951; minister in the Rajasthan government 1954-55, 1964-67; founder, Panchayat Raj Sangh, 1957-58; member, Rajasthan Legislative Assembly, 1952-57; and 1964-66; member, Rajya Sabha, 1960-64 and 1968-74.

5. Fighting the Elections [1]

Congressmen should fight the elections with all their strength aggressively, not defensively, and without demeaning themselves by trying to gain the support of this or that undesirable group. Nothing would be more fatal for the Congress than to lose its soul by making compromises with other groups for gaining local ends in elections.

We must approach the Indian people absolutely frankly, without inhibitions, frankly confessing what we have not done, what we ought to have done and telling them what we have done. I have no doubt that every single type of trouble will be played up by our opponents. All this has to be faced, but not by adopting an attitude of compromise on principles.

I am not prepared to say that the soul of the Congress is bright and shining at the present moment. I don't think so. Nevertheless, we still possess a bit of it and that gives us some strength. The moment we lose that bit, we go to pieces completely. It is important, therefore, that we should not demean ourselves in any way, merely for the sake of some election, either general or local.

1. Speech at a meeting of the Congress Parliamentary Party, New Delhi, 29 December 1956. From *The Hindu*, 5 January 1957.

With all our strength, I am sure, we shall win. But I really do not care very much if we win or lose. It is because I do not care whether we win or lose that I am stronger and can fight better and hit hard and be aggressive.

It is the mentality of fear, that makes one defensive, that makes one compromise, that makes one give up this or that and speak in a low voice. Our approach to this question should be a courageous approach, not an approach of fear. It should not be a defensive approach, not an apologetic approach, not a compromising approach. It should be an approach which is fair and square. But you can take that approach only if you are clear about what you stand for and if you are convinced of the rightness of your position. If you yourselves are in error or are trying to gain the support of this or that undesirable group, merely for some local advantages, you cannot take up that brave attitude, because there is a chink in your armour.

I am more conscious than anyone of the difficulties which the Government has had to face and of the Government's failures and failings. But I do not face the Indian public with any shame or apology in regard to the work of the Government, in spite of my knowledge of our many failings. I want to approach them with the fullest strength, talking to them about our failings as well as our achievements, treating them as comrades and taking them into my confidence. This is the most paying approach from the strictly practical point of view. Once you trust the people, they trust you. If you like them, they like you. It is a law of nature.

The rule of life is that if one is gentle, others will be gentle too. I do not mean to say that I behave in that way because I have innumerable failings, but I do believe in that and I want to treat and have tried to treat the Indian public and the Indian masses in this way.

I have often spoken harshly to the Indian masses. For me they had put up with what they might not have put up with for others. Even when I have spoken somewhat harshly to them, I have spoken with affection for them and they know it.

The conception of cooperation is much better than the conception of service. I do not mean that service is bad; it is good, but it may be a dangerous thing too. For the person who is doing this service has a superiority feeling and he conveys that feeling to others: "I am superior, you see, I am doing this for you", "I am morally superior", and thereby the true relationship of two human beings which should be one of cooperation is somehow put aside and one becomes dependent on the other and, being dependent, rather resents that dependence.

The elections should be faced frankly without inhibitions. Do not merely go about bragging about our deeds; confess the other things too and discuss these matters with the people with not only frankness but so as to make them feel that you are treating them as equals in intelligence to you. They may not be equal in intelligence to you, but the mere fact that you approach them as equals will bring you nearer to them.

We are not going to vanish from India, even if the election results go against the Congress or it loses an election or two. Indeed it might be a very good thing for those who lose the elections. They will be pulled up from their complacency. The fact, however, remains that the Congress is going to fight the elections aggressively.

6. International Affairs[1]

The All India Congress Committee, at its meeting held in November 1956 in Calcutta,[2] referred to the critical situations that had arisen in Egypt and Western Asia and in Hungary and expressed its grave concern at these developments which had brought the world to the verge of widespread war. It pointed out that compulsion and armed intervention by one country in another could no longer be tolerated and, if persisted in, would result in world war. The Congress endorses the views contained in the resolution of the All India Congress Committee and approves the policy of the Government of India in regard to these crises.[3]

2. Recent events have led to tragedy in Egypt and Hungary and to the suffering of large numbers of human beings. But they have also brought an element of hope in that they have demonstrated that the spirit of freedom in men cannot ultimately be crushed by even superior force and that where such an attempt at coercion is made, world opinion opposes it. They have also shown that military pacts and alliances come in the way of peace and that the stationing of armed forces of one country in another leads to ill will, conflict and the fear of war. The old military approach to the problems of world has thus failed and it becomes necessary to adopt a different approach if real peace is to be established and the recurring fear of war is to be removed.

1. Draft resolution for the Indian National Congress session at Indore, 2 January 1957. JN Collection.
2. See *Selected Works* (second series), Vol. 35, pp. 275-306.
3. For AICC resolutions see *Selected Works* (second series), Vol. 35, pp. 275-277. For the Government of India's policy, see ibid. pp. 346-388.

3. The Congress welcomes the withdrawal of the Anglo-French forces from Egyptian territory[4] and trusts that the foreign forces in Hungary[5] will also be withdrawn and the people of Hungary will be given freedom to decide their own future by peaceful methods.

4. The Congress realises that fear and suspicion have led to competition in armaments and to the maintenance of foreign armed forces and bases in a large number of countries. Each country is naturally anxious for its own security and some have sought to secure this by the addition to their own armed strength and by military pacts and alliances. And yet this very policy of reliance on armed forces and military pacts has led to an increase of that fear and suspicion and to a greater lack of security and the world moves in a vicious circle seeking a way out, and finding none.

5. It has become essential, therefore, for new policies to be framed and for new approaches to be made with courage. These should be based not on threats or the use of armed forces in other countries, but a recognition that each country must have freedom to live its own life without interference from others whether this interference is by way of military force or economic sanctions or is based on some ideology. The events in Egypt and Hungary have shown that military force does not yield results and even an ideology cannot be imposed by the help of armed forces.

6. The Congress had previously welcomed a relaxation in world tensions and the progress made towards democratisation in some countries of Central Europe. It regrets that these hopeful trends have been checked. Any reversal of these normal processes will only take the world further towards disaster. It trusts, therefore, that the march of freedom in all countries and the normalisation of peaceful relations between countries will be encouraged and recent events will not be allowed to come in their way.

7. It is essential that progress should be made towards disarmament. Recent developments have indicated that the gap between the rival viewpoints in regard to disarmament is somewhat less than it was previously and some success might be achieved if steps to that end are taken. The Congress recognises that a complete solution of this, as of other important problems, cannot be achieved at one step,

---

4. In accordance with their statements of 3 December 1956, the British and French began a progressive withdrawal of their troops. The evacuation of their forces in Egypt was completed by 22 December 1956. The withdrawal was phased with the progressive takeover by troops of the United Nations Emergency Force (UNEF), which moved into areas evacuated by the British and French forces.
5. The Soviet forces that had entered Budapest on the 24 October 1956 began withdrawing on 30 October but re-entered Budapest on 4 November ostensibly to maintain order.

but every step taken in the right direction will lower world tensions and tend to produce a climate of peace which will help in further advances towards solutions.

8. The Congress adheres firmly to its policy of non-alignment and of friendship with all nations and expresses its conviction again that international affairs should be governed by the principles of Panchsheel.

7. Conduct of the Election Campaign[1]

In the Election Manifesto of the Congress attention is particularly drawn to the importance of moral values and of the maintenance of high standards in public as well as in private life. Congressmen are therefore specially enjoined that their election campaign should be conducted on a high level and without any personal recrimination or bitterness. The campaign should be based on the objectives, ideology and programme of the Congress, as stated in the Election Manifesto. The object of widespread democratic elections is not merely for individual candidates to gain success in them, but also to educate public opinion and the masses of India. Because India enjoys adult suffrage for both men and women, a general election offers a unique opportunity to reach the vast masses of India and to carry out an educative campaign in regard to objectives, ideology and domestic and international problems. It is these subjects, as well as the achievements of the Congress Governments since independence, that should be emphasised before the public. This should be done with dignity and without personal attacks on opposing candidates and always remembering that every Congressman has to set a high example of personal conduct.

1. Draft resolution for the Indian National Congress session at Indore, 2 January 1957, JN Collection.

8. To V.K. Krishna Menon[1]

The Residency,
Indore,
January 4, 1957

My dear Krishna,

I am here in Indore. I hope to return to Delhi on the 8th January. On the 12th morning I shall leave Delhi again for various places, returning on the 17th morning.

The question of your elections has been discussed here and we do not quite know what to decide. I shall probably send you a telegram about it in a day or two.

As I informed you, S.K. Patil[2] has told me that he will be glad to have you stand from north Bombay, i.e., the suburban area. He thinks that this should not be a difficult seat for you to win. The people there are willing to have you. Kamaraj Nadar[3] is also prepared to give you what he calls a 'safe' seat but not in Madras city. Some Kerala people have also offered to put you up as a candidate. If you have to stand for the Lok Sabha, I imagine that the north Bombay seat would be the best of these three. It would, of course, involve some work for electioneering as there is bound to be some opposition. But we expect to win the seat. In any event you would have to come here for the nomination. I believe this takes place about a month before the elections. I do not know the exact date of the elections in Bombay, but I presume they will be some time early in March. This means that you should be here in the first week of February at the latest.

Some of my colleagues feel, however, that it is not worthwhile for you to stand, especially at this stage, for the Lok Sabha. Even Indu[4] feels that way and thinks that you should continue in the Rajya Sabha. Indeed she says that she talked about this to you and you had then agreed to her suggestion.

There is one other aspect of this. If you stand for the Lok Sabha, you would naturally have to resign from the Rajya Sabha. The vacancy in the Rajya Sabha is likely to be filled by an opposition candidate.

---

1. V.K. Krishna Menon Papers, NMML.
2. President, Bombay Pradesh Congress Committee.
3. Chief Minister of Madras.
4. Indira Gandhi.

WITH U.N.DHEBAR AT THE CONGRESS SESSION, INDORE, 4 JANUARY 1957

WITH K. KAMARAJ NADAR AT THE CONGRESS SESSION, INDORE, 4 JANUARY 1957

I am writing to you but I shall be sending you a telegram soon and we shall decide finally after hearing from you.

Bakhshi Ghulam Mohammad[5] is here. I showed him the message you had sent about the Kashmir matter coming up before the Security Council on the 15th January.[6] He was quite clear about not sending any representative of his Government to New York on this occasion. He took up the attitude that so far as he and his colleagues were concerned, he had finalized the matter and he saw no reason why he should get entangled with the Security Council discussions. In any event, as you have yourself indicated, you do not want anyone so far as the work is concerned. From the political point of view there is no need for anyone else to go. If any particular development takes places, perhaps we can consider this question.

You must have been informed by M.J. Desai[7] of the talk he had with someone from the UK High Commission. In the course of this talk, a suggestion was thrown out that the Security Council might send some kind of an observer to have a look round in Kashmir and report to the Council about the situation there. This suggestion, it was said, was an entirely personal one and not from the UK Government. But I imagine that it must have come from the UK. I suppose that the UK Government is not keen on this discussion in the Security Council. Perhaps the UK is also not anxious about it. I do not know what attitude they might adopt, but it is quite conceivable that they might think of suggesting to despatch an observer to gain time.

I do not like the idea of an observer coming but it is not clear to me what we can say in reply. Of course, anybody can go to Kashmir and in fact vast numbers of tourists and others have gone there in the last year.

The question of displaced persons from Eastern Pakistan coming to India is not related to Kashmir but it is very much related to our relations with Pakistan. I do not know if you will find it necessary to mention this fact in the course of the debate. I think it is very relevant. These refugees continue to pour in at the rate of about 20,000 a month and they are creating a stupendous problem for us which is really worse than the millions who came from West Pakistan. In the west there was really a major exchange of population; in the east it is almost entirely one-way traffic.

I have just received a letter from Mehr Chand Khanna, our Minister of Rehabilitation, in which he has given some up-to-date facts about this problem

5. Prime Minister of Jammu and Kashmir State. He was a special invitee to the 62nd session of the Congress Party at Indore.
6. See *post*, pp. 337-338, for Nehru's reply to Krishna Menon's message of 5 January 1957.
7. Commonwealth Secretary, MEA.

of the refugees from Eastern Pakistan and how we have thus far dealt with it and what remains to be done. I am sending you a copy of this as this will give you some idea of the magnitude of this problem. The worst of it is that there appears no end to it; it is a continuing one. Some time ago we calculated that since the partition, four million refugees had come from Eastern Pakistan into India (this of course excludes those who came from Western Pakistan). The four million figure must now have gone up.

Yours affectionately,
Jawaharlal

9. The Democratic Spirit[1]

...Well, the first thing is that this Election Manifesto is, in a sense, to be attached to our Five Year Plan, the whole Plan. It is quite impossible to put everything that we are going to do in this Manifesto. The Second Five Year Plan gives this in great detail. The Second Five Year Plan itself is not absolutely rigid or final. We may change it, but it is a balanced document. It is important that we do not simply put down all the things that we wish to do – we want to do many things— but we have to put them down, first of all, by saying what we intend to do within these five years. Secondly, in a balanced way so that each step might balance the other.

Planning essentially consists in balancing; of industry and agriculture; the balancing between heavy industry and light industry; the balancing between cottage industry and other industries. All these are balances. If one goes wrong then the economy is upset. If you concentrate too much on industry, leaving agriculture to look after itself, the country gets into difficulties.

You may have noticed that in some of the East European countries where there have been some inner conflicts and trouble, probably the real basis of this struggle has been economic because their economy was not, as it happens, a

1. Speech while introducing the Congress Party's Election Manifesto, at the sixty-second session of the Indian National Congress, Indore, 4 January 1957. AIR tapes, NMML. Extracts.

balanced one and too much stress was laid on rapid development of industry and especially heavy industry. As a result, agriculture suffered, and consequently the whole economy suffered.

A very eminent economist[2] of one of the East European countries delivered a speech two or three months ago in which, criticizing their own plan, he recommended to the people in those countries to look at India's Second Five Year Plan, which was a much more balanced effort, and curiously enough recommending the people of East European countries to lay greater stress on village industry and handicrafts. It is an extraordinary thing how the wheel has gone a full circle. From complete emphasis in these countries on heavy industry they have suddenly found that while heavy industry is necessary and important, you must have some other basis for the economy otherwise difficulties would arise. That is a lesson for us.

We believe firmly that industrial progress in India will depend and must depend on the growth of heavy industry. There is no industrial progress unless you have machine-making industry; unless you have iron and steel here, and therefore we lay stress on that. We have always to remember that unless we balance that with the growth of village industry, we will produce an unbalanced structure which may crack up and fall down. The importance therefore of village industry, of household industry, cottage industry, and small industry is very great. It is great from the employment point of view; it is great also from the point of view of balanced production; it is great from the point of view of producing commodities for daily use. Therefore all these things have to be balanced. Maybe some people who think of one aspect, agriculture or heavy industry or cottage industry, want all the emphasis to be laid on that particular aspect. But we have to balance the three. The economy of a country and specially of a developing country must be balanced. In a static economy some kind of balance is achieved at the cost of poverty and the starvation of the people, but once you are developing, as we are developing our economy, we have to take care at every step to balance it lest one step outstrips the other and you get into difficulties. We have laid stress on this, on the utmost importance of food production and agriculture, which must form the base of industrial development. We have laid stress on heavy industry. We have also laid stress on cottage and village industry.

Many of our friends and colleagues and many friends who belong to other parties talk about socialism, in what I would say with all respect, a very rapid way. Now, I do not criticise others and I do not wish to say that what we say about socialism is the final word on it because I do look upon this as a dynamic

2. Professor Oskar Lange of Poland.

conception, as a growing conception, as a thing that is not rigid, as a thing which must fit in with the changing conditions of human life and activity in every country, and it may not take the same shape in one country or the other. I do believe that socialism can be of many varieties; that a socialism in a highly developed industrial community may be of one type, in an agricultural country, not so much developed industrially, it may be of somewhat different type. So that I do not see why one should try to copy something else. But obviously one should take advantage of the experience gained in other countries. If I wish to industrialise my country I have not only to learn the techniques, the higher techniques of industrialisation, from the countries where the higher techniques are adopted and are flourishing, but I have also to learn many other things – the way they industrialized, to copy their successes and avoid the pitfalls.

I do not see why I should be asked to define socialism in precise, rigid terms. Well, it is something which should not be rigid. Broadly speaking, I want every individual in India to have an equal opportunity of growth, equal opportunity of work according to his capacity and so on and so forth. I want a welfare state.

Now Kaka Sahib Gadgil[3] differentiated between a welfare state and a socialist state. It is true that a welfare state need not be a socialist state, but a socialist state must be a welfare state. That is obvious. That is, socialism is a welfare state plus something else.

When we talk of socialism, that is the true transformation of society according to the broad principles of socialism, we must remember that this is not something that is merely a legal process of passing laws. Laws are necessary but it really affects all the ten thousand or hundred thousand operations of human beings in India—not only in production, in transport, in distribution, in consumption and everything. The whole life of a country, if you analyse it consists of millions of contacts, whether it is between the shopkeeper and the buyer, or the big machine and the small machine. There are hundreds of thousands of these contacts of human beings to carry on the business of society.

All those contacts are based on some basic assumption of the social structure. Let us say they have been based more or less on the capitalist assumption. Capitalism was an advance on the feudal conception of society. Capitalism was in advance in another way because it undoubtedly added greatly to the wealth of the world by exploiting machines and the like, apart from exploiting human beings. Capitalism therefore did a great deal of good to the world. I am saying this because people seem to imagine that some things are innately evil and have always been evil and some things have been innately good and will always be

---

3. N.V. Gadgil, Congressman from Maharashtra and a former Union Minister.

good. There is no such thing as that in human society. At each stage of human society something is adapted to that stage and it does it good. Then as society advances that thing may become out of date. That thing which is good in itself becomes harmful and restrictive and prevents the growth of society. Then some other thing has to be adapted. Capitalism did a great deal of good but society outgrew it or is outgrowing it. Therefore it is out of date; therefore it is weak and injurious. And we want the socialist structure basically.

One thing I should like to stress is that the whole of the capitalist structure means some kind of an acquisitive society, acquired at the expense of someone else. It may be that that tendency is to some extent inherent in ourselves, though it depends, of course, on our environment and how we grow up and all that. Now a socialist society must try to get rid of this tendency to acquisitiveness and replace it by cooperation more and more.

Now if you think of these two phrases, acquisitiveness and cooperation, you are not going to bring about a change by passing a law. It is a long process of training and till you bring it about you will not wholly succeed. You will partly succeed. But even from the very limited point of view of changing your economic structure, apart from your minds and hearts, even from the limited point of view of your industrialisation and all that, it takes time. And the countries that have grown quickly, even they have taken time. If you consider that the Soviet Union has industrialized quickly; well, it has taken thirty-five years or more over it, thirty-nine years now.

I remember – Chairman Mao[4] saying about three or four years ago, that it will take China twenty years to achieve some kind of socialism. Mind you, they have got an authoritarian state. They have got people who are exceedingly industrious, who are disciplined, and in spite of all these factors he said it will take twenty years. He said that three years ago, because he was not merely indulging in wishful thinking. He was speaking as a practical idealist, as a practical person.

We cannot afford merely to repeat slogans which have no meaning. We must realise that this process of bringing socialism in India, more especially in the way we are doing it, that is, by the democratic way, will take time. It will take time inevitably, whatever processes we may adopt, even authoritarian processes, or any other process.

We have definitely accepted the democratic process. Why have we accepted it? Well, for a variety of reasons. We think that in the final analysis it promotes the growth of human beings and of society. As we have said in the Preamble to our Constitution, we attach great value to individual freedom. Because in the

4. Mao Tse-tung, Chairman of the Communist Party of China.

final analysis we want the creative and the adventurous spirit of man to grow. It is not enough for us merely to produce the material goods of the world, although we want to produce the material goods of the world, to have high standards of living but not at the expense of the spirit of man; not at a expense of his creative spirit, his creative energy; not at the expense of his adventurous spirit; not at the expense of all those fine things of life which have ennobled man throughout the ages.

I am not entering into any argument but I am merely showing you that this democracy is not merely a question of elections and getting people elected for Parliament to meet. Something infinitely more than that. The democratic spirit, it is that that I value, and that which we hope will grow with outward forms of democracy.

How to combine this democracy with socialism is the question before us and to combine both these with peaceful and legitimate methods. That is the problem India has got before it. It is a difficult problem and yet I think we can face it with a measure of confidence. We have achieved many things in the past which were difficult and there is absolutely no reason why we should not achieve this also. We have to win the goodwill of the people, we have to win the cooperation of the people; even an authoritarian government cannot function without a large measure of goodwill and cooperation. Therefore, it is important that we take our people into our confidence, be frank with them, frank about our failings, frank about our difficulties, frank about our hopes and aspirations, so that they may understand.

I want you to go to them. Make this election campaign a great campaign of comradeship with our people, of friendship with them, of talking, discussing with them these problems. Not merely delivering a speech, a brave speech, and reciting some slogans. That is not enough. Telling them what we have done, telling them what we have to do, telling them of our difficulties, telling them of our strength to overcome these difficulties.

Now, we know our failings. They are great even as our virtues are considerable. We fall out very quickly whether it is on the basis of religion or province or language or caste. We are always splitting up into bits, fissiparous tendencies. That is the terrible enemy we have to fight and every intelligent man in India has to fight whatever party he might belong to.

People talk of the Congress being, what they call, a monolithic party. People say that the Congress is perpetuating a one-party system in India. I just do not understand what they mean. So far as the Congress is concerned, it is after all the mirror of the Indian people, and because it is the mirror of the Indian people it mirrors all their failings. And we have plenty of failings in the Congress. We represent those failings as well as those virtues. True, we should try to get over those failings and get others to get over their failings. I do not say the Congress has no failings. It has plenty. And we see that all these failings assume more importance and more prominence at election time.

Elections bring down the standard of a human being. Everywhere, whether it is England or France or America or India. Election time bring down the standards of human beings. Whatever elections that may be and probably the worst elections are the municipal elections here, where people function in such an extraordinary way that they forget all common standards of decency. That is so. We must try to fight this.

The Congress has many failings because the Indian people have failings. But when it is said that it is a monolithic party, well, it is patently wrong. This Congress is essentially, and I say more so than almost any party that I can think of in any country, a democratic institution. True, in a huge institution all kinds of things may grow up, even tendencies of bossism, which are bad, which I disapprove of. Also, local leaders, other leaders trying to perpetuate themselves. All these things are unfortunately the unfortunate companions of democracy. And that is why sometimes people do not like democracy because of the growth of all these things. We suffer from the ills of democracy as we have the virtues of democracy.

People talk about the Congress having a one-party government. In other countries presumably they do not know what our constitution is and how we function. But when people in India talk about that, it surprises me. After all, here are these elections. Anybody can stand, anybody can get elected if, that is to say, people vote them. Our Election Commission is independent of government, it can do what it likes. It has often come to decisions which have been not at all pleasing to the Government, I can tell you. But there it is. We have deliberately made it an independent Commission so that it may conduct our elections impartially and with no favour to government or to the party controlling government.

What more can one do? I think Pantji referred to this yesterday. Are we to go and support the candidates of the opposition parties or are we to put up dummy candidates to oppose us? What are we to do about it? Is this the way a democracy functions? The whole thing would become bogus. The only way to function is to fight hard. The only way is to give the other man, the other party every opportunity to have his say and to fight hard against us. Then the results come that the Congress has a great majority. Well, that does not mean that it is a one-party government. If at any time, after an English election, it so happens that one party gets a tremendous majority, nobody says that it is a one-party government in the country. The fact is that we are the inheritors of history. The history of the last seventy years, of the last forty years, the history in the making of India in which the Congress has played an important and sometimes a dominant part. It

287

is inevitable that it should be so in India as it is. We cannot start from scratch now and make other people the inheritors of all this tradition in history. Therefore, I should like you to bear this in mind....

One thing more. Some amendments have specifically dealt with the question of fixing minimum standards and maximum standards of income. The whole conception of socialism is, broadly speaking, an egalitarian conception of society. Equality can be of many kinds. You cannot impose equality, of course, because human beings are essentially different. But you can and should lay down conditions of equality of opportunity, of equality of certain standards of living, certain minimum standards, so that everybody should enjoy the benefits of those standards of living, whether it is food, clothing, education, health, work, etc., education most of all. But if you start trying to produce equality by cutting off heads or reducing the height of a person to the average height of the human being in India, that is an exceedingly artificial process which, as a matter of fact, can hardly be done.

What is more important is this that one proceeds by legislation, by taxation to prevent the accumulation of wealth. What is important, is not what a man may earn today, but the prevention of a person gradually to earn without working for it. You can never stop. Oh, I won't say never, but it is difficult to stop. A great writer earns more because his books sell more; you may tax him. That is a different matter. Of course you can tax. You cannot stop a great actor from earning more because the actor is popular, that is, except by taxation again. Unearned income is bad essentially from the social point of view. Therefore the sources of unearned income should gradually be dried up. But this kind of official saying that a man should not have more than so much a month is totally impractical. It cannot be done. You can say, of course, that every man above a certain income, the tax is hundred per cent. You may say that. But you won't be able to enforce it, and you will encourage all the wrong tendencies of deception, of hiding, of avoidance and all that, which is bad. Let us have a tax system, which can be implemented. Apart from this, the question of incentives is important. It is a fact that today we have to pay sometimes lakhs and lakhs a year to an expert we get from abroad. We pay some people as much as five lakhs a year for their services in India because we think it is worthwhile paying them five lakhs a year, because they save us a hundred lakhs thereby, or fifty lakhs in a huge river valley system or something like that. But that is very rare....

In a dynamic society like this, it is very difficult to say what would happen if you take away the incentives to special effort. And I have seen it in every country I have been to, communist, socialist or other, that the moment they took away these incentives they suffered and they had to go back to providing the incentives.

I should like you to remember one other fact. Socialism in a highly

288

industrialised economy is one thing. If you have built-up the country, industrialised it, you have to convert only the social relationships. But in a country which has got to do both the building up and the socialization, you have to face difficult problems. And you have always to balance the two in a way so that one may not come in the way of the other. If the socialism you are seeking to introduce comes in the way of your industrialisation or growth, then it is preventing growth, it is preventing socialisation. Because socialisation is not the socialisation of a poor country remaining poor. That has no meaning. If you take steps which prevent the country from progressing rapidly and making wealth to invest more and more, you will not progress. Therefore, one has to balance these factors. And looking at it in this way, I suggest to you that while we concentrate on the one hand by taxation and otherwise in reducing higher incomes, in making unearned income less and less important in our social structure, the real thing on which we should concentrate is this minimum standard for everybody. If you attain that, of course automatically you attain much of the other things. It may not come in regard to a few persons but so far as 99.9 per cent of the population is concerned it will come.

When you have achieved that you can take the next step. So I beg of you to consider these problems in a realistic way. We have tried to frame this Manifesto in as realistic a fashion as we can. That realism does not mean our aiming low. We do not aim low. We are aiming high. If in the course of these five years we achieve what we have laid down in our Second Five Year Plan, it will be a great victory, one of the greatest that India has won. And not only will it be a victory, but it will be the prelude to other victories, because then we would have established our feet soundly and we can then march without relying too much on others. It will be very difficult; five years will not end our progress, of course, but I say we would have crossed that dangerous barrier which separates an undeveloped country from a developing country. Once we have done that, it will be easier going, and faster going, and I commend to you this resolution.

10. Integrity of Thought and Action[1]

In this rapidly changing world, when one crisis follows another, any individual or organisation, which cannot adapt itself to changing circumstances, tends to become static and out of date. Congressmen should remember this. We have a fine record of achievements in the Congress during its long history, but that very success has added to our responsibilities and burdens.

In this age of atomic weapons and cold war, with all its undesirable consequences and the hatred and violence that it produces, I have come to believe more and more that the basis of our action must be integrity in thought and activity. Unless we have thought and courage, we shall drift about and find no haven. This applies to the whole country and not merely to the Congress. I believe that we have succeeded in a large measure because we have had some integrity. In the measure we have not succeeded, we have lacked integrity of thought and action.

While this is the foundation, the superstructure is also important. That superstructure has to deal with international problems as well as domestic problems. On the whole, we have maintained some standards in our international policies. In the domestic sphere, the problems are in a sense more complicated and more difficult. We have produced a Second Five Year Plan after a great deal of thought and I believe it is a good plan. It requires all our effort. But no plan is static and we must keep wide awake all the time and in line with changing conditions. In addition to basic character, we must have an intellectual understanding of this changing world and its problems and a practical application of our thinking to existing issues.

I do not expect every member in the Congress to be an economist or a specialist, but I do expect them to try to understand where we are today, where we want to go to and the main path which will lead us to our goal. I want him to be earnest and to avoid as far as possible the failings which come from living in an acquisitive society. To the extent that he will serve others, he will do good to the country and to himself.

We meet in Indore at a difficult time in the world's history. We shall require all our wisdom to face the crises that encompass us.

1. Message to the souvenir brought out by the Reception Committee of the Indore session of the Indian National Congress. From the *National Herald*, 4 January 1957.

11. Problems Facing Us[1]

A number of problems face us but I would refer to only two or three. Firstly, we have to face the international situation. We have to constantly think of the developments in the international field because our entire future is intimately linked with preservation of world peace. I would not, however dilate on this point at any length. The second question relates to our Second Five Year Plan and how Congressmen should work for its implementation. The third question, of course, is the question of general elections. All these are interrelated.

I am happy that in this Congress we have passed a few resolutions.[2] In fact, a number of things are always happening, but we cannot express ourselves on all questions in our resolutions, for that would mean a very large number of resolutions. Actually in the earlier stages, the Congress generally used to pass resolutions on almost everything. There used to be as many as forty to fifty resolutions and the whole lot used to be published like a book. When Gandhiji came to the Congress he did not approve of this practice. He actually said that there should be only one resolution in a Congress session. Furthermore, whereas earlier the resolutions mostly voiced demands, Gandhiji insisted not on voicing demands but on telling what is our duty and what we should do.

Our organisation has the task of leading the nation. We have presented to the nation a picture of this advance in the Second Five Year Plan. I would really like to know how many of you have studied the Second Five Year Plan. I call upon all of you to thoroughly study the Plan, if not the big edition then at least the summarised one. It is your responsibility to explain the Plan to the people, and you can do it only when you thoroughly understand it. The Plan is not merely a list of what we have to do. It has a philosophy and an approach to the problems of India's development. I hope that all of you will take great care to thoroughly study it. Only then will it be possible for you to conduct the election campaign in a manner as to make it a mighty campaign of mass education.

1. Address to an informal meeting of delegates at the Plenary session of the sixty-second session of the Indian National Congress, Indore, 5 January 1957. From *The Hindu*, 19 January 1957.
2. The Congress at its session held at Indore on 5 and 6 January 1957 adopted a resolution on the 1857 centenary celebrations. A resolution amending Article I of the Congress Constitution was also adopted. Also adopted were resolutions on the Congress Election Manifesto, a code of conduct for the elections and on International Affairs.

I can tell you on the basis of my experience that generation of heat and controversy does not lead anywhere. If a thing is said peacefully, with restraint, it creates a greater effect. If this method of peaceful explanation is given up and the method of calling each other names is adopted, then the whole exercise degenerates into how loudly the contestants can talk. I must tell you that in a competition of speaking loudly you cannot have the better of your opponents.

Elections are not the main thing. The main thing is the task to be completed after the elections. The biggest thing before us is the Second Five Year Plan. We must know that greater the effort we make lift today the further we will advance. The election campaign must be made a great educative campaign for our people.

Let us be very clear about what we want. There is a lot of talk about democracy everywhere. But if you look round, you will come across very few countries which are really democratic. There may be not more than half a dozen countries which are really democratic. Parliamentary democracy is not very firmly placed in the world of today. Parliamentary democracy demands that we continuously serve the people and explain to them patiently.

Further, parliamentary democracy demands that we must have tolerance. We must have the capacity to patiently listen to what our opponents and critics tell us. Under parliamentary democracy we must be prepared to accept a decision even though it may be against us. Without this the country would be involved in a deadlock. Similarly, we need democratic practice in our own organisation. The organisation may comprise of people of different shades of opinions, but once a decision has been arrived at, it must be unquestionably accepted.

The whole world is today looking at us with astonishment. Though inexperienced, we have taken our country forward on the path of democracy during the last few years. It is a vast country and so diverse; yet we have successfully conducted its affairs democratically during the last few years. But if you look at it in another way it can be said that the democratic idea is not quite novel to us. On a small scale, we had this democratic method in our villages through the ancient panchayat system. Then the British also introduced some democratic methods during their rule. But more important than all this is the fact that the Congress organisation during the last thirty to forty years of its history has worked in a democratic manner and has moulded our masses in a democratic style. The Congress had to fight a mighty power and it adopted the democratic method for arriving at decisions. At the same time it had to be a mighty disciplined organisation to be able to fight the battle.

It is true that after our freedom, we became a bit slack. But really speaking the battle is never over and let us not forget that we still have many weaknesses. We had a glimpse of it last year when so many disputes arose in the country on the question of reorganisation of states. A country which quarrels like this can be pocketed by another country.

This quarrelling like children is most undesirable. But why should we accuse our children when we ourselves indulge in this. Our children are really very good. We must develop among ourselves the capacity to patiently listen to the criticism of our opponents and to tolerate them.

12. To Lal Bahadur Shastri[1]

The Residency,
Indore,
January 5, 1957

My dear Lal Bahadur,

As I mentioned to you, I have received a number of papers relating to elections. I am sending most of these to you. You can deal with them as you consider proper.

I enclose a letter from Hayatullah Ansari.[2] I should have liked him to come to the Lok Sabha where, I think, he would have been helpful. But I do not know what we can do in the matter.

Indira tells me that there is some talk of Bahuguna[3] being asked to stand from Karchana. So far as I remember, he was specially asked to take in hand some time ago the constituency in which he has been working and which we lost in the last election. He has done a lot of work there and I think it will not be right for us to push him back to Karchana. Indeed, I am not quite sure if he will win the seat if Bahuguna goes away to some other place.

Yours affectionately,
Jawaharlal

1. JN Collection.
2. Member, UP Legislative Council, 1952-66.
3. H.N. Bahuguna, member, UP Legislative Assembly, 1952-1971.

13. The Evolution of India's Foreign Policy[1]

It is evening and the work of this session is almost over. Yet I have been presented before you like an exhibit, not to speak about any resolution. I am here before you because you often make me feel overwhelmed with your show of affection. Just now you have adopted a resolution on international affairs. I did not speak, nor do I do so on such resolutions in the AICC sessions generally. But I speak on the subject because I am the Minister for External Affairs and in that capacity have a special relationship with our foreign policy. So I do not think it proper for me to say anything about foreign policy resolutions. However, I shall draw your attention to another matter. I have a complaint to make about the various people who spoke on this resolution. The complaint is that they mentioned me so often and praised me so loudly as though our foreign policy is my brainchild. This is a misunderstanding which Indiraji tried to correct just now. I want to continue that effort. Please do not think that I am saying this out of a sense of modesty. You must know that I do not have any false sense of modesty. But we are assembled here to discuss matters of grave importance and it is wrong to allow our attention to be distracted by personalities. The real issues tend to get hidden. By praising me, whether you deceive yourselves or not, you certainly deceive others in the country and outside too. It gives rise to the feeling that our foreign policy is something new whereas the fact of the matter is that it is a very old one and is deeply embedded in the psyche of the nation. To my mind, it reflects the very heart and soul of India.

This is something which should be understood and explained to others. I have often said in the Lok Sabha and elsewhere too that whether Jawaharlal is around or not, and no matter who comes in the future, I can say with full confidence that we cannot go very far from this policy. We may veer a little this way or that, or the emphasis may shift slightly. That is a different matter. The principles on which our foreign policy has been based have formed part of India's thinking during the last thirty to forty years and in a sense, they reflect the thought of thousands of years. Anyhow, let us leave that aside. I would say that it has been the thinking in the Congress during the last thirty years. It blossomed during the years of our freedom struggle and now forms our official policy. You will find that all these things have been said in the various Congress

---

1. Speech at the sixty-second session of the Indian National Congress, Indore, 6 January 1957. AIR tapes, NMML. Original in Hindi. Extracts.

resolutions of the last forty years. It is because our foreign policy is a part and parcel of our internal policies. No nation can have a foreign policy which is diametrically opposed to its internal policy. If that were the case, it would cause great harm. One or the other would be suppressed and certainly neither would succeed. Therefore it is essential that the two should be in harmony. It may not be hundred per cent so and the emphasis may shift. But fundamentally they must be in harmony. You may feel that our entire internal as well as foreign policy ought to be completely changed. That may or may not be right or not. But you must understand that our internal as well as foreign policy spring from the same roots.

As I said various resolutions on foreign policy have been adopted during the last thirty years. But it is true that until India got independence, the Congress resolutions were somewhat in the air, in the sense that they were not the official government policy. We used to speak merely on behalf of the party. But even that had a great impact. In 1938, and before and after that too, we had raised our voice against Hitler's Nazism or when Japan attacked Manchuria in China, or when there was a civil war in Spain. We sent whatever help we could by way of food-supplies and medicines. The invasion of Czechoslovakia in 1938 shook the world profoundly. But the Congress resolutions by no means represented the official line and other countries look at the government's line only. The official Indian policy in those days used to be framed not in Delhi but in London. It is only during the last ten years that our foreign policy has become the official Indian policy. But its roots go back many years. Therefore I want you to understand clearly that our foreign policy is not new. It is not a product of my brain or that of any of the others seated here. If we had adopted any other policy, we would have strayed from the old traditions and thinking of the Congress. In fact, I shall go a step further and say that it reflects the thinking of India for the last hundreds of years. We would have strayed away from that.

I want you to remember that I do not want it to be mentioned again and again that our foreign policy has something to do specially with Jawaharlal. Jawaharlal is merely a mouthpiece for our policy. It is a product of the Indian tradition and will continue for years to come with minor changes. What I am saying is of fundamental importance. Some people especially in other countries are often deceived into thinking that our foreign policy is one person's brainchild or a temporary, superficial thing. They may be under the impression that they can intimidate us by threats and pressures into abandoning our policy. I want you to understand this because it is very important.

That does not mean that every aspect of our foreign policy has been laid down in a tome. It is obvious that that is not so. But our fundamental policy remains firm and blends with our domestic policy. Otherwise it would not be effective at all. When new problems crop up, it is obvious that fresh thinking has to be done. But it has to be done within the basic framework. When new issues arise in Egypt or Hungary, Algeria or elsewhere, the stand that we take has to take into account the circumstances. It cannot be laid down in advance. But it cannot be too far removed from our fundamental policy. You must bear this in mind.

What is this fundamental policy that I mentioned? It is a broad fact that even we fought for our freedom by peaceful, non-violent methods. We struggled against the representatives of the British empire for a couple of generations. But Gandhiji always pointed out that we had no enmity with England or the English people but only with British imperialism. He laid great stress on this. As you know, even at the height of the struggle, when people were full of anger and there used to be firings and lathi charges, an Englishman could walk through an Indian crowd and not a hand would be lifted against him. This was the discipline which Gandhiji had instilled among us. It is a pity that we have forgotten that lesson to some extent in our domestic affairs. But we had been taught to regard not an individual or a nation but colonialism as our enemy. Secondly, we were taught to draw even our opponents to our way of thinking by patience and not to do anything to create a gulf or spread bitterness. I do not say that we learnt this lesson fully and, as I said, even now we often forget it in our day-to-day affairs. But we had been taught this lesson and proved to the world that we could stick to this path.

You must bear this in mind and think how it can be applied to foreign affairs. You will find that our policy of friendship with all nations fits in very well with the path chalked out by Mahatma Gandhi for our freedom struggle. All this talk of increasing military expenditure, military aid and alliances, etc., does not fit in in any way with our thinking. How can we forget the lessons we have learnt during the last fifty years? Moreover, why should we forget them? There is nothing new when we say that military alliances are bad and that peace cannot be maintained at the point of a sword. It does not mean that we have enmity with any country. These lessons have been dinned into our heads from the time we started doing public work and began to face the problems of the country and the world. I want everyone to understand this.

People often complain that we are against this or that nation. That is not so. I am convinced that at least at this point of time in history, people of all nations want to live in peace and amity and are against war, with the exception of a few mad men here and there. At the same time the peoples' minds are filled with fear, fear of one another, of the enemy and of showing weakness in case it gave the enemy a leverage. There is a pall of fear everywhere. I do not know if you think fear is a good thing or not. The question is that when everyone wants peace, how is the fear to be removed? It cannot be done by brandishing swords and weapons for that only increases the fear and makes the other side take out their swords too. It becomes a vicious circle to which there is no end. Fear cannot be removed in this way and so long as it is there, weapons and bombs will keep on accumulating. What then is the alternative?

I would like to point out humbly that there is no other way except to reverse the trend. I do not say that nations should disarm completely and put their trust in god. I do not think any responsible man can say such things, particularly when the defence of the nation is at stake. Therefore we have to keep our army. But the effort should be to change the atmosphere in which the arms race goes on unceasingly and nations hurl abuses and threats at one another. We have learnt from our own experience of the cold war during the last ten years that it solves nothing. On the contrary, it has created new and knottier problems. We have seen the effect of military alliances in international relations. When there is a military agreement between an extremely powerful nation and weaker ones, it acquires a wholly different character. A military alliance can be formed between equals, not when there is great disparity between the parties.

So we raised our voice against this system. We do not wish to interfere in the affairs of independent countries but we expressed our views for what they were worth because we felt that such things were not helping the cause of peace. We expressed our views quite clearly against the SEATO and the Baghdad Pact, etc., which are likely to have a direct impact upon us. We are not directly concerned with the NATO. You may remember that the matter came up once during the Goa affair, but it died down. The Baghdad Pact and SEATO are around us. What are they in aid of? There are conflicting views about this. On the one hand, it is said that they are directed against the Soviet Union. The Soviet Union, on the other hand, is assured that they are directed not against that country but against India. There is no secret about it. This is said quite openly.

How can we close our minds to these things? Our neighbours are accumulating huge arsenals and openly threaten to use them against India. I am aware that wherever American military aid has been given, we have been assured in writing that it would not be used against us and if an effort was made to do so, the United States would put a stop to it. I have no doubt about it that the Government of the United States is fully aware of the need to prevent the wrong use of the aid it gives. But the fact remains that the arms are being piled up all around us. India simply does not have the resources to invest in military expenditure, nor do we wish to give up our Five Year Plans in order to pile up arms. We have refused right from the beginning to get arms from others. We buy what we need which is very little. We try to invest as much as we can for development. But

297

circumstances compel us to change our attitude. How can we be complacent when the United States is supplying Pakistan with the latest weapons? We too have to think of some arrangements. I do not think that any wise administration in Pakistan will go to war with India. But the problem is that one cannot always rely on the wisdom and common sense of the other side. Nobody knows what may happen. The result is that our burden increases.

Other countries talk of helping us and we will gratefully accept whatever we get. But far from helping us, American aid to Pakistan is casting an additional burden upon us. We are compelled to spend our precious resources on buying arms or producing them here which we do not want. This is the dilemma that we are facing.

We believe that military pacts and alliances will not prevent war but only increase tensions. The world knows that there are only two great powers today which can start a world war – the United States and the Soviet Union. The other countries lag far behind them in every way. There can be no world war unless it is started by one or the other superpower. That much is quite clear. If anyone else took the lead the superpowers can put a stop to it. It is also obvious that the superpowers can inflict incalculable damage on each other and destroy the world in the process.

Two significant developments have taken place recently. One was in Egypt and the other in Hungary. I think I have mentioned this earlier too. But let me repeat it. Both these developments have been extremely painful. But we also caught a glimpse of something heartening. Firstly, we saw that it is no longer easy for a big power to suppress the weaker countries as used to happen in the colonial era of the 19th century. Secondly, we saw how valiantly a small country like Hungary fought for its freedom against insuperable odds. These incidents have been painful but at the same time show some hopeful signs. The fear of suppression by the superpowers has been lessened to some extent because we have seen that it is not easy to suppress the weaker countries. We have seen the reaction of world public opinion when such incidents occurred. So it is reassuring that this type of aggression have become more difficult to pull off. I do not say that it is impossible. But whether it is colonial aggression or communist aggression, it has been proved that they have become extremely difficult. In my opinion, these incidents have cleared the air to some extent.

I had felt that we had arrived at a crossroads when we could bring a new approach to world problems, instead of continuing in the old ruts. I am sorry to say that leaders and statesmen in other countries do not seem to have recognized the fact that this is a special opportunity. We must grasp the opportunity to branch off boldly on a new course instead of brandishing swords and weapons. I repeat, no responsible individual can say that we should all disarm completely.

But at least we can keep our swords sheathed instead of brandishing them around. I want you to understand these things.

I want to discuss one thing more. There has been talk, sometimes openly and at others, hints are thrown out, that we raised our voice about the Egypt incident but were silent about Hungary and made half-hearted protest. I do not consider this criticism to be valid. As far as Egypt was concerned, we were involved at every step. We were participating in the talks and knew up to the minute every new development that took place. So we could express an opinion when it was necessary without any hesitation. The developments in Hungary have been painful and out of small beginnings, had escalated out of all proportion. But what is more significant is that our effort at all times was to try to find a peaceful solution to the problem. As we have said in this resolution, we have demanded that foreign troops should leave Hungarian soil. Now somebody said we should have said "Russian troops". Well, everybody knows that most of the troops were Russian. Dr Rai has pointed out that "foreign forces" was not the right expression. We did not want to say or do anything which would stop the troops being withdrawn.

Now if you consider the incidents in Hungary – they started on the 23rd of October. On the 30th of October, a statement was made by the Soviets that the troops would be withdrawn. The movement for withdrawal began. But then certain incidents occurred which forced the Soviets to send back the troops. What I am trying to point out is that decisions have to be taken at a delicate stage in a crisis. The attack on Egypt was of course a grave incident. But take the case of Hungary. We had to decide whether we would help Hungary by making a great deal of noise. We are not a silent party to the painful events which have occurred in Hungary.

Then there is the issue of Algeria and South Africa. We are not saying very much about the problems of other African countries. But that does not mean that we have forgotten about them. The thing is that we cannot help very much by repeating the same things. We want to help. These issues are before the United Nations. We have to deal with them in various ways. The principle remains the same. There are some countries which believe in sabre-rattling, whatever the result may be. We are not among those. We may make mistakes sometimes because we may not be able to understand an issue properly. But I want you to understand that we cannot conduct our foreign policy by passing resolutions daily or abusing other governments. There are grave faults in us. We too face great difficulties. Who are we to judge others? We want to remain silent as far as possible about the affairs of others. We have to speak out when there is some fundamental principle involved or we are directly concerned in any way.

Take Pakistan, for instance. There have been tensions between our two governments over various issues. On our part we have made great efforts. I will not go into all that. But right from the beginning our efforts have been to see to it that our relations with Pakistan should be good. We have said this again and again. It is laid down in our Manifesto also that we neither wish to go to war with Pakistan or to swallow it. We have accepted partition and do not wish to see it annulled. The fact is that any such step would lead to great upheavals in India and bring all our plans for development to a halt. We do not wish to go to war with Pakistan under any circumstances or to undo the partition. There are one or two parties, like the Jana Sangh, which say such things. But please bear in mind that there can be no greater wrong than this. The only possible basis of relations between India and Pakistan is mutual cooperation. We will achieve that somehow. Otherwise both the countries will suffer. That is why we have tried to lay the foundations of civilized conduct between us. The Foreign Minister of Pakistan says that India is the greatest enemy of Pakistan.[2] We cannot help that. But such statements make matters worse. We refrain from saying things like this because we are convinced that it will not solve any problems.

So I have tried to explain to you that our foreign policy is by no means vague or in the air. It has not sprung up suddenly but is rooted in India's ancient past. Secondly it is in tune with the policy chalked out by Gandhiji during the freedom struggle. Thirdly, it has to be in step with our domestic policy. If we follow any other foreign policy, it is bound to have repercussions on our domestic policy. There will be great upheavals. The two should go hand in hand. Fourthly, even if you leave aside the question of principle and look at the situation in the world from a purely practical point of view, there is no alternative before us. Any other country situated as we are today would have chosen this course. For instance, people in the United States remember that 250 years ago when they became independent, they too had adopted a more or less similar policy. This is what I wanted to explain to you. You must not bring in Jawaharlal into it. It is absolutely wrong. I simply cannot understand it. This is not the way to look at any issues seriously.

People often raise the question as to who will direct the foreign policy when Jawaharlal is no longer there. It is absolutely absurd. Some of our colleagues have also raised this question to which our President has replied very gently. He should have been more firm. But anyhow, the whole thing is absurd. How can

2. Speaking at Rawalpindi on 21 October 1956, Feroz Khan Noon said "there was only one country in the world inimical to Pakistan and that was Bharat on account of her intrasigent policy in Kashmir."

any nation grow if we think like this? A new India is emerging. But it is not due to any single individual but because of activities such as our Five Year Plans. Millions of people are engaged in these tasks and it is they who will shoulder the burdens of the country. Those who ask futile questions do not understand the true meaning of democracy. It is only the mind which is not democratic that looks for answers to such questions....

14. To Sundarlal[1]

The Residency,
Indore,
6th January, 1957

My dear Sundarlal,[2]
Thank you for your letter of the 29th December which I have read with interest. It is rather difficult to reply to it at any length because this would involve a consideration of a large number of problems.

You refer to the Congress organisation[3] and suggest the formation of what you call a national government.[4] You also suggest certain economic measures.[5]

1. JN Collection.
2. Freedom fighter and Congressman from Uttar Pradesh.
3. Sundarlal drew Nehru's attention to the fact that "at present", everyone in the Congress, the government and the country appeared to be united. But this he said was only because of Nehru's personality, which kept the disruptive anti-social elements in check. Additionally, Sundarlal warned of the increasing influence of communal elements within the Congress party, adding that they were more of a menace than those in "openly communal organisations." He noted that their real interest was "anti-Congress and anti-national."
4. Sundarlal suggested the formation of a National Government, with members from all political parties. The one essential overriding qualification to be a part of such a government, according to Sundarlal, "should be their unshakable faith in secularism and an unrelenting opposition to all types of communalism." He felt that if such a system were replicated at the state level, it would go a long way in "automatically" organising and strengthening the anti-communal forces in India.
5. Sundarlal opined that it was necessary to provide employment for all rather than increase the total wealth of the country or raise the standard of living. With this objective in mind, he suggested giving a free field to the development of cottage industries, "under the control of men who believe in them quite on Gandhiji's lines." He added that such governmental activity would also satisfy men like Vinoba Bhave and the Gandhian economist, J.C. Kumarappa.

301

The latter proposal presumably means that we should set aside the Second Five Year Plan and start anew on the basis you have suggested. This is rather a large proposition and surely you will not expect me to go back on all the concentrated work of some years which has resulted in this Plan. Personally I think that the Plan is, by and large, a very good plan. It gives a big place to cottage industries, in fact as big a place as can be absorbed. I am sorry I do not agree with Dr Kumarappa's view at all. Your proposals are isolated suggestions about certain matters which can hardly be considered by themselves. The whole Plan and the economic approach to our problems would have to be completely revised. That is not a practical proposition.

As for your proposal to have an anti-communal and progressive national front based on secularism, I do not quite see how any effective government or organisation can be formed of people who may agree on the question of anti-communalism but who disagree about many other things. No government can function in that way and no economic policy can even be enunciated. We shall all be at sixes and sevens.

The Congress is of course a large and the biggest organisation and undoubtedly there are many people in it who pay only lip service to the Congress ideals. In any system of democracy that is inevitable in a large organisation. The point is what the organisation as a whole is aiming at and what it is trying to do. This educates not only the organisation but others also. I have no doubt that the Congress has right aims and has done a great deal to further them and impress them upon the people.

I do not take the view that I am the only person who can hold the Congress together. The Congress roots are much deeper and so far as I am concerned I am trying to make them as firm as possible. I cannot guarantee the future.

Perhaps I am partial to the government of which I am a member. But I do think that it has a very creditable record of work and that our progress has been in some ways quite remarkable. We have not solved India's problems nor will those problems be fully solved for a considerable time. I suppose that can be said about any country. It is rather extraordinary that people coming from abroad, who began with a prejudice against India and our work, have been greatly impressed by what they have seen being done here. This applies, oddly enough, to communist and anti-communist.

Yours sincerely,
Jawaharlal Nehru

15. To Lal Bahadur Shastri [1]

The Residency, Indore,
January 7, 1957

My dear Lal Bahadur,

Bakhshi Ghulam Mohammad had a talk with me this evening. He had visited today Mhow and addressed a public meeting there, chiefly of Muslims. He also talked to the Muslims there. Later, he addressed a Muslim meeting in Indore and again had a talk with them.

When he came back, he told me that he was much concerned at the frustration he found among Muslims in India wherever he went. Also that they seemed to be completely out of touch both with the Congress and the governments. Quite apart from the important questions of relieving their distress or difficulty, such as lack of employment, what distressed Bakhshi Sahib most was this lack of contact with them. He told me that he found much the same thing in Calcutta where, increasingly, the Muslims in sheer despair were drifting away from the Congress and often going to the Communist or other like parties. It was not communism that attracted them but just the feeling of frustration. He thought that much the same process was happening in the UP, Bihar and elsewhere.

In Calcutta, there are a large number of Muslim voters in Dr B.C. Roy's[2] constituency. Possibly it is taken for granted that they will vote for Dr Roy. But this is by no means sure unless they are properly approached.

The Muslims who met him in Indore and Dhar told him that no one seemed to care for them or to come to them, not even their representatives in Parliament or the Assembly. In fact nobody visits them at all except perhaps just at election time asking for votes. The Ministers also ignore them or see them from a distance. Bakhshi Sahib walked some little distance in Mhow in the streets. People said that they were surprised at his doing so as they thought that Ministers never walked and never visited people in their houses. They only went about in cars.

What Bakhshi said has been for long my own impression and I have been much worried about it. But I did not know what to do. There are certain matters of considerable psychological importance, even though in practice they might not be so important. One of these major matters is the question of Urdu. There

1. JN Collection.
2. Chief Minister of West Bengal.

can be no doubt that this has affected Muslims, more especially in the UP and Bihar, very acutely. Then there is the question of employment in government services. It has become increasingly difficult for them to get employment in the Army or the Police. I do not know what the position is in the Railways and the Posts & Telegraph Services. But I rather think that the number of new Muslim entrants is very few even there.

We have still Muslims in these various services, but they are really relics of the past. New persons have fewer chances of coming in, both in the Centre and in the States.

However, these are governmental matters. I have only mentioned them as a kind of background. What I am writing to you about is the Congress aspect and the election aspect and, more especially, the question of contacts. This is really important. Congress leaders as well as the organisation have lost touch with the Muslim mind. We have hardly any real links. Maulana Azad, of course, is a powerful leader but owing to his ill-health he can meet very few persons and seldom goes to public gatherings. I fear he has lost touch also with new forces among the Muslims. His health does not improve and we cannot rightly ask him to do much more than he is doing.

Then there is Dr Syed Mahmud.[3] He is certainly helpful to a certain extent, especially in Bihar. But he is also rather feeble and cannot be expected to do much. Among the younger Muslims in Parliament are Abid Ali[4] (not very young) and Shah Nawaz Khan.[5] Abid Ali may or may not be helpful in Bombay among the Muslims but I doubt if he is of any help elsewhere. Shah Nawaz Khan is a good and earnest person but again not helpful from this point of view.

We lay stress on a sufficient number of Muslims being nominated for election. This, of course, is good. But I doubt if we always select the right persons. Some old Congress Muslims may be good in their way but do not appear to have much influence with their own community. Some of our old Muslim colleagues who are in the Jamiat-ul-Ulema have been, for instance, useful in certain circles, but they think in a particular way which is not always ours.

I do not know any obvious remedy for all this and I am merely unburdening my mind. The real difficulty is that ever since 1947 the Congress has lost touch with the Muslim mind in India and has made no real effort to improve the situation. Our resolutions are good, our speeches may be good and we put up

---

3. Congressman from Bihar and Minister, Ministry of External Affairs, 1954-57.
4. Congressman from Mumbai and Deputy Minister for Labour, 1952-62.
5. Former member of the INA and at this time Parliamentary Secretary to the Minister of Railways.

some Muslim candidates now and then, but still the fact remains that we are just out of touch. What is more, we tend to think of the Muslims as some extraneous group which has to be appeased to some extent by seats in the Legislatures and sometimes otherwise. There is really no attempt to understand the problem, much less to solve it. Most Congressmen just forget the Muslims except from the narrow election point of view.

What can we do about it on behalf of the Congress? To a slight extent, we might improve matters in the choice of our candidates, though I suppose we will ultimately not do much. The candidates who are put up will be usually either some people connected with the Congress in the past who have lost touch with their own community, or some other feeble Muslims who do not count for much. What we should aim at is to get some bright young people with ideas and vigour. That was why I was rather anxious that Hayatullah Khan Ansari might be chosen by us, as well as other people like him.

But, apart from this question of elections, I think the Congress and, more especially, the AICC and the Working Committee should think about this matter. Bakhshi Sahib suggested that the Congress should have some kind of a department to deal with it. This will at least keep the matter in the forefront before our eyes. I rather doubt if such a special department would be advisable. But I think that one or more really competent young Muslims of the right way of thinking might well be associated with the AICC fully. They need not just do work among the Muslims or about them. They can be engaged in other activities also. But they should be asked to keep in touch with what is happening to Muslims in various parts of the country.

Also our Ministers should be roused to some action. Quite apart from our being able to remove any grievances, the mere fact of meeting them and giving them our friendly sympathy goes a good way.

This letter, though a longish one, is vague and nebulous. That presents the state of my mind in this matter. All that I can say about this is that this deserves our very careful attention. Constituted as most of us are, we are just apt to forget this problem. I think we are likely to see a considerable number of Muslims turn away from the Congress during the elections.

I should like you to show this letter to Dhebarbhai and Pantji. I do not wish to trouble them by writing to them separately.

Yours affectionately,
Jawaharlal

16. To U.N. Dhebar[1]

New Delhi,
January 9, 1957

My dear Dhebarbhai,

After our talk at Indore about Krishna Menon's seat and our decision that he should stand from Bombay North, I sent a telegram to Krishna Menon informing him of this. He has replied to me[2] accepting this and has, I believe, sent telegrams of acceptance and thanks to Bombay also.

I hope this matter will be finalised now. If Krishna Menon has to take any particular step in the near future about it, kindly let me know so that I can inform him.

Yours sincerely,
Jawaharlal Nehru

1. File No. 4, Secret correspondence between U.N. Dhebar and Jawaharlal Nehru. AICC Papers, NMML.
2. Menon in his reply of 8 January said he respected Indira Gandhi's advice on his standing for elections. He added that he did not want to run away from a contest, or shirk PSP opposition in Bombay. Menon said he was prepared to accept the consequences of a defeat. "You have rightly said that the decision must be mine and I alone am making it so far as I am concerned", added Menon.

17. To U.N. Dhebar[1]

New Delhi,
January 11, 1957

My dear Dhebarbhai,

Master Tara Singh[2] came to see me this evening and, as usual, talked vaguely about various matters. He began by complaining of the growing corruption in the Punjab. As an instance, he showed me some papers relating to Choudhury Devi Lal,[3] Parliamentary Secretary from the Haryana. These papers did not seem to establish anything conclusive.

Then he talked about a list prepared by the observer for Gurgaon District, Shri Durga Das Bhatia[4] of Amritsar, having been tampered with. Some pages and contents were substituted. Apparently, Durga Das said so to Sardar Baldev Singh.[5]

He complained of the attempts to create division among the Sikhs and was particularly excited about Gian Singh Rarewala.[6] He talked about Gian Singh Rarewala having been purchased by the High Command by some promises made to him, and he said that Maulana Azad had told him so.

I told him that I felt sure that Maulana Sahib could never have said this. Gian Singh Rarewala joined the Congress without any kind of promise or assurance being given to him. Probably, he was told later that he would be consulted as regards the seats from PEPSU.[7] I saw nothing objectionable about this.

He then gave me a paper which I enclose.

1. JN Collection.
2. Akali leader, who was associated with the Sikh Missionary College in Amritsar.
3. Member, Punjab Legislative Assembly.
4. (1908-1972); Congress member of the Fifth Lok Sabha from Amritsar.
5. Former Union Defence Minister.
6. Former Chief Minister of PEPSU and at this time leader of the United Front opposition in the Legislative Assembly.
7. Tara Singh said that Rarewala had joined the Congress "in indecent haste", with a handful of his followers in the Pepsu Legislative Assembly elected on the Akali ticket. Rarewala, according to Tara Singh, had entered into a bargain with Partap Singh Kairon, Chief Minister of Punjab by which "not only was Rarewala to get certain number of seats but was to be consulted in the selection of candidates for the Pepsu area and particularly the Akalis." The Congress President was also aware of this commitment, observed Tara Singh.

I need not say in detail as to what Master Tara Singh said to me because he has no doubt repeated it to Gulzarilal Nanda and others and, perhaps, you also. If you like, you can send this letter to Gulzarilal.

Yours sincerely,
Jawaharlal Nehru

18. Cable to V.K. Krishna Menon [1]

...Since my return from Indore Congress I have been terribly busy with accumulation of work, election matters and Dalai Lama's visit. Most leading Congressmen including Patil are travelling about on election work. Hence often delay in answering messages.

Your Bombay seat has been finalised.[2] I have no doubt that you will win it. Nomination probably about 28th January though I am not sure yet. Your presence for nomination not necessary but usually considered desirable. Patil will send you further particulars.

Please do not worry about odd statements in press by irresponsible writers. They have no importance. I had one such statement contradicted.[3]

1. 12 January 1957. JN Collection. Extracts. The message was sent by Nehru from Rajgir in Bihar to M.O. Mathai in New Delhi, who then transmitted it to Krishna Menon.
2. Krishna Menon in his cable of 10 January announced that his decision to contest from Bombay was "final". He added: "I am convinced that the course I had decided is the right one irrespective of whatever may happen in the future."
3. Krishna Menon wanted "those concerned" to refrain from arranging leaks to the press and to avoid giving the impression that he was " nearly persona non grata" with Nehru. The Prime Minister had apparently arrived at "certain adverse conclusions" about him and had even mentioned this to others.

We quite realise great pressure on you on Kashmir, disarmament and generally deteriorating world situation. We are happy that you are dealing with these matters.[4]

Here, as usual, election is dominating other and far graver problems.

Patil has telegraphed today to say that your candidature for North Bombay has been unanimously accepted and finalised and that he has cabled you accordingly. I understand privately that Peter Alvares[5] of PSP is standing against you and that Democratic Research Service and other organizations sponsored by Masani and others as well as the organised Catholic Church will work against you. Foreign agencies might also be indirectly involved. Though personally I would have liked you to contest a by-election somewhat later to the Lok Sabha, I should now like to ask you to hold your chin up. Your contest will have great significance and I have no doubt that the robust good sense of our dear people will triumph and you will get elected by a thumping majority. There shall be no question of defeat.

4. Krishna Menon claimed that his work in the UN and "the position we have established here and in world affairs...result in being continually called in and approached on most things by a multiplicity of parties and persons at all levels."
5. President, National Congress, Goa and a member of the Praja Socialist Party's Executive Committee. He contested the Bombay North Lok Sabha seat in the general elections and lost to Krishna Menon.

19. To B. Ramakrishna Rao[1]

Raj Bhavan,
Calcutta,
January 15, 1957

My dear Ramakrishna Rao,[2]
Your letter of the 12th January[3] has reached me here in Calcutta.

I know very well of the difficulties in Kerala, more especially for the Congress. I also realise that it is quite possible for the Congress to fare badly in the elections. We have discussed this matter at some length with Kerala Congress people, S.K. Patil and members of the Central Election Committee. We have indicated to them how far we can go. It is dangerous for us to agree to any arrangement which goes against our basic policies. That will bring down the reputation of the Congress all over India and we shall then deserve to lose. Short of any kind of an arrangement which is against our principles, we have suggested what might perhaps be done. But we must be prepared for a defeat if that comes our way and not get too excited about it.

Yours sincerely,
Jawaharlal Nehru

1. JN Collection.
2. Governor of Kerala.
3. Rao warned of the real danger of the communists emerging as the single largest party in Kerala in the forthcoming general elections. With the aim of averting the unholy alliance between the PSP and the Communists, he suggested that the Congress should arrive at an understanding with the PSP and the Muslim League.

20. To Amrit Kaur[1]

New Delhi,
January 21, 1957

My dear Amrit,[2]

You wrote to me some time ago about your seat for Parliament.[3] I did not know the position then, and so did not reply to you. I returned to Delhi today and had a talk with the Congress President and some other members of the Central Election Committee of the Congress.

As you know, Swaran Singh is also anxious to stand from Jullundur. That is his home town and normally he will stand from it as he has done in the past. The Akalis do not like him at all and will no doubt create grave difficulties for him elsewhere. It is not easy to deal with them.

Because of this, we have found it difficult to choose another suitable constituency for Swaran Singh. It is important that he should be elected to Parliament. Unfortunately, there are not too many Sikhs of high calibre in Parliament. The Election Committee, therefore, had decided, even before I returned,[4] that it would be better for Swaran Singh to stand from this constituency. When they told me of the position, I felt that I had to agree.

It should be easy for you to find another constituency for the Lok Sabha. If you prefer it, there will be no difficulty in your coming to the Rajya Sabha.[5]

Yours sincerely,
Jawaharlal Nehru

1. File No. 1, Secret correspondence between U.N. Dhebar and Jawaharlal Nehru, AICC Papers, NMML.
2. Union Minister for Health.
3. In her letter of 29 December 1956, Amrit Kaur said she wanted to stand for election to the Lok Sabha from her home state, Punjab. She added that Partap Singh Kairon had "readily agreed" to her standing from Jalandhar, a few months ago. Amrit Kaur noted that Swaran Singh "since a month or so" started saying that he had a "prior claim to the constituency" and suggested giving Ambala to the Minister for Health. She contended that she had lived and worked in Jalandhar for years as a member of the Municipality and in the villages as Gandhiji's first agent for the village industries association. In Ambala, Kaur said: "I have no such record and being a Hindu area, I shall not be able to pull my full weight."
4. Nehru returned from a tour of the USA and Canada on 28 December 1956.
5. Amrit Kaur concluded by saying: "The scramble for seats is deplorable and therefore if *you* (emphasis in original) feel that I should not ask for a constituency this time I am willing to stand down altogether." Amrit Kaur was a member of the Rajya Sabha from 1957 to 1964.

21. To R. Shanmuga Rajeswara Sethupathi[1]

New Delhi,
January 22, 1957

Dear Raja Sahib,[2]

I have your telegram and your brief letter in which you say that the non-inclusion of your name in the list of candidates for election is a slur and you ask me to permit you to vindicate yourself to stand as an Independent.

First of all, the non-inclusion of a name is not a slur for anybody. The Congress Election Committee has to consider a large number of factors and then to come to a choice. Many good people are not included. Many decisions have been made in this respect which are not very much to my liking. It is obvious that if no changes are made, the same persons are perpetuated in our Parliament and Assemblies. This is not a good thing. So far as I am concerned, I accept decisions even though I may disagree with them.

I do not know what you mean by my permitting you to stand as an Independent. There is no question of permission for you to do something with which I disagree. If you want my advice, I would say that you should not stand. We must get used to observing discipline even though we may not like it. If you stand as an independent you, instead of vindicating yourself, would really indicate that your not being chosen was justified.

But I should like to repeat that there is no question of any slur on anybody in this matter.

Yours sincerely,
Jawaharlal Nehru

---

1. JN Collection.
2. (b.1909); joined the Congress Party in 1949; member, Madras Legislative Assembly, 1947-62; Minister for Public Works, Government of Madras, 1952-57; member, All-India Congress Committee.

22. To Tara Singh[1]

New Delhi,
January 23, 1957

My dear Master Tara Singh,

I have just received your letter of January 23rd.

I am sorry to learn that you are dissatisfied with the allotment of tickets for Parliament and the Legislative Assembly in the Punjab. I have had practically nothing to do with this matter and do not even know who have been chosen. But I do know that my colleagues took enormous pains over this matter and tried their utmost to choose the most suitable persons, keeping various points of view in mind. I doubt if such great care has ever been taken before. As you know, they had the advantage of frequent consultations with you and your colleagues.

You refer to merit and then say that merit seems to be the last thing considered.[2] As an example, you mention the case of the Chief Minister Sardar Partap Singh.[3] I am rather surprised to learn this as I have known Sardar Partap Singh for many long years and have a high opinion of his capacity and integrity. You say that he interferes illegally in the administration of the State in very small matters. As I do not know to what this refers, I can give no opinion. But a Chief Minister may often interfere in small matters if, in his opinion, something goes wrong. Even I interfere in the smallest matters if I think it necessary. Of course, there should be no interference with law courts and their work.

In any event, if there has been some interference which was not desirable, this has little to do with the basic merits of a person. It may be due to some error in judgement where two views can be held.

Yours sincerely,
Jawaharlal Nehru

---

1. JN Collection.
2. Tara Singh noted that the word "merit" served "as a smoke-screen only" adding that merit "seems to be the last thing considered" in the allotment of tickets in Punjab.
3. Tara Singh alleged that Partap Singh Kairon interfered illegally in the administration of the state and added that he was guilty of contempt of court in one case.

23. To Amrit Kaur[1]

New Delhi,
January 26, 1957

My dear Amrit,

I have just seen your letter of the 25th, on the evening of the 26th January. I am distressed to read it. I can well understand that, as you wrote to me, you wanted to stand for the Jullundur constituency. That was a natural desire. I can also understand that you did not like the decision of the Central Election Committee. But I really do not understand why you should have taken this decision so much to heart.

So far as I am concerned, I have practically not participated in the meetings of the Central Election Committee. I attended some meetings right at the beginning when some general principles were discussed, and I attended one of the last meetings about three days ago when the work had been nearly finished and only some odd questions remained. In between, I had made some suggestions to the Central Election Committee. As it happened, some of my suggestions were not accepted by the Committee, and I did not like it at all. But I informed Dhebarbhai that I had done my duty in making the suggestions. It was for him and for his Committee, who are going into all the aspects of the question, to decide finally, and I would accept their decision whether I agreed with it or not. I have done so in all matters, some of which have not at all been to my liking.

When you wrote to me some time ago about your seat, I informed Dhebarbhai and Pantji about your letter, though I did not send the letter to them. Your last letter to me, I did forward to Dhebarbhai, although it was marked 'personal and confidential'. Dhebarbhai is my chief in this matter, and I thought it only right that I should place your letter before him. I am sorry if you think that this was a breach of confidence.[2]

I might mention also that Swaran Singh has not been to see me at any time about his seat for Parliament. I learnt from other sources that he also wanted to

---

1. JN Collection.
2. Amrit Kaur said she was "deeply hurt" for not being asked in a friendly manner to give up Jalandhar in favour of Swaran Singh. Kaur observed that if she had not written to Nehru (see *ante*, p. 311, for Nehru's letter of 21 January.) "I would have received no word at all from the Congress Committee." She added: "Common courtesy requires that where I had asked for a constituency months ago and where my name was the only one sent up by the Pradesh Committee I should have been apprised...even before the decision was taken...."

stand for Jullundur because this was his home town and he had always stood from Jullundur for the Punjab Assembly. Only once at the end of a Cabinet meeting when we were walking out, Swaran Singh mentioned to me that he was rather embarrassed that he and you should want the same constituency. That was all he said.

Dhebarbhai once mentioned to me about the difficulty they were having in regard to this seat as two colleagues of ours both favoured it. It was indeed because of this delicacy as between two colleagues, that Dhebarbhai did not approach you about this earlier. You think apparently that you were ignored in this matter. Indeed, it was the other way about. It was consideration for you that prevented him from broaching a personal question to you. There were no facts to be obtained, and nor was there a question of giving up a seat because that has not been your seat up till now. The question might have arisen if you had continued in the Mandi seat. A decision had to be taken, and the facts were fully known. Dhebarbhai naturally wished, and all others agreed with him, that both you and Swaran Singh should be given good seats. The only question was which seat to give to each.

I was away from Delhi when all these matters were considered. No final decision, however, had been taken about the Jullundur constituency because of this difficulty that all the members of the Committee felt. When I came back to Delhi, I was asked to attend one of the last meetings of the Committee. I went there. This question came up and some of the members discussed this question quite objectively and expressed their opinion that it would be better for Swaran Singh to have the Jullundur constituency and for you to be given another good constituency in the Punjab. In the balance, I agreed with them, because I felt that any constituency was an easy one for you, while that might not be so for Swaran Singh. Dhebarbhai said that he would meet you himself and tell you about it.[3] I also mentioned to him that I would write that evening.

I really do not understand why you should consider that any courtesy has been denied to you. The Election Committee has had to consider a vast number of cases and has worked terribly hard. The problems they faced, were very difficult ones, involving not only the choice of the candidates on merits, but the appropriate constituency so that the candidate might get in. It is not merely a formal matter to nominate a candidate, but to see that he gets in, and changes

---

3. Dhebar and Shriman Narayan called on Amrit Kaur at 9 p.m. on 25 January. Dhebar offered her Kaithal, which she refused. Kaur claimed that Dhebar had told her that she would not have been given even that seat, if Nehru had not shown him Amrit Kaur's letter of 21 January. Amrit Kaur wrote to Nehru that she then told Dhebar that "the blame for discourtesy lies on the shoulders of everybody including yourself."

have been made in many constituencies because of this. It may be that the change was not a good one. But, there was no lack of consideration and courtesy anywhere. You had previously stood for Mandi and it never struck me that there would be any particular reason why you should not accept another good constituency nearby. There is no question of anybody having a right in such matters, and I think you are completely wrong in saying that it was your right to stand from Jullundur. It may have been desirable for you to do so. Who is to be a judge of this in any organisation? As I have told you, my opinions have been overruled several times, and I have accepted the decision of the Committee, chiefly for the reason that they had every factor before them, and I did not. And, also, of course, there is such a thing as discipline in an organisation.

I am really very sorry that you should talk in this connection of a spirit of intrigue and lack of integrity in the Congress ranks.[4] I have been in the Congress for a pretty long time. Ever since the question of elections has cropped up in the Congress, Congress Election Committees have considered the choice of candidates, and they have had difficulties to face. I have never known greater care having been exercised in this matter than during this present occasion. I do not know of a single person in the whole of India who has greater integrity in these matters than Dhebarbhai. And yet, without even enquiring into what has happened, you refer to intrigue and lack of integrity. The fact that wrong choice may be made or wrong constituency ordered or other mistakes committed, may be so here and there, but your charge is something more serious than that. I am deeply grieved that you should look upon this matter in this way. I hope you will think about it again and realise what a grave injustice you are doing to Dhebarbhai and me as well as to my other colleagues in the Committee.

My personal advice to you would have been and is that you should accept the proposal put forward by Dhebarbhai to you to stand for another constituency. Kaithal was mentioned in this connection, and it is a good seat. But there were other choices too.

You have raised the question of Christian representation.[5] I know nothing about this matter, as I have not been working in the Committee. But, in this

---

4. Amrit Kaur said she was filled with sorrow by the "spirit of intrigue and lack of integrity which have crept into Congress ranks".
5. Amrit Kaur wrote that "not one Indian Christian has been proposed by the Congress for the Lok Sabha" from any state. "Is this the secular state that you speak so often of?" asked Amrit Kaur. She added that Christians had lost confidence in the Congress and its leadership and that she had advised them "not to vote against the Congress" in the elections but they were free "to refrain from voting at all should they be morally strong to show their displeasure in that way."

matter, I take it that the Pradesh Congress Committees usually have a very large say. They have to run the elections, and they have to think always of a person who can get in and not merely a person who is put forward and is bound to lose. No one thought of you as standing for a seat because you were a Christian. You were thought of as a colleague, just as Rafi Ahmad Kidwai[6] was chosen because he was a colleague, not because he was a Muslim.

We may have made some mistakes. But, to be accused of communalism by you is, to say the least, surprising. If the Christians wish to vote against the Congress to show their displeasure, I cannot help it. They would injure their cause. As you know, Christians in Northern India are a very small minority. It is different in South India.

You refer to what Master Tara Singh told you.[7] Master Tara Singh's behaviour in the last few days has been far from commendable.

Yours sincerely,
Jawaharlal Nehru

6. Former Union Minister for Food and Agriculture.
7. Tara Singh had said: "If we behaved as the Christian community does and never raised our voices in protest, we would be nowhere."

24. To S.K. Patil[1]

New Delhi,
January 30, 1957

My dear S.K.,[2]

I have tonight issued an appeal to the people of India to vote for Congress candidates. This is being sent to the Press here. I am enclosing a copy of it.[3]

As Krishna Menon is away, busy in the Security Council, I do not know when it will be possible for him to come back. Obviously, he cannot leave the Kashmir issue in midstream. Perhaps, he can come here later, in the third week or so, of February. Because of his absence, I have thought it desirable to issue an appeal for him specially. There are many misrepresentations being made about him especially, and I gather that the Socialists and the Democratic Research Service and other organisations are working hard against him.

I have, therefore, drafted an appeal,[4] and I enclose it. I am not issuing this from here. I should like you to issue it in Bombay.

Yours sincerely,
Jawaharlal Nehru

---

1. JN Collection.
2. President, Bombay Pradesh Congress Committee.
3. See the next item.
4. See *post*, pp. 321-322, for this appeal.

25. National Integration: Historic Function of the Congress[1]

The first stage of the general elections is over and nominations have been made. Inevitably, some have been chosen as candidates and some have been left out. So far as the Congress organisation is concerned, the burden of choosing candidates has fallen on the Pradesh Congress Committee, and the Central Election Committee headed by the Congress President. I am afraid I could not share that burden much. This was a difficult and thankless task and some deserving persons have been left out. Not to be chosen involves no discredit, for it is not possible to accommodate even all the deserving persons. Those who have been left out have my sympathy. But I am sure that there will be many avenues open to them for national work.

In the Congress, as in any organisation, a certain discipline has to be observed and all of us must accept the final decisions with good heart and in good spirit. As a soldier of the Congress, I accept the decisions made on behalf of the Congress and I appeal to the voters all over India to support the Congress candidate.

I support them not merely because I am a Congressman but because I am convinced that at this moment in our history it is important that we should have strong and disciplined parties of the Congress in the Central Parliament as well as in the State Legislatures. The parliamentary democracy that we have got in India can only function effectively through disciplined parties with clearly stated objectives. Otherwise there is no stability, and effective work cannot be done, nor can there be any real planning.

Both in the domestic and national sphere as well as in the international field, we face vital problems of far-reaching importance. Our most important task is to fulfil the Second Five Year Plan and thus lay the foundations for rapid growth in the future. Every effort has to be bent to this end and for this purpose it is essential that a strong and well-organised party like the Congress, having the people's confidence, should implement this plan. Any doubt or confusion on this issue will prevent the plan from functioning as it should and delay India's progress.

In international affairs, our policy of non-alignment and of friendship with all countries has been firm and straight and in accordance with our national

---

1. Statement to the Press, 30 January 1957. From *The Hindu*, 1 February 1957.

approach to these questions during the last many years. We have not pleased everybody because of this and sometimes some countries have even expressed their displeasure because we could not line up with them. It is not possible to please all countries when our policy is an independent one of non-alignment and of judging on the merits of each question. But India's views count in the world and her stature has grown. With that growth, further responsibilities have come upon us. We cannot follow adventurist policies, nor can we give up our independence of thinking and action by attaching ourselves to some group of nations or military alliance. We have worked for peace and our work has sometimes produced definite results in the furtherance of the cause of peace. It is our intention to continue this policy and to devote ourselves to the maintenance of peace and friendship between nations. Even though we differ in our policy from that of some countries, we bear malice to none and seek their friendship. I am convinced that both for the sake of our national interests as well as the larger cause of world peace, there is no other policy open to us.

In a world full of torment and trouble, we have pursued these policies unflinchingly and engaged ourselves in the mighty task of building a new India as well as in the great adventure of man. Great and difficult problems confront us in India and abroad. It is only by adhering to our principles and having faith in our people that we can face them and progressively solve them.

I believe that it is the historic function of the National Congress to integrate India not only politically and economically but also emotionally so that our country might become a symbol of unity and progress with no ill will to any other. The general election is a challenge to the people of India. I trust that they will answer this challenge by rising above all petty differences and giving their verdict in favour of the high principles for which the Congress stands.

26. An Appeal for Krishna Menon[1]

At the conclusion of the first stage of our general elections when nominations have been filed I have appealed to the people of India to give their verdict in favour of the National Congress and the principles and policies for which it stands. It is not necessary for me to issue appeals on behalf of each Congress candidate. I appeal not for votes for individuals, though individuals deserve them, but for the great organization to which I have had the honour to belong for the last forty-five years. I have asked, therefore, that Congress candidates, whether for Parliament or the state legislatures, should be supported. Congressmen especially and all those who support them should work in a disciplined way, forgetting and setting aside any internal differences that they might have.

Although I am not issuing any appeals for individual candidates, many of whom are my old colleagues and comrades I am issuing this particular appeal to the voters of Bombay, that great city which has played such a memorable part not only in our struggle for freedom but also in the growth of our industry. I hope that all Congress candidates in Bombay city as well as State will receive the vote and support of voters. My principal reason for issuing this appeal is to mention especially the name of my old and valued colleague, Shri V.K. Krishna Menon, who is standing from part of Bombay city for the Lok Sabha. I am doing so because he is at present engaged abroad in a difficult task of high national importance.

We have asked Shri Krishna Menon to stand from Bombay city so that the citizens of Bombay may have an opportunity to give their verdict on the major international policies of the Congress and the Government of India. With these policies Shri Krishna Menon has been intimately connected for many years. We felt that it was right that the voters of Bombay which is in many ways the political nerve centre of India should pronounce on them and give their verdict generally on the policy of non-alignment which India has followed. It has been in furtherance of this policy that Panchsheel has grown, that we adhered to the declaration of the Bandung Conference, that we are close friends with the countries of South East Asia as well as of the Arab world. It is because of them that we have friendly relations with the great powers and other countries in the various continents of the world, and seek to cooperate with them even when we

---

1. Statement to the Press, 30 January 1957. From the *National Herald*, 7 February 1957.

disagree in some matter. We have believed in a peaceful and friendly approach to countries which differ from us and have laid stress on our points of agreement rather than on those on which we disagree. Because of this policy, India has grown internationally and has served the cause of peace and cooperation among nations.

Shri Krishna Menon represents this policy in the fullest measure. As I issue this message, he is stating India's case brilliantly before the Security Council in a matter of great import not only to us in India but to others also. I should like to state that in the fine exposition of his case in the Security Council, he has had the full approval and support of our government, and we wish him every success.

Shri Krishna Menon could have easily continued in the Rajya Sabha, of which he has been a member or been chosen from some other constituency. But we thought it eminently desirable that our international policy should be put to the test in the great city of Bombay itself so that its intelligent citizens might proclaim to the world where we stand and what we believe in. Shri Krishna Menon, being engaged in the Security Council, cannot easily undertake an election campaign which otherwise he should have done. It is for this reason that I have issued this appeal.

I trust that the citizens of Bombay will, by giving their enthusiastic support to Shri Krishna Menon, give a fitting answer to the challenge that has been thrown to us from various quarters.

27. To Sri Krishna Sinha[1]

New Delhi,
February 9, 1957

My dear Sri Babu,[2]

I understand that Masani is standing from Jamshedpur for the Lok Sabha. No doubt he hopes that the Tata interests will support him. My concern is that the INTUC organization should not even passively give him any support. In fact they should oppose him fully. I am writing to you because I heard that John was rather lukewarm about this matter. I think he should be told that Masani is opposed to every major policy of the Congress as well as of the INTUC.[3]

Yours sincerely,
Jawaharlal Nehru

---

1. JN Collection.
2. Chief Minister of Bihar.
3. The same day Nehru wrote to Khandubhai Desai, Minister for Labour, that Michael John, a member of the AICC and former INTUC President was "inclined" to support M.R. Masani, "possibly because of pressure from Tatas." Nehru wanted it made clear to John that it would not be proper for any INTUC organization to support Masani. On 18 February, John clarified that Nehru's information was wrong.

28. To Shriman Narayan[1]

New Delhi,
February 12, 1957

My dear Shriman,[2]

Manmohini Sehgal[3] came to see me this evening. I advised her to withdraw. I told her that from the purely Congress point of view, it was a matter of little concern to me whether she withdraws or not. It made no great difference if we won or lost one seat. But, from the point of view of her future work in the political field, it seemed to me very unfortunate that she should stand against the Congress candidate. I told her also that all of us recognised that we had not treated her very fairly in this matter. But a set of circumstances had arisen, which led us to certain decisions. I had much sympathy for her and I knew that she had done very good work in this constituency throughout these years.

She was impressed by my argument, but she said that she had committed herself to so many people and so many workers that it was not very easy to withdraw suddenly and put these people in a false position. Against some of them, action had been taken by the Delhi Congress Committee. Some had actually resigned some temporary jobs that they were holding, in order to devote themselves to this election work.

I told her that if she withdrew, it would not be right for anyone to suffer because he had supported her, and we would try our best to see that there was no unfair treatment of this kind. I left it at that and told her to think over it and act as she thought proper.

As I told you on the telephone, I think that Sucheta Kripalani[4] must issue a statement about these rumours that she had been promised a Ministership,

---

1. Shriman Narayan Papers, NMML. Extracts.
2. General Secretary, AICC.
3. Manmohini Sehgal, Nehru's niece, resigned from the Congress on 25 January 1957 after the Delhi Pradesh Congress Committee bypassed her in favour of Sucheta Kripalani for the New Delhi Lok Sabha seat. Four days later Mrs. Sehgal filed her nomination as an Independent candidate. On 4 February, the Delhi Pradesh Congress Committee expelled her for six years from the party for breach of party discipline. Mrs Sehgal said at a press conference on that day that it was "unfair" to give a Congress ticket to Sucheta Kripalani, who had opposed the party in 1952.
4. Wife of J.B. Kripalani; left the Congress in 1951 and joined the Kisan Mazdoor Praja Party; rejoined the Congress in December 1956.

etc.[5] These rumours are injuring her. Maulana Sahib is strongly of the opinion that she should issue a statement. I agree. The statement should be clear and explicit....

Yours sincerely,
Jawaharlal Nehru

5. On 8 February 1957, Nehru wrote to Sucheta Kripalani that she had openly declared in public that the Prime Minister had offered her a ministership. Nehru denied having done so. Mangal Dass, Secretary, Delhi United Refugee front in his telegram to Nehru had alleged that Sucheta Kripalani was threatening refugees with dire consequences if they did not vote for her.

29. To Mehr Chand Khanna[1]

Raj Bhavan, Cuttack,
February 13, 1957

My dear Mehr Chand,[2]
Some people wrote to me the other day saying that Sucheta Kripalani was telling people that she had been promised a Ministership by me, presumably the Ministership of Rehabilitation. I was surprised and distressed to learn this, and I wrote to her about it.[3] She replied that she had never said anything of this kind and could not possibly say it as it was not true. Her opponents were putting this in her mouth in order to humiliate her.

I am writing this to you so that you might not believe these rumours that are spread.

Yours sincerely,
Jawaharlal Nehru

1. JN Collection.
2. Minister for Rehabilitation.
3. See the preceding item.

30. An Appeal to the Electorate[1]

Five years ago general elections for the Lok Sabha and the Vidhan Sabhas were held. Once again similar general elections are being held in which the Congress has set up its candidates in all the states.

Our brothers and sisters, who have a vote, should exercise their right after mature consideration. Voting does not merely connote one's preference for a particular candidate. Voting also implies as to which party's policy is liked by the electorate and which particular party is considered by them to serve the country rightly.

I have been associated with the Congress for long and I think that the Congress policies have been for the good of the country. In future also the Congress alone can run the affairs of the country with firmness and on right rails. Therefore, I hope the people will give their votes only to the Congress candidates.

I am sending this message particularly to the eastern districts of UP because I wanted to go there and meet the people, but I am sorry that I do not have the time to do so. While sending this message, I hope that my brethren in the eastern districts will show that they like Congress policies by casting their votes in favour of the Congress.

---

1. Message to the people of the eastern districts of Uttar Pradesh, 14 February 1957. From the *National Herald*, 15 February 1957. Original in Hindi.

31. To Lakshman Singh Bahadur[1]

Raj Bhawan,
Patna,
February 14, 1957

Dear Lakshman Singhji,[2]

I have received your letter of the 9th February today.[3] I agree with you that no one, least of all a Congressman, should make any general charges against ex-rulers and ex-jagirdars and state that they have connections with Pakistan or any other country. Such general charges are always objectionable.

I am terribly busy at present, but I have glanced through the Hindi notice that you have sent me. I do not like its wording or its content, but as far as I can see in a hurried reading, the statement about Pakistan is not connected with you. Objection is taken to your working against the Congress. As I have said above, I do not approve of this notice, but I think that you have drawn an inference from it which perhaps is not justified.[4] I am sending your letter and this notice to the AICC Office for them to deal with it.[5]

1. File No. SN-19, AICC Papers, NMML.
2. (b. 1908); Maharawal of Dungarpur; Independent member of the Rajya Sabha, 1952-58.
3. Lakshman Singh stated that a Hindi pamphlet issued by the Dungarpur District Congress Committee alleged that the ex-rulers and ex-jagirdars of Rajasthan had a "unholy connection" with Pakistan or the USA. Singh said that if any person was found guilty he should be tried as a traitor and punished. He observed that this was tantamount to "hitting below the belt." Singh felt that such allegations "without any semblance of truth behind it" were hardly worthy of the Congress.
4. Lakshman Singh argued that some of them had suffered under chief minister Mohan Lal Sukhadia and added that they would use all the constitutional methods to bring about a change in the existing set up of Rajasthan.
5. Nehru wrote to Shriman Narayan that even if information was available about the links of ex-rulers and *jagirdars* with Pakistan, it should not be published or broadcast. It was for the AICC to take appropriate action.

327

You refer to Shri Jai Narain Vyas.[6] As you know, he is an old friend of mine whom I respect. He is at present the President of the Rajasthan Pradesh Congress Committee, and the choice of Congress candidates for Rajasthan was made in consultation with him and with his approval.

I am sure that you will not say anything unworthy of me or anyone else.

Yours sincerely,
Jawaharlal Nehru

6. Lakshman Singh observed that it was a great pity that the services of a "fair-minded man" like Jainarain Vyas, a former Chief Minister of Rajasthan, were lost "through the intrigues of the present ministry."

32. To Shriman Narayan[1]

New Delhi,
February 16, 1957

My dear Shriman,
Your letter of the 16th February.[2]

I think that it would be desirable for Sucheta Kripalani to issue a brief statement.[3] It does not matter who has spread it, but others have heard about it

1. From, *Letters from Gandhi, Nehru and Vinoba*, Shriman Narayan, pp. 76-77.
2. Shriman Narayan admitted that without Nehru's intervention it would have been impossible to get Manmohini Sehgal to withdraw from the contest in New Delhi. Mrs Sehgal had released to the press a statement to this effect on 15 February, but Shriman Narayan expressed his displeasure over her adding a sentence to the already agreed upon press release without informing him. Narayan met both Mrs Sehgal and her co-workers to convince them of the "desirability of her withdrawal" from the contest and assured them that disciplinary action taken against them would be withdrawn.
3. Shriman Narayan had told Sucheta Kripalani that it was "in her own interest" to issue a statement about the alleged offer of a ministership to her. Mrs Kripalani expressed a desire to meet Nehru before she did so and added that "only a few persons who were interested in Mrs Sehgal's candidature" had spread such a rumour.

and they asked me.[4] In fact, I have written even to Mehr Chand Khanna telling him that this is false.

I do not know when I can see Sucheta as I am completely occupied tomorrow and day after tomorrow morning I go away.

I understand that you have been asking Bakhshi Ghulam Mohammed to do some election touring in India. D.P. Dhar[5] came to see me today and mentioned this and asked what my advice was. I told him to convey to Bakhshi Sahib that his first duty was in Kashmir and he must not allow anything to come in the way of that. If, however, he felt he could go away for a short time, then he might visit Bombay and Calcutta and no other place. It is quite wrong to take him away from Kashmir at this moment. He wanted me to tell you about this, so I am mentioning it.

Yours sincerely,
Jawaharlal Nehru

4. Shriman Narayan informed Nehru that Mangal Dass, who had sent the telegram regarding Sucheta Kripalani was a Jana Sangh worker and ran "some kind of bogus Delhi Refugees organization."
5. Deputy Home Minister, Jammu and Kashmir Government.

33. To Sucheta Kripalani[1]

New Delhi,
February 17, 1957

My dear Sucheta,

Your letter of the 17th February.

Perhaps it will be enough if, in the course of some speech that you deliver at Delhi, you refer to this rumour that some people have spread and deny it.[2] In that case, you need not issue a statement to the press. This is a simple way of dealing with this.

Yours sincerely,
Jawaharlal Nehru

1. JN Collectcion.
2. See *ante*, pp. 324-325 and the preceding item.

34. To Abul Kalam Azad[1]

Camp: Anand Bhawan,
Allahabad,
February 20, 1957

My dear Maulana,

You will remember my suggesting to you that it would be desirable for you to pay a visit to Gurgaon. I hope that you have got this in mind and propose to go there fairly soon. I suggested this not because it was necessary for you to go and seek votes for your election, but because I felt that it would be right and necessary for you to show to the people there that you are interested in them. It was more

1. JN Collection.

of an act of courtesy than anything else. It would be in keeping with democratic procedure.

I have visited Allahabad twice during the last two weeks,[2] although there is no doubt about my election. Indeed there is no real opposing candidate. There are three persons standing against me, but none of them has the least strength. It was thus not necessary for me from the point of view getting votes to come here. As a matter of fact, I have visited every *tehsil* of this huge constituency. One small part is left out and I hope to visit it during the third visit. The whole object of these visits has been not only to show this courtesy to the people here who are my voters, but also to gain some touch with them, so that they may not feel that I am an outsider not caring for them. I think that one of the chief virtues of these big elections is for this contact to be established between the candidate and his electors. The voters feel happy that they are treated in this way and that we care for them.

It is for this reason that I had begged of you to visit Gurgaon, so that people may not say that you do not care for the voters there. I have no doubt that you will be easily elected, but I should like this friendly feeling between you and your voters.

I propose to address a meeting in Gurgaon on the 28th of February in the afternoon.

Yours affectionately,
Jawaharlal

2. On 6 February and again on 20 February.

KASHMIR

1. Cable to V.K. Krishna Menon [1]

Your telegrams 542[2] and 544[3] of December 28th. I agree that it is not possible for you to come to Delhi in the circumstances and you will have to go back via London to New York. Chou En-lai is arriving here tomorrow, visiting Bhakra-Nangal and then going back straight to China. He is not visiting Nepal or any other country I am accompanying him to Bhakra-Nangal to have time for talks.

2. You will remember our receiving an aide-memoire from Pakistan about Kashmir in which some questions were put.[4] Copy of this was sent to you to New York.[5] We have sent no reply yet and a reminder has come. I think that some brief reply should go now avoiding commitments. I agree with you that this matter should not be discussed too much with other delegations at this stage.

3. I understand from Patil that Lok Sabha seat is available for you in North Bombay.

1. New Delhi, 29 December 1956. JN Collection.
2. Krishna Menon, who arrived in Cairo on 27 December for talks with President Nasser, cabled to Nehru that "it would have been quite impossible to cover the essential topics and to receive any useful account of Egypt's position (on Suez) from Nasser to leave for Beirut this afternoon to meet you in Delhi before you leave for Bhakra." Thereafter, he decided to return to New York. He felt it was better to utilise the remaining time "to cover the field of essential and urgent questions" regarding Suez with Nasser.
3. Referring to Arthur Lall's meeting with the Soviet Counsellor in New York who had made general queries about Jammu and Kashmir, Krishna Menon wrote: "It is not necessary that we should promote any resolution or allow the impression to get around that we are relying on them even though that may well happen ultimately." Discussions, at this stage, with other delegations in the UN, according to Menon, would "either lead us into the position of discussing compromises or appearing intrasigent," and would come in the way of dealing with the primary issue of aggression by Pakistan in Kashmir.
4. See *Selected Works* (second series), Vol. 35, pp. 328-329, for Nehru's note on talks with the Pakistan High Commissioner on 22 November 1956. On this day, Pakistan handed over the aide-memoire regarding the framing of the new Constitution of Jammu and Kashmir to Nehru.
5. Menon in his reply of 30 December said he had already informed the Commonwealth Secretary M.J. Desai about his preference "for a short courteous acknowledgement" to the Pakistan aide-memoire confirming that nothing had occurred in Jammu and Kashmir that was contrary to the Constitution of India or any international obligation undertaken by India. Menon added that as Pakistan had taken the matter to the UN Security Council, it would be appropriate for India to state that "arguing the matter in different forums does not seem purposeful."

2. Reply to Pakistan[1]

The Government of India have considered the Aide-Memoire presented by the High Commissioner for Pakistan[2] in India on November 22, 1956.

2. The Government of India have since learnt that the Permanent Representative of Pakistan to the UN has, in his letters of the 16th[3] and 26th November,[4] 1956, to the President of the Security Council brought this matter to the notice of the Security Council and asked for action. In view of this reference, the Government of India do not wish to make any detailed comments on the Aide-Memoire.

3. The Government of India would, however, like to make it clear that whatever they have done in regard to Kashmir is not only in accordance with the Constitution of India but also with the Charter of the United Nations and does not, in any way, infringe any agreements entered into by the Government of India. The infringements of the UN Resolutions of August 1948 and January 1949 appertain to the actions of the Government of Pakistan who, for over nine years, have been in unlawful occupation of Indian territory.

4. The process of constitution making in Kashmir began nearly six years ago.[5] The latest decision[6] of the Constituent Assembly of the State of Jammu and Kashmir is a logical development of that process and does not involve any contradiction with what Government of India's representative said in the UN or elsewhere some years ago.[7] It is a development necessitated by changing circumstances and a succession of events which Government of India had pointed out from time to time.

---

1. Aide-Memoire, 31 December 1956. File No. KS-22/56, MHA.
2. Mian Ziauddin.
3. In its first letter Pakistan said that the adoption of a new Constitution by Jammu and Kashmir on 17 November 1956 and its entry into force on 26 January 1957 would nullify the Security Council's resolution of 30 March 1951 and run counter to its objective that Kashmir's accession to India or Pakistan should be decided by a plebiscite under UN auspices. Pakistan wanted India to desist from integrating Jammu and Kashmir into its Union as this step would violate the UN resolutions.
4. The second letter confirmed that the constitution of Jammu and Kashmir had been adopted by the "so-called" Constituent Assembly and urged the President of the Security Council to seek clarifications from India.
5. In 1951.
6. Section 3 of the Constitution of Jammu and Kashmir confirmed the State's accession to India.
7. B.N. Rau informed the UN Security Council on 1 March 1951 that the opinion of the Constituent Assembly would not be binding on the Government of India or prejudice the decision of the Security Council.

3. Cable to V.K. Krishna Menon[1]

Kashmir issue.[2] We have had prolonged discussion at full meeting of Foreign Affairs Committee about your proposal to write to Security Council to consider our complaint.[3] As I have informed you, my immediate reaction to this was in favour of your proposal.[4] Also we have all felt that since you are dealing with the case and are acquainted with Security Council procedures your opinion must be given every weight.

2. Nevertheless, almost every member of our Foreign Affairs Committee was very doubtful about advantage to be gained by our writing to Security Council as suggested.[5] Such letter immediately before the Security Council considers Pakistan's complaint will appear to be an artificial step reviving our original complaint with a view to obstruct consideration of Pakistan's complaint and as a narrow legalistic approach. We have often been criticised for trying to avoid dealing with merits by adopting legalistic tactics. This may well create adverse opinion against us not only in Security Council but also elsewhere.

1. New Delhi, 8 January 1957. File No. 14-KU/57, MEA.
2. On 2 January, Pakistan wrote to the President of the Security Council requesting him to convene a meeting of the council at an early date to resume consideration of the Kashmir question, in view of the intention of the Constituent Assembly of Jammu and Kashmir to adopt a new constitution for the state on 26 January 1957.
3. Krishna Menon informed Nehru on 5 January that the Security Council was to meet on 16 January. He added that his purpose of telling the Council to "formally or informally" communicate this date to the Government of India was "not to accept the position that a meeting can be unilaterally fixed." According to Krishna Menon, the meeting of the Security Council, having been called by Pakistan, placed India on the defensive. Therefore, he suggested that India should write to the Security Council for a meeting to consider India's complaint. He said: "...it is strongly felt that we would make a bad error if we do not submit such a letter."
4. On 7 January 1957, Nehru approved Krishna Menon's suggestion, adding that he had consulted the Prime Minister of Jammu and Kashmir State, Bakhshi Ghulam Mohammad, on the issue also.
5. The draft letter sent by Menon for Nehru's approval dealt with "Pakistan's acts of aggression" in Jammu and Kashmir as first elaborated in India's complaint of 1 January 1948. India's basic contention was that Pakistan's forces had illegally occupied a part of Jammu and Kashmir. Therefore, the letter stated, that India had "hitherto engaged in discussions in the hope that evacuation of their territory would take place" and since this had not occurred in the last nine years it was "constrained to ask the Security Council to call a meeting and direct Pakistan to bring an end to their invasion and desist from further acts and threats of aggression against India."

3. The arguments you have used are valid and should be fully utilised. The question is whether this should be done by way of independent letter or in dealing with Pakistan's complaint. While it is true that procedurally it is better to be positive rather than on the defensive, psychologically this may have reactions against us and our attitude might be considered undignified and petty. It would not be in keeping with broad attitude taken up by us during last few years. In our attempt to gain procedural advantage we might well lose a measure of goodwill.[6] Security Council being driven into a corner might react in a way harmful to us.

4. By our formally reviving our old complaint by letter we shall be compelling Security Council to treat this matter de novo and possibly take some intermediate steps of enquiry which will lead again to uncertainty and frustration in Kashmir.

5. It is true that this may happen even on Pakistan's complaint, but chances are less. If both sides present their complaints, then Security Council must come to decisions which will be based more on political considerations than legal.

6. For the last two or three years our general attitude has been that no step should be taken to create upsets in Kashmir. This has been widely appreciated. But if we ourselves formally insist on whole matter being taken up afresh, then our argument about upsets does not hold, and other considerations will apply.

7. Even if we do not send proposed letter, our full case, including Pakistan's original aggression and subsequent activities, should certainly be presented to Security Council. It might even be desirable, should you approve of this, to give this case in writing when Security Council considers Pakistan's complaint. But that is for you to decide.

8. I have indicated briefly some points raised during our discussions. There were many other aspects also which were considered. In view of strong opinion of all our colleagues here, I would suggest to you not to send proposed consideration of all you have written.

---

6. Replying to Nehru on 13 January, Krishna Menon wrote: "I must mention that there is no goodwill for us on the Kashmir issue so that there should be no complaint from any of your colleagues afterwards that I dissipated the goodwill. It is the other way round."

4. The Game Plan in the UN[1]

The following message was received at 7.30 a.m. on Tuesday, 15th January 1957 (today) by telephone from PM for SG[2]:

I have received by telephone various messages from Krishna Menon about Kashmir which you must have seen. There is some mutilation, but the general argument is quite clear.[3] Krishna Menon has studied every aspect of the case thoroughly and I agree with his broad approach. In fact there appears to be no other approach open to us at present.[4] We should, therefore, inform him of our general agreement and leave details to him.

You should consult Cabinet members of Foreign Affairs Committee, more especially Maulana Saheb and Pantji, and then send message to Krishna Menon of our general agreement with his approach.

I agree also that you should see UK, USA and other Heads of Missions concerned and explain our position briefly but firmly to them.[5]

1. Camp: Kolkata, 15 January 1957. JN Collection. The message was received by N.K. Seshan, a member of Nehru's personal staff.
2. N.R. Pillai.
3. In his cable of 13 January, Krishna Menon noted that India's efforts had thus far been directed towards "obtaining the vacation of aggression" by Pakistan in Jammu and Kashmir and added that these efforts "were not for the purpose of testing the validity of the accession or for determination of sovereignty of the territory." Therefore, he felt that India should take the position in the UN that the accession of Jammu and Kashmir "is complete and final." Referring to India's "plebiscite involvements", he emphasised that "whatever we may have said yesterday has only validity in that context." He contended that "it would be a political error" to offer any proposals. Any such step, warned Menon, would lay India open to charges of breaches of promises and commitments.
4. Krishna Menon said he had "thin hopes" of India winning this case and expected that the matter would get "talked out" in the UN.
5. Krishna Menon suggested this owing to Nehru's frequent absence from Delhi for conducting the general elections.

339

You might also inform Krishna Menon that we have received many reports of possible trouble by Pakistan. We are vigilant and have taken such precautions as are possible in existing circumstances.[6]

6. In his second cable on 13 January, Krishna Menon spoke of rumours that Pakistan contemplated direct intervention in Kashmir, in addition to her Security Council initiative. Direct action "synchronised with the proclamation of the Kashmir Constitution on 26 January, may lead to a disturbed situation" and eventual UN intervention, warned Menon. Given the "whispers" in the UN about the superior air force of Pakistan, Krishna Menon felt the time had come for India to assess her relative air strength and capacity. He stated: "Kashmir would be a frontier for long and irrespective of whatever impression you have carried the air strength of Pakistan will see augmentation." He doubted the US would exercise its restraining influence on Pakistan.

5. To Bakhshi Ghulam Mohammad[1]

New Delhi,
January 17, 1957

My dear Bakhshi,
Your letter of January 16th.

Krishna Menon is having a very difficult time in the Security Council. Practically everybody there is against us except the representative of the Soviet Union.[2] In particular, much play is made of something happening on the 26th January, which must be stopped. As far as I understand, nothing dramatic is going to happen. The Constitution has been passed, and it just comes into effect on that day. I would suggest that you might not have any elaborate ceremonial just at this moment.

1. JN Collection.
2. Arkady A. Sobelov.

Because of all this also I think I better not send you any message on this occasion.

I have also received your letter giving me population figures of Jammu and Kashmir.

Yours sincerely,
Jawaharlal Nehru

6. Cable to V.K. Krishna Menon [1]

Your telegram 64 January 16.[2] As many errors in transmission we are waiting for corrections.

As far as we can find out, Noon's references to statements by me all relate to certain messages sent by me to Liaquat Ali Khan[3] within the first ten days or so of invasion of Kashmir in 1947.[4] Full texts of telegrams sent by me then are given in White Paper on Jammu and Kashmir issued by our Government.[5] During those days we had no knowledge of part that Pakistan Army was playing in this invasion except that it was obviously helping the raiders. It was later in November

1. New Delhi, 18 January 1957. File No. 14-KU/57, MEA.
2. The cable referred to Pakistan's first speech at the opening of the Kashmir debate in the Security Council on 16 January 1957. In the opinion of Krishna Menon, "Pakistan feels assured of support of all except Russia who would vote against any resolution which does not have our approval." He stated that the Indian delegation had privately let it be known that if support for India came only from the Soviet Union "it would not be of our desire or our making."
3. Prime Minister of Pakistan, 1947-51.
4. According to Krishna Menon, Pakistan's foreign minister Feroz Khan Noon referred in his opening speech at the Security Council "to matters which did not come in Security Council proceeding but purport to have been said between Prime Ministers." Krishna Menon also reported that some of the statements by Noon were "inaccurate in regard to the Kashmir Constitution." He said he had gathered from US sources that Noon's suggestion of sending a UN force to Kashmir "has much support in the Council."
5. Refers to White Paper on Jammu and Kashmir, Government of India, 1949.

that we came to know of presence of Pakistan Army itself in Kashmir because our troops came in contact with them there.

You will notice that at that time I had suggested to Pakistan to make a joint request to UN to undertake a plebiscite in Kashmir. Pakistan did not accept this and in fact continued its aggression for more than a year subsequently, that is throughout 1948.

We went to Security Council to avoid all out war with Pakistan. Later, fact of Pakistan's aggression came out clearly and military situation in Kashmir State began to be unfavourable to them. Resolution of UN Commission of August 13, 1948 was agreed to by India subject to clarifications made by us to the Commission in my letter dated 20th August, 1948.[6] Pakistan did not agree to this Resolution and continued its aggression. Owing to further deterioration in military situation from Pakistan's point of view, they agreed to UN Commission's Resolution of January 5 which supplemented August 13 Resolution.

Further correspondence between Prime Ministers of India and Pakistan from July 1953 to October 1954 including Joint Communique of August 1953 is given fully in second White Paper with you.[7]

6. See *Selected Works* (second series), Vol. 7, pp. 301-304.
7. Refers to *Kashmir: Meetings between Prime Ministers of India and Pakistan (July 1953-October 1954), White Paper*, Ministry of External Affairs, Government of India.

7. Cable to V.K. Krishna Menon[1]

Your telegram 66 January 17th.[2]

I have already informed you about paragraph 1.[3]

You can refer to the fact of the US supplying considerable quantities of arms to Pakistan. This fact had added to our difficulties and apprehensions.

Pakistan Radio announces that Shaikh Abdullah has written to Security Council.[4] You have also referred to some communication from Abdullah. Is this the letter which he wrote to President of Constituent Assembly to which Sadiq replied[5] or is this some other message? No communication from Abdullah has passed through normal channels.

1. New Delhi, 19 January 1957. File No. 14-KU/57, MEA.
2. This cable carried reports from two newspapers containing extracts from Nehru's public speech in Kolkata on 16 January in which he criticised US arms aid to Pakistan. See *ante*, pp. 25-43 for Nehru's speech.
3. Nehru cabled to Krishna Menon on 18 January asking him to quote from his public speech. He added: "There is no doubt that Pakistan leaders told both Soviet and Chinese leaders that arms received by them from US were intended to strengthen themselves in the context of India ... while saying something entirely different to the US," i.e., that they needed arms to defend themselves against possible communist intervention.
4. On 25 January the Pakistan High Commission in London released the text of a letter purported to have been written by Shaikh Abdullah. This letter denounced the Jammu and Kashmir Constituent Assembly's ratification of the State's accession to India as a "fraud upon the people, a betrayal of their right to self-determination and a gross breach of international commitments." The letter is also said to have declared that only a free plebiscite could end the agony of the people of Kashmir and eliminate a grave danger to peace.
5. See *Selected Works* (second series), Vol. 35, p. 327. G.M. Sadiq was President of the Jammu and Kashmir Constituent Assembly.

8. Shaikh Abdullah's Letter[1]

I enclose a copy of a letter I have received from Mridula Sarabhai.[2] I am not sending any answer to it.

There is reference in this letter to *The New York Times* of the 15th January. Please try to find out from this number of *The New York Times* what this is. I suppose you have received a copy of it. If not, perhaps you could get one from the American Embassy.

Any letter from Shaikh Abdullah[3] would normally pass through the hands of the Kashmir authorities as he is under detention. The Prime Minister of Kashmir has informed me that no such letter has passed through their hands. It also appears that the so-called letter is unsigned. I think we should make full enquiries about this insofar as we can.

In my telegram to Shri Krishna Menon, I referred briefly to this letter and asked him to tell us what it is. After our enquiries have been made, you might send him such information as may be necessary.

1. Note to the Secretary General, MEA, 19 January 1957. File No. KS-43/57, MHA.
2. Mridula Sarabhai, a close associate of Mahatma Gandhi and at this time a supporter of Shaikh Abdullah, claimed that Abdullah's letter to the Security Council was "fictitious" and added that the contents were really abstracts from his correspondence with either G.M. Sadiq or P. Subbarayan. She alleged that "some sort of document" had been acquired from local state sources, and added that she would counter the allegation about Abdullah's letter because "every effort of his has been distortedly used and given publicity to by the press in India." To this end she sought Nehru's permission to correspond with Abdullah.
3. Leader of the National Conference and a former Prime Minister of Jammu and Kashmir.

9. Cable to V.K. Krishna Menon[1]

I met Malcolm MacDonald[2] today and spoke to him about Kashmir. He expressed his concern and at the same time pointed out the difficulties and complexities of the case. He suggested that you might keep in touch with UK Delegation as well as others so that they might be kept informed of our point of view. Pakistan was carrying on insistent propaganda with other delegations in UN. While we cannot follow their tactics, we should keep in touch with other delegations.

2. I shall be seeing US Charge'[3] soon.

3. While very little can be expected from UK or USA, it appears desirable to maintain contacts with them and keep them informed.

4. Following information supplied by Kashmir Government:

At time of partition State was presumed to become independent and choice for accession to either of the two Dominions rested with Ruler. In August 1947 Ruler entered into Standstill Agreement with Pakistan. Pakistan violated this by withholding essential supplies and sealing borders, later committed aggression. After accession of State to India, Ruler in March 1948 installed in office a popular Interim Government and declared his determination to establish a fully democratic constitution to be framed by an Assembly based on adult suffrage. Government of India, on their part, reciprocated by providing a special status to the State under Article 370 of Constitution of India which envisages convening of a Constituent Assembly for the purpose of framing the Constitution of State. This Article was framed in consultation with representatives of the State including Shaikh Abdullah and Afzal Beg.[4]

Owing to military operations continuing and other discussions, there was delay in convening Constituent Assembly. Ultimately elections held in August-September 1951 and Assembly came into being on 31st October 1951. Tasks Assembly set itself were:

(a) to devise Constitution for future governance of the country;

(b) decision on question of State's accession;

1. New Delhi, 19 January 1957. File No. 14-KU/57, MEA.
2. UK High Commissioner to India.
3. F.P. Bartlett.
4. Founder of the Plebiscite Front in Jammu and Kashmir.

(c) determine future of Royal Dynasty; and

(d) decision on question about compensation to be paid to landowners whose lands have been taken over under land reforms.

During past years decision taken on some of these matters progressively. Final decisions were taken on 17th November 1956 and most provisions of Constitution came into force then. Remaining provisions which will come into force on the 26th January relate to internal democratic set up, such as responsibility of executive to legislature, composition of legislature and elections based on adult suffrage, independent judiciary, a Public Service Commission and a statutory machinery for holding elections.

Thus any postponement of these provisions would only delay functioning of internal democratic structure of State.

Constituent Assembly has finished its work. It is meeting on 25th evening for some formal valedictory speeches and will automatically dissolve itself at midnight of 25th January.

In regard to question of accession, Constituent Assembly's decision which came into force on 17th November 1956, was only restatement of the position as it existed.

It is worthwhile noting that in response to a demand from political parties of "Azad Kashmir", Ministry of Kashmir Affairs of Pakistan decided to establish responsible Government through an elected Legislature in that territory. Justice Din Mohammad[5] was appointed primarily to prepare such a constitutional arrangement, but no progress was made.

Refugees: Provision has been made by law to accept refugees coming back to the State who will then be deemed citizens of India. Of the large number of persons who were uprooted by Pakistan's aggression, there has been a resettlement of nearly 450,000 Muslim refugees in the areas of Poonch, Mendhar, Rajouri, Darhal, Budhil and Nowshera and they have been restored to their possessions. Adequate financial grants and loans were given to them for this purpose. Similarly over 1,16,000 Hindu refugees uprooted from Pakistan occupied Kashmir have also been completely resettled.

It will thus be seen that the State Government have gone very far in rehabilitating and settling the refugee and other displaced population.

Civil Liberties: Under old hereditary Ruler there was practically no civil liberties in State. These have been progressively enlarged and are now more or less in line with civil liberties guaranteed by the Indian Constitution.

5. (b. 1886); practised law at the Lahore High Court, 1916-33; Judge, Lahore High Court, 1933-47; member, Indian Delimitation Commission, 1935-36; served in the Radcliffe Boundary Commission, 1947.

In regard to Preventive Detention Law, person affected has a right to make representation against order and to be heard by Advisory Tribunal consisting of persons eligible for appointment as High Court Judges. At present, altogether 49 persons are detained throughout the State under various provisions of the Preventive Detention Act. All of these have made or can make representations to tribunals whose advice is acted upon by State Government.

Previous to 1953 there were 15 daily and weekly newspapers in the State. Since then, this number has increased to 48, including seven monthlies.

10. Cable to V.K. Krishna Menon[1]

I saw Bartlett,[2] American Chargé today. He told me after his talks with Pillai and Desai he had kept State Department informed of our viewpoint. Yesterday he saw Sadiq, President, Constituent Assembly and as results of his talks with him informed Washington that nothing special was going to happen on 26th January.

He gave me message from State Department that they were anxious not to do anything in regard to Kashmir matter which would impair US-India relations. They were not yet clear in their minds what course to adopt and would like to hear both sides. According to their policy, they wanted to support UN and its decisions. They had instructed their delegation in UN to keep in close touch with you.

He also said that State Department, while realising that our views were against recently announced Eisenhower policy for Middle East,[3] had appreciated that our comments had been restrained.

1. New Delhi, 19 January 1957. File No. 14-KU/57, MEA.
2. F.P. Bartlett; US diplomat; First Secretary and Consul of the Legation in Vietnam until September 1952; Chief of the Mutual Security Agency Mission at Saigon, September 1952-July 1953; detailed to the US National War College, July 1953-June 1954; Counsellor for Economic Affairs, New Delhi, 1954-58; Director of the Office of South Asian Affairs, State Department; 1958-60.
3. The Eisenhower Plan, placed before the US Congress on 5 January 1957, authorized the US President to extend economic and military aid to any country in West Asia that sought aid "against armed aggression from any country controlled by international communism."

11. Cable to V.K. Krishna Menon[1]

Your telegram 82 January 22nd.[2] I understand that Mridula sent identical telegram to you, President Security Council[3] and Noon. Further that she is following this up with some kind of letter enclosing her circular letters to members of Parliament, which are pretty bad.

2. I do not think she has any idea of going to New York.[4] She is so unbalanced, confused and unhappy that it is difficult to say what she might do.

3. I have heard that she sent telegram to Shaikh Abdullah in prison telling him that she had denied authenticity of alleged letter for Security Council. To this Shaikh Abdullah replied by cryptic telegram thanking her for her message, whatever that might mean.

4. We are enquiring further into this matter and might send you another message.

1. New Delhi, 23 January 1957. File No. 14-KU/57, MEA.
2. According to Krishna Menon, Feroz Khan Noon, the Foreign Minister of Pakistan, had submitted as annexures to his speech on 16 January a number of letters of Mridula Sarabhai relating to Kashmir. In the meantime, Mridula cabled to Menon that these letters had been taken out of context and were "misrepresentations and distortions" of her views. She requested him to wait for her "representation before taking note of extracts presented by Noon."
3. Carlos P. Romulo of the Philippines was President of the UN Security Council.
4. Krishna Menon said it was not clear as to what Mridula Sarabhai meant by "my representation." He assumed she had plans of visiting New York. He wanted Mridula Sarabhai to send a telegram directly to the Security Council President and say that the letters appended by Noon to his speech "do not represent her views."

12. Cable to V.K. Krishna Menon[1]

Your telegrams 87[2] and 88[3] January 23. Fairly full reports of your statement before Security Council on the first day have appeared in the press here. We have all greatly appreciated your manner of handling this difficult position. I entirely agree with line that you have taken up.[4]

When I was in Washington,[5] I did expect from what Eisenhower told me that US attitude on Kashmir issue might be more reasonable. But lately I felt rather sure that UK's attitude would be bad and USA would line up with them.[6]

1. New Delhi, 24 January 1957. File No. 14-KU/57, MEA.
2. Krishna Menon stressed the necessity of viewing developments "in the context of the world picture." He said: "In Kashmir the issue is not one of resolutions or even Pakistan but of bases and we have to hold on at least to our legal position to thwart that." Menon observed that the British and Americans were still prepared to pretend that the Constituent Assembly and 26 January were the crux of the present situation, even though they knew that their position was untenable.
3. This telegram gave details of the draft resolution on Kashmir jointly prepared by the UK and US. Menon stated: "It treats both parties as equals as though we were both sinners and the usual sanctimonius adjuration to both." He said that the US was "fully in all this" and its stand had little to do with the Security Council "but is concerned with our policy, particularly Suez and also represents an active phase in the new alignment of the US" West Asia.
4. Krishna Menon informed the Security Council that India's approach to the Kashmir problem, since 1 January 1948, had been based on the following considerations, among others: (i) The State had legally acceeded to India. (ii) It was a constituent unit of India and the only authority that could legally separate Jammu and Kashmir from the Union was the Indian parliament. (iii) The territorial integrity of the State was inviolable and Pakistan had committed aggression against the State and therefore it must "vacate that aggression." Menon also said India stood by its commitments under the UNCIP resolutions in the light of its understanding of them and of the explanations and assurances given to it by the UNCIP as regards the provisions of the resolutions.
5. From 14-20 December 1956.
6. Krishna Menon said that since Nehru's US visit all efforts had been made by the Indian delegation to the UN "to be in the good books of the Americans". But he had no reason to believe that "the US attitude towards Pakistan or India has changed one bit." The US, according to Krishna Menon, were looking to the time when there would be trouble in Kashmir and "their great power will be necessary for us to survive, either by offering to restrain Pakistan or coming to our aid."

Nevertheless Dulles's letter[7] and now the draft resolution[8] they have put in are even worse than I expected. I am a little surprised to learn that the Russians may abstain.[9]

Anyhow you should certainly pursue the line you have adopted. There is or can be no question of our changing our broad policies because of pressure tactics from others.

7. John F. Dulles, the US Secretary of State, cabled on 23 January that he and President Eisenhower were "distressed" over the India-Pakistan dispute over Kashmir. He asked Nehru to understand that "as a minimum, we cannot disregard the prior decision of the UN with reference to a plebiscite, unless the parties concerned agree on some other solution." Dulles said the US was engaged with the British in trying to evolve a draft resolution, "which we hope will be considered moderate and generally acceptable."
8. The draft resolution shown to Krishna Menon on the night of 23 January reiterated the earlier UN resolutions and stated that any action that the Constituent Assembly of Jammu and Kashmir "may have taken or might attempt to take" to determine the future shape of the state "would not constitute a disposition of the state in accordance with the principle of a plebiscite under UN auspices."
9. Menon wrote in his first cable that the Soviet Union would abstain from voting "because they fear that the US would promote a move to have the matter referred to the Assembly if they exercised their veto. Menon said he had not advised the Soviet representatives how to vote.

13. To N.C. Chatterjee[1]

New Delhi,
January 26, 1957

My dear Shri Chatterjee,[2]

Thank you for your telegram about Kashmir. I quite appreciate the significance of the Security Council resolution.[3] But I do not think that an immediate summoning of Parliament at this stage would be helpful. Thus far, the decision of the Security Council, though a bad one for India, is really rather general and a kind of preliminary to a further consideration of this problem. Probably this further discussion will take place within a week or two.

Yours sincerely,
Jawaharlal Nehru

---

1. JN Collection.
2. Hindu Mahasabha member of the Lok Sabha from Hooghly, West Bengal.
3. The Security Council passed a resolution on 24 January 1957 on Kashmir by ten votes to nil, with the Soviet Union abstaining. This resolution, while recalling the earlier UN and UNCIP resolutionsm declared that any action that the Jammu and Kashmir Assembly "may have taken or might attempt to take to determine the future shape and affiliation of the state" would not constitute a disposition of the state in accordance with the principle of a "free and impartial" plebiscite that might be conducted under the auspices of the UN.

14. Cable to V.K. Krishna Menon [1]

Your telegram 97 January 26.

I entirely appreciate what you say. Indeed even before your telegram came, I came to that conclusion about Soviet abstention. [2] I do not think there is any misapprehension here on this subject. You need not bother about the Rosenthal's despatches. [3]

I had already previously asked Secretary General to see UK and US and Australian representatives. [4]

Today, 26th January passed off well both in Jammu and in Srinagar and other parts of Kashmir. [5] The day was celebrated with a good deal of fervour. In Srinagar weather was bad and it was snowing. Nevertheless very large meeting was held to celebrate the occasion and processions were taken out. There were no counter-demonstrations. In fact, it is said that the Security Council Resolution rather added to the vigour of the celebrations.

News from various centres in Pakistan is of hartals and demonstrations before Indian High Commission Offices. [6]

1. New Delhi, 26 January 1957. File No. 14-KU/57, MEA.
2. Krishna Menon believed that the Soviet Union would have voted against the Security Council Resolution of 24 January, if India had specifically asked them to do so. Menon stated: "We did not give them advice as we did not want at this stage to raise the cry of veto." V.V. Kuznetsov, the deputy foreign minister of the Soviet Union, told Krishna Menon that he was disturbed that there were "some surprises" in India at their abstention. The Soviet official also told Krishna Menon that they would vote against any resolution that came up again, if India so wished.
3. Krishna Menon noted that A.M. Rosenthal, the correspondent of *The New York Times* in India was exploiting the importance being attached in New Delhi to the Soviet Union's abstention. Menon said it was "best to show no concern whatsoever about the Soviet vote and not to attach any importance to their abstention in any public demeanour."
4. See *ante*, p. 339.
5. On this day the Constitution of Jammu and Kashmir was adopted.
6. See *ante*, p. 83.

352

15. The Soviet Abstention [1]

The Soviet Ambassador[2] came to see me today with some Soviet engineers to discuss the question of building up a heavy industry plant in India. After that he stayed on and told me that he had just received a message from Moscow explaining their abstention from voting on the Kashmir question in the Security Council.

2. He told me that it was the intention of the Soviet representative to vote against the resolution put forward. He gave me some dates. Later Arthur Lall[3] saw the Soviet representative and discussed the matter with him and suggested that, in view of all the circumstances, it might be better for the Soviet to abstain from voting. Later again the question arose whether the Soviet representative might move an amendment to the Five Power resolution. This amendment was to relate to the last sentence about the matter being kept pending. After discussion however it was decided not to move the amendment.

3. The reason for abstention, as suggested by Arthur Lall, was that in the case of voting against the resolution the matter would go to the General Assembly of the UN and might be passed there even by a two-third majority.

4. This message from the Soviet Government, meant to be conveyed to us, indicates their anxiety that we should not feel that they had done anything against our wishes in this matter and that they would like to support us fully on the Kashmir issue.

5. I am noting this down for record.

---

1. Note to the Secretary General, Foreign Secretary and Commonwealth Secretary, MEA, 29 January 1957. JN Collection.
2. Mikhail Menshikov.
3. Member of the Indian delegation to the UN, 1954-59.

16. To Bakhshi Ghulam Mohammad [1]

New Delhi,
January 29, 1957

My dear Bakhshi,

Thank you for your two letters of January 29.

We shall certainly convey to Krishna Menon your appreciation of the way he presented the Kashmir case in the Security Council.[2] We have not yet received the full text of his speech. We shall try to send you a copy of it.

I am very glad that Republic Day was celebrated adequately both in Srinagar and Jammu.

I am leaving Delhi on the 31st January morning on an election tour. I shall be touring a good deal in the month of February. This is somewhat inconvenient as we do not know when the Kashmir matter might come up again before the Security Council. But I shall keep in touch.

Yours sincerely,
Jawaharlal Nehru

1. JN Collection.
2. Bakhshi Ghulam Mohammad wanted Nehru to convey to Krishna Menon his "sincere thanks" for his "excellent performance" at the UN. He said that India's position had been stated categorically and unequivocally. He observed that the "issues have been clinched" by Krishna Menon's firm stand adding that he "touched comprehensively all aspects of the question."

17. Cable to V.K. Krishna Menon[1]

I am leaving Delhi for Madras and other places on 31st morning returning 3rd afternoon. Leaving again on 6th, returning 8th. I shall be away from Delhi frequently for election work during February.

2. Please let us know your estimate of when Kashmir matter coming up again before Security Council, how long it will take and what probable developments are likely to take place.

3. In Pakistan there has been an orgy of hatred against India. To some extent this has taken place also in Iraq, Iran and Turkey. Even in England our Republic Day celebrations were not attended this year by many diplomats and members of government even after accepting invitations. We are informed that public opinion in England is hostile to us since Security Council resolution. Even Labour friends are rather cool.[2]

4. Our advice is sought by our various Missions as to what line they should adopt. I should like to have your suggestions about this.[3]

5. In view of developments in Security Council, what is your programme likely to be about return to India?

1. New Delhi, 29 January 1957. JN Collection.
2. Vijayalakshmi Pandit, India's High Commissioner to the UK, cabled to Nehru on 29 January to this effect. She added: "It seems obvious that we are being punished for our stand on Suez."
3. Krishna Menon replied on 30 January that foreign missions should only state that India had no intention of going back on any international commitments, but point out that its commitments to a plebiscite were provisional and based upon conditions precedent. He noted that India's representatives must explain "with great intensiveness" that the action now proposed by Pakistan was against the UN Charter. Krishna Menon added that India was being put in the position of an aggressor "while we are the aggressed." He added that if "we are abjured to respect one resolution of the UN then all resolutions should have been obeyed."

18. Cable to V.K. Krishna Menon[1]

I have just received your telegram 107 January 29.[2] We have not yet received full report of your statement in Security Council on Kashmir. UN Information Centre here also cannot supply it as it was much mutilated in transmission. We have thus far only seen reports in press which, though fairly long, are still very limited and sketchy in parts. Press and public opinion here have entirely supported line taken up by you and we wholly agree with it.

You should certainly point out our great difficulty in participating in proceedings during period of general elections here which are on a vast scale and in which all Ministers, including you, are taking part.[3] But perhaps it would be better not to make too categorical a statement about this. Also this might induce Pakistan to insist on decision before date you mention.

I agree with what you say in paragraph 6 of your telegram.[4] Legal aspect cannot be ignored but even more important aspects are political and factual and, more especially, consequences of any action which might lead not only to great upsets in Kashmir but also worsening of Indo-Pakistan relations and possibly leading to conflict.

Tomorrow evening I am speaking at public meeting in Madras in English.[5] There I shall briefly but firmly refer to some of these aspects and more particularly to our full agreement with line you have taken up.

This evening Foreign Affairs Committee is meeting. I shall telegraph to you later again.

---

1. New Delhi, 30 January 1957. File No. 14-KU/57, MEA.
2. Krishna Menon sought Nehru's reactions to his marathon speech in the UN Security Council on 23/24 January and asked "whether yourself or colleagues and the country generally are satisfied about the position taken..."
3. Krishna Menon said that the Security Council had been informed that India was not in a position to depute any one to participate in the proceedings in New York between 15 February and 1 April 1957 because of the general elections.
4. Krishna Menon observed that the bulk of his speech was not legal, but political, factual and a rebuttal of allegations against India and based on Security Council or UNCIP material. He termed as "propaganda" the criticism that India was taking "legal positions" on Jammu and Kashmir. It was necessary to do so "because the present initiative by Pakistan is in regard to the allegation that changes are illegally brought about by us by the Constituent Assembly procedure," observed Menon.
5. See *ante*, pp. 51-71.

19. Cable to K.P.S. Menon[1]

Your telegram 50 January 29.[2] You can certainly tell Khrushchev that we have understood and appreciate attitude of Soviet representative in Security Council on Kashmir issue. When first news came to me of possibility of Soviet abstention on resolution I was a little surprised and enquired about it.[3] Further information coming to me made the position clear. I am grateful to Soviet Government for their appreciation of India's attitude and their help in this matter.

1. New Delhi, 30 January 1957. JN Collection.
2. Nikita Khrushchev, First Secretary of the Communist Party of the Soviet Union, asked K.P.S. Menon, India's Ambassador in Moscow, to "specially" inform Nehru that the Soviet Representative in the UN had abstained from voting on the 24 January resolution on the "advice" of Arthur Lall.
3. Khrushchev's information was that Nehru was displeased at the Soviet abstention. Menon therefore asked if he could "reassure" Khrushchev that the Soviet action had not "lent itself to any misunderstanding" on Nehru's part.

20. Cable to V.K. Krishna Menon[1]

Khrushchev has sent message to me through K.P.S. Menon saying that Russian representative had been instructed to vote against resolution on Kashmir in Security Council. It was on advice of our people that he abstained.

2. I have replied to say that I quite understand this and have expressed my appreciation of Soviet help in this matter.

3. Following appreciation of military situation for your personal information. About three years ago we had repeatedly stated that in case of further aggression by Pakistan in Kashmir, this will be considered as aggression on India and we shall be entitled to consider it as Pakistan's war against India. I believe this declaration helped in preventing further aggression. At that time Pakistan was militarily much weaker than India. Position today is different, and Pakistan has gradually crept up to parity with sometimes better and later weapons and aircraft.

4. Question however is how far they can use these weapons. Our Military Advisers are of opinion that they will require six months more to be able to use them to some extent and twelve months more to use them most effectively.

5. Chances of military operations in Kashmir or against India appear very unlikely in near future. But there is always possibility of so-called satyagraha by pushing in large numbers of apparently unarmed people or petty raids.[2] We have information that tribal people are being collected and trained as also groups in Azad Kashmir.

6. Azad Kashmir army has been increased to 35 battalions with some artillery. Presumably they are well armed. They have also three airfields in Azad Kashmir, Kotli, Muzaffarabad and Gilgit.

7. It is conceivable that Pakistan might say that it is not taking any military action but cannot restrain Azad forces from entering Kashmir. It is always possible, especially after snows melt in early summer, for these forces to penetrate in some places in northern sector which is mountainous and difficult to patrol all over. In southern sector climate is always favourable for this, but international boundary is quite near and may be crossed.

8. Tribal people can also be pushed in various places. All this can cause some embarrassment to us though from a military point of view this may not be serious. Question may well arise as to what steps we should take to meet this menace.

1. New Delhi, 30 January 1957. File No. 14-KU/57, MEA.
2. See *Selected Works* (second series), Vol. 30, pp. 338-340.

Should we consider this as attack on India as a whole or to be dealt with locally? Any action we may take elsewhere would then be declared by Pakistan to be Indian aggression justifying their full use of American arms and equipment.

9. Our instructions to Army are that while any local aggression must immediately be resisted, no widespread action should be taken without our full consideration.

10. Large-scale arming of Pakistan forces with armour and aircraft has made great difference to military position. In about six months time our new supplies of armour and aircraft are likely to reach us. This will equalise matters somewhat.

11. American Ambassador[3] told us last year that they would keep us informed of US aid given to Pakistan. Some information was given then. No further information given since then although considerable quantities of military equipment supplied to Pakistan.

12. We do not expect any serious military development in near future, but Pakistan people have been so roused up by campaign of hatred and misrepresentation that it will be difficult for Pakistan to lie low and do nothing at all.

3. John Sherman Cooper was the US Ambassador to India till August 1956.

21. Cable to V.K. Krishna Menon [1]

I returned to Delhi this afternoon and we had meeting of Foreign Affairs Committee. Unfortunately, most members are away touring. Maulana Azad was present, also fortunately Bakhshi. Some other members will be returning to Delhi within two days, and we shall confer with them also. Meanwhile, we gave careful consideration to your telegram 110 of January 30th. [2]

2. We realise fully the complexities and difficulties of the situation and how world opinion, chiefly for political reasons and, to some extent, because of ignorance of basic facts of long story of Kashmir, is ranged against us. We have to face this situation as best we can, without giving in on any vital point.

3. As regards legal point that you have raised and the resolution proposed [3] being illegal, you can certainly point this out, but we are all of opinion that any reference of legal issue under article thirty-six to International Court would be unwise and would entangle us badly. [4] The reference presumably would be mainly on question of accession. This could be countered by saying that whatever legal merits might be, subsequent statements had produced new situation which had to be dealt with. Also, our stress on this legal aspect would lead to conclusion that we were raising legal issues because we were weak on merits and were thus merely prevaricating. But the main thing is that we shall get hopelessly entangled in long procedures, and yet, at the same time, may be tied up with Security Council which may still continue to take some steps.

1. New Delhi, 3 February 1957. File No. 14-KU/57, MEA.
2. Krishna Menon opined that international opinion would always be against India on Kashmir. The West, he added, invariably mentioned the Indian promise to have a plebiscite in Jammu and Kashmir and the inherent right of self-determination of the people of Kashmir. Krishna Menon observed that the Security Council's attitude "had nothing to do with the merits of the question", because they had decided on that even before the debate opened on 16 January 1957. India would have to "grin and bear the position" that "our territory and rights cannot be bartered away," concluded Menon.
3. On 30 January, Krishna Menon cabled that he had secured a copy of the draft resolution circulated by Pakistan. It focussed on two aspects; first, demilitarization of Kashmir and, second, the despatch of a UN force to the region. This force would monitor the demilitarization and ensure the conduct of a plebiscite.
4. Krishna Menon noted that G.S. Pathak, a lawyer and a member of the Indian delegation to the UN, had opined that Pakistan's new proposal was ultra vires of the UN Charter. He sought Nehru's consent to invoke Article 36 of the Charter on Pakistan's proposal.

4. We agree that we should avoid any further commitments. If this question is to be considered afresh, then whole matter must be viewed from the beginning onwards. We have not gone back and have no intention of going back on any international commitments. Those commitments were conditional on certain action being taken by Pakistan. You have already dealt with this in detail. That action was not taken by Pakistan, and much else has happened since then. It is in the context of these subsequent developments as well as present position that the question has to be viewed. It has been and is our desire to have peaceful settlements and relations with Pakistan. Any attempt at settlement which ignores situation as it has developed, will not lead to a settlement but will cause large-scale upsets and much worsening of our relations with Pakistan. It is clear that in view of hatred campaigns, incitement of religious passions, which have already led to vast migrations from East Pakistan, military threats, etc., it would be wholly unreal to think of a plebiscite. Such an approach is likely to lead to large-scale civil strife not only in Kashmir itself but also in Pakistan and India.

5. The course you suggest in paragraph eight[5] would certainly be agreeable to us. We might even go a little further, if necessity arises, and agree to Secretary General being asked to deal with this matter with a view to arriving at a peaceful settlement.[6] If so, he should deal with it in all its aspects. This latter course is not free from difficulty, but in view of all the circumstances, it might be accepted. If Secretary General comes here, we shall of course give him facilities for meeting people.

6. In Moscow, Pakistan Ambassador[7] called on Gromyko[8] and requested Soviet Union mediate between India and Pakistan on basis of compliance of Security Council's old resolutions or alternatively plebiscite under UN supervision with assistance of militia formed out of selected Kashmiris. He did not indicate whether Pakistan would withdraw its troops from occupied part of Kashmir.

---

5. Krishna Menon said the Indian delegation was "endeavouring" to put the "idea into people's heads" that the only resolution that could be passed was that both parties should honour all UN resolutions and seek peaceful ways of resolving difficulties in accordance with the Charter. He however noted that such a move was not likely in the face of pressure from Pakistan. He also posited that if a strong resolution was introduced, the Soviets would veto it.

6. The next day Nehru cabled that both Bakhshi Ghulam Mohammad and G.M. Sadiq were unhappy with the suggestion to invite the UN Secretary General to visit Kashmir. Nehru said he was conveying the wishes of the leaders of Kashmir, who feared that such a move would open out a fresh series of visits and consultations about Kashmir. He wanted to avoid such a development.

7. Akhtar Hussain.

8. Foreign Minister of the Soviet Union.

Gromyko told him that Russian Government's attitude had already been made clear.

7. In public speech[9] in Delhi this evening, apart from repeating our general attitude, I stated that on no account could we agree to foreign forces coming on Indian territory.

9. See *ante*, pp. 72-88.

22. Cable to V.K. Krishna Menon[1]

Malcolm MacDonald has just seen me and conveyed message from his Government that they were anxious if possible to finding solution of Kashmir problem which was agreeable to India and Pakistan. The Council was naturally bound by its previous resolutions. What was our attitude about plebiscite? If all conditions laid down previously were fulfilled could we then envisage plebiscite or do we think that new developments and present conditions rule out plebiscite altogether? MacDonald said that he himself felt that there were considerable risks in having plebiscite which would upset things and he had pointed this out to his Government. If this was our attitude, then it would be desirable to make this clear to Security Council pointing out all these dangers.

Apart from this, he said that some constructive approach on part of India as to what should be done now would be helpful.

I told him that owing to our eagerness to find some way of peaceful settlement we had put forward numerous suggestions in the past. Now these were held up against us and real basis of dispute forgotten or passed over. We did not wish to get entangled any more in such procedures and we had therefore to lay stress on basic facts.

As for plebiscite, I was sure in my mind that any such attempt would lead to very grave consequences. I could not, therefore, think of a plebiscite now or in foreseeable future as a solution. In theory I could not rule it out but in practice it offered no solution to me.

I then suggested that some course of action such as you have mentioned in paragraph 8 of your telegram 110[2] of January 30 might be advisable. He said he would communicate this to his Government.

1. New Delhi, 4 February 1957. File No. 14-KU/57, MEA.
2. See *ante*, p. 361, fn no. 5.

23. Cable to V.K. Krishna Menon[1]

In your telegram 110 of January 30, you said that my telegram 21024[2] had somewhat unnerved you. I do not know what you read into it, but there is no reason for you or for me to be unnerved about anything.[3] I had reported to you information received by us. I am naturally rather unhappy at many people in England who ought to know better suddenly showing their teeth to us, but that cannot affect our thinking or our policy.

1. New Delhi, 4 February 1957. File No. 14-KU/57, MEA.
2. See *ante*, p. 355.
3. Replying the same day, Krishna Menon stated: "I am not affected, much less rattled, by people outside but I tend to get shaken when anything rightly or wrongly gives me the feeling that all is not well on our side."

24. Cable to V.K. Krishna Menon[1]

Kashmir. Our own information from some foreign missions here, which fits in with what you have told us, is that UK is taking lead in supporting Pakistan in Security Council. USA is undecided. Sweden somewhat inclined in our favour.

2. There is rising feeling in India against UK due to general knowledge of UK's attitude in this matter as well as hostile comments in British press. It is only through our influence that we have prevented this feeling taking shape of demonstrations. There have already been large-scale student demonstrations against Pakistan.[2] I have discouraged them.

1. New Delhi, 4 February 1957. File No. 14-KU/57, MEA.
2. On 2 February, students demonstrated in front of the Pakistan High Commission in New Delhi.

3. It seems to me that most countries are now realising dangers of any precipitate step by Security Council hostile to India and beginning to appreciate grave risks involved in it. This point should continue to be pressed home. There is no reason why we should weaken at all in our attitude in regard to Kashmir issue.

25. Cable to V.K. Krishna Menon[1]

Your telegram 137 February 5th. I agree with the line of action you have proposed in paragraphs 7 to 10 of your telegram.[2]

We are not taken in by what Macmillan said.[3] British policy in regard to Kashmir has been aggressive against India throughout this period. This is reflected also in the press there as well as in many individual statements. Practically everyone in England except for Nye Bevan[4] has been attacking India.

Your paragraph 4 is based on a misapprehension.[5] Macmillan and Selwyn Lloyd have been told quite clearly that what you have said represents our

1. New Delhi, 7 February 1957. JN Collection.
2. In view of the Security Council deliberations, Krishna Menon opined that India should take the position that its only commitments were those arising from the 13 August 1948 and 5 January 1949 resolutions, together with the assurances given by the UNCIP. He said he would continue to stress the legality and finality of accession, assert the sovereignty of Jammu and Kashmir, and "rebut" the charge that the Constituent Assembly was a "coup and not legitimate."
3. Harold Macmillan, sworn in as the British Prime Minister on 10 January, told Vijayalakshmi Pandit on 4 February of "his desire" to help solve the Kashmir problem. Macmillan hoped that there was no thought in Nehru's mind that the UK was "using the present situation" to retaliate for India's stand on Suez. He also told Mrs Pandit that Selwyn Lloyd, UK's foreign secretary, was upset by Krishna Menon's "unnecessarily strong attack" in the UN General Assembly on the Suez issue.
4. Aneurin Bevan, British politician and Labour MP.
5. Krishna Menon stated: "I do beg of you to do something which will prevent our Ambassadors sniping at me all the time." He added that Mrs Pandit had a duty as India's representative to point out to Macmillan that India was not "out to attack them and had not done so." Menon felt that India should not take what Macmillan was reported to have said at face value. He said it was necessary for India's representatives to "forget personal animosities" in the interests of the country.

Government's view and that we wish to be friendly with the British and have tried to restrain the strong public feeling in India against the United Kingdom. I had reported to you only what Macmillan said for information, and not the obvious replies.

You have a difficult position to face in the United Nations. So have we in India and elsewhere. I am sure that all of us have to support one another and not to distrust.

You can certainly meet Macmillan on your way back.

26. Cable to Vijayalakshmi Pandit[1]

From all accounts British attitude in UN over Kashmir continues to be as bad as ever in spite of what Macmillan told you. In fact our information is that they are exercising great pressure on United States, Sweden, etc., to side with Pakistan completely even on certain basic matters as well as stationing of UN forces, etc., there. Meanwhile Pakistan's threats about war continue and cannot be considered bluffs. Situation is very serious and responsibility for it must rest largely on UK.

2. Because of this urgency, I have asked Pillai immediately to point all this out to Malcolm MacDonald as a personal message from me.[2] He will be told that we entirely agree with line taken by Krishna Menon which is in full consultation with us and we are going to adhere to it.

1. Camp: Allahabad, 7 February 1957. File No. 14-KU/57, MEA.
2. On the same day, the Secretary General in the Ministry of External Affairs, N.R. Pillai, sent for the UK High Commissioner and explained India's position.

27. Cable to V.K. Krishna Menon[1]

On return to Delhi I have just seen Malcolm MacDonald. Yesterday Pillai had met him and talked to him fully on subject on lines indicated in your telegram of February 7. Pillai spoke to him on my behalf and asked him to convey my message to Macmillan.

2. I have again emphasised what Pillai said to him and dangers of situation in event of Security Council passing any unfortunate resolution. I spoke to him about strong feeling in India on this issue which I have seen for myself during my tours and how we are trying to restrain it. Also of great strain on Indo-British relations and general belief that UK was not only fully supporting Pakistan, but trying to stampede others in Security Council.

3. MacDonald said that he had been receiving messages exchanged between UK Government and their representative in UN[2] regarding Kashmir during the last two weeks. While UK's general attitude may be said to incline towards Pakistan they had been trying to restrain Pakistan not only in regard to the content of the resolution but especially about bellicose statements and threats. He also said that UK Government had felt the weight of the argument that it would not be desirable to proceed with this matter during our elections. He could not commit himself as to what his Government might finally decide, but said that they were anxious that this question should be decided with the consent of parties concerned.

4. I laid stress on growing danger of situation and grave risk of some false step or incident leading to far-reaching consequences.

1. New Delhi, 8 February 1957. File No. 14-KU/57, MEA.
2. Pierson Dixon.

28. Cable to Vijayalakshmi Pandit[1]

Your telegram 0476 February 7.[2] I am sending you separately copy of my reply to Macmillan which MacDonald is forwarding to him. I presume you have received copy from Commonwealth Office of Macmillan's message to me[3] which came today.

My reply to Macmillan states our position briefly but I hope clearly.[4]

My speech in Allahabad was evidently mis-reported.[5] I said nothing about accepting plebiscite. You should make this perfectly clear.

In the course of the past eight years, we have made many suggestions for peaceful settlement. They have all been rejected by Pakistan and meanwhile basic issues are sought to be ignored and we are treated as guilty parties. We do not intend to make any further proposal which is treated as a commitment by us so long as these basic issues are not dealt with and our honour as a country is not vindicated.

At present high passions have been aroused on all sides and it is impossible to consider this question calmly. All that can be done at present is to allow some time to lapse without further commitment of any kind.

We do not accept UK Government's or Pakistan Ambassador's estimate of position in UN, though it is quite possible that some Asian countries might vote against India and some others might abstain.

1. New Delhi, 8 February 1957. File No. 14 -KU/57, MEA.
2. Mrs Pandit said that Douglas-Home, British Secretary of State for Commonwealth Relations, had assured her that "far from exercising any pressure on other delegations or taking a pro-Pakistan attitude themselves UK Government were all along striving to avoid matter being taken to the General Assembly." Douglas-Home opined that the best that could be done was for the Security Council to pass a 'holding' resolution taking particular note of the 24 January resolution and suggesting a report within a period of couple of months.
3. Macmillan assured Nehru that there was no truth in the suggestion that the UK was forcing the pace over Kashmir or giving encouragement to Pakistan to try to secure the passage through the Security Council of a resolution which would be embarrasssing to India, in advance of her general elections. He also "justified" Pakistan's taking back the Kashmir issue to the Security Council.
4. See the next item.
5. See *ante*, pp. 89-105, for Nehru's speech of 6 February 1957.

367

29. Message to Harold Macmillan[1]

I came back to Delhi today from my election tour and met Malcolm MacDonald soon after. In the afternoon he sent me your personal message. I am grateful to you for this message and appreciate your frankness. I am resuming my election tour after another day. I am, however, taking the liberty of sending this reply to you so that there might be no misunderstanding in your mind about our position in regard to the Kashmir issue.

2. I am thankful that you appreciate our difficulty in dealing with this matter while our countrywide election campaigns are in progress. Not only I but practically every Minister is touring in his own as well as other constituencies. It is very difficult to get them to meet together. Elections in India are unlike anywhere else because of the vastness of the country and the colossal number of voters. We have nearly two hundred million voters and the elections are not only for our Parliament but for all our State Assemblies. For both of these there are over 3,500 constituencies.

3. I confess that your message has not made me happy because of the basic assumptions underlying it. These assumptions appear to me to be unrelated to facts and to ignore not only the original cause of this dispute, but also what has happened since then.

4. You refer to the constitutional issue.[2] That constitutional issue is the legal accession of the Jammu and Kashmir State to India. This was subsequently followed by armed aggression by Pakistan on this territory of India. These facts cannot be challenged and govern the entire situation. Throughout the consideration of this problem by the United Nations Commission and other UN representatives, the sovereignty of the Jammu and Kashmir State over the entire territory of the State and the responsibility of the Government of India in regard to defence and other matters have been accepted by the Commission and others and all arrangements proposed were based on this. The resolutions of the Security

---

1. New Delhi, 8 February 1957. File No. 14-KU/57. MEA.
2. The British Prime Minister said the UK Government had announced in the House of Commons in December 1956 that they stood by the existing resolutions and "we indicated that we would support Pakistan on the purely on the constitutional issue." Macmillan said "any further resolution in the Security Council should be formed "with the maximum possible regard to its acceptability to both parties." Macmillan claimed that "support for Pakistan was very general and the result cannot be ascribed to United Kingdom lobbying."

Council dated 13th August 1948 and the 5th January 1949 are the basic resolutions which have to be considered, together with subsequent developments. In these resolutions stress was laid on a new situation being created by the intrusion of Pakistan forces into the Jammu and Kashmir State and the first step indicated was the withdrawal of those forces from Jammu and Kashmir State territory.

5. Subsequent to that every effort was made by us to find a way to a peaceful settlement. But, as you know, these efforts failed and not even that first step mentioned above was taken by Pakistan, which continued to hold and consolidate its position in a large part of the State. All these intervening stages of discussions and proposals have not led to any result. We have to go back to the original position and at the same time consider the great changes that have taken place since then. Our efforts at finding a solution are now treated as final commitments regardless of the basic facts of the situation. You will appreciate that in these circumstances we are quite unable to make any fresh suggestions as these might again be treated as commitments. We feel there can be no just or satisfactory solution of the Kashmir problem unless those basic facts are accepted.

6. I am glad that you do not accept the two-nation theory on which the whole of the Pakistan case is based.

7. The Constituent Assembly of the Jammu and Kashmir State came into being over four years ago.[3] The statements made by us at that time in the Security Council made clear our basic position. We have not resiled from that position at all. The Assembly has been gradually drafting its constitution and giving effect to parts of it during these four years. It is not the Assembly that has brought about the accession of the State to India. That was done in October 1947. The Assembly finalised this constitution in November last. Nothing was going to happen or did indeed happen on the 26th January or later.

8. While we are quite clear about the legal and constitutional position which must govern the consideration of this problem, we have pointed out the practical consequences of any wrong step being taken now. From your message it appears that you consider that India is in the wrong and Pakistan was the aggrieved party and that therefore India must make some kind of a gesture to put itself right. I confess that I am wholly unable to understand this argument which completely ignores the facts of the case. Pakistan has undoubtedly been the aggressor and we have been the aggrieved party. Because of our desire to have peaceful settlements and friendly relations with Pakistan we have made every effort not to lay too much stress on Pakistan's wrong doing. That is now brought up against us.

---

3. In 1951.

9. You have indicated that you appreciate the deep sense of Pakistani frustration and can understand even their talk of war in these circumstances.[4] If this problem is one of vital importance to Pakistan, it is of equally vital importance to India and the Government and people of India have endured this agony of nine years because we have always wanted to adhere to peaceful methods and approaches. Pakistan has continually threatened us with war on this issue and indeed has concentrated, with the help of others, on building up its war apparatus till it is a danger to India. We, in India, are a more restrained people and believe more firmly in peaceful methods. But the attitude and activities of Pakistan in regard to Kashmir have raised very deep feelings in India. No government in India can possibly think of giving up what it considers right from every point of view, both legal and practical, and continue to exist.

10. You have referred to press comments in the United Kingdom and the United States. I am aware of these and can only regret that opinion should be expressed without a careful consideration of facts as well as the circumstances that exist today. During the past years successive British Governments always assured us that they adopt a neutral attitude in this matter. It appears from what you have said in your message that the UK Government's attitude is far from neutral and is in fact in support of the basic position taken up by Pakistan.[5] I deeply regret this from the point of view of the Commonwealth as we have valued Commonwealth cooperation in our mutual interest as well in the interests of world peace.[6]

11. I have not seen any draft resolution that might be moved in the Security Council and so I am unable to express any opinion in regard to it.

12. In view of the grave dangers involved in any decision being taken which creates upsets and upheavals I would earnestly request you to consider this question in all these aspects.

---

4. Referring to the talk of war in Pakistan, Macmillan observed that this was "bound to arise when people feel that all peaceful efforts, whether by direct talks or through the machinery of the United Nations have not brought them any nearer to the solution of problems of vital importance to them." Macmillan wanted Nehru to offer a gesture to "help to allay this sense of frustration."

5. Macmillan said the UK's aim was to produce a 'holding' resolution so that the deadlock could be broken soon after India's general elections. He added that if Pakistan were to accept a suspension of discussion in the Security Council for two or three months, "they must be able to satisfy their own people that everything is not being dropped entirely in the meantime."

6. Macmillan stated: "I feel that in the interest of all the Commonweaith we must find a way out of this intractable problem."

30. Cable to V.K. Krishna Menon[1]

Lord Home[2] saw Vijayalakshmi last night. He was full of assurances of goodwill, During conversation he made some rather remarkable proposals which I am passing on to you to indicate the UK Government's attempt to draw us out. I have made it clear to Vijayalakshmi that we are not prepared to consider or to make any proposal which is later treated as a commitment, so long as basic issues are not dealt with and our honour as a country is not vindicated.[3]

2. For your information, I give below some of his suggestions. He enquired if we would agree to plebiscite under any circumstances, such as if Pakistan withdrew its troops from Kashmir and allowed Jammu and Kashmir to take over entire State. Another suggestion was whether it was possible to have plebiscite in Jammu on one side and Azad Kashmir on the other leaving the issue of the Valley to be considered separately.

3. Yet another was whether India would agree to appointment of a commission or tribunal or arbitration board which might consider rectification of the present cease-fire line so as to form eventually the Indo-Pakistan frontier. If so, what territorial latitude would India allow to such a Commission? Would it be only question of a few hundred yards for the purpose of rationalising the border for administrative and strategic purposes or would it be more?

4. Canadian High Commissioner, Robertson[4], also saw her and said that Sweden was thinking on lines of making a reference to The Hague Court on question of Kashmir accession. Britain, however, was not keen on such reference as it might place her and Lord Mountbatten in an embarrassing position.

5. Home did not refer to this Swedish proposal but said that there was a suggestion that Swedish Delegate[5] as current President of Council might perhaps be asked to visit India and Pakistan on a fact finding mission.

6. Pakistan High Commissioner went to canvass Burma's vote. He was told that Burma would vote for India. Thereupon, Ikramullah[6] retorted that only Asian States to vote for India would be Burma and Ceylon.

1. New Delhi, 8 February 1957. V.K. Krishna Menon Papers, NMML.
2. A.F. Douglas-Home, Secretary of State for Commonwealth Relations, 1955-60.
3. See *ante*, pp.
4. Norman A. Robertson (1904-68); Canadian diplomat; entered Department of External Affairs, 1929; under secretary of State for External Affairs, 1941-46 and 1958-64; Clerk of Privy Council and Secretary to the Cabinet, 1949-52; High Commissioner to the UK, 1946-49 and 1952-57; Ambassador to the USA, 1957-58; Director, Graduate School of International Affairs, Carlton University, Ottawa, 1965.
5. Gunnar Jarring.
6. Mohammad Ikramullah, Pakistan High Commissioner to the UK.

31. Cable to V.K. Krishna Menon[1]

Your telegram 154 February 8.[2] What you have mentioned is no longer much of a secret as you will realise from my last night's telegram to you.[3]

2. The question is what our reaction to such a proposal should be. Of course, it is open to the Security Council to make a reference to the International Court of Justice whether we agree or not. Such a reference, presumably, is to help them to consider this question further. If they want to do so it is difficult for us to object. We may be sure of our position about accession, but if others want the highest legal advice, how can we say no.

3. I cannot consult my colleagues who are touring about but my own present reaction is that if such a proposal is made we cannot oppose it. At any rate, this will remove subject temporarily from the present supercharged political atmosphere and give everyone time to think more calmly. What is your own reaction?

1. New Delhi, 9 February 1957. File No. 14-KU/57, MEA.
2. Krishna Menon was informed by the French delegation that the Swedes were thinking of of asking the International Court of Justice to advise on the "validity or otherwise of the Maharaja's accession to India."
3. See the preceding item.

32. To Habib Ali Bourguiba[1]

New Delhi,
February 9, 1957

Dear Mr Prime Minister,[2]

Our High Commissioner in London has informed me that your Ambassador, Mr Taieb Slim[3], called on her[4] and gave a message for me on your behalf. This message expressed the distress of the Tunisian Government at India's disregard of the UN resolution on Kashmir and emphasised that in their view I had fallen from my high moral position and this was a blow to Asia and Africa. I understand you have also issued a statement to the press on these lines.[5]

This unusual message would have been a surprise to me if any other Government had sent it. Coming from you and your Government with whom we have been on terms of close friendship before and after attainment of Tunisian independence it was an even greater surprise and distressed me. You will appreciate that it is not a friendly message to a friendly country.

I am not aware of the justification for this message but presumably you satisfied yourself before coming to this decision. I shall be glad to know on what grounds you came to this decision. I am not aware of India having disregarded any UN resolution on Kashmir. It is of course not for me to judge my moral position either before or now. For over nine years now India has been a victim of Pakistani aggression in Kashmir and that aggression has continued in spite of UN resolutions asking Pakistan to withdraw her forces from Kashmir. I should have thought any person conversant with the facts would have come to the conclusion that India had not only acted correctly but over generously during these nine years.

---

1. File No. HC(S)-20/57, MEA.
2. Habib Ben Ali Bourguiba, Prime Minister of Tunisia, April 1956-July 1957.
3. Tunisian Ambassador to the UK, 1956-62.
4. Vijayalakshmi Pandit wrote on 8 February that Taieb Slim who had been in New Delhi some years ago to open the Tunisian office, "was obviously uncomfortable at the mission entrusted to him and seemed in a hurry to leave."
5. The official communique issued from Tunis on 8 February expressed "surprise" at India's "refusal to bow before the UN decision on Kashmir." The communique, signed by Bourguiba, "regretted that the Indian Government could even for a moment be among those governments which refuse to bow to the decisions of international jurisdictions."

I shall be grateful to you if you will kindly let me have an early answer[6] as we do not wish our friendly relations to be interfered with by any misunderstanding.

Yours sincerely,
Jawaharlal Nehru

6. Replying on 12 February, Bourguiba said that Tunisia would have been pleased had the people of Jammu and Kashmir expressed their will to accede to India through a plebiscite. He added: "... what we sincerely deplored is that India, listless to the Security Council recommendation, declared Kashmir as already part of India." Bourguiba feared that the common position both nations held as anti-colonialists on issues like Cyprus and Algeria "might be seriously impaired by the impression your attitude created." The Tunisian Prime Minister felt that it was not enough that Nehru satisfied himself "to do what is right in your own view; the world at large should be convinced that it is right."

33. Pakistan's Approaches to the Soviet Union[1]

The Soviet Ambassador came to see me yesterday and told me that he had been asked by his Government to inform me of numerous approaches that the Pakistan Government had made to the Soviet Government on the subject of Kashmir. He gave me some kind of a chronological account.

2. On the 24th January, the Pakistan Ambassador went to the Soviet Foreign Office and put forward a proposal that the Soviet might mediate. They did not agree to this. Next day, the 25th January, he again went to see them and said that since the Soviet could not serve as mediators, a new formula could be considered. This was that the UN forces should go to the Pakistan side of the Ceasefire Line. The Pakistan Army on that side will then withdraw. India would also withdraw the bulk of her forces from Kashmir and a plebiscite should take place under the supervision of the UN and a Plebiscite Administrator. He also said

1. Note to the Secretary General, Foreign Secretary and Commonwealth Secretary, MEA. 9 February 1957. JN Collection.

374

something about reducing the Azad Kashmir forces to 6,000. Definite dates should be fixed for each phase of the operations including the plebiscite.

3. The Soviet reply was that they had already made their position quite clear and they were opposed to foreign forces intervening.

4. On the 28th January, the Pakistan Ambassador again called and put forward another proposal. This was to the effect that the Soviet Government should exert friendly influence on the Government of India so that the latter might carry out the old resolutions, presumably about the plebiscite. If the Soviet Union did not succeed in getting India to act in this way, and as foreign forces were not agreeable, local forces should be raised to supervise the plebiscite.

5. To this the Soviet Government replied and informed the Pakistan Government that their attitude remained as before. There had been no change in it. The Soviet Ambassador added that this attitude had already been made clear by the statements made by Bulganin and Khrushchev to the effect that the Kashmir question had already been solved by the Kashmir people themselves.[2] The Soviet representative in the UN had also made a statement to this effect on the 24th January.

6. The Soviet Ambassador then referred to an entirely different question. This was about a direct passenger air service between Delhi and Moscow on a mutual basis. He wanted talks to begin on this subject. I told him that talks could certainly take place, but they must wait till the end of the elections. We were much too busy during election time to consider this or any like matter.

7. I am sending this note for record.

---

2. At a civic reception in Srinagar on 10 December 1955, Nikita Khrushchev said that the people of Jammu and Kashmir had decided the status of Kashmir as one of the states of India.

34. To S.W.R.D. Bandaranaike[1]

New Delhi,
February 11, 1957

My dear Prime Minister,[2]

I have received today through your High Commissioner[3] in Delhi a message from you relating to Kashmir.[4] I thank you for this message and appreciate your friendly approach.

I need not tell you that it has been our desire throughout these troubled years to seek a peaceful solution of this difficult question. We shall continue to strive to this end.

It was more than nine years ago that this dispute arose. The origin of this trouble, as you will remember, was an invasion of the territory of Jammu and Kashmir State by armed forces from Pakistan which came without warning and committed arson, rapine and murder. The Jammu and Kashmir State thereupon acceded to India through normal legal and constitutional processes. At that time Lord Mountbatten was the Governor General of India, and as the Head of the State, he was also naturally associated with these processes. It became our legal duty, as it was our moral obligation, to protect the State from this invasion. It was with the greatest reluctance that we undertook this very difficult task. This developed into military operations between India and Pakistan in the territory of Jammu and Kashmir State.

It would have been legitimate for us to carry these operations into Pakistan territory as Pakistan was the aggressor State and was using its territory as a base for these operations. We refrained from doing so because we did not want to spread the area of conflict. We made various appeals to the Pakistan Government to withdraw their forces, but these were rejected. In order to avoid any large-

1. JN Collection.
2. Prime Minister of Sri Lanka, 1956-59.
3. Edwin Wijeyeratne.
4. In his message delivered on 9 February, Bandaranaike said he was "deeply distressed" by the "unfortunate situation" developing between India and Pakistan regarding Kashmir. He appealed to Nehru to strive for a "peaceful settlement" in the interests of Asian and African solidarity.

scale war, we then went to the Security Council requesting them to ask Pakistan to withdraw her forces.[5] Later, the Security Council sent a Commission here.[6]

In August 1948, the United Nations Commission for India and Pakistan passed a resolution which we accepted,[7] but Pakistan did not.[8] Early in January 1949, a further resolution was passed[9] by the Commission reaffirming and supplementing its earlier resolution. This resolution was accepted by us and later by Pakistan. In the August resolution it was stated clearly that a new situation had arisen as Pakistan had sent her forces inside Jammu and Kashmir State territory.[10] The first step laid down by the resolution was for the withdrawal of Pakistani forces from the State territory. India was asked to withdraw the bulk of her forces from the territory as the aggression of Pakistan had been vacated. It was recognised, however, by the UN Commission and the Security Council that India had the constitutional right to help in preserving the integrity of the State and, therefore, to keep some of its forces there. Several other steps were enumerated. The first one, of course, was the ceasefire, then a truce, and then, after several stages, a plebiscite.

I might mention that the offer of plebiscite was made by us in the earlier stages and rejected by Pakistan. Later, we agreed to this plebiscite, but subject to a number of conditions among which was not only the withdrawal of the Pakistan forces, but also the recognition of the sovereignty of Jammu and Kashmir State and its special relation to India.

None of the steps indicated by the resolution of the Commission was taken by the Pakistan Government. In fact, the very first step, that is, the withdrawal

---

5. On 1 January 1948.
6. The United Nations Commission for India and Pakistan (UNCIP) was constituted by the Security Council resolution of 21 April 1948.
7. This was the resolution of 13 August 1948, which India accepted on 20 August. See *Selected Works* (second series), Vol. 7, pp. 301-304.
8. Pakistan did not accept the 13 August Resolution as the Commission had not agreed to its contentions about the legitimacy of the "Azad Kashmir" government and about the withdrawal of tribesmen only after it was satisfied that the Muslims in the State were safe.
9. On 5 January 1949.
10. Part II of the 13 August Resolution stated: "As the presence of troops of Pakistan in the territory of the state of Jammu and Kashmir constitutes a material change in the situation since it was represented by the Government of Pakistan before the Security Council, the Government of Pakistan agrees to withdraw its troops from the state." The foreign minister of Pakistan, Zafrullah Khan, had admitted to Joseph Korbel of the UNCIP that Pakistani troops had been operating in Jammu and Kashmir since May 1948.

of Pakistan forces, was not taken and these forces still continue in Kashmir territory.

These nine years have naturally seen numerous developments in the State. One third of the State is still under unlawful occupation of Pakistan forces. We have, at no time, agreed to this occupation, although we have stated that we will take no military measures against it.

Throughout this period, all kinds of wild charges have been brought against India by Pakistan and we have been accused of fraud, aggression, suppression, etc. As a matter of fact, the Jammu and Kashmir State has very full autonomy and some three or four years ago they had an election for a Constituent Assembly which also functioned as a Legislative Assembly and has brought about far-reaching land and other reforms. The Constitution was framed gradually during these three or four years and given effect to in parts. The final Constitution was passed in November last. Contrary to statements made in various places, nothing was done by us on the 26th of January last.[11]

There can be no doubt about the legal and constitutional position. In spite of this, we have repeatedly discussed this matter with Pakistan to find some way out. We were and are naturally anxious that no steps should be taken which might lead to upheavals not only in the Jammu and Kashmir State, but also in India and Pakistan. That such upheavals can happen is clear from the fact that there has been in past years a continuous stream of refugees coming from East Pakistan to India. Altogether, nearly four million refugees have come over from East Pakistan (this is in addition to those millions who came from West Pakistan). These refugees are a tremendous burden upon us and they continue to come daily. It would be a terrible thing if any further step were to lead to vast migrations from one country to the other. This is the practical aspect.

The Jammu and Kashmir State has made very great progress during the last few years and its people have not been so well off at any time in historic memory. We are anxious naturally that all this progress should not be nullified and the people of the State brought to the verge of ruin.

It is not possible for me, of course, to give you all the facts of this long story in a letter. I shall send you, however, the full reports of the speeches of our representative in the Security Council on this issue as they give most of these facts in some detail.

11. Elections to the Jammu and Kashmir Constituent Assembly were held in 1951. On 17 November 1956, the Constitution of Jammu and Kashmir was adopted. It came into force on 26 January 1957.

We are always willing to discuss this matter with the Pakistan Government, but we cannot be a party to accepting anything which directly or indirectly casts a slur on our honour and ignores the fact that we have been the victims of aggression.[12] Further, we do not want anything to be done which leads to upheavals and misery all round.

In Pakistan there has been—and this still continues—constant cries for jehad and holy war against India, and all kinds of preparations are made for these. Very large-scale supplies of the latest type of arms and aircraft have been obtained by them from abroad, and it is largely because of this that they have taken up an aggressive and threatening attitude. You will appreciate that it is very difficult for us to ignore the real facts of the situation and to surrender to these threats and calumny. No government in India would exist for a day if it did so. In fact, our Government has been studiously moderate and has tried to restrain public opinion.

I shall be sending you soon the material referred to above.

Yours sincerely,
Jawaharlal Nehru

12. On the same day Nehru, replying to Bandaranaike's letter of 8 February stated: "The odd thing is that all the moderation we showed in the past and our efforts to bring about a settlement are turned against us today."

35. UK Attitude on Jammu and Kashmir[1]

Vijayalakshmi Pandit rang me up from London this evening and spoke to me for nearly half an hour. She told me that Macmillan had sent for her again and she had had a talk with him for an hour and a half to two hours. Selwyn Lloyd was present throughout.

2. Macmillan was anxious to impress upon her the great importance he attached to the Commonwealth. This was for him something more important than almost anything else.

3. He referred to Suhrawardy's[2] statement in which he said that the UK had helped Pakistan very much over the Kashmir issue and expressed his gratitude to the UK.[5] Macmillan was very annoyed at this statement and said it was not true. He further said that Suhrawardy was a very bad man and he had no doubt made this statement deliberately to embarrass the UK.

4. He then went on to say that Selwyn Lloyd and Krishna Menon had quarrelled. The UK Government was in no sense responsible for this quarrel, and this should not be allowed to come in the way of Commonwealth relations.

5. Macmillan then referred to some kind of a holding resolution on Kashmir. Vijayalakshmi pointed out that our basic position must be guarded in any resolution. If this was not done, then we could not agree to it.

6. Macmillan said that he was groping for some solution and he was thinking aloud. Could a Commission go to Kashmir, or could there be a condominium? He said something about a moral issue being involved, and presumably that the UK was influenced by the moral aspect. Vijayalakshmi replied that certainly there was a moral issue, and this was exactly what India felt, and that was why they wanted the basic position to be stated.

---

1. Note to the Secretary General and Commonwealth Secretary, MEA, 11 February 1957. JN Collection.
2. Suhrawardy, while addressing a gathering of students at Dhaka on 6 February 1957, stated: "I would like to pay tribute to the amount of assistance which we have received from the UK on Kashmir ... the result is that not only have we been supported by other countries, great countries like the USA, but another great country like Russia has considered it fit and proper to remain neutral."

7. Macmillan then said something about the canal waters dispute and that Nehru should make an imaginative gesture. He went on to talk about a possible partition of the Jammu and Kashmir State. Vijayalakshmi asked: are you prepared to support such a partition. (Presumably, but I am not sure, the partition meant more or less on existing ceasefire line). Selwyn Lloyd interrupted Macmillan and told him that they could not agree to such a partition, but there might be a partition on the basis of Azad Kashmir going to Pakistan and Jammu going to India, while the Valley presumably would have a plebiscite.

8. Macmillan then said what should be done after our elections. A Commission could then go to Jammu and Kashmir. He (Macmillan) said that he was going to talk to Hammarskjold[3] on the telephone.

9. Macmillan then referred to the reports we had had that the UK Government were completely siding with Pakistan and trying to push others to do so. He said this was not true. The Americans probably had told us so. They were bad. Or, perhaps, our own representative had told us so.

10. Macmillan then talked about Kashmir's history. What was the past history of Kashmir? Apparently, he was referring to the more or less distant past, unconnected with the present. Vijayalakshmi offered to send him the book of Kalhana, which gives the history of Kashmir up to about 1000 A.D.

11. This book was translated from Sanskrit by Ranjit Pandit[4] (Vijayalakshmi's husband) and is called *The River of Kings*. It is a fascinating book.

12. Macmillan then asked if our family was Kashmiri. What was our connection with Kashmir? Vijayalakshmi told him that our family had come from Kashmir long ago, but we had been settled in the UP for a long time.

13. Macmillan referred to the Pakistan or Azad Kashmir army and said that the old British Indian Army was chiefly recruited from these areas. These men were very tough and the best in the army. If they attacked India, he seemed to think that India would crack up.

14. Vijayalakshmi told me that Macmillan was evidently much confused and perplexed and not at all happy at the various developments that had taken place. This morning's newspapers in London, more particularly the *Daily Telegraph* and the *Daily Mail,* had scare headlines about the great excitement in Pakistan and the call for war against India—"the people's war", it was stated. Apparently, some British correspondents had visited Azad Kashmir and been told so. Also, reports in Pakistan newspapers. A correspondent named Anthony Mann had

---

3. Dag Hammarskjold was the Secretary General of the UN.
4. Ranjit Sitaram Pandit, a lawyer by profession, translated Kalhana's *Rajatarangini.*

sent a message to this effect. These Press reports had also created some excitement in London.

15. One of the London papers had referred to the UK selling an aircraft carrier to India and said that this was very unfair to Pakistan.

16. It appears that the UK Government is rather worried about the possibility of a reference to the International Court of Justice, of the issue of the accession of the Jammu and Kashmir State to India. They are particularly worried at the prospect of Lord Mountbatten being summoned to give evidence on this issue. They do not at all like the idea of the ex-Viceroy being summoned as a witness on this issue, and probably will tell him not to go.

17. Lord Mountbatten is also rather agitated because of this Press propaganda in London and the general impression created that India was doing something wrong and her moral authority was going. He, in fact, asked Vijayalakshmi to go to India to explain the position in England to us here.

18. I told Vijayalakshmi that there was no need to get excited about these matters and that we here were quite calm and collected, although we realised the possible dangers that might confront us. Unlike us, however, there appeared to be great excitement not only in Pakistan but also in the UK. So far as we were concerned, we were not going to budge from our basic position, and this had better be made perfectly clear to Macmillan. I suggested to her to tell Macmillan to read Krishna Menon's second speech[5] in the Security Council. She said that she had suggested this and Macmillan had replied that nobody had time to read an eight-hour speech.[6]

19. I further told Vijayalakshmi that we were fully acquainted with Press opinions in England as well as other reactions there. We did not propose to get swept off our feet by this kind of unthinking and agitated approach. We shall hold to our position. She said that she had made this perfectly clear to Macmillan.

20. Macmillan told her that he would like to see her again soon.

21. This note is for secret record only. There should be no circulation whatever.

5. On 24 January 1957.
6. On 23-24 January 1957.

36. To Lord Mountbatten[1]

New Delhi,
February 11, 1957

My dear Dickie,

I had a talk[2] with Nan[3] on the telephone this evening. The talk was of course in Hindustani. Among other things, she told me that she had met you and you were rather worried about various developments and more especially the reactions of the British Press and others in the United Kingdom. You even suggested to her to go to India to explain the situation to us.

We are very fully acquainted with the British Press reactions. We get them daily. Naturally they are rather distressing. I do not think Nan or anybody else could add to our knowledge of the position in England vis-a-vis the Kashmir affair.

It seems to me, however, that there is greater excitement over this issue in England than even in India. At any rate, the Press has worked itself up to a pitch. In Pakistan, of course, the Press has become almost delirious. And yet, oddly enough, the people of Pakistan are not terribly excited. As for "Azad Kashmir", most of the people there are fed up with the Pakistan Government and there have been demonstrations against it in spite of considerable repression.

It is true that a difficult situation has been created and it is not pleasant for us to be told constantly that we are the guilty party and that we are not honouring our international commitments. I have no doubt in my mind that the Pakistan case is not only wrong but based on falsehood. I do not say that we have been perfectly justified in everything that we have done in Kashmir. But I am quite clear in my mind that basically we are right both in law and in fact. I see no reason why we should allow ourselves to be bullied or threatened into doing something wrong. No Government in India could last more than a few days if it succumbed to these pressures.

Our Government has restrained itself through all these years and tried to be as accommodating as possible. We have always wanted a peaceful settlement with Pakistan, subject always to certain basic points being safeguarded. It is quite absurd for anyone to say that for the sake of peace we should make generous

---

1. JN Collection.
2. See the preceding item.
3. Vijayalakshmi Pandit was affectionately called by this name in the family.

gestures, generous gesture presumably meaning that we should admit the error of our ways and ask Pakistan to be gracious enough to forgive us.

Quite apart from the merits of the question, any wrong step by us at present will lead to upheavals in Pakistan and in India and the ruin of Kashmir. Instead of solving the Kashmir problem, it will create a problem infinitely worse.

Please remember that there has been a constant stream of refugees from East Pakistan throughout these years. Nearly four million refugees have come over from East Pakistan alone during these years. This is apart from the millions which came from West Pakistan in 1947-48. Only three or four months ago this rate of refugees coming from East Pakistan was 30,000 a month or more. Now it has gone down considerably, but it still continues. Just imagine this kind of thing happening on a colossal scale.

I do not wish to say this in public, but the fact is that Pakistan is controlled today by a set of persons among whom some gangsters play the most important role. They only subsist on the Kashmir cry, otherwise they would go to pieces. Therein lies a certain danger in the situation.

Since we are dubbed as the guilty party, surely we have a right to have the full question examined and a clear decision made on the origins of this dispute, that is, accession and invasion. It is no good telling us that this is past history and then to be told that we are the sinners. In the course of these long negotiations every attempt that we have made to come to terms, every accommodation offered, every suggestion made, is now brought up against us as a commitment, when all these suggestions were subject to certain basic positions being accepted and to the withdrawal of Pakistan forces from Jammu and Kashmir State.

I am quite sure that if the Kashmir issue was settled even to the satisfaction of Pakistan, our troubles with Pakistan will continue. The issue is a much deeper one. Anyhow, we are rather tired of being cursed at and bullied and threatened. Our minds are full of our five year plans and, just at present, with our colossal elections. We will not allow ourselves to be diverted from our main task. If trouble comes, we shall face it.

Please do not worry about this situation. We shall come through and then perhaps those who are criticising us so vigorously will think again and perhaps see some light.

Krishna Menon's first speech in the Security Council was a very long one, but all that had to be said, because we want it on record and we do not want others to forget it. Unfortunately these long speeches are not read by most people. His second speech, though fairly long, was shorter and is a much more concise account of our position. I wish people would read it. We are having these speeches printed and I shall send you copies or you can get them from our High Commission.

Edwina will be leaving us very soon, day after tomorrow morning. I am afraid we have been so busy with our elections that we have not looked after her as we should have. However, it has been very good to have her here and I hope that she has had some rest. She would not have much when she goes to Cyprus.

I hope to send you some mangoes with Edwina. This is of course not the season for them, but we shall raise some in Bombay, where Sri Prakasa is now the Governor.

Yours,
Jawaharlal

37. To Vijayalakshmi Pandit[1]

New Delhi,
February 11, 1957

Nan dear,

After our talk on the telephone this evening, I wrote a letter to Dickie. I enclose a copy for your personal information. Do not send it to your office.

You said something about the scare headlines in the British Press about "Azad Kashmir" suddenly pouncing upon India and "a people's war", etc. I am afraid that the British people have undergone a considerable transformation. They have lost their old balance. The process has been a gradual one, but the Suez crisis and what followed has upset their mental equilibrium completely. I am sorry. What we see in England today and especially in the Press there is some kind of perverted thinking backed by passion and preconceived notions which we normally see in war time. This of course has its dangers, because it leads people to do foolish things.

Anyhow, it is up to us not to get excited and not to lose our heads and certainly not to allow ourselves to be bullied. I am quite clear in my mind that we should not budge an inch from our basic position in regard to Kashmir. I am prepared to admit that in the past we made a mistake in being too accommodating to

---

1. JN Collection.

Pakistan over this issue and making all kinds of suggestions which now are put up before us as commitments which we must honour. Even from the narrowest point of view, those so-called commitments were subject to all kinds of conditions which have not been fulfilled. I am concerned naturally with India's interests and I bear no ill will to Pakistan and wish it well. But most of all, I am concerned with the good of Kashmir and her people. I have no doubt at all that Kashmir would go to wreck and ruin if Pakistan sets its foot there.

Krishna Menon's second speech was a very fine one and well worth reading in order to understand our position. He may have irritated people and obviously he has fallen out with Selwyn Lloyd. But Selwyn Lloyd has behaved badly and not truthfully. The real anger against us in the United Kingdom is due to the sudden realisation that we have dugged in our toes and are not going to be pushed about. They had perhaps expected to unnerve us. They have not succeeded.

We shall be sending you soon some copies of Krishna's speeches which we have had printed in book form. It is too long and few people will read it. But governments certainly have to read it. Please send copies of it to Macmillan, Home and Dickie, apart from any others. It is really the second speech which is more concise and readable. We are having this printed also and it would be sent to you.

Except for a couple of days after tomorrow, I am likely to be almost continuously absent from Delhi till the end of the month.

I spoke to you on the telephone about Nye Bevan. Keep in touch with him and give him the impression that you want to be friendly with him. Like all of us, he is a little vain and likes to be made something of.

I was much worried some time ago about all these recent developments in regard to Kashmir but have got over that phase and I am quite calm about it. I know how difficult it must be for you to face in a cool and detached way all the attacks that are being made on India and to some extent on me. Still I hope that you will not allow yourself to be swept away by any of them. Set an example of calm and detached behaviour.

Today I had Malcolm MacDonald and his wife to lunch. It was a quiet lunch. I was glad to have them here just to show that we have no ill-feeling against him.

Love,
Jawahar

38. To Enaith Habibullah [1]

New Delhi,
12th February 1957

My dear Habibullah,[2]

Your wife has sent me the record of your talk to the cadets about Kashmir. This subject has become so tremendously complicated that certain simple aspects of it are apt to be forgotten. In order to bring out all the facts in this long story, Krishna Menon made a very long speech. Unfortunately the very length of it makes it very difficult for people to read it. But it was necessary to put all these facts on the record. His second speech was more concise and effective. The point[3] you have brought out in your talk has a very important aspect and you have done it very well. I am giving your address to N.R. Pillai. I hope you don't mind my sending copies of it to various people. Your name will not be publicly used.[4]

I enjoyed my visit to Kharakvasla, brief as it was.[5]

I enclose a note for Hamida.[6] Will you please give it to her?

Yours sincerely,
Jawaharlal Nehru

1. JN Collection.
2. (b. 1910); commissioned in the Indian Army, 1930; graduated from Staff College, Quetta, 1942; during the Second World War held staff appointments in the Middle East; fought in Burma, 1944-45; post-war, served at Army HQ and Southern Command till January 1948; promoted to Brigadier and commanded the Shillong Independent sub-area; at Staff College, Wellington, 1950; appointed Commandant, National Defence Academy at Khadakvasla, January 1955.
3. Habibullah in the course of his talk stated: "The accession of Kashmir to India is not only a counter to any demoralising influence among the Muslims of the rest of India, but its rightness cannot be denied by any democratic or right-minded people." He also noted that there was a need for an "ever growing" intimacy with India of an Indian Kashmir and the very friendliest of relations between India and Pakistan. "Nehru is a man to welcome and to lead such a move", concluded Habibullah.
4. On the same day, Nehru sent copies of Habibullah's talk to Vijayalakshmi Pandit and Krishna Menon. He wrote to Mrs Pandit that she could show it or even send a copy to some members of the UK Government, the only condition being that the author's name should be "privately" mentioned.
5. On 1 February 1957.
6. (b. 1916); General Habibullah's wife; member, Uttar Pradesh Legislative Assembly, 1969-74; Minister in Uttar Pradesh Government, 1971-73; Congress (I) member of the Rajya Sabha, 1976-82.

39. Cable to V.K. Krishna Menon[1]

Your telegram 161 February 11.

We are in broad agreement with your analysis and criticism of the four points[2] given in para 2.

2. Point 2. Use of word "demilitarisation" is vague and presumably refers back to previous resolutions which lead up to plebiscite. Our view of demilitarisation is that it should be on Pakistan side and should thus put an end to aggression. Proper wording of point 2 would be "to stress the importance of a peaceful settlement".

3. Point 3. is totally unacceptable to us.

4. Point 4. Use of word "demilitarisation" here, as in point 3, is vague and confusing. Reference to Pakistan proposal is in fact a repetition of point 3 and is objectionable.

5. You can bear these suggestions in mind in considering any revised draft. We do not mind any variation in wording provided our objective is attained.

6. There have been no communications about these points between me and the Prime Minister of Britain.

7. We agree with your comments in para 4.[3] I made this clear in my last message to Macmillan.

---

1. New Delhi, 12 February 1957. File No. 14-KU/57, MEA.
2. Krishna Menon stated that he had received a note from Pierson Dixon, the UK's permanent representative to the UN, listing four points to be tabled as a resolution on 16 February. They were:
   (i) To recall its previous resolutions.
   (ii) To stress the importance of demilitarization.
   (iii) Note Pakistan's suggestion about a UN force and say that it merits consideration.
   (iv) Ask President of Security Council to examine quickly any proposals which will contribute to demilitarization or help towards a settlement, bearing in mind the previous resolutions, the statements of both parties, and the Pakistan proposal.
3. While handing over the four points to Krishna Menon, Dixon had said that the UK was willing to take into account India's election difficulties and would "help to tide over that period to enable India to resolve the deadlock." Krishna Menon replied that the Government of India had not said anything about resolving the deadlock. Instead it pointed out that it would not be possible to be present in strength at the Security Council until a new government was formed after the elections.

8. We agree with the arguments you advanced, which are given in your paragraphs 5 to 9.[4]

9. Your para 20. I do not see how we can oppose the visit of the President of the Security Council.[5] But his visit can only be helpful if certain basic positions, as stated by us, have been clarified. Otherwise he can only talk vaguely about goodwill or demilitarisation as Graham[6] did. Past eight years have shown that this approach yields no results chiefly because those basic issues are slurred over. Effect of his coming here will naturally to some extent depend on nature of resolution passed, though in any event it is bound to have some unsettling effect.

10. We are making immediate protest to Washington and London, as suggested by you in paragraph 15.[7]

11. Regarding Swedish proposal[8] for reference to World Court, we shall await your further opinion. We are not anxious for it, but we cannot object to it. Reference, however, will have to be properly framed.

4. Krishna Menon observed that: (i) India was committed to only the UNCIP resolutions of 13 August 1948 and 5 January 1949 to which the Security Council was a party; (ii) by saying that Pakistan's proposal to send a UN force 'merits consideration' the proposed resolution ignored India's case of Pakistani aggression; (iii) the sending of UN forces to Pakistan occupied Kashmir would be a violation of India's sovereignty; (iv) and that the resolution being put forward by the US and the UK was a "joint offensive."
5. This visit had been proposed in connection with the resolution introduced by the US and the UK. Krishna Menon observed that "the attitude of Mr Jarring (President of the Security Council for February 1957) though he talks of impartiality cannot be regarded as favourable to us."
6. Frank P. Graham, UN mediator on Kashmir, 1951-52.
7. Krishna Menon suggested pointing out to both the US and the UK that "their suggestion" of a UN force for Kashmir was "illegal" under the UN Charter and one-sided.
8. See *ante*, p. 372.

40. To Vijayalakshmi Pandit[1]

Raj Bhavan, Cuttack,
February 13, 1957

Nan dear,

I received your handwritten letter of the 4th February yesterday in Delhi. I would have liked to reply to it immediately, but I just could not manage it. I sent you, however, a brief telegram in reply and then, a little later, I started for Cuttack in Orissa.

You refer to a rumour going around to the effect that it was your handling of the Kashmir case in the Security Council in 1952 that spoiled it.[2] I have not heard of this rumour at all, although there is plenty of criticism about our errors and omissions in the past. No names have been mentioned so far as I understand, but the general impression is that our initial mistake was made when Gopalaswami Ayyangar[3] and B.N. Rau[4] were dealing with it. It may be, of course, that some mischief makers in London bring in your name in this connection.

As a matter of fact, if anybody is to blame for the policy we adopted then, it is our Government. I am completely responsible for it and next to me, Gopalaswami Ayyangar, who was specially dealing with the Kashmir case. You do not come into the picture at all because you dealt with this at a much later stage when we were merely carrying on with the policy laid down previously in the statements made by Gopalaswami Ayyangar and B.N. Rau.

It is all very well for people to criticise us about what happened in the past. We can all be wise after the event. It may well be that if we had adopted a somewhat more rigid policy right from the beginning, that is, from 1948 and

---

1. Vijayalakshmi Pandit Papers, NMML.
2. Mrs Pandit stated that a rumour doing the rounds in London and "gathering volume" was that her handling of Kashmir in the Security Council made it necessary for Krishna Menon to salvage it "so to speak". That is apparently why he had to speak at such great length and earn the unpopularity of the Security Council and other interested parties, observed Mrs Pandit. She said this was not an isolated thing, "but another link in a chain which is being systematically forged to lessen the effectiveness of my work here."
3. Union Minister without Portfolio, 1947-48; for Railways and Transport, 1950-52; Representative to the UN, 1948.
4. Prime Minister of Jammu and Kashmir State, 1945, Constitutional Adviser to the Constituent Assembly, 1946-49; Representative to the UN, 1949-52.

later, we might have been in a better position to deal with this question now. The mistake, if any, occurred in 1948 and 1949. I do not personally think that the broad policy we adopted was in any sense a wrong one in the circumstances then prevailing. We went all out to be cooperative and to seek a settlement, subject always to certain basic issues. As usual, those who want a settlement are always at a slight disadvantage as compared to those who do not want it except on their own basis, that is, surrender by the other party. In the old days of the Muslim League, we had to face the same difficulty. The Muslim League was out to break and separate and could indulge in every kind of hate propaganda. We wanted to keep together and did not approve of this hate campaign. Naturally, we had to speak in a gentle and cooperative manner. Perhaps this weakened our position, but there was no help for it.

You have referred to Krishna Menon and to various forces that work in London trying to discredit you. I think I am well aware of all this and, of course, I strongly disapprove of it. So far as Hari Handoo[5] is concerned, I think that his behaviour has been bad and I did not at all approve of him. I wish that when I was in London on previous occasions I had sent for him and spoken to him, but I was too busy and did not attach much importance to him. It is also, I imagine, true that he goes about telling Krishna all kinds of things which are not true and Krishna readily lends his ears to them. Krishna is peculiarly susceptible and credulous in this respect. He will believe almost anything without enquiry and make that the basis of his thinking in such matters. I have spoken to him about this, and I propose to speak again.

I have known Krishna now for a long time and have a fairly good appreciation of his abilities, virtues and failings.[6] All these are considerable. I do not know if it is possible by straight approach to lessen those failings. I have tried to do so and I shall continue to try. This is a psychological problem of some difficulty and has to be dealt with, if at all successfully, by rather indirect methods. I propose to deal with it both directly and indirectly.

I hope I have the capacity to judge people and events more or less objectively. I am not swept away by Krishna; nor would I like my affection for you to influence

5. According to Mrs Pandit, these rumours were started by Handoo, a Kashmiri medical practioner "who is Krishna Menon's right-hand man here." She said Handoo's own utterances to her brought home "how deeply rooted is the hatred in this group for anyone who even unconsciously competes with Krishna Menon for your favours."
6. Mrs Pandit observed that Nehru knew nothing "of that other side" of Krishna Menon's character "which is in such complete contrast to the one you see." She added that Krishna Menon's growing unpopularity was not because of his stand on Suez or Kashmir, "but his twisted approach to problems and his manner of dealing with them."

my judgment to any large extent, though to some extent, of course, affection does make a difference and indeed should. Krishna has often embarrassed me and put me in considerable difficulties. If I speak to him, he has an emotional break-down. He is always on the verge of some such nervous collapse. The only thing that keeps him going is hard work. There is hardly a person of any importance against whom he has not complained to me some time or other. Later he has found out that his opinion was wrong and he has changed it.

So far as you are concerned, you should know that, apart from my deep affection for you, I have a very high opinion of your capacity and ability. To that, of course, we must add the great value of your personality, to which you yourself have referred. You have my complete confidence in this matter.

I would gladly express this confidence in public. In fact, at a very large meeting in Cuttack today I said something about it, though it was not perhaps the right occasion. I shall say so again. If Parliament had been sitting, it would have been easy, but I shall find other opportunities. You will have my full support. It is a quality which not many persons possess—I think you and I possess it—that is, to speak in straight and firm language and yet not be personally disliked.

So far as the Kashmir matter is concerned, we are in the middle of a very critical situation. Every attempt is being made to bully and frighten us. We have taken a strong line and we refuse to be bullied. Indeed, no one in my position or in our Government's position could possibly give up our main issues. The whole of India will shout out against him.

Last night I sent you a message for Macmillan. This was a criticism of the proposed resolution in the Security Council. That resolution, though supposed to be a holding one, really went pretty far in favouring the Pakistan standpoint. We cannot agree to any such thing. If and when they pass a resolution to which we cannot agree, we shall have to consider what to do. One thing is quite clear, and that is that we will not permit foreign forces to come to Kashmir. We are not even going to agree to these forces going to "Azad Kashmir", though, of course, we cannot physically prevent them from doing so. I think that the UK, the USA and Pakistan are likely to come to some such agreement, that is, to send foreign forces to the area of Kashmir occupied by Pakistan.

You mentioned in your telephone conversation about the scare messages in the *Daily Telegraph* from its correspondent in "Azad Kashmir". You also said something about Macmillan warning us about might of the Pakistan Army. So far as conditions in "Azad Kashmir" are concerned, they are pretty bad from Pakistan's point of view, and we are not at all worried about what the people there might do. It is true, however, that Pakistan has built up a large and well equipped army of about 40 battalions in "Azad Kashmir". Our main concern about the Pakistan Army is the new equipment from the USA. We do not think too much about their officers or men.

I am dictating this from Raj Bhavan, Cuttack, which is presided over now by Bhimsen Sachar. Tomorrow morning I proceed to Bihar.

Love,
Jawahar

41. Cable to V.K. Krishna Menon [1]

Your telegram No. 169, 171 and 173 of February 13th.[2] Also text of Resolution on Kashmir proposed by UK and USA.[3]

This Resolution is even worse than was indicated in four points.[4] We cannot agree to it as it is. I need not give reasons as you know them well.

As regards visit of President of Security Council to India, it will serve no purpose if he comes with terms of reference given in Resolution. We cannot stop his coming if he wishes to do so and we are always prepared to discuss any other proposals towards peaceful settlement. Perhaps it will be best not to commit ourselves to any course of action in discussing this Resolution. If it is passed, then you might say that you will refer it to your Government for instructions.

1. New Delhi, 15 February 1957. JN Collection.
2. In the first cable, Krishna Menon said that he was in no doubt whatsoever that the UK was the "intiator" of the resolution on Kashmir and added that the UK "has not merely responded to Pakistan but is cooking everything."
3. The text of the resolution handed over to Krishna Menon by the US stated that demilitarization preparatory to the holding of a plebiscite had not been achieved and added that Pakistan's suggestion of the use of a temporary UN force in connection with demilitarization "would merit consideration." This resolution was tabled in the Security Council on 16 February.
4. See *ante*, p. 388.

As regards Soviet veto,[5] I think that we should not come in the way of it. The veto will be about Resolution as a whole, not against President of Security Council visiting India.

These are my reactions; but in changing situation you will have to exercise your judgement.

I think that you should stay on in New York for a few days more if necessary to see the end of this business in Security Council and even more so if it goes to General Assembly.[6] Do not worry about your election here. Polling in Bombay City will take place on 11th March.

5. In his first cable, Krishna Menon observed that the Soviet Union would vote against any resolution which went beyond "recalling" earlier resolutions and sought "further consideration" of the Kashmir issue. He noted that the Soviet Union would come out strongly against any mention of sending UN forces to Kashmir.
6. Krishna Menon said he was leaving for India soon, but was uncertain about events in the Security Council. He feared a postponement, "because US is not ready or even more because of the Israel question."

42. Cable to Vijayalakshmi Pandit[1]

I have received your telegrams 533[2] and 541[3] of February 13th. I have also seen draft Resolution[4] on Kashmir for Security Council sponsored by UK and USA. It is even worse than four points which I indicated to you. It is clear UK is wholly supporting Pakistan. We shall have to adhere firmly to position we have taken up. If Resolution passed by Security Council or General Assembly we shall then consider what we shall do.

Meanwhile please convey to Macmillan my surprise and distress at this draft Resolution which goes much further in supporting Pakistan's position than even four points mentioned to us previously. I regret deeply that this partial and unfair attitude has been taken up by UK regardless of facts and law or of what we have said repeatedly both in Security Council and personally to him. This is a matter of serious consequence, and I am particularly distressed at fact that repeated assurances given to us on behalf of the UK Government have not been fulfilled. We cannot possibly agree to this Resolution.

1. New Delhi, 15 February 1957. JN Collection.
2. Mrs Pandit said she had told Douglas-Home that India was probably better off without the kind of assistance which the UK was giving through their resolutions. Regarding Pakistan's "favourable position" in the Security Council, she said India had taken her stand on certain principles and could not be swayed by arguments that India would be defeated.
3. Mrs Pandit stated: "There is no doubt Government (UK) position rapidly crystallising all out for Pakistan."
4. See the preceding item.

43. The Legality of Kashmir's Accession[1]

Vijayalakshmi Pandit telephoned to me this evening from London and told me that Lord Home and others were pressing her to get us to make some kind of constructive proposals about Kashmir. She had said, according to our instructions, that we were not prepared to make any proposal. Whatever we had said previously becomes a commitment, even after it is rejected. We had been insulted and our honour brought into question. Therefore the basic issues must be dealt with before any other step could be taken.

2. I told her that this was the correct attitude and she must persist in it.

3. She also told me that Aneurin Bevan was likely to go to Burma, probably some time in March. He would like to pay a brief visit to India either on his way to Burma or on his way back and wanted my reactions. I told her that he would be welcome here whenever he comes, but that we were busy till about the middle of March with the elections.

4. She also said something to the effect that UK Government had taken legal advice from their advisers about the accession of Kashmir. I did not quite follow what this advice was, but evidently it was not very much in our favour and in any way it was up to the UK Government to interpret their Independence Act and its consequences. I told her that we were not prepared to accept any interpretation of the UK. In these matters and if necessity arose, the matter will have to be decided by the International Court of Justice.

---

1. Note to the Secretary General and Commonwealth Secretary, MEA, 16 February 1957. JN Collection.

44. A 'Holding' Resolution on Kashmir[1]

India is opposed to the latest resolution before the Security Council on Kashmir as it opens the door to entirely misconceived proposals, which are wholly wrong.

The proposal to send a United Nations force to any part of the Jammu and Kashmir State is against international law and the Charter of the UN unless India accepts it. We have made it clear that in no circumstances will we accept any foreign force on our territory. And yet, this UK and US resolution mentions this also.

In the present proposal reference is made to demilitarisation. Certainly there should be demilitarisation. But what does this mean? Surely, if there has been aggression, this must be ended and Pakistan must withdraw her forces from Kashmir territory. If there has been accession of the State to India, then it is our duty and obligation to protect it from aggression and attack. In fact, this was all along admitted by the UN Commission that visited Kashmir. The way this is put now is to equate India and Pakistan and indeed to indicate that India is at fault. Thus step by step the position is altered in people's minds and India is blamed later.

The question of plebiscite when it was raised was made conditional and the first condition was Pakistan's withdrawal of all her forces from Kashmir. Even that first and essential condition has not been fulfilled and Pakistan's aggression is still a continuing fact. It is not we who have come in the way. Meanwhile many years passed and many vital developments have taken place in Kashmir and elsewhere. Pakistan, with outside aid, has built up a big war machine which threatens India.

The Security Council has bypassed basic facts relating to Kashmir and has not even given any consideration to the arguments of facts and law as well as practical consequences which had been placed before it.

I am amazed at this repeated slurring over of basic facts and the attempt to advance step by step in a direction which we consider wrong and unfair. The present resolution is another such step.

---

1. Statement issued to the Press Trust of India correspondent aboard the Prime Minister's plane while returning to Delhi from an election tour of Orissa and Bihar, 16 February 1957. From *The Hindu*, 17 February 1957.

The draft resolution sponsored by the United Kingdom, the United States of America and some other countries on Kashmir in the Security Council is stated to be a holding resolution.

We have no objection to a real holding resolution so that the entire question may be fully considered later. But the present proposal is much more than a holding resolution and opens the door to a number of other proposals which we think are entirely misconceived. Throughout these past nine years, the Security Council has not given consideration to the major and basic issues governing Kashmir, that is, Pakistan's aggression and Kashmir's accession to India. It is only when these basic issues have been dealt with that other questions arise. Unfortunately this procedure has not been adopted and because of this all subsequent difficulties have arisen. We have always made this clear but in our desire to arrive at a peaceful settlement we have discussed many proposals which have failed to produce any result.

Now we are told that those intermediate proposals and discussions were commitments by us and we need not go back to the real causes of the dispute. This is manifestly unfair and ignores realities. Those realities are based on facts, as well as a basic difference between Pakistan and India on the two-nation theory, and on a religious or a secular State. Any decision on these issues has far-reaching consequences. In spite of this, the Security Council bypasses them and does not even give any consideration to the arguments on facts and law as well as practical consequences, which have been placed before it.

We are told that we have ignored UN resolutions and especially the last one.[2] I am not aware of this. It was we who went to the UN and have consistently sought their assistance and cooperated with them. We have done nothing at all since the last resolution. This has been repeatedly pointed out but the unfair charge continues to be made. Nothing happened on January 26, except some valedictory speeches in the Jammu and Kashmir Assembly. The accession took place in October 1947. The finalisation of the Jammu and Kashmir Constitution took place in November 1956.

Thus we oppose the UK-USA proposal because it is much more than a holding resolution and, in fact, it goes much further and opens the door to and encourages certain proposals and suggestions which are, according to us, wholly wrong. And this is done without considering the basic issues.

2. Of 24 January 1957.

45. Cable to V.K. Krishna Menon[1]

Please refer to your telegram No. 180 February 16th. We agree with your making a positive approach before the Security Council and putting forward our demands. We agree also that only commitments between Pakistan and ourselves are contained in the two resolutions of UNCIP. Naturally the demands have to be considered in view of subsequent developments and all that has happened during succeeding years which have basically altered the then existing situation.

2. Your para 9 we agree to Clause (1).[2] But dealing with this only and not with Part II would mean that Pakistan can maintain some forces there as at that time of ceasefire and only withdraw additional forces. This would not be very helpful.

Clause (2): There appears to be some misapprehension about this.[3] No territory belonging to Kashmir State has been incorporated in the Pakistan Constitution except perhaps Chitral. Chitral previously was autonomous State recognising suzerainty of Kashmir Maharaja and paying nominal tribute. Round about end of 1947 it acceded to Pakistan informing Maharaja's government of this. Chitral's case is a very doubtful one as it was not essentially part of Kashmir State.

Northern areas such as Gilgit Agency, Skardu, Astore, Chilas, Hunza and Nagar are directly administered by Pakistan. Southern area known as Azad Kashmir and consisting of Muzaffarabad, part of Poonch and Mirpur has a nominal government of its own but this is nominated by Pakistan. None of these Northern or Southern areas have been incorporated into Pakistan by its Constitution.

Clause (3): This is not at all clear.[4] While it is true that sovereignty of Jammu and Kashmir State is accepted in practice all along it was clearly stated in August 13 Resolution Part II (B) that ceasefire line will be maintained. I have no doubt that according to this resolution we could not send forces across ceasefire line. If that is so then we cannot demand now that our garrisons should be placed on other side of ceasefire line.

1. New Delhi, 18 February 1957. V.K. Krishna Menon Papers, NMML.
2. Krishna Menon said it was necessary to ask Pakistan to start abiding by Part I of the 13 August 1948 UN Resolution. This related to the observance of ceasefire by both sides.
3. Krishna Menon suggested that Pakistan should 'disgorge' all the territories that had been incorporated into Pakistan by the new constitution adopted in early 1956.
4. Krishna Menon pointed to the need to resuscitate the demand of having check posts, and garrisons on Kashmir's western and northern frontiers, "which are the frontiers of the Union of India."

I should like you to refer specially to our aide-memoires of 20th August 1948 and those giving discussions with Lozano on December 20th and 22nd, 1948.[5]

If we confine ourselves to Part I of August Resolution we cannot ask for complete removal of Pakistan forces from invaded territory which we have been pressing for all along.

3. Question of partition does not arise now and must not be raised.[6] But the fact remains that even from our security point of view it would be no gain and might well be a loss for us to include some areas which can only give us continuous trouble. It is true that readjustment of present ceasefire line including some strategic points would be advantageous to us. These questions do not arise now but some time or other later we may have to face them. When I first made a proposal for a settlement on basis of ceasefire line I made it clear that this would be subject to adjustments on geographical, strategic and like grounds.[7]

4. Our position should be as you say that ceasefire agreement has been violated by Pakistan; in spite of this we are not rejecting the two UNCIP resolutions and are actually repeating the demands made therein and making no fresh demands. It is true that in accepting these two resolutions we accept the implication of a possible plebiscite subject to various considerations then existing. It is clear that in any succeeding step that may have to be taken later every factor and subsequent development will have to be taken into consideration. Your para 13 states position clearly.[8] You will bear in mind that Kashmir Government as well as some leading persons here have been saying that plebiscite is out of the question now.

5. Broadly speaking therefore we agree with the approach you have suggested subject only to your not making any claim which might run counter to what we

---

5. See *Selected Works* (second series), Vol. 7, pp. 301-304. Also see *Selected Works* (second series), Vol. 9, pp. 221-224. Alfred Lozano was the personal representative of the UN Secretary General at that time.
6. According to Krishna Menon, the option before India to accept the partition of the Jammu and Kashmir state along the ceasefire line was "eminently dangerous to the security of India". He clarified that it was not India's intention to take back the occupied territory by force.
7. See *Selected Works* (second series), Vol. 28, pp. 246-263.
8. If the Security Council asked India to "perform" the rest of the 13 August 1948 resolution, in case Pakistan fulfilled her part of the conditions, Krishna Menon said, he would state that "we will carry out our international obligations." He added that the "pre-condition is that the other side must remedy its default." Krishna Menon observed that, "if all other conditions are carried out and we do not carry out our side then they would be in a position to charge us with a violation.

have said previously more especially at the time of the UNCIP resolutions. You can of course repeat that we do not in any event propose to use force in order to bring any changes though of course if any further aggression takes place we shall resist.

46. To Vijayalakshmi Pandit [1]

New Delhi,
February 19, 1957

Nan dear,

I returned to Delhi today from a tour in Rajasthan. Tomorrow morning I am leaving Delhi again for a rather long tour which will include Allahabad, Nagpur, Akola, Vijayawada, Warangal, Hyderabad, Bangalore, Mysore, two days in Kerala, Mangalore, Raipur, Jabalpur and then back to Delhi. I expect to return to Delhi on the 27th February afternoon. After that I shall be mostly in Delhi except for a day's visit to Kanpur and brief afternoon excursions to roundabout areas. Anyhow the election business will be over by the 12th March, when I go to Allahabad just to vote.

These past days and weeks have been full of strain, not so much because of elections and touring, but because of the Kashmir affair. All of you have no doubt suffered from this same strain. I suppose that in another day or two the Security Council will finish its present discussions on this issue.

It seems very likely that Jarring,[2] the Swedish member of the Security Council, will visit our part of the world some time in March. The situation will remain a

---

1. JN Collection.
2. Gunnar Jarring (b. 1907); Swedish diplomat; Associate Professsor of Turkic Languages, Lund University, 1933-40; chargé d'affaires in Addis Ababa, 1946-48; Minister to India, 1948-51, concurrently to Sri Lanka, 1950-51, Iran, Iraq and Pakistan, 1951-52; Director, Ministry of Foreign Affairs, 1953-56; Permanent Representative to UN, 1956-58; representative on Security Council, 1957-58; Ambassador: to USA, 1958-64, to USSR, 1964-73, and to Mongolia, 1965-73; Special Envoy of UN Secretary General on Middle Eastern situation, 1967-91; author of several books including *Materials for the Knowledge of Eastern Turkestan* (Vols. I-IV), 1947-51, *An Eastern Turki-English Dialect Dictionary*, 1964, and *Literary Texts from Kashghar*, 1980.

difficult one, but I think that we have rather passed the pitch and people are thinking again. That is the impression I gather even about England and to some extent the USA. We have no intention of weakening in our stand, though of course we shall have to adapt it to changing circumstances.

During my eight days tour beginning tomorrow, I shall not be very easily accessible to our Ministry. Possibly, I shall get telegrams and papers, but they may well be delayed. If a reference is made to me, the answer may not be sent soon.

Malcolm MacDonald came to see me today as he is leaving tomorrow for Bombay and after two or three days for England for consultations. He has a fair understanding of our position and I believe he has sent strong messages to his Government. But I doubt if they carried much weight. It is obvious that Selwyn Lloyd is full of bitterness and even malice against India. However, as passions tone down, people may look at the facts again.

I received an interesting letter today from Norman Cousins[3] of *The Saturday Review* of America conveying a message to me from Dr Schweitzer.[4] As this may interest you, I am enclosing a copy together with my reply.[5]

Rita[6] is here. So also is Avtar Krishna[7] and the babe. Indira is wandering about various places. I learn about her travels from newspapers, but I am going to meet her in Allahabad tomorrow morning.

I think you might meet Malcolm MacDonald while he is in London.

I am glad that Nye Bevan is taking up a clear line in regard to Kashmir. As I told you, he will be welcome here whenever he comes. There will be no difficulty. Keep in touch with him.

Love,
Jawahar

3. Editor, *The Saturday Review*, 1940-77.
4. Albert Schweitzer; missionary surgeon; awarded the Nobel Prize in 1952.
5. See *post*, pp. 468-471.
6. Rita Dar, Vijayalakshmi Pandit's daughter.
7. Avtar Krishna Dar (b. 1918); appointed in the IFS as a War Service recruit, April 1947; Third Secretary, Washington, June 1947; Second Secretary, November 1948; Vice Consul, San Francisco, August 1949; First Secretary, Indian Legation, Berne, 1950-51; Under Secretary, MEA, 1951-53; First Secretary, Indian Legation, Damascus, 1953-54; First Secretary, Peking, 1954 to August 1956; OSD and later, Director, Chief Controller of Imports and Exports, Ministry of Commerce and Industry, January to December 1957; First Secretary, Singapore, 1957-59; Consellor, Cairo, 1959; Joint Secretary, MEA, 1965.

47. No Foreign Troops in Kashmir [1]

The four-Power resolution in the Security Council on Kashmir which was vetoed by Russia yesterday,[2] is collective aggression or collective approval of aggression.

India will not allow, in any circumstances, foreign troops to land on her territory. We are committed to peace and the ways of peace but if our freedom is threatened, then we must protect it in every way open to us.

The attitude of some countries in the Security Council is one of deliberate hostility to India. A peaceful settlement with Pakistan was possible if other countries did not interfere and encourage aggression and a policy of hatred, fanaticism and violence.

Mr Krishna Menon has spoken with passion in the Security Council on the four-Power resolution on Kashmir. In speaking thus, he has represented the passion of India. In this matter there are no differences in India between parties and there is full unanimity among all, for it affects not only the honour and integrity of India but also its security and independence. It is also a matter of grave concern to the United Nations. Does it accept and approve of aggression on India by Pakistan and the violation of UN resolutions by Pakistan?

India has not violated a single international commitment. It is Pakistan that has violated the ceasefire agreement in Kashmir and refuses to withdraw her forces from the territory forcibly occupied by her.

These and other questions have been explicitly placed before the Security Council on behalf of India. But they have been ignored and there has not even been an attempt to answer them. Does aggression mean something different in India than what it does elsewhere in the world?

1. Statement issued to the Press Trust of India correspondent on board the Prime Minister's plane en route from Allahabad to Akola in Maharashtra, 21 February 1957. From *The Hindu*, 22 February 1957.
2. This resolution, introduced in the Security Council, called for demilitarization of Kashmir and the sending of a UN force to the region. It also called upon Gunnar Jarring, the Swedish representative, to visit the subcontinent and discuss the issue with India and Pakistan.

Even the issues raised by the distinguished delegates of Colombia had been ignored.[3]

Are we wrong in assuming that the attitude of some countries in the Security Council is one of deliberate hostility to India, ignoring patent facts and past history and even forgetting the provisions of the Charter of the United Nations? We are told that the four-power resolution was meant to lead to a just and fair solution and to prevent mistrust and misunderstanding. If that is so, then words have lost their meaning or there is a singularly perverse attempt not to understand what has happened or what is taking place now.

India looks upon the proposal to send foreign troops here as an act of hostility to India.

We have stated categorically that in no event will we allow any foreign forces to set foot on Indian territory and yet this has been mentioned in the four-power resolution as a matter for consideration. I do not know if this is supposed to lessen tension or help in removing mistrust. We can only look upon it as an act of hostility to India and a breach of the UN Charter.

In the old days we struggled against the attempts of the British Government in India to encourage divisions and separations in India in order to weaken the nationalist movement. We refused to accept the two-nation theory and later gave a secular basis to our Constitution. After independence we tried to forget the past and laboured not without success for close and friendly relations with the United Kingdom. Now the old past raises itself again and policies are being pursued by other countries which promote separation and imperil India. I am convinced that, as in the past, so now, peaceful settlement and friendly relations between India and Pakistan are possible if other countries do not interfere and encourage aggression and a policy of hatred, fanaticism and violence.

We are committed to peace and the ways of peace. But if our freedom is threatened, then we must protect it in every way open to us.

While India talks of peaceful solutions, military aid flows into Pakistan and the campaign of hatred and threats of war continue to fill the air.

We have been told that the four-Power resolution is in furtherance of collective security. It looks to us perilously like collective aggression or collective approval of aggression.

3. Francisco Urrutia, Colombia's UN representative stated in the Security Council on 17 February that the UNCIP's agreement with India in 1948 over Kashmir was arrived at through direct negotiations and was not provided for in the Commission's resolution of 13 August 1948. He also revealed that it was Admiral Chester Nimitz's appointment as the Plebiscite Administrator and not India's attitude as was generally believed, that obstructed the conduct of a plebiscite in Kashmir. Pointing to the UNCIP's recognition of India's sovereignty over Jammu and Kashmir, Urrutia observed that the Commission had never accepted the presence of the Pakistan Army in the state.

48. Keeping the Missions Informed[1]

You will see the telegram I am sending to Krishna Menon; and also the statement I issued to PTI today.[2]

I am glad that you are informing our Heads of Missions in foreign countries to withhold approach to governments there in regard to Kashmir issue. But later on I think that we should approach all these governments to explain to them our position in regard to Kashmir. They should be kept informed of this and we must not lose touch with them; but this will have to wait till some further development now. Meanwhile I suggest that airmail letters be sent to all these Missions explaining to them the new situation that is arising and telling them that we propose to hold firmly to our position. We do not intend making any proposals and we want them to explain this Kashmir matter from our point of view to the governments concerned. But as we are expecting some new development in the course of a day or two, they should wait till then. We shall send them brief telegram to ask them to approach the governments on the lines indicated.

I notice that our circular telegram was not sent to Shri A.C.N. Nambiar, our Ambassador in Bonn. It may be because West Germany is not a member of the United Nations. But may I suggest that it is desirable to forward the telegram (by air mail) to Ambassador Nambiar for his information? That will be helpful to him. I also notice that the circular telegram was not sent to our Ambassadors in what might be called Communist countries. I think that it is desirable to send them also copies for information. There is nothing more precious than authentic information to our representatives living far away and have to answer questions on all kinds of subjects.

PS: No Head of Mission has been asked to approach the Spanish Government. Perhaps our High Commissioner in the UK can do this through the Spanish Ambassador[3] in London.[4]

---

1. Telephonic message for Secretary General, MEA, as conveyed to M.O. Mathai from Nagpur, 21 February 1957. JN Collection.
2. See the preceding item.
3. Mignel Primo De Rivera.
4. At the end of this typescript Mathai added in his own hand: "Also how about Tunisia, Morocco, Liberia?"

49. Cable to V.K. Krishna Menon[1]

I have received your telegram 198 of February 20th in Nagpur. We all think you have put up a magnificent fight and congratulate you upon it. You have drawn far too much on your health and we are anxious about it.[2] You should take care of yourself now.

I quite agree with you that we should not weaken in any way and should not indicate that we have other proposals. I do not propose to say anything about them; but I issued a statement[3] today which you will no doubt have seen. This was really in criticism of Four-Power proposal. I have not yet seen text of new Resolution to which you refer.[4]

I am sending message to Arthur Lall for Dr Hitzig.[5]

1. 21 February 1957. File No. 14-KU/57, MEA.
2. Krishna Menon suffered from low blood pressure and had on occasions suffered breakdowns during the proceedings of the Security Council.
3. See *ante*, pp. 403-404.
4. On 21 February, the four-Powers introduced a new resolution that referred to sending Gunnar Jarring to visit India and Pakistan to examine proposals, "which in his opinion, are likely to contribute towards settlement of the dispute." This was passed by 10 votes to nil with the Soviet Union abstaining. There was no mention in it of either demilitarization or the sending of a UN force to Kashmir.
5. W.H. Hitzig, the doctor who treated Krishna Menon in New York.

1. To M.K. Vellodi[1]

December 26, 1956

My dear Vellodi,[2]

I had a talk with Lord Mountbatten yesterday about the aircraft carrier. I understood from him that he had written to you at some length in answer to your letter.[3] I need not, therefore, repeat what he said to me. He gave me a note which really contains no new information and refers to previous stages. I enclose this note.

As a result of this talk, I feel convinced that we should go ahead with the refitting or reconversion of the carrier, as arranged, through British agencies.[4] Lord Mountbatten was definitely of opinion that we should not go in for a long stroke catapult and, perhaps, one or two other things, which, from our point of view, were not really necessary and which meant a great addition to the price. I agree with this. As you know, I have long been of opinion that too great complications in technique are not suited to a country which has not got the technical background for them. Also, from the point of necessity, this seems unnecessary.

I feel sure that the estimate given to us by the Dutch firm cannot be for the same reconversion as we had asked for from the Admiralty.[5] Further, it is clear that the Dutch themselves have to rely very greatly on British designs and British help at every stage. They have not enough competence for this work, and we are likely to get into a great deal of trouble if we deal with them. The responsibility will be divided between the Dutch and the British, and each party may well blame the other for all the failings. Lord Mountbatten appeared to be fairly sure in his mind that the Dutch just could not do the work entrusted to them properly.[6]

---

1. Camp: London. JN Collection. Nehru stopped in London on 24-25 December 1956, while returning to India after his visit to the USA and Canada.
2. Defence Secretary.
3. Vellodi wrote to Mountbatten on 9 December.
4. See *Selected Works* (second series), Vol. 34, pp. 201-202, for details of India's plans to acquire the *Hercules* aircraft carrier from the UK.
5. Vellodi had told Mountbatten that a Dutch shipyard had offered to modernize the *Hercules* for about 4 million pounds. The UK Admiralty had estimated that the same work at the British shipyard in Belfast would cost around 10 million pounds.
6. Vellodi had informed Mountbatten that the Naval HQ in Delhi felt that the Dutch could not do the work of reconversion of the carrier. Vellodi wanted Mountbatten to use his influence to get the UK Admiralty to reconsider its prices for refitting as finances were a worry for the Government of India.

Apart from all this, it would be politically an unwise thing for us to shift over at this stage from the British to the Dutch. We can be quite sure that we will get what we have bargained for, from the British. We cannot be sure of this from the Dutch. Possibly, the price charged by the Dutch for the same type of work may be a little cheaper, but I cannot conceive of the difference being so great as has been suggested.

It appears that we have to make our final decision soon. I am writing this letter to you from London, although I am returning tomorrow, because I am not quite sure when I might be able to see you. I should, of course, like to see you before I go out of Delhi again, which is likely to be on the 30th afternoon. In any event, I should like you to talk about this matter with N.R. Pillai.[7] You might show this letter to the Defence Minister.[8]

Yours sincerely,
Jawaharlal Nehru

7. Secretary General, MEA.
8. K.N. Katju.

2. To Joachim Alva[1]

New Delhi,
23rd January, 1957

My dear Alva,[2]

Thank you for your letter[3] of the 21st January.

We are not unaware of the developments in the Maldives Islands.[4] But I do not quite understand what you expect our High Commission in Ceylon or our Ministry here to do about this matter. We have no Monroe doctrine for the Arabian Sea, the Indian Ocean or the Bay of Bengal. Nor can we develop such a doctrine in the present day world. Naturally we do not like bases being set up roundabout our country.

The Maldives Islands have been under British suzerainty by treaty for a considerable time past[5] and we cannot possibly stop these islands from being used as transit and refuelling centres, even though we might not like this.

As for submarines, I think that such resources as we have can be employed to better purpose in developing our Navy for the present. These resources are limited.

Yours sincerely,
Jawaharlal Nehru

1. JN Collection.
2. Member of Lok Sabha.
3. Not available.
4. The Commonwealth Relations Office announced in London on 3 January that it had been decided, after consultation with the Maldivian Government, that "the United Kingdom Government will re-establish and operate the airfield in Addu Atoll as a staging post." A spokesman of the Office said that flying directly across the Indian Ocean would make practicable a shorter, direct route from Britain to Australia, New Zealand, and the Far East for long-range aircraft.
5. The Maldives Islands, an independent Sultanate, had been under British protection since 1887.

3. To M.K. Vellodi[1]

New Delhi,
February 3, 1957

My dear Vellodi,

Lady Mountbatten[2] has received a letter from Lord Mountbatten in which he refers to the Canberra deal.[3] I give below an extract from this letter:

"Will you tell Jawaharlal how delighted I am that he has given a firm decision about their carrier—now we can go ahead. Nothing ever seems to be done unless he sees to it himself. You would hardly believe it, but the great Canberra deal which I discussed and negotiated with him last March and by which the RAF actually gave up orders they had for first line Squadrons because I said it was essential to have the Canberras in service in India before the summer this year, has not yet been clinched by India. The UK were genuinely ready for a high speed deal because I explained to Anthony Eden that unless he could release Canberras very quickly it would be of no help to India. Yet ten months later the British are waiting patiently for the Indian Government to confirm the order for which they were in such a tearing hurry."

I had an idea that we had finalised this Canberra deal. What is the position?

Yours sincerely,
Jawaharlal Nehru

1. JN Collection.
2. Edwina Mountbatten.
3. See *Selected Works* (second series), Vol. 32, pp. 290-291.

412

7
PORTUGUESE POSSESSIONS

1. To S. Nijalingappa[1]

New Delhi,
21st January, 1957

My dear Nijalingappa,[2]

I was in Bombay yesterday. I discussed Goa matters there.

It seems that since the formation of the new States the old arrangements have not been working very satisfactorily. Even before these States had been formed, we had decided that the Government of India should take direct charge of the security of the Goan border and the effective implementation of our policy there.[3] It is essential that this policy should be uniformly applied all along the border whatever the State boundary might be. Previously, the Ministry of External Affairs dealt with the Bombay Government which was the only State Government concerned with Goa and there was full cooperation. Now there are two State Governments. Your Government has not been in touch with our previous policies in regard to Goa and I was told that some difficulties had arisen, and to some extent Goa affairs had got entangled in the coming elections.[4] This is very unfortunate.

I gather that some of the Mysore leaders have been in contact with the various Goan parties of which there are many. We have had a great deal of trouble with these Goan parties which refuse to pull together and often act contrary to our own policies. In Bombay there are, I believe, fourteen Goan parties, all pulling in different directions. Peter Alvares of the National Congress, Goa has sometimes functioned in a way we did not approve of. Indeed, hardly any of these parties has functioned responsibly and our efforts at bringing them together have not succeeded.

The whole Goa question is an exceedingly difficult one and has wide international implications. The question may seem small because Goa is small, but the great powers are all interested in this question and we have thus all to

---

1. JN Collection.
2. Chief Minister of Mysore.
3. The Government of India had taken a number of measures to stop contacts between India and the Portuguese possessions in India. These measures included restriction on money transfer, stricter control on import of essential goods like steel and textiles, a ban on import of Indian labour, and suspension of posts and telegraph services.
4. The second general elections took place from 24 February to 14 March 1957.

415

move very warily. In any event, we shall have to consider our policy very fully in all its aspects and it might be that we have to vary it somewhat. We cannot do this in the course of the elections. Also, because there are various other world issues at present coming in the way. There is Kashmir for one.

We have thus to wait till April in order to consider this matter in all its aspects. Meanwhile, we are having full particulars collected and papers prepared. We shall naturally consult the Mysore Government at the time.

A piece of news has reached me which has surprised me much. This is to the effect that Peter Alvares was made an offer that he should stand from Karwar for the elections and he would get an uncontested seat, provided he accepted the idea of Goa's eventual merger with Mysore. I do not know who made this offer, but whoever it was he did a very wrong thing and entirely in opposition to our policy, both Congress and Government. We cannot possibly leave a seat uncontested in this way in favour of a PSP candidate or indeed any candidate. Apart from this, there is no question of Goa being merged into Mysore or Bombay or into any State. This is our firm and decided policy which has been proclaimed on many occasions.[5] We are committed to Goa remaining a separate entity and not being merged in an existing State. This should be made perfectly clear to everybody concerned. We had tremendous difficulties in the past because some Maharashtrian leaders had proclaimed that Goa would become part of Maharashtra. This made the Goa question much more difficult and our opponents made much of it.

I gather that a number of leaders of various Goan parties have been paying frequent visits to Mysore and discussing this question with them. Some of them have apparently also given the assurance that they will work for the merger of Goa with Mysore. This is very irresponsible behaviour. Goa can only be dealt with by the Centre and nothing should be done by any State which comes into conflict with the Centre's policy.

Please make this quite clear and discourage any Goan people from having separate talks in Mysore. They should be referred to the Centre.

Yours sincerely,
Jawaharlal Nehru

---

5. For instance, see Nehru's address to a rally of Goans at Mumbai on 4 June 1956, printed in *Selected Works* (second series), Vol. 33, pp. 411-412.

2. Help to Purushottam Kakodkar[1]

Asoka Mehta[2] spoke to me briefly in Bombay yesterday and, at my request, gave me the attached note. I have written a letter[3] to the Chief Minister of Mysore, copy attached.

2. I am greatly troubled about the Goa question and I think all our policy requires reconsideration. I am afraid we cannot give time to it at present. But towards the end of March or beginning of April we should consider this fully in the Ministry first and then in the Foreign Affairs Committee. All necessary papers should be prepared.

3. I am not at all satisfied with monies being apparently given for work inside Goa. This has brought us no good results and has in fact, I believe, complicated the situation and made the people there more frustrated. This matter will have to be gone into.

4. I met in Bombay Kakodkar[4] whom we have been giving an allowance for some months past. I do not know how effective he is, but I like him because he is a man of integrity and his previous association with Gandhiji has given him a proper outlook. Unlike him most of the other Goan leaders are very irresponsible. I had asked Kakodkar to see me from time to time, chiefly because I wanted to encourage him. He has an impression that our Ministry does not like his coming and seeing me. In fact, Asoka Mehta has told me something to that effect, perhaps thinking that I should not be troubled in this way. I think Asoka Mehta should be informed that I had particularly asked Kakodkar to see me sometimes and he should not be discouraged from doing so.

5. Kakodkar was greatly worried about the extensive smuggling that, according to him, is still going on between Goa and India. He often visits the border and he said that he was quite sure of this.

6. Kakodkar's wife is ill and is probably suffering from T.B. She is going to be sent to a hospital. He mentioned to me that these hospital expenses are likely to be heavy. At present he is paid an allowance of Rs 400/- a month plus Rs 100/- as travelling expenses. We might consider the question of paying any hospital expenses separately.

1. Note to N.R. Pillai, Secretary General, MEA, and Subimal Dutt, Foreign Secretary, 21 January 1957. JN Collection.
2. A leader of the Praja Socialist Party.
3. See the preceding item.
4. Purushottam Kakodkar, a Goan nationalist leader who was arrested in Goa in 1946 and kept in a Lisbon jail for several years.

7. Once when Kakodar was here, he suggested that perhaps he might be paid the allowance not through the Ministry, but through the Prime Minister's Secretariat, or in some other way. I had agreed to this, but later we decided to carry on with the old practice. Evidently, he is not happy about this and he asked me if it was not possible to have the cheque sent direct, preferably from the PM's office, to his wife to the Bombay address as Kakodkar is often travelling about. I think this might be agreed to.

8. A copy of this note might be sent to FS in Calcutta. When he comes here, we could have a talk.

3. Cable to V.K. Krishna Menon[1]

... Your telegram 78 January 21.[2] I agree with you that it would be undesirable to raise the question of Goa and India specifically in the debate about non-self-governing territories. But it would be desirable to mention Goa lest it be thought that we do not consider it a colonial territory. It is for you to decide how best to deal with the matter.

Portuguese Government has announced release of Indian satyagrahi prisoners in Goa.[3] We do not know yet who and how many are going to be released. There are over forty Indian prisoners there and one or two who claim to be Indian nationals are not accepted as such by Portuguese Government. There are, of course, hundreds of Goans in prison for political reasons. These will not be affected by order of release.

There is no doubt that this release of Indians in Goa has been brought about by pressure on Portugal by US Government.

1. New Delhi, 23 January 1957. File No. 14-KU, Vol. I, MEA. Extracts.
2. V.K. Krishna Menon, India's representative to the UN General Assembly, reported that Portugal had refused to submit information about Goa to the Fourth (Trusteeship) Committee of the Assembly. Pointing out that there was "reasonably wide demand for insisting that she should do so." He asked Nehru whether "we should speak about Goa as one of the colonial territories without going into the issues concerning Goa and India" in the debate about non-self-governing territories. He argued that "not mentioning the word Goa at all could be tantamount to acquiescence in the view that Goa is part of Portugal and not a colony."
3. Thirty-two Indian prisoners in Goa were released on 2 February 1957.

8

EXTERNAL AFFAIRS

I. GENERAL

1. The International Situation—I[1]

Jawaharlal Nehru: Mr Deputy Chairman,[2] Sir, I beg to move:

"That the present international situation and the policy of the Government of India in relation thereto be taken into consideration."

I welcome, Sir, this debate in this House on international affairs for a number of reasons: firstly, because in such a debate the comments made by honourable Members are very helpful to Government in considering the situation; secondly, because we feel that in regard to this question of international affairs and these developments in regard to them Parliament should be kept in as close touch, as possible, in fact not only Parliament but the people of India. Indeed I have an idea that probably our people generally in the country are more internationally conscious than the people of many other countries. They take interest in these international problems. Our press, I think, devotes more space to them relatively speaking than the press of many other countries. I think that is good because these international problems not only affect our own internal problems—we have therefore to see our own internal problems in some relation to them—but also because thinking of international problems tends to widen our own vision which is right. Otherwise we become perhaps overconscious of the little circle of problems with which we have to deal daily forgetting the larger context in which they function. So, I welcome this debate. At the same time I have a sense of slight unhappiness in not being able to place before this House, on this occasion at least, any very clear-cut information or clear-cut ideas about many things that are happening. We react moderately or powerfully to events, we criticise them, sometimes we condemn them and we express our disapproval of things. That is fairly easy—whether it helps or not is another matter. It is always easy to condemn others. It is a little more difficult to condemn ourselves or to see our own errors.

1. Statement in the Rajya Sabha, 3 December 1956. *Parliamentary Debates* (*Rajya Sabha*), Vol. XV, 1956, cols. 1315-1341. Extracts.
2. S.V. Krishnamoorthy Rao, Deputy Chairman, Rajya Sabha, 1952-62.

Much has happened in the past few months which, as the House well knows, has been disapproved of by us and we have expressed our concern and disapproval about it. Much is happening today which we feel very greatly concerned about, not only in its individual context of good or evil but, even more so, in the consequences it has or may have on world peace. We are, in fact, going back or have gone back to the concept of the 'cold war' in its intense form. Because of these happenings, a certain process of drawing away from it which has been observed during the last two or three years has not only been halted but, for the moment at least, reversed. I do not personally believe that it can be wholly reversed. Too much has happened for us to go back to two or three years ago, but it is a fact that, for the moment, passions have been rising because of some deplorable happenings and the result is something which comes in the way of any cool thinking or dispassionate and objective consideration of events. I can very well understand those strong passions that have been roused and in fact, our own tendency is to react in that way. Nevertheless, we have tried, to the best of our ability, to understand these problems not with a view merely to express an opinion in regard to them, but with a view to help in controlling a deteriorating situation or in finding some peaceful methods for its solution. The governing factor in our thinking and in our action has been this—how can we help in improving the situation, not merely how we can express our reactions or feelings strongly in regard to it? That is relatively easy.

Now, broadly speaking, there are two major problems before the world, or rather two sets of problems. One might be said to concern Egypt and all that has happened there including the Israelite invasion, the Anglo-French intervention and invasion and all the rest that has happened. The other concerns Hungary and all that that has happened there or may be happening now. These two sets of problems have rather put in the shade many other things that are happening in the world—many other things to which, normally speaking, I would have drawn the attention of this House and spoken about, whether it is Indo-China or whether it is our relations with our neighbouring countries or other matters. And so, today also more or less I shall concentrate my remarks on these two major issues that are giving us so much trouble.

I should like to say just a few words about Pakistan right at the beginning and I am saying these words because, only this morning or yesterday, I read the report of a speech by the Prime Minister of Pakistan in which India found a prominent place.[3] India finds a prominent place, indeed, in many speeches in Pakistan as well as in the press of Pakistan. Normally speaking, one might have

---

3. For Suhrawardy's remarks at Lahore on 2 December 1956, see *post*, p. 427.

felt a little flattered at the attention that is being given to India. But it is really most unfortunate how some leading authorities in Pakistan and the press there have developed certain obsessions and complexes which make it difficult for them to consider any matter in a straightforward way. The other day, a prominent paper of Karachi which refers to India almost in every issue and leading article called India the greatest enemy, of course. And frequently, I read in those papers from Pakistan articles or comments which amaze and distress me. I can understand their not agreeing with us or their disapproving us or their criticising us. But there are certain standards which, I do hope, might be maintained—certain standards of relatively objective consideration of problems.

Now when we have these major problems outside whether it is Egypt, whether it is Hungary or whether it is any other problem and we are busy in our own country with our Five Year Plan or other matters, we do not go on discussing our relations with Pakistan. Maybe, in this House or in the other, we answer questions about it. We may not agree with them, but anyhow, we are relatively cool about it. We are not excited about it and I do submit that, however bad or difficult a problem may be, excitement does not help. And it amazes me—this state of affairs in Pakistan which finds expression in these exuberant speeches or articles. The Foreign Minister of Pakistan,[4] in the course of the last few weeks or some months, has occasionally made statements which, if I may say so, have almost set a new standard in regard to statements of foreign ministers of any country. I do not wish to revive it or maintain their standard. But it is regrettable that even the normal courtesy and decorum on international affairs, on international controversies or contacts are being forgotten in Pakistan in regard to these matters. What has happened after all? Many things have happened in the world. What has happened vis-a-vis India and Pakistan in the course of the last few weeks that in speeches, statement after statement is being made by their prominent men attacking India? I have thought and thought over it. Of course, you may say, "Oh! In Kashmir they have passed the Constitution." Well, that is so. They have passed the Constitution—and a good thing too. But they have been considering this in the same Constituent Assembly for the last three or four years—four years, I think. Step by step they have gone over it and it has functioned not only as a Constituent Assembly, but as a Legislative Assembly also and they have, as the House knows, passed a number of laws, made land reforms and all kinds of things. And now, as a final step, they have finalised the Constitution.[5] They have every right to do it. And it may be that this has come as a shock to some people in Pakistan who do not keep pace with events, with the

4. Feroz Khan Noon.
5. On 17 November 1956.

changed conditions. I am sorry if they are so backward in their thinking or in feeling as to what is happening in the wide world. And now there is a barrage of propaganda, attack on India, because of that—if it is because of that. I do not wish to say much about Kashmir now, because we have to consider other issues today. But I should like to say that all this talk which is so often repeated in Pakistan and sometimes in important sections of the foreign press about Kashmir to the effect that India is breaking its pledges, India is going back on her assurances and so on and so forth is, I may say with all respect, so absolutely devoid of any foundation or any objective consideration of the course of history during the past nine years that I am surprised that any responsible person should go on repeating it.

The first thing to remember, and remember it always, is that Pakistan is the aggressor in Kashmir, and it is about time that everybody knew about it. In India it is not necessary, but in Pakistan and in foreign countries it is about time that people who go on criticising India should give us their explanation of this fact. Do they deny this fact? Let us have a factual understanding with regard to these points. Opinions may differ. But let us have a clear understanding of all the facts, and the major fact is that Pakistan committed aggression, and still continues aggression in part of the Kashmir territory. That is the major fact. And I may remind the House that when they talk about plebiscite and about India going back on this first Resolution and the major Resolution of the United Nations Commission they completely forget that the first thing that was put down in that Resolution was—I do not remember the exact wording—that Pakistan's armies were there.[6] That had been denied by Pakistan. The first thing that the Resolution said was that Pakistan's armies must be withdrawn from the territory of Jammu and Kashmir. That was eight years ago, but that has not been done even up till now. Now, who has failed in carrying out international obligations? Every other obligation followed from that. For instance, we were asked not to withdraw all our armies, but to withdraw—what was that word? I think it was 'bulk'—the bulk of our armies from there. But it was admitted and clearly understood that it was India's duty to give protection to Kashmir. That was made perfectly clear. And after our experience of this utterly unprovoked and unjustified aggression on the Pakistan side, we were not going to leave Kashmir a vacuum for anybody to walk in like that. And after the accession of

6. The 13 August 1948 UNCIP Resolution stated that the presence of Pakistani troops in Jammu and Kashmir constituted a "material change" in the situation, "since it was represented by the Government of Pakistan before the Security Council, the Government of Pakistan agrees to withdraw its troops from the State."

Kashmir it was our constitutional and legal duty to protect Kashmir. So, that is admitted by everybody and by even the Commission. But when they said that Pakistan's armies must be withdrawn, we agreed to withdraw part of our armies— if you like, the bulk of our armies—and to maintain adequate numbers for the protection of Kashmir. That was our duty.

So, that is the position. Now, eight years have elapsed, and they have not yet withdrawn their armies; they sit there still. We went—maybe we were wrong in this, but because of our strong desire for peace and in order to come to terms with our neighbouring country we went—very far in our talks. It may well be that many honourable Members sitting here might think that we went too far in our talks, but it exhibited the length to which we were prepared to go to settle this question peacefully. And we discussed the question of withdrawal of our armies and other things, although we could well have said: "No, no. We would not talk to you till you have withdrawn your armies." That was a perfectly legitimate question. We could have easily said, "At least put an end to the aggression by withdrawing your armies." We were perfectly justified in saying that we would not talk to them. Still, we talked to them, and even then we could not come to any agreement with them. Even after the withdrawal of their army, I challenge anybody to deny what I say that Pakistan committed aggression in Kashmir. Secondly, that aggression is a continuing aggression, because they have got their armies in one-third of the whole territory of Jammu and Kashmir. And it is true we have moderated our position and we have tried to come to terms with them, and we have even given up the strong position that we had.

But these two basic facts remain. The original Resolution of the United Nations Commission laid down as a first thing that Pakistan must withdraw its armies. That has not been done, although eight years have passed. Now, when this Resolution was passed, most of us thought, and certainly I thought that in the course of a year or eighteen months the Resolution will be given effect to and we will try to solve the problem. And because of that, we rather held our hands in regard to various developments in Kashmir. Well, a year passed, two years passed, three years passed, and like that so many years passed, but no kind of a settlement or even an approach to a settlement came, and Pakistan would not even withdraw its army. Therefore, ultimately we said: "We cannot wait for ever or wait till Pakistan agreed to do something, and we have to go our way in Kashmir." It was then that the Jammu and Kashmir Government decided to convene a Constituent Assembly, after two or three years had elapsed and nothing had been done. They asked us, and we said: "You are completely welcome to do it—not only a Constituent Assembly, but a Legislative Assembly." They were anxious to have land reforms and various other reforms. So, they went ahead with it. At that time, there was an outcry in Pakistan, when this Assembly was going to meet, and they said something about India going behind her assurances and promises. Our representative at that time—I think Shri B.N. Rau or Shri Gopalaswami Ayyangar, I am not sure, one of them anyhow—said that the Jammu and Kashmir Government had a perfect right to have an Assembly—Legislative or Constituent Assembly—and they had perfect right to frame their own Constitution, but the Jammu and Kashmir Government or their Assembly cannot bind down the Government of India or our Parliament.[7] That was patent. But we did not wish to come in their way to go ahead. So, we said that any undertakings that we have given, we shall stand by them, that is to say, any action in Kashmir will not come in the way, although other matters may come in the way. And so, we made that clear statement. Now, if I may repeat, the very first part of that joint undertaking between the two countries and the UN Commission about the withdrawal of Pakistan's troops was never given effect to. But we cannot wait for ever before we take any action. Secondly, eight years have passed, or even more than eight years since this Kashmir trouble in its present form started. And after all there is such a thing as an assurance not going on for ever and holding things up. Therefore, we certainly allowed and encouraged the Kashmir Government to go ahead with framing their Constitution. I stated, either in this House or in the other, about the beginning of this year or last year that there must be some finality about these things. It cannot be kept open because Pakistan won't act in a particular way. So, that much about Kashmir.

And may I add that we are not at all alarmed at the prospect of this matter being taken up in the Security Council? If it is taken up, well, we shall have to go back to the whole ABC of this problem, and ask the Security Council, before it does anything else, to examine the aggression issue. Let it examine that issue fully as well as the other connected issues and not just take it somewhere midway, because in our desire to have a settlement, we had made various suggestions, and in fact various proposals were made.

H.C. Dasappa[8] (Mysore): What about the Pakistan Prime Minister's reference to an attack from India?

JN: Yes, the honourable Member is perfectly right. What he says is rather amazing to me. It has been stated here[9] as follows:

---

7. B.N. Rau said this in the UN Security Council on 1 March 1951.
8. Congress member of the Rajya Sabha, 1954-57.
9. As reported in the *Dawn*, 3 December 1956.

The Pakistan Prime Minister, Mr Suhrawardy, declared here today that Pakistan would continue to seek alliances—military and otherwise—as long as there was "even a remote danger from India to the country's safety and territorial integrity."

He stated that Indians as a whole had not accepted Pakistan's existence and there was every possibility of a leadership arising in India which might work for 'greater India' by undoing partition and annexing Pakistan.

He took pains to defend Pakistan's membership of the Baghdad Pact and said: "Even if there is a five per cent or a two per cent chance of an attack (from India), I must be strong enough to see that that chance should be zero per cent!".

It is entirely for the Prime Minister of Pakistan and his Government to decide what alliances or pacts they sign with other countries. They are an independent country, but it is for us to decide as to what our reactions should be to what they do. The House will remember that this question of Kashmir itself was powerfully affected by the fact that Pakistan came to an agreement with the United States of America for supplying arms, armaments. That changed the situation completely from our point of view and we made it perfectly clear. In fact, talks were going on with the Pakistan Prime Minister and they suddenly came to an end. I do not object in the slightest; how can I? Pakistan is a completely independent country, and I do not wish to come in the way of their alliances at all, but if those alliances in my opinion affect my country, I have to shape my country's policy accordingly; I have to shape our attitude in regard to any world question accordingly.

Mr Suhrawardy thinks that Pakistan stands in danger of an attack from India. What can I say about that except that this kind of thinking itself, I think, is the result, shall I say an obsession, some kind of obsession or complex that they may have developed? Anything more remote from reality I cannot imagine in this wide world. I cannot speak obviously for every individual in India. I do not know what certain persons with perverted ideas may wish or may not wish, but I do say that it is completely wrong to think or to say that people in India have not accepted Pakistan. They have completely accepted Pakistan, and they have accepted it not only because we agreed to Pakistan, the partition of India—Pakistan came into existence therefore with our agreement—but also because all that has happened in these past years has made it perfectly clear to my mind—and I hope to other minds too—that any kind of the slightest reversal of that partition would be highly injurious certainly to India. Here we are busy with our plans, Five Year Plans, and all kinds of schemes for development, and it would be a person who can only be described as a fool or a lunatic who would put aside all these problems and work of ours and indulge in adventures of that kind. Apart from any other point of view, from the strictly opportunist point of view in favour of India, it would be completely wrong for anyone to think of any kind of adventure or action against Pakistan. I want to make this perfectly clear. It is not a question, as Mr Suhrawardy seems to imagine, that some kind of alternative leadership might do it. Honourable Members are sitting opposite here and in the country, and I am quite sure that there is no alternative leadership which thinks in those terms. The fact of the matter is that the complete failure of Pakistan's policies, international and national, have led them to find some excuse for their public. About their national policies, it is not for me to talk about them, but we know what the economic and political conditions there are—they are not conditions on which one can congratulate anyone. We know, and here a fact which is more important than any other fact, certainly more important than the Kashmir issue, is this fact of the continuous exodus from East Pakistan to India. Let Pakistan explain. Let the great journals of the Western world who talk so much about Pakistan and India explain. They moralise to us and tell us what our duties are. This is an amazing phenomenon. Years have passed; year after year passes, and the exodus continues and three and a half million people have come from East Pakistan to India, maybe more.

Mehr Chand Khanna (Minister for Rehabilitation): More than four millions.

JN: My friend says more than four millions. It is an amazing number. One can understand the original exodus from India to Pakistan and from Pakistan to India. There was an upheaval, and it happens, but this is a kind of continuing thing. Surely there is something very sick there, some illness, some disease, which afflicts the people there, which makes this happen, but we are talking about Pakistan's policies.

Mr Suhrawardy talked a great deal about military alliances and pacts. So far as I am concerned, he is welcome to his military alliances. He can have a few more if he likes, because if there is anything that is absolutely clear, that has become clear in the last few months: it is the weakness or futility of these military alliances and pacts. I do not quite know what has happened to the SEATO. Nobody has mentioned about it from India for a very very long time, but mention is certainly made of the Baghdad Pact. A good deal of mention has been made of the Baghdad Pact, but the Baghdad Pact has undergone a strange transformation. In some ways, the most important member of the Baghdad Pact and certainly the biggest country, the most powerful country in the Pact is the United Kingdom. Now, we find some of the other members of the Pact meeting together and proclaiming: "We have not invited the United Kingdom. We do not want it in this." And it is going to be something in the nature of what is called a Muslim bloc. They are welcome to it, but the House will see it is changing its character. It is hinted that the United Kingdom may not be in it but that they would like the United States of America to come in as the leading Muslim power, I suppose, in the world. It is really extraordinary, the way these things are explained. I doubt very much—I cannot speak for the USA—but I would certainly imagine that the USA is not happy at its being dragged into this peculiar position.

Take this Muslim bloc idea. What was the result of the Baghdad Pact right at the beginning? The first result of the Baghdad Pact was mainly to bring security to the Mid-Eastern countries. After all—what was it meant against? It was presumably against the Soviet Union. Now I am not quite clear what Mr Suhrawardy or his predecessors in the Prime Ministership of Pakistan thought about it, because they have spoken in differing voices. They have spoken with great assurance to the United States and to the other countries that in this Pact, of course, we join you in your fight against communism. This Pact is not meant to be against India. I know they have said so both to the United States and to the United Kingdom and other countries: "It is entirely against the danger from the North that we have this." I know also that they have said to the leaders of the Soviet Union: "This has nothing to do with communism. Not at all. We are not afraid of you. It is against India." So these kinds of different statements have been made. I don't know. Whatever it was, the fact remains that the Baghdad Pact was one of the major reasons, I think, for the countries of Western Asia and Egypt falling out among themselves. There was a split in the Arab League which had been holding together.[10] On the one side Iraq and Pakistan and Iraq and Turkey and one or two other countries and on the other side, Egypt, Syria and Saudi Arabia. Jordan was, to some extent, on this side then. Since then it appears to have shifted somewhat. So this famous attempt at securing security of the Mid-East resulted, first of all, in this breaking up of the Arab League and the conflict between those countries is there and it served almost as an invitation for the Soviet Government to take greater interest in Mid-East. Of course the mere fact of geography, the fact that the Soviet Union is there also inevitably makes it take interest. You cannot expect to ignore a great power when it is sitting at your doorstep and decide on major policies without the slightest reference to it, but anyhow this was the result of the Baghdad Pact.

Gradually many other things happened. I cannot—I am not giving you the history of this but there was the sale of arms, aircraft, etc., from the Soviet

10. The League of Arab States was established in Cairo in March 1945 by seven Arab States, then independent or on the threshold of independence—Egypt, Iraq, Saudi Arabia, Yemen, Trans-Jordan (later Jordan), Syria and Lebanon. The split in the Arab League was caused by Iraq's adherence to the Baghdad Pact in 1955-56.

Union, from Czechoslovakia and others, to Egypt and to Syria, and maybe to one or two other countries, which created a great deal of consternation. I say even that was at least partly due to the system of alliances. If you have an alliance on the one side, inevitably it produced reaction in the other and they try to do that themselves or without an alliance they try to help countries which might serve their purpose. This is the normal way in international affairs. You build up a system of military alliances on the one side. Another system grows up on the other. You build up NATO and the Warsaw Treaty comes up on the other so that you cannot deal with these questions by the system of alliances and we have seen it today how it broke down. It is breaking down. There was the Baghdad alliance and there were others. They broke down in the stress of events; between Greece, Turkey and Yugoslavia, other factors came in. So, as I was saying, one of the great things that has happened is the futility of this system of alliances, but if Mr Suhrawardy pins his faith in the Baghdad Pact, he is welcome to it. Anyhow what can I do about it except to say that it is our conviction that these systems of military alliances come in the way of peace, promote insecurity, do not bring about security for which they are intended and actually help in the race for armaments?

So, now, as I mentioned it at the beginning, there are two major areas of trouble—Egypt and Western Asia, and Hungary. The two are, of course, entirely different in kind. In Egypt and in the Western countries, a great deal has happened subsequent to the Anglo-French invasion. But if you wish to prevent yourself getting entangled in all these matters, I think you will come to the conclusion that the very basis of the present trouble is the presence of foreign forces in Egyptian territory. Of course I can go back to before they came, but I am not going back to it. It was on the one hand the Israeli invasion of Egypt that started the new and acute phase of this trouble and on the other hand the Anglo-French bombing of Cairo, etc., and subsequent landing of forces there. Now so long as those forces are not withdrawn, whether they are the Israeli forces or the Anglo-French forces, so long you cannot get on with any kind of a settlement of any problem there, even mainly dealing with the Suez Canal. We are anxious to have the Suez Canal function as other countries are, but you cannot just do it. You cannot do it till you get rid of these forces which always keep the situation tense and on the verge of war. That, I think, is the core of the problem. Now, if one looks at the present state of affairs in some of the West Asian countries one sees confusion. One sees, to some extent, a process of disintegration going on. It is an extraordinary state of affairs, each country complaining against the other. It is difficult for me, with all the sources of information at my disposal, to find out exactly what is happening. It must be much more difficult for honourable Members who have fewer sources of information. We read reports of armies being massed on the borders of countries. Russia, it is said, is massing armies on the borders of some countries. Turkey is massing armies somewhere else or Iraq is massing somewhere. All these are newspaper reports. I don't say that they are correct. I am not saying it. But newspapers every day contain reports of troop movements to this border or that border; whether Russia is massing her armies there or Turkey's armies are massed on the Iraqi border or on the Syrian border or some other border or the Iraqi armies on the Syrian border or Iraqi armies are sitting in Jordan, it is a most confusing situation. And behind these movements are all kinds of intrigues to pull down this Government or even ideas of, well, putting an end to one or two odd countries and annexing parts of their territories, possibly ideas encouraged sometimes by other more distant powers but anyhow affecting the policies of those countries there.

Meanwhile, there have been internal troubles. There is no doubt about it that all over the Arab countries there has been intense feeling against the Israeli invasion of Egypt and the Anglo-French action in Egypt. There is no doubt about it. Nevertheless an attempt has been made by some Governments to oppose Egypt in many ways, to oppose the feeling for Egypt in their own countries. There has been trouble in Iraq because the people are pro-Egypt and the Government does not like it. There has been a good deal of trouble there. Only this morning, honourable Members may have seen the strange arguments advanced by the Prime Minister of Pakistan which are critical of Egypt.[11] After all that has happened, for Pakistan to say that is surprising indeed. It shows the confusion that exists. For the sake of this argument, we may treat Pakistan as a country of the Middle East because its politics and the rest are more or less on those lines though rather more backward than those of the countries of the Middle East.

What am I to tell this House about this confusing situation except that one sees, by the Israeli attack on Egypt and by the Anglo-French attack on Egypt a certain process of disruption and disintegration having started there. The first thing to check this process is for the Anglo-French and the Israeli troops to be withdrawn. Then only can you deal with the situation. Fortunately, the United Nations have taken swift steps to form an international force and we have

---

11. Speaking in Lahore on 2 December, Suhrawardy criticised the policy of neutrality followed by some countries, including India, and stated: "Egypt thought and said she was neutral. That is why nobody came to her assistance. She had to pay for her neutrality. Not a single Arab stirred from his home to assist her in spite of her military alliances with some Arab countries."

contributed to it; our detachment is there.[12] If I may put it in another way, vacuums have been created and are being created in the Middle East and a vacuum cannot exist for long, especially a power vacuum, and there is rivalry as to who will succeed in filling that vacuum. Previously, all this area was supposed to be an area of British influence. Now, the British influence has greatly lessened, to say the least of it. Now, who is to fill that vacuum? It may be either the countries themselves or some outside countries. Naturally, we want these countries to be independent, to profit by their resources and to be on friendly terms with other countries, but not to be under the subordination of other countries. Now, there is that vacuum at present and whenever there is a vacuum in such a way, dangers arise. Dangers are not local because, if anything further happens there in the shape of any conflict, immediately it may affect the whole world situation; it may develop into a world war and because of this—the same thing applies to Hungary—we have to be very careful as to what we say and what we do.

Our primary object is to prevent war and the secondary object is to help in improving the situation and lessening tensions. If really to satisfy some inner urge in us, we take some action and that action results in worsening the situation, well, that is poor satisfaction that we have condemned the world by giving expression to our strongly-felt opinions but have helped the world go towards the pit of disaster. This is what often checks us and has checked us. Many honourable Members here and the public naturally are not in almost daily contact with things happening and with the dangers of the situation. They react as any normal human beings would react in expressing their opinions, but a government cannot easily react in that way of expressing itself strongly when it feels that the situation is not so simple. It is not black and white; there are shades of grey and one just cannot say "yes" or "no". After all, the objective is not the condemnation or the praise of a government but the settlement of a problem or the easing of tension.

May I repeat that in regard to Egypt, the first thing is the withdrawal of these troops. Unfortunately, there has been great delay in this. After all, there was great speed in bringing them there, and therefore there should be no physical difficulty in taking them away. I am glad to say, as far as I can say, that it is agreed that the Anglo-French and the Israeli forces are going to be withdrawn. They have agreed to that. I am not saying anything from secret knowledge; this is what has been said repeatedly. I hope they will be withdrawn soon. I believe

12. The UN General Assembly on 5 November 1956 adopted a resolution for the setting up of a United Nations Emergency Force for Egypt. See *Selected Works* (second series), Vol. 35, p. 435 and p. 444.

that the Foreign Minister of the United Kingdom is going to make a statement[13] this afternoon in the British House of Commons and I hope that he will make this point clear in his statement. Therefore, I shall not say much more about it now.

I should like to say a few words about Hungary. Again, here is a question which has powerfully affected people and has raised passions. It has been a terrible tragedy; there is no doubt about it, as I stated in the other House. I have no doubt in my mind that in Hungary there has been a popular movement, a popular rising in which large numbers of the people there including—not only including but more especially including—the workers there, the trade unions there have participated. It is admitted by everybody that in the past numerous grave mistakes were committed in Hungary by the ruling authorities there and it is admitted that these people—everybody again—were justified in raising their voice and objecting to those things happening which are now admitted to be mistakes. But, it is said that they went too far in that direction; maybe they went too far, but the point is that it was undoubtedly a popular upheaval against certain leading people in their own country and later, it took the shape of an upheaval against the Soviet forces sent there. Well, this great tragedy occurred. Right from the beginning, I stated repeatedly two things: one is that the people of Hungary should be allowed to fashion their own destiny, and secondly, the Soviet or all foreign forces should be withdrawn from there.[14] Now, these two things have been said right from the beginning. It may be that having accepted a certain policy, it may have to be faced. Whatever it is, the practical politics of it might be considered, provided the policy is understood and is given effect to with fair speed. Things cannot disappear overnight and when these upheavals have taken place, one should like to bring about the changes in a way so as to leave not only as few scars as possible but also so as not to bring about big reactions on the other side which will again create something else. These difficulties occurred but the basic thing was that.

Now, in this matter we have been addressing the Hungarian Government and the Soviet Government as well as the other Governments who are interested and we have expressed our viewpoint and our concern and we have had replies. I shall not go into all these developments. The House will remember that we sponsored a Resolution[15] in the United Nations together with Indonesia

13. See *post,* pp. 452-453, for details.
14. See *Selected Works* (second series), Vol. 35, p. 276.
15. On 21 November, the UN General Assembly adopted this resolution by 57 votes to 8 urging Hungary to permit the entry of UN observers.

and Ceylon and maybe one or two other countries, suggesting that the Secretary General of the UN should go there or should be invited there and allowed to go there, and UN observers also, I believe, because very grave charges were made about deportations on a large-scale.[16] Now, those charges were denied by the Hungarian Government. Now, when charges are made and denied, it does not seem to us to be becoming for any responsible organisation to pass judgement without enquiring. Even though one may be inclined to believe something, one ought to have some kind of an enquiry and that is what we suggested, that the Secretary General and the UN observers might go and report. It is not a question of deliberate falsehood being spread but it is so easy in an excited atmosphere that must prevail in Hungary or in Budapest, for all kinds of petty happenings to be exaggerated, for all kinds of rumours to take the shape of facts. Honourable Members know sometimes if there is any trouble here or anywhere what wild rumours circulate about it and we find later that there was little substance in them so that it is difficult to separate the truth from the part that is exaggerated. Anyhow, we took up the position in the UN that the UN—the UN is gravely concerned with this matter—should not decide finally that this has been so, that deportations have happened when it is clearly denied, and it must enquire into it.

Now, we were anxious that opportunities for the Secretary General to go there should be afforded and we addressed the Hungarian Government on the subject pointing out to them and pleading with them that this should be so.[17] Unfortunately, our Ambassador to Hungary is also the Ambassador to the Soviet Union[18] and he fell ill just at that moment and he could not go there. We had a representative in Budapest throughout, the First Secretary, and I should like here to express my high appreciation of the way this First Secretary, Mr Rahman,[19] functioned throughout these very difficult times. I think he was one of the very very few diplomats who functioned at all in Budapest. Others were there but I do not think they functioned at all during this period, but Mr Rahman continued to function and continued to report although it took many days for the report to reach us. Because our Ambassador to Hungary, Mr K.P.S. Menon could not go there, we asked our Ambassador in Prague, Mr Khosla,[20] to proceed there immediately as my personal representative to meet the Hungarian authorities

16. See *Selected Works* (second series), Vol. 35, p. 352.
17. For Nehru's messages in this regard, see *Selected Works* (second series), Vol. 35, pp. 476-477.
18. K.P.S. Menon.
19. M.A. Rahman, Charge d'Affaires, Budapest.
20. Jagan Nath Khosla, Ambassador to Czechoslovakia, 1955-58.

and he has been there and is still there now. I believe now Ambassador K.P.S. Menon has also arrived there yesterday. So we tried our utmost to explain our position to the Hungarian authorities because we attach great importance to the Secretary General of the UN being invited to go there as well as UN observers. Now, normally it is not a good thing for a country to accept outside observers to come in but in the peculiar circumstances of the case and this question of deportations having been raised, we thought it would be desirable. But I am very, very sorry that up till now neither the Hungarian Government nor the Soviet Government has agreed to the Secretary General going or to the observers going there. They have said, "this will be an infringement of our sovereignty and these people coming from outside might unsettle settled things in the public mind". Well, it is very unfortunate and they say that there are hundreds and hundreds—600 I believe—of foreign correspondents and "it is not that we are hiding anything"! But the fact remains—I think that is most unfortunate—that they are not allowing the Secretary General of the United Nations to go there. And the natural inference from this is that people begin to think that the charges brought against them in regard to deportations and others are true or partly true. I hesitate even now to pass final judgement because they have denied them but I cannot hide the fact from this House that the inference which is created in people's minds is that there is some truth at least in those charges and that perhaps they may have been exaggerated.

Then, again, there has been this case which I consider most unfortunate, the case of Mr Nagy[21]—it is spelt Nagy but it is pronounced, I believe, as 'Nodge'— the previous Premier of Hungary. Now, he took refuge, sought asylum in the Yugoslav Embassy in Budapest; he and some colleagues of his. I will not go into that question as to how and under what circumstances he did that but he did it. Later the Yugoslav Government and the Hungarian Government of Mr Kadar[22] came to an agreement and written assurances were given about Mr Nagy returning to his house there. While he was returning, he was arrested by Soviet authorities and sent to Rumania. Now, I must confess....

H.N. Kunzru[23] (Uttar Pradesh): Is it certain that Mr Nagy is in Rumania now?

---

21. Imre Nagy, Prime Minister of Hungary, October-November 1956; took refuge in the Yugoslav Embassy on 4 November, and on 24 November he was deported to Romania; executed by the Russians in 1958 for his part in the Hungarian uprising
22. Janos Kadar, Prime Minister of Hungary, 1956-58.
23. Congress Member of Rajya Sabha, 1952-62.

JN: I believe he is. I believe he is in Rumania; not only in Rumania but in the Carpathian mountains. He is being kept in a very healthy spot—one of the health resorts of Rumania in the Carpathian mountains. The fact is, I believe, that he is there, he and his colleagues. Also some letters have come from him to his people, I believe, in Budapest. But even though he may be kept comfortably in a health resort, the fact remains that this breaking of an assurance given by the Kadar Government, either breaking it itself or being unable to keep to it, is a very serious matter and I am not surprised at the Yugoslav Government feeling indignant over it and very unhappy about it. I believe that they have published certain documents. All this does create a very unfortunate impression about the way things have been done in Hungary.

Now, I might mention that today the General Assembly of the UNO is likely to consider a Resolution on Hungary.[24] I am mentioning this just to put before the House how difficult our position becomes when a complicated position is dealt with in a simple way and you have to say 'yes' or 'no' to it when neither 'yes' nor 'no' is a correct answer in our opinion. I shall just briefly tell the House what the resolution is. I think it has appeared in the press. I don't remember. Anyhow, here the resolution refers to all the previous resolutions on Hungary passed by the General Assembly and indirectly, if not confirms them but in a sense does confirm them. Of all the previous resolutions, one was our own resolution. In regard to one we were partly agreeable; in regard to some we disagreed completely. Now, in this in the preamble there is this general sweep about all the other resolutions. We do not agree with all the other resolutions that had been passed. We may explain this, of course, but I am saying about the difficulty when we have to vote. If we vote 'yes' we vote for something which we disagreed with in the past. If we vote 'no' then we vote against something which we want to vote for and this difficulty arises. Then, again, in this resolution the Hungarian Government is repeatedly referred to as the Hungarian authorities, that is, the Soviet Government and the Hungarian authorities. That, of course, is deliberate. Now, the Hungarian Government, it may well be so, is not a government which is functioning entirely with its own will and power. That might well be so. I am inclined to think so myself, but deliberately not to call it a Government means that you are not going to deal with it as a Government and they will not deal with you and other steps you have to take later. In fact, you are closing the ground for dealing with them as a Government and preparing the ground for dealing with them in some other way. Now, that may or may not be justified; but that certainly comes in the way of any peaceful approach to this

24. See *post*, pp. 559-560.

problem by consent of the Hungarian Government and the Soviet Government—whether it is in regard to the removal of the Soviet troops or anything else. So that, it is not a wise approach, even though the statement itself may have some truth in it. Then there is a reference to this deportation of Hungarian citizens, as if it is a continuing process. Now, again I say this is denied completely by the Hungarian Government and the Soviet Government. For us it is true that their refusal to allow the Secretary General or others to go there does put a great deal of blame on them and it is for them to justify all this. Nevertheless, for the UN to accept as a fact something which is denied stoutly in this formal way seems to us not quite correct. Then the resolution goes on. It says that they must be called upon—the Hungarian authorities and the Soviet Union—to send a final reply in the next four days. That is all right except that in such matters an ultimatum of four days—the time and the date—does not help. The point is what are we aiming at? We are aiming at some kind of a solution on the lines which I have indicated, that is, the removal of the Soviet armies from there, that is, the Hungarian people should decide for themselves. Now, if we create conditions which prevent this that is not a wise move.

Then, another thing it says, ask the Secretary General immediately to despatch observers to Hungary and other countries. Now, observe, we ourselves are in favour of the despatch of observers to Hungary, but obviously they can only go to Hungary if the Hungarian Government lets them. They cannot go at the head of an army to observe and to force the Hungarian Government. If the Hungarian Government does not let them go, obviously they cannot go into Hungary. To send them to other countries, to observe what is happening in Hungary, seems rather odd. It means really to go to the refugees from Hungary, to the emigres from Hungary, and get their accounts. Now, their accounts are valuable—I do not say they are not—but obviously the accounts of the refugees are one-sided, very excited accounts and it is difficult to form an objective judgment of the situation from that. It only will probably give us a more exaggerated view of a very bad situation and anyhow it will be a view of something that has occurred not of the present.

K.S. Hegde[25] (Madras): What is the alternative that we are suggesting?

JN: "What is the alternative that we are suggesting"—to whom?

---

25. (1910-1990); Congress member of the Rajya Sabha, 1952-57; Vice-Chairman, Rajya Sabha, 1953-54; Speaker, Lok Sabha, 1977-80.

K.S. Hegde: The course that may be adopted by the United Nations.

JN: It is not up to me to suggest alternatives. I say this does not work and I say this Resolution could have been easily improved upon with a view to making it constructive and functioning. I can improve upon it. I want this process to go on. I want the Secretary General and the UN observers to go there. But this thing, at least part of it, I agree with. I have mentioned to you this resolution because the difficulty that arises is that with part of it we agree and part of it we do not. Now, we cannot say 'yes' and we cannot say 'no'. We get into these difficulties. They cannot easily be solved.

Now, I do not know how things will shape themselves there, but here is a situation which may well drift to war whether in the Middle East or in Hungary, because whether you like or you do not like, the fact remains that you cannot take steps which involve the sudden humiliation of any country—sometimes you have to, that is a different matter—whether it is England, whether it is Egypt, whether it is any country. The way to get things done is to lay stress on what you want done avoiding humiliation. Then a country gradually agrees to it. But if in our passion and anger we wish to humiliate a country into the bargain, then it resists that and creates more difficulties and the very solution we desire becomes more difficult.

There is just one thing more I should like to mention here before I end. The House might know that I received a communication from Mr Bulganin in regard to disarmament. He had sent it to some of the great powers. He has sent me a copy. We are grateful for that. And I sent him a brief reply thanking him and saying that this really is a matter for the big powers to determine. There is nothing much for us to do about it, but we shall gladly help if our help is needed. Now, the unfortunate fact of it is that these proposals had been made at a time when these passions are excited and people think in terms of war. You really have to deal with this atmosphere and improve it and lessen the tensions before you sit down and talk about disarmament. When we read everywhere that forces are being massed on this frontier or that frontier, to talk about disarmament becomes rather unreal. That is what I say. As for the rest, the whole disarmament problem is a most vital problem of the day and until that is done I think nothing much will happen. But again there, there is China—a great country, a powerful country. Is it conceivable that some orders issued by other countries or by the UN are going to be accepted by China as orders? You cannot have it both ways, ignore China, keep China outside the pale of international society and then issue orders to China. I am quite sure that China wants peace and China would gladly agree to any reasonable proposal, but neither China nor indeed a smaller country is prepared to accept this kind of orders even though among the group giving orders might be the Soviet Union. Therefore, it gets tied up, these questions about China's recognition and the rest.

In the last few weeks we have had very eminent visitors here, as the House knows. Only yesterday or the day before—I am getting mixed up—Premier Chou En-lai was here and has gone on a tour of India for ten days or so.[26] I had occasion to talk with him about various matters. They were very profitable talks showing a very large measure of agreement, showing also a measure where we did not agree or where we agreed to differ. There is nothing very surprising about that. The surprising part is that in spite of various differences we do agree on so many matters that we can cooperate, and even where we disagreed in some matters, it is a friendly disagreement and it does not affect our friendship and cooperation. Now this afternoon we are having the Prime Minister of Nepal reaching Delhi.[27] We shall welcome him of course in a friendly and cordial way, because Nepal is particularly and closely associated with us in history, geography and culture. We want it to flourish as an independent country and to develop and progress. But quite inevitably our relations with Nepal have to be closer than those of many other countries because, as I said, of this bond of history, geography and culture.

Sir, I ventured to take a lot of time of this House, and now I move. . . .

26. Chou En-lai was in India from 28 November to 10 December 1956.
27. Tanka Prasad Acharya was on a state visit to India from 3 to 18 December 1956.

2. The International Situation—II[1]

Jawaharlal Nehru: Mr Deputy Chairman, may I, to begin with, respectfully express my appreciation of the level of debate in this House on this motion which I proposed yesterday? Certainly I have profited by it and I am sure a wider circle of people outside this House will also profit by it, because the questions before us are really complicated and they concern matters which cannot easily be dealt with in a phrase or a slogan. It is all for the good, therefore, that various aspects of these questions are put so that to some extent people might be enabled to get a right perspective.

May I, right at the beginning, also refer to what the honourable Member, Mr Bimal Ghose,[2] said about my imputing motives to people? I hope I have not done so. I do not think I have done so and so far as I remember, what I said in the Lok Sabha was that some people are influenced and swept away by, well, propagandist activities. In fact we have been swept away or influenced. We are influenced, but influenced to what extent is another matter. But that is not imputing a motive to anybody. It is merely saying that we have not, perhaps, been on the alert, or not careful enough to retain our foothold in regard to any particular matter. I referred to certain organisations and I mentioned that there are in India a number of organisations often going under rather attractive names, of freedom and democracy, but whose purpose appears to be propagandist rather than a search for truth, rather than, I would even say, a passion for freedom or democracy. Now, it is open to any organisation to do propaganda or pursue any line of action. There is freedom in this country for that to be done. I cannot object to that, although I may disagree with them. But it is necessary for us to be reminded that some of these are organisations whose membership contains many estimable persons, as the honourable Member himself says, some Ministers, Congress members, Members of Parliament and others, and estimable members of the Socialist Party. It is true that they are there. I am not quite sure that all of them often realise, or have realised in the past, that perhaps the basic purpose is rather propaganda and not so much as search for truth or democracy or freedom. That is my view and I cannot impose it on others. We know also that there are

---

1. Statement in the Rajya Sabha, 4 December 1956. *Parliamentary Debates (Rajya Sabha)*, Vol. XV, 1956, cols. 1527-1546.
2. Kisan Mazdoor Praja Party member of the Rajya Sabha, 1952-57.

organisations going by the name of, well, literary or artistic or cultural organisations, which essentially want to do propaganda under the guise of literature or culture or dancing or singing. That is so. It is open to them to do it. But I do not want to be deluded by it. I want to know where I stand and then I can accept them enjoying their dancing, singing, etc. Also, without being misled by them. That is my main point.

Another thing, if I may say so with respect is that it is the right not only of the Opposition but of anybody in the country, and even the duty, to criticise the Government. I do not object to it at all. But sometimes, the criticism seems to me to be not only wide of the mark, but, well, very much ill-advised and perhaps not quite decorous, if I may use the word, and sometimes very personal. Indeed, the other day in an English newspaper of repute, it was stated that among the various activities in India, the one activity which is very popular, most popular, is the criticism of Government, including not only by their opponents, but by their own members. I think the *Manchester Guardian* had an article by one of its correspondents to that effect. It said it is astonishing what the Government puts up with in the shape of criticism in this country. Well, I do not mind that at all. But when I retaliate in more or less moderate language, then there is a hue and cry. Then I am told that I am not fair to the other party.

This does surprise me. After all, many of us here, certainly I, we have had some experience in the past of the smell of battle, and if we indulge in a few strokes here and there, or in a battle of debates, use some language which is rather pointed, why should people talk about motives? If I may say so, it is not quite fair for some people to talk from a high moral plane to us and not expect us to reply to them. It is not fair. Either we speak on the political plane to each other or, if you like, on the moral plane to each other, if we are good enough to speak from that plane. But this mixture of the political plane with high morality, does not seem to me to be very becoming. Anyhow, this conception that the Government is there or the Members of the Government are there to be hit and sat upon, without their replying, appears to me to be a wrong conception.

In the famous fables of La Fontaine[3] in French there is a couplet:

Cet animal est tres mechant:
Quand on attaque, il se defend.

It means: This animal is wicked: when any person attacks it, it presumes to defend itself.

3. Jean De La Fontaine (1621-1695); French poet, orator and historian.

Therefore I invite friends opposite not only to oppose but certainly to criticise Government's activities—and I think it is essential that they should be criticised—but also I beg them to accept criticism too or replies to that criticism and be prepared for that.

Now, before I go on to any particular subject, there is a certain larger perspective that I should like to place before the House. The honourable Mr Bimal Ghose expressed his surprise and pleasure at the fact that he found in a document issued by a leading Communist an attempt to reason. He said that he hoped this will continue. Well, there has been something much more than that, as he knows, and that is, for the past many months or more, a repeated confession of past errors and past mistakes. That is something even more than reason. Now, if grave mistakes had been committed once, there is no particular reason why they might not be committed here and now even though the language used in justification of the here and now may be stout language. It was stout language previously too and yet it is admitted now that it has covered up numerous mistakes for which people had to suffer later. In the case of Hungary if one thing is admitted by everybody concerned, it is this that very serious and very grave mistakes were committed in Hungary in the past—I do not know, for how many years—till recently. President Tito of Yugoslavia, who is so situated both by experience and by geography as to be able to form an opinion which deserves notice—whether you agree with it or not—in a very long speech delivered last month[4] dealt with this past of that area, the many mistakes, and pointed out that it was the continuation of those wrong policies that brought about this situation in Hungary.

So that what we see today is undoubtedly a major change happening not only in outward policies which are sometimes clouded by words but something deeper in the minds of men and I have no doubt, even before the events of the last few months, quite considerable changes in thinking have taken place in the Soviet Union. In the other Communist countries of Eastern Europe, there were obstructions and difficulties in the way of their self-fulfilment, if you like, and hence this has arisen. Now there is one side of the picture, which is called the process of democratisation or liberalisation and which process of course I presume that practically every Member of this House would welcome. He may think it is going too fast or too slow but he would welcome that because this huge gap—I am not for the moment thinking of the particular merits or demerits of the process—that process was helpful in reducing the gap which separated

---

4. On 11 November 1956. For Nehru's remarks on this speech, see *Selected Works* (second series), Vol. 35, pp. 478-479 and p. 470.

the world into two major or various parts. It made it easier to keep out of this terrible climate of cold war that had persisted during the last ten or eleven years.

That was one side of it. On the other side also there were many movements visible which went towards the lessening of that cold war. That is to say, gradually people were getting a little tired of living on slogans; whether they were communist slogans or anti-communist slogans, it led them nowhere. There was coming a progressive realisation that this will not solve any problem. It was patent, looking at it from the political or military plane, that these great countries or great blocs of countries were just not going to be liquidated, neither was going to liquidate the other without being liquidated itself—that war would not settle this business. If war would not settle it, then some other way must be found, other than war. The way other than war could not be cold war because cold war itself kept up the atmosphere and climate of war and prevented any approach and might at any time develop into war. Therefore cold war too in theory was discarded not in practice so much, but people realised that it did not help. And so all this thinking and ferment in people's minds went on everywhere.

We in India—I do not mean to say the Government or the Congress Party but generally speaking we in India—are situated a little more favourably than many other countries in considering these matters, not because we are not swept away by these passions so much, pro-communist or anti-communist. Therefore we can keep our feet on the ground to some extent. We may have our sympathies this way or that way; that is a different matter. We may have our convictions but we are at least devoid of the tremendous passions of some of the protagonists of the cold war, this side or that side. Therefore we can look at things perhaps in a clear perspective and the fact that we have adopted a policy of non-alignment—of course, it is non-alignment; I do not know why Prof Kabir[5] asked for it to be called non-alignment; it is there; that is what we call it; we do not call it neutrality; neutrality is a completely wrong word in this connection—that does not mean that we have not got views of our own on various problems. But it means that we are not going to be pushed hither and thither by other countries. As far as possible we would not allow ourselves to be swept by gusts of passion, communist, pro-communist or anti-communist, but try to find our own way according to the light of our own reason and try at the same time to keep friendly relations with the rest of the world. So, that is our approach and I believe that that approach told; it did good to us and it enabled us to serve other countries or other situations at a time when it became rather difficult to find a suitable unaligned or uncommitted country. Also,

5. Humayun Kabir, Congress member of the Lok Sabha from West Bengal, 1956-62.

whatever governments might or might not feel about it, I would say even governments progressively appreciated our attitude; even governments which were themselves committed strongly to this side or that, appreciated our attitude progressively. But quite apart from them, I have no doubt at all in my mind that peoples in every country appreciated it very greatly, not, again, because India was specially virtuous or specially clever, not that, but because these people in every country hunger for some way out of this deadlock and this cold war. They wanted not to be suppressed all the time by these slogans and cries this way or that way. They were tired of it. They saw no hope in it. And they felt that a country like India—and there are other countries too—did suggest some kind of a way out of this tangle. Now, these processes, not because of India but because of the natural evolution of events, have been bringing about changes—whether it is in the Soviet Union, whether it is in the East European countries or West European countries or the United States of America, everywhere. In brief, people began to think that way, not giving up their basic convictions but feeling that that was not the way to set things right. We welcomed that.

Now, when these crises arose in Egypt or in Hungary—apart from judging the crisis as it was, condemnation or disapproval—in whatever we did or said, always at the back of our mind was this: what will help the basic objective we have? We were gravely shocked at these events. What shocked us more than the events or what alarmed us was, are these things going to come in the way of that process of development—whether it was in the Soviet Union or the United States or England or France or anywhere. That was a major thing—the various forces in the world gradually coming together and the big gap getting less and less. Now, this alarmed us that this was a setback, and while we condemned or expressed our disapproval, always we were thinking, let us not do something which encourages this setback, which puts an end to those progressive or liberalising tendencies that are functioning. And that conditioned our behaviour to some extent.

It is a little difficult for me to discuss internal happenings in countries, whether it is America or England or the Soviet Union or China, but any honourable Member who has at all studied these matters will see the changes all over occurring of ferment and change, taking place, whether it is in the so-called capitalist countries or the communist countries or others. You can see it from China to Peru, if I may say so, to use an old phrase. So, this consideration has always to be borne in mind if you want to keep the entire picture before you. How can you help the forces going towards some kind of a settlement in Europe? Now the attack on Egypt, the Israeli attack to begin with, immediately followed by the Anglo-French attack, came as a great shock to us, because

444

apart from its inherent wrongness, it was something entirely opposed to the whole current as we thought ought to go. It was undoubtedly and absolutely a reversal to pure colonial methods. There is no doubt about it. Now, it may be due, of course, to various fears and apprehensions in the mind of the United Kingdom Government. They might lose their oil, they might lose their influence in the Middle East; whatever it was, no doubt there were some reasons which had appeared to them to be adequate. Even before the setback, all that argument—for two months or more about the Suez Canal, after the nationalisation of the Suez Canal[6]—was an extraordinary argument and we expressed ourselves clearly and forcefully on many occasions in regard to that. Then came this attack at a moment when just almost on that very day of the attack, they were supposed to meet and talk in terms of their resolution in the Security Council.[7] It was an amazing thing. And if by any chance it had succeeded, it would have been a disaster. We know that it would not have succeeded. Before success came there would have been a world war and the arguments advanced—I shall perhaps deal with that a little later—about the objectives of this having been more or less achieved, seem to me really very extraordinary. However, then came Hungary—of course, not then; they overlapped rather. The Hungarian thing gradually grew up towards the end of October and November. Now, of course, I am not comparing the two in terms of badness. The two were essentially different. They represent different types of things, though equally bad. But they were different and different problems were involved in both. Above all, the question in Hungary—apart from this killing that took place—as in Poland was whether these processes of democratisation and liberalisation should continue in a stable and peaceful way and gradually bring about the changes desired by the people of the country or whether any attempt should be made perhaps to speed them— maybe they stumble and fall down and bring greater conflicts in their train. There was that danger all the time. In Poland they escaped that danger because of the leadership of the country and because of various other factors. I imagine that in Hungary they would have escaped that danger also if exactly at that time the Anglo-French invasion had not come in the other place. That is guesswork, of course; I do not know. It is a possibility. But somehow that upset

6. Nasser proclaimed the nationalization of the Suez Canal on 26 July 1956 and set up an Egyptian Canal authority to replace the existing privately owned international stock company. See *Selected Works* (second series), Vol. 34. p. 318.
7. See *Selected Works* (second series), Vol. 35, pp. 421-422.

the apple cart in many places and led to conflict in a big way and intervention by the Soviet forces. Now, let us try to understand the position.

H.N. Kunzru: May I ask the Prime Minister whether as a matter of fact it is correct to say that what happened in Egypt affected the situation in Hungary? I seek this information only for my enlightenment. The Hungarian trouble started earlier. The invasion of Egypt came about eight or nine days later and the First Secretary of the Communist Party, Mr Erno Gero, had already asked for the intervention of the Russian troops in the Hungarian revolution. Is it factually correct to say that happened?

JN: I have got the honourable Member's point. May I answer that in the little time I have got? These things were overlapping right through October. The original trouble in Hungary—in a sense, conflict—took place on the 3rd October. This led in the next two or three days to conflict, shooting, killing and something. It led later to the withdrawal of the Soviet forces and declaration on the 30th October—a declaration of policy of the Soviet Government which, considering everything, was a satisfactory and hopeful declaration. Now, the curious point is that three days after that they returned. Now, I cannot go into the whole position. Honourable Members will remember that on the 3rd November, I think it was that date, Mr Bulganin issued his famous warning to the various countries involved. We received that too, not as a warning to us but for information. I remember we got it at about eight o'clock in the evening. And I confess we were rather alarmed at that, seeing the prospects. And we sat up till a very late hour in the night, with the senior officers of our External Affairs Ministry, considering all papers and evolving a reply for Mr Bulganin, which was sent that night, in the small hours.[8] Of course, war seemed to be very near. It is difficult to disentangle all these things, because the situation was developing even before the Anglo-French attack. We know now that people had been asked, even Americans had been asked to go out of Egypt. Several days before British nationals had also been asked to leave. However, I cannot lay down these things as something which I can prove. I am merely putting something before the House as to how action and reaction takes place in these matters.

There can be no doubt that the Soviet Government, when it indulged in the second sending back of troops into Hungary, must have realised—because they are highly intelligent people—that it would go against them in world opinion,

8. For Nehru's reply of 6 November to Bulganin, see *Selected Works* (second series), Vol. 35, pp. 436-437. Also see pp. 439-440 for related references.

that they would be criticised and condemned by many people.[9] Why then did they do it? I do not know. I cannot go behind their minds. But according to them there must have been some very strong reasons; it may be fear, it may be apprehension, whatever that may be, because the whole system of Europe in the last ten years has been built up in a balancing of armies and armaments, and there is this cold war, there is the boundary of the cold war, what is called the "Iron Curtain" and what not.

Now one of the basic facts of the situation in Europe has been, when you consider disarmament or anything else, the fear of German rearmament. There is all over Eastern Europe, whether you go to Czechoslovakia or Hungary or Poland or the Soviet Union, this overriding fear of German rearmament. Twice in our generation German armies have roamed over these countries and brought infinite destruction. It may be that in some of these countries there might be two rival fears as they are because of past history, fear of Germany and fear of Russia. But there it is. There is undoubtedly in every country of Eastern Europe fear of German rearmament because they know that in the science of war as in industry Germany is top-ranking, and once they get built up a huge war machine nobody quite knows what it might do. That is governing the situation. NATO comes into existence[10] to begin with—and they may be justified—I do not know if anyone criticised them at the time. Then questions of German rearmament come in. Then Germany joins NATO.[11] All this produces the fear complex elsewhere. Then the Warsaw Treaty[12] comes in trying to balance each other.

Now the problem presumably arose that this balance was going to be upset by what was happening, the apprehension was there. The problem no longer remained—I am trying to analyse—of the freedom of Hungary or anybody but of the survival of nations in a great war. Or it might be that because of all this, whether it was in Egypt or Hungary or elsewhere, war came into the picture, and no country wants to take risks in war. They risk unpopularity but not security.

9. On the morning of 4 November 1956, the UN Security Council met in a special emergency session to discuss a resolution which (i) called upon the Soviet Union to desist immediately from its military action in Hungary and withdraw its troops without delay from Hungarian territory (ii) reaffirmed the rights of the Hungarian people to a Government "responsive to their national aspiration" (ii) explore the need of the Hungarian people for food and medicine and (iv) asked all UN members to cooperate in making such supplies available.
10. NATO was established under the North Atlantic Treaty signed in Washington D.C. on 4 April 1949 by the Foreign Ministers of Belgium, Canada, Denmark, France, Great Britain, Iceland, Italy, Luxembourg, the Netherlands, Norway, Portugal and US.
11. West Germany (Federal Democratic Republic) joined the alliançe in 1955.
12. The Warsaw Pact was established in May 1955.

I am trying to analyse it; I do not know if my analysis is true or not, but I am trying to put a wider picture before the House. The other day it was said on behalf of the Soviet Union: "We will withdraw all our forces from every other country. You withdraw yours from every other country, you stationed them there." I agree that that is not an adequate justification for what they have done in Hungary, for keeping their forces there. But there is something in it. "Let everybody withdraw, let every country go its own way. Why should we on one side become weak from the point of view of any future conflict?" So, this is the background of these events.

But behind that background, again, all these forces are at work, these liberalising forces, as much in the Soviet Union as in any other country. Today take Poland, for instance. Poland is on very friendly terms with the Soviet Union, but Poland is a different country from what it was a year ago, there is no doubt about it, absolutely different. Anybody who goes there can see it. Even for the first time the Polish representative[13] at the United Nations votes separately and differently. That shows how these forces that are working in these countries are going in the right direction. Now unfortunately that did not take place in Hungary and the terrible tragedy occurred there, and everyone of the Members here has expressed and feels very deep sympathy with the Hungarian people because they have gone through hell. It is a terrible thing and it makes little difference whether there are some people there who might be called subversive elements or not, some people there who are anti-socialists or not. There is very little difference. There probably were, I have no doubt there were. I have no doubt that people came from outside to encourage them, in fact we have evidence of it, but basically and fundamentally in Hungary it was a great popular rising. That is the basic thing. Others joined it, and this was suppressed—it has been suppressed now in a military sense, not in any other sense; even now the trade unions and the workers and others are well disciplined and are putting forth their demands, political demands, and they continue to do so; they are not at all put down.

Right from the beginning when the Hungarian question came up before us, for some days I was not quite clear. We laid down two elements of our policy in regard to it: that the Soviet forces should withdraw, and that the Hungarian people should be left to fashion their own destiny—right from the beginning. The leader of our delegation at the UN said that repeatedly, and I said it here too. The only thing we did not do at that time was to go into a long disquisition about it and particularly to condemn the Soviet Union or any other country at that stage, because we did not wish to do so before we had facts, etc. And also

13. Jerzy Michalowski.

because there was a sudden wave, a passionate wave, of condemnation everywhere, and we wanted to stick to our feet and not be swept away by it—and that passionate wave was justified, but it was caused not only by the fact of the story of Hungary but as a reaction to Egypt; that is to say, people had felt, so many people in England and elsewhere, so humiliated by what happened in Egypt that they felt relieved that they could curse somebody else and not be themselves the guilty party. This was a psychological change in the situation, and everything that could be said regarding Hungary was justified. But it appeared to us that an attempt was made almost to suppress the Egyptian problem in the UN, to push it aside and replace it by the Hungarian problem. We wanted to resist that not in any sense to push aside the Hungarian problem but to keep the Egyptian problem to the fore all the time, and we succeeded in doing that. There was this danger of the Egyptian problem being pushed aside because people felt strongly about Hungary—it was right that they should feel that way—but there was that political motive, not in the people who felt it but in the authorities who wanted rather to push aside the people's mind from the Egyptian problem which had exercised them so much. Now we wanted to resist that. This has nothing to do with our opinion about Hungary. But we wanted to resist this movement to push out the Egyptian problem from people's minds. It was really pushed out.

Now, Shri Bimal Ghose referred to that resolution on Hungary[14]—the one which has been much argued about. It is quite right that he objected to our representative abstaining from voting on a certain clause of that resolution which said that the Soviet troops should go out. Now, I have not got the resolution here; I cannot find it immediately. But if you read the speech that our representative delivered and published in the press and circulated—it is a fairly long speech—you will find that throughout that speech, the stress laid by him was on the evacuation of the Soviet troops, on the people of Hungary deciding their future. He was stating our policy in the speech in the United Nations. But as I said before in the context of that resolution and the phrasing of this, I do not approve of this particular phrasing. Therefore, I shall abstain. But we stand for it. There is no doubt about this statement being repeatedly made as to what we stand for—that is, the withdrawal of the Soviet troops.

B.C. Ghose: There is nothing wrong in the phrase.

JN: Mr Ghose, I have not got it with me. You cannot get out of certain atmosphere the whole thing. But the only thing is to read the speech. This kind of voting

14. Of 9 November 1956.

449

takes place because of the time there and it may be that one has to decide so many times in the course of the day and night as to how to vote in the particular circumstance prevailing there. We are not surrounded by that environment or that circumstance, the effect of this or that. People have to judge on the spot making clear their own position almost immediately. I am quite sure. I do not know if the honourable Member has read that speech. When I read it, I found it a very powerful argument indeed. That clause was adopted. And I should like to say—because in spite of having tried to clear the subject the other day, I find there is some element of confusion or doubt about this matter—that earlier our representative, or the leader of our delegation, Mr Krishna Menon, and we have been in close touch with each other. He knows thoroughly what our policy is and how our mind works. We are discussing these matters repeatedly and he represents it with complete accuracy and precision. And whatever he has done there—naturally it was not possible for him to refer to us on every vote—has been done in accordance with our wishes. After all, he is not only the leader of the delegation, but he is also an important member of our Cabinet. He knows the mind of the Government. He is part of the Government. And so, I am surprised that some people talk without trying even to find out what is happening. I do not blame them—to some extent—because they do not have the material. But still a responsible person does not jump into the fray without knowing what the effects of it are.

An honourable Member, Mr Sapru,[15] said that we do not give publicity. Well, he is right.

P.N. Sapru: I did not say that we do not give publicity. I said that our publicity might be better.

JN: We do not give adequate publicity. All right. Well, partially he is right. But publicity of what? These are the emergency sessions of the United Nations sitting all night and day. Everybody is exhausted there. We get a report; we get reports several times a day. But we did not have the actual figures of voting, etc., immediately. They came to us four or five days later. And in the meanwhile, we were caught up and surpassed by a lot of publicity on the other side. That is perfectly true. However, that is unfortunate.

May I just briefly say what the Hungarian position is now? The Hungarian Government has now said that they have invited the Secretary General of the United Nations to visit Hungary, the date of his visit to be fixed in consultation

---

15. Congress member of the Rajya Sabha from Uttar Pradesh.

with the Hungarian Minister for Foreign Affairs in New York.[16] He will visit as the Chief Executive of the United Nations, with no terms of reference. That is the point. I am not telling something new. That has appeared in the morning newspapers. You seem to think that I am reading out something new. Maybe, the language is slightly different.

The point is that they do not want him to go there in pursuance of a United Nations resolution, but as the Chief Executive of the United Nations. They said, "You can come; and fix a date with our Foreign Minister," while they have categorically refused to admit any United Nations observer saying that this is an infringement of their sovereignty and that there are already 500 or 600 newspapermen there. Well, I am sorry that they did not go much further and did not admit the observers because in this matter, it is not a question of sovereignty that is involved; it is really a question of the good name of a country when such charges are made—the charge, apart from others, being about these deportations. Now, we have been told—we have been given solemn assurances—that there have been no deportations.

K.S. Hegde: Have you received any report from Mr Khosla in that connection?

JN: What can poor Khosla say about deportations? He does not watch these things. Nobody can. He can only report on popular rumours about so and so. He went to the Government. The Government denied it solemnly. "No, it is not true. We will show you that it is completely wrong." The Soviet Government denies it with solemn assurances. What is wanted today? In the circumstances existing, the right thing is, let the Secretary General go there; let the United Nations observers go there and let them see and report. But we know undoubtedly that one fact stands out and that is the treatment given to Mr Nagy. I do not see how in any way it can possibly be explained away. I think it is a shocking thing that has happened to him.

16. On 3 December, Hungary informed the UN Secretary General, Dag Hammarskjold, that, although it would not permit UN observers to enter the country, the Secretary General would be welcome in Budapest. After discussions with Imre Horvath, the Hungarian foreign minister, Hammarskjold informed the General Assemly on 4 December that it had been agreed that he should arrive in Budapest on 16 December for a three-day visit. On 5 December, however, Budapest Radio announced that the date fixed by the UN Secretary General was "not suitable" and therefore the visit would "not take place."

Humayun Kabir: There was a report that the President of the Workers' Council in Budapest also has been arrested yesterday or this morning.

JN: May be, many people have been arrested, I suppose. But here, as the honourable Dr Kunzru and others pointed out, apart from other things—this question of an assurance being given to him and that assurance being broken or the Hungarian Government being not able to give him protection or whatever it was—this fact stands out. And I do hope that he will go back soon to Hungary if he likes to go back. In spite of these facts, in spite of all these tragic events that have occurred I do not believe that the processes to which I have referred—those of liberalising—have stopped or are going to be reversed.

In fact, two major facts stand out. One is that any attempt to bring back colonialism is doomed to failure. The strong country tries it on a weaker country. Colonialism exists in many places in the world still. It is true. But bringing it back from where it has gone, I think it is quite clear, cannot be done in the future. The second thing is—I think it is equally clear—that communism, or if you like, socialism, cannot ultimately be imposed by force. I entirely agree with Mr Bimal Ghose—whatever his opinions or mine may be—that if I try to impose socialism on another country, well, that ceases to have any virtue, obviously. And this attempt, however well meaning people might have considered it, to make people good socialists by force has failed. If we look at this picture again from a different perspective, we find that the feeling of nationalism is still a very powerful feeling. Maybe, in a country like the Soviet Union—I am not judging it, I am merely mentioning it casually—the feeling of socialism and nationalism may be combined giving strength to the country; or maybe, in a country like China, it is a combined feeling giving strength to the country. But where you separate the two, then it is not easy to suppress nationalism. It just comes up, and it will come up, as it has come up in Hungary. I do not think the nationalist movement in Hungary was anti-socialistic. I do not think so, although there may have been probably some anti-socialist elements in it. But there was no reason to think that it was anti-socialistic. And there is no doubt that the dominating urge was for freedom.

Now, reference has been made to Mr Selwyn Lloyd's statement[17] which appeared in the newspapers today. Naturally, we welcome his statement in so far as he says that the Anglo-French troops will be withdrawn rapidly, through no date has been mentioned. But I must confess that when I read his whole speech carefully, I was distressed somewhat by the many statements that he has

17. In the House of Commons on 3 December 1956.

made. Well, perhaps he has to justify all that has happened, and he still makes out that by the Anglo-French action that they took, they conferred enormous benefits on humanity—the language is mine, not his—that is to say, they prevented a world war and they prevented all kind of things and they prevented a much worse disaster happening. Now I need not say all that, but I regret that this wrong conception still holds his mind. He says that they took great care to minimise casualties and damage. Last night I saw some photographs of Port Said, and they brought home to me the horror of war. A good part of Port Said and huge fine buildings were all in ruins and large areas were all in ruins. And probably all was not due to bombardment, but to burning as well, because when incendiary bombs are thrown, fire starts and a good part of the city is burnt down. But the fact is that damage in Port Said is very, very great, both human and to the city. And once you start this kind of thing, you cannot limit it. Mr Selwyn Lloyd goes on to say that the situation was deteriorating and it was one sooner or later likely to lead to a war. Why? I cannot imagine it. In fact, the situation was well in hand, and they were going to meet together to decide about the Suez Canal when this happened. Secondly, he says that by their timely action they not only rapidly halted local hostilities but forestalled the development of a general war. I just do not understand this. And then he says that their second purpose was to interpose a force to prevent the resumption of fighting. Now I want to make one thing perfectly clear, because he lays great stress on this. The United Nations has now put a force there, and we made it perfectly clear when we sent our detachment that we were not going there as a kind of continuation of the Anglo-French force, but we were going there because the Government of Egypt had agreed to our going there. And we also told them that we would remain there only so long as the Egyptian Government was agreeable, and in any case this was not in continuation of that Anglo-French force and we were not going to seize hold of the Suez Canal, but we were sent there more or less to keep ourselves on the borders—the ceasefire line.

Well, there is another, and rather odd fact that Mr Selwyn Lloyd mentions. First of all he says: "I believe we shall reach an agreement..." That is, about the future of the Suez Canal. He says that he believes that there will be an agreement providing adequate guarantee that the six requirements—six principles—will be met.[18] "Her Majesty's Government, of course, adhere to their view as expressed in the Resolution voted on by the Security Council on the 13th October with regard to the 18-Power proposals". Now this is a most amazing remark to make. The 18-Power proposals are as dead as mutton—cold mutton—and talking about

18. See *Selected Works* (second series), Vol. 35, p. 419.

or going back to these 18-Power proposals, which were made and which were also rejected before all this fighting and bombardment arose, seems to be quite amazing. As a matter of fact, the whole background of the Middle East situation has changed because of this upheaval and fighting. It is not particularly easy to go back at all. Naturally, so far as we are concerned, we have felt and we feel today also, that the very first step that is to be taken is the withdrawal of the Anglo-French and Israeli forces. After that step only one can take up other questions. We are anxious, and most anxious, that the Canal should be cleared. It should resume its functions for the good of everybody, for the good of Egypt and for the good of everybody. But we just cannot discuss or take up these matters effectively till this first matter is finally settled, not by a declaration, but actually by the fact of withdrawal. Then alone we can consider these other matters and deal with them.

Then much has been said about Pakistan. There is just one thing that I should like to remind the House about. Mr Suhrawardy talks about an invasion from India or India wanting to do this or that to Pakistan. The House will remember that four years ago, or maybe, five years ago, I offered a no-war declaration[19] to guarantee that neither country would go to war and each country would settle these problems peacefully, and even if there is no settlement, they would never go to war with each other. But they never accepted that offer. That offer still holds good. And I went a step further and I said that even though Pakistan did not accept that declaration, I, on behalf of India, made the declaration that I would not go to war with Pakistan unless we were attacked, because after all we have to defend ourselves. So I cannot imagine really what this type of propaganda that is being carried on by Mr Suhrawardy actually means. I fear that it is a prelude possibly to some little trouble. The House may remember, or perhaps may have forgotten, that Goa is a special protege of Mr Suhrawardy. He visited Goa[20] and he visited Lisbon, etc., in this connection. I have no right to object. He is a lawyer, a practising lawyer, and he had every right, as a lawyer, to be briefed by anybody. Now he is Prime Minister. The whole attitude of Pakistan, apart from Mr Suhrawardy, in regard to Goa—well, it is difficult to explain except to say that they dislike India so much that they want to injure India wherever and however they can. Then some honourable Members read out his speech or statement in regard to Egypt. Now, the Bandung Conference, the Colombo Powers' declaration—all of that goes by the board if Mr Suhrawardy's policy is the policy to be pursued by Pakistan.

19. In December 1949.
20. See *Selected Works* (second series), Vol. 30, p. 387.

Mr Bimal Ghose said something about the United States' military help to Pakistan. It is certainly true that the USA declared very firmly that any help they would give must be on condition that it was not used against India and that presumably Pakistan gave that assurance, but the fact is that from the statement of Mr Suhrawardy he seems to think that those arms can be used against India if he so chooses.

Now, Mr Bimal Ghose asked me about Goa. I am afraid I cannot give him a very satisfactory reply except to say that so far as our thinking goes, we have no doubt that Goa must and will have to come to India, but if he asks for any date, I cannot tell him. If he asks me whether there is any change of policy, I cannot help him: there may be slight changes. The fact is of course that Goa cannot just be isolated from all these big problems that we are discussing. It comes in somehow. It is not a simple thing that can be dealt with separately, but it is a matter of deep sorrow for us that not only Goa is under Portuguese rule but that some of our men, including a Member of Parliament,[21] are still incarcerated there.

Finally, as the House knows, in about ten days' time or less, I am going to the United States at the invitation of President Eisenhower. Now, the United States has played a very important part in the last month or two and more especially, if I may say so with all respect, President Eisenhower has played a very important part. It is a great privilege to me to be invited by him, for me to go there and discuss all these important matters that are happening in the world, at any rate those that concern us. There is a difference of opinion on many topics between the United States Government and the Government of India, as there are differences with almost any country to some extent, but I do believe that there are many basic similarities in approach also, and I am glad to find that greater emphasis is being laid on those common points and less on the differences. I do not think any country—India or any country—can really function with grace or effect unless it functions in its own way, after the manner of its own thinking. The moment you lose grip about yourself and your own thinking, you do not count for much ultimately. If we differ with any country, well, we should agree to differ in a friendly way. The other day I stated in the other House that I had long talks with the Prime Minister of China, Mr Chou En-lai. We were pleased to find a large amount of agreement, but in some matters we did not agree; we agreed to differ, but that does not affect our friendly relations, our cooperative relations with China. In the same way with other countries; after all, we have our own way of thinking and doing things. Our background, whatever it is, it is

21. Tridib Chaudhuri.

not opposed to any other and we can only find satisfaction in self-fulfilment in working out our own destiny in our own way. In doing that, it is good to learn from others, to cooperate with others, and be influenced by others where you can be influenced. I am therefore greatly looking forward to my visit to the United States and to my meeting President Eisenhower. I am sure that I shall profit by it; whoever else does not I cannot say.

I beg to move the motion that stands in my name.

3. Relevance of Commonwealth Membership[1]

S.N. Mazumdar[2] (West Bengal): Sir, I move the following resolution:

"This House is of opinion that India's further continuation of her membership of the Commonwealth is inconsistent with the principles of Panchsheel."...

Mr Deputy Chairman: Motion moved:

"This House is of opinion that India's further continuation of her membership of the Commonwealth is inconsistent with the principles of Panchsheel."

Jawaharlal Nehru: Mr Deputy Chairman, this Resolution deals with a subject which has frequently come up in this House and in the other House and indeed which was referred to in the recent debate on international affairs we had in this House. It is a hardy perennial and every argument that the honourable Member has used has been previously mentioned and previously replied to. I find, therefore, some difficulty in saying anything new about it. I appreciate the honourable Member's, if I may use the word with all respect, very moderate approach to this problem and his language. He refers to the feelings of a strong section of the public in regard to this matter. I am prepared to admit that there

---

1. Statement in the Rajya Sabha, 7 December 1956. *Parliamentary Debates (Rajya Sabha)*, Vol. XV, 1956, cols. 1773 and 1782-1795. Extracts.
2. Satyendra Narayan Mazumdar (d. 1987); Rajya Sabha member of the Communist Party from West Bengal, 1952-57.

are many people in his country who, for sentimental or other reasons, would advocate this or would approve of it if it takes place. I don't deny that. I think also that those very people, or many of them if we once explain the position to them, may change their views on the subject. It is very easy, in any issue of this type, to get people to agree to a sentimental approach to a problem of this type but it would be a bad day when a government's policy in such matters is governed by sentiment only and by the sudden passion of the moment.

The honourable Member has referred repeatedly to Shri Rajagopalachari and in fact has based his argument mainly on what Shri Rajaji has stated in this connection.[3] Now anything that Shri Rajagopalachari says deserves our closest and most earnest attention. He is one of our wise men who has had great deal of experience but, nevertheless, I feel that even when wise men become unconnected with public affairs and do not have all the aspects of the particular problem, then their wisdom is likely to go astray simply because it is not based on a factual appreciation of the situation, apart from other aspects of it, and it is a little dangerous in such cases to offer an opinion which is really based on the reaction to some event. Now actions and reactions take place but if we started functioning as a government or as a country merely on reactions as to what other people did, then we would be pushed from this side to that. There are all kinds of reactions. We have very powerful reactions sometimes, not only in the present instance, on what happened in Egypt as a result of the invasion and attack of the Anglo-French forces, not only on what happened in Hungary and Budapest as a result of the intervention of foreign troops or what Pakistan said; we shall always be reacting. But to think of a brave gesture of defiance or anger, that surely is not the way a country's foreign policy can be conducted. We become the puppet of other people.

Let us consider this matter again in this larger perspective of war and peace which the honourable Member quite rightly laid stress on. What helps our objective, the main objective of world peace? What helps our main objective of cooperation between the nations of the world? There is a negative aspect of it, that of avoiding or preventing war. That is satisfactory in the sense that it is urgent and imperative to avoid war. But there is a positive aspect too, of trying to root out the causes of war and gradually bring the nations together, to cooperate

3. S.N. Mazumdar quoted C. Rajagopalachari from an article in *Swarajya* dated 24 November 1956 in which Rajagopalachari opined that India should "part ways" with the Commonwealth over the Anglo-French attack on Suez and stated: "India's lead in this matter will signify much especially if followed by Ceylon and Pakistan and the totality of that effect will go to strengthen the Resolution of the United Nations Assembly and give moral consolation to Egypt."

together even though they disagree a great deal. It is absurd to imagine that every country in the wide world will adopt a single policy and agree with every other. That is totally unrealistic. Therefore, we aim at countries carrying on their different policies and yet cooperating with other countries, finding a large measure of agreement even though in some matters they may differ. That is to say, first of all internally they may differ as much as they like. The question only comes up when countries function outside the internal sphere. Then there is likely to be something in the nature of conflict, when two countries do that, or when one country does it. And it is to avoid that that those principles embodied in what is called Panchsheel were stated to the public and to the world. The honourable Member opposite protected himself by stating that this question of the Commonwealth has nothing to do with Panchsheel. Of course, it has nothing to do with it. Then he said that this Resolution was drafted before various things happened. Now, that is, if I may say so, one of my grievances, that honourable Members opposite are always left behind by events. They try hard to catch up....

S.N. Mazumdar: I anticipated them.

JN: ... but the events escape them and go ahead. But in a changing period we have to keep abreast of events, keep in tune with them. Now, it is easy to break anything, it is much more difficult to join or build. You break in a moment. An artist or creator works hard at a piece of art; whether it be a beautiful vase, a potter's work, or a building or an architecture, enormous labour and creative instinct go to build it, but with a blow you can break that beautiful vase or with a bomb you can destroy that piece of architecture. It is easy to break. There is enough breakage in this world not to add to it, and our broad policy has been not to break with any country but to ever get closer to it.

It so happened that in the course of the development of events and of history we were associated with the Commonwealth. Now, let us be quite clear about this matter to which the honourable Member referred, that India has always stood for dissociation. I do not think that is a correct statement. India has always certainly stood for independence as opposed to dominion status. It is perfectly correct. We stood for independence. Now the honourable Member is confusing these two ideas, the association with a country whether it is in the nature of alliance or in any other way—there are hundred and one ways of association of independent countries—that is one thing; and the old idea of dominion status. There is this difference between the two. When in the year 1947 we became independent, a certain period passed when we were what is called a dominion, till we framed our Constitution and we became a republic. We accepted the dominion status as a provisional stage, till we framed our own Constitution. In a way, we accepted it. But to have accepted dominion status as a more or less permanent basis would certainly have been in contravention and in defiance of what the national movement stood for. We stood for independence. We stood for a Republic of India. But that has nothing to do with what association the Republic of India has with any other country, whether it is England or Russia or China or Burma.

We have today many types of associations and probably we are one of the very few countries in the world which have the fewest legal associations with any other country. Apart from treaties about cultural associations, apart from trade and cultural treaties, we have no political associations which bind us in the slightest with any country. I cannot immediately think of any other country, perhaps Switzerland is one such, but I don't know. Almost every other country has binding treaties, tying itself up with some other country whether it is political or military. There are these groups or alliances on the one side, like NATO alliance, the Baghdad Pact, the SEATO, the Warsaw Treaty, the Balkan Treaty and so on, and there are other treaties too. These tie up other countries not to do this or that. But we are the freest among them. From that point of view we are less entangled, less committed than almost any country anywhere. But at the same time, curiously enough, we have the closest association with many countries, sometimes opposing countries. We have, as I have stated, very close relations with our neighbour Burma. Our relations with Burma are closer, if I may say so, than our relations with many of the Commonwealth countries— with Indonesia, Ceylon, and, in varying degrees, our relations with other countries. Well, there is Russia and there is China. We do not agree with much that they do; but our relations are friendly. There is the Prime Minister of China at present in India and he is rightly receiving warm welcome, not only in his own personal capacity, but as a representative of a great and friendly people. In a week from today I am going to the United States of America, one of the great countries, one of the most powerful and most influential countries in the world, to meet the President of that country who has recently again been elected and who can undoubtedly be said to represent the vast mass of the American people. They have shown their confidence in him and they have done it because, I think, fundamentally they think that he strove for peace. I shall have the privilege of meeting him and I am happy that our relations with the United States are friendly. That does not mean that we agree with everything in the policy of the United States or that they agree with our policy. This idea, this conception, that you can only be friendly with a person or with a country whose policy is completely in line with yours is a bad conception. It is a dangerous conception.

S.N. Mazumdar: I have never said that.

JN: I do not say that the honourable Member said that but I am merely carrying this idea a little further. I do not say that the honourable Member said this. The opposite of that conception is that you must be in conflict with the countries which differ from you.

H.D. Rajah[4] (Madras): Will the honourable Prime Minister kindly say whether his relationship with Britain is on the same level as that of America? Or, does the American Government have the same relationship with Britain as we are having?

JN: Relationship with whom?

H.D. Rajah: With Britain in the Commonwealth.

JN: Obviously the honourable Member knows the answer. America is not in the Commonwealth but is more closely associated with the Commonwealth than we are, in many ways; in a military sense. America is associated with the Commonwealth countries; in the economic sense and in every sense, their association—Anglo-American association—is infinitely closer than the associations of some of the Commonwealth countries inter se. Everybody knows that.

Now, let us consider this question of war and peace. The honourable Member said something about broad masses. Well, whether they are broad masses or narrow masses, one is apt to get a little lost in these phrases which come down to us from the past few decades and we lose ourselves in these slogans. Recent events and recent developments have shaken up many of the old slogans. Whether they have been shaken up by events in Egypt or by events in Hungary, they have both shaken everybody up completely and we have to think anew as to what the right course is—not to express our condemnation. It is open to us to condemn everybody, this nation or that, but the right course is to help the cause of peace; this is of the most vital consequence. In the course of the last, let us say, year or two, there has been a great deal of relaxation of what was called the cold war. We all welcomed that. And then there was another thing. There was a great deal of relaxation of the internal, shall I say, not structure, but organisation or whatever you may like to call it—internal happenings in the Soviet Union and the East European countries, a process which was called the process of democratisation, of liberalisation. We welcomed that and we welcomed it because all this was

---

4. (1904-1959); Republican Party of India member of the Rajya Sabha, 1952-59; founder President, Republican Party of India.

happening in a normal, peaceful way and without bringing in grave upsets in its train. It was obvious to those who studied the situation in any part of the world—I am not talking about the Soviet Union but any part of the world—that there were certain forces which had worked against the cold war and towards normality, internally in countries and extremely in their relations with other countries. We welcomed that and, in a very small measure no doubt but nevertheless in some measure, we played our part in encouraging those forces. I do not presume and I do not wish this House to imagine that India played a very brave part in all this—every country does to its capacity and ability—but I certainly do respectfully say that whatever little part we played was played to encourage the forces towards better relations between countries and for peace.

Now at the present moment, in the course of the last few months, something has happened which has unfortunately put a stop to those forces for the moment and we are back again or are going back again to a rather intense phase of the cold war. It is a dangerous development, a bad development. I do not personally think that it is going to be a lasting development—there is a hopeful aspect—but there it is and once we go back to the stage of cold war, then you always have the hot war round the corner if something happens. In this last month of November, on one or two occasions, we came very near a big war. Suppose the war had come, the historians in future might have sat down—if there were any historians alive then—and said, "Oh, it was so and so's fault, this country's fault", but the point was that war did come with all its destruction and terror in spite of the condemnations, the slogans and the pious platitudes that we might utter. It brought little comfort to anybody for us merely to condemn.

Therefore, while we have naturally to express our opinion, whether it is in the United Nations or in this House or elsewhere, about what is happening and express them in a straight way, in a clear way, we have always to remember that every word that we say should be weighed and balanced and should not be such as makes the situation more difficult, as tends to break existing things and not mend and to join them. It has been India's privilege and honour to help in joining countries, to be a bridge between them and not to break the bridges that already exist. So, in these last troubled days, the last month, six weeks or more we have always had this problem before us. A right step, a right movement, if carried too fast, too speedily, might upset things and lead to a reaction which is very very wrong. Merely talking about the right is not good; the right has to fit in into the local circumstances and must not produce a powerful wrong reaction, a wrong reaction meaning war. That has been the grave problem in Hungary, and that was the problem in Egypt. If you drive a country to a stage when it becomes very difficult for it to do something without sacrificing its entire prestige and self-respect, that is if you wish to humiliate a country, well—I do not say it is necessary: it depends on the country—the possible result is that that country, in its reaction and anger and to avoid humiliation, will even indulge in war. If you create a condition in a country when rightly or wrongly it feels that all its future security is endangered, then it does not care whether it is popular or unpopular. There, it is a struggle for survivorship—so it is thought by the people of the country—and all the national passions of that country come up. So that it is not merely enough to sit in a judgement seat for us, for any country and piously dole out praise and condemnation. We have to take all these very difficult factors into account, and see what will be the result and whether it will really help the cause that we seek to encourage. So whether it has been Egypt or whether it has been Hungary, we have always had to keep that in mind.

People had sometimes criticised us saying, "Oh, you have double standards" or "You do not speak up your mind clearly" or "You try to minimise in something and exaggerate something else." It may be that sometimes the expression of our views was a little cautious and sometimes it was less cautious. We are not perfect people, but always we had that fact in mind and I certainly do repudiate the idea that we have ever followed any double standards or different standards anywhere. We have followed this. But certainly we have always kept in view this factor that anything that we say does not encourage that tendency which we wish to discourage, the tendency to war. That we have had in view most certainly and we keep it in view still. It is all very well in this House or in the other place to pass resolutions which may even be justified but if the result of that resolution which is logically justified is to create a worse and more difficult situation in the world, then it is not justified.

So that when I see all these things in this large perspective, if we see this world, how this cold war resulted in these great armed blocs of nations, each calling itself a defensive bloc, not, shall I say, without some reason, not without some justification—at any rate, they felt, I think, honestly that they were a defensive bloc, one afraid of the other but each felt the same way and each said the same thing—then it is totally immaterial what they say; it is totally immaterial if I am told that the SEATO pact was a defensive pact and "why does anybody worry?"; or that the Baghdad Pact was a defensive pact, "why does anybody worry?" May be that in the minds of some of the members of the Baghdad Pact or the SEATO it was a defensive pact. I do not challenge their bona fides but I do challenge their logic. Any pact, whatever you may call it, is an offensive thing and produces the results of an offensive pact in the minds of other countries. But then it does not matter what you have in mind; you have to judge this by the effect it produces in the world or in the other countries. What is the effect in other countries? Looking at it, considering it as an offensive thing, as something that threatens them, they immediately start doing something which threatens the other party, whether it is increasing armaments or any other thing. Anyhow, the atmosphere is vitiated; the cold war atmosphere comes in. The SEATO came. When did SEATO come? Just after a great improvement had taken place in South East Asia; after the Indo-China war was over. There was an improvement and people breathed with some relief. Soon after comes SEATO. It was totally unnecessary. Nobody in his wildest stretch of imagination could say any war or any attack was going to take place in the near future; of course, nobody could talk about the distant future. Then this thing comes in; people who straightened, who began to relax, start again, full of tension: "This is going to happen; we shall prepare"—and a tension of war preparations is created. Take the Baghdad Pact; what is going to happen there. I do not know, of course because the Middle Eastern region or Western Asia has always been rather a difficult place with plenty of conflicts. That is true: but there comes the Baghdad Pact, a pact for defence and security. Well, the first effect of the Baghdad Pact was to split up the Arab nations, to bring dissensions among the countries of Western Asia. I leave out the effect on us because we have often discussed it. We have also often said this. The very region where it sought to have security, lost or began losing that sense of security and one may say that, at any rate, one of the proximate causes of subsequent developments in Western Asia was the Baghdad Pact leading to a...

Radha Kumud Mookerji[5] (Nominated): May I know why the UNO should permit pacts in the interest of collective security?

JN: The honourable Member should ask the UNO; I am not the UNO. But if I may say so, it is my humble opinion that many of these pacts are against the Charter of the United Nations. The United Nations Charter provides for regional organisations certainly but not of the type that have taken place. And look at the regions too. Is this a region? Let us say, I can understand the Atlantic region. Even in the Atlantic region a number of Mediterranean countries come in, thus extending the Atlantic rather far. If Turkey comes in, what has Turkey got to do with the Atlantic region? Geographically I mean. But that is another matter. But I think they are not in tune with the Charter—these pacts, etc. Leave that out.

As I was saying, take every single alliance and pact and you will find that by and large the effect of it has been to induce the opposite party to have pacts or to have more armaments and the result is that in the balance we do not have greater

5. Member, Rajya Sabha, 1952-58.

security so far as armaments are concerned and we only have the cold war and fear. Now, that is the position.

Now, all over the world today there are foreign forces spread out—foreign bases, forces—everywhere. I do not know how many countries are there. There are scores of countries with foreign bases today. Well, it is my belief that the right approach to this problem—that is the basic approach—is for the removal of all foreign forces and all foreign bases from every country. But for me to say it today, looks absurd because I know it cannot be done today; it merely irritates people. I do not want to irritate the countries; it is merely showing off that I am very pure and all that. I am not; I do not know how my country would behave when faced with danger. Sometimes people say that we in India presume to moralise too much, presume to be holier and purer than others. Well, I do not presume that; I do not think we are holier or purer or more moral than anybody else in the wide world. We talk about morality or purity or holiness; I do not think we are more moral or purer or holier. I dislike this kind of egregious unctuous talk by people wherever they may be. If we are good, we may be. But let us think more of our failings and improve them than about the virtues that we may possess. But we have one virtue and that is an important virtue and that is due to a number of factors; geography, for one thing for which we are not responsible. Whoever is responsible for the geography of the world is responsible for it—as to where India is situated in the present context of the world. That is one thing. Then history and other things are also responsible, our past, the history of our national movement which has conditioned our thinking. And Mahatma Gandhi is responsible who also conditioned our thinking. So, so many factors are responsible. But the point is that the virtue that we possess is this, that not being in immediate danger, so far we have a sense of security; not a perfect sense but a greater sense of security than many countries of Europe or many countries of the Middle East or many countries of the Far East. Geography and other factors give it to us and of course I will say it is purely geography; it is our own structure, a certain feeling of reliance on ourselves, and that gives us a certain measure of security. It is our thinking that has prevented us from joining up or from hating any country or considering that any country is our enemy, any country in Europe, in America or in Asia. I know we are not on good terms with Pakistan; leave out Pakistan for the moment. But even with Pakistan we do not—we try hard not to think of Pakistan in that way. We may get angry at something they do, but we do not think of it in that way. We are really not good, if I may say so, at hating. We may get angry but we as a people are not good at hating, national hate especially. . . .

A fairly remarkable example of that is how after all this long period of British domination in India, after we became independent and came to terms with them, we forgot, we did not get angry. Anyhow, we were not moved by a great passion against the British. We became friendly with them. I think it is rather a unique example in history and I think that apart from our past traditions, the person most responsible for developing that outlook in the Indian people was Gandhiji. That is true. Anyhow the point is that, as I said, we have one virtue and that virtue is that we are not hostile to any particular country. And we are not moved by those passions which afflict other countries whether it is the passion of fear, say, some countries in Europe or some countries in Western Europe are terribly afraid of the Soviet Union's mightily strength. They are afraid. The Soviet Union is afraid. I tell you it is afraid of a re-armed Germany, terribly afraid of a rearmed Germany, having atomic weapons, more afraid than almost anything, and its policy has been shaped so as somehow to stop this. If it comes, then it has to prepare for that. Anyhow the main basis of these actions is this fear. Why all these East European countries? What is the Soviet Union's chief interest in them? Because they are between it and Germany which might be rearmed. Immediately you see the fear complex coming on either side. Now, India has not got that fear complex for a variety of reasons which we need not go into. India is not hostile to any country. Therefore, when any event occurs, we are not swept away by passions, as other countries are. That is no virtue in us. I do not say that we are better. But because of geography and other causes—we get angry, we disapprove—but we are not suddenly obsessed by that fever of fear and other things as other countries are. Therefore, we can judge world events a little more objectively. We may judge wrongly. That is a different matter. I do not say that we are cleverer or more intelligent, but we are not swept away by passions in these things so much—and that too chiefly because of geography and Gandhiji and this and that. We can judge these things more objectively and, therefore, we can often make suggestions which are helpful. We can soothe other countries. We can act as a bridge to some extent and bring them together. That I say is the sole virtue that I suggest we have, and that is not a real virtue; it is the result of circumstances that I have mentioned.

Now, in everything that we do we keep this in view: are we helping the cause of peace or not? I do not want to make a brave gesture—all right, so and so has done wrong and we condemn that country. I am quite sure that every kind of contact that we have got with a country—whether it is the Commonwealth association, the Commonwealth group or whether it is any other contact—helps the cause of peace. It does not hinder my adopting any policy, as the House knows. It helps the cause of peace and brings us together; and I am for everything that bring us together, without tying us up in any way. After all we are tied up much more in the United Nations, by the Charter. That is really being tied up to some extent. We welcome that tying up. I am not complaining, but that is some tying up. And the Commonwealth is no tying up at all, of that type or any type. What is tying up is all this array of alliances from the Warsaw Treaty to NATO, Baghdad, SEATO and the Balkans. The whole world is full of these knots which tie up and we want to unravel these knots, to open them out, so that people may live, as far as possible, without fear, and live their own lives.

I submit that while normally I would have opposed such a resolution, as I have done in the past, in the present circumstances, I would oppose it still more.

4. To K.M. Panikkar[1]

New Delhi,
February 4, 1957

My dear Panikkar,[2]

I have just received your letter of the 1st February and have read the report attached to it.[3] This makes very interesting reading. The tendencies you mention are obviously there, and I have little doubt that the pressure of events will add to them. There is no future for Western Europe except in some form of a union, whatever that form may take.

Nevertheless, I rather doubt if the process will be as rapid as you have indicated. The major difficulties will be from Germany, which you have mentioned, as also from the United Kingdom. But Europe, or rather Western Europe, will

---

1. JN Collection.
2. India's Ambassador in France.
3. Panikkar stated in his letter that he had studied "the major changes that France is planning, in association with others, to re-establish a balance in the affairs of the world." He said he had "tried to analyse... the three basic proposals which are about to take shape—the European economic union, known as the Common Market, Eurafrica and Euratom, the three together constituting in a solid base for a new European structure." He added: "Whether it takes 5 years or 10 years, it is now fairly obvious that the three major European countries—France, Germany and Italy—together with the Benelux area will come together for economic and industrial development and naturally their political orientation will also undergo a radical change... It will undoubtedly mean a shift in the balance of power", with Europe achieving "in a short time under Franco-German leadership...a position at least of equality with the other two Great Powers."

inevitably be driven in that direction. What happens in the future will primarily depend on the avoidance of war, because a war will create entirely new conditions for the people that survive. Also in the course of the next ten years or so many other developments will take place in Asia and elsewhere. Any European Union is bound to be dominated by Germany. Apart from everything else, the Germans are a very vital and hard working people, and I fear that the French and the British have, to some extent, lost their vitality and capacity for hard work. in any event, Germany will not take any step which comes in the way of her reunification, and that reunification will not take place till there is some major understanding between the Eastern and the Western blocs.

I think that your note deserves circulation to some of our major Missions.[4]

The question of the de jure transfer of Pondicherry to India has been pending for a long time.[5] The present position is very unsatisfactory and it comes in the way of many things being done. The other day I was in Madras[6] and met many people from Pondicherry who complained of this delay. I think that you should keep on reminding the French Government of this. It is hardly becoming for a decision to be arrived at and not to be given effect to for years.

Yours sincerely,
Jawaharlal Nehru

4. The same day Nehru minuted S. Dutt, Foreign Secretary, that Panikkar's note should be printed for circulation to members of the Cabinet and to the major missions. Nehru added: "Shri Panikkar is a keen observer, but he tends rather to go ahead of facts and difficulties and slightly to dramatize events. What he says is, I think, true in essence, but I rather doubt if his timetable is at all correct."

5. The de facto transfer of Pondicherry and three other French territories took place on 1 November 1954. On 28 May 1956, India and France signed a treaty providing for the de jure transfer of these territories to India. While the Government of India ratified the treaty on the same day, the Government of France did so on 27 July 1962.

6. On 31 January 1957.

5. To Norman Cousins[1]

New Delhi,
February 19, 1957

My dear Norman Cousins,

Thank you for your letter of the 13th February, 1957,[2] which I received today. We are in the midst of our general elections and I have to do a good deal of touring. I returned to Delhi only this morning and am going out again for a few days tomorrow morning.

I am happy to learn that Dr Schweitzer is in good health. I can well understand his distress at the present drift in the world. I suppose every sensitive person feels that way. I confess that I do not see any easy way out of this drift towards disaster. Apart from the actual dangers involved, what is distressing is the gradual acceptance by most people of this state of affairs as normal and almost inevitable.

None of the outstanding political leaders of today appears to have the vision or the strength to stop this drift. Every step that the leaders of the United States or of the Soviet Union might take, even though it may be a good one, is suspect by the other. That applies to the other big powers like the UK, France and China. The world atmosphere is thick with suspicion and fear. Everyone, I believe, recognizes that a major nuclear war is out of the question. And yet, in spite of this, the armament race goes on and atomic and hydrogen bombs are piled up. The testing of nuclear weapons continues, even though many eminent scientists believe that this may be poisoning the atmosphere.

I doubt if there is anyone in the world today whose opinion can carry more weight in these matters than Dr Schweitzer. No one can accuse him of partiality, and whatever he says will at least command world attention. I welcome, therefore, his intention to try his utmost to deal with the present crisis. What steps he can take about this is difficult for me to suggest. His proposal for some outstanding

---

1. JN Collection.
2. Norman Cousins, editor, *The Saturday Review* (New York), who had "just returned from Africa", wrote that Albert Schweitzer, German missionary surgeon and Nobel Peace Prize winner (1952), was deeply distressed by the "present drift" in the world and would like to do something about it. But Schweitzer "refused to involve himself in matters concerning the politics of one nation or another for he wanted to identify himself with membership of the human family at its largest rather than with any of its groupings."

political leaders to meet is, in theory, excellent.[3] But I would be greatly surprised if the persons he mentions, agreed to get together at present. Almost everything would depend on President Eisenhower. If he suggested such a meeting, it would come off. Obviously, no meeting would have much value if President Eisenhower was opposed to it or did not attend it. If, by some miracle, the meeting could be held, I think it would produce good results.

It would be difficult enough to get President Eisenhower to meet Khrushchev or Bulganin. It would be, I think, next to impossible for him to agree to meet Chou En-lai at present. When I had my talk with the President during my recent visit to Washington, the only subject on which he grew quite warm and rather excited was on the subject of China. He was angry at China's behaviour and, more especially, at their refusal to release ten Americans. I think that the Chinese attitude in this matter is quite extraordinarily foolish. I have a high opinion of Chinese intelligence and foresight, quite apart from their policies. And so, it has surprised me that they still hold on to these ten Americans. The President told me quite definitely that he would have no truck at all with the Chinese so long as these ten were not released. Even after that, he would go very slow, but some small step might be taken.

It appears certain to me, therefore, that there is not the least possible chance of the President agreeing to meet Chou En-lai. That will mean a complete upsetting of American policy and a tremendous uproar in the United States. Personally I do hope that the Chinese Government will release those ten and thus break this deadlock. Even if that happens, I doubt very much if the President or Dulles will take any forward step in a hurry.

Early last year, it seemed that the world was gradually getting out of this dreadful drift to war. There was a lessening of tension all round, and certain changes in the Soviet Union and the East European countries were full of promise. Hungary put an end to this and, as you know, produced violent reactions in the greater part of the world. It was a great misfortune that what happened in Hungary synchronised with the Anglo-French attack on Egypt. It is possible, I think, that if this had not happened, Hungary might have come out of the crisis as Poland did. The Soviet Union was convinced at the time that the Anglo-French attack on Egypt had the approval of the United States and presaged a major war. This

3. Cousins wrote that it had been suggested by some of Dr Schweitzer's friends that the political leaders of the world including Nehru, Eisenhower, Khrushchev, Chou En-lai and Macmillan might come together to meet with Schweitzer, perhaps in Vienna, "to consider the world problem not in terms of the conflicting national interest but in terms of the overriding common interests of the human community."

was not true, of course, but I have no doubt that the Soviet Union thought so at the time. Because of this, they decided to take no chances in Hungary and were prepared to face the odium which their cruel repression of the Hungarian nationalist movement brought them.

There has been a reaction in the Soviet Union and they have gone back to some extent on the more liberal policy that they had embarked upon. Personally I do not think that they can ever really go back upon it, because there are too many forces at play in the Soviet Union which will not ultimately tolerate this. I do not mean that the people of the Soviet Union want any basic change in their political or economic structure. Nearly all of them have grown up since the Revolution and accept that structure. But they want greater individual freedom and a lessening of the tensions in which they live. Also, more of the good things of life, commodities, etc. They do not want the secret police. There has been some improvement in these directions, in spite of Hungary. The measure of freedom and liberalization in the Soviet Union or the East European countries is directly related to war-scares and tensions.

The question, therefore, is how to lessen these tensions and remove the ever-present fear of war. I suppose this cannot be done at one jump, but step by step one may go in that direction.

Unfortunately, almost everything is thought of in military terms, and even the good deeds that are done, have a military wrapping. The Soviet Government talks crudely and aggressively about their military might and indulges in cruel repression if this is challenged. At the same time, they do sometimes put forward proposals which appear to be reasonable and logical. But, because of this background, those proposals are rejected and are not even considered. The United States has given a great deal of much needed help to other countries. But, again, the military aspect is dominant. Also, the help often goes to the most reactionary ruling groups in backward countries. Thus, this help does not bring in a sense of liberation or relief.

I do not know what to suggest. I have almost begun to feel that attempts at improving the world situation merely result in distressing entanglements which do little good to anybody. And yet, one cannot remain a passive spectator. Anyhow, Dr Schweitzer is the one man who can take a lead. Perhaps, he could privately and informally make the approach he has suggested and then judge the results. I think he should first write to President Eisenhower. Any kind of a joint letter to a number of persons will probably irritate and make some of them feel that they are being embarrassed.

So far as I am concerned, I would gladly help in any little way that I can. But I have no exaggerated opinion of what I can do. Recent developments in regard to Kashmir have not added to my belief in my capacity to do anything worthwhile in international affairs. I do not think that we have been in the wrong in what we have done in Kashmir. And yet, as you must know, we have been attacked with anger and malice, and every attempt has been made to humiliate us. I suppose this will pass. But this does demonstrate how every person who does not fall into line, is suspect and is in peril.

This would not apply to Dr Schweitzer. That is why I say that he is the one man who might bring some light into closed minds.

In this matter, I would like Dr Schweitzer to trust to his own judgement or, if I may use Gandhiji's phrase, to his "inner voice". That will be a better guide than anything that I can say.

If you write to Dr Schweitzer, please convey my deep regards to him.

Yours sincerely,
Jawaharlal Nehru

II. VISIT TO THE USA AND CANADA

1. On Arrival[1]

Mr Vice-President, I am deeply grateful to you for your welcome and for what you have said. It is a great happiness to me to come here for the second time to this great country[2] and I consider it a great privilege that I should have the opportunity to meet the President[3] and talk to him at this rather important and even, perhaps, critical moment in our history.

You mentioned, Mr Vice-President, the ideals that govern this great Republic, the ideals of independence and individual freedom. I can assure you that we, in

---

1. Reply to Vice-President Richard M. Nixon's welcoming remarks at National Airport, Washington D.C., 16 December 1956. From *Nehru Visits USA*, The Information Service of India, Washington, p. 2.
2. The first visit to the USA was in 1949.
3. Dwight D. Eisenhower.

India, adhere to those ideals and that we are going to continue to adhere to them, whatever else may befall us.

We believe in the freedom of the individual, the freedom of the human spirit. And in many other things, too, I have found that there is so much in common, even though we are separated by half the world, between this great Republic and the Republic of India.

And so I thank you again, Mr Vice-President, and I should like to express my gratitude to the President for his gracious invitation to me to come here.[4]

---

4. In his reply to President Eisenhower's welcome at the White House on the same day Nehru said: "I have been looking forward to this visit for a long time and now that I am here, I feel happy to be not only your guest, Mr President, but among the American people who are so very friendly and hospitable."

2. A Perspective on India[1]

I feel happy and a little surprised to see so many of our compatriots in Washington. As you know, I have come to the United States after seven years and will be here for six days—four days in Washington and about two days in New York. It seems rather absurd that I should travel thousands of miles and come to a large country like this, which is playing a very big role in world affairs, and spend only six days here. I am helpless; nowadays it is not so easy to come here from India. But it was an old promise and I was rather keen to meet the President and so I came. I was scheduled to come in July but I had to postpone my visit because President Eisenhower was indisposed.[2] I have come now and am happy to have the opportunity of holding talks with him at leisure. There were many things to talk about and as you are aware, even during the last two, three months, many

---

1. Address to members of the Indian community, Embassy of India, Washington D.C., 16 December 1956. AIR tapes, NMML. Original in Hindi.
2. For Nehru's correspondence relating to his proposed visit to the USA in July 1956, see *Selected Works* (second series), Vol. 34, pp. 309-310.

WITH PRESIDENT DWIGHT D. EISENHOWER, WASHINGTON,
16 DECEMBER 1956

WITH PRESIDENT DWIGHT D. EISENHOWER, 18 DECEMBER 1956

significant things have happened in the world. There have been wars, turmoil and the danger to the world still persists. So, I am sure that these talks will clear my mind and perhaps of others too. I do not wish to say very much about these talks except that you must realize their significance and how they affect India and the world.

The events which have occurred in Egypt and Hungary and in neighbouring areas are pretty historic. They shed light on a number of new factors and the new forces that are emerging in the world. We must understand them well. Our work lies in India and we do not wish to interfere in other countries. The task of uplifting the 36-37 crores of people in India is a gigantic one and all we wish is to be allowed to do this work peacefully. We are not interested in interfering in the affairs of other countries or to play a role on the world stage. I am telling you this because newspapers in the United States and elsewhere often mention that India wants to be the leader in Asia. That is absurd. India is not interested in becoming a leader neither is she keen to take on a leadership role. But our effort has been to maintain friendly relations with everyone, whether we agree with their views and policies or not. That is the real test of friendship. When two individuals hold similar views, there is no problem about their becoming friends. The question is: can there be friendship even when there are differences of opinion, whether it is between individuals or countries? It would be unrealistic to expect that all the countries of the world must think and act alike. Peoples are different, countries are different and it is not surprising that each one must seek its own path. If there is a clash of ways which creates conflict, it affects the whole world.

You must have heard about Panchsheel, which has been talked about for the last two or three years. Panchsheel is a very old concept which has been prevalent in India for over two thousand years, from the times of the Buddha or even earlier. Perhaps in those days it used to refer to the character of human beings. Now we are using it in the political field, to lay down a code of conduct for the countries of the world. That too involves a question of character—the character of nations. So we are not saying anything new. Many people have said this earlier. It has been said in India for thousands of years. But it needs to be reiterated once again because until the countries of the world accept the principle of non-interference in the internal affairs of one another, of mutual friendship and consultations, aid and advice without any pressure, of non-aggression, etc., the world cannot be rid of wars. What is the reason for the conflict in Egypt and Hungary at the moment? It is a matter of external aggression. Anyhow, it is a very big thing and you must understand it. We have been successful to some extent to maintain friendly relations with everyone whether we agreed with all their policies and views or not. We have friendly relations with the United States, which is a great power in the world, even though sometimes our actions have displeased them and the American newspapers criticize India. But the fundamental thing is that we wish to maintain friendly relations with them and will continue to make efforts to do so, whatever the ups and downs.

As you know, about ten to fifteen days ago, the Chinese Prime Minister Chou En-lai visited India.[3] He is a great Communist leader and we gave him a hearty welcome. If President Eisenhower comes to our country, as I hope he will, we will accord a hearty welcome to him also. In this way India follows her own path and helps a little in clearing the way for others. In this world which is full of fear and hatred against one another and armies are getting ready, any country which maintains friendly relations with both sides helps a little towards clearing the air and may even act as a bridge between two countries. Though we do not wish to interfere in international affairs, it is a fact that in today's world, no nation can remain isolated. So we participate in the activities of the United Nations and other world forums and express our views.

But our real work lies within the country and respect for India will go up in the world to the extent that she progresses. At the moment there is great respect for India in the world. Why? It is not because India has a population of thirty-six crores of people or that she is a large country, because that was there even earlier. But now three things have happened. One is that people saw that in the last ten years since freedom, we have worked very hard and succeeded to a large extent in making some progress. By we I mean the people of India. The countries which are capable of such achievements are respected in the world. Secondly, the world feels that if we continue to progress at this pace, within a few years India will become a force to reckon with, not militarily but in other ways. So we are respected. Thirdly, in the beginning our foreign policy was not much liked by many countries. They felt that we were neither here nor there. So they did not like it. But gradually they have seen that we do what we like with complete freedom and do not yield to any pressure, while maintaining friendly relations with all countries.

Now I will come to what is happening in the country. India is a very ancient country and it is not easy to change her. Yet India is changing very rapidly and anyone who visits India even after two-three years will find many new things. Those who go after an interval of five or six years are amazed at the transformation that is taking place, in the cities and the rural areas. The First Five Year Plan came to an end about six months ago. It was not very ambitious but we had to work very hard and succeeded to a large extent. It has increased

---

3. From 28 November to 10 December 1956

the self-confidence of the people as happens when an individual or a nation takes up a task and completes it successfully.

We are now taking up a bigger and more ambitious project, the Second Five Year Plan, and we will have to work much harder than before, bear hardships, shoulder many burdens and try to save. This is a great testing time for the country. We are determined to complete these tasks though the difficulties are far greater than what we had imagined and the Suez Canal crisis and other international problems are causing complications. Yet we are fully determined to face them and overcome them. Every Indian must realize that he has to participate in them for these things cannot be done by government orders alone. No government can bring about changes by passing a few laws or ordinances. This is a great task in which millions of people must take part for only then can a country change. The government has to lead the way by making proper laws and plans. But they will remain on paper unless the people participate in them. At least so far we have had the full cooperation of the people wherever they have been given an opportunity.

Great things are happening all over the country which you must be aware of. If you are not, you should try to understand them. But the most revolutionary schemes are the Community Projects and the National Extension Service. They are not for show but are really transforming the rural areas and uplifting the people and buoying up their self-confidence, which is a big thing. It has been India's way in the past too but especially so since Mahatma Gandhi came on the scene. As you know, Mahatma Gandhi was a peace-loving and non-violent man. But at the same time he was a great revolutionary too. So he did a great thing by combining revolution and peaceful methods. If you adopt peaceful methods and you are unable to achieve results, it is not enough. We have to achieve results. But we cannot afford to achieve our ends by violent methods for their consequences would be bad, as we have often seen in other countries. So he combined these two things—doing revolutionary things by peaceful methods, which is a great achievement.

We achieved independence by similar methods more or less. We had opposed the British for years but the moment we became free, our quarrel was over for we have no desire to fight with anyone. So in a sense we solved the problem without any bitterness.

Then we took up the problem of the princely states. In other countries problems of this nature have led to great violence and the others expected that the same thing will happen in India too. But the merger of five to six hundred Indian states took place peacefully which amazed everyone. Similarly, we abolished the zamindari and the *jagirdari* systems without any violence. The issues connected with land have always led to a great deal of violence and quarrels in

475

other countries. We have nearly settled it peacefully. All sorts of revolutionary changes are taking place in the country. We are facing great challenges in the economic and social field. As you know, laws have been passed to improve the status of the Hindu women—concerning their marriage, divorce, inheritance, etc.. These are very difficult things to do in a country steeped in old customs and prejudices. We have achieved all this peacefully.

I am trying to show you how we brought about a political revolution and are now trying to bring about revolutionary economic and social changes in the country. A country can progress only when these three things go hand in hand. I do not say that we have done everything that we wished to do. A great deal remains to be done. But whatever we have done is something that we can be proud of and can compare favourably with any country. But when a country embarkes upon a journey of this kind, it cannot afford to stop. There is an old saying that the man who rides a tiger cannot get off because if he does, it is likely that the tiger will be upon him. So when a country is engaged in such revolutionary tasks, there can be no rest for anyone. We have to keep going until we reach our goal. Anyhow, that is what we wish to do. But some people caution us against the dangers of going too fast. That may be so but it is even more dangerous not to go ahead. So we have to keep going and succeed in whatever we have undertaken. We need the understanding, help and cooperation of everyone in his own way in this.

I shall not go into what you should do or not do. But the first thing that you must understand, and to some extent explain to others, is what our goals and ideals are and then do whatever you can in helping to reach them. This is the duty of every Indian. Ours is a poor country and we wish to remove the poverty. There is no doubt about it that we are poor and it is absurd and silly to boast about ourselves. We want our people who go abroad to be able to maintain a civilized standard of living. But we cannot compete with others as far as wealth goes because we are a poor country. Even here in Washington you will find the citizens of many poor countries trying to live up to false standards which they cannot afford. We do not wish to do so. We must prove our mettle by our actions and the greatness of our culture. Anything else is false and not particularly civilized. We will be held in respect if all the Indians who live here remember that they are representatives of India and the honour of India lies in their hands. They must not do anything which is a blot on India's name. We must always remember this. Our Ambassador is not the only person who has been designated as such, but all Indians are ambassadors in their own way, because their way of living and behaviour has an impact. You are an example of what India is all about to people who have not visited India. Therefore your conduct must be worthy of India's name and honour. I would like all of you to think about these things. If you can occasionally visit India, it is well and good. But if you cannot, you must strive to understand, even from this distance, what is happening in the country not merely in the political field but the task of nation-building which is going on in the cities and villages of India. Only then will you get a clear picture and be able to explain to others.

Today I had talks with President Eisenhower for a short while. He wanted me to explain what our Five Year Plans and all about, and I was very happy to do so. I shall be talking to him again in the next few days. A great deal depends on our succeeding in our plans for they are not something on paper but with which the lives and the very future of thirty-six crores of people—men, women and children—are tied up. So you have to look at it from this point of view and not as a tome to be read. When I go to our villages, I find that our children are not being looked after properly. They do not get enough to eat, clothes to wear, houses to live in and proper education. I feel very upset and somewhat angry with myself that I as Prime Minister am unable to do anything for them. We talk a great deal about India and her future. After all, what is India? India is her men, women and children, not something made out of bricks and mortar. Mountains and rivers are also part of India but so are her men and women. When we talk of India's future, it is the children of today who will grow up to be the India of tomorrow. Children, boys and girls, are the country's greatest treasure. Therefore it is extremely important to look after them well, give them enough to eat, clothes to wear and, above all, provide opportunities for their education so that they can grow and develop well in later life into useful citizens. So these are the problems which confront us.

It is obvious that we cannot change the entire system overnight by some magic. But we have to move very rapidly in that direction so that we may reach our goal in five, ten or fifteen years at the most. Please remember that the Five Year Plans are not something on paper drawn up by great economists and planners. That too has to be done but behind it is the picture of crores of men and women, their lives and happiness and frustrations. If you think about it in this way, all our plans will come alive for they concern living men and women and are not mere documents on paper. What is happening in India at the moment is an exciting venture. We have a lot at stake in this venture and it is imperative that we should win. *Jai Hind.*

SELECTED WORKS OF JAWAHARLAL NEHRU

3. Talks with John Foster Dulles[1]

I had about an hour's talk with Secretary Dulles[2] this afternoon.

2. After an enquiry by me about his health after the operation, he referred to the recent NATO meeting in Paris[3] and said that it was not at all easy going. Some of the other countries represented in NATO wanted an assurance that no major step would be taken by any country without consulting the others. Mr Dulles could not agree to this proposition. He said that he had made no issue of not being consulted by the UK Government before the Anglo-French ultimatum to Egypt. In fact, for a couple of months before that there had been constant consultation over the Suez Canal issue between the UK Government, France and the USA. It was true that the actual ultimatum and attack on Egypt came as a surprise to him. He made no issue of not being consulted in this. His grievance was that the ultimatum and the attack on Egypt were basically wrong and if approved of, this would result in similar things happening elsewhere. The United Nations would hardly have any function left. It was because he considered this Anglo-French action in Egypt basically bad that he objected, and not because they were not consulted.

3. As for the proposal by some of the NATO powers for previous consultation in regard to any action on major issues, he could not possibly give this guarantee. The US had contacts and agreements with a very large number of countries many of which were not in the NATO. He could not bypass them or come to any decisions affecting them in which they were not consulted. Mr Dulles said that the idea behind some of the NATO powers appeared to be that the NATO, fully supported by the USA, should be a dominating influence in all world problems. He, Mr Dulles, did not agree with this. He said that NATO was a defensive organisation and not for any such offensive purpose or to dominate over the rest of the world.

4. Mr Dulles further said that he did not want the Middle East mentioned in the NATO communique. Under pressure, however, from others, he had agreed to some mention. It seemed to him odd to mention the Middle East and not mention the question of Cyprus which was of much more intimate concern to

1. Note to V.K. Krishna Menon, N.R. Pillai, Secretary General, MEA and G.L. Mehta, India's Ambassador to the USA, Washington D.C., 16 December 1956. V.K. Krishna Menon Papers, NMML.
2. US Secretary of State.
3. From 11 to 14 December 1956.

478

the NATO powers. He then said that he was worried over the Cyprus issue. The British Government's proposals for a constitution had apparently been rejected by the Greek Government although the Greek Government was anxious to come to some settlement.[4] In effect, these proposals gave a great deal of power to the British Governor who would not only control foreign affairs and internal law and order, but could decide as to what questions might affect either of these two subjects. Thus he could enlarge the domain of his own authority as far as he wished.

5. Secretary Dulles referred to the position in Egypt and the Middle East and said that this was not at all satisfactory. The British had this morning issued some kind of an ultimatum about their six salvage ships. They had laid down some conditions for the use of these salvage ships for clearing the Canal. In the event of their offer not being accepted within twenty-four hours, the salvage ships would be called back. Some of these ships had actually done some salvage work and had raised some of the sunken ships. If they went away suddenly, they would drop these ships back into the Canal, which would be unfortunate. The conditions which the British had laid down were:

(i) that the salvage ships should be manned by British crew,

(ii) that they would have the right to fire in self-defence if they were attacked, and

(iii) that the United Nations force should guard the full length of the Canal to protect the salvage ships.

6. Mr Dulles said that the conditions were not very unreasonable and might perhaps be modified somewhat; but what he objected to was this method of issuing ultimatums. This kind of thing added to one's difficulties and did not help the solution of any problem. The State Department had been in telephonic touch with London, apparently trying to get this period of the ultimatum increased.

7. Mr Dulles also said that Nasser was not very cooperative. The Secretary General of the UN, to whom the British ultimatum had been sent, was also unhappy about it and was apparently trying to persuade the British to extend the period and perhaps also to agree to some modifications of the ultimatum.

---

4. Anthony Eden, the British Prime Minister, announced in the House of Commons on 12 July 1956 that the UK would grant Cyprus self-government and that Lord Cyril Radcliffe had been asked to work on a draft constitution for Cyprus. Radcliffe's proposals were published on 19 December. The Greek Government rejected the proposals saying they were neither democratic nor liberal since the elected majority principle was strangled by the unbridled powers of the Governor.

8. Mr Dulles referred to the ten American prisoners in China[5] and said that their continued detention was preventing any progress being made in regard to the improvement of US-China relations. He realized that the present situation in regard to these relations was unsatisfactory and some time or other they had to be improved. So far as the entry of China into the UN was concerned, for the present the US had to oppose it because of the strong public opinion against it. But, it might be possible to influence public opinion step by step in the right direction. The first step that seemed essential was the release of these ten American airmen. If that was done, he could assure me that the US Government would remove the prohibition preventing Americans from going to China. Any American could go there, journalist or other, and the reports of these people about internal conditions in China would greatly influence American opinion.

9. I told him that we had all along been anxious to get these prisoners released and, in fact, I had spoken to Premier Chou En-lai on this subject when he came to Delhi recently.[6] In answer, Chou En-lai gave a long account of how they had taken several steps, including the release of many prisoners, but the US Government had not responded by any similar gesture. It was up to the US Government to do something, and then they would consider the release of these prisoners. More particularly, Chou En-lai had referred to the difficulties placed in the way of Chinese, students and others, in the United States. Mr Dulles said that it was quite open to any Chinese to go back to China, if he wanted. Under the agreement, he could apply to the Indian Embassy, who would fix this up. In fact, however, only about fifty or sixty had gone back, including two Chinese prisoners. It was not possible for him to make lists of all Chinese in the United States. He had made enquiries from the various prisons and he had a list of those Chinese. There was another reason for his not supplying the names of all the Chinese here, because this might lead to pressure being exercised on their relatives in China.

10. I told Mr Dulles that during his recent visit to India, Premier Chou En-lai refrained from any attacks and, in fact, was very moderate in his speeches. He

5. On the same day Nehru sent a note to G.L. Mehta, stating: "When I mentioned the question of the Chinese prisoners and the Chinese in America, Secretary Dulles said that so far as they were concerned, they had given every facility to any Chinese person here (in USA) to go to China, if he wanted to.... The subject is a difficult one on both sides, China and the US. I do not think the Chinese attitude in this matter has been very helpful. Nevertheless, we should do our utmost both with a view to achieving some result and, secondly, to impress upon the Chinese that we have done everything."
6. From 28 November to 10 December 1956.

expressed his wish to improve relations between China and the USA. He seemed to me to be anxious to do so.

11. In discussing Anglo-French action in Egypt, Mr Dulles mentioned that if this kind of thing was condoned, Syngman Rhee[7] would immediately want to attack North Korea or Chiang Kai-shek[8] might indulge in military adventures also.

12. I mentioned to Mr Dulles about the position in Laos where after long arguments, the two parties, that is, the Government and the Pathet Lao, had come to an agreement. Under this agreement, the Royal Laotian Government was prepared to take a representative of the Pathet Lao in their Government. But the American Ambassador[9] had strongly objected to this and had said that, in case it happened, American aid would not be forthcoming. I said that it was unfortunate that this agreement was being objected to. Mr Dulles said that he was not in intimate touch with the latest developments as he had been in hospital, but it was true that the US Government did not approve of a representative of the Pathet Lao joining the Laotian Government. If a communist came in this way and, more particularly, if he was in charge of the police and law and order, he would strengthen his own group's position and create trouble. Mr Dulles promised, however, to let me have further particulars about these matters before I left Washington.

13. Mr Dulles made some brief reference to the refugees from Hungary.

14. I pointed out to him that the Egyptian and the Hungarian crises had brought into light significant movements. They had made it clear that it was no longer easy for the biggest of powers to revert to a colonial policy. Further, they had made it clear that communism could not be imposed on a country which did not want it. In effect, international communism had broken down and even internal communism in any country had received a big shock. Members of the Communist Party in any of the non-communist countries were hard put to it how to understand or explain recent happenings in Hungary. They were facing great frustration and confusion, and some leading ones had resigned from the Communist Party.

15. I added that both these happenings had created a new position in the world. In spite of the tragedies involved, there were hopeful signs provided they could be taken advantage of. There were liberalizing movements in the Soviet

7. President, Republic of Korea (South Korea), 1948-60.
8. President, Republic of China (Taiwan), 1950-75.
9. J. Graham Parsons, US Ambassador in Vientiane, Laos.

Union and in the East European countries and if they were allowed to continue, many of the fears of today would end or at least lessen, and door would be opened for peaceful solution of some of the existing problems. What I was anxious about was that they would not have a chance of peaceful development and, in fact, that war might result.

16. Mr Dulles said that he agreed with me and that, in fact, some two years ago, he had expressed his opinion that unless the Soviet Government went ahead in these East European countries to liberalize them and to avoid interference, there would be a blow-up. That had happened now, a little sooner than he had expected. It was clear that the liberalizing forces I had referred to could not ultimately be reversed. What he was afraid of, however, was that war might come. There was more likelihood of it now than there had been in the past two years or more. Russia feeling itself in the wrong, might plunge into war to prevent what they consider humiliation.

17. The Baghdad Pact was referred to, and Mr Dulles said that great pressure was being exercised on him by some countries to join the Baghdad Pact. His own Defence Services Chiefs also wanted him to join it. But he had resisted this pressure though he was not sure what the ultimate decision might be. He thought that the UK had been very precipitate about this Baghdad Pact and, therefore, led to many unfortunate developments as in Jordan.

18. I told him that, as he knew, I was not in love with Baghdad Pact and since that Pact had come into existence, it had only led to troubles and divisions in the Middle East. He said that it was the British Government that had pushed this through in spite of their advice. Now, although not members of the Pact, they were helping those countries. The question of joining the Baghdad Pact or not was a very difficult one for him. He was opposed to it, but he could not guarantee what the future might bring.

19. He mentioned the possibility of anti-Russian demonstrations in East Germany and, as a result, volunteers from Western Germany going to the Eastern part. This might well lead to war.

4. A Friendship to Treasure[1]

Mr Vice-President, ladies and gentlemen, just before this very pleasant and agreeable meeting I was talking to the Vice-President and telling him that I began what might be called my public speaking late in life, and under rather unusual circumstances.

I was very shy of speaking at college and at the university; in fact, in my university, at Cambridge, I joined the Debating Society, and there if a person did not speak, he paid a fine. I gladly paid the fine, and years passed after that and then I had got rather entangled with the peasantry of my province, who were living very unhappy lives, and I got to meet them and I had to say something to them, and I was not shy of them, as they were very simple. I started to talk to 200, and then to 500, and a thousand, in a casual way and thus got over a little of my reluctance to speak, but I have never quite got used to speaking at such functions. I don't mind very large audiences of peasants and those in my country who cannot help but put up with what I say, and who will not criticize what I say; it's easy; but here, it's very difficult.

The Vice-President repeatedly warned us or told us that this was not a formal affair and there was no toast, and that if I wanted to do so I might do so, and if I didn't, I needn't do so—I don't quite know what the difference is.

Anyhow, I am very grateful to you, Mr Vice-President, and to you, Madam,[2] for this opportunity to meet so many eminent people here in Washington. I really am sorry that I should come all the way from India to Washington and to New York, just for a few days. It seems rather absurd to take all that trouble, although it is worthwhile, no doubt; but, unfortunately, as the Vice-President realized, in spite of what he said, comparing his own duties to those of ambassadors, elections and the like are important things in politicians' lives, and very soon we are going to have a big election in India, the general elections. It will absorb a lot of time and energy and also a little bit of anxiety, occasionally.

So, I am sorry I have come here for a very short time. Nevertheless, I am glad I could come and have the opportunity of renewing my acquaintance with Washington, this very beautiful city, and most especially the President and the eminent leaders who live here. It is not adequate to say, but it gives one such a

---

1. Speech at a luncheon given by Vice-President Richard M. Nixon, Washington D.C., 18 December 1956. From *Nehru Visits USA*, The Information Service of India, Washington, pp. 3-8.
2. Patricia R. Nixon.

new lease of life, if I may say so, in thinking and having certain pictures in one's mind upon which you can hang so many thoughts.

The Vice-President referred to Ambassadors. I entirely agree with him that the work of Ambassadors is both difficult and very heavy nowadays—perhaps not in every country, for sometimes I find ambassadors have a very easy time. But that only applies, maybe, to some; others have to work very hard indeed, and deal with all kinds of new things happening in the world, some pleasant, very often unpleasant things. But ambassadors' work grows, and an ambassador not only must work hard but at the same time not with complete assurance, because there is perhaps some sort of a ministry or department at the back of him that may pull him up at any time; he both tries to go ahead and he is also afraid of being pulled back. So it is not an easy task at all.

The Vice-President referred to his visit to India.[3] I am glad he referred to that because that gave him some little picture of our people, more especially, not of the people he might have met in New Delhi, but I think he did visit some villages round about New Delhi that are more typical of India than New Delhi, and I think the villagers he met gave him an Indian welcome, and that, probably, was more representative of India than any banquet or function he might have participated in.

Our people are friendly, and one thing that has surprised me, and many American visitors who have come to India have spoken to me about it, it surprised them more than it surprises me, because, after all, I am used to my own people, and that is: in spite of poverty, distress, and all kinds of things, our people have not forgotten their dancing and laughing, which is a great virtue. They have not been oppressed, but they are depressed occasionally, but still they do not take life in such a heavy way because of the obvious disability they suffer from. Well, I suppose that insofar as economic standards are concerned, they will make progress. We are working to that end, but I am very, very anxious that in making progress they do not forget how to sing and dance and laugh. That is more basic and important even than perhaps economic progress. Of course, there is no conflict between the two, certainly.

Anyhow, so far as we are concerned in India, we are engaged in a pretty big task. I can tell you that it is heavy, naturally, and one feels sometimes rather disappointed, but it is a big exciting job, and I feel exhilarated, not all the time, but very often, because of being tied up with this great work.

Previous to this business, we spent long years, many of us in India, in our struggle for independence. That had a powerful effect on us, conditioning us,

3. Nixon visited India from 29 November to 4 December 1953.

484

moulding us, to some extent, in a particular pattern. Then, too, it was an exciting thing. I must say my life has been full of excitement. Some people sometimes express their sympathy over my ten years in prison. Yes, I spent about ten years, off and on, in prison, but I can tell you, I cannot say that I enjoyed them, because that would not be true, but nevertheless it was all a very exciting time, and that is perhaps more worthwhile than some kind of just empty enjoyment of other things, because when one is mentally and otherwise tied up with something that one considers big, a great undertaking, well, it has an effect on him. I think one grows more by being engaged in big undertakings than otherwise. Some of the shadow of the great things falls on the persons working for those things.

That is a very satisfying feeling, in spite of a thousand difficulties and occasional heartbreaks. The same way, we are engaged in this tremendous task in India, we have an achievement of independence behind us, we have the enormous satisfaction and joy of seeing something that we had worked for years and years to come true, dreams coming true. It doesn't often happen that dreams come true, but the moment it came true, immediately we realized that, it was only a stage of the journey and we had to pack up our knapsacks and start afresh. Well, we did it, and it is a longer and more difficult journey, but even so, great dreams do come true, and maybe as time goes on, the big dream will also come true, and the thought of that is exhilarating.

I must not go on in this way. I do not know if it is a proper way for me, but I do wish to say that I am tremendously grateful to the President, of course, but to others here, for your very genuine hospitality and friendly way in which you have accepted us as friends. That is an honour and a privilege, and a friendship which I shall treasure.

I am grateful, very grateful to you, Mr Vice-President, and to you, Madam, for your kindness.

5. Continuity and Change[1]

Mr Secretary, Mrs Dulles, ladies and gentlemen. I have been in Washington now, this time, for barely three days, and yet, I have a sensation that I have been here a long time.

It has often seemed to me that this reckoning of time by the clock is a very feeble way of measuring its passage. On other occasions, when time seemed to me to stand still, when I was incapacitated from any particular activity by being kept in detention in prison, time had a different quality. There is nothing to measure it by, nothing in the sense of sensation or change—everything was the same day after day, every sight was the same.

On other occasions, time seemed to run fast because there were new sensations, new sights, so that the clock seemed to be a very poor way of measuring it.

Now, these less than three days I have been here, I have had so many, not novel experiences, but still experiences, sensations, feelings, that it gives me the idea that I have gone through a great deal.

And among the major experiences and sensations has been the extraordinary warmth of the welcome my daughter and I have had; and, if I may use the word, the affection we have experienced wherever we have been to here.

I came here on the kind invitation of the President, and yesterday I had the unique opportunity of being with him the whole day and discussing all manner of topics and subjects, and realizing again what I knew—what a great man the President of the United States was and is, and how it is to the great advantage of the world that in this crisis in world affairs, the head of this great country should not only represent the power and might of the United States, but a certain moral quality which in the ultimate analysis is something bigger.

I do not know how to thank you, Mr Secretary and others, and especially the President, for all the kindness and friendliness that we have experienced since we came here.

You mentioned just now about the fact that sometimes in regard to some matters there may not be complete agreement.[2] It has always surprised me that

---

1. Speech at a banquet given by John Foster Dulles, the US Secretary of State, Washington D.C., 18 December 1956. From *Nehru Visits USA*, The Information Service of India, Washington, pp. 10-15.
2. Dulles stated that Nehru stood for the inevitability of change and the importance that the process of change should be a peaceful one, with non-violence as its theme. He added that, "...there is, I think an instinctive recognition on the part of all, even though they disagree in some respects with the application of your views, a recognition of the fact that you stand for something which is basic and indeed indispensible for our world as it is today."

in this world of ours there is so much agreement in spite of its extraordinary diversity and variety. Also, we hear such a great deal about conflicts in the world—and of course there are conflicts and very bad ones sometimes—and yet the fact remains that the world wouldn't carry on for a day but for an enormous amount of cooperation—it would just collapse. If there were more conflicts than cooperation in the world, then the world just would not work.

But, unfortunately the element of conflict, the elements of disagreement and friction, somehow stand out and are made to stand out even more by the modern methods of publicity. Somebody said that virtue may be very good, but it is not news. Vice is news. A disaster is news. Nobody writes about the peaceful conditions prevailing in a humdrum family. But if there is any trouble or any flood or any earthquake, it is news. But earthquakes nevertheless are few and other things happen which are not recorded.

So that if one looks at it that way, it is extraordinary and satisfying that in spite of the fact that probably no two human beings are alike, these 2,000 or 2,500 million human beings do pull on in this world more or less with a measure of cooperation, sometimes quite a great deal of it.

Perhaps, I have often wondered, when people disagree, how far that is due, among other causes, to geography. Of course, it may be due also to, in a sense, history, or tradition, that is, the past conditioning of people which has made them what they are. They can't get out of the shells wholly, to some extent they might.

But let us take geography only. I imagine myself sitting at the North Pole and I look around and I see a particular picture of the world before me. If I go to the Equator, I see something different, apart from climate. The map of the world is different. If I sit in Washington, well, the world is the same but the perspective is different. In Delhi, it is somewhat different again.

And so, it seems to follow that because all these determining factors which give us this perspective or that, we form somewhat different ideas of things. I don't mean to say basically different, but the emphasis is different. Mr Secretary Dulles is in charge of the foreign policy of the United States, I am in charge of the foreign policy of India. We are concerned in our ways—his is a much bigger way, mine is a smaller way—with the problems of other countries. But inevitably my problems with my neighbour countries loom large before me, not because they are bigger or greater countries, but because they are at my threshold. Even though it might be a small country, well, I have to think more about it because it is there, whereas Mr Secretary Dulles need not necessarily think so much, because in itself that country may not be important. But because it is my neighbour I have to think more of it.

So that these perspectives differ, because of geography and this and that; and they lead, they appear to lead, to certain differences of opinion, or perhaps, more so, not so much to differences but to the emphasis one lays on a particular factor; one may lay more of it because from his viewpoint it is more important where he stands, what problems he deals with, than another person who may give some emphasis to something else.

I merely put this because I feel that we tend, all over the world, rather to give undue emphasis to certain factors which are important, no doubt, but perhaps do not deserve that amount of emphasis.

Then, Mr Secretary, you talked about change and the inevitability of change. Well, I suppose there are two factors which are inevitable in history; one is change and the other is continuity—both are essential. Without continuity, well, you break up, and it takes some time to join the broken threads. If we had only continuity, it is stagnation, you don't grow, so you must have change. If we have all change and no continuity, well, you don't seem to profit by the accumulation—our wisdom of the past is a break, and again you have to build anew. So I suppose the ideal state would be where there is continuity and change, both. Even the biggest revolutions, really, cannot break that ultimate continuity, and if they seem to break it, they go back to the continuity after a while, because otherwise they would be rootless, the people of a country.

In my country's philosophy, in Indian philosophy, life is often compared to, shall I say, a running river or a flame in the sense that the river is constantly changing, the water is flowing away, and yet, it is the same; the flame is the same, and yet, it is a continuously changing thing, thus bringing about a certain idea of seeming continuity and yet change.

Well, sometimes the process of change seems sudden and we call it a revolution or an earthquake. And yet, probably the bigger changes are not the earthquakes but, speaking in geological terms, these are the infinite changes that are taking place on the earth's crust, or inside, which only sometimes give place to an earthquake.

And so, I suppose, in human society something, some kind of a violent revolution takes place, attracts attention, seems very big, and yet probably the biggest revolutions ever since the world began, if I may say so, have been the changes which have followed the Industrial Revolution. Those are the real revolutions which have changed human life completely and go on changing it. And now we stand on the threshold of the atomic age, which is likely to bring another tremendous revolution, and yet they come in step by step without, apparently, any big break.

The United States of America are, well, particularly a dynamic society, always trying to better themselves, to change and go forward. India, I suppose, has a

WITH JOHN FOSTER DULLES AT BLAIR HOUSE, WASHINGTON,
16 DECEMBER 1956

AT THE INDIAN EMBASSY, WASHINGTON, 16 DECEMBER 1956

reputation of being somewhat static. And that reputation is partly correct, at least in the past. Yet, if you examine India, it is not so static, after all, and if you examine the United States it is not hopping about, it is continuous. It is not that they don't break with anything, both the elements are there. Only maybe sometimes the society appears to go rather fast ahead because of various circumstances.

Anyhow, this is not an occasion to philosophize, Mr Secretary, but we do seem to be living during a period of history when, because of the inherent workings, not because of so-called human revolutions, but inherent workings of the social organism, of science and its developments, enormous changes come and the pace of change increases.

And sometimes, although these changes take place and we profit by them, we really don't fit into them. What I mean is, probably the intellectual and mental and, if you like, the moral make-up of the individual doesn't quite catch up with the technical changes that come in. Just as you may fly today from the coldest climate to a very hot climate in a very short time, and your physical body might not easily adapt itself to it. So, the problem today is how far human beings are mentally, intellectually and morally adapting themselves to the tremendous changes that science and technology have brought about and are bringing about.

Maybe many of the political problems of the day can be explained by this difficulty in the process of adjustment and adaptation of society. Well, anyhow, it will have to adapt itself, find some equilibrium or else—well, it will break.

The one dangerous, and at the same time hopeful, feature of today is that the possibility of this break is evident unless something is done or unless something is prevented. That has at least woken up people and it may be that they might devise means to find proper adjustments for human society and proper restraints, so that these tremendous forces might not be used for evil purposes.

Anyhow, these problems will go on afflicting men, and when we solve one problem, no doubt others will arise. We who live today are pressed by the problems of the day. Probably, I suppose in the past, if we can place ourselves in the position of those who lived then, they thought that their age was the most terrible and difficult of all and the most dangerous. Old newspapers, say, in Napoleon's time make very interesting reading. There was terror in some countries of Europe, say, England and elsewhere, because of Napoleon. This devil incarnate was upsetting everything. Well, the world survived, and it seems a relatively almost sedate time compared to other times which came later.

So I presume the world will go on and adjust itself. Nevertheless, I suppose we have to help the world to adjust itself and not leave things to chance.

Meanwhile, as Mr Secretary Dulles said, well, some of us, most of us in India and I suppose most of us in other countries of the East, are very much engrossed in the work of getting their countries out of that period of stagnation, that morass in which they were stuck. It is hard work and exciting work, and it is worthwhile work and I have no doubt that we shall make good.

I am very grateful to you, Mr Secretary, and the other eminent ladies and gentlemen who are here, for their welcome and for their leadership.

May I ask you to drink to the health of the President of the United States?

6. The Democratic Way of Life[1]

I am emboldened to address you in this intimate fashion because of the friendship and hospitality which you, the citizens of the United States, have showered upon me. I have come to your great country on a brief visit, at the gracious invitation of your President, whose humanity and whose distinguished and devoted services to the cause of peace have won for him a unique place among the statesmen of the world. I am happy to be here, and my only regret is that I can only stay a few days and have no opportunity of meeting many of you personally.

Five years ago, a professor of an American university visited me in Delhi, and gave me a gift which I have treasured greatly. That was a mould in brass of Abraham Lincoln's right hand.[2] It is a beautiful hand, strong and firm, and yet gentle. It has been kept ever since on my study table, and I look at it every day and it gives me strength.

This may perhaps give you some idea of our thinking and our urges in India. For, above all, we believe in liberty, equality, the dignity of the individual and the freedom of the human spirit. Because of this, we are firmly wedded to the democratic way of life, and in our loyalty to this cause we will not falter. Nearly seven years ago, we constituted our country into a Republic, and gave to ourselves

1. Television and radio address from Washington D.C., 18 December 1956. From *Nehru Visits USA*, The Information Service of India, Washington, pp. 15-19.
2. Arthur E. Morgan gave this gift on 13 April 1949. See *Selected Works* (second series), Vol. 10, p. 98.

a Constitution based on these principles, and guaranteeing the fundamental human rights of freedom of the individual, equality of man and the rule of law.

Five years ago we had general elections in our country for our central Parliament as well as for our State Assemblies. These elections were organized on a vast scale by an authority free of government control so as to ensure that they were free and impartial. Early next year we are again going to have general elections in which two hundred million voters are entitled to participate. You will realize the vastness of these elections when I tell you that there will be one million two hundred thousand polling booths, so that no voter will need to go far to cast his vote.

As you know, India is a big country with a population of 370 million, one-seventh of the total population of the world. It is a country steeped in history and tradition, with a civilization nearly as old as recorded time and a culture nourished on its own soil and blended happily with those of other peoples and of other lands. This year we celebrated in India and in many other countries the 2,500th anniversary of a very great son of India, the Buddha, who gave us the message of peace and compassion.

Through the centuries India has preached and practised toleration and understanding, and has enriched human thought, art and literature, philosophy and religion. Her sons journeyed far and wide braving the perils of land and sea, not with thoughts of conquest or domination, but as messengers of peace or engaged in the commerce of ideas as well as of her beautiful products. During these millennia of history India has experienced both good and ill. But throughout her chequered history she has remembered the message of peace and tolerance. In our own time, this message was proclaimed by our great leader and master, Mahatma Gandhi, who led us to freedom by peaceful and yet effective action on a mass scale.

Nine years ago, we won our independence through a bloodless revolution in conditions of honour and dignity both to ourselves and to the erstwhile rulers of our country. We in India today are children of this revolution and have been conditioned by it. Although your revolution in America took place long ago, and the conditions were different here, you will appreciate the revolutionary spirit which we have inherited and which still governs our activities. Having attained political freedom, we are earnestly desirous of removing the many ills that our country suffers from, of eliminating poverty and raising the standards of our people and giving them full and equal opportunities of growth and advancement. India is supposed to be given to contemplation, and the American people have shown by their history that they possess great energy, dynamism and the passion to march ahead. Something of that contemplative spirit still remains in India. At the same time the new India of today has also developed a certain dynamism and a passionate desire to raise the standards of her people. But with that desire is blended the wish to adhere to the moral and spiritual aspects of life.

We are now engaged in a gigantic and exciting task of achieving rapid and large-scale economic development of our country. Such development in an ancient and underdeveloped country, such as India, is only possible with purposive planning. True to our democratic principles and traditions we seek free discussion and consultation as well as the willing and active cooperation of our people in the implementation of the Five Year Plans. We completed our First Five Year Plan eight months ago, and now we have begun, on a more ambitious scale, our Second Five Year Plan, which seeks a balanced development in agriculture and industry, town and country, and between factory and small-scale and cottage production. I speak of India, because it is my country and I have some right to speak for her. But many other countries in Asia tell the same story, for Asia today is resurgent and these countries which long lay under foreign yoke have won back their independence and are fired by a new spirit and strive towards new ideals. To them as to us independence is as vital as the breath they take to sustain life, and colonialism in any form or anywhere is abhorrent.

The vast strides that technology has made have brought a new age of which the Untied States of America is the leader. Today the whole world is our neighbour and the old divisions of continents and countries matter less and less. Peace and freedom have become indivisible and the world cannot continue for long partly free and partly subject. In this atomic age, peace has also become a test of human survival.

Recently, we have witnessed two tragedies which have powerfully affected men and women all over the world. These are the tragedies in Egypt and Hungary. Our deeply felt sympathies must go out to those who have suffered or are suffering, and all of us must do our utmost to help them and to assist in solving these problems in a peaceful and constructive way. But even these tragedies have one hopeful aspect, for they have demonstrated that the most powerful countries cannot revert to old colonial methods or impose their domination over weak countries. World opinion has shown that it can organize itself to resist such outrages. Perhaps, as an outcome of these tragedies, freedom will be enlarged and we will have a more assured basis for it.

The preservation of peace forms the central aim of India's policy. It is in the pursuit of this policy that we have chosen the path of non-alignment in any military or like pact or alliance. Non-alignment does not mean passivity of mind or action, lack of faith or conviction. It does not mean submission to what we consider evil. It is a positive and dynamic approach to such problems as confront us. We believe that each country has the right not only to freedom but also to decide its own policy and way of life. Only thus can true freedom flourish and a people grow according to their own genius.

We believe therefore in non-aggression and non-interference by one country in the affairs of another and the growth of tolerance between them and the capacity for peaceful coexistence. We think that by the free exchange of ideas and trade and other contacts between nations, each will learn from the other and trust will prevail. We, therefore, endeavour to maintain friendly relations with all countries even though we may disagree with them in their policies or structure of government. We think that by this approach we can serve not only our country but also the larger cause of peace and good fellowship in the world.

Between the United States and India there had existed friendly and cordial relations even before India gained her independence. No Indian can forget that in the days of our struggle for freedom, we received from your country a full measure of sympathy and support. Our two Republics share a common faith in democratic institutions and the democratic way of life, and are dedicated to the cause of peace and freedom. We admire the many qualities that have made this country great and more especially the humanity and dynamism of its people and the great principles to which the fathers of the American Revolution gave utterance. We wish to learn from you and we plead for your friendship and your cooperation and sympathy in the great task that we have undertaken in our own country.

I have had the great privilege of having long talks with the President and we have discussed many problems which confront the world. I can tell you that I have greatly profited by these talks. I shall treasure their memory and they will help me in many ways in my thinking. I sincerely hope that an opportunity may be given to us before long to welcome the President in our own country and to demonstrate to him the high respect and esteem in which we hold him.

We have recently witnessed grievous transgressions of the moral standards freely accepted by the nations of the world. During this period of anxiety and distress the United States has added greatly to its prestige by upholding the principles of the Charter of the United Nations.

The danger of war is not past, and the future may hold fresh trials and tribulations for humanity. Yet the forces of peace are strong and the mind of humanity is awake. I believe that peace will triumph. We are celebrating in this season the festival of peace and goodwill, and soon the New Year will come to us. May I wish you all a happy New Year and express the hope that this year will see the triumph for peace and freedom all over the world. Good night.

7. The Global Picture[1]

Frank Holeman, President of the National Press Club: On behalf of all the officers and members of the National Press Club, I want to give a warm welcome to our guest today. This is his second visit to the National Press Club. In 1949 he addressed a luncheon here.[2] This time he preferred to give his whole time to questions. Somebody must have told him that reporters would rather talk than eat..... Let me then introduce to you Jawaharlal Nehru of India. The Prime Minister would like to start with the first question.

William F. McGaffin, *Chicago Daily News*: Mr Prime Minister, in your speech last night, sir, you said the talks you had had with the President will help you in many ways in your thinking. Sir, could you spell that out a bit? In what ways do you expect that these talks will help you.

Jawaharlal Nehru: Well, it is not an easy question to answer. Primarily by getting a much better understanding of American policy, and more especially of the President's background of thinking in regard to it, which is very important.

Bill Downs, CBS News: Mr Prime Minister, in your speech last night to the American people you said that "the forces of peace are strong; the mind of humanity is awake." How do you apply this to the Soviet Union in light of the events in Hungary?

JN: Well, I applied it, that phrase, more especially to the events in Egypt and Hungary, that is, the reactions to those events in the minds of people, whether they are represented in the United Nations or elsewhere, whatever means of judging one had about public opinion.

If you are referring to the minds of the people in the Soviet Union, obviously I have no sure indication. But I imagine that people in the Soviet Union are not very happy about events in Hungary, if I may put it mildly in that way.

1. At the National Press Building, Washington D.C., 19 December 1956. AIR tapes, NMML.
2. On 14 October 1949. See *Selected Works*, Vol. 13 (second series), pp. 305-307.

David P. Sentner, Hearst Newspapers: Do you believe that the technique of Mahatma Gandhi of passive resistance could be used successfully by the Hungarian people?

JN: I cannot give a reply about what might happen in Hungary or any particular place because I am not adequately acquainted with the background in the sense of when people apply a technique they must, to some extent, be trained in it; they must, to some extent, understand it. There is always a danger of superficially applying a technique and not adhering to it and thereby falling between two stools; but I do believe that that type of technique is not only effective but, if I may say so, in the long run more effective than other techniques, if people have understood it and can do it in an organized way.

Raymond P. Brandt, *St Louis Post-Dispatch*: Mr Prime Minister, competent authorities have said that the Asiatic countries, notably India, Ceylon and Burma, will be more adversely affected by the closing of the Suez Canal than England. Will you work with the United States, France and Great Britain for the immediate clearing up of the Canal regardless of what personnel and machinery is used?

JN: No, sir. First of all, while it is true that the closing of the Suez Canal affects India in the sense that it sends up the prices of our exports and imports, and delays things coming, I don't think it would be true to say that it affects us more than the other countries you mentioned. But quite apart from that, the real question is not how much it affects us, but what steps should be taken to get back to normality there; and we are anxious, of course, that steps should be taken, subject always to the sovereignty of Egypt, and we don't want to ask for steps to be taken which offend that sovereignty in any way.

Chalmers M. Roberts, *Washington Post*: As a result of your talks with the President, is it possible that you will stop in Cairo on your way home to discuss with Colonel Nasser either the Canal settlement issue or the Palestine problem?

JN: I am afraid there is no chance of my stopping in Cairo on my way back. Well, for two reasons: one is, it is just a question—it is very difficult for me, practically speaking, to do so. I have to be back by a certain date in Delhi. If I had the chance I would gladly have stopped there. . . .

Chalmers M. Roberts: Do you have any other plans for Indian participation with the United States to settle either of those two Middle East problems?

JN: No, we have no particular plans. We function, as you know, in the United Nations, and we function on the diplomatic plane where there are frequent consultations. We have no particular magic plan to do it.

John L. Steele, *Time*: Did you bring to President Eisenhower any message from Chou En-lai. If not, would you give us your appraisal of Chou which you may have given the President?

JN: These personal appraisals are rather embarrassing.

I did not bring any particular message from Mr Chou En-lai. But naturally, I have had talks with him and I gave the President the gist of our talks in regard to some matters of common interest.

As many of you know, Mr Chou En-lai is a rather remarkable man and impressive. He gave me the Chinese viewpoint in regard to certain problems of Asia and—well, I conveyed it to the President, not as a message from him, I mean, but in explaining what their thinking was.

John L. Steele: Can you give us the gist of that, sir?

JN: The gist of that, I would say that they have certain complaints, complaints in the sense of steps taken or not taken. They say—I am merely repeating—that we have gone several steps forwards, but there has been no favourable reaction on the other side. Broadly speaking that is the gist of their position.

Now, you may have a different opinion, that is a different matter.

May Craig, *Portland Press Herald*, Maine: Would you agree to a Suez settlement which would allow Egypt to continue to bar Israeli ships?

JN: I shall answer that question slightly indirectly. That is to say, I think that the Suez Canal should be opened to all ships without exception.

The question that has arisen there, that is, before these recent developments, was about Israeli ships being barred, and as to the interpretation of the old Convention of 1888. I believe President Nasser said that he accepted the 1888 Convention completely, but his interpretation of that was that if he is at war with a country, then it does not apply.

Now, it is a question of interpretation of that Convention. I should imagine that some court, like the World Court, should be asked to interpret it, and whatever interpretation they give should be accepted. That is one way of it, so far as the past is concerned. So far as the future is concerned, we can sit down and have a new Convention.

Charles W. Roberts, *Newsweek*: Sir, last night you spoke of India's dedication to liberty, equality and dignity of man, and freedom of the human spirit. How do you reconcile this concern and dedication to freedom of the human spirit with India's refusal to condemn Russia's aggression in Hungary?

JN: There is no question of India refusing to condemn anything. If you are referring to one of the recent resolutions of the United Nations Assembly, you will remember that a resolution was put forward by India, and amendments were moved. Now, that resolution put forward by India expressed in fairly strong terms India's views about what had happened in Hungary. The whole point was: are we going to satisfy ourselves by a strong denunciation or condemnation or are we to have some constructive approach to the problem?

India attempted to put forward a constructive approach which, in effect, was that the Secretary General of the UN should move in the matter himself on behalf of the UN to get things going, otherwise people sit apart from each other, condemn each other, and nothing is done.

The point was: Here is a very serious issue, we want to help Hungary, we want to do many things. Well, how are we going to do it? If we think that by condemnation it will resolve itself, well and good. But we thought that some other constructive approach—we expressed our disapproval of what had happened there in very strong terms. It is a question of the context and the wording and how you end up.

Milton Friedman, Jewish Telegraphic Agency: Sir, do you believe the establishment by India of normal diplomatic relations with Israel would contribute towards the status of India as an objective force working towards Middle Eastern peace?

JN: About a year or two after Israel came into existence the Government of India recognized Israel. But it is true that we did not exchange diplomatic missions with Israel, and we have not done so yet. Frankly, the reason was that we felt that we would be able to help in this matter more by not going a step further and having these—exchanging diplomatic missions. You know that our relations and contacts with the Arab nations are very considerable, and in this matter there is considerable passion, and we thought that was the better course. Of course, we sympathize with many of the claims of the Arabs, their territory, in regard to refugees, and in regard to other matters.

Anyhow, we felt that the only way to settle this matter is for those people to come together and settle it. Now, after recent occurrences, it is infinitely more difficult for the present, at least—I am not talking about the future.

Edward T. Folliard, *Washington Post*: You have expressed the hope that President Eisenhower will visit India. Do you think he will go over there or did he give you any indication that he might or that he would like to?

JN: You don't want me to commit the President. This is the President's.... I should be very happy if he comes. I hope he will come.

I.H. Gordon, International News Service: Why do you advocate membership in the United Nations for Red China; and if Red China comes into the United Nations, what would you advocate doing with Nationalist China?

JN: Well, legally and constitutionally speaking, there is only one China. What I mean is the mainland of China does not recognize a separate Formosa Government, and the Formosa Government does not recognize the other Government. They both claim to be one. It is not that either claims to be two. Each claims to be the real article, the other not. So the question of two does not arise. Neither of these two claim to be two or want to be two, and I do not think that in the circumstances of today or in the context of history, it is likely that two can continue.

Obviously, the Formosan Government, at the most, is the Formosan Government, it is not China. Let me say, the map will show you it is not China, whatever else it is. It is Formosa, and to call it China is slightly stretching language.

Richard L. Wilson, *The Register*: Have your discussions with President Eisenhower led you to believe that the United States has a new policy toward neutralist nations which, basically, is more acceptable to India?

JN: That is a difficult question for me to answer because you are wanting me to tell you what American policy is, what is United States policy.

What I say is this: that I gathered the impression that the policy of the United States—I am not referring to any basic change—it is a flexible policy adapting itself to circumstances. How it will adapt itself I cannot say, but it is not as rigid as I thought.

Sarah McClendon, *El Paso Times*, Texas: Sir, you are familiar with our programmes whereby we sell our surplus commodities to the foreign governments in exchange for their local currencies, and then we loan part of this local currency back to you. I wonder if you find this programme helpful or harmful?

JN: Well, that is a kind of broad question, which I can't answer broadly; but insofar as it has happened in India, it has been helpful, very helpful to us. Recently, there was a wheat deal[3] which was very helpful to us.

John M. Hightower, Associated Press: Do you find that the policy of the United States with respect to Red China is less rigid than you thought?

JN: No, I am afraid I can't answer that question because I really cannot say yes or no to that.

Paul A. Shinkman, Radio Station Wash-Wdon: You said in your address to the American people last night that your economic programme in India calls for purposeful planning and the willing and active cooperation of your own people. Are we to understand from that that you don't require any material support from outside, for example, from this country?

JN: We have to face such a tremendous problem—the problem may be divided up into two parts. One is the major part, really, what we have to do in our own country, and the resources we have to raise in our own country, which inevitably must fall on the people. The other is when you industrialize, you have to get machinery from abroad, which involves foreign exchange and the like, which, whatever the effect on the people, the countries accept unless they export and get things in exchange.

However, a brief answer to your question is that foreign help in this matter can be and is of great assistance, even though the quantum of foreign help compared to what the country does, is small. The real burden falls infinitely more on the people of the country, but even the relatively small help that comes is of vital importance. It can make a difference; therefore, it is very welcome.

A.D. Rothman, *Sydney Morning Herald*: In view of the fact that India has constantly stressed its belief in the self-determination of nations, there is a considerable feeling that there is inconsistency between that point of view

3. An agreement was signed on 29 August 1956 with the US for the purchase of American farm surpluses mainly, wheat, rice and cotton.

and India's actions in relation to holding a referendum in Kashmir. Can you clarify that for us?

JN: Well, I will answer your question briefly, but you do not expect me to clarify a question which has rather baffled people for the last eight years. The papers on that question run into a large number of volumes.

You must remember the beginnings of the Kashmir trouble. The beginnings were unabashed aggression, armed aggression on Kashmir, and unless you keep that in view, you would not understand the rest of it.

We talk about aggression a great deal. There is no doubt that that was aggression, and there is no doubt that the United Nations Commission that went there acknowledged the fact, too. It must follow from that—you talk about a plebiscite or a referendum—the first thing laid down by the United Nations Commission was that Pakistan armies should withdraw, and the aggression should cease.

Well, it is eight years, and they have not withdrawn yet. Nothing else follows unless that is done. As a matter of fact, in Kashmir there have been elections, there is an elected Assembly, there are going to be elections on an adult basis in about three months' time, and I really would invite any of you gentlemen who care to go and have a look around there, and then form an opinion.

William McGaffin: Could we go back for a minute to your answer about US policy being not as rigid as you thought it was. Could you give us some instances of that, sir—not as rigid on the question of Asian neutralism, perhaps?

JN: I can't give you instances because I am giving impressions of approaches. I may not have got a correct impression quite possibly, because it is not in regard to any particular subject we discussed, and I found a change there, but the general approach to these problems seems to me to be governed by an appreciation of a changing world, and trying to fit in with these changing conditions.

Joseph Chiang, Chinese News Service: In regard to the question of China, sir, as you know, the United Nations, the American Government and other free nations of the world recognize the Chinese Nationalist Government in Formosa. Do you think they are wrong?

JN: Surely you do not expect me to be rude to anybody. The fact that we do not recognize it or we recognize the government on the mainland should indicate our views on the subject.

500

Edward P. Morgan, American Broadcasting Company: India is held up as an exponent of moral force in the world. How does the Soviet Union fit into your definition of moral force, and whether it fits or not, do you judge that the present policies of the Soviet Union add up to a force for good in the world?

JN: Well, first of all, I disclaim entirely any claim to moral force for India as a country. I do think that our leader, Mahatma Gandhi, was an exponent and a very powerful one, of moral force, and that he has influenced India greatly in the right direction, and we try to some extent to follow what he said. Sometimes we fail, sometimes we succeed in a small measure, that is, I do not wish anyone to imagine that we in India think ourselves more moral, higher or better in any way than others. We do think that our leader set us a very fine example, and we try to keep it in mind, to the best of our ability.

About the Soviet Union, as about any country, including India, I think you will find that there is a great deal of good and bad, both. The proportions may vary. I don't know if you want me to discuss Communism as such or the application of it, these are big questions; obviously there are many things in the Soviet Union, in the past and in the present, with which I do not agree.

Many things have happened; but I have found, taking the present conditions as they are today, the people of the Soviet Union are an extraordinarily friendly people, hospitable people, and passionately desirous of peace.

I believe also that many recent tendencies in the Soviet Union have been in the right direction of liberalization, democratization, and I should like those tendencies to function in an increasing measure. I believe they will function. I don't think it is possible, because of a variety of reasons, for them to be stopped or for the Soviet Union to go back to conditions, say, a few years back, before these tendencies came into evidence.

Now, what the future will show I do not know.

Edward P. Morgan: Are you saying by that, sir, that you believe it is you own judgement that the so-called Stalinist element of the Russian Government is defeated?

JN: Did you say defeated? Defeated?

Edward P. Morgan: Yes, that is what I said.

JN: Well, I would put it this way: that the post-Stalin policy cannot, I think, be suppressed or made to revert to the pre-Stalin—to the previous policy; I don't think—it may be delayed. It may be obstructed occasionally, because that policy is not a question really of a few people at the top merely thinking so, but something representing broad opinions and developments.

For instance, take the Russian people as a whole. During the last generation or so, a people who were largely illiterate have become very literate; they read tremendously. It makes a difference to a whole people if they are reading a great deal, even if the literature they read is limited. It makes them think; it broadens them.

Then they have become technically minded. They are all working machines now. The old muzlik is there no longer. At present he works a tractor.

All these have made a difference, and these differences ultimately show themselves in political organization and other matters or political views; they affect them. I think the changes are fundamental, the changes towards democratization and liberalization.

Chalmers M. Roberts: Do you think it is possible, and you are a student of Marxism from way back, do you think it is possible that those changes or that liberalization can go in a Communist country to the extent of its becoming democratic in the sense you spoke of last night about India and the United States?

JN: If by democratic you mean some kind of parliamentary system of government, well, I don't think so. I don't think anybody in Russia has experienced, has had in the past experience of it or thinks of democracy in terms of parliamentary government. After all, parliamentary government is even today not extended to too many countries in the world. But I should imagine that the other forms of democratic expression, that is, the people's will prevailing, will almost inevitably take shape.

You ask me about Marxism. I am no authority on Marxism; but I should like people to remember always that Marx, who was a very big man, lived and wrote a hundred years ago, wrote about conditions in Europe, in Western Europe, in the early nineteenth century.

Surely conditions have changed in the last hundred years, and any argument based on what happened in England in the early nineteenth century is not applicable today; and any person holding on to that argument, well, they are not living in the present; they are living in the past, and insofar as they have closed minds, they do not go ahead in their thinking or in their action.

Herb Gordon, International News Service: How would you propose that the world today take an initial step towards disarmament, and what should that step be?

JN: That is rather an intricate question; but disarmament, I take it, means lessening of the arms possessed or the armies, reduction of the armies, lessening of the armies, restrictions on the use of atomic warfare, all these are various steps.

But behind all that is the necessity to create a certain confidence that no party will misuse that. That is the important thing really and, therefore, I suppose it is essential that arrangements should be made for some kind of checking and inspection to satisfy oneself that the agreement is not broken.

I can hardly discuss the details of it, but I do feel that after this long argument about disarmament, the two main parties concerned are remarkably near each other; actually, factually what was put forward is not very different, and can easily be ironed out.

There is, of course, the background of lack of confidence. That is the real thing, not the proposals.

Ruggero Orlando, Italian Radio and Television: Do you consider Russia and China a single bloc?

JN: No, sir, not at all. I think they are very different from a single bloc.

R.H. Shackford, *Scripps-Howard*: Last night you said colonialism in any form or anywhere was abhorrent to India. Do you consider the Soviet Union a colonial power, that is, a nation which imposes its will upon other nations, such as in Eastern Europe?

JN: Well, it depends on what meaning you attach to words in the English language. The word colonial has a certain meaning, which I do not think applies in that context; but it does apply in other contexts, that is, if you say the Soviet Union dominates over another country, it is perfectly correct, of course—and it is a bad thing, I agree with you. You may use the word colonial in a restricted way or in a wider way, whichever way you like, but the point is that, apart from words, the Soviet Union, as it has been seen quite clearly in the case of Hungary, has exercised a dominating influence and power there.

Frederick Kuh, *Chicago Sun Times*: Can you say in what form we can cooperate with India's Second Five Year Plan a little more fully?

JN: In the main it is in certain forms of aid and in the form chiefly of loans, long-term loans, which India can pay back gradually later.

Milton B. Berliner, *Washington Daily News*: Would you say that the United States policy today is more sympathetic than it ever has been to India's non-alignment policy?

JN: I should imagine that there is more understanding of it and, if I may say so, well, perhaps, a little appreciation of it.

John L. Steele: Some of us are slightly puzzled as to what two gentlemen meeting for twelve hours straight on a rather muddy Gettysburg Farm could think to talk about. I wonder if you could at least tell us the topics you discussed with the President.

JN: You see, in India we are supposed to be a people given to contemplation and leisurely talks. Perhaps some of that affected the President, too, that day.

John L. Steele: Can you enlighten us as to the topics that you did discuss, sir, not as to the substance of them?

JN: No—But there was a large variety of topics. I really would not even suddenly remember all of them. I have to think. Various things came into our minds. We discussed the past, we discussed the present, we even had a peep into the future.

Richard Harkness, National Broadcasting Company: Will you tell us, sir, if the speeches and votes of Mr Krishna Menon at the United Nations express properly and precisely the foreign policy of you and your Government?

JN: Mr Krishna Menon and his delegation naturally keep in the closest touch with the Government of India, and they know exactly what the Government of India's mind is on the subject.

Naturally, as from day-to-day things happen, the delegation have to decide— they cannot confer every minute—and their decisions have been in accordance with our policy.

I do not know to what particular thing you refer. Speeches—well, whether things are expressed more strongly or less strongly, unless I see it I cannot say anything. I think there has been, perhaps, some misunderstanding about a vote or about a phrase or a speech here and there, because it has been considered apart from the context. If the context is seen it would appear to have a somewhat wider and different meaning.

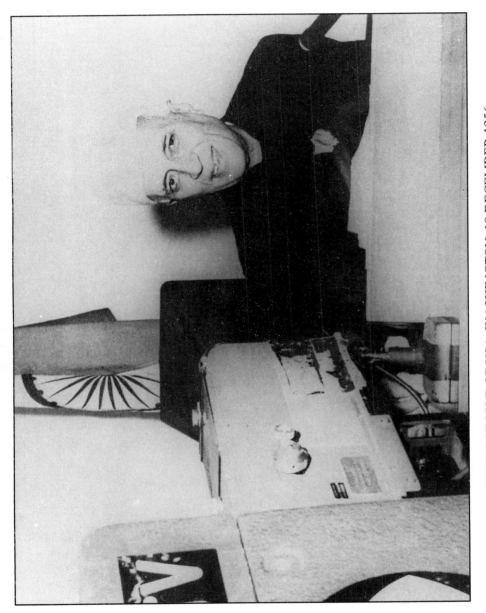

BROADCASTING TO THE PEOPLE OF USA, WASHINGTON, 18 DECEMBER 1956

ON ARRIVAL AT LA GUARDIA AIRPORT, NEW YORK, 20 DECEMBER 1956

Lillian Levy, *National Jewish Post*: In your considered judgement, sir, how can India help resolve the differences and difficulties, between Israel and her Arab neighbours, particularly Egypt, and thus contribute to the stability in the vital area of the Middle East?

JN: This question has become so very much more difficult after recent occurrences, that is, after the Israelite invasion of Egypt, that I honestly do not know what one can do at the present. Of course, I hope and believe that something may be done in the future, but just at the present moment, the question hardly arises or can hardly be considered in a normal way.

Spencer Davis, Associated Press: Can you say what prospects there are for the release of the ten American prisoners who are still being held in Communist China?

JN: Well, I should very much like them to be released. I hope they will be released some time, but it would not be right for me or fair for me to say anything more because I am not responsible. How can I commit anybody?

Spencer Davis: Sir, in the context of India being a bridge between the United States and Communist China, and your....

JN: I know that. But I find any statement made may be embarrassing because I can say anything I am going to do, but for me to talk about any other government is not only embarrassing to me but also to other governments, and it may not be true, so I get into a false position.

Warren Rogers Jr, Associated Press: Do you plan to take up this question of the Americans in China with Chou En-lai?

JN: Obviously, we have discussed this with him, and we will discuss it with him.

Frank Holeman: I am sorry that is all the time we have for questions this morning.
I want to thank you again, Mr Prime Minister, and present the National Press Club Certificate of Appreciation for appearing here and making news wherever you go.

JN: Thank you.

8. Fostering a Climate of Peace[1]

Mr President,[2] Mr Secretary-General,[3] and distinguished delegates to the United Nations. The President has just said something about my giving a message. He gave me no clue as to what the message should be. And I am in some difficulty. It is true that one can talk about many things, but all of you, ladies and gentlemen, have been busy, and probably more busy than usual, in facing very difficult and intricate problems.

Now you are shouldering the burden of the world, if I may say so. I am a mere Prime Minister of a country. The United Nations in the eleven years of its existence has grown, and this year particularly it has assumed, I believe it is correct to say, an even more important position in world affairs than previously. Of course, even if the United Nations did not do anything wonderful, the mere fact of the United Nations itself is of the greatest significance to the world. But recently it has shown that it can face problems courageously and deal with them with a view to their ultimate solution.

I think perhaps, of the many things that have happened in recent years, this is one of the most hopeful. It may be that the United Nations decides something occasionally which is not agreeable to some of you or to me. That is bound to happen. But the point is that there is some forum like this, representing the world community, which can deal with problems and, if not solve them suddenly by magic, it can positively try to solve them and ultimately, I hope, succeed, and negatively prevent the disastrous consequences of no solution at all.

So this great responsibility and burden has fallen upon you. Although I have many burdens to carry in my country—and in a distant way all of us are associated with the work of the United Nations—nevertheless I have not had the privilege and honour of ever coming here as a delegate. I have heard of your activities and how, in spite of difficulties, in spite of apparent conflicts, gradually this sense of a world community conferring together through its elected representatives is not only happening but seizing the minds of people all over the world.

1. Address to the delegates to the eleventh session of the UN General Assembly, UN Assembly Hall, New York, 20 December 1956. File No. 1(2)-UN-II/57, MEA.
2. K.N.B. Wan Waithayakon of Thailand was President of the eleventh session from 12 November 1956 to 8 March 1957.
3. Dag Hammarskjold.

That, I think, is a great event. I hope that, gradually, each representative here— while, obviously, not forgetting the interests of his country—will begin to think that he is something more than the representative of his country, that he represents, in a small measure perhaps, the world community. I hope that this thinking in terms of the whole will gradually take the place of separate thinking, in terms of each country.

Now, quite apart from the problems which you have to face, the thing that worries me often—if I may say so with all respect—is the manner of facing these problems. It is because of that that I welcome this development—gradual, no doubt, and difficult—of a sense of facing the problems from this larger point of view, this point of view of the world, of the principles which are laid down in the United Nations Charter and which should gradually be translated into effect in the world.

You will forgive me if I refer to something which has very powerfully influenced my own country. I represent a generation in my country which struggled for freedom, and which struggled for freedom in a particular way, under the guidance of Mahatma Gandhi. Now, the one major lesson that Mahatma Gandhi impressed upon us, in season and out of season, was how to do things, apart from what we did: objectives and ends we all have, but what is important is how to proceed in attaining an objective, how to proceed so as not to create a fresh problem in the attempt to solve one problem; never to deal even with the enemy in such a way as not to leave a door open for friendship, for reconciliation.

I think that in this matter our country and the United Kingdom—whatever our past history of conflict may have been—did set a good example when we came to an agreement resulting in the independence and freedom of India, and resulting, further, in friendship between the two countries. It is rather a unique example that we who, for generations past, had come into conflict with each other, with resultant feelings of ill will and hostility, nevertheless—having solved the problem of the independence of India—could forget that past of hostility and could be friends. Certainly, credit for this is due to both parties, but to some extent it is also certainly due to the manner of approach that we had under the guidance of Mahatma Gandhi. Always he was telling us: "You are fighting for a principle—for independence. You are fighting against, let us say, British imperialism; you are not fighting the British people; you are not fighting anyone British; be friendly with them."

I may tell you that there were occasions in India—and many occasions— when there was tremendous anger and bitterness at something that had been done; our people may have been shot down or beaten up in the public streets. But on no occasion do I remember, even when passions were excited, that an

507

Englishman could not walk unharmed through even a hostile crowd in India. That is rather remarkable.

I do not say that Indians are more peaceful or better. It is not that at all. They are as feeble specimens of humanity under stress and strain as any, but it was this repeated lesson that was driven into our heads. And once or twice, when our people misbehaved, Mahatma Gandhi took a step which enraged us younger people at the time. He stopped the whole movement. He said, "You have misbehaved. Stop it. I do not care what the consequences are."

So, year after year, decade after decade, he trained us. I do not know if we became any better for the training, but a certain habit grew—a habit of thinking as well as a habit of action.

I gave that instance because I do feel that there is something in it, whether dealing with national problems or international problems. Wars come, and whether wars have been good or bad in the past may be argued. But after the war we often find that the problems that we have to face are more difficult than before the war. The problems have not been solved, even though victory has come. The question, therefore, is to solve problems and not have other problems— and perhaps more difficult problems—afterwards.

We cannot afford to take a short-term view. We must look ahead, and the only way to look ahead assuredly is for some kind of world order—call it what you will; "one-world", or whatever it may be—to emerge in this world of ours. There is no other way. That is obvious.

If that is so, nothing should be done, even in the excitement of the moment, which comes in the way of the evolution of that order. Nothing should be done which increases hostility and hatred and bitterness. There is plenty of hatred and bitterness in the world today. We all feel it. I feel it; you feel it. We cannot become angels, but nevertheless the actions we indulge in—in a larger way as nations, or as individuals—might perhaps be so controlled, without giving up a single principle or any single opinion that we may hold, as not to make the path of reconciliation difficult.

Recently we have had, apart from the normal problems of the world, two major developments, incidents, tragedies—call them what you will—which have engaged the attention of this august Assembly. You know them: whether it is in Egypt or roundabout, or in Hungary or roundabout—both very important and very unfortunate happenings, and yet both of them, perhaps, having and element of good in them too, not in the act itself but in the consequences.

Many things have emerged from that which personally I welcome—apart from the sorrow at the tragedies—and the one big thing that has emerged is that world opinion is today a strong enough factor not to tolerate what it considers wrong—and world opinion chiefly represented in the United Nations Assembly, and elsewhere too in other ways. That is a very important factor, I think—an important factor which, in future, will probably deter or make more difficult any such aberrations from the path of rectitude by any nation, if I may use that word, and every country, weak or strong, will have to think twice before it does something which enrages world opinion. That is a good thing, and that itself shows this development of some kind of conscience of the world.

After all, wars and other conflicts take place not because something may happen, but essentially because something happens in the minds of men. I believe that in the constitution of UNESCO it is stated that wars begin in the minds of men. It is perfectly true. Therefore, if I may venture to suggest to you, who are much more experienced than I am in these matters, it becomes important, I repeat, that any decision we may arrive at—and it should be according to principles no doubt—must not lead to greater bitterness as far as possible.

To some extent it might. An attempt should be made to avoid that. The attempt should be to solve the problem and not merely to exhibit our anger at something that has happened, although there is anger there of course; there is annoyance. But, after all, we are working for the future, and that future can only be of cooperation between countries based on freedom of nations and freedom of individuals.

Now there are these two problems before you, and they are being dealt with by the Assembly. I can offer no suggestion except what I have said in the way of an approach to them, that is, the way of tolerance. Tolerance does not mean carelessness; it does not mean just passivity. It means something active. It does not mean forgetting any principle that you stand for that is laid down in the Charter.

I think it is of the greatest importance that the United Nations, as should all of us, should keep in mind always the Charter of the United Nations. That is the basis. It may be that you cannot give effect to the Charter quickly or suddenly because the world is imperfect. Nevertheless, step by step one should move in that direction and keep that fresh in our minds. If so, then you will advance in the right direction. At the present moment and always—perhaps more at the present moment—I think the first thing to remember and to strive for is to avoid a situation getting worse, to avoid finally a situation leading to major conflict because, as we all know, a major conflict means the destruction of all the values one holds, however justified one party may think in having it.

Because of the development of various new types of weapons, war has really become an impossible proposition for any sane world or any sane country. Wars have been terribly bad previously, and we have seen that wars have not solved any question. Negatively they might have done something; positively they have not solved anything. Now it is clear that far from solving anything, they may bring enormous destruction. So the very first thing to remember is the avoidance of war, and the avoidance of creating a situation which might drive the world into war. Nobody wants war, but perhaps we do not always think about creating situations which might ultimately result in the madness of war. That may perhaps be the rather negative side to this question.

The positive is working actively for peaceful solutions based on principle and at the same time based on the future cooperation of the world. We have to live at peace with our neighbours. There is no other way to live. And today, with various developments, every country is practically the neighbour of the other. No country is far removed. In other words, we therefore have to work for cooperation among all countries of the world.

Unfortunately, we have had what is called the cold war. Perhaps the cold war is better than a hot war or a shooting war; undoubtedly it is. It can be pulled back. When a shooting war begins, nothing can be pulled back until it exterminates a large part of the world. Nevertheless, surely the idea of the cold war is the very negation of what the United Nations stands for.

It is the negation of what the Constitution of UNESCO, says: that wars begin in the minds of men. Cold wars mean nourishing the idea of war in the minds of men. If we go on nourishing the idea of war in the minds of men, then obviously there is always the danger of its bursting out from the minds to other activities.

I remember Mahatma Gandhi telling us something, which may not be applicable here on this occasion—it was said in a different context. Mahatma Gandhi, as you know, was devoted to non-violence and preached non-violence all his life, and yet he said, "If you have a sword in your mind it is better to use it than to nurse it and nourish it in your mind all the time. Take it out, use it and throw it away, instead of being frustrated in yourselves and always thinking of the sword or the use of the sword and yet superficially trying to avoid it."

Therefore, I submit to you that this idea of cold war is essentially, fundamentally wrong. It is immoral. It is opposed to all ideas of peace and cooperation. It may be, of course, that, because human nature is weak, countries may quarrel. That is a different matter. But let us at least be clear in our minds as to what the right way is and try to follow that.

We have, as we know, all kinds of military alliances. It is not for me, especially on this occasion, to criticize them or to say that they are justified or unjustified. Nevertheless, since you have been gracious enough to ask me to speak to you, it would serve little purpose if I talked empty platitudes to you, and I want to place before you what I have in my own mind. I am quite sure that at the present moment, as we stand today—I am not talking about whether something might have been justified in the past or not, but today—all these pacts and military alliances are completely out of place. I would go a step further. They are unnecessary, even from the point of view of those people who have those pacts and alliances. I may admit for the sake of argument that they were necessary at an earlier stage when conditions were different, but for the moment I would like you to consider circumstances as they are today, and I do submit that these pacts and alliances do not add to the strength of any nation. They only make that country or some other country hostile. Thereby armaments are piled up, and disarmament becomes more and more difficult. Hatreds continue; in fact, a cold war continues.

If it is our objective, as it must be of any reasonable person, that we must have peace, then it follows necessarily that we must not have cold war. If we must not have cold war, then it follows necessarily that we must not buttress our idea of peace by past military establishments and pacts and alliances. All this seems to me to follow logically. It may be that you cannot suddenly give effect to your wishes. That is a different matter, and you must face it. But you must aim at that and state that you aim at that.

I have no doubt that all the peoples of the world, wherever they may live, are passionately desirous of peace. I doubt that there are any people anywhere—even those who sometimes talk rashly about these matters—who desire war. Certainly the common man all over the world, in every country, desires peace passionately. If that is so, why should we not follow that path? Why should we be led away by fears and apprehensions and hatreds and violence? That is logical, and yet I know that life is not logical. Many other things come in. Nevertheless, an attempt might be made to follow the logic of this argument.

We have seen and we know that the presence of foreign forces in a country is always an irritant; it is never liked by that country; it is abnormal. It may be that an abnormal situation takes place because life is sometimes illogical and abnormal. But the point is that the presence of foreign forces in another country is abnormal and undesirable. And it does not conduce even to producing that sense of security—now, at any rate—which it is meant to produce. It does not give a sense of security today. I am a layman, of course, and I know nothing about warfare—but, after all, I do possess some intelligence to consider these matters. And I know that with the development of warfare as it is developing today, as it has developed and will develop, any war that takes place is likely to be a world war, with missiles hurled from vast distances. If that is so, then even the military practice of having places dotted all over with armed forces and bases becomes unnecessary and becomes simply an irritant and an invitation to some other party to do the same—and, if I may use the word with all respect, to enter into competition in evil and wickedness.

How are we to face this problem? I know that you cannot pass a resolution, even in the United Nations General Assembly, to put an end to this. You may pass a resolution, of course—but it will not put an end to it. However, if we are clear that that should be our aim, then surely we can work toward that end, even though it may take some time.

Connected with that, naturally, is the very important problem of disarmament. We all know how difficult it is. I remember that long ago the old League of Nations had a Preparatory Commission for Disarmament. It worked for years and produced I do not know how many dozens of fat volumes of argument and discussion and so on. And then the League of Nations itself considered all of it. And it came to nothing.

You cannot, by any manner of disarmament, make a weak country strong or a non-industrial country the equal of an industrial country. You cannot make a country which is not scientifically advanced the equal of a country which is.

You can lessen the chances of war, the fear of war. Ultimately, of course, the entire question is—or, at any rate, partly is—a question of confidence and of lessening the fears of one another. For that purpose, disarmament helps, although it does not equalize conditions. Dangers remain. But there is a powerful feeling for peace in every country and vast areas of the world which are backward and poverty-stricken and unhappy, and which passionately want progress, are having the world's attention directed to their development. Surely, that is not only good in itself, but it will reduce the sense of fear that pervades the world and oppresses us.

What, then, can our possible steps be? Honestly, I cannot tell you exactly what steps you might take, because so many factors are involved. But I certainly feel that we must aim at two or three things.

One is that, according to the Charter, countries should be independent. Countries that are dominated by another country should cease to be dominated by that country. No country in the wide world—or, at any rate, very few countries in the world—can be said to be independent in the sense that they can do anything they like. There are restraining factors—and quite rightly. In the final analysis, the United Nations itself is a restraining factor in regard to countries misbehaving or taking advantage of their so-called independence to interfere with the independence of others. Every country's independence surely should be limited in the sense that it should not interfere with the independence of others. The first thing, then, is to have this process of the independence of countries extended until it covers the whole world.

Secondly, there is this idea—these ideas are all allied and overlapping—that we can ensure security by increasing our armaments; this notion has been rather exposed recently, because obviously the other party can increase its armaments and so, in a sense, the balance of arms would vary but little. In any event, total destruction may well be the result. Therefore, this maintenance of armed forces all over the world on foreign soil is basically wrong, even though such maintenance is with the agreement of the countries concerned. These countries may agree to it through fear of somebody else, in order to seek protection, but it is not a good way of thinking.

If we could remove these armies and, together with such removal, bring about some measure of disarmament—although I admit a difficulty in doing so suddenly—I believe the atmosphere in the world would change completely. I think the natural result would be a much more rapid progress towards peace and the elimination of fear. Furthermore, I do not see how you can make progress so long as you, I and all of us are constantly afraid and are thinking of becoming more powerful than the other country, and thus speaking to the other country from a position of strength. Obviously, the other country thinks in the same way and there can be no great improvement in the situation while it is approached from this standpoint.

I know that it can be said that all this involves risk to a particular nation or group of nations. I do not think there is any way to avoid this risk. Human life is full of risk and uncertainty and, certainly, the existing situation is full of risk and danger. So therefore, even if you look at it from the point of view of taking a minor risk to avoid a major one, such minor risk is an improvement. For my own part I am quite certain there is no risk.

We have seen in the world in the last two or three months how it reacts to what it considers evil-doing. That is one of the healthiest signs apparent. After all, even a country which might seem for the moment to be indulging in wrongful actions does so because it believes it can carry some part of world opinion with it. If it cannot carry such opinion, it is difficult for it to proceed. We have seen that even the biggest and strongest of nations cannot impose their will against world opinion.

Therefore, we have developed a very strong protection against a country which acts wrongly. Why not adopt this protection instead of these armies and armaments and so on? Instead of countries having armed forces in other countries, ostensibly to protect them, why not do away with the system of military alliances and pacts, and face each other frankly and openly and, if there is a quarrel, deal with it in a normal way, such as a quarrel between individuals, endeavouring to settle it by argument—either in the United Nations or elsewhere.

I submit to you that we have come to a stage in the world when a choice has to be made—not today, not tomorrow, if you like the day after tomorrow—but we really cannot go on following the old path which leads to no particular

513

destination except the preservation of force and hatred. The choice has to be made.

I do feel strongly that these two events in Egypt and Hungary have introduced in their own way a certain new phase in historical development. Of course the thing has been developing for some time past, but this has suddenly laid bare this development for everybody to see and think what it means. And this phase of historical development must be dealt with by this august Assembly and by all countries with understanding, with sympathy, not with anger nor with the desire to humiliate anybody, for the moment you have that you get the psychology of cold war or war fever, when the other party tries to humiliate you. In any situation it is made difficult for the other party to agree where you drive a party into war and the choice becomes one of humiliation and surrender—which few countries are prepared to accept—or war. That is a bad result to produce even though our motives may be good, even though we may be justified in saying what we do or in acting as we do. If it leads to something wrong, something that we do not want, then we have erred.

So, to go back to what I ventured to suggest at the beginning, means are at least as important as ends; if the means are not right, the end is also likely to be not right, however much we may want it to be right. And therefore, here especially in this world Assembly to which all the nations of the world look, I hope an example will be set to the rest of the world in thinking always about the right means to be adopted in order to solve our problems; the means should always be peaceful, of course, but not merely peaceful in an external way in the non-use of armaments, but peaceful in the approach of the mind, and that approach of the mind, I have no doubt, will create a reaction in our minds and an entirely different atmosphere will be created—a climate of peace will be created which will help greatly in the solution of our problems.

I ventured to say something which is not remarkable; maybe I am repeating platitudes to you, who are much wiser than I am in dealing with these problems, but as I have said it would have meant little if I had not spoken what I had in my mind. That would not have been fair to you or fair to me. I hope you will forgive me for this impertinence. I thank you.

9. Facing Responsibilities[1]

Commissioner Patterson,[2] Mr Mayor, Mr Governor,[3] Excellencies and gentlemen, I find it a little difficult to find words to express my gratitude to you, sir, Mr Mayor, and to all those who are present here, for their warm and friendly welcome and for the honour you have done me by giving me this opportunity of meeting so many distinguished leaders of this great city and of this great country.

I feel overwhelmed on this occasion, and listening to the words which previous speakers have uttered, I feel that in the warmth of your heart you have said many things about me which I hardly deserve. But, perhaps, that does not matter much. What matters is what you feel, and what I feel. Words are important, certainly, but the thought behind the words is more important. And, I have sensed, even in this very brief visit to the United States, the warmth and the cordiality of the people of this country and their goodwill towards my country.

Somebody told me once that nobody should go to the United States for the first time. Well, I have come the second time, now. And, although, the second time is brief, it has been full of so many things that, as I said yesterday, it seems quite a long time since I came here.

Time is measured by the clock, but really that is not a very satisfactory way of measuring time. Time, ultimately, is the succession of sensations, feelings, and sometimes hangs heavily, and it does not seem to end at all, and sometimes it passes very quickly.

I have had experience with both, having had the opportunity—and, if I may say so—the good fortune of spending many years in prison from which, I think, I profited considerably. There were long periods when time seemed to stand still because nothing happened there. There was no way of measuring it by any sensation or experience. It is true that the sun rises and the sun sets. And you know the day is over. But, it was very extraordinary that, after months and years in jail, the record of yesterday, and yesterday's history came to a standstill because the intervening period had no special element in it to strike the imagination. And so time remains still and, again, outside activity I tried to make up by this intensive activity.

1. Speech at a luncheon hosted by Robert F. Wagner, the Mayor of New York, at the Waldorf Astoria Hotel, New York, 21 December 1956. From *Nehru Visits USA*, Information Service of India, Washington, pp. 54-61.
2. Richard C. Patterson, Jr, Department of Commerce and Public Events, New York City.
3. William Averell Harriman, Governor of New York.

Anyhow, I was referring to my few days' stay in Washington, and now in New York, which are not merely full of engagements—that is a minor matter—but full of deeply felt impressions which will remain and will come back to my memory again and again—impressions of the American people, of leading citizens of this country, of the ability in various departments of human activity, and something more, something which, perhaps, is almost more representative of American life than the great activities and progress America has made.

It is quite true, I think, as Prince Wan once said, "America is supposed to be a leader in scientific and technical advances, in business and in many other departments of human activity." And, yet, I suppose if there were not something more basic about the American people, they would not be in the position they are in today. That basic thing is a quality of humanism, generosity and warmth of heart, and certainly adherence to what I would call the basic principles of the American Revolution.

I referred the other day in my television broadcast[4] to a fact which has meant much to me. Some years back an American friend came to my house in Delhi and gave me a cast of Abraham Lincoln's hand, a bronze, and ever since then I have kept it on my study table, and I gaze at it every day, partly because it is a very beautiful hand, beautiful art in many ways—there is a certain extraordinary expression of strength and gentleness in it – but more because it reminds me of a celebrated figure, not only of the United States but of the world who has been a hero of mine since my childhood, and the immortal words he uttered on various occasions often remind me, in a sense, of my own duties, what I should purport. And, so, this quality of the American people is what has appealed to me most.

It is obvious that any people, whether American or Indian, or any other, are a mixture of good qualities and bad qualities. We are not saints; we are not perfect beings. We try to progress, and it may be that some qualities that we have in India are perhaps more evident in India than in any other country; it may be also, and indeed it is, that our failings are very evident also. Anyhow, we seem to learn from each other.

We, in India, as you know, have been absorbed in a tremendous adventure, to begin with, the adventure of gaining and achieving independence. And, we were fortunate enough to achieve that which we had striven for, and dreamed about year after year. We achieved it.

The moment of our achievement was also the moment of our starting on another journey and another adventure, the adventure of building up India and

4. See *ante*, pp. 490-493.

raising her hundreds of millions of people, and that was a bigger task than the one of gaining independence.

Well, we are engaged in that adventure, and we are good hearted, and we realize even as we go forward, how difficult it is, how responsibilities increase; the more one grows the more the responsibilities of that individual or country grow with it. So, we are growing in strength, and we grow in many other ways. And, at the same time, our difficulties grow, and our responsibilities grow. And that is inevitable. That is the price of growth, to face our responsibilities, because the United States has grown in hundreds of ways, and its responsibilities grow a hundred fold. And, that is the price we have to pay; we cannot escape it.

So, we are engaged in this tremendous adventure, an adventure, if I may say so, against our own failings, our own poverty, not against any people or any country. And, naturally, we are seeking the goodwill and sympathy of other people. I remember vividly the sympathy and help that we had from the people of the United States, when we were struggling for freedom, and we are sure that in this new adventure of ours we can have, and indeed we have had, that sympathy and help.

Sometimes it is said that there are great differences between the United States and India in the international field and in other fields. I believe this is greatly exaggerated. Very obviously there are sometimes differences in outlook and opinion. Indeed, I imagine in the United States of America, among the people here, there are differences. In India I know there are great differences of opinion. Yet we come together. Yet we have all these people of the same ideals. We talk about democracy, and the very nature of democracy is, whether within a country or outside, to have a variety of opinions and out of clashes of opinion the truth tries to emerge to the people, and the country, both together. It varies from the totalitarian countries where differences of opinion are not allowed to prevail. Only a single opinion comes up which precludes from the truth arising out of the clash of opinions and battle of ideals, from which comes progress.

So, it is a gross exaggeration, and I think, and I might say, it is wrong to say there are vital differences of opinion between the United States and India. There is a basic ground of principle on which we agree.

It is true that we have been conditioned and nurtured in a particular way, geographically, historically and traditionally. And even our recent struggle for independence has conditioned us in a particular way. And we would be untrue to ourselves if we did not accept that condition and improve and change it, if we can, but work in accord with our faith and beliefs. If we did not work in accordance with our faith and beliefs, we would not be worthy. Nobody is worth much if he cannot function according to his own nature and belief and principle.

Prince Wan Waithayakon, referred to the great son of India, the Buddha, whose birthday has just been celebrated, the two thousand five hundredth anniversary, and we are trying to regain his message of peace and compassion.

Two or three hundred years after the Buddha, there was an Emperor of India named Asoka, a rather extraordinary man even though he was an Emperor. In the full tide of victory in a war, it suddenly came to him how terrible war was. He heard accounts of hundreds of thousands of people slain and made captives, and so on, and it came to him as a shock that he had won victory at that cost. He stopped the war, and he, himself, has related how he felt about it, and inscribed it on stone tablets and pillars, not only on one, but they are strewn all over India. And, on them are inscribed his various inscriptions on how he came to the decision to put a stop to his own war after he had learned of the cost of human suffering caused by it, and he said: "No more war for me." He stopped the war in the middle of it.

There are interesting inscriptions of his in which he teaches his people all the time about the cause of righteousness. He had reverence, he said, to his own faith, but also reverence to the faith of others. And he said: "Unless you revere the faith of others, your own faith will not be revered." So, he goes on repeating again and again the message of tolerance which he got from the Buddha.

I mention this because in spite of innumerable failures in our history, the history of India and the Indian people, this kind of message has been repeated again and again, generation after generation, and it has sunk in, to some extent, into our minds. And, in our own day, Mahatma Gandhi repeated it. And that is the background of our thinking to some extent.

Maybe sometimes it enfeebles us, it is possible, and we want to be dynamic, and I hope we will become dynamic as, perhaps, in the past. It may be that, because of these tactics our life became stagnant and did not move, but stopped. Well, that is a bad thing for a nation. And we felt it and became subjugated to other countries and did not make any protest. We began to dream of the past, forgetting the present. That is not good.

Well, we pulled ourselves out of it, and now, I hope, we are gaining a measure of vitality, but behind all that vitality and dynamism, still behind all that, the message of the Buddha remains in our minds. It tells us that it is better to be friendly than to be inimical and that it is better even to win the enemy over than to beat your enemy not by giving up your principles, because that is not winning him over, but while holding on to your principles, to hold the other party over.

Thus we come back to what Mahatma Gandhi used to tell us always, and which he exemplified in his own conduct, and his conduct towards the British people against whom we were struggling.

518

We were weak and feeble and we misbehaved often enough, but the fact is that the feelings we had toward the British people were friendly while fighting them. Mahatma Gandhi said: "Even if you wish to push British rule out of India we have no enmity against the British people." And so a remarkable thing happened, and I do believe it is very remarkable that the minute the British rule went from India, there was no enmity against the British people, and we are great friends today.

There are other examples in the world, millions of examples, where people having become free still nurtured a dislike and even hatred. We are not, by and large, a people who hate deeply. That is not our nature. We are grown up enough to know, and sometimes it may be a weakness, too. I have to admit it. But perhaps, if you think of this, you may get something of the background of what we are thinking because we are, in numbers, a great many people with a great variety and diversity, but a proud history, and even when we were split up, as we were and have many people with many languages, and all that, still throughout our history we have been bound together by some strange ideas, strange things, cultural and others, which have never allowed India to go to pieces even in her subjugation and misery, and we held together in that sense.

So, the basic ideas become reflected to some extent in our activities today, whether internal, external or international; not always, but nevertheless they are there in the back of our mind, in what we say and what we do.

Previous speakers mentioned the fact that, today, the world is facing great problems, crises, which is perfectly true. I suppose that in almost every generation people have thought their generation is facing a great crisis. Naturally, they think of today. But, I think it is true today to say that the world, today, does face a very important stage or phase of human history.

Whatever the ideas and technical advances that have taken you so far, it still poses new problems, and new developments in atomic energy, machinery, automobiles and other means of communications are terrific. There are new vistas opening up, the human race has tremendous power at its disposal, and it depends on how one uses this power, whether for good or ill. To solve, the problem of our age, apart from this question that we are facing, the immediate problems, international and national, and quite apart from what solution we have formed, there may be many different solutions offered; one may decide which one to take.

The real foundation, if I may respectfully beg to suggest it to you all, is the attitude of approaching this problem, whether in solving the problem you do not leave behind half a dozen new problems.

Obviously the path of wisdom is to solve the problem in such a way that the solution of one problem does not to lead to other, more difficult problems, as it has often happened in the past, often after wars that have happened. One wins a war—wins a war completely—and then one finds enormous problems have arisen, more than before the war. That is victory, no doubt, but it is not real victory of having solved the problem, but rather victory in a military sense.

Therefore, the point always is, how to achieve certain objectives. If you go to war it is for the purpose of achieving something. Who wants to go to war for the pleasure of it? You go to war to achieve something, you go to war because an enemy is obstructing something, or it is something you don't like. What do you do after victory? You have defeated the enemy, and that is only a small part of the job. The real job was to achieve something—the main objective being not the war, but the achievement of reaching a peace, something constructive.

The major thing that is to be avoided is to sow the seeds of future problems, of future conflict, and future wars.

Now, that leads one to think that the approach should be such as not to sow the seeds of future conflict, and does not mean, as I stated at the beginning, giving in on any point and surrendering a single principle. But, it does mean that in following one's principle one does that in a way to solve the problem and not merely to serve a satisfaction of expressing ourselves in a strong way, expressing our opinion in a strong way. That may bring momentary satisfaction, but our objective is to solve the problem and in accordance with the principles one holds, and see that it does not lead to others.

I am sorry, but I hope you will forgive me for my rather philosophical generalizations but, as you have done me the honour of inviting me here, I thought I should say something I had in mind, which troubles me.

There will always be basic difficulties. There is the prophet. The prophet is a person who, I imagine, holds to the truth regardless of all consequences, and usually because he holds to the truth, regardless of all consequences, he is stoned to death. He is honoured afterwards, no doubt, but for the moment he is stoned to death. The prophet can seldom be what can be called a leader of men, because the men have stoned him to death and honoured him afterwards. He holds to his principles regardless of the consequences.

Then, there is the political leader, and I talk about the best type of leader. There are all kinds of leaders. The political leader certainly wants to hold to principles, but he has to get these principles through to his people. He may have a certain conviction, but he has to convey that conviction to the others, especially in this democratic age. Unless there are other people who feel the way he does, he is helpless. So the leader always has a problem how far he should compromise with his principles.

The prophet does not compromise his principles regardless of the consequences. The political leader always has that problem, and should decide

520

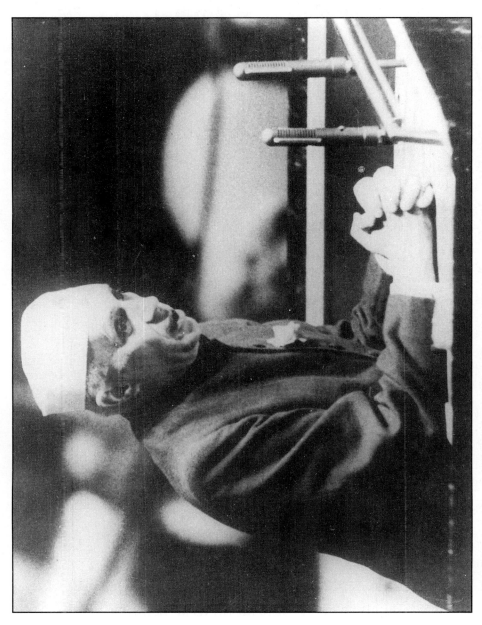

ADDRESSING THE UN GENERAL ASSEMBLY, NEW YORK, 20 DECEMBER 1956

RECEIVING A WRISTWATCH FROM RICHARD M. WAGNER, MAYOR OF
NEW YORK, 20 DECEMBER 1956
Governor Averell Harriman is also seen

on how much of his principles to compromise to achieve something for his people. If he compromises too many of his principles, he has lost; and he has lost his leadership.

So, it is a difficult problem which the leaders of human communities have to face, and therefore have to strike a balance. So, that is not an easy matter, and more especially it becomes difficult in democratic communities because it is by no means sure that in democratic communities, what might be called men of high principles come always to the top. Other people of more varying qualities come up.

Nevertheless, we have found and I do believe most earnestly that, with all the failings and difficulties we have to face in a democratic way, that is by far the best and only way that I can conceive of for human progress. It is not perfect, by no means, but it does allow people to become perfect and gives them opportunities to become so.

And I am anxious that every people have an opportunity to reach and be allowed to reach stature. Having done that, then, whatever the people do we have to accept, but give them opportunities to reach growth. If you take that from them, you have a totalitarian regime and you take something away from a people that is of most vital significance to human growth, and I dislike that intensely.

I have ventured to put some thoughts rather vaguely before you. You will forgive me, Mr Mayor, but I really am infinitely grateful to you, Mr Mayor, and all of you distinguished gentlemen, and I carry away with me the memory of this occasion for a long time. I thank you.

10. Building for the Future[1]

Friends, I have no special message to offer to you but I wish to express my gratitude to you for this opportunity to meet the members of this group which has played such an increasing part at the headquarters of the UN, and which represents the great continents of Asia and Africa. I am grateful to you also, Sir,[2] for the very kind and generous sentiments that you have expressed.

I do not quite remember when this group was first started. I am told about five years age or more and, as with everything which has reality behind it, it did not start artificially, but grew out of circumstances which delegates from these countries had to face. Anyhow it has grown now, which is something obviously important not only for our respective countries, but also for the United Nations.

It can powerfully affect the decisions of the UN this way or that way, and it can affect the policies of our respective countries to some extent. Some differences arise, I suppose, with all of us, in regard to various policies, which each country naturally has to determine for itself, and its representatives here may sometimes find it difficult to say or do something, which might commit their country without that country having an occasion to consider the questions that come up from day-to-day. But it is obvious that all of us who sometimes differ from each other, facing different problems in each country, have some common bonds, some common approaches to important questions which has led us to form this informal or formal group and discuss these matters here.

I think to some extent this group, took shape and form after the Bandung Conference,[3] which itself represented countries of Asia and Africa. Now I have no doubt that this group representing Asia and Africa performs a historic function.

I am not myself very anxious for groups to be formed on a continental basis or a regional basis, which while on the one hand bringing some countries together, inevitably results in separating them to some extent from the others, who are outside that group. But I think that argument, which may be valid in certain circumstances, does not apply to this particular group. This is a big enough

1. Address to the Twenty-seven nation Asian-African group at the United Nations, New York, 21 December 1956. From *Nehru Visits USA*, The Information Service of India, Washington, pp. 61-65.
2. Hashim Jawed of Iraq, Chairman of the Asian-African group in the United Nations.
3. The Asian-African Conference was held at Bandung, Indonesia, from 18 to 24 April 1955. For details, see *Selected Works* (second series) Vol. 28, pp. 97-158.

group, it is a geographical group, even though there might be some differences amongst them, but representing more specially countries that might be called underdeveloped—the countries that demand great attention should have greater attention for their development—the countries which in the past were, if not ignored, at any rate not enough importance was attached to them.

One of the major changes of the last few years or since the war, is a certain shift, well, in the balances in the world, due to changes in Asia and Africa, specially Asia. Although these changes are obviously taking place—there are many countries independent now, which were not independent—there is a tendency still for questions, relating to even Asia and Africa, and much more so for questions outside that region, to be decided by countries outside Asia and Africa. I can understand that other countries are interested in those questions, and have every right to participate in the solution of the problems of Asia and Africa.

I do submit that the old habit is not so evident today as in the past. The old habit that Asian and African problems could be decided by others has no meaning at all today. But the old habit persists, and it is not an easy matter for people and countries to get out of the ways of thinking to which they had grown accustomed to in the past. I think that this inclination is due to the fact that the people have not adjusted themselves to the reality in Asia and Africa. Of course Asia and Africa are not static, but changing, and developing. But this basic fact, I think, should be kept in view, not by us; I am talking of other countries.

I had the privilege of addressing the UN General Assembly about six or seven years ago in Paris,[4] and I laid stress even then on this fact. I imagine the necessity for stressing this fact is not great today. The people realize that the different conditions and developments, demanding special attention, specially require that the settlement of all problems affecting Asia and Africa not be made without the consent and approval of countries in Asia and Africa.

Recent months have seen many things happening in the world and more especially one particular matter which powerfully affects countries in Asia and Africa and others—a situation that arose in Egypt owing to invasion and intervention, etc. That has been something of world significance—that is something even more, I believe, in regard to consequence of certain historic significance. I have no doubt it will powerfully affect the future.

Now, may I say a word or two with all respect about how perhaps we might help in the solution of these problems that affect us in Asia and Africa and even world problems which are outside our region but which affect us.

4. For the full text of Nehru's address to the UN General Assembly on 3 November 1948, see *Selected Works* (second series), Vol. 8, pp. 290-295.

This group consists of distinguished representatives of countries functioning in the UN who have to grapple with problems with a view to their solution, not merely with a view to expressing opinion and leaving to chance and not merely with a view to expressing opinion strongly this way or that way. Because, after all, we are grappling with problems. We want to avoid war. We also want economic and political and social progress. We want to develop a feeling of good fellowship, certainly among ourselves, and all other countries of the world.

When we had the Bandung Conference, we laid stress on that fact. The Bandung Conference was held for us to get together. It was not meant to be some kind of conference opposed to Europe or America. That was not its intention. Some people were afraid that it was so. We had no intention, if I may use the expression, of 'ganging up'; otherwise our voice was ignored and the voice of Asia and Africa was not effective.

I do hope that while we function together, these facts might be kept in mind, because we are building for the future—a future not merely one of deciding problems on which votes might be taken in the UN today or tomorrow—but we are building up a future not of conflict between continents, but a future of cooperation and good fellowship of free and independent nations. And certainly we should take no steps that take us into another direction. Things have happened in the world which have moved us greatly and have angered us, yet again it is true that anger does not help us in solving the problems. Still the fact remains that the angered actions of today may be stumbling blocks of tomorrow. Are we to put up stumbling blocks on our path to face the difficulty tomorrow?

Therefore, I do submit that this juncture of history, which I consider a very important juncture, because I do believe that we have arrived at a certain phase in historical development which is of great importance, may well lead us away from all the troubles of the cold war and conflict between nations towards a somewhat better and cooperative future.

I do not say that this will happen suddenly, but I do say that something has been happening, which has been more evident lately, and we should take advantage of it. It is obvious that each country can play a helpful role, and the UN can play the most helpful role of all. This group can play the important role, not only by pressing the claim of Asian and African countries, but in doing so we must impress the world that we have in view the future of the world—that we are working not merely in any angry way reflecting the passions of the moment, but the future which we and others will inherit.

I do trust that this may be kept in view, that the prestige of this group will rise and wield more influence than its votes in the General Assembly, because we stand for something constructive and not destructive. After all we want constructive efforts to solve the problems of the world.

May I finally express my great pleasure at some of the recent admission of members in the UN and to this group, including Japan which came in a few days ago. A little before that Morocco and Tunisia and Sudan came in,[5] and I have no doubt that these countries will play a very important part in the UN and more especially in this group.

I am very grateful to you, friends, for this opportunity to meet you and say a few words to you. Thank you.

---

5. The General Assembly unanimously adopted resolutions on 12 November 1956, admitting Sudan, Morocco and Tunisia to the UN. On 18 December 1956 the UN admitted Japan.

11. Tackling India's Economic Problems[1]

Mr Chairman, I am glad and grateful for this opportunity to meet the members of the board of directors of the Far East-America Council.[2] What you have just said in explaining our own approach and attitude represents more or less in broad outline what we ourselves think about it.

We are naturally very anxious to make progress rapidly, to increase the standards of our people. Apart from our desire to do so, there is the compulsion of events which forces us to do so. That is to say, social forces, social upsets. All kinds of things might happen if we don't proceed rapidly enough. So that is what I call the compulsion of events.

We have approached this question in the strictest, if I may say so, practical way. What I mean is, with no ideological or doctrinaire approach. We want to get things done. We just don't mind what ideology the people may be concerned with, but one thing we have to preserve is the democratic structure of our politics and economy.

---

1. Speech at a conference of the Board of Directors of the Far East-America Council of Commerce and Industry, New York, 21 December 1956. From *Nehru Visits USA*, The Information Service of India, Washington, pp. 66-71.
2. The Far East-America Council of Commerce and Industry was an organization of American businessmen with interests in India.

Planning, what is it after all? It is getting people to do voluntarily what we want them to do. There is no compulsion. If they don't do it, then they don't do it, and the matter ends. So any idea of associating compulsion would not be correct. Again, we feel that any kind of a rigid approach is not right. A rigid approach is not right because the conditions of countries differ, the backgrounds of countries differ.

Now, it is quite absurd, let me say, in the United States, to suggest some other way than you have here. It fits in, you have grown into it, you have prospered and all that. There it is, the example of growth and prosperity is there, and no question arises of your trying some other method.

But you have had very, very special advantages, apart from a period of time— a vast country to explore and develop and all that. Well, we just have not got that time at our disposal because if we waited, if our progress was slow, we would be overwhelmed, overwhelmed by two things: one, as I said, the social forces and the second is just the growth of population.

Now, I don't mean to imply that our population is growing at a terribly fast pace; it is not. It is rather that our pace of growth is not big; but in totality. Because it is a big population to begin with. Well, even relatively small growth makes a difference. I don't think our pace of growth is more than the European countries; in fact, it is less. But when we start with a base of 360 million, well, additions become considerable and each growth adds to our problems, whether it is food or commodities or anything.

So we are compelled by these circumstances to find an urgent solution to these problems. Greater production of goods is our immediate aim so that people may have them. Generally all industries should flourish, big industries, small industries, little industries, any type of industry. Employment should grow; there should not be any type of unemployment which, apart from its being a bad thing in itself, again creates dangers for us.

So we have to face these problems. And when we sat down to think about them we did not have any ideological approach. In fact, we avoided even terms which connote ideology. We just said, well, here is food. We must produce at least enough food for our people, not only today, but five years, ten years later, when the population is more. Clothing, housing and the other necessities, you might say, because, remember, that the problem in India, or the problem in any country in Asia is, first of all, to provide the necessities of life to all. The luxuries, or even those things that are not luxuries, but which are not absolute necessities, really come after that. So we sit down and we say, we have to provide these necessities. How are we to do it?

Well, first agricultural production. Then, because we have to give employment to people, we always have to face the problem that with higher techniques, which we must have—naturally, you can't have primitive methods of production; but the immediate effect of higher techniques is unemployment. The immediate effect of having fewer persons to do it would be that more are thrown out of employment, and then the social difficulties would rise.

That does not mean we are against higher techniques; we are not. We think that progress can only come through higher techniques. But the changeover has to be so planned that it does not create a new problem for us. We invited quite a large number of people from various countries—economists, industrialists and financiers, and all kinds of people—to consult with us and to advise us.

It was peculiar, interesting, that they started off by telling us ideas which they had brought with them. What they gave us were good ideas, but gradually, after studying the problems for about two or three months, they became shaky about their own ideas being applicable to India. They said, "We realize that the problems of India require some special treatment and not merely the treatment we had thought of."

In fact, they told us—they warned us—economists from abroad—English, Canadian, French, Poles, quite a number of people—they said: "You can profit by the examples, by the experience of other countries. Please do so. But please do not copy them. Develop your own economic approach in regard to your own problems. Because if you get something from abroad, it may not meet all your particular and special problems." And we tried to do that.

We are trying to do that, in effect. Our approach is one of trial and error. We have tried to do something. If it does not succeed, we will retract our steps and function somewhat differently.

Also, the main problem of a country like India, that is, an underdeveloped country, and which follows from its underdevelopment, is the paucity and lack of resources for development. The surplus for investment is very little, and you have to, well, do without things in order to create greater surplus for investment, and you must have more for investment. Otherwise you don't go ahead.

Now, how to do it? On the one hand, people want higher standards. On the other hand, in order to invest we want to save on this and that, and in a sense, in a way of forgetting their higher standards for the moment.

If we have a steel plant – well, a steel plant is essential, but it takes about four or five years before it starts producing steel. Meanwhile it goes on absorbing money. And we have to guard against inflationary tendencies.

So all these problems we have to consider, trying to profit by the experience of others, but in the particular context of India as it is today, and always with the flexible minds, so as to vary the plan or vary our approach, where we think it might lead us into difficulties or the wrong direction. That is our broad approach to this problem.

As I said our resources are limited. We cannot afford to see them applied to things which are not of the first importance. They may be applied, well, for something that is good, but something else may be more important or more desirable. If our resources go into something that is otherwise good, but for the moment does not solve our problems, it takes away the resources from the actually important things. So that is a problem for a country with lack of resources. It is not a problem which arises in a country of big resources, because you can do everything at the same time. We have to choose what to do and channel our resources to the more basic things. That again requires this kind of economy, for the purpose of planning, so as to channel our resources in particular directions which we consider absolutely urgent, leaving the rest of the field, naturally, for free enterprise, etc.

Now, the field for private enterprise is very large and very considerable. From this point of view—all our land, of course, is privately owned and we will continue to do that—we do want to develop on our land as many cooperatives as possible, because there are too many small holdings—absurdly small. But if the small farmer comes together with a number of others, then they can have modern methods and profit by them.

A very big sector of our economy we are developing pertains to the small-scale cotton industry. We have been going into the cotton industry, chiefly, I may tell you, because of the employment problem; it may be that the cotton industry will not be profitable after some years. I don't know. But for the present, it becomes important, both to add to our production and to give employment to people. So that a small-scale cotton industry with higher techniques, insofar as we can introduce them—we don't want primitive techniques, but we do not want suddenly to throw our people from employment wherever they may be, unless we can absorb them some way, and if the process of absorbing goes, it is all right. But if we are to industrialize as we must, we must lay the base of that industrialization, the base for producing iron and steel, producing power, hydro-electric power, etc. We are concentrating on that.

Talking about agriculture, which is also of first importance for us, greater production, better irrigation methods, not so much mechanization of agriculture—we dare not do that, because it is all very well for mechanization in a country with much land and few people. Whether it is the United States or the Soviet Union, there is much more land than human beings, relatively speaking. But in a country where human beings abound, we have to go cautiously in letting them work and not throwing them out by too much mechanization. So the land comes first. One of the biggest things we are doing now is this community development scheme in our rural economy, villages, with which is also attached the small industry. But for major industrialization, it becomes essential that we have a base for that, a base, as I said, of iron and steel plants and certain other basic industries—the machine-making industry—and all that. That is what we are taking up, leaving the other fields—most of it—for private enterprise to carry out. The State can go directly or in conjunction with private enterprise or both. So that is the problem.

We realize, of course, that we have to, in a large measure, necessarily shoulder the burden for this, both for practical reasons and for psychological reasons. By psychological, I mean, I want the people to bear the main burden—the mere fact of their shouldering the burden makes them develop, hardens them into doing a job. If somebody else does a job for them, well, they would not be capable of carrying it on afterwards.

But the fact remains that it is a terrific burden in many ways and some relatively—relative to the full effort—small help goes a long way, in easing, if I may say so, the labour pains of industrialization. And so we very much welcome your cooperation and help. I cannot of course, discuss in detail; that is beyond me.

12. Common Approaches in the Cause of Peace[1]

As you know, I have come to this great city and great institution just for two days, and I have had a large number of engagements, but I am particularly glad that it was possible for me to come here for a short time and meet the representatives of the Commonwealth at the UN. I know of course that the Commonwealth group here meets from time to time to discuss matters and express their respective opinions. I think that is a good thing. But it is not enough merely to deliver formal speeches at the UN. It is much more important that we should discuss problems and matters in a more informal way amongst ourselves. Maybe sometimes we do not convince each other or hold different opinions. Nevertheless it is important that this should be done. It helps at least to understand the other's position, even if one does not wholly agree, and that is a great thing.

You have just referred, Mr Pearson,[2] to certain statements of mine in regard to the Commonwealth during the last two or three months. I spoke in our own

1. Address to the Commonwealth group at the United Nations, New York, 21 December 1956. From *Nehru Visits USA*, The Information Service of India, Washington, pp. 65-66.
2. Lester B. Pearson, Secretary of State for External Affairs, Government of Canada, and head of the Canadian delegation to the UN.

parliament on several occasions about the Commonwealth and made perfectly clear what the attitude of our Government is to it, in spite of differences of opinion on important matters. I do attach importance to this Commonwealth connection which I think is not only good for ourselves, but is good also to the larger cause of peace that we represent.

There are far too many disruptive tendencies in the world, that any tendency which brings together than separates is to be welcomed. The Commonwealth represents such a powerful tendency and shows vitality, that in spite of these differences, it can hold together and help in our having many common ways of working and common approaches in spite of our differences.

I hope that these meetings of your group here will continue and we will help each one of us to thrash out problems, and reach agreements if possible, and even if we differ, we will agree to differ and remain friends and associates in the Commonwealth.

Thank you for inviting me.

13. Reducing the Risk of War[1]

Edgar McInnes: (This question related to India's role in the Suez crisis.)

Jawaharlal Nehru: India would like to help to end the Suez Canal dispute between Egypt and, Britain and France. Our advice is listened to as that of a friend.

In that sense, we can help a little and we would like to help if we can. The canal, blocked during the Anglo-French attack on Egypt, must be cleared and a political settlement obtained with Egypt before any attempt could be made to bring about peace between Israel and the Arab States.

EM: China in detaining ten American civilians on the mainland, is committing a 'small thing' to affect its relations with the United States.

---

1. An interview with Edgar McInnes, President, Canadian Institute of International Affairs, Ottawa, 23 December 1956. From *National Herald*, 25 December 1956.

JN: Sometimes even small things begin to represent some major controversy.

EM: Did you find any common ground between President Eisenhower and the Red Chinese government?

JN: It seems inevitable that two great countries like the US and China should have an understanding, whether they agree or not. I hope that understanding will grow.

EM: Is it possible that a country like China can be friendly with the West?

JN: I don't think totalitarianism has much to do with this matter. The thing that comes in the way of good relations between two countries is fear and suspicion.

EM: (This question related to India's policy of non-alignment.)

JN: We would be false to our traditions and methods of achieving independence if in the international sphere we followed a policy of military pacts and alliances. There is even some doubt in our minds if we should have much to do with military means in our own country. We don't take to the idea very lightly.

EM: Is it not possible that the Western nations, by maintaining the balance of power, are helping India to pursue its foreign policies?

JN: I don't take that that affects the question of India's policy very much.
As far as India is concerned, I don't think any sensible person has the slightest fear of an attack from any big country, although as far as other countries are concerned in Asia it is conceivable.
Any kind of an attack on a weak country probably would lead to a major war. No country is going to take the risk of a major war unless by some circumstance it is forced into it.
We have arrived at a stage where everyone wants to put an end to the idea of a major war and realizes that a minor war might lead to a major one. If that is so, it follows that the atmosphere which might create a major war should be avoided. The cold war business is totally and absolutely illogical once you decide not to have a war. I am not advocating a surrender of principle. There is no question of becoming weak. But why shout war, or make gestures about war under these circumstances?

531

EM: (This question related the withdrawal of Anglo-French troops from the Suez Canal.)

JN: I agree that Britain and France have responded to the force of world opinion by ending their attack on Egypt.

EM: Do you agree that the Soviet Union has responded to world opinion which condemned its intervention in Hungary?

JN: There is something in what you say. I have long waited for a gesture from France in Algeria where matters are worse than they are in Hungary. In Hungary, the passive resistance used by the people will help solve the problem. I have no doubt that the Hungarian episode has shown the way to greater national freedom of many countries. The Hungarian revolt demonstrates that a great country, even with the strength of the Soviet Union, no longer can impose its will on a relatively weak country.

The Egyptian and Hungarian crises have increased tension and brought nearer the danger of war, but, at the same time, they have cleared the air.

Therefore, if you can survive the present, the future might be good.

It is true to a certain extent that India's basic principles have brought our country nearer to the democracies, rather than to the totalitarian countries. At the same time, we are out for social ends and broadly speaking we are socialistic—but through democratic processes and not through authoritarian processes.

In that sense, we are naturally much nearer to countries with parliamentary democracies. On the other hand, countries in the East and our own country have been attracted not to communist regimes but to many economic socialistic experiments from which we wish to learn.

14. To Dwight D. Eisenhower[1]

December 26, 1956

Dear Mr President,

Your letter of December 20th[2] reached me at Ottawa. I am now on my way back to India, and I hasten to write to you from London to thank you for your letter.

I cannot tell you adequately how much I appreciated your and Mrs Eisenhower's[3] great kindness to me and my daughter. I am quite sure that this meeting of ours and the talks we had were of great benefit to me and, I hope, to my country, and I shall treasure their memory. I am also very glad of the opportunity I had to discuss important matters with Secretary Dulles and other senior officers of the US Administration.

My visit to Washington and New York was a very short one. And yet, it was rich in new experiences which have left a great impress on my mind.

Although I have not reached my country yet, I feel sure that this visit has greatly impressed my own countrymen. They will welcome the closer knowledge of each other that we have obtained, and look forward to ever-growing avenues of cooperation and friendship.

I earnestly hope that it will be possible for you and for Mrs Eisenhower to visit India and see for yourselves some parts of our country and the work we are doing there.

May I wish you and Mrs Eisenhower a happy New Year.

Again, thanking you, and with the deepest regards,

Yours sincerely,
Jawaharlal Nehru

1. JN Collection.
2. President Eisenhower wrote: "We were delighted to have had the opportunity to know you better, and to learn more of India's outlook and problems, and of your own thoughts. Our talks were most helpful to me personally. I am pleased that you met at some length with Secretary Dulles and other important officers of the Administration. Thank you again for the beautiful rug that you presented to Mrs Eisenhower and me. We shall always treasure the rug with fond memories...."
3. Mamie Eisenhower.

15. A Report on the Foreign Tour[1]

The Prime Minister gave a brief account of his foreign tour and the talks he had with President Eisenhower and the Prime Ministers of Canada[2] and the United Kingdom[3] and Chancellor Adenauer[4] of West Germany.

2. His talks with the President were extensive and covered a variety of matters concerning several countries. The President had been taken by surprise by the aggression against Egypt and had taken a strong line against England, France and Israel, contrary to the advice of some of his own party men. All the same, he could not approve of some of the actions and utterances of President Nasser. He desired that the West Asian problems should be solved in a peaceful manner and to the satisfaction of all the parties concerned. The Prime Minister had indicated that a peaceful settlement would be facilitated by proceeding in the matter step by step. The first thing to do was to get the Suez Canal cleared for traffic. Secondly, a long-term settlement of the Suez problem could be taken up. When the atmosphere was more favourable, the problem of Israel could also be settled in consultation with the Arab countries.

3. The Prime Minister had further pointed out that the recent events in Egypt had shown that world opinion was strong enough to prevail against aggression of stronger powers against weaker countries. The events in Hungary had revealed that communism could not succeed in a country unless it was allied to nationalism. Over ten years of Soviet propaganda in Hungary could not prevent the Hungarian revolt which was the result of resurgent nationalism.

4. With regard to the peaceful development of West Asian countries, the Prime Minister had urged that it was necessary for strong powers, like the United States, to back forces of democracy in these countries while giving economic aid and not merely set up puppet heads of government who did not have support of the people. In this connection, he disapproved of military pacts, like the Baghdad Pact, which merely gave military assistance to the countries and did not help in the improvement of their economic condition. The failure of such pacts had become clear from the aggression against Egypt by one of the members of the Baghdad Pact.

1. Minutes of a meeting of the Cabinet, New Delhi, 29 December 1956. JN Collection.
2. Louis St Laurent.
3. Anthony Eden.
4. Nehru met Konrad Adenauer on 27 December 1956.

5. With regard to Hungary, the Prime Minister had told the President that Soviet Russia had sent her troops for the second time[5] after the Anglo-French aggression against Egypt had taken place. For one thing, Russia had been concerned about the developments in Poland and the other Eastern European countries and did not want the trouble to spread. When Egypt was invaded, Russia naturally thought that the Anglo-French action had the approval of the United States and it might develop into a third world war. Russia, therefore, resorted to strong action in Hungary. A great deal of changes were taking place, both inside Russia and her satellite countries, and it was the Prime Minister's opinion that an ending of the cold war would facilitate such changes and result in the easing of tensions.

6. The Prime Minister had also given the President an idea of our position regarding Kashmir. He had pointed out that Pakistan leaders had been saying openly that they would use American arms for any purpose they considered legitimate and they would talk with India from a position of strength. President Eisenhower had given the assurance that any attempt by Pakistan to use American arms for aggression against India would be met by strong action on the part of the United States.

7. Another subject which figured in the talks was Goa. Apart from the question of accession of Goa to India, the Prime Minister had particularly referred to the Indian prisoners in Goa who were undergoing a lot of hardship. The American attitude with regard to this matter had been sympathetic.

8. About India's Second Five Year Plan, the President had expressed great enthusiasm and promised his support.

9. With regard to China, the President had expressed the view that the policy of the United States was not likely to change as long as the American prisoners in China were not released. The people of the United States still remembered their suffering in Korea and felt strongly on the subject. If the Chinese Government released the American prisoners, it would be possible for the United States to let American journalists and others visit China, which might ultimately pave the way for better relations between the two countries.

10. The problem of Laos in Indo-China was also one of the subjects discussed by the Prime Minister with President Eisenhower. A government was about to be formed in Laos, including one or two communist members, but the United States had got alarmed and threatened to withhold economic aid to Laos. The United States was afraid that the formation of such a government would

5. On 4 November 1956.

ultimately result in the assumption of complete control by the communists. The Prime Minister had pointed out that the action of the United States would be against the Geneva Accord and, in any case, it need not be assumed that inclusion of one or two communist members would result in the assumption of all the powers by the communists. The United States Government had agreed to continue economic aid to Laos for the time being.

11. With the Prime Ministers of Canada and the United Kingdom, the talk related mainly to the clearance of the Suez Canal and the ultimate settlement of the Suez dispute.

12. Chancellor Adenauer had told the Prime Minister during his talks with him that if the communists would give up their idea of world domination, some satisfactory settlement was possible in Europe. The Prime Minister had explained that in the light of the events which had taken place recently in Poland and Hungary, the question of world domination by communists did not arise. West Germany was intending to raise the question of re-unification of Germany in the United Nations, and the Prime Minister had said that while he was of opinion that the re-unification of Germany was necessary for a stable peace in Europe, this could not be brought about by threats or coercive methods. The cold war must end first and the atmosphere of fear dispelled.

13. Finally, the Prime Minister said that an aide-memoire on Kashmir had been received about a month ago from Pakistan and an answer was proposed to be sent in a few days.[6]

6. See *ante*, p. 336.

16. To G.L. Mehta[1]

The Residency,
Indore,
January 6, 1957

My dear Gaganvihari,

I am writing to you from Indore where I came for the Congress session. This session ended tonight. I am, however, staying on for another day and returning to Delhi on the 8th morning.

The session has been, I think, a good one. Naturally, it was devoted chiefly to the election manifesto.[2] You will, of course, see this in the newspapers. I shall send you printed copies later.

Although this is a party manifesto, since the party happens to be the Government party, it represents the Government's viewpoint about various matters. I think it will be desirable for you to send copies of this manifesto to some important journalists and others.

I have received here today two letters from you dated 29th[3] and 31st December[4] and a note[5] on my visit dated December 25. Thank you for them. In the note you

---

1. JN Collection.
2. For full text of the Congress Election Manifesto, see *ante*, pp. 260-273.
3. Mehta wrote: "Dulles told me that the President was very pleased with the visit and so was Dulles. I reliably understand that Dulles told the officers of the State Department that he had been most impressed by your analysis of the situation in Eastern Europe. Apart from the fact that there was a basic similarity in the conclusions drawn by you and by American leaders for events in Eastern Europe, the Americans, he said were fascinated by your presentation."
4. Mehta wrote that the State Department had declined to include, a lunch or dinner by Governor Harriman for Nehru "presumably because" early in December 1956 Harriman had strongly criticised President Eisenhower, in the presence of Selwyn Lloyd, for letting down Britain and France in the Middle East. "The President is rather touchy about these matters" noted Mehta. When the US State Department found that an engagement with Governor Harriman had been made directly by Krishna Menon they accepted it.
5. Mehta wrote: (i) "The American public was immensely impressed with the fact that the Prime Minister and his daughter were invited to a private family lunch at the White House—something that has not been done before for any foreign dignitary."; (ii) "No other foreign statesman has yet been taken to Gettysburg for informal talks by the President."; (iii) "The duration of talks held by the President with the Prime Minister is the longest since he assumed office over four years ago."; and (iv) "Press coverage was larger than I have seen in the case of anyone not excluding Churchill."

mention that the honours shown to me are usually given to the Head of a State. I noted this at the time. Indeed, the gun salute is always reserved for Heads of States. In India we would not think of giving it to anybody but a Head of a State. It was the first time in my life that I received such a gun salute in India or abroad and I was rather embarrassed by it.

I appreciate very much the intimate and friendly way that the President met me, both at his house at Christmas time and at Gettysburg. I hope you will, when opportunity offers, express my great appreciation to the President and Mrs Eisenhower.

We have been reading the message of the President to the Congress about giving military and other aid to the Middle East countries. I confess I am disturbed by this as I am convinced that this gives the present situation a wrong direction. Newspapermen have been after me to say something about it. I have, however, refrained from expressing any opinion. At the Congress session today, however, I referred rather indirectly to the President's message in terms of our own policy and said that I regretted the military approach.[6]

All good wishes to you,

Yours sincerely,
Jawaharlal Nehru

6. See *ante*, pp. 294-301.

17. Talks with the US President[1]

This is a brief note of my talks with the President which occupied fourteen hours on two or three occasions.

2. The President had asked me about our Five Year Plan. I gave him the background of it and he appeared to be greatly interested. I also gave him some pamphlets dealing with the Plan. He told me later that he would 'boost' our Plan.

3. I discussed the Indo-China situation and especially the new developments in Laos. At that time an agreement had been reached between the two contending parties in Laos, namely, the Royal Laotian Government and the Pathet Lao. The American Government had, however, not approved of this agreement and had indicated that they would stop aid to the Laotian Government. I pointed out to the President how unfortunate any such action on the part of the US Government would be and how it would be exploited against them. I gave a number of reasons to him and later to Secretary Dulles. These reasons apparently produced some effect, as the US Government varied their policy and decided to continue their aid to Laos in spite of the agreement. They said they would wait and see what further developments took place.

4. I explained to him the background of our relations with Pakistan and the main problems between the two countries. I referred to the canal water dispute, the evacuee problem and the tremendous exodus from East Pakistan which was continuing from day-to-day and causing us a great deal of trouble and anxiety. In particular, I spoke about the Kashmir issue and gave him some background information. What appeared to impress him most was that it would be unwise to take any step now which would upset things as they are and create further difficulties.

5. I spoke to him about Goa and pointed out the great restraint we had exercised on the face of continued provocation and in spite of strong feeling in our own country on this issue. He seemed to be impressed somewhat, but he said that the Portuguese Government was a very difficult one to handle. He also pointed out that the US Government had its hands full with major problems and it was not easy for them to add to them at present. In regard to one matter, however, he said that they would try to do something. This was the continuance in prison in

---

1. Note, 8 January 1957. JN Collection. Nehru had talks with President Eisenhower at Gettysburg Farm on 17-18 December and in Washington on 19 December 1956.

Goa of a number of Indian nationals. He agreed that they ought to be released, but again added that the Portuguese Government was difficult. Subsequently we have heard that the US Government have mentioned this matter to the Portuguese Government. But we know nothing about the effect of this intervention.

6. The principal subjects discussed were, however,

      (i) the situation in Egypt and the Middle East,

      (ii) the Hungarian situation, and

      (iii) Sino-American relations.

7. As regards Egypt and the Middle East, he said that the Anglo-French action against Egypt had come as a great shock to him and he had insisted on the United States disapproving of that action, even though this meant going against their allies. His own advisers had tried to restrain him, as they were afraid this might affect the Jewish vote in America, but the President had made it clear that this was a matter of principle for him and, whatever the result, he would stick to the principle.

8. He was obviously thinking a great deal about the position in the Middle East, although he did not put forward then any definite proposal. He expressed apprehension about the Soviet creeping in and filling the vacuum caused by the ending of the British and French influence. He spoke to me rather in terms of economic aid. I pointed out that so far as I knew, the reports of Soviet intervention in Syria were greatly exaggerated. He agreed that later reports received by him had also been to this effect. Nevertheless he was anxious about the future.

9. He asked about President Nasser. I told him that I had a high opinion of him. Colonel Nasser had impressed me not only as a man of integrity but also as one anxious to learn. Sometimes he tended to speak at a public meeting in rather aggressive terms because he got excited. Also he had to face a very difficult situation in Egypt and had been fighting fanatical elements there. He was probably the most reasonable of the members of the Egyptian Government and in any event there was no one to replace him.

10. I gave him briefly my views on the general situation in the Middle Eastern region ever since the fall of the Ottoman Empire at the end of the First World War and the way that some West European Powers had played about with these countries in West Asia. The process of consolidation had been interfered with. Conditions there had been very bad both politically and economically. Social conditions were largely feudal, except in Lebanon. The Baghdad Pact had created more divisions and conflicts in that area as well as had been a challenge to the Soviet Union, which was next door. The help given to these countries of West Asia had not resulted in any improvement of conditions there. Even the money that was given for economic development had produced little result. In effect,

outside help had often strengthened unpopular and feudal regimes, and no real reforms of any kind had been introduced. The land question was important in many of these countries. The countries giving the help thus appeared in the eyes of the people there to side with these feudal and unpopular regimes and themselves shared in this unpopularity. The President agreed that there was some truth in what I said, but he did not know how to avoid this difficulty.

11. We discussed the immediate issues. I said that the first question to be tackled was that of the clearance of the Suez Canal. It was not much good trying to deal with other problems before this was cleared up. The next question would be the future of the Suez Canal. The third and the most difficult question was that of Israel. This was bad enough previously and now it had become much worse because of the passions roused. It would do no good to raise this question at this stage. I agreed, however, that some time or other later, this will have to be tackled, though how I did not know. Israel could not disappear from the map and, at the same time, the very existence of Israel infuriated the Arabs. Yet I thought that conditions might arise later when this question could be tackled in a more reasonable atmosphere. But prior to that, the Suez Canal issue should be satisfactorily settled, and some return to normality in the Middle East should take place. The existence of Israel was not only disliked in itself, but also because Israel was considered as an outpost of the Western Powers. I mentioned that a suggestion made some years ago, that there should be some kind of a federation or a confederation in Palestine with an autonomous Israel a member of it, had been a good one, but it was hardly possible to revive it.

12. I dealt at some length with the general situation which had arisen as a result of what had happened recently in Egypt and Hungary. The failure of the Anglo-French attack on Egypt made it clear that it would be very difficult in future for any power to try to use old colonial methods in a country in Asia or Africa which had become independent. Also, it had become clear that it was not at all easy to enforce communism with the help of foreign arms. That had been the lesson of Hungary. Indeed, Hungary had demonstrated that international communism was no longer a force.

13. During the last two years or so, changes had been taking place in the Soviet Union itself and in the communist countries of East Europe in favour of democratization. This was a natural development and the surprising thing was that it had been delayed so long. Every revolution toned down after a while and could not continue for long at a high pitch. But the First World War, intervention in the Soviet Union, civil war, Hitler and the Second World War and, finally, Stalin had prevented a return to normality. By normality, I did not mean that the Soviet Union would adopt the parliamentary system of government. I did not think there was any going back in regard to the broad economic structure of the

Soviet Union. Nor was there any demand for it from the people. But the people were certainly tired of living at this high pitch and wanted a quieter life. They wanted especially a freer life and not to live in fear of the secret police. Also, they wanted many commodities which they could not easily get.

14. In the East European countries, all these factors prevailed plus the very important one of resentment against some measure of foreign domination. That is, nationalism was opposed to Soviet domination. As soon as changes became evident in the Soviet Union, the process of change was swifter in the East European countries. In Poland, it was just possible to come to terms peacefully. In Hungary, there was no adequate leadership, and just then the Anglo-French invasion of Egypt took place. It is just possible that but for this Anglo-French action, the Hungarian problem would have been solved on the lines of Poland. As it was, it developed into a terrible tragedy.

15. My main contention was that the progressive forces in these communist countries which were working towards democratization, could not be turned back, although they might be delayed and obstructed because of recent happenings. The real danger was that the Soviet Union might be driven into a corner because of Hungary and war might result. If war could be avoided, developments would be natural and in the right direction. Therefore, not only should war be avoided but an atmosphere of war should also not be kept up.

16. I pointed out that we had really reached an important historical phase in the development of the Russian Revolution and we should take advantage of this fact by changing our old approaches which were in the main military. President Eisenhower did not appear to disagree with much that I said, although his emphasis was different and he laboured continuously under the fear of the Soviet Government extending its field of activities and, more especially, getting a grip of the Middle East. I tried to reason with him that this was not feasible at present and, indeed, the Soviet Government had been hurt so much by the Hungarian rising that it was not at all likely to invite further trouble.

17. The events in Hungary had not only undermined the whole conception of international communism but had also, at the same time, weakened national communisms. They had shown that while communism might grow in a country, it could not be imposed on other countries.

18. What had happened was very important in regard to communism, because Hungary had underminded the mystique of communism. Communism, apart from its violence, coercion and other bad features, had certain idealistic elements in it which had attracted some very fine men and women, who only saw the idealistic part and ignored the other brutal parts of it. It is this idealistic part that had been undermined and communists everywhere were perplexed and feeling frustrated. The way to deal with this situation was to allow these forces to function

and not to have a climate of war which gave an excuse for the suppression of views and checked the growth of these forces.

19. With much of this, the President agreed, but his agreement was of course limited and conditioned by other factors and more especially the obsession about the dangers of communism spreading and his desire to check it.

20. In the course of our talk I had pointed out to the President that in Russia the basic fear was that of a re-armed Germany. So also in the East European countries who had two fears—the fear of Germany and the fear of Russia. Everyone of these countries had suffered terribly at the hands of Germany. Ever since its inception, the Soviet Union had grown up in circumstances which made them feel that they were in a state of siege. This had powerfully affected their mental outlook. That outlook would not change by military threats. Indeed the military approach increased that outlook. Now, partly because of the strength of the Soviet Union and partly because of the growth of the more liberal forces there, changes were taking place which was all to the good, provided nothing came in their way.

21. I developed these arguments at some length.

22. We discussed Sino-American relations. The President was particularly excited about the retention of the ten American prisoners in China. I agreed with him that these persons should be released. But at the same time I gave him the Chinese viewpoint. This latter was to the effect that China had released many American prisoners, but no response had come from the US, and therefore the Chinese Government did not see why they should go on acting unilaterally. The President said that he recognized that the present lack of any relations between the US and China was abnormal and could not subsist for long. Even countries at war established peace some time or other. But he made it clear that America would not move her little finger so long as the American prisoners in China were not released. If they were released, then the US might remove the ban on Americans, journalists and others, going to China. If their reports of present conditions in China were satisfactory, the opinion of the people of the US would gradually change. But at present nothing could be done because of the strong feeling against China.

23. I invited the President to come to India. He was obviously keen on doing so and said that he would try to arrange it some time late in 1957. Nothing more definite was said about it.

24. I might mention that the US Government went out of their way in showing me honour. For the first time in my life I was received with a nineteen gun salute which normally is given to Heads of States. Although it was Christmas time, my daughter and I were invited to lunch at the White House immediately after our arrival. This kind of thing is not usually done. My being taken to the President's farm at Gettysburg was also very unusual.

543

III. SUEZ CRISIS

1. Cable to V.K. Krishna Menon[1]

Your long telegram No. 509 of December 2nd.[2] You need not have taken the trouble to explain in detail what happened. There was no question of our being critical of step(s) taken on our behalf. I have entirely agreed with them.

A message was sent by Pillai merely to inform you of an informal communication to us from UK High Commission.[3] MacDonald is ill partly I think because of shock of recent events.

There can be no question of our changing our basic policy which you have repeatedly stated. I am by no means sure myself of what United Kingdom will do ultimately, but I have a feeling that they realise their folly and wish to save face. It is quite possible that if events take a better turn for them they may resile. We should therefore keep alert but at the same time not make it impossible for them to retire with dignity.[4]

1. New Delhi, 3 December 1956. V. K. Krishna Menon Papers, NMML.
2. Krishna Menon had explained why he had spoken so strongly in the General Assembly on 24 November 1956 on a Belgian amendment, which sought to minimize criticism of the UK and France, as embodied in two resolutions introduced the same day. These resolutions dealt the withdrawal of Israeli and Anglo-French forces from Egypt and the clearance of the Suez Canal.
3. Krishna Menon asked Nehru if India was going to acquiesce in a conditional withdrawal as reportedly suggested by the UK High Commissioner, Malcolm MacDonald, to N.R. Pillai. Referring to Nasser's refusal to accept the six principles of 13 October 1956 as one of the conditions for an Anglo-French withdrawal from the Suez Canal, Krishna Menon stated: "They (Egypt) will not give any assurances with regard to Britain and France unless they make peace." For the six principles, see *Selected Works* (second series), Vol. 35, p. 419.
4. Referring to MacDonald's communication to Pillai on "conditions for withdrawal", Krishna Menon stated: "There is little doubt that we should not seek to humiliate any one or to prevent face saving. I submit, however, that these conditions are not face saving. They save the whole body of the aggressor."

Our position continues to be what it has been, that is, that foreign forces must withdraw from Egypt without any conditions attached.[5]

5. Selwyn Lloyd, British Foreign Secretary, told the House of Commons on 3 December that Britain and France would withdraw from the Suez Canal Zone "without delay." Lloyd claimed that Britain's objectives in Egypt—to halt Israeli-Egyptian warfare and expose Soviet penetration in West Asia—had "been achieved." He also indicated that in return for the Anglo-French withdrawal Britain expected immediate reopening of the Suez Canal and negotiation of a Suez settlement on the basis of the "six principles."

2. Message to Gamal Abdel Nasser[1]

I am happy to find that the Anglo-French and Israeli troops[2] will at long last be withdrawn entirely from Egyptian territory. I feel sure that this would not have been possible had not world public opinion overwhelmingly stood by Egypt. It was a great relief to us to find that despite their long and close alliance in many matters of international policy, the United States of America also stood firm on the question of the withdrawal of the aggressor forces from Egyptian soil. While we can permit ourselves the hope that the worst will soon be over, there will still be need for continuous vigilance for some months to come at least. I am anxious that the revulsion of feelings caused by aggression against Egypt should not be sidetracked by extraneous factors. As it is, developments in Hungary[3] have to an extent come in the way of concerted action against aggressors in Egypt. I feel, therefore, that it is more than ever important to prevent other things coming in the way of the sympathy of the world expressing itself fully in favour of Egypt.

In this context I venture to draw your attention to the reports which are circulating abroad that considerable pressure, direct and indirect, is being brought

1. New Delhi, 5 December 1956. JN Collection.
2. On 8 November 1956, Israel agreed to withdraw its troops after a set of agreements with the UN Emergency Force. By 22 January 1957, it had evacuated all occupied territory, except for the Gaza Strip and the Sinai Coast. Concerning these areas, Israel insisted on safeguards for free navigation and freedom from attack across her borders.
3. See *post* pp. 555-579.

to bear on the large number of British and French nationals[4] and persons of Jewish origin[5] in Egypt. Some of the latter have, I am told, been resident in Egypt for generations. As you may be aware, I asked our Charge[6] in Egypt to mention the matter informally to your Government and I am told that he has already done so and had a discussion with Ali Sabry.[7] I would repeat the assurance which Rajwade has already given to Ali Sabry that it is farthest from our mind to interfere in any matter which is in the full discretion of the Egyptian Government. But, Mr President, I feel sure that you will be concerned as much as I am at anything being done which might create an unfortunate impression on world opinion and alienate sympathy from Egypt at a time when most countries in the world are supporting your cause. You have in the recent past shown exemplary patience in the most provocative circumstances. If I may say so, this has impressed the world almost as much as your courage throughout this critical period. I would request you, therefore, not to take steps which would compel a large number of persons to leave Egypt in penurious circumstances. Considerations of security have of course to be borne in mind. But it would not be in the interest of Egypt herself to allow impression to grow that an attempt was being made to recoup losses suffered by Egypt as a result of aggression by UK, France and Israel by sequestrating the properties of British and French nationals. Action is certainly justified against those who have abused the hospitality of Egypt by subversive activities. But the large majority of the people are, I believe, innocent victims of the wrongs committed by their Governments and I would request you to show them compassion. If you do not wish any British or French national to remain in your country, they might, I suggest, be given reasonable time to wind up their affairs and not be forced to leave immediately.[8] Even from the short term point of view a little patience and tolerance at this stage would help in the discussion of bigger issues concerning Egypt in the United Nations and elsewhere. I would not have made this appeal to you had I not felt sure that you would not misunderstand me.

4. Small groups of French and British residents of Egypt landed in Europe by 2 December. The Swiss Minister to Egypt, Max Koenig, said on 9 December that expulsions of individual British and French citizens from Egypt and sequestration of their property continued "relentessly" on a large-scale.
5. At least 1,000 Egyptian, foreign and stateless Jews had been imprisoned in Egypt. The European Director of the American Jewish commission, Zacharia Shuster, said that hundreds had had their property sequestrated and others given individual orders to leave the country.
6. R.G. Rajwade.
7. President Nasser's political aide.
8. The Egyptian Interior Minister, Zacharia Mohy Eldin, stated on 9 December that of the 18,000 British and French citizens in Egypt, 1,452 had been expelled from the country.

3. Cable to V.K. Krishna Menon[1]

French ambassador[2] saw me this evening and said that French Government were rather distressed at our general attitude in recent weeks towards France. What distressed them was not that we were critical, which we had every right to be, but that we appeared to be hostile to France. As an instance, he said that relations of the French delegates in the UN during this crisis had actually been more friendly with the Egyptian representative[3] than with the Indian.

I told him that there was no question of hostility against France. It is true that we had reacted strongly to what had happened and had criticized it, but whether it was England or France, there was no question of hostility. Public feeling was strong and in fact we had tried to check it and to distinguish between countries as such and some of their acts that we disapproved of. I could not say what had happened in the UN, but there was so much burden on our delegation there during these days that it might have been difficult for them to keep up normal contacts.[4]

I assured him that we were as friendly as ever to France. In fact during recent speeches I had especially refered to our friendly agreements in regard to Pondicherry, etc. As a matter of fact criticism of England had been much sharper here than of France.

1. New Delhi, 7 December 1956. JN Collection.
2. Stanislav Ostrorog.
3. Omar Loutfi.
4. In his reply of 9 December, Krishna Menon regretted that the information given by the French Ambassador was incorrect and pointed out that there was "a concerted attempt here in view of issues and the importance of Asia and India to put us in the wrong." He stated: "Ali (Yavar Jung) tells me that he gets on very well with the French representative on the Second Committee...(Arthur S.) Lall often talks to the people he knows ... Several members of our delegation meet them socially as well as any other. When Pineau was here during the Security Council meetings I asked to see him more than once. Various excuses were given including that he had a cold. He saw me more than once but he would not recognize me. The same thing happened this time also .... their delegation sits right in front of us in the Assembly and we smile to each other .... last week or so when Ambassador Alphand came here from Washington, I went up and spoke to him and renewed our acquaintance." Krishna Menon added: "The Egyptians having broken off the diplomatic relations do not want (to) talk to the French and also avoid them."

4. Cable to Ali Yavar Jung[1]

I saw Eden today. He spoke about the clearance of the Canal and about British nationals in Egypt.

2. About Canal clearance,[2] he said that they had placed their salvage ships under the UN and if they were used, he was informed that the clearance could be done very rapidly. He hoped this would be done. I told him that we were all anxious to have the Canal cleared and working as soon possible.

3. He expressed his apprehension about their nationals there. I told him that I had sent a message[3] to President Nasser on the subject and that he had denied taking any step for mass removal.[4] It was possible that conditions were difficult and this induced people to go away.

4. As you well know, I feel that pushing out of foreign nationals from Egypt will be injurious to her interest. Home[5] said that Fawzi[6] had also expressed his apprehension on this matter. I hope you will be able to ease this situation. You need not bring my name again, unless you feel it necessary.

---

1. London, 15 December 1956. JN Collection. Nehru made a stopover in London on his way to Washington for talks with President Eisenhower. Ali Yavar Jung was India's Ambassador in Cairo.
2. According to British Admiralty, 49 vessels and bridges had sunk in the Suez Canal, with 11 sunken vessels blocking the main channel. Raymond A. Wheeler, advisor to UN Secretary General Dag Hammarskjold on Suez Canal problems, estimated on 11 December that full clearance would be accomplished in less than a year. See also *Selected Works* (second series), Vol. 35, p. 448.
3. See *ante*, p. 479.
4. The Indian Charge d'Affaires R.G. Rajwade reported on 5 December that Nasser had contended that British, French and Jewish interests had dominated the Egyptian economy for decades and, in recent months, tried to paralyze the country's economic life. Nasser told Rajwade he could not ignore these interests, particularly in the context of British and French radio propaganda aimed at his overthrow; and he was therefore attempting to rid Egypt of them.
5. A.F. Douglas-Home, British Secretary of State for Commonwealth Relations.
6. Mahmoud Fawzi, Egyptian Foreign Minister.

5. The Situation in the Middle East[1]

The Syrian Ambassador, Dr Farid Zeineddine[2], said that recent events in the Middle East had demonstrated a close connection between Zionism and Colonialism. It was evident that Israel had the backing of Britain and France in its act of aggression against Egypt. The Canal problem was not, therefore, the real issue. The real issues were (a) Zionist expansion; and (b) the Baghdad Pact. The USA was supporting the Baghdad Pact without formally joining it. Western Powers did not want Arabs to act collectively and wanted them to revolve round a Turkey-Pakistan axis. They wanted to create a scare about communism on the one hand and offer aid with US help on the other. The aim was to make the Arab States forget Israel and turn them against Soviet Russia.

2. The Syrian Ambassador further said that Syria had been a target of this policy because of her geographical position, because she was a centre of Arab nationalism and because she wanted to follow a policy of non-alignment. Pressure was being applied against her and there had also been a concentration of British troops on the border. Syria did not have adequate power to defend herself. The possibility of military action could not be excluded. The flow of oil was important for Syria herself and she was prepared to help in restoration of the pipeline provided a settlement was reached about the Gaza Strip and assurance were given against hostilities by Israel. The Syrian Government had sent a message to President Eisenhower on the eve of Prime Minister's visit to enable him to discuss the Syrian point of view with Prime Minister.[3] He also referred to the purchase of arms by Syria.

3. Prime Minister said that Israel's recent attack[4] was inexcusable but Israel could not be made to disappear. He felt that no immediate settlement was possible because of recent events and the passions that had been roused by them. India

1. Record of talks with the Ambassadors of Syria, Israel and Iran to the USA, Washington, 19 December 1956. This was cabled by G.L. Mehta, India's Ambassador to the USA to N.R. Pillai, Secretary General, MEA on 29 December 1956.
2. Syrian Ambassador to the USA since 1952 and its permanent representative to the UN.
3. President Eisenhower recalled that Nehru gave him a letter from the President of Syria during their talks at Gettysburg Farm on 17-18 December 1956. Eisenhower stated: "While Nehru said he had not read it carefully, he did agree when I spoke to him about it that it is mere repetition of the Arab complaint as voiced by Nasser in some of his speeches."
4. On 29 October 1956, the Israeli army launched an attack on Egyptian positions in the Sinai Peninsula in violation of the Armistice Agreement of 1949 between Israel and Egypt.

was prepared to assist in clearing the Canal and in arriving at a peaceful settlement of the Canal problem as also the withdrawal of foreign troops. Prime Minister felt that fear of Soviet intervention in the Middle East was unjustified. The Baghdad Pact had given unnecessary provocation to Soviet Russia.

4. There was some discussion on the question of border between Israel and Arab countries and the desirability of UN guarantee. The Syrian Ambassador felt that a guarantee by the United Nations would not be desirable but the Prime Minister thought that a satisfactory border settlement was essential for stability in the area.

5. The Israel Ambassador, Dr Abba Eban,[5] saw Prime Minister. He said that Arab nationalism had triumphed in twelve countries since the last war and these Arabs had thrown off the Western imperialistic yoke. Israel had supported independence of these countries and was prepared to work with them on a free and equal basis. The problem was mainly psychological. There were emotional conflicts which prevented a sane solution. If India could exert her influence for a settlement, the situation could be remedied.

6. The Israel Ambassador, said that it was essential to recognise that (a) Israel was a sovereign state that had come to stay; it might require an educative and psychological process to recognise this; (b) the Arab States in their resistance to Israel should not receive the indiscriminate support of Asian countries which should judge and determine these problems on their merits; and (c) peaceful settlement could be achieved in this area only by stages. In the first place, there would have to be a period of non-belligerency. While Israel troops should be withdrawn, Israel should also be given certain guarantees. The Israel Ambassador mentioned four points in this connection; (a) militarisation of Sinai; (b) Gulf of Aqaba should be occupied by the UN; (c) no discrimination against Israel in the use of Canal which should be open to all countries if the principle of universality was to be effective; and (d) guarantees against commando raids.

7. Prime Minister said that he was glad to get a first-hand account of Israel's point of view but emphasised that there were practical difficulties in the way of a settlement at present as the situation had been rendered much more difficult because of military action. He said that there was no anti-Jewish feeling in India but he should frankly state that there had been considerable feeling against Israel because of recent events and its alliance with imperial Powers. It was felt that

5. (b. 1915); Israeli diplomat and politician; Liasion Officer with the UN special commission on Palestine, 1947; representative, provisional government of Israel to the UN, 1948; permanent representative, 1949-59; Ambassador to the USA, 1950-59; President, Weizmann Institute of Science, 1958-66. Minister without Portfolio, 1963-66; Minister for Foreign Affairs, 1966-74; guest professor, Columbia University, 1974.

Israel was allowing to be used as a colonial foothold. He hoped, however, that after the withdrawal of troops and a settlement of the Canal issue, better atmosphere would prevail. The UN forces were placed whereas conflict was likely. Prime Minister said that the best way to avoid exploitation by outsiders was to come to a settlement between countries themselves.

8. The Iran Ambassador, Dr Ali Amini,[6] also saw Prime Minister and briefly explained (in French) the stand of his country on the Baghdad Pact. He said that the Iran Government was really afraid of Soviet aggression and recalled the Azerbaijan incident. Prime Minister reiterated his opposition to the Baghdad Pact and said that it had divided the Arab World, aroused Soviet Russia's suspicions and had not ensured security in the region.

6. (1907-1992); Iranian politician; appointed economic director to the Ministry of Finance, 1938; elected to Iranian Parliament, 1940; named under-secretary to Prime Minister Ahmad Qauam es-Saltaneh, 1948; Minister of National Economy, 1950-51; Minister of Finance, 1953-55; Minister of Justice, May-November 1955; Ambassador to the USA, 1955-58; re-elected to Parliament, 1960; Prime Minister, May 1961-July 1962.

6. To Ali Yavar Jung[1]

December 26, 1956

My dear Ali,

My sister[2] has received a letter from Sir Ifor Evans,[3] enclosing a letter he has written for President Nasser. I am sending this to you for delivery, together with a copy which you can keep. I hope it will be possible for the Egyptian Government to permit these archaeologists to continue their excavations.

1. Camp: London. JN Collection.
2. Vijayalakshmi Pandit, India's High Commissioner to the UK.
3. British scholar and administrator; Provost, University College, London, 1951-66.

I am now on my way back to India. Krishna Menon will be reaching you soon[4] and before this letter gets to you, he will tell you of our talks and our general views about the present situation. This is complicated and difficult, and I fear that the Egyptian Government will have no easy task. They will require a great deal of wisdom and restraint to deal with the problems facing them. After the first flush produced by the Anglo-French and Israeli operations against Egypt, which brought world opinion on the side of Egypt, there is naturally going to be some reaction. England and France have been humiliated by this world opinion, and they are deeply frustrated. The United States as well as some other countries feel that they have done all they could to help Egypt, and now there is a tendency for them to help the others to retrieve their position somewhat. We have, therefore, to be very careful in how we deal with the situation and not allow it to drift away in a wrong direction. That is why I have said that this will require all the wisdom that Egyptian authorities possess. True wisdom consists in knowing how far we can go, to profit by the circumstances and to create a feeling of generosity which again results in a change in one's own favour.

I cannot discuss details as I am not competent to do so, and the situation changes from day-to-day. While firmness is necessary in dealing with principles, it is not wise to get stuck up in regard to details.[5]

All good wishes to you and your wife[6] for the New Year.

Yours sincerely,
Jawaharlal Nehru

4. Krishna Menon arrived in Cairo on 27 December. On 21 December, Nehru had telegraphed to Yavar Jung from New York: "I hope you have expressed my regret to Nasser about my inability to visit Cairo on my way back. I am, however, anxious that Krishna Menon should go there soon and have asked him to do so. Please inform President Nasser accordingly."

5. On 5 January 1957, Krishna Menon sent Nehru a long report of his conversations with Nasser. With regard to the future of the Suez Canal, he wrote: "I stated and restated our position several times about moderation and your view that essential firmness and generosity as well as moderation had to be exercised. I did not find any resistance to this except that I felt Nasser's mind is a little confused on the question in regard to finding a method of settlement." Krishna Menon added: "He accepts your advice that a negative attitude will not do."

6. Zehra Ali Yavar Jung.

7. Cable to V.K. Krishna Menon[1]

Your telegram No. 4 of January 2nd.[2]

2. When I passed through Dusseldorf Chancellor Adenauer told me that Hammarskjold had asked USA for five million dollars for Canal clearance and had asked German Federal Government for loan of one million dollars which Adenauer had accepted in principle.

3. As you have pointed out there are many difficulties and complications about this matter.[3] In any event we cannot commit ourselves at this stage to any payment for clearance of Canal. Indeed so far as foreign exchange is concerned our position is a very difficult one and we cannot afford any payment. We should therefore inform Hammarskjold about our difficulty in regard to principles as also the practical difficulty of our paying anything in near future.

---

1. New Delhi, 5 January 1957. V.K. Krishna Menon Papers, NMML.
2. Krishna Menon reported that the UN Secretary General Hammarskjold had written to the Permanent Missions in New York on the subject of the cost of the Suez Canal clearance. He asked for 10 million dollars and requested member governments to make available "loans" to this amount. He added that the total cost of clearance would be about 30 million dollars.
3. Krishna Menon said that Hammarskjold was thinking of proposing to the General Assembly that repayment to governments who contributed to the cost of clearance should be from the proceeds of a surcharge on canal tolls. He thought that the effect of the toll surcharge would be that the cost of clearance would be paid by the consumers including those countries who were not parties to the aggression, while such countries which either did not use the canal or used it to a very limited extent would be exempted. Pointing out that Egypt did not agree to make good the damages caused by aggression against her, Krishna Menon added: "Since Egyptian ships and a great part of their trade go through the canal, surcharge proposal would also mean their sharing in clearance cost...."

8. Cable to V.K. Krishna Menon[1]

Your telegram No. 99 27th January.[2] We agree that it is desirable for us to take us positive and constructive attitude and with your general approach to this question. But as you say, we should not adopt any line without consent of Egypt. It would be preferable to have simple resolution without details.

You must have seen Ali Yavar's telegram No. 57 26th January. UN papers referred to by you in your telegram No. 101 of 27th January not yet received by UN Information Centre.

1. New Delhi, 28 January 1957. V.K. Krishna Menon Papers, NMML.
2. Krishna Menon wrote that American officials had shown him a rather detailed draft resolution for the General Assembly which "in many respects represents our views and our impact", though he disapproved some of its clauses. He added: "The resolution need only demand immediate withdrawal and full compliance by all parties with the terms of the Armistice Agreement. . . . It should be restated that there should be no question of UNEF occupying either Gaza or any other place under Egyptian sovereignty or administrative authority."

IV. HUNGARY

1. To Josip Broz Tito[1]

New Delhi,
2 December 1956

My dear President,

Thank you for your letter of 28th November[2] which I received this afternoon through your Ambassador.[3] Like you, I am very unhappy at developments in Hungary as well as in the Middle Eastern region.

In some ways there have been indications of improvement in Egyptian situation and I believe that the British Government feel now that they cannot ignore world opinion and are prepared to withdraw their troops soon. All they want now appears to be to avoid humiliation.

But situation in other Arab countries has gravely deteriorated and several of them are intriguing against each other. Indeed there appears to be a process of disintegration going on there. This is dangerous from the point of view of both the Egyptian situation and world peace.

The Hungarian situation has also had a very bad effect on the position in Egypt. All the strong feeling against Anglo-French aggression is now being turned against Soviet Union.

We have tried our utmost both in Budapest and Moscow to induce Governments there to permit UN Secretary General Hammarskjold to visit Budapest as well as, later, UN observers.[4] In spite of every effort of ours, this has been refused again. This will have very bad reactions in United Nations where strong resolution is likely to be passed by great majority against Soviet Union. Possibly credentials

---

1. JN Collection.
2. For a summary of Tito's letter, see *Selected Works* (second series), Vol. 35, p. 478, fn. 3 and p. 479, fn. 6.
3. Boglan Crnobrnja.
4. For Nehru's messages of 22 November 1956 to N.A. Bulganin and the Hungarian Prime Minister, Janos Kadar, see *Selected Works* (second series), Vol. 35, pp. 474-477.

of Hungarian Foreign Minister[5] who is in New York might be withdrawn. This will add greatly to seriousness of situation and make it calamitous. I deeply regret that Soviet Union should take up a position which appears to be patently wrong and could have only bad consequences.

In regard to Nagy's arrest and deportation,[6] I quite agree with you that that was utterly wrong and a breach of international conventions.[7] We shall say this when occasion arises.[8]

While expressing our views in the United Nations, we have endeavoured not to say or do anything which may add to the difficulties and tensions of the world. Our primary object has been not to condemn but to help in finding a way out of this dreadful situation. I must confess that I am greatly disappointed, but we shall continue our efforts for peace, whatever happens.

With sincere regards,

Yours sincerely,
Jawaharlal Nehru

5. Imre Horvath.
6. Imre Nagy, Prime Minister of Hungary at the time of the popular uprising in October 1956, sought refuge in the Yugoslav Embassy on 4 November 1956 following the entry of Soviet tanks into Budapest. He left the Embassy on 22 November after Kadar had given written and verbal assurances to the Yugoslav Government for Nagy's safe conduct to his home. Despite this promise, Nagy was abducted by Soviet troops shortly after leaving the Embassy and deported to Romania.
7. Tito described the deportation of Imre Nagy and his group to Romania as "most deplorable".
8. See *ante*, pp. 435-436.

2. Cable to V.K. Krishna Menon[1]

Your telegram No. 494 dated 30th November.[2] We have also had long report from Khosla[3] after repeated talks with Kadar.[4] Newspapers announce refusal by Hungarian Government to permit Hammarskjold or UN observers to go to Budapest. I quite agree with you that this is disastrous from every point of view. We have tried our utmost in persuading, entreating and bringing pressure on parties concerned without result. So far as Hungarian Government is concerned, my impression is that they would have agreed. It is really a Soviet veto and the Hungarian Government has no independent existence.

2. After their public refusal there is no point in my approaching Russian Government again. We just have to face the consequences.

3. I have received a message from Tito. He feels strongly, as I do, about Nagy's arrest and deportation by Soviet authorities after written agreement and assurance(s) by Hungarian Government. The Russian Government have little reputation left after all these incidents, and the Hungarian Government stands totally discredited. Russian Government having taken one wrong step continue to take more wrong steps. I have no doubt that this is harmful to them and to the cause of world peace. As you say, it is powerfully by affecting Egyptian situation. It is clear to me that if question of their refusal to admit Hammarskjold or UN observers comes up before General Assembly also question of Nagy's arrest and deportation we have to express our regret and disapproval of both. About Nagy we should support Yugoslav's protest.[5] We should do all this politely if

---

1. New Delhi, 2 December 1956. V.K. Krishna Menon Papers, NMML.
2. Krishna Menon said it was important to let the Russians know that India had no desire to gang up with the West or just blame them. "But we feel that the consequences of a total refusal by the Russians to anything about Hungary is calamitous and will come in the way of things," stated Krishna Menon. He said that "further efforts" should be made to get the Soviet Union to agree "at least in principle" to let Hammarskjold visit Budapest.
3. Jagan Nath Khosla, Minister in Prague, was at this time in Budapest as Nehru's personal representative.
4. Janos Kadar, appointed Prime Minister of Hungary on 4 November 1956.
5. Nehru received a cable from the Indian Embassy in Belgrade on 3 December which stated that the "general approach" of the Yugoslav Government on the deportation of Imre Nagy was to seek a settlement through diplomatic channels. The Yugoslav officials said that as their government had received no reply from Moscow to the publication of the correspondence between the two countries on Nagy's future, they would be "compelled to speak out in the UN."

possibly but firmly. We cannot be parties to acquiescing in something that is patently wrong and which will lead to further wrongs.

4. I had long discussions with Chou En-lai about various matters including Hungary. While there was broad agreement about other matters we agreed to differ about Hungary. Chou En-lai admitted that Hungarian position was difficult and complicated but to the extent of his knowledge he supported Soviet's view point. Ultimately he said somewhat reluctantly that it might be desirable for Hammarskjoeld to go there and promised to ask his Representative in Budapest[6] to enquire.

5. In Arab countries in Western Asia there appears to be complete confusion and gradual disintegration. Indeed this process of disintegration applies to other parts also.

6. Recent reports about proposed deportation of large numbers of persons has been denied by Egyptian Government. But reports from our Embassy does not support this denial. I fear Egyptian Government is also drifting in wrong direction.

7. Pillai sent you telegram 24045 today. It appears that Selwyn Lloyd's report to his Government after returning from New York has rather shaken them and convinced them that they must climb down. Whether they will do so or not after new developments in Hungary is another matter. In any event, while we stick to our principles, we need not use strong language.

8. This applies to other matters also. We cannot put ourselves in the wrong and do something which is against our own convictions. But we should try to avoid giving needless offence or aggravating a situation that is bad enough.

6. Ho Te'Ching.

3. Cable to V.K. Krishna Menon[1]

Your telegram 505 December 1st[2] just received. We have considered the matter as carefully as we can in short time. Draft resolution[3] certainly contains certain assertions which we do not approve. To move numerous petty amendments appears undesirable. To abstain throughout also appears undesirable and likely to give wrong impression of our general attitude. In view of all that has happened this will be difficult to explain either to our own public or to others.

We feel that you should make clear statement to begin with drawing special attention to (1) our objection to use of phrase "Hungarian authorities" instead of "Hungarian Government".[4] (2) Reference to deportations of Hungarians as if it was continuing process when it is categorically denied and no impartial enquiry has taken place adding however that in view of refusal Soviet and Hungarian Governments to facilitate such enquiry inference is against their contention. There is also admitted case of deportation of Nagy and undoubtedly there are some others also. (3) Despatch of observers to Hungary cannot take place without agreement of Hungarian Government despatch to other countries cannot be helpful at all and may merely add to confusion. (4) Date December 7 is also undesirable as this may well lead to creating further difficult situation.

---

1. New Delhi, 3 December 1956. V.K. Krishna Menon Papers, NMML.
2. Krishna Menon sought instructions from Nehru on India's vote on a draft resolution on Hungary placed before the UN General Assembly on 2 December 1956 by 14 nations, including the USA. Menon felt that "detailed instructions were required in view of the previous history and misrepresentation that would be made of anything that is said." He warned: "Either one remains uncommitted or gets drawn into one power bloc or the other."
3. The 14-nation draft resolution, (1) called upon the Soviet Union and the "Hungarian authorities" to comply with all the previous resolutions on Hungary and to permit UN observers to enter Hungary; (2) requested the Soviet Union and Hungary to agree, not later than 7 December, to the visit of the observers; (3) recommended that in the meantime the Secretary General arrange for the immediate dispatch of observers to countries bordering Hungary.
4. Krishna Menon wrote that paragraphs 2 and 3 of the preamble of the resolution referred to the Hungarian "authorities" instead of Government since the sponsoring countries objected to the word "Government".

Regarding withdrawal Soviet troops we cannot refer to any "solemn assurances" given by Bulganin to K.P.S. Menon.[5] But we may generally refer to Soviet Government's statement that they will withdraw their troops[6] and express our hope that this will be done speedily. In this context it is not desirable to refer to Western withdrawals.[7]

Having made our position clear we should abstain from voting on preamble as well as on operative paras 2, 3 and 4 of resolution.

We should vote for operative para 1 of resolution even though we make clear that we do not agree with parts of it more especially date.

Finally on whole resolution we should abstain.

Thus we make clear statement explaining our position. Then we abstain on separate parts of resolution except operative para 1 for which we vote. We abstain on whole resolution at the end.[8]

We should certainly not remain silent and we should express ourselves fully and critically about attitude taken up by Soviet Union.[9] Of course you must yourself deal with this matter.

I shall refer to this resolution briefly on above lines in debate in Parliament today.[10]

5. Krishna Menon asked whether India should state in the UN General Assembly that Bulganin had given "solemn assurances" to K.P. S. Menon, India's Ambassador in Moscow, that no deportations had taken place in Hungary.
6. The Soviet Union issued a statement on 30 October agreeing to discuss with the other countries which were party to the Warsaw Treaty for the withdrawal of Soviet forces. The statement also said that it would withdraw its troops from Budapest as soon as the Hungarian Government recognized that it was necessary to do so.
7. Krishna Menon wrote: "Our position on withdrawal is difficult because we cannot argue in the UN that withdrawal must or may be conditional on Western withdrawals from their foreign bases and yet, as you have said in Parliament, that is the context in which this problem exists." For Nehru's statement in Parliament, see *Selected Works* (second series), Vol. 35, p. 358.
8. The resolution was passed by 54 votes to 10 by the UN General Assembly on 4 December. India and 13 other countries abstained.
9. Krishna Menon thought "that this is an occasion when, independent of the resolution, we should express ourselves fully and critically about the Soviet Union. Kindly say whether you would prefer some other member of the Delegation to speak or handle this matter. I have no objections."
10. See *ante*, pp. 436-438.

4. Cable to V.K. Krishna Menon[1]

Khosla informs us reliably that our suggestions to Hungarian Government about invitation to Hammarskjold were acceptable to them but were not acceptable to Russia.[2]

1. New Delhi, 4 December 1956. V.K. Krishna Menon Papers, NMML.
2. J.N. Khosla cabled to Nehru that the "Hungarian Government in written reply expresses inability to alter position regarding observers." As regards the UN Secretary General, Khosla stated, they "persist that their representative negotiates with him in Rome or New York without delay" and that they would welcome him in Budapest at a "later date convenient for both parties." However, Khosla added, it was "reliably learnt" that Nehru's suggestions regarding the visit to Hungary by Hammarskjold and UN observers were acceptable to the Hungarian Government but not to Moscow.

5. Cable to V.K. Krishna Menon[1]

I have received message from Bulganin about Hungary.[2] This is being separately repeated to you. There is nothing new in it.

2. I am much disturbed at report that Hungarian Government have gone back on its invitation to Hammarskjold[3] or at any rate wants to delay it. Please let me know your appreciation of this new development.

3. It appears clear to me that apart from legal quibbling Soviet authorities do not want people connected with UN to go to Budapest for fear of major demonstrations against present Hungarian Government.[4] As a matter of fact these demonstrations appear to be continuing though peacefully and rather in the form of passive resistance.

4. Yesterday I sent a long message[5] to President Nasser appealing to him to show consideration in treatment of British and other nationals in Egypt.

1. New Delhi, 6 December 1956. V.K. Krishna Menon Papers, NMML.
2. In reply to Nehru's message of 22 November [*Selected Works* (second series), Vol. 35, pp. 474-476], Bulganin wrote on 4 December that in the existing conditions, "the Hungarian people need tranquility above all" in order to bring about normalization of every aspect of economic and political life of Hungary. He added that his government agreed that the arrival of UN Observers in Hungary would violate its sovereignty and contradict the principles of the UN Charter.
3. Krishna Menon replied on 6 December that it was not correct that the Hungarian Government had "gone back" since no official communication had come from Hungary. After discussions with Imre Horvath, Hammarskjold had informed the General Assembly on 4 December that it had been agreed that he would arrive in Budapest on 16 December for a three-day visit. On 5 December, however, Budapest Radio announced that the date mentioned was "not suitable".
4. Krishna Menon stated that in the general debate on 6 December, he "spoke firmly about the duties of (the) Soviet Union irrespective of all legalities." He added that "apart from downright condemnation and vituperation against the Russians I have said everything critical that can possibly be said."
5. See *ante*, pp. 545-546.

6. K.P.S. Menon's Presence in Budapest[1]

I am surprised to see in the evening paper that K.P.S. Menon[2] and Khosla have both left Budapest, one for Moscow and the other for Prague. I think it is of great importance that K.P.S. Menon should be in Budapest now and in the near future. All kinds of developments are going to take place there. If, unfortunately, he has gone back to Moscow, he will have to return to Budapest almost immediately.

1. Note to the Secretary General, MEA, and Foreign Secretary, 7 December 1956. File No. 5(5)-Eur E/56, MEA.
2. K.P.S. Menon, India's Ambassador to the USSR, was also accredited to Hungary.

7. Cable to V.K. Krishna Menon[1]

Your telegram No. 529 of December 7.[2] You should vote against repeat against any resolution asking for expulsion of the Hungarian Delegation. Such action would be most extraordinary, if not highly irregular. We cannot understand how a delegation can be expelled so long as it has credentials from its government which have already been accepted by the General Assembly. Even if it is admitted that the Hungarian Delegation gave certain assurances to the Secretary General which later could not be implemented we have to remember that the Hungarian Government are free to revise their decision, if not to overrule their Delegation. There is also no evidence that the Delegation deliberately gave misleading assurances to the Secretary General. If the question is one of expelling Hungary from the United Nations it must be resisted by all means since apart from constitutional or legal aspects this would create a most dangerous precedent.

2. There is no question of a shift in our policy.[3] You should explain our position saying that we consider it most unfortunate that the Hungarian Government should not yet have agreed to admit the Secretary General of UN to their territory and complied with the resolution of the UN on this point. You should express disapproval of the Hungarian refusal or delay and then explain on the grounds mentioned in the preceding paragraph why you have to oppose the resolution. You should add that the General Assembly should not take any step which would worsen the present position, intensify cold war and rule out all avenues of peaceful approach to the solution of this difficult problem.[4]

1. New Delhi, 8 December 1956. V.K. Krishna Menon Papers, NMML.
2. The US had proposed informally on 7 December a resolution calling for the suspension of Hungary's delegation to the UN General Assembly. Krishna Menon sought instructions from New Delhi on this.
3. Arguing that abstention would be "both undignified and undesirable", Krishna Menon stated: "Vote for (the resolution) would be represented as a shift in or reversal of our 'neutralist' policy and also as the result of reproach by the Government of position I have taken, which is spoken of as 'misrepresentation' of Nehru."
4. Krishna Menon informed Nehru on 9 December that the idea of expulsion or refusal of credentials of the Hungarian delegation had been kept in suspense as it "encountered opposition in an appreciable body of the Assembly and a resolution would have had adverse votes and not merely abstentions from many countries which hitherto have only abstained."

564

8. Cable to V.K. Krishna Menon[1]

You must have received copy of K.P.S. Menon's telegram from Prague about events in Hungary.[2] We are asking him to go to Moscow and see Soviet leaders and then return to Budapest where he should remain for some time. Khosla returning to Budapest immediately.

2. From all the reports that we have received about Hungary, it is clear that national revolution took place there widely supported by almost all classes including especially workers. To say that some reactionaries brought about this revolution, is patently wrong though, no doubt, they took part in it. It is further clear that, in spite of terrible losses of Hungarians in human lives and property, they have not been cowed down and are continuing to resist, though on the whole peacefully. This may however lead at any moment to violent conflict resulting in heavy killing.

3. Soviet account of events in Hungary and their justification for their action cannot be accepted by us, even though we understand fear motive behind them, and apprehension that Hungary might become hostile country as it is, Soviet action has made Hungarians more hostile than ever to Russians, and there is no likelihood of their changing this attitude because of repression and armed pressure. Even though they submit for a while this will be sullen submission on surface only with inner fires burning, and likely to break out from time to time. There can be no progress towards solution in Hungary now unless Soviet reverse their policy and gradually withdraw their troops and their imposed rule. No one can consider Kadar's Government as free to frame its policies and in any case, it has not got Hungarian people behind it.[3]

1. New Delhi, 9 December 1956. V.K. Krishna Menon Papers, NMML.
2. K.P.S. Menon wrote to Foreign Secretary S. Dutt on 8 December: "Soviet intervention specially in second stage was ruthless. Parts of Budapest city looked like areas ravaged by war. Government have admitted that 40,000 tenements were destroyed. Estimates of casualties vary considerably. We reckon that 25,000 Hungarians and 7,000 Russians were killed. Nevertheless spirit of people has not been crushed." He added: "Consider it important that I should communicate my own observations to Soviet Government and if possible open their eyes to realities. Trust Prime Minister approves."
3. K.P.S. Menon wrote: "I met Prime Minister Kadar for one and half hours. . . . He trotted out familiar reasons such as existence of fascist elements, absolute need for restoring law and order, etc. Kadar does not realize that [the] presence of Soviet troops is [a] constant irritant and that continued arrests may lead again to [an] explosive situation. Doubt whether Kadar is [a] free agent."

4. Soviet argument apparently is that they might permit some kind of national communism as in Yugoslavia or Poland, but they will repress ruthlessly any attempt to go beyond this. This may be understood from Soviet point of view, but we cannot support argument. In effect it is intervention and imposed rule supported by armed forces from abroad. This is certainly contrary to Panchsheel.

5. From practical point of view, we have to consider always that nothing should be done which leads to war, and therefore even a right action should be deferred to more appropriate time, if result of it is immediately bad. This consideration has rightly governed our attitude. But difficulty arises when we appear to be opposing right action and thus comprising our principles and, at the same time, not succeeding in averting the greater evil which we wish to avoid.

6. We have tried our utmost to influence Soviet and Hungarian Governments to permit Hammarskjold to visit Budapest. We have failed thus far. We should certainly go on trying but it appears it is almost too late now for that to make much difference. No one can justify Soviet obstruction in this matter.

7. Further Nagy's arrest and deportation was completely unjustifiable.

8. As I understand it the policy Soviet is pursuing will not lead to any improvement of situation even from the practical point of view of avoiding conflict. They have got themselves entangled and there is no way out except for them to be courageous enough to reverse this policy. They are unlikely to do so at present at least.

9. We shall have to face this dangerous and developing situation from day-to-day and it is important that we do not allow ourselves to get entangled in a way which leads people to think that we have given up our basic principles. While we do not wish to condemn and make situation more difficult for us and others, we cannot remain silent when silence itself becomes acquiescence in patent wrong. We have always said that our policy is independent and we judge each situation from the point of view of our general principles. We have to follow that policy.

10. I am quite clear in my mind that withdrawal of recognition from Hungarian Representative in UN would be completely wrong and we should oppose this. But if question of expressing opinion on Soviet action arises we have to disapprove of it or even condemn it subject to suitable language being used.

11. I do not know how matters will shape themselves in course of the next few days. But I thought I should let you know how my mind is working. Naturally we are continuously giving a great deal of thought to these matters as they are of vital importance both for us and for the world. I am very much concerned with maintaining peace of the world but I am equally concerned with our acting rightly and in conformity with the principles we have proclaimed.

9. Cable to Arthur S. Lall[1]

Reference our telephonic talk yesterday, Prime Minister agrees that while it is right for our Representative in New York to suggest to the Hungarian and the Soviet Delegates that Hungary should agree to receive the Secretary General on a specified date, it would not be desirable for him to send a special message to Bulganin on this subject. He received a long reply from Bulganin[2] on the subject on Hungary only a few days ago. To put the same suggestion again with specific date, etc., to the Soviet Government so soon after this negative reply would be embarrassing both to the Prime Minister and to Bulganin.

1. New Delhi, 9 December 1956. The cable was sent by Subimal Dutt, Foreign Secretary to Arthur Lall, member of the Indian delegation to the UN General Assembly. *Notes, Memoranda and Decisions of Jawaharlal Nehru (September 1946-May 1961), The Hungarian Crisis, 1956.* File Nos. 59/3/NGO/56-Vols. I & II, 59/5/NGO/57 and 59/7/NGO/57, MEA.
2. See *ante*, p. 562.

10. Cable to V.K. Krishna Menon[1]

We have received this morning American draft resolution[2] on Hungary and are awaiting your comments on it.

2. It is clear that some countries are trying to push USSR relentlessly. At the same time it is equally clear that USSR is in the wrong in regard to its activities in Hungary and is thus giving opportunities to other countries to put it more in the wrong. To say that Hungarians and their Government should be given time to settle down is not helpful considering that Hungarians and their present Government are in conflict and large majorities of Hungarians refuse to accept present conditions. In effect it means that time should be given for people of Hungary to be suppressed.

3. The only real and abiding solution of wider problem is for all foreign forces to be withdrawn from various countries of Europe and specially of Central Europe. But to make this condition precedent to withdrawal of Soviet forces from Hungary does not appear to me legitimate in existing circumstances when there is acute crisis in Hungary and demand for immediate withdrawal of Soviet forces is made by people there supported by constant demonstrations and call for general strike.

4. American draft resolution is provocative in some phrases and we would have preferred it otherwise. References in operative clause 2 to violation of Charter and clause 4 to withdrawal under United Nations observation are certainly objectionable.

5. Apart from this however substance of operative clauses generally flows from broad attitude we have taken up asking for withdrawal of Soviet forces and allowing Hungarian people to determine their own future.

---

1. New Delhi, 10 December 1956. V.K. Krishna Menon Papers, NMML.
2. The US and fifteen other countries introduced in the General Assembly on 9 December a draft resolution condemning "the violation of the (UN) Charter by the USSR in depriving Hungary of its liberty and independence." The resolution also called for the withdrawal of Soviet armed forces from Hungary under UN supervision and the restoration of an independent Hungarian state. Four more countries subsequently joined in sponsoring the resolution which came to be known as the Twenty-Power Resolution.

6. On receipt of your message about this on the resolution we shall telephone to Arthur Lall.[3]

3. On 10 December, Foreign Secretary S. Dutt sent Arthur Lall a cable in which he stated: "Our delegation should make our position clear, namely, that our acceptance of the preamble would not mean our agreement with the substance of the resolutions which we either opposed or on which we abstained in the past. We are also not willing to commit ourselves to the view that the Soviet action amounts to a violation of the UN Charter. In any case we are opposed to UN observation of the withdrawal of the Soviet forces. After having made our position clear, the resolution should be supported. Prime Minister... approves of this message and wants this to be conveyed to Krishna Menon immediately."

11. Cable to V.K. Krishna Menon[1]

Your telegram No. 536[2] of December 9th came this afternoon. We have considered it very carefully with our colleagues. As you know we feel strongly that Soviet policy in using their armed forces in suppressing Hungarian people is wrong and is likely to entangle them still further. They have not even accepted our earnest request to allow Secretary General and UN Observers to go to Hungary. Exponents will realise that American resolution may lead to grave consequences such as declaration of Soviets as aggressor country, sanctions and possibly War. We are thus placed in a very difficult position. Popular feeling here is strongly in favour of Hungarian people and condemns Soviet action.

2. We are against your suggestion of making statement and then declining to participate in voting or otherwise. We are also opposed to your voting against this resolution.

1. New Delhi, 10 December 1956. V.K. Krishna Menon Papers, NMML.
2. Krishna Menon sought guidance on the Twenty-Power resolution initiated by the US. He stated: "The purpose of this resolution is to draw everyone on one side or the other in the cold war by putting them in the position that you are for or against the Hungarian people..." He also said: "It is quite obvious that a Yes vote for the resolution as it stands is impossible with any sense of responsibility."

3. We should have liked to know what is the attitude of the Asian-African Group. We do not wish to be isolated in this matter from them.

4. We suggest that the following attitude should be adopted. You should make statement at an early stage saying that you deplore the attitude of Hungarian and Soviet Governments in not (not) allowing Secretary General and UN Observers in accordance with Assembly resolutions and our own earnest request. You are also of the opinion that Hungarian problem cannot be solved unless foreign troops are withdrawn and people left to decide their own future without intervention. This was also stated by Colombo Powers.

5. We are anxious to bring about this result and help the Hungarian people but resolution as drafted is likely to produce contrary results and come in the way of any peaceful settlement favourable to Hungarian people's wishes. It may well lead to accentuation of cold war at the expense of Hungarian people and even to major war. We have above all to avoid any such disastrous development. Therefore while there are parts of the resolution with which you are in complete agreement, there are other parts which are wrongly conceived and whose consequences are unpredictable and likely to be dangerous.

6. You may move some amendments which presumably will be defeated.[3] Finally if resolution remains as it is, you should abstain from voting.[4]

---

3. On 10 December, India, Indonesia and Sri Lanka jointly submitted three amendments providing for substantial changes in the operative paragraphs of the Twenty-Power resolution. One of the amendments provided for replacement of the sixth preambular para by a provision: "Noting the overwhelming demand of the Hungarian people for the cessation of intervention of foreign armed forces and the withdrawal of foreign troops." The sixth preambular para read: "Considering that recent events have clearly demonstrated the will of the Hungarian people to recover their liberty and independence." However, the General Assembly only agreed to include the suggested provision as an additional preambular para.

4. On 12 December, the General Assembly adopted the Twenty-Power resolution by 55 votes to eight, with 13 abstentions. India abstained along with twelve other countries, viz., Afghanistan, Cambodia, Egypt, Finland, Indonesia, Jordan, Morocco, Saudi Arabia, Sudan, Syria, Yemen and Yugoslavia. Iran, Iraq, Lebanon, Laos, Liberia, Myanmar, Nepal, Pakistan, Sri Lanka, Thailand and Tunisia, voted for the resolution.

12. Events in Hungary[1]

Jawaharlal Nehru: Mr Chairman,[2] I understand that an honourable Member, Dr H.N. Kunzru, made some reference yesterday to the reports which we are said to have received from our Ambassador in Hungary. We have not as a matter of fact received his or Mr Khosla's full report yet. It is coming by bag, so we have been informed. But we have naturally received a number of telegrams almost daily from Mr K.P.S. Menon and previously from Mr Khosla. It is rather contrary to normal practice for me to place before the House these confidential telegrams that we have received which include the results of talks with the people in authority in Hungary and others. It would be not only contrary to practice but likely to prove embarrassing to those people who talked to them. I regret I cannot do that. But, broadly speaking, what our Ambassadors have reported to us has really been stated publicly on various occasions, and there is no doubt that the revolution in Hungary was what is called a national one, a widespread one. There were, they said, elements in it which might be called counter-revolutionary or reactionary. There were elements in it which came from outside too. But those formed a small part of this essentially because it was a national movement in which the great majority of the workers, industrial workers, and students took part in the city of Budapest and elsewhere. That is the basic fact. Then many things happened.

This phase of the revolution in Hungary started on the 23rd October, and on the 30th there was conflict soon after in which the Hungarian Army also partly participated. And then, the House may remember that on the 30th of October the Soviet Government issued a statement about their general policy not only in Hungary but in those States of Eastern Europe, and they referred to the Warsaw Treaty under which they kept their forces there, and they said that they would withdraw them from Budapest immediately and, as for the rest, after consultation with the Warsaw Powers. Now, it does appear to us and to our Ambassador that that was the position then, and in fact the Soviet Government did withdraw their troops outside Budapest. After that other events happened in Budapest and there was a good deal of fighting internally. Just about that time, within a day or two, events took place in Egypt which brought a new factor possibly into

1. Statement in the Rajya Sabha, 13 December 1956. *Rajya Sabha Debates*, Vol. XV, cols. 2353-2361.
2. Sarvepalli Radhakrishnan.

consideration. Now, after that initial withdrawal from Budapest there was a return of the Soviet forces, and a return in large numbers. And then took place the other aspect of this great tragedy in Budapest. There are various estimates of the people who were killed in these shootings. It is difficult to have any accurate estimate. But from such information as we have received, it would appear that about 25,000 Hungarians and about 7,000 Russians died in this fighting. The Russians were presumably largely men of the forces. Maybe some others too. Since then, there has been no big scale fighting. There have been occasional incidents involving some petty shootings and maybe, some one or two or three people were killed. But there has been no major fighting. But there has been a considerable measure of passive resistance, workers not going back to work. Then many of them or a good number of them went back to work, but worked only to a small extent. And it may be of interest to hon. Members here to know that our Ambassador told us that the atmosphere he found in Budapest at this time was reminiscent of the Civil Disobedience days in India.[3] I do not know whether I am right in this matter or not, but a word has come into use in Hungary, especially in Budapest, in connection with the suspension of work, etc.—the word is 'kartal'. Whether it is derived from 'hartal', I do not know. Maybe.

Now, our special instructions to our Ambassadors, Mr Khosla and Mr Menon, at that time were that they should speak to the Hungarian Government about the visit of the Secretary General of the United Nations and the observers of the United Nations. They reported about past events. But when events are taking place from day to day, it is more important to know what step to take than to go into the past history except to understand the situation. They had long talks with the present Prime Minister of Hungary, Mr Kadar, and with others,[4] and presented our viewpoint with such argument and force as they could. Mr Kadar informed them that they had no objection to the visit of the Secretary General of the United Nations, but that that should take place later, with no time fixed. But they took strong exception to the United Nations observers coming there, as they considered it an infringement of their sovereignty. I am mentioning this

3. In his report of 8 December on events in Hungary K.P.S. Menon stated: "Almost daily there are processions and demonstrations occasionally leading to clashes with police and army. Atmosphere in Budapest reminiscent of our civil disobedience days. Only Hungarians have to face tanks and not lathis."
4. K.P.S. Menon wrote: "In Budapest met Prime Minister and Foreign Minister and representatives of various political organizations such as Revolutionary Workers' Central Council, Association of Intellectuals, Writers' Union, Revolutionary Students Union, etc. Also had talks with Soviet, Chinese, British, French and Yugoslav ministers. Khosla met even [a] larger circle."

past history also. Other things have happened in the United Nations, as the House knows.

Now, in the course of these developments, our great anxiety and the anxiety of many people has been that they should not be allowed to drift towards a war situation. Naturally, this House and all of us have the greatest sympathy for the people of Hungary and have witnessed the gravest tragedies that have been enacted there. But we have also kept in mind that this tragedy might be infinitely greater if war comes not only elsewhere, but in Hungary itself. Therefore, our approach has been to prevent this happening in so far as a country like ours has any weight in the councils of the world. It is with this object in view that the recent activities of our delegation in the United Nations have taken place.

Honourable Members may have seen the resolution[5] that was moved on behalf of India and some other countries and the amendment[6] moved also on our behalf there to the other resolution sponsored by some countries. The major changes were not in regard to any judgement of the situation in Hungary, but rather as to whether the approach should be as we thought it should be—a constructive one somehow to get over these difficulties and bring about the result, the result being not only an avoidance of war and the establishment of peace and more or less normal conditions, but the withdrawal of foreign forces from Hungary. We thought that that constructive approach was more important than merely a negative approach which might lead to more dangerous consequences. That is the main difference between these two Resolutions—the one put forward by a number of countries—twenty, I think—and the other put forward by India, and, I think, three other countries. Well, that is over now.

The latest news is that the resolution put forward by the twenty countries—the United States and others—was passed with one amendment. I think one of our amendments was adopted in it. Otherwise, it was passed and thereupon, our representative did not press our resolution. He might have pressed it separately. But since that had been passed, he did not think it worth while pressing the other resolution.

5. A draft resolution submitted in the General Assembly on 10 December by India, Indonesia, Myanmar and Sri Lanka "deplored" Soviet refusals to withdraw troops from Hungary and noted that the suppression of the revolt had brought "violence and bloodshed" in Hungary. Calling for the "cessation of the existing foreign intervention" in Hungary, the resolution urged that Hammarskjold should travel to Moscow "without delay" to discuss a solution of the Hungarian crisis with the Soviet Government.
6. See *ante*, p. 570.

Now, I find that the hon. Dr Kunzru quoted some sentences from the speech of the Leader of our delegation in the United Nations and wanted to know whether he was expressing the opinion of the Government of India in this matter. I shall read out a part of his speech as reported in the press —we have not got it separately.

> My Government does not want, in the present context of existing circumstances in the world – although it does not conform to its own policies— to go into the question of withdrawal of foreign forces in the sense of forces which are tied to defence alliances in this context.

May I explain this? In our opinion, the way to bring about real stability and peace in Europe and in the world and to put an end to the tensions and the armaments race, in fact, to endeavour to solve these very grave problems, is for the withdrawal of all foreign forces from every country – certainly in Europe; at the moment, I am dealing with that. I think the major problems of Europe such as the very important problem of Germany which is the heart of Central Europe would be much nearer solution if this element of foreign forces on both sides was removed. It is our opinion and we hold by it. Nevertheless, we did feel that for us to press that opinion at this juncture in Hungary, when there was a deep crisis there would not be legitimate in this context. I hope it will be considered that that is what Mr Menon has said—that was removed. It is our opinion and we hold by it. Nevertheless we did feel that for us to press that opinion at this juncture in Hungary, when there was a deep crisis there would not, although we want that, we are not pressing that general proposition at this stage, but are rather pressing Government does not want, in the present context of existing circumstances in the world the existence of foreign troops in any country is inimical to its freedom, is a danger to world peace and cooperation. But in the particular circumstances that obtain there are different alliances ranged one against another." There is NATO, there is the Warsaw Pact, there is the Baghdad Pact and SEATO and so many others.

That is why he says:

> "....—although it does not conform to its own policies – to go into the question of withdrawal of foreign forces in the sense of forces which are tied to defence alliances in this context. We believe here are different alliances ranged one against another, policy of power balance which is rapidly pushing this world into a state of war. We are, therefore judging the situation in the limited context of the use of Soviet forces in regard to internal affairs in Hungary. The only justification, if there was one, would have been for the Soviet forces to have been called to the aid of civil power in conditions where there was an attempt at a coup d'etat.

574

My Government is convinced that the original revolt against the Hungarian regime that existed was a movement of national liberation, by which is meant not national liberation as a colonial country but movement to overthrow or rather to bring about the kind of changes that are taking place in Eastern Europe."

Now, as the House will notice, the burden of the argument is that first of all with these defence alliances, etc., which have prompted foreign troops to be placed in foreign countries, we disagree but we are not going into them—alliances under which one country helps another with troops. According to these alliances, it may be justified in a strictly legal way when that alliance permits troops to be there and permits them to be utilized if there is a coup d'etat. That is the legal argument. What is a coup d'etat? It is not a national uprising of somebody trying to seize power rather against the nation's wishes. Mr Menon has pointed out that even if one agrees with this, it does not apply to Hungary, because this was a national rising. This is the burden of the argument, a perfectly legitimate argument and an argument which strengthens the main contention that the Soviet forces should be withdrawn from there. The Soviet intervention was not a case of their intervening according to their treaty obligations, because there was no coup d'etat but there was a national rising. That is the whole burden of the argument. Perhaps the hon. Member thought that some kind of high principles were being laid down about intervention. This question only arises when under some alliance foreign troops are present and there is a coup d' etat. Then, the question arises what the legal implications are under the treaty. But our position and Mr Menon's position is that they should not be there at all, foreign troops should not be there at all. There is a difference and you ought to consider this question, apart from the facts, from the legal point of view of what the alliance permits and from the practical point of view of facts.

H.N. Kunzru (Uttar Pradesh): May I put a question? Would the Prime Minister mind being interrupted? Would any of the countries that are members of the NATO be justified in a case of serious civil disturbance in asking for the aid of another foreign power which was a member of the NATO?

JN: So far as I am concerned, that would not at all be justified. That is my whole argument, that the Soviet troops functioning there was not justified. The whole argument was that, even if by some strict interpretation in a coup d' etat some people may say it is justified, it is not so. It was really strengthening the whole argument. In fact when foreign forces are placed in a country, you put them and that country in a very difficult and embarrassing position. What are they there for? All kinds of difficulties have arisen, not of this type, but in every country difficulties with the local population and all that. The whole thing is unnatural and should not be encouraged.

I would suggest to the honourable Member and other honourable Members to read the full speech of Mr Krishna Menon. It does not appear in all the papers fully. We have not yet received it fully. It has appeared in one newspaper rather fully. It is a very powerful plea in this matter with which we wish to associate ourselves fully.

HNK: May I ask for information on one point? The leader of the Indian delegation stated in the course of his speech that the information received here—I quote now—"led India to believe that the one factor which was preventing the unity of various Hungarian elements was the presence of foreign troops." Another statement made by him is: "The amount of damage to Budapest, India was informed, was in the scale of what would take place in wartime." Is this correct?

JN: The honourable Member is trying to draw me out about the reports of our Ambassador.

HNK: Our representative has said it openly.

JN: It is true that our Ambassador reported to us that the damage in Budapest was heart-rending and it was in the scale of what occurs in wartime.[7] That is true. As far as the other statement is concerned, I do not precisely remember what our Ambassador said, but the whole point is this: Our position—and I believe that hon. Member's position—is that so long as foreign troops remain there, it is difficult for the local people to come together and function properly. That is quite correct.

7. See *ante*, p. 565.

13. Cable to Vijayalakshmi Pandit[1]

Your telegrams 3708 December 19th and 3721 December 20th.

2. As regards Labour resolution,[2] you will observe that I have been speaking on those lines in Washington as well as in the United Nations here. I wish Labour people had not dragged my name into this resolution. That does not help....

1. Camp: New York, 21 December 1956. JN Collection. Extracts.
2. Vijayalakshmi Pandit, India's High Commissioner in the UK, informed Nehru that 117 Labour MPs had jointly given notice of a motion in the British House of Commons urging "Her Majesty's Government to ask the Prime Minister of India to use his good offices to secure a withdrawal of Russian military forces from Hungary, and to use his influence to effect a reconciliation between Russia and the Western Powers, which would make possible a new approach to a peaceful solution of world problems."

14. Cable to V.K. Krishna Menon[1]

Your telegram 27 of January 8. US Resolution on Hungary.[2] We agree with your suggestion that our delegation need not speak in this debate and should abstain at the time of voting.[3]

1. New Delhi, 9 January 1957. File No. 29/1-XP(P)/57, MEA.
2. Krishna Menon stated that the US proposed to submit to the General Assembly a resolution seeking to establish a five-nation investigating committee to gather information on the situation created by the intervention of Soviet armed forces in Hungary. The committee was expected to collect evidence either in Hungary or elsewhere, presumably from those Hungarians who had escaped to the West.
3. Krishna Menon wrote: "It is wholly difficult to maintain any sense of integrity in any statement we can make without causing offence to both sides which latter is not our purpose." On 10 January, the Assembly passed the resolution.

15. To Herbert V. Evatt[1]

Raj Bhavan,
Poona,
February 1, 1957

My dear Mr Evatt,[2]

Your telegram of the 31st January has been forwarded to me and has reached me at Poona. Thank you for it.

I need not tell you how distressed my colleagues and I have been at the events in Hungary. There can be no doubt that a national uprising took place in Hungary against domination by the Soviet Union. It is true, I think, that some foreign agencies as well as individuals intervened and this intervention worked very much against the Hungarian people's rising. It is also true that just at that time the developments in Egypt, including the Israeli invasion of Egyptian territory and the Anglo-French action, gave the whole situation there an international turn and had some effect on the situation in Hungary. Probably it made the Soviet think that a major war was likely and they wanted to take no chances in Hungary as they had done in Poland. But the fact remains that there was a liberation movement in Hungary started by the great majority of the people there and that this was cruelly crushed.

Apart from our Representative in Budapest, we sent our Ambassador in Moscow and our Minister in Prague to Budapest. Both in Budapest and in Moscow we tried our utmost to plead for the Hungarian people.

So far as the case of the four English students is concerned, and more especially Judith Cripps,[3] we have already asked our Ambassador in Moscow as well as

---

1. JN Collection.
2. A former Foreign Minister and Deputy Prime Minister of Australia and the leader of the Parliamentary Labour Party.
3. Judith Cripps, aged nineteen and the grand daughter of the late Sir Stafford Cripps, was one of the four Oxford University students arrested in Hungary on 24 January on the charge of being in possession of false passports. Lady Isobel Cripps requested Nehru to approach the Soviet authorities for the release of the students. She pointed out that Judith possessed a valid passport and the only reason for her visit was on humanitarian grounds to help refugees.

our Representative in Budapest to intercede on their behalf.[4] I do earnestly hope that these brave young students will not have to suffer for their courage and humanity. We have not given any publicity to our efforts because I thought this might perhaps come in their way. But these efforts will continue.[5]

Yours sincerely,
Jawaharlal Nehru

4. Nehru telegraphed to K.P.S. Menon on 30 January in this regard: "I think this is a suitable case for you to approach (the Soviet Government)." He added: "You might also approach [the] Hungarian Government. Pillai will be telegraphing to Rahman in Budapest also on this subject."
5. The four British students were released and expelled from Hungary on 2 February 1957.

V. THE NEIGHBOURING COUNTRIES

(i) China

1. To Chou En-lai[1]

New Delhi,
5 December 1956

My dear Prime Minister,

We have been following with great interest the account of your visits to Poona, Bombay and Bangalore. Today you must have reached Madras.[2] I am very anxious that you should not tire yourself too much. I am blaming myself for having made a programme for you which is rather heavy and takes up all your time. The desire of our people to have the privilege of meeting you or seeing you was so great that I gave in in several instances. I hope you will forgive us for this weakness that we showed in drawing up your programme.

I trust that you will have some rest in Madras which is a city known for its peaceful and soothing atmosphere. Please do not hesitate to indicate that your programme should be shortened or any item should be left out, if you so desire. It is more important that you should not have to undergo too much fatigue than for you to see some extra place. The pressure of our people who want to meet you or see you is naturally great. But where necessary this has to be resisted. You will, I am sure, have already formed an impression of the great friendship of our people for you and for your country.

I am writing to you specially and sending my letter with T.N. Kaul[3] to Madras. The reason for my doing so is that I have received an urgent message[4] from my colleague, V.K. Krishna Menon, who is in New York. In this message he says

---

1. JN Collection.
2. The Chinese Premier arrived in New Delhi on 28 November. On 1 December 1956, he left for Pune to visit the National Defence Academy at Khadakvasla. On 7 December he travelled from Chennai to Asansol and then to Kolkata. On 9 December he left for Myanmar.
3. Joint Secretary, Ministry of External Affairs.
4. Of 3 December 1956.

that one Mrs Downey, the mother of one of the American prisoners in China, came to see him. She thanked him and our people for all that had been done about the prisoners and begged us again to do what we could to obtain the release of her son. Krishna Menon says that she behaved with dignity and understood all the difficulties. She made a special request that her appeal might be conveyed to you and to me.

In transmitting Mrs Downey's appeal to us, Krishna Menon has earnestly pleaded for the release of all the ten American prisoners in the next few days. He says that such action on the part of the Chinese Government will be widely appreciated and would help in clearing the atmosphere. He believes that any such step would be in the Chinese interest and calculated to help in lowering tensions. It would on no account be considered as any weakness on the part of the Chinese Government. The fact that ten Americans are kept in China under detention does not result in any marked pressure on the American Government but it does enable people to make a charge that they are kept in order to exercise that pressure. Krishna Menon has added that an announcement of the release of the prisoners might be made before I go to the United States.

I am taking the liberty of forwarding Krishna Menon's message to you. I trust that you will not misunderstand my doing so. We have no desire to interfere in China's internal affairs of which you are the best judge. But I do feel with Krishna Menon that an announcement of the release of the American prisoners in China, at this moment of difficulty and crisis in the world, would prove helpful not only in the context of Chinese-American relations, but also in a wider context. I venture to suggest to you that this matter might engage your consideration.[5] If it is possible for you to take the action suggested, it would make us very happy.

With all good wishes to you,

Yours sincerely,
Jawaharlal Nehru

5. Nehru cabled to Krishna Menon the same day stating: "I spoke about American prisoners to Chou En-lai when he was in Delhi. He replied at length blaming the Americans for various misdeeds and said nothing definite about [the] possible release of prisoners."

2. Cable to V.K. Krishna Menon[1]

I sent T.N. Kaul with a personal letter to Chou En-lai at Madras pleading for the release of the 10 American prisoners. You must have seen Chou's reply to questions at a press conference after he received my letter describing you as an optimist and a friend. Last night he talked to Kaul for about two hours tracing history of the whole case. He mentioned your assessment of May last year when you were in Peking[2] that release of fifteen US airmen would lead to a Foreign Ministers' meeting. He said this had not happened and their own assessment was that Sino-US relations are not likely to improve during the next year or so in view of Eisenhower's declaration during election campaign that US Government would support Chiang Kai-shek.

2. Chou En-lai said that neither you nor Hammarskjold nor US Government had ventured to ask for the release of Downey and Facteau who are not US airmen but pure and simple spies against whom the charges were serious and overwhelming. In any case Chou En-lai would like to have fresh assessment by you as to whether release of American prisoners at this stage is likely to lead to a meeting of the two Foreign Ministers even informally without any specific agenda. He would also like to know whether you have had any talks with US authorities which lead you to suppose that such a step might lead to improvement of Sino-American relations. It is possible a few prisoners excluding Downey and Facteau may be released if your assessment is favourable.

3. I would however not like to create false hopes in Chinese minds and would therefore appreciate your cabling your definite views on the subject immediately.[3] Chou En-lai has referred matter to his Government and will send written reply on 9th.

1. New Delhi, 7 December 1956. V.K. Krishna Menon Papers, NMML.
2. Krishna Menon, in his reply to Nehru on 11 December, recalled that during his visit to Beijing from 11 to 21 May 1955 he had repeatedly requested Chou En-lai to release all US prisoners, but the Chinese Premier agreed to releasing only four. He believed that the Sino-American talks at Geneva would not progress, unless the prisoners' issue was resolved. "It is a mere irritant and and it does not help the Chinese in any way," observed Menon.
3. Krishna Menon said that he did not suggest taking up the issue of prisoners with the Americans "on the basis of a bargain of prisoners in return for agreement to negotiate." Menon assessed that the Chinese were holding on to the prisoners "as effective pressure on the US." He concluded that the psychological effect of a release would be considerable and would help Nehru in his talks with Eisenhower.

4. It would appear therefore that there is little chance of release of remaining American prisoners unless he gets some kind of the assurances that he requires. If no assurances coming now he will wait for my talks with Eisenhower and return here. He asked why we were not pressing the US Government also for return of Chinese students and others.[4]

4. Krishna Menon observed that India needed to do more regarding Chinese prisoners in the US. He noted that if Nehru mentioned this matter to Eisenhower, the latter would say "he does not want to retain one person here." He felt it was up to India "to make the implementation more operative than hitherto."

3. Talks with Chou En-lai—I[1]

Prime Minister opened the talks by giving a gist of his talks with President Eisenhower.[2]

Jawaharlal Nehru : I had talks with Eisenhower at his Gettysburg Farm for one day.[3] Only two of us were present. We discussed a variety of subjects. In the main, Eisenhower was interested in the Middle East situation and the question of how to handle it. There were three questions: (1) clearance of the Suez Canal; (2) future of the Canal; and (3) some kind of settlement in the Middle East which will include Israel. At first, Eisenhower thought that all these questions could be taken up together. I, however, said that we must take them separately. To solve first and the second and when passions had calmed down, then take up the third question. Eisenhower mentioned that although US was in close contact with Britain and although US knew that Britain was excited over the Suez issue,

1. Record of talks with Chou En-lai at Sutlej Sadan, Bhakra-Nangal, between 3 and 6 p.m. and partly on the train from Nangal to Delhi, between 10.30 and 11.30 p.m. and from 00.30 to 2.30 a.m., 31 December 1956 and 1 January 1957. *Chou En-lai's Visit to India (December 1956- January 1957),* File No.F.12 (109), NGO/56 and F.12/132/NGO/59. MEA.
2. See *ante*, pp. 539-543.
3. On 17-18 December 1956.

WITH ARNOLD J. TOYNBEE, NEW DELHI, 16 FEBRUARY 1957

Eisenhower said that he had taken a strong line against Britain and France on the question of Egypt and they were now humiliated and had suffered financially also but they were still friends and he did not want them to collapse financially and, therefore, he was giving them considerable financial help. At the same time, Eisenhower said, that he was anxious to help Egypt economically and find some way out of the Middle East problem and to raise the living standards. Eisenhower mentioned about his idea to use all avenues to help the people of these countries, but it is not quite clear to him. Eisenhower finally asked me to use whatever influence I had with Nasser to help solve these internal and external questions regarding Egypt.

Would Chou like to say something?

Chou En-lai: What possibility is there in the opinion of Your Excellency of settling the Egyptian dispute on the basis of six points passed by the United Nations[6] some time ago?

JN: There is good chance of settlement except for one point which says that the Canal should be isolated from politics. Nasser did not like it, though his Foreign Minister[7] agreed to it. Nasser asked as to what this provision meant. But I feel that, with some variation, some acceptable solution might be found. One difficulty is that Egypt says that Israeli ships would not be allowed to go, because Israel is at war with Egypt. This is not quite correct because the Convention[8] says that, even in war, it should be kept open. It is true that in the First and Second World Wars it was closed, but that was done by Britain and the fact remains that all ships should pass through the Canal and that Nasser has accepted the Convention. Since it is matter of interpretation of the Convention, it may be sent to the Court at The Hague and the burden of decision would then lie on the International Court at The Hague. Nasser has indicated that even if the decision is against him, he would still accept it. Nasser is not prepared to say so himself because he is afraid that people of Egypt would not like accepting this interpretation if he did so on his own and, secondly, because he is afraid that it would give a handle to other Middle East countries to work against him. Apart

6. On 12 October 1956, UK, France and Egypt agreed on six principles as the basis for resolving the Suez Canal issue. The next day, a resolution based on them, was passed in the UN Security Council. See *Selected Works* (second series) Vol. 35, pp. 418-419 and p. 563.
7. Mahmoud Fawzi.
8. This refers to the Convention of Constantinople of 1888.

from this, there seems to be no other difficulty. Nasser had also said previously that he would treat Britain and France in the same way as Israel, but he had later on modified it by saying that British and French ships may be allowed to pass since these two countries had not openly declared war against Egypt. For these subjects, I had sent Mr Krishna Menon to Cairo and he was to come here to see you also. I have, however, received a telegram yesterday saying that he could not come to Delhi and that he was proceeding to New York for the UN Session.[9] As regards clearance of the Canal, Britain has probably the greatest experience in the salvage work and it had collected a big salvage fleet at Port Said, but Nasser would not allow them to do the work. Britain had said that they could send their ships under UN flag and their men in civilian uniforms with UN badges, but Nasser did not agree to this. Even so, some understanding seems to have been arrived at between Egypt and Hammarskjold, but I do not know the details. Even so, it is difficult to salvage ships which were carrying concrete. It is, however, expected that in about 2½ months the Canal could be cleared.

Although Egypt has pushed Britain, France and Israel out and they appear to be strong, the position of Egypt and Nasser is not really so strong. If they have been able to push out Britain, France and Israel, it is not on account of Egypt but mainly on account of world opinion. Militarily, they were defeated by even Israel. Egypt could succeed only because a majority in the UN including the United States, supported them. Devoid of this support, Egypt is weak. So, it is in the interest of Egypt to settle the question quickly before people start realising Egypt's weakness and start feeling that Nasser is obstructive.

Chou En-lai: Guaranteeing of free international navigation is one of the principles, but it is different from international control as proposed by Western Powers. We wonder whether in the talks between Egypt and India any concrete content has been given to it.

JN : Nothing very concrete. Nasser has agreed privately to an International Advisory Council from the users who can be consulted and who can give advice. So to that extent, some measure of international cooperation would come in. There again is one more difficult question about Egypt's claim to compensation for several kinds of losses which she has suffered. There are military losses which are heavy. Then there is damage to Port Said and elsewhere and also losses to the Canal.

Nasser is taking the attitude that he would not talk to Britain and France on this, but one must talk. Even in war, people do talk. I feel that he will eventually

9. See *ante*, p. 335.

talk, although it may not be feasible now. Recently, some suggestions have been made that a large group of powers may take up the subject. This proposal is in line with the Soviet proposal in the Security Council. I told Eisenhower that, before any Committee discusses it, it is necessary to clear the Canal and that there should be informal contacts before a formal approach is made.

Eisenhower then discussed the situation in Hungary. He said that a large number of refugees is coming to the US and Canada. Already 1,50,000 refugees have come in this way, and there is more and more pressure of more people coming in. Eisenhower said that, while Britain and France have finally accepted the UN resolution and have withdrawn their armies, the Soviet Union has not done so and has not approved of Hammarskjold going to Hungary. This has created, he said, tremendous feeling in the US. Eisenhower said that he and his Government did not wish to push things too far there and would like to avoid war at any cost and that he wanted a peaceful settlement. Eisenhower added that it was obvious that no settlement was possible when large Soviet forces were in Hungary against the wishes of the Hungarian people. Eisenhower also spoke about the situation in Central Europe and particularly in Germany and said that the Soviet Union had not lived up to the agreements with the Central European countries and many East European countries were not satisfied and that the USSR was forcibly suppressing them. He felt that there was great instability and, if there would be instability, in East Germany also a grave situation will arise.

Chou En-lai : As to the East European question, we discussed it last time. I pointed out that the two questions (viz., Hungarian question and the Egyptian question) are different in character. In the last two years or so, the East European countries are trying to improve their internal conditions and their relations with the Soviet Union. This is permissible and necessary and they have already made some achievements in this task. Some imperfections are however bound to exist and the people are bound to express some discontent. It has happened in Poland, in Germany and in Hungary and similar situations might also arise in future. If the question is limited only to internal question, then the question is easy to settle. We cannot say that socialist countries do everything well in making progress. Secondly, however, the Western Powers were carrying out subversive activities in East European countries. There were also landlords and capitalists who had lost and some of whom had fled and some of whom had stayed behind. If an opportunity presented itself, they would naturally start their activities and if it was supported by subversive activities of Western countries, the situation would be grave. Your Excellency also agreed that in Hungary also there were subversive activities designed to overthrow the socialist government and to throw her in the Western camp. The socialist countries concerned and majority of people in Hungary itself were however opposed to it. If there is a strong government, it can cope with such difficulties; but, in Hungary, the government was weak and could not control the situation and therefore asked the USSR to come in under the Warsaw Treaty and that is the only way out of it. Even if the subversive activities are put down, still the efforts to improve the internal situation have got to be made and they are being made and, as far as my information goes, situation in Hungary is improving. Our view is that the Soviet Army's going to Hungary cannot be compared with the British and French invasion in Egypt.

One thing which deserves attention is what Eisenhower told you about East Germany. East Germany is closely connected with West Germany and there are also people who do not like the system in West Germany. If they got foreign help and started activities, then troubles would start also. As a result of the Second World War, troops of three Powers have been stationed in West Germany while Soviet troops came in to East Germany. The Soviet Union had proposed withdrawal of troops but this has not been agreed to. If some trouble arose in East Germany, East Germany would also ask the Soviet Union for help to put it down, because East Germany's armies are weak. In West Germany, there are people dissatisfied with the system there and West Germany would also use troops to suppress the people there in case of trouble and the Western Powers would also assist them in doing so.

There is a difference in systems and there is difference in objectives. In Poland, however, this kind of situation did not arise. There was not much subversive activity and they could themselves control the situation without foreign assistance. So, the conditions were better and there was quick improvement.

JN: These questions, namely, the situation in Hungary and Poland, largely depend on factual appreciation. We have been receiving full and practically daily reports from our Ambassador and representative in Hungary and on the strength of these reports the situation seems to have been something like the following:

While it is true that some external subversive elements were there, they formed only a small part of the trouble. It was mainly a national uprising of the workers, students and the youth. The object was not so much to change the internal regime as to get rid of foreign domination, namely, that of Soviet Union. The same thing happened in Poland too. But, as you have said, there the leaders were strong enough to control the situation. The question factually, therefore, is whether the large majority of people in Hungary want to assert their independence or not. That some subversive elements took advantage of the situation and raised slogans is not enough to ignore the actuality that a strong national uprising took place. In the riots that took place, 25,000 Hungarians are reported to be dead. That, in a city like Budapest, it required 1,000 tanks would show the extent of the uprising. Our information is that originally it was a strong national uprising, not directed against the USSR; but when the demonstrations took place and workers were shot, it became anti-Soviet. Even the Workers Councils wanted the socialist system but not foreign domination.

The question is whether this system has been imposed on them or not. If it is imposed, then it will mean that there is no national freedom. On October 30, the Soviet Government made a policy statement announcing the withdrawal of its troops; but, after a few days, the Soviet troops went back with a large number of tanks. We had asked our Ambassador[10] in Moscow to speak to the Soviet leaders of his impressions in Budapest. And although it has not been made public, he has done so. We have also seen that, for over a month after fighting had stopped in Budapest, workers did not go back to work and they stated that they will resume work on end of foreign domination and withdrawal of foreign troops. A great majority of Hungarians do not oppose socialism, but they want their own people to run the Government and the feelings are very strong on the point. A very large number of people have come out as refugees. How can this problem be solved? It is a continuing cancer. The minds of the people have not been won over till now. How will they be won?

I agree that foreign troops should be withdrawn from Germany. When we discussed this matter, Eisenhower said that they will withdraw the American troops as soon as the West German Government wanted them to withdraw. Otherwise, they would withdraw them after the situation improved. You say that in Hungary the Soviet troops were asked to go there. But the Kadar Government was formed under very peculiar circumstances. The former Prime Minister was pushed out and then Kadar came into power.[11] Kadar could not go out of his office building because of strong feelings against him. He is reported to be on the upper floor of the Government building, while the Soviet troops occupied the lower floor. He may be a good man; but, in the eyes of the people, it is not he who is governing but the Soviet Union which is governing. I do not doubt that the majority of the Hungarian people do not want foreign authority. Is there any way of finding out what the great majority of people want? For over thousand

10. K.P.S. Menon.
11. Imre Nagy was ousted on 4 November. The Soviet Union announced the same day the appointment of Janos Kadar as the Premier.

years in the past, the Hungarians and the Poles have very strong nationalist feelings and a fear of either Germany or Russia. Therefore, one can understand their aspirations. Even if they want to have socialistic system, they want to be free.

I told Eisenhower that, looking at it from the Russian point of view, the Soviet Union is afraid of hostile frontiers coming nearer to them and their security being endangered. Eisenhower said that he could understand it and that he could discuss ways of removing all fears. But the difficult problem to solve was that Hungary was occupied by Soviet troops against the wishes of the people and it went against every principle that the Americans stood for.

I feel that something has to be done and something can be done only after gradual withdrawal of Soviet troops which, I am sure, they will do. Otherwise, they will retain Hungary but will lose the people, which is bad.

The most unfortunate part of the Hungarian episode, it appears to me, is that it has harmed the cause of socialism in Europe and elsewhere and many of us who are friends of USSR are very much distressed and find it difficult to justify what has happened there. There is an unfortunate conflict between nationalism and socialism. Socialism has to be based on nationalism or otherwise it is weakened.

Now, there are hundred and thousands of refugees from Hungary who have become active propagandists against Russia. Even European countries have hundreds of them, and they are anxious that his matter should be settled. The main thing is to find a settlement acceptable to the large majority of Hungarian people. Otherwise, it is also going to have a bad influence on other East European countries. In Poland also, there is much sympathy for Hungary.

Chou En-lai : Yes, the situation in Hungary is very complicated. You have underestimated the trouble which took place between the 23rd October to the beginning of November. USSR did promise and in actuality also withdrew her troops from Budapest. But precisely at this time anti-revolutionary elements gained control of Nagy's Government and asked the West for help and for abrogation of Warsaw Treaty. Nagy was going towards the West. This constituted a great danger because this could not guarantee that socialist system would be maintained in Hungary. We in the East do not so much feel the seriousness of the situation but other socialist countries in Europe felt very much concerned and disturbed over this threat. Even Yugoslavia and Czechoslovakia felt very much concerned and Tito's report also bears this out. At this time, the Hungarian armies were completely disintegrated and reactionary elements had gained control of the situation. People's nationalism and desire to be free from foreign domination could be utilised for anti-revolutionary ends. History has proved it and Nagy had pushed the government on to the counter-revolutionary road. At this time, Kadar left Nagy, and those who left Nagy formed a government and asked USSR for help. Since it was the Soviet troops that suppressed anti-revolutionary activities and not the Hungarian People's Armies themselves, it was not naturally very powerful. But at that time there were only two ways out, namely, (1) that the Soviet troops leave Hungary and push it into Western camp. This would have meant large-scale massacre and in fact it did happen. Or, otherwise, (2) that USSR should send her troops and suppress counter-revolution. There was no third way.

Nagy also had to depend on the Soviet armies to put down the uprising. But because it depended on the Soviet armies, he felt weak and could not carry out his work. And in three days, many revolutionaries were massacred. Without Soviet support it is obvious that the socialistic system could not be maintained.

In Poland also, the government made certain mistakes, but the leaders there could handle the situation. In China, this kind of situation cannot take place. But even if it occurs, we are strong enough to control it. I am going to talk to you about Tibet in a short while where also our inimical countries are trying to carry out subversive activities, but they will not be successful. Finally, the present government in Hungary is a temporary measure. There will still have to be organised a popular government; but unless subversive activities are put down, the country will go in an entirely different direction. Even among the workers, from the beginning there has been some dissatisfaction. Many of the workers' leaders are saying they want to maintain socialistic system, but it may be merely superficial expression and they are saying things on behalf of counter-revolutionaries. We must wait and see. We feel that the majority of people in Hungary want socialism. All the same, it is a difficult and complicated question. There were only two roads – either to allow Hungary to go West or to preserve socialistic system. I have been travelling all this time and had no time to study all the details, but after going to Peking, I will look into the details.

JN: A great deal depends on knowledge and appraisal of facts. I agree that Nagy took a wrong line at the last moment and created difficulties. The whole trouble is not accidental but is the result of past mistakes, but it is someone else's fault and not Nagy's fault. Nagy proved incapable of dealing with the situation. But subsequent events have not proved the ability of others to meet the situation. Shooting down is not any solution. No one doubts Russia's might and naturally Hungarians cannot stand against it. But can socialism succeed by military force, without freedom? Is it compulsory socialism? These problems arise. The Hungarian uprising may have been suppressed, but the Hungarian people cannot be won over that way. The only way is through friendly cooperation.

Chou En-lai: Yes, to win over the people one must use persuasion and socialism will win, if only people accepted it. This is one thing. But to put down internal or external forces of reaction which are originally oppressing people, it is necessary to have military strength. Counter-revolutionaries can also be a part of the people or sent from outside and hidden among the people.

When people are being oppressed by reactionary governments, they have to use arms as in the case of bourgeois democratic revolutions, as in the French Revolution and the American Revolution or in socialist revolutions as in the Soviet Union and China. After the success of the revolution, again military strength is necessary to defend socialism from foreign aggression and internal subversion. So, these are two different matters.

As regards the working class, there should always be persuasion and never imposition. But in Hungary armed forces were disintegrated by Nagy and he allowed haughty elements to gain control of the army. It was a special situation and under it a new government was formed and outside assistance was requested. But this was necessary under the circumstances.

JN: Premier Chou has used the philosophy of force. Every Government uses force. Although we are opposed to force, we too use force although very small. But we do hope that we can reduce and even do away with our armies one day. In Hungary, Nagy Government acted wrongly. That is true. It could not control the situation. That also is true. But the situation arose out of past mistakes, which had angered the people. There was no economic betterment and then there was the foreign domination which went against all their traditions.

Chou En-lai: The question before us is an appraisal of the past and a way out for the future. Regarding the past, our view is that, if action had not been taken in Hungary, she would have fallen in the Western camp. As to the future, it depends on developments there. If the Hungarian Government gets stronger, the situation will improve. It is impossible and impermissible to restore Nagy. So, we must try to support the present Government and improve the situation there.

JN: I also discussed other matters with President Eisenhower. We discussed Pakistan and I told him that the now considerable arms supplied to Pakistan was causing us considerable apprehension. Eisenhower said that he never had the intention that Pakistan should use the arms aid against India; but in case Pakistan did so, he would not only stop the aid but would also take very strong measures.

As regards, Goa, President Eisenhower said that the Portuguese were a very difficult people to deal with. They lived in a different world.

My information is that the agreement[12] in Laos is not liked by the USA. It was after months of efforts that we brought the two sides together in Laos and it would be unfortunate if the agreement breaks down. Both President Eisenhower and Dulles said that they did not like that Pathet Lao representatives should be in the Government. But, after my talks with them, they said that they would not obstruct but would watch what happens and they have informed the Laos Government accordingly.

I spoke to the Canadian Government also about Laos and they were anxious that the agreement should go through. They told me that they would try to impress upon the US Government that the agreement should go through.

Chou En-lai: We told Prince Souvanna Phouma[13] that they should settle their internal questions by themselves. We would like to see them peaceful and neutral like Cambodia. We told them that all our relations with Laos will be with the Laos Government and that we stick to this policy. In Cambodia, we were told that Laos Government understood that we have only good intentions towards them. We are glad to know that through India's efforts an agreement has now been arrived at between the two parties in Laos and that Canada is supporting it and that US has promised not to obstruct it. What the Americans probably mean by "watching" is whether Chinese influence comes in Laos.

JN: Eisenhower said that it was illogical not to recognise each other (i.e. China and America) but it was a result of certain circumstances. Even in war, countries deal with each other. And he implied that some time or other China and America would deal with each other; but, Eisenhower said, at present there is a strong feeling in US and that he shares it. Even if he had not shared it, he (Eisenhower) could not override popular feelings in this regard. Eisenhower said that America had suffered great losses in the Second World War and they had forgotten it, while they still remember the losses in the Korean war. Eisenhower further said that there was strong feeling in United States about the ten US prisoners in

12. On 28 December 1956, the Royal Government of Laos and the Pathet Lao regime in northern Laos signed an agreement establishing a government of national union.
13. Laotian Prime Minister.

China and that it was not possible for him to take any steps until this question was settled. I told him what you had told me in details that there were forty-four or so prisoners in China out of whom all except ten have been released. Although so many prisoners have been released, still the US made no adequate response to this gesture of the Chinese Government and it was for the US Government to make some move. Eisenhower repeated that there was strong feeling in his country on the question.

I also mentioned to him about the Chinese nationals in America. Eisenhower said that any Chinese in America, whether in prison or outside, could go back. He (Eisenhower) had asked the Indian Ambasador[14] to interview anyone in or outside the jail. But this was not done. What more could he do, he asked. He said perhaps one more statement could be made by the American Government saying that all Chinese who wished to go can do so. Eisenhower added that America had no desire to retain any Chinese, who wanted to go back, in America, but if some did not want to go back what could he do.

As regards a Foreign Ministers' conference, I told Dulles about it. Dulles said that all this might happen when conditions were created. He said that there was strong feeling in the US specially about the prisoners in China. Therefore, he cannot meet the Chinese Prime Minister.

Eisenhower told me that he had heard that great changes and improvements had taken place in China and he thought that, if the US people knew about them, they might change their views. Both Eisenhower and Dulles said that their hands were tied down especially on the question of prisoners. If the prisoners were released, Eisenhower said, that he would allow journalists and other nationals to go to China and their reports from China might perhaps bring about a change in the view of the Americans and would normalise feelings. He said that if the prisoners were released, they would lift the ban upon journalists and other persons going to China and things might improve slowly.

Chou En-lai: We will talk about the Sino-American relations tomorrow. I would first like to speak about the Tibet question. India is clear about the situation in Tibet. Tibet is a vast territory with only one million population. They are of the same nationality, viz. Tibetan. Throughout history, Tibet has formed a part of China; but, unlike Sinkiang which is also a national minority area, it was never made into a province of China. The religion of the people is Lamaistic. In dealing with Tibet, we take a very careful attitude. In the past, religion and politics were combined into one, that there was the same religious

14. G. L. Mehta, India's Ambassador to the USA.

594

and political leader. But in actuality, political power was vested in the government (*Kashag*) under the Lama, since a new Lama was always an infant (less than one year old) and could not look into political matters till he came of age. Therefore, for more than ten years, political power rested in the hands of the government. Besides, the temples also wielded powers. There are three large ones in Lhasa and there are living Buddhas there who have power. Therefore, those who have power are the living Buddhas and the persons in government.

Tibet is divided into three parts: Inner Tibet: Outer Tibet; and Chamdo area. In the past, Chamdo was sometime made a part of Sikang. Sometime, it was not a part of Sikang. Now, all these three parts are made into one autonomous region. In this area, there has been formed a preparatory committee[15] with Dalai Lama as Head and Panchen Lama as Deputy Head. Next year, the autonomous area will be formed. These three parts still have some distance (differences) among them, because the reactionary government in the past have created discord among them. We have always advised unity. Our policy has always been to give them an autonomous government under the Central Government, enjoying a large measure of autonomous rights. The Central Government consults it on all related matters and local matters are handled by themselves. We fully respect their religion; everyone lives in religion there and every family has to give one or two of its members to the temple. At present, we do not talk of democratic reforms to them; but when other parts of China become economically better and if Tibetans feel the need and agree to it, then we can introduce them. At present, there is a semi-feudal and semi-slave system in Tibet with compulsory service to government and temples. China can help them in improving their living conditions, but then there is the difficulty of communications. Therefore, it will have to be done slowly.

The two Lamas (Dalai and Panchen) are young and able. They have their own views on subjects. Since their tour of various places in China, they want to improve conditions in Tibet. We, however, advised them not to go too fast but to take all the government and Lamas with them first. There are bound to be people who are dissatisfied and people who are afraid that their religion would be affected. It is natural because they do not understand the policy of the Central Government. We take an attitude of waiting and seeing. But there is also a minority under foreign influence which does not like Tibet to be

15. This was the Preparatory Committee for the establishment of the Autonomous Region of Tibet (PCART). It was inaugurated on 22 April 1956 in Lhasa.

under the Central Government and wants to have an independent Tibet. Their activities are mainly carried out from Kalimpong and these include some Tibetans who have returned from the USA. In the past, some trouble was started in Tibet once or twice, but Dalai Lama pacified it. Towards them, we take a mild attitude. We disbanded their organisation, but made no arrests. We let Dalai Lama persuade and educate them. This was the situation in the past. There is, however, a group in Lhasa which has kept constant contact with Kalimpong and has never stopped its activities. When Dalai Lama went to Peking for People's Conference[16] (and when Your Excellency met him there[17]), these people started rumours that Dalai Lama was not going to return and this caused disturbances. Only when Dalai Lama went back the rumours stopped.

This time, when India invited Dalai Lama and Panchen Lama[18] the Chinese Government knew that some trouble would start in Tibet after they left Lhasa. But, on the other hand, the Chinese Government considered the friendly relations existing with India and they also knew that Dalai Lama would be well received in India and the visit would help religious contacts. Dalai Lama decided to come and also to bring more people with him. Then we also advised Panchen Lama to accept the invitation; because if only Dalai Lama came, it would show disunity between the two Lamas. We also knew that when they came to India they would meet many Tibetans who had never returned to Tibet after liberation. There are thousands of Tibetans near Kalimpong. And although Dalai Lama did not go to Kalimpong, these Tibetans did not give up hope and the US agents have encouraged such and other subversive activities. Dalai Lama's brother,[19] who has recently returned from the US told Dalai Lama that the United States would support independence movement in Tibet or failing that would welcome him in the United States.

Now the Kalimpong Tibetans want Dalai Lama to go to Kalimpong in order to preach to them. And it is difficult for him to decide. If he does not go, then it would not be good from the religious point of view. But if he goes, there is bound to be some trouble. At the same time, some of the officers

---

16. The first session of the First National People's Congress met in Beijing from 15 to 28 September 1954. The Dalai Lama was one of the participants. He returned to Lhasa on 29 June 1955, after a year's stay in China.
17. Nehru visited China from 19 October to 30 October 1954. See *Selected Works* (Second Series), Vol. 27, p. 78 where Nehru mentions his meeting with the Dalai Lama.
18. To participate in the 2,500th Buddha Jayanti celebrations, held in India from 26 to 30 November 1956.
19. Thubten Jigme Norbu.

accompanying the Dalai Lama this time have also been influenced in their Indian visit. The influence comes from two sources; (1) Kalimpong Tibetans, including Dalai Lama's brother. Among these officers, there are some backward elements who fear reform and are easily susceptible to propaganda. (2) Local officers in India: some of these local officers are quite unfriendly to China. In welcome speeches to the two Lamas, they called Tibet a separate country and made no mention of China at all. For example, the Mayor of Bombay[20] and the Mayor of Madras or some nearby town referred to Tibet as a separate country without mentioning China. In the case of the latter Mayor, he was going to say it but the Chinese Embassy officials came to know about it and protested and therefore that part of the speech was dropped. Calling Tibet a different country gives an impression that Tibet could be independent.

Dalai Lama is really faced with a problem. The Chinese Government had advised Dalai not to go to Kalimpong; but if he does not go to Kalimpong, it would show that Dalai has some prejudice against the Tibetans in Kalimpong. But if he goes to Kalimpong, all sorts of embarrassing questions would arise. If Panchen goes, it would be much more awkward, because Panchen comes from Outer Tibet (Hou Tsang) and there is historically some animosity between the Inner Tibetans and Outer Tibetans. But if Panchen does not go, then also again it would give ground to spread rumours that something is wrong between them or that the Chinese Government is not allowing him to go there. Actually, in one of the big temples in India, something unpleasant between the two Lamas also occurred. Therefore, the matter is very complicated and the chief cause is the instigation of USA. Taiwan has also a hand in it because another of his brothers[21] (married to a Chinese) has come from Japan.

At the same time, since Dalai left Lhasa, those bent on trouble are preparing for an incident in Lhasa. These people have some armed forces. Some three temples in Lhasa have also armed forces and they want to create an incident with the People's Liberation Army there. If it happened, then there would be bloodshed. This plot was, however, discovered and then an open meeting was called where the representatives of the Central Government declared that they should not try to create an incident; but if they did so, People's Liberation Army would definitely take measures to put it down. People's Liberation Army on its part, would not take any provocative steps. The local government and the People's Liberation Army representatives have formed a committee to handle this matter. So, for the time being, the matter is over;

20. Salebhoy Abdul Kader.
21. Gyalo Thondup, elder brother of the Dalai Lama.

but, as long as Dalai Lama is away, something might happen. The Kalimpong people are thinking of keeping Dalai as long as possible so that his absence could be taken advantage of. This is chiefly instigated by the USA and Taiwan. Since Dalai Lama is in India, if anything happens it will be unfortunate. We will, of course, take measures to put down any incident in Tibet, but still it is not good if something happens.

Newspaper reports say that Dalai Lama might stay in India. He can if he wants to as long as he abides by Indian Government's regulations. Whether he wants to go to Kalimpong, he is going to decide tomorrow. He has to consult his Government. This is the whole situation. If anything should happen in Tibet or in Kalimpong, of course the Chinese Government would be directly concerned. Since Dalai Lama is in India, I thought I should also inform Your Excellency about this. The situation is a complicated one.

JN: Your Excellency has said a good deal. You said that I know a lot about Tibet but I don't know. Something of what you told me is news to me. I know nothing about Dalai Lama's going to Kalimpong. I am hearing it for the first time. It is a matter primarily for Your Excellency and Dalai Lama to decide. It would be embarrassing for us to say anything either way.

About Kalimpong, I am surprised to learn that there are tens of thousands of Tibetans there. I know that there was a large number but not to this extent. There are many kinds of Tibetans and the people are akin to Tibetans. I have heard also for a long time that Kalimpong has a nest of spies and the spies are probably more than the population. In the past, we have turned out some of the people from Kalimpong, including Americans. I have not met any of Dalai Lama's brothers. I have met one eight or nine years ago. And the second time I have met him was when Your Excellency introduced me to him recently. I do not know that his brothers were in Delhi. The Government of India's policy has been not to allow anti-Chinese propaganda to be carried out here.

I am thankful to Your Excellency for the background material given to me. But I do not quite understand what you meant when you said that Tibet in the past had not become a province of China.

Chou En-lai: That Tibet is part of China is a fact, but it as never an administrative province of China but kept an autonomous character. Therefore, when we started negotiations for peaceful liberation of Tibet, we from the first recognised the autonomous character of the region.

When I said that India knew more about Tibet, I meant about the past history. For example, I knew nothing about McMahon Line until recently when we came to study the border problem after liberation of China.

JN: Historical knowledge is not important but is useful as background information. History is gone. My impression was that whatever it may be in theory, for all practical purposes Tibet has all along been autonomous. But at the same time, whatever government there might have been in China, Tibet has always been claimed by the Chinese Government. The British tried to create some trouble on account of their fear of Czarist Russia but this is past history. We recognise that China has, in law and in fact, suzerainty over Tibet even though it may not have been exercised sometime. As your Excellency has said, Tibet has behaved in an autonomous way and was cut off from other countries. The criterion of an independent state is that the state should have independent foreign relations and Tibet had no foreign relations except with England.

The McMahon Line was put forward in the 1913 Conference between the Chinese, the Tibetans and the British.[22] That Conference decided not only the McMahon Line but also two other points. The Chinese Government raised objection only to the other two points. Surely, the Chinese Government always knew about it (i.e. the McMahon Line).

As regards Dalai Lama, we do not want any incident to take place about Dalai Lama in Kalimpong or while he is in India. We will do as Your Excellency and Dalai Lama decide. What kind of incident does Your Excellency fear might happen? If you can give some specific idea about the trouble, we can prevent it.

Chou En-lai: The situation is really very complicated and it is difficult for me to say as to what specifically might happen. Dalai Lama is also concerned about this matter and he also said that the situation is complicated. There are two possibilities: (1) We have already raised this matter seriously with the Dalai Lama. Now Dalai Lama will naturally go back and talk to his officials and maybe perhaps nothing would happen except some small quarrels or verbal exchanges and he returns to Lhasa safely. Alternatively, (2) a possibility is that attempts might be made at Kalimpong to detain Dalai Lama. In fact, that is exactly the slogan raised there : "Won't let Dalai Lama go back".

Panchen Lama does not want to go to Kalimpong. If he goes, he might be treated discourteously or some other trouble might be created. These are some of the possibilities.

If such incidents happen, Indian Government has power to intervene and check them, because such incidents partake of the nature of anti-Chinese activities or activities designed to create an independent Tibet or espionage or encouragement to subversive activities. We are mentioning these

22. This was the Simla Conference held between October 1913 and April 1914.

possibilities to your Government in advance so that, if anything happens, the Government of India could take preventive measures.

As regards the Tibetan question, even during the Ching dynasty, Tibet was indeed part of China and, at the end of the 19th century, when China was defeated in war with France and other countries, all Western Powers wanted to divide China; but they could not agree among themselves and so agreed to have separate spheres of influence. This was especially true after the Boxer Uprising. That is why Tibet was always kept as a part of China, not only in law but in fact, with a view to keep balance between Powers.

The relations of Sikkim and Bhutan with China differ from those between Tibet and China, because Sikkim and Bhutan were never under China and even the Imperial Power did not recognise Bhutan and Sikkim as being under them. But in the case of Tibet, it was a different case. The Ching Emperor appointed Governors to Tibet and troops were also stationed in Lhasa. The British wanted to go into Tibet under the pretext that Russia wanted to get into Sikang. Russia also made the same pretext, namely, that Britain was trying to get into Tibet, to get into Sikang. Exactly because of this rivalry and balance of power, Sikang and Tibet were never taken actually. But there are many still who are not acquainted with these facts. Even the Pakistan Prime Minister recently[23] told me that he always thought Tibet to be independent. Even the Simla Conference admitted Chinese suzerainty over Tibet.

McMahon Line—What I meant was that people like me never knew about it till recently. The then Chinese Government, namely, the warlords in Peking and the KMT naturally knew about it. Perhaps U Nu might have told Your Excellency that we studied this question and although this Line was never recognised by us, still apparently there was a secret pact between Britain and Tibet and it was announced at the time of the Simla Conference. And now that it is an accomplished fact, we should accept it. But we have not consulted Tibet so far. In the last agreement which we signed about Tibet[24], the Tibetans wanted us to reject this Line; but we told them that the question should be temporarily put aside. I believe immediately after India's independence, the Tibetan Government had also written to the Government of India about this matter. But now we think that we should try to persuade and convince Tibetans to accept it. This question also is connected with Sino-Burmese border and the question will be decided after Dalai Lama's return to Lhasa. So, although

23. H.S. Suhrawardy was in Beijing on a state visit from 18 to 29 October 1956.
24. Refers to the Agreement on Trade and Intercourse between India and the Tibet Region of China. It was signed in Beijing on 29 April 1954.

A FAREWELL HUG FOR CHOU EN-LAI, NEW DELHI, 1 JANUARY 1957

WITH SHUKRI EL-KUWATLI, PRESIDENT OF SYRIA, NEW DELHI, 17 JANUARY 1957

the question is still undecided and it is unfair to us, still we feel that there is no better way than to recognise this Line.

JN: The border is a high mountain border and sparsely populated. Apart from the major question, there are also small questions about two miles here and two miles there. But if we agree on some principle, namely, the principle of previous normal practice or the principle of watershed, we can also settle these other small points. Of course, this has nothing to do with the McMahon Line.

Chou En-lai: Yes, the question can be solved and we think it should be settled early.

JN: I would like to mention one thing in connection with what you said about some Mayors trying to make out Tibet as an independent country. Reference by a Mayor has no significance. He does not know much politically and probably very little about China and Tibet. They would generally only know about the great religious significance of Tibet to Indians and that is all that they must be stressing.

Our policy has been to deal with the Chinese Government about Tibet and the treaty on Tibet was also signed with the Chinese Government. We are naturally interested in what happens in Tibet as one of our near neighbours but we don't want to interfere. Our main interest is from the point of view of the pilgrims—not only Buddhist pilgrims but Hindu pilgrims too for whom Kailash and Manasarovar are sacred places and abodes of God. A Dalai Lama is always a mythical figure and a great deal of mystery is attached to him in the mind of an Indian. So, when Dalai Lama came, the people were naturally greatly attracted to him. But the only significance is that the people would be interested from a religious point of view. Your Excellency has said that Tibet is backward and cut off. But it cannot remain long that way. They are a deeply religious people and they are naturally afraid that their religion and customs would be upset. I myself personally think that changes are inevitable in Tibet, but I would like Tibetans to feel that they themselves have brought about the changes. As Your Excellency has said, Tibet is a part of China but with full autonomous powers. Then I don't understand why there should be any trouble in Tibet at all.

Chou En-lai: Basically, I am in agreement with your views but there are certain specific matters which may be clarified. We have always held the view that purely religious contacts should not be limited or restricted by State boundaries. Thus, in Asia, there are many Buddhist countries and they should have more contacts with each other. We have established relations in religious matters even with Thailand. Chairman Mao also said that there should be increasing contacts between Chinese Buddhists and Buddhists from other countries and that we should remove restrictions. This would also increase the confidence of Buddhists in Tibet that we respect their religion. So we also approved of Dalai and Panchen Lamas visit to India. But purely religious contacts is a difficult matter. Some try to exploit it for political ends, as in the West some call themselves Buddhists and try to instigate movement for the independence of Tibet.

Your Excellency said that Tibetans should feel that the reforms are brought about by themselves. It is correct, but this does not mean that there would be no trouble because there are some who are open to foreign influence and there are some who lack understanding. They feel that since China is a socialist country, religion may be restricted; but actually it is not so. We respect religion. On the other hand, the Ching dynasty used religion to decrease the populations of Tibet and Mongolia, while we want to increase population in Tibet without putting any restrictions. Furthermore, among the Tibetans there are many who are not so progressive. Those who are progressive want quick reforms, but this makes the non-progressive ones suspicious of the progressive elements and they feel that the latter are being influenced by the Hans. For example, in Szechuan province the progressive Tibetans wanted early reforms and there was resistance. The backward elements started agitation and one armed lamasery surrounded the People's Liberation Army troops and this People's Liberation Army detachment had to be fed by means of air-dropped food and thus finally they were able to beat back the attack. Some of these Tibetans later ran away to Lhasa. So, even if we agree that Tibetans themselves should carry out reforms, such problems and difficulties do arise. If it is a question of internal dissatisfaction alone, we would like to adopt a policy of waiting. But if there is foreign influence in it, then it becomes troublesome. Therefore, we maintain that religious contacts should be developed in Asian countries, but at the same time we should stop subversive activities. Espionage activities are carried out in the open in Kalimpong and we feel that the Government of India should intervene because these activities will interfere with religious contacts and exchange.

JN: If any fact about espionage comes to our notice, of course we will take steps. But if it is only a vague suspicion and no proof, then it is difficult to take action.

Chou En-lai: It is quite true. What we sought by informing the Government of India before hand was to help the Government of India to deal with the situation in case something happens.

As regards Dalai Lama's going to Kalimpong, I should be able to let you know something by tomorrow morning after I have seen Dalai Lama.

4. Talks with Chou En-lai—II[1]

Chou En-lai : This morning I had talks with both Dalai Lama and Panchen Lama and I have also told them about our yesterday's conversation. They told me that yesterday they held a meeting. Dalai Lama still finds it difficult to decide. The people with him also know the complicated situation; but there are over 10,000 people waiting for him at Kalimpong and if he does not go, it may not also look nice. Therefore, his party also find it difficult to make up their mind. Dalai Lama wanted me to have a talk with his officials this afternoon and then perhaps something could be decided. Panchen Lama will not be going to Kalimpong. Firstly, it may be embarrassing for him and it may not also be safe because the Tibetans there are mostly from Lhasa and they are hostile.

So it is more important for Dalai Lama himself to decide. It won't be good for us to tell him. So, I can tell Your Excellency the final decision later. The Dalai Lama's retinue always make him waver. If, however, they agree to go directly to Lhasa, then a trial flight to Lhasa will first have to be carried out.

JN: Yes, if they agree to go straight; still they will have to go separately for ceremonial purposes. They can go to Lhasa from Calcutta. Perhaps the Tibetans from Kalimpong could come and see him at Bagdogra on the way.

Chou En-lai: I also wanted to tell Your Excellency something about my visit to Burma and Pakistan.

1. Record of talks with Chou En-lai at New Delhi, 2.30 p.m. to 5.00 p.m., 1 January 1957. *Chou En-lai's Visit to India (December 1956- January 1957)*. File Nos. F12 (109), NGO/56 and F.12/132/NGO/59, MEA.

I first went to Burma.[2] In Burma, the situation is, generally speaking, good. Leaders of the Burmese Government also went with us to Mohnyin, and the Kachin leaders were also there. As regards the border question, the Burmese Government leaders told me that the final decision could be arrived at only in February when the Burmese Parliament opens. Through this visit we have been able to understand the Burmese Government leaders and I think we can get along better.

In Pakistan[3] I found proof that the people of Pakistan want peace and friendship. But immediately the Kashmir issue was raised, they asked many questions. As Your Excellency told me, I told them that if the UN Resolution which was adopted eight years ago is to be carried out, then Pakistan should withdraw her forces and then India would also withdraw her forces to certain limit and then plebiscite could be held. I have also told them that throughout the last eight years Pakistan had not carried out this. Pakistan's reply was that they would carry this out but there must be simultaneous withdrawal of troops. If this is difficult, then Pakistan is ready to withdraw first, but UN troops should be asked to enter the part vacated by Pakistan troops. This is the view of some of the Pakistani leaders, but others do not necessarily share it. There is no definite solution thought of, to the problem. They also gave me lot of material on Kashmir. I told them that I will study it later. I told them that the Chinese attitude was to advise amity and direct talks with India. I only advised them to be peaceful and to have direct talks with India and nothing more. I listened however to a lot of people who came and told me many things. But basically they were the same as I was told in Peking by the Pakistan Prime Minister.

Sino-American Relations—President Eisenhower mentioned to you about the feelings of the American people. He has said that they have forgotten their losses in the Second World War but they still remember their losses in Korea and have strong feelings about them. We can quite understand it, because in Korea Americans did not win. They did not gain victory. Therefore, it is difficult for them to forget and the feelings are constantly aroused in the people by the China lobby; but Eisenhower has taken no steps to lessen this kind of feeling.

China also has very strong feelings. Though we succeeded in defending our security and maintaining the 38th Parallel, still we had to make great

2. From 10 to 19 December 1956.
3. Chou En-lai visited Pakistan from 20 to 30 December 1956.

sacrifices in Korea. But, in the process, Taiwan was occupied by the Americans and they are also interfering with our liberating the shore islands.

In Korea, although at the front we destroyed a large number of Rhee's[4] troops, still in the negotiations we made a great concession on the question of PsOW. Despite the fact that the United States and Rhee did many provocative things, including detention of PsOW, we tolerated it all. The NNRC's report on this was never even presented to the United Nations. All these hurt the Chinese feelings and yet we tolerated it and did not connect them while dealing with the cases of the American prisoners in China, nor did we feed the Chinese people on this and arouse their feelings in the matter. What the US wants is to make China make concessions from the beginning to the end, and this is difficult for us to accept. Eisenhower himself said that the present state of relations is illogical, unreasonable. And this proves that the relations are unreasonable. It takes both sides for having a rapproachement. America wants China to make concessions and then only they would allow journalists and other nationals to come to China. This is an unreasonable situation. This cannot last long. A solution this way is unlikely. It goes against the feeling of the Chinese. There are many Chinese nationals in the United States who want to come but are not allowed to come back. If more can return, then the situation can change. There is no need to say more about it. You represent us on the question of Chinese nationals in the United States and we will send you some more material about it.

While in the United States, you put forward very just views and we are thankful to you; but we feel that as far as improvement of relations with America are concerned, time is still not ripe. We clearly know that there is not much possibility of the United States creating more tension in the Far East. I don't say that there is no possibility at all. For example, they might try to do some subversive activity in Tibet. And if we get hold of any evidence of US espionage activities in Kalimpong, we will inform the Indian Government in order that you might be able to take action. Of course, these activities should not prevent improvement of Sino-American relations; for in fact, if relations are improved, then the United States will have to be more careful in their dealings with us and they will have many inhibitions before they do a thing. So we would like to wait and see.

The Geneva talks are still on. If America is genuinely interested in rapproachment, then they can agree on at least one or two points. In the Geneva talks, it was never stipulated that China should release all prisoners,

4. Syngman Rhee, President of South Korea, 1948-60.

but America may not implement the Agreement at all; nor was it decided that it is only after agreement on the first agenda that the second item should be discussed. We have fully carried out the terms of Agreement. Those of the American nationals wishing to return have all gone away and a majority in the jail has been released but, on the other hand, a large number of Chinese nationals in America want to come back but cannot come back. Improvement of relations can be done from different angles and that will increase the possibility of release of the remaining Americans. There will be more chances of testing the intentions of the Americans.

JN : I have told all this to Eisenhower. There is great divergence of views between the two sides. I doubt whether either can persuade each other and it is hard to suggest any definite steps.

Your Excellency said that in China too there is great feeling as in the United States. It is true that in the US there is a China lobby but I may mention what Eisenhower told me. He said : "These people (Senator Knowland[5] and the rest) take an extreme attitude. I do not care what they do, but they create strong feelings in the American people and I cannot go against it". Now the question is whether matters should be allowed to drift or something should be done. My impression is that the United States is not likely to do anything unless the prisoners are released. About the Chinese nationals, they said that they have openly allowed them to go. They have also allowed the Indian Ambassador to meet them in prison or outside; but if they would not go, what can they do about it? The question again is whether anything is to be done or nothing is to be done. These ten prisoners are hardly a part of a major issue, but the Americans feel that they have become a symbol of humiliating the United States and the Chinese not wanting any change. As I said, it is not for me to suggest any major policy change by the Chinese Government, but I am anxious that something is done to solve the deadlock and get things moving.

These prisoners are young men in their twenties and they cannot be considered guilty of anything important. It does not make much difference if they are in prison or not but their being kept in prison makes a difference. On the prisoners

---

5. William Fife Knowland (b.1908); American publisher and Senator; editor, *Oakland Tribune*, member, California Assembly, 1933-35, and California Senate, 1935-39; member, Republican National Committee, 1938; Chairman, Republican Executive Committee, 1941-42; served in the US Army, 1942-45; appointed US Senator,1945; elected full term, 1946; re-elected 1952; majority leader, 1953-54; minority leader, 1955-58; member, US delegation to the 11th session of the UN General Assembly.

question, there is great sympathy with the United States in other countries and the release will help soften the atmosphere. Apart from the question of right and wrong, it is clear to me that, because of the question of prisoners, the United States is not likely to make any move; but I feel that in the short run and in the long run the Chinese would stand to gain by showing generosity to the prisoners and releasing them. The release would not be a sign of weakness on the part of China; but, on the other hand, the deadlock would be somewhat relaxed. To what extent it would be relaxed I do not know except for what Eisenhower and Dulles told me, viz., the Americans would be allowed to go to China. It would be a pity if major developments are held up for this rather small matter.

Chou En-lai: Here, a question of reciprocity by both sides is involved. In the Geneva talks, we reached one agreement and we carried out and even exceeded from what was expected of us; but what the United States is doing is to give empty promises. They say 'who wants to go may go', but actually laws and regulations prevent a person from going away. On the question of release of nationals, we must have some more guarantee. It is proved that agreement itself is no guarantee. Because we released three-fourths of the prisoners in our hands and in return there was no guarantee from the American side and there was no response. Therefore, the remaining prisoners in China would serve as a guarantee for the return of our nationals from America. Your Excellency said that the United States cannot do anything beyond a public announcement. But these are empty words. In fact, they can do much. If American nationals can return to America, Chinese nationals should also be able to return to China and we require some kind of guarantee. We will study how it can be done and let you know later.

As to what you said about the prisoners being young, probably you were thinking of the airmen; but all the airmen are released. Among the ten prisoners now remaining, only two are military people and were caught from a plane which was shot down and while they were trying to get in touch with the ground personnel. The United States has denied that they are army men. The remaining eight are American nationals and some of them are old and some quite grown up. If we talk about these eight, then we must talk about Chinese residents in the US who are in jail. If these eight are to be released, then both should be released. Even if the prisoners are released, no one can say how far the situation will improve because the US policy changes and wavers and Eisenhower cannot completely decide it. Therefore, we will take a step and see what happens. Since nothing can be done, then reciprocal treatment may be given on both sides giving freedom to nationals from both countries to return home. The Chinese do not regard the question of their nationals in

America a small matter because they form a large number. Whatever propaganda the United States may make we cannot help it because United States has large news agencies in the world to spread such news while we have no such facilities. So, the issue of prisoners is quite important. The United States talk of its public opinion. But while thousands of Chinese prisoners were detained by the United States, it evoked no comments. So we must see what kind of public opinion it is. As regards Sino-American relations, on the question of release of prisoners we feel there should be reciprocal treatment. After going back from here, we will study what specific proposals could be put forward taking into account the views that you have expressed.

JN: What are the specific laws and regulations preventing Chinese nationals from leaving the United States that you just mentioned?

Chou En-lai: I have already mentioned about them to Mr Kaul. One is a provision by Immigration authorities for obtaining entry permits to Taiwan before they can leave, but these Chinese have families on the mainland and this would virtually make them Taiwanese. (2) Besides, they create difficulties also for the Chinese if they want to leave. There are many Chinese in America on contract and they are not allowed to leave before the expiry of their contract. (3) Chinese nationals have to report constantly to Immigration authorities and there are moreover many other peculiar regulations.

JN : Are these regulations meant specially for the Chinese ?

Chou En-lai: We do not know whether they apply to others or not, but what we have learnt is from the notices sent to the Chinese nationals in America.

JN : I was repeatedly told in America that the Chinese can go back any minute they want and that nothing will come in the way of any person leaving America, provided he wants to go back. In fact, the Americans said that they do not want to retain any Chinese. As regards the permit system, I understood that it has not prevented any man from returning to the mainland. It was introduced, I understand, mainly because the Americans do not recognise China proper. As regards the US prisoners in China, I was told that one of them is fresh from the college and he is not an army man at all because he was physically weak to be admitted to the army. He was working only on the clerical side and understands only English.

Chou En-lai : Your Excellency is probably referring to the case of the two American prisoners who were involved in espionage. It is indeed a case of espionage. They are convicted and the case is made public and their Chinese agents have also confessed. If necessary, we can disclose the details of the case to the entire world. It will create a huge uproar, but it would not harm us. Even Hammarskjold did not touch this case. He only touched on the case of other nationals. If these two are to be released, then the question is to be taken up along with the other eight and on the basis of reciprocity. If the oral promise of the United States is indeed true, then we can put forward a formula.

JN: Americans are not terribly worried about these people. In fact, there are every day hundreds of people dying in the States and it is not so much a question of human feelings. In a way, the China lobby is happy that these prisoners are there, because then they can exploit their imprisonment.

Chou En-lai: Even if the prisoners are released, they can find another pretext. Probably a formula has to be found on the basis of reciprocal treatment and giving some guarantee to us. Only this way can we explain our action to the Chinese people. We feel that probably Sino-American question will remain as it is for a long time. For, as soon as one question is over, another crops up.

(At this stage the talks were concluded and then the two Prime Ministers talked about Premier Chou's third visit to India. Premier Chou said that he would be coming to India on the 24th and will leave for Nepal on the 25th. Premier Chou said that it was a pity that he would be missing the Indian Republic Day only by a day. PM said that the Chinese Prime Minister was welcome to India any time. Premier Chou said that now that he was not going to Nepal, the two Lamas had also dropped the idea of going to Nepal. Before going to Nepal, Premier Chou said, he would like to discuss the question of relations between China, India and Nepal with Premier Nehru and would like to ask if Premier Nehru would like to make any suggestions to the Chinese Prime Minister regarding his visit to Nepal. Premier Chou added that he would like to talk about this matter when he comes to India next time. Premier Chou said that he was shortly meeting the two Lamas and that he wanted to have a talk with the two brothers of Dalai Lama. Premier Chou added that he wanted to tell Dalai Lama's elder brother that he could have his different views, but it was unnecessary for him to carry on his activities).

5. Talks with Chou En-lai—III[1]

On our journey to Nangal and back, in Nangal and today in New Delhi, I had long conversations with Premier Chou En-lai. During his previous visit to Delhi, I also had long talks with him.[2] The present talks were in continuation of those talks.

2. Apart from a number of minor matters, I discussed especially with him:
    (i) The crisis in Egypt and the Middle East
    (ii) The Hungarian situation
    (iii) Tibet
    (iv) Sino-American relations

3. Our talks were through interpreters, the Chinese interpreter[3] and Shri Paranjpe.[4] No one else was present except today when Marshal Ho Lung[5] was a silent witness of them. Paranjpe has taken fairly copious notes and it would be desirable to get a copy of these notes for record in our Ministry. I do not want these records to be circulated even in the Ministry and only the persons actually concerned should see them. They should, therefore, be kept under Top Secret cover.

4. I made also fairly long notes of my talks with him about Tibet and Sino-American relations. I shall attach these to this note. Below I am giving a summary of some of these talks.

Tibet

5. Premier Chou En-lai said that Tibet was a vast territory with only a small population, about one million. It has always been a part of China, but never a province of China as Sinkiang. I asked him to explain this and he made it clear that Tibet had always been, though a part of China, a separate and autonomous part, presumably having a special status which was much more than that of a province and that it had a well-defined nationality, namely, the Tibetan. Politics

---

1. Note to N.R. Pillai, Secretary General, MEA, R.K. Nehru, India's Ambassador in Beijing and Apa Pant, Political Officer in Sikkim, 1 January 1957. JN Collection.
2. Chou En-lai was in New Delhi from 28 to 30 November 1956. He had a series of private discussions with Nehru during this visit.
3. Pu Shou-Chang.
4. V. V. Paranjpe.
5. Deputy Prime Minister of the State Council of China.

and religion were interconnected and the *Kashag,*[6] a kind of Cabinet, held political power. The new Dalai Lama was always an infant and seldom lived of good age. Therefore, it was the *Kashag* that really was the chief authority in Tibet.

6. Other seats of power were the big temples with their living Buddhas. There were three large temples in Lhasa.

7. Tibet was divided into three parts: (1) Outer Tibet; (2) Inner Tibet and (3) Changdo area. The Changdo area had been sometimes part of Sikang Province and sometimes part of Tibet proper. Now all the three had been joined into one.

8. A Preparatory Committee with Dalai Lama as its head and the Panchen Lama as Vice-Chairman had been established and next year Tibet would become an autonomous region.

9. There had been often previously discord between the three parts. The policy of the Chinese Government now was to have an autonomous region with considerable rights, under the leadership of the Central Government which would consult Tibet in all matters relating to Tibet. So far as local matters in Tibet were concerned, they would be decided mainly by Tibetans themselves. Their religion would be fully respected. It was not proposed even to talk of democratic reform in Tibet at present. At some future time, when other parts of China were more developed and the Tibetans agreed, a beginning might be made with democratic reforms in Tibet.

10. At present the living standards in Tibet were very low and there was a lack of transportation facilities.

11. Both the Dalai Lama and the Panchen Lama were very young and very able. They had their own views. Since their tour in China, they wanted to go ahead in Tibet with reforms. The Chinese Government had advised them, however, not to go ahead too fast. They should carry their advisers and others with them. In spite of this advice, some people in Tibet were afraid that their religion would be affected. They did not understand the policy of the Central Government which was to wait and see.

12. Some people under the influence of foreign governments did not want Tibet to be under the Central Government of China and talked about the independence of Tibet. Their activities for independence were mainly carried on from Kalimpong. Some of these people had returned from the USA. In the recent past, there had been some trouble in Tibet, but the Dalai Lama had pacified these people and the Chinese Government had adopted a mild attitude. They

6. The Dalai Lama's Council of Ministers consisted of four officials, three aristocratic and one monastic.

disbanded the organisation claiming independence, but did not arrest anyone. They left it to the Dalai Lama to persuade these people.

13. There was a group of people in Lhasa who had kept constant contact with the group in Kalimpong and had never stopped their activities. When the Dalai Lama went to Peking, this group spread the rumour that the Dalai Lama would not return to Lhasa. Only when the Dalai Lama returned to Lhasa was this story ended. This year, when India and Nepal invited the Dalai Lama, the Chinese Government knew that if the Dalai Lama went out of Tibet, there would be some trouble in Tibet. Still, because of religious reasons as well as the friendly relations with India and Nepal, the Chinese Government left it to the Dalai Lama to decide. After the Dalai Lama had decided to visit India and Nepal, with a large number of companions, the Chinese Government advised the Panchen Lama also to accept.

14. There were tens of thousands of Tibetans round about Kalimpong and US agents were all the time inciting them. The Dalai Lama's brother recently returned from the US. He told the Dalai Lama that the US would give support to the independence movement and welcome the Dalai Lama to the US.

15. As the Lamas did not go to Kalimpong, the Tibetans there were disappointed, but they had not given up hope and were now insisting on his going there nominally to preach. If the Dalai Lama did not go to Kalimpong, this would not be good from the religious point of view. If, on the other hand, he went there, there was bound to be trouble.

16. Among the officials accompanying the Dalai Lama to India, some had been influenced in India by two sources: (1) Tibetans in India including the Dalai Lama's brother in Kalimpong, and (2) local officials in India, some of whom had been unfriendly in their speeches of welcome, calling Tibet a separate country and not mentioning China. The Mayor of Bombay was mentioned in this connection and there was another case elsewhere. (I pointed out that all these people were concerned with the religious ties between India and Tibet and were not referring to any political aspect.)

17. Premier Chou En-lai went on to say that this encouraged the Dalai Lama's officials and the Dalai Lama was faced with the difficult problem of going or not going to Kalimpong. The Chinese Government advised them not to go there. It was even more difficult for the Panchen Lama to go to Kalimpong as the Tibetans there were mostly from the Lhasa region which had been opposed, historically, to the Panchen Lamas in the past. If the Panchen Lama did not go to Kalimpong, this would give rise to misunderstanding about Chinese Government preventing him.

18. Premier Chou referred to some unpleasant incident in some temple in India which had embarrassed the Lamas.

19. One brother of the Dalai Lama who had just returned from Japan and had contacts with Taiwan was also creating trouble.

20. Since the Dalai Lama left Lhasa, those who were out for trouble were preparing for some incident of armed conflict with the Chinese forces. If this happened there would be bloodshed. This plot was discovered in time and an open meeting was held in Lhasa. Representatives of the Central Government announced that no one should try to have such an incident. If any armed attack took place, it would be put down. The Chinese forces, however, would not take any provocative steps. A joint committee of Chinese and Tibetans was formed to deal with this situation. So long as the Dalai Lama was away from Tibet, there was always the danger of some such kind of conflict taking place. But the Kalimpong Tibetans wanted to keep the Dalai Lama in India for as long as possible. Their activities were chiefly instigated by the US and Taiwan. If any untoward incident occurred in Tibet while the Dalai Lama was away, this would result in unfortunate consequences.

21. Premier Chou continued: The Government of India had stated that Tibetans might stay in India provided they did not agitate against China and obeyed the laws of India. If anything happened in Tibet or Kalimpong, the Chinese Government would be directly involved.

22. At our second meeting, we continued the talk on Tibet and I wanted further clarification about Tibet's position in China in the past and in the present. Premier Chou repeated that Tibet was always a part of China, but it was never made an administrative part of China and had always been autonomous. Hence the present Government in China recognised this fact. He referred to past history and the activities of British Imperialism in Tibet. In this connection he said that the present leaders of China had not even heard of the McMahon Line till after the Revolution.

23. I asked Premier Chou as to what his fears were about an incident in Kalimpong. So far as the Government of India was concerned, we wanted no trouble there or anywhere else in India and we could certainly prevent any disorder.

24. Premier Chou replied that he had a talk with the Dalai Lama who had agreed that the situation in Kalimpong was complicated and something might happen there if he went there. The Dalai Lama was conferring about this matter with his officials. It was possible that nothing serious might happen now. But there was another possibility that the Tibetans in Kalimpong might demand independence for Tibet. They might also try to keep the Dalai Lama in Kalimpong and prevent him from going back. Also, the Panchen Lama did not want to go there as he might be treated with discourtesy. The Indian Government could of course deal with any disorder. Premier Chou was informing them so that they could be prepared to deal with any contingency that might arise.

25. Premier Chou then went back to past history and said that even during the Ching dynasty Tibet was part of China. At the end of the 19th century, when China suffered defeat at the hands of Western Powers, the latter wanted to divide up China, but could not agree among themselves. Hence only separate spheres of influence were established. Tibet was always considered by these Powers as part of China.

26. The relations of Sikkim and Bhutan with China were different from Tibet's relations with China. Sikkim and Bhutan were never under China and even the imperialist powers never considered them as such, as they did in regard to Tibet. The Ching dynasty appointed Governors and stationed troops in Tibet.

27. Premier Chou said that in his talks with the Prime Minister of Pakistan, the latter had said that he had always thought Tibet to be independent. Premier Chou then told him the facts.

28. Premier Chou referred to the McMahon Line and again said that he had never heard of this before though of course the then Chinese Government had dealt with this matter and not accepted that line. He had gone into this matter in connection with the border dispute with Burma. Although he thought that this line, established by British imperialists, was not fair, nevertheless, because it was an accomplished fact and because of the friendly relations which existed between China and the countries concerned, namely, India and Burma, the Chinese Government were of the opinion that they should give recognition to this McMahon Line. They had, however, not consulted the Tibetan Government about it yet. They proposed to do so.

29. In 1954, when India and China were discussing their Treaty, the Tibetan Government wanted the Central Government of China to raise the question of the Indian frontier with them. They were told by the Chinese Government that this question should be postponed.

30. Premier Chou said that about 1948, soon after the Indian independence, the Tibetan Government wrote to the Indian Government on this subject of the frontier.

31. Premier Chou added that the Central Government tried to convince the Tibetan Government to recognise the McMahon Line as an accomplished fact in India and Burma.

32. I pointed out that, apart from the McMahon Line, there were certain very minor border problems between India and Tibet. These should be settled soon to put an end to these petty controversies and so that everybody should know that there was no dispute left about the frontier. The settlement should be based on established practice and custom as well as the watershed if there was any such thing there. In these small border problems very small pieces of uninhabited territory in the mountains were involved. They had no importance and the border

should be a geographical one as far as possible. Premier Chou agreed that these should be settled soon on this basis.

33. I pointed out that Tibet had been important for India because of a religious bond which applied both to Buddhists and Hindus. It was from this point of view that references were often made to Tibet. The Dalai Lama was considered some kind of a mythical figure and was greatly respected and attracted crowds. Tibet had been backward and cut off. It was deeply religious. There was fear there of religion and customs being interfered with. If an assurance was given that Tibet would have full internal autonomy, then there was no reason why there should be any trouble. Tibet would undoubtedly change as it could no longer remain isolated. If these changes came on Tibet's own initiative, then they would be wholesome and stable. If there was any sense of imposition, then there would be trouble.

34. Premier Chou said that he was basically in agreement with what I had said. But he wanted to clarify certain matters. The Central Government of China had always been of the view that religious contacts should not be limited by boundaries of states. For this reason they favoured the present visit of the two Lamas to India. Chairman Mao had said that Chinese Buddhists should have greater contacts with Buddhists elsewhere and the Chinese Government was now seeking ways to facilitate these contacts and remove any restrictions which came in the way. This would increase the confidence of the Tibetans also. But there were some people who wanted to exploit this for other purposes. Thus some Buddhists in Western countries had other objectives. The Chinese Government did not wish to encourage such persons to go to Tibet.

35. Premier Chou said that it was right that reforms in Tibet should be carried out by Tibetans themselves. But, even so, there might be some trouble in Tibet because of foreign influence.

36. Tibet's religion had caused decrease of population. The Ching dynasty aimed at this through religion. The present Government of China wanted to encourage religion without any obstruction. Some people in Tibet were more progressive, but others would suspect them of being influenced by the Han people.

37. Premier Chou referred to some Lamas in temples, probably in the east, having taken to arms and surrounded a detachment of the People's Liberation Army.[7] For a number of days the detachment had no contacts with outside. Finally the Chinese Government had to send supplies by parachute so that resistance could be carried on.

---

7. Perhaps Chou En-lai was referring to the revolt in the Changtreng Sampheling monastery, one of the largest monasteries in Kham.

38. Thus, although it was agreed that internal problems should be dealt with by the Tibetans themselves, in practice difficulties arose. Foreign influence came in and created trouble. But for this, the Chinese Government would leave the matters wholly to be settled internally.

39. Premier Chou said that if espionage activities took place in Kalimpong or any other place in India, he hoped that the Indian Government would take action. I replied that if we had proof we would certainly take action, but we could not act unless we had proof and on merely vague rumours.

40. In my talk today with Premier Chou En-lai, he mentioned that he had talks with the two Lamas and told them about my conversation with him. The Dalai Lama was still perplexed about going to Kalimpong. The Panchen Lama had no intention of going there as he felt he would be embarrassed there and also there was some risk to his person.

41. I mentioned that it might be desirable for the two Lamas to go back to Tibet by air. Premier Chou liked this idea and said that there should be a trial flight before the travel by air. He was going to talk again to the Dalai Lama about this question of going to Kalimpong and let me know more definitely tonight.

42. I discussed the programme of the two Lamas in India—their going to the place near Mandi and later to Nalanda and then to Chittaranjan, etc. He agreed. The Nepal visit has been given up. I said that I agreed that it would be better for the Nepal trip to be taken up on some later occasion. I have also indicated that in all the circumstances it would perhaps be better for the two Lamas not to go to Kalimpong during this visit. They might go there on some other occasion. If they fly to Lhasa, their planes would stop at Bagdogra and an opportunity might be given to people to gather there and worship them or take their blessings. This should not be inconvenient for people in Kalimpong which is not far from Bagdogra.

43. In regard to my conversations with Premier Chou En-lai on other subjects, I shall write a separate note. These, I repeat, must be treated as Top Secret. Copies should be given to our Ambassador in Peking, Shri Apa Pant and one copy for the Ministry which SG should see and then pass on to Foreign Secretary.

6. Talks with Chou En-lai—IV[1]

The talks on this occasion began with Premier Chou En-lai asking me about my visit to Washington and my talks with President Eisenhower. I told him that I had had long talks with the President covering a variety of subjects. Among these subjects were the Middle East, Hungary, Pakistan and Kashmir, Goa, Indo-China and especially Laos, and Sino-American relations, apart from a broad consideration of the world problems. I did not say much about these talks relating to Pakistan and Kashmir, and Goa.

2. About Indo-China, I referred to the recent agreement in Laos between the Royal Laotian Government and Pathet Lao and said that the US Government were not very pleased with this agreement. However, I had explained this to them and pointed out how it would be very harmful for this agreement to break down right at the beginning. I think I produced some effect on their minds. They said they would not come in the way and would wait and see what happened.

3. The first subject I dealt with was the situation in Egypt and the Middle East. I explained this at some length to Premier Chou, who asked me certain questions for elucidation. There was no particular discussion on this subject.

4. We then moved on to Hungary. On this subject, there was a long discussion which I need not repeat here. Premier Chou practically repeated the Soviet argument and stood by it. His main contention was that, whatever the previous faults and errors committed, a crisis arose when Nagy asked for the help of Western Powers. The Hungarian Army had disintegrated and there was chaos. The choice, therefore, lay in Soviet intervention or allowing Hungary to become an ally of the Western Powers. In these circumstances, the Soviet had to intervene, and they were right in doing so. I argued with Premier Chou at considerable length and pointed out that, however Nagy might have erred, the situation created in Hungary was deplorable and, in effect, it was the Soviet Government that was dominating the scene there, and Kadar was helpless and counted for little. This had produced a strong reaction in many countries of Asia and Europe against the Soviet. It was clear that the great majority of the Hungarian people were opposed to Soviet domination and demanded the withdrawal of Soviet troops. We discussed this question at great length without apparently producing any effect on each other. We left it at that.

1. Note to N.R. Pillai, Secretary General, MEA, R.K.Nehru, India's Ambassador in Beijing, and Apa Pant, political officer in Sikkim, 1 January 1957. JN Collection.

5. Sino-American relations were also discussed at length. I enclose a note I took on that occasion.

6. I pleaded hard for the release of ten American prisoners and made it clear that there could be no progress in bettering these relations unless these people were released. Premier Chou repeated his old arguments and would not budge an inch. He said that the only approach could be reciprocal. He would think about this matter again and let me have further suggestions about such a reciprocal approach.

7. There our talks more or less ended. I asked Premier Chou if there was any other subject which he wished to mention. He said no. Then I asked him if he intended visiting Nepal later. He said yes, and he wanted to talk to me about Nepal. If I wanted to talk about that subject now, he was prepared to do so. I said I had nothing special to say in regard to Nepal.

8. He then told me that he would be going to Afghanistan from Moscow and then to Nepal, passing India on the way.[2] Probably, he would reach India on the 24th January and leave for Nepal on the 25th. He said he would be sorry to miss our National Day on the 26th January. I told him that he would be welcome on any day, and we would be glad if he was here on our National Day. So far as I was concerned, I would be in Delhi from January 22nd to the 30th.

9. Later in the evening, I met the Dalai Lama. He told me that he had not yet decided about the visit to Kalimpong. He felt that it would be difficult to miss it. I suggested to him to fly back to Lhasa from India. He did not like the idea much and said that he had promised to visit some monasteries in Tibet on the way to Lhasa. Therefore, it was better for him to go by road.

10. I told the Dalai Lama that his brother at Kalimpong often spoke very foolishly and it seemed to me that he was rather unbalanced. I told him that as he had already agreed by a Treaty[3] to Tibet being part of China but autonomous, it was not easy for him to break this agreement. Indeed, any attempt to do so would result in a major conflict and much misery to Tibet. In an armed conflict, Tibet could not possibly defeat China. I also pointed out that we had a treaty with China in regard to Tibet. Our position all along had been that sovereignty rested with China but Tibet should be autonomous. Therefore, the best course for the Dalai Lama to adopt was to accept this sovereignty but insist on full autonomy in regard to internal affairs. He would be on strong ground on this, and he could build up the Tibetan people under his leadership.

2. Chou En-lai was in Moscow between 17-19 January 1957. He was in Kabul between 19-23 January 1957.
3. The 17-point agreement signed on 23 May 1951.

11. I told the Dalai Lama also that I had been surprised to learn that some people had advised him to remain in India and not return to Tibet. That would be the height of folly and it would harm him as well as Tibet. This was not the way to serve the cause of Tibet. He must be in his own country and give a lead to his people. He listened carefully to what I said and did not say much himself. I am likely to meet him again a week or so later.

12. On my way to the airport to see Premier Chou off, he told me that no decision had been arrived at about the Kalimpong visit of the Dalai Lama. Premier Chou had met the *Kashag* or Cabinet of the Dalai Lama and spoken to them about it. He had also met the Dalai Lama's two brothers and spoken to them frankly, telling them that they could hold any views they liked but they must not create trouble in Kalimpong or elsewhere.

13. Apparently, the Dalai Lama will indicate his final decision about the Kalimpong visit to the Chinese Ambassador in Delhi later.

14. I think it is desirable, whether the Dalai Lama goes to Kalimpong or not, for someone on our behalf to make it clear privately to the brothers of the Dalai Lama that we do not approve of any agitation or trouble in any part of India in regard to Tibet. We sympathise with the people of Tibet and are prepared to help them in any legitimate way. But we cannot tolerate any mischief in Indian territory. In the event of the Dalai Lama going to Kalimpong, some special steps should be taken for the prevention of any trouble there.

7. To S.W.R.D. Bandaranaike[1]

New Delhi,
January 21, 1957

My dear Bandaranaike,[2]

As you know, Premier Chou En-lai has visited India twice in the course of the last few weeks and I have had fairly long talks with him about various matters. He will be coming here just for half a day and a night on the 24th January and will go from here to Nepal. From there, I understand, he will proceed to Ceylon

1. JN Collection.
2. Prime Minister of Sri Lanka, 1956-59.

via Calcutta. I have not received his exact programme yet and even the Chinese Embassy here do not know much about it. But it does appear that he will be going to Ceylon and you may have some indication of when he is likely to reach there. Probably we shall have fuller particulars in the course of two or three days.

2. As you are likely to have talks with Chou En-lai when he goes to Colombo, you might be interested in some brief account of my talks with him. These talks covered a great deal of ground and we discussed many subjects. Among these subjects were:

(i) Egypt and the Middle East
(ii) Hungary
(iii) Sino-American relations
(iv) Indo-China
(v) Our relations with Pakistan and Kashmir question
(vi) Goa, and
(vii) Tibet

3. On the occasion of his second visit, he was particularly interested in the talks I had had with President Eisenhower when I went to Washington. I gave him a brief account of them, more particularly in regard to Sino-American relations.

4. I need not write to you about our talks in regard to Indo-China, Pakistan, Kashmir, Goa and Tibet. As regards the Middle East, there was, at the time, not much in the nature of a discussion. I told him of my appraisal of the situation. We did discuss, however, at considerable length the Hungarian situation and Sino-American relations.

5. I am afraid we disagreed about Hungary and what had happened there.

6. As regards Sino-American relations, everything has got stuck up because of the non-release of ten American prisoners in China. It has seemed to me for some time past that China gained nothing by keeping these ten prisoners in detention and could well afford to release them. I have been pressing this on Chou En-lai for some time. He has, however, reacted strongly and said that they had already released more than thirty Americans and there had been no response from the American side. He saw no reason to carry on in this unilateral way and there must be reciprocity. The American answer is that every Chinese person in the United States can return to China if he so wishes. They cannot force him to leave the United States against his will. I shall not here enter into any detailed account of this complicated subject. I think there is some justification for what the Chinese Government says, but it is not enough for them to take up this non possumus attitude in this matter. Eisenhower told me emphatically that he would take no step at all vis-à-vis China, so long as these ten prisoners were not released.

Feeling in the United States was too strong on this subject. If they were released, he would take one step and that is, allow Americans, including American journalists to go to China. Their reports might well help to mould American opinion and make it less anti-Chinese. I informed Chou En-lai of this, but he stuck to his point. At last he said that he would try to evolve some suitable formula based on reciprocity and would tell me about it later. Perhaps when he comes next, he might say something about this matter.

7. About Egypt and the Middle East, he naturally took up a strong line against the UK and France. I largely agreed. About the USA also he felt that it was secretly backing England and France. I did not wholly agree about this, at any rate, in so far as the initial stages were concerned. The US had taken a strong line against England and France after the ultimatum and invasion of Egypt. It had also expressed itself strongly against the Israeli invasion of Egypt. It was true, however, that subsequently the US had taken up some kind of a middle attitude.

8. After this had come the Eisenhower speech laying down what is called the Eisenhower doctrine about the Middle East. When I talked to Chou En-lai last, very little of this had come out and so we did not discuss it.

9. I might mention here that in our opinion this Eisenhower doctrine about the vacuum in the Middle East and the threat to the Soviet Union contained in it are not at all to our liking. I have indicated as much privately to President Eisenhower.

10. Coming to Hungary, Chou En-lai supported the Soviet thesis completely. I could not agree with him, although I admitted that some of the Western Powers had certainly intervened in Hungary and instigated the people there to rebel. But essentially the Hungarian rising was a national movement widely backed by the workers, students and others. I could understand that the Soviet was placed in a difficult position, more especially as just at that time, the Anglo-French invasion of Egypt took place. Nevertheless I could not reconcile myself to the forcible imposition of Soviet policy in Hungary with the help of a thousand tanks, etc. Budapest is a city in ruins today and, according to our information, at least 25,000 Hungarians were killed. Apart from our representative in Budapest who has remained there throughout all these troubles, we sent our Ambassador in Moscow there as also our Minister in Prague. We have had very full reports from them and they have made very distressing reading. I have had little doubt the Kadar Government was only carrying on because of Soviet troops. It had very little backing in Hungary itself. It may be of course that the rising having been suppressed, the Kadar Government can function more or less on its own with less help from the Soviet. But to call it an independent national Government is hardly correct.

11. Anyhow, the Russian action in Hungary seemed to me to be opposed to the Five Principles about which we talk so much. Also from the longer point of view, this action could not possibly solve the Hungarian problem. The Hungarians might feel defeated, but they would remain sullen and discontented. What impressed me more than the fighting in Hungary was the passive resistance of the workers there which continued for a long time in spite of the terrible time they had passed through.

12. Chou En-lai did not agree with me in this analysis at all and was of opinion that Hungary was faced with a critical situation. If the Russians had not acted as they did, Hungary would have fallen into the lap of the Western Powers and this the Soviet could not tolerate. There was something in this, but I did not wholly agree. I think with a somewhat wiser policy Hungary could have remained a friend of Russia, although more independent like Poland. In any event these aggressive methods would hardly gain friendship in the future.

13. It seems to me that the Hungarian tragedy has brought out an essential weakness in the policy pursued by the Soviet Union in the East European countries. The same type of reaction has taken place in Poland and in other countries. In Poland, fortunately, some kind of an agreement was arrived at.

14. In all these East European countries, there are two major fears – fear of an armed Germany and fear of the Soviet Union. I have no doubt that there is increasing dislike of Soviet domination there and no amount of coercive tactics will change this dislike into love and affection. Some other policy has to be followed to make them friends and reliable allies. But evidently the Soviet Union got very frightened at these developments and decided to come down on them with a heavy hand. The Chinese Government have lined up with them completely and supported them.

15. What is particularly unfortunate is that the new trends towards liberalisation and democratisation in the Soviet Union and elsewhere in the Communist countries have been checked and to some extent reversed. The anti-Stalin movement now has given place to moderate praise of Stalin. I do not suppose that these powerful new trends can be stopped. But meanwhile all this adds fuel to the fire of cold war. On the American side also, the cold war is being encouraged.

16. These recent developments indicate certain inherent contradictions in the communist regimes. They also indicate that it is no easy matter to impose communism on another country. Communism may grow out of internal conditions as in Russia or China, but it cannot be imposed. Even eleven years of propaganda, education and indoctrination in Hungary did not win over the Hungarian people. Nationalism and the desire for national freedom was stronger than an imposed communism. As a matter of fact, I think that the Hungarian

people do not at all want to go back to the capitalist system. They want socialism, but they want freedom also.

17. For the present, however, we are again in the thick of the cold war and countries like ours, Ceylon and India, have to face the inevitable difficulties of unaligned countries. We get the worst of both worlds.

I hope these odd jottings will give you some idea of my talks with Chou En-lai.

I hope you are keeping well.

Yours sincerely,
Jawaharlal Nehru

8. Talks with Chou En-lai—V[1]

First Session[2]:

At the outset, Premier Chou En-lai mentioned that after his visit to Nepal he would be reaching Calcutta on the 29th January and would like to visit Santiniketan as he had received a cabled invitation from Professor Tan Yun Shan.

PM replied that it would be an excellent idea. He suggested that it might be convenient for the Chinese Premier who would be reaching Calcutta about noon on the 29th to leave for Santiniketan the same afternoon, spend the night and the next morning there and come away on the afternoon of the 30th.

PM said that he presumed that the Chinese Premier was aware of the latest programme of Their Holinesses Dalai and Panchen Lamas. PM mentioned that Dalai Lama was at the time at Kalimpong and after attending the Republic Day

---

1. Summary of talks with Chou En-lai held at New Delhi on 24 January 1957. JN Collection.
2. The talks began at 4.00 p.m. at Teen Murti House in New Delhi.

celebrations at Darjeeling on the 26th, would return there and then proceed to Tibet via Gangtok. We had taken precautions that there should be no trouble or incident in Kalimpong.

Chinese Premier mentioned that before Dalai Lama left Delhi, a Tibetan called Shagapa[3] presented a document to the Dalai Lama, but Shagapa had been spoken to firmly and warned that there must be no trouble at Kalimpong. The Chinese Premier recalled that this Shagapa had left Tibet long ago and was now staying at Kalimpong.

PM handed over to Chinese Premier a note from Mr Bartlett, US Charge d'Affaires at Delhi, on Chinese nationals in USA and US prisoners in China, adding that this document appeared to be a sequel to PM's recent talks on the subject in Washington.

PM also handed over a letter from Ella Maillart,[4] a Swiss lady who was coming to India in March and wished to visit Tibet. This lady had, some years ago, made a journey through Sinkiang, Kashgar, etc., in company with the well-known writer, Peter Fleming.[5]

The Chinese Premier received these documents without any comment.

Jawaharlal Nehru: Your Excellency has visited many places recently and will perhaps like to talk on Your Excellency's impressions.

Chou En-lai : I would like to talk about the situation in Europe, but before that, I would like to acquaint Your Excellency with the details of our talks with the Prime Minister of Nepal. I have already informed Ambassador Nehru about these talks, but would like to mention them to Your Excellency also.

The first question raised was regarding exchange of Ambassadors between China and Nepal. The question was should the Chinese Ambassador be in

---

3. Tsepon W.D. Shakabpa (b. 1907); Tibetan government official; entered government service, 1930; subsequently, headed finance department; spokesman, Tibetan National Assembly; headed, Tibetan Trade delegation, 1948; moved to India, 1951; appointed personal representative of the Dalai Lama, 1959.
4. Ella Kini Maillart (1903-1997); Swiss explorer, skier and Olympic sailor whose six-month journey into Soviet Turkestan is described in *Turkestan Solo* (1934). Her expedition across the Gobi desert with Peter Fleming is described in *Forbidden Journey* (1937).
5. Robert Peter Fleming (1907-1971); British journalist and travel writer; remembered for his journeys up to the Amazon and across the Gobi desert, recounted in *Brazilian Adventures* (1933) and *News from Tartary* (1941).

Kathmandu or concurrently accredited from Delhi. We (Chinese) insisted that the Ambassador should be in Delhi as this might deprive US of the excuse for insisting on having their Ambassador in Kathmandu.

The Prime Minister of Nepal pointed out that as Nepal was already in the UN, it would like to have diplomatic relations with other important countries in the UN. As it might be difficult for Nepal to have a concurrent accreditation at Washington, it may ultimately be difficult for her to refuse to accept a US Ambassador in Kathmandu.

We (Chinese) said that in any event, China would not like to be the first to have an Ambassador in Kathmandu. In case US takes the first step in sending an Ambassador to Kathmandu, China may then reconsider the matter in the altered circumstances.

The Chinese Premier stated that this question may come up again during his ensuing visit to Nepal when he proposed to reiterate that in any case China would not like to be the first in having an Ambassador at Kathmandu.

PM agreed with this approach.

Chou En-lai : The second question was that of exchange of Consul Generals. We (Chinese) have already agreed that Nepal can have a Consul General at Lhasa and Trade Agents elsewhere in Tibet. Though under the agreement, China has a reciprocal right to have a Consul General at Kathmandu, she does not at present see any necessity to send a Consul General there but may do so later if she feels necessary.

The third question was that of economic and financial aid to Nepal from China. China agreed to Nepal's request but made it clear that the amount of aid must be less than those given by India and US.

This aid will have no strings attached to it. Its purpose was not that Nepal should refuse aid from US, but that US should be obliged to refrain from attaching any strings to their aid. In other words, the purpose was to assist Nepal in maintaining her independence.

Fourthly, Nepal also wanted technical assistance from China. She wanted machinery and experts for starting new industries and installing factories. We (Chinese) pointed out that China could provide technical aid only in light industries but in these India was more advanced. In any case, while China was willing to provide machinery and technical equipment for industries in Nepal, we (China) advised Nepal to approach India for technical experts as such experts from India were likely to be more acquainted with local conditions in Nepal. China has, therefore, decided not to send any experts.

The Government of Nepal had not yet furnished a list of machinery and technical equipment that they required from China – but this would probably be confined to light industries. In any event, China would keep India informed about Nepalese requirements as soon as they were received from the Government of Nepal.

As regards China's general relations with Nepal, the view of the Chinese Premier was that they should be built on:

(a) The Five Principles; and

(b) On the basis of friendship between India and Nepal.

In other words, the Sino-Nepalese relations should be based on friendship between these three countries. Both our countries, India and China, wished to improve and strengthen their friendship with Nepal and neither wants anything from Nepal. My ensuing visit to Nepal will also be in the same spirit and I would keep India fully informed of developments.

I would, however, like to have Your Excellency's views on the subject.

JN: Nepal and India have very close contacts geographically, culturally and linguistically. Nepal can be roughly divided into three regions. The first is the *Terai* consisting of the forests and plains at the foothills of the Himalayas. In this region the people were 100 per cent like Indians.

Then there is the middle valley inhabited by the Newars. Finally, there were the mountain people consisting mainly of Gurkhas. The politics of Nepal was dominated by the people of the Kathmandu valley.

Is Your Excellency aware of the recent history of Nepal?

Chou En-lai : No.

JN: About hundred years ago, the Prime Ministers of Nepal revolted against the King and for the last 100 years the Prime Ministers' clan, the Ranas, have been the rulers of Nepal. The King virtually became a prisoner in his palace without any powers, though he was left in enjoyment of his personal property and wealth. The Prime Ministers' clan—the Ranas—intermarried with Indians.

Until about seven years ago, the Prime Ministers were autocratic rulers with practically no restrictions on their powers. They used the revenues of the State as their privy purse. The history of their rule has been stormy. There were several assassinations and three or four ex-Prime Ministers were exiled to India. Even now they are in India. They brought so much money with them that they are still living on it.

The British Government in India got on very well with the Ranas and completely ignored the King. Nepal had no foreign relations with any country except UK. She had only an Agent – not a fully accredited Ambassador—in

Delhi. It was only five or six years ago that Nepal appointed her Ambassador in London concurrently to Washington.[6]

The British, as they did not consider Nepal independent, sent no Ambassador to Nepal, but only a Resident, viz., a dignitary with the same powers and functions as the British Representatives in "native States" of India. The Resident was all powerful in Nepal. The chief interest of the British was to use Nepal as a recruiting ground for their army. The Gurkhas, when properly trained, make very good soldiers, though without the proper training, as in the Nepalese Army, they are no good.

When we became independent, we and the British had a Tripartite Agreement with Nepal under which we were authorised to recruit twelve Gurkha battalions in Nepal and the British eight. Under this agreement the Gurkhas so recruited by the British were also permitted transport and transit through India if they were in civilian dress.

Recently, there has been some opposition in Nepal to the recruitment of these Gurkhas as soldiers for countries other than Nepal. The Government of Nepal, however, finds the arrangement economically advantageous.

The British also had some Gurkha Recruiting Depots on Indian soil which we have asked them to remove.

No truly national Government could grow in Nepal under the Ranas and under British tutelage, firstly because Nepal was politically backward and secondly because leaders of nationalist and democratic movements were ruthlessly suppressed and heavily punished. The present Prime Minister, Tanka Prasad, was himself in prison for twelve years and was actually in chains.

A nationalist movement, however, grew up among Nepalese young men in India who participated in our national movement.

The King of Nepal had more liberal views than the Rana Prime Ministers. He was, therefore, more popular, was widely respected and almost regarded as a divinity.

About five or six years ago, there was some internal trouble in Nepal. As a result one day the King with his entire family actually took refuge in the Indian Embassy.[7] Only one grandson was left behind. The Ranas officially deposed the

6. An agreement on commerce and friendship between Nepal and the United States was signed at Kathmandu on 27 April 1947, and the Nepalese Ambassador in London was accredited as Minister to the US and US Ambassador in New Delhi as Minister to Nepal.
7. On 6 November 1950, King Tribhuvan, his two queens and three sons and some other members of his family sought refuge in the Indian Embassy. See *Selected Works* (second series), Vol. 15, Part II, pp. 356-357.

King and proclaimed the two-year old grandson[8] as the new King. Though UK was inclined to recognise the new King we refused to do so. The Royal family then came over to India and the revolt in favour of the King spread in Nepal. The UK sent an observer[9] to report on the situation. This agent reported that the situation was fluid and advised the British Government to wait and see how the situation develops before recognising the new King. As a result of the revolt the entire Government began to disintegrate and the Rana Prime Minister[10] could not control the situation. The Ranas who had lost much of their power and authority then approached us. There were talks in Delhi. As the popular movement was not strong and as the King was the only stable and cementing factor, the result of the talks was that the King was reinstated in power. The Rana Prime Minister continued as PM for some months and was then replaced by a popular Prime Minister with a promise of elections in a year or two. Since then there have been several changes of Prime Ministers, but the political situation still remains unsettled.

About six years ago, we had a treaty with Nepal recognising Nepalese independence and regulating Indo-Nepalese trade, etc. We also exchanged letters to the effect that Nepal would consult us in foreign affairs and defence and would coordinate their foreign policy with our own.[11]

The last King died about two years ago. The new King Mahendra appointed the present Prime Minister a few months ago.[12] At present the Prime Minister holds office entirely at the King's pleasure and without any big popular organisation backing him. No elections have been held yet, though they have been promised in October 1957. The present Prime Minister's party is one of the smallest in Nepal. The biggest political party there is the Nepali Congress which is now in opposition.

For the last few years, we have been helping Nepal technically, administratively and educationally. There is a development plan in which we are helping. While some good work has already been done, progress has not been satisfactory, due

---

8. On 7 November 1950, Prince Gyanendra, the second son of Crown Prince Mahendra, was installed as the King of Nepal. The Government of India was officially informed of the installation of the boy King on 10 November 1950. *See Selected Works* (second series), Vol. 15, Part II, pp. 357.
9. Maberly Esler Dening.
10. Mohan Shamsher Jung Bahadur.
11. On 31 July 1950. See *Selected Works* (second series), Vol. 16, Part I, p. 485.
12. Tanka Prasad Acharya, leader of the Praja Parishad Party, was the Prime Minister of Nepal from January 1956 to July 1957.

largely to the weak administration in Nepal. The Nepalese Army was useless. At their request, we sent a military mission of only about 200 persons two or three years ago, which has been training the Nepalese Army.

Until recently Nepal was completely isolated. It had no roads and no airports. People were actually carried in baskets and even motor cars were carried for miles on the shoulders of hundreds of persons. We have, however, built a highway which is nearing completion.

Economically, there is great inequality of wealth in Nepal between the Ranas on the one hand and the people on the other.

The Americans, though they have no Embassy in Kathmandu, have many technical experts working there, on road projects, etc. They also have a library. The British and the UN are also helping in some development schemes.

Chou En-lai : I would like to know the present position of K.I. Singh[13] in Nepal.

JN: Singh who is liked by the King has now formed a party which is fairly popular. I met him three or four months ago. On the whole he impressed me as a fairly intelligent and honest man.

Chou En-lai : I thank Your Excellency for this background information on Nepal. I should, however, like to have a similar picture about Ceylon—a country which I shall be visiting for the first time.

JN: Ceylon and Pakistan got independence at about the same time as India. Ceylon has no history of national struggle. Therefore for some years, even after independence, the change was only at the top. Kotelawala, the previous Prime Minister, was himself a very wealthy man and a rich landlord.

Bandaranaike—a typical Oxford University product—won the election partly because the previous ministry was unpopular and partly because of the Buddhist support. He is a good man and is an old friend of mine. He has, however, got himself tied up with a language controversy. Tamils in Ceylon are agitating against him.

We, on our part, are concerned not only about the old Tamils settled in Ceylon but also the new generation of Indian workers who really built up the tea and

13. A rebel leader who took part in the 1950 uprising and later sought asylum in China. He returned to Nepal in 1955 after receiving a royal pardon, and founded the Samyukta Prajatantra Party.

rubber plantations in Ceylon. Ceylon wishes to drive out most of these Indians. The matter is under discussion with us.

The Singhalese are in many ways very close to us. Even the old Singhalese trace their descent from India. Their standards of living are however somewhat higher than that of average Indians due largely to their rich, tropical resources like tea, rubber, copra, etc. If Indians are driven away, I think the tea industry would collapse.

Chou En-lai: Was Ceylon ever a part of India ?

JN: Not quite a part of India, though for some periods in their history, kings from Southern India have ruled in Ceylon.

Ceylon, like Burma, has been experiencing a strong Buddhist revival. The scriptural language—Pali—which is understood in Ceylon is very much like Sanskrit.

Chou En-lai: I thank Your Excellency for all this information.

JN: I would like to ask Your Excellency whether the cash aid to Nepal that Your Excellency talked about will be in foreign exchange.

Chou En-lai: Yes. It will partly be in foreign exchange.

JN: Will any part be given in Nepalese or Indian currency?

Chou En-lai: Entirely in Indian currency. When I said foreign exchange, I meant Indian currency.

I would now like to talk to Your Excellency about my visit to European countries. I stayed in Budapest for only one day[14] but met Hungarian leaders in Moscow also.[15] I found the situation much better than I had expected. The law and order situation in particular was much better than I had thought. I would say that the situation was now stable. It is true that the Soviet armed forces are still stationed in a few places. One sees signs of destruction in only one or two streets of Budapest. I had lunch as well as meetings with Hungarian leaders in the Assembly hall. Travelling from the airport to the city, I saw smoke from every factory chimney. Shops in Budapest were

14. On 16-17 January 1957.
15. Chou En-lai met Janos Kadar on 10 January 1957 in Moscow.

open till late hours. Automobiles were plying on the streets. According to the Hungarian leaders, the wheels of industry were working again. The same was true of agriculture. Farmers' cooperative had been formed by the administration.

President Dobi[16] told me that Nagy became reactionary and even appealed for help from Western Powers. Many genuine revolutionaries, including the Secretary of the Party who was in sympathy with Kadar, had been killed. On the 31st October reactionaries were released from jail. They beat the Secretary of the Party and grievously injured him. Before the Secretary died on the 1st November, he sent a message warning Kadar. Nagy completely went over to the side of reactionaries—that is why Kadar broke with him.

I attended a meeting of active workers of the party at which Kadar himself was present. I got the impression that the workers and peasants supported the present Government and the situation was becoming stable. I therefore feel that the views expressed by me in my previous talks that the Kadar Government should be supported is the correct view. I have received a cable from Yugoslavia today according to which Tito is likely to support Kadar Government. So will Poland. The only way to consolidate and improve the present situation was to support the Kadar Government. I do not think they will allow past mistakes to recur. Of course, difficulties still remain such as the stoppage of work in factories and the fall in production, but that is all the more reason why we should support the Kadar Government.

Last time Your Excellency told me that some 150,000 refugees had left Hungary. I found this correct. Some are in Yugoslavia with whom the Government of Hungary is negotiating in order to persuade the refugees to return. Nothing can, however, be done about those refugees who went over to western countries. Some of these refugees are now realising that the standard of living of workers in Hungary is actually better than those of workers in Western countries. Some refugees who went to Belgium found that Belgian factories did not even have canteens for workers. I found the standard of living of Hungarians even better than those of Poles.

In Poland, I visited Warsaw[17] and four other places. The new leadership there has close contacts with the masses. This has been confirmed by the

16. Istvan Dobi (1898-1968); Hungarian politician; served as a labour battalion guard during the Second World War; elected to the National Assembly after the war; minister of agriculture, 1945-46; leader, Smallholders Party, February 1947; minister without portfolio, May 1947; Prime Minister, 1948-52; President, 1952-67; joined the Hungarian Socialist Workers Party, 1959.
17. From 11 to 16 January 1957.

recent elections. The new leadership impressed me. They have close ties with the Government and the party. They are, however, keen on socialism and wish to remain in the socialist camp. They are facing two difficulties:

(1) Unfavourable balance of payments: In order to restore this balance they even have to export coal. The production of coal in. Poland is highest in the world but because of the necessity to export, they themselves have to use less coal. The per capita consumption of coal is only two and a half tons per year. The consumption of meat is forty-six kilos per month. Even those quantities are inconceivable in Eastern countries. Of course, there have been mistakes in the adjustments of planning. Poland would at present welcome investment from Western countries.

(2) Difficulties arising out of mistakes of past leadership: Education which has been too doctrinaire does not encourage independent thinking on the part of the individual. As a result, democracy has not been able to fulfil itself. The present Government is now giving attention to these matters. I think, however, that the counter-revolutionaries will not be able to use Polish socialism to stir up trouble. Both Poland and Hungary are correcting past mistakes, but not in the way that the West would like them to. There is little possibility of their taking a neutral stand which is equivalent to going over to the Western camp. Although there has been some recent confusion, future development is likely to be healthy. Other socialist countries will also learn from the difficulties of Hungary and Poland.

Second Session[1]

Chou En-lai: I would now talk to Your Excellency about Afghanistan. We have exchanged Ambassadors with Afghanistan. Though in ancient times China and Afghanistan had cultural contacts, there have been no contacts recently.

The country is mountainous. This has enabled the people to resist foreign aggression.

Agriculture and Irrigation: They, however, have economic difficulties. Agriculture is backward. The main problem is to increase agricultural production. The Royal Government is now paying attention to irrigation. We saw two dams—one near Kabul and also a smaller one near Kandahar. The dam at Kabul has a potential of 240,000 kW. It has been constructed by German engineers. The Government is going to have a bigger dam constructed by Russians.

Considering that they have no railways, their achievements in the field of development are quite considerable.

The principal products are hides and skins, cotton, wool, fruits and copper. Their exports are mainly to India, Pakistan, Czechoslovakia, Japan, etc. They must however have economic relations with more countries.

The foreign policy of the Royal Government is neutral. They do not like military blocs and are guided by the Bandung spirit. They have two Baghdad Pact countries on their border, viz., Iran and Pakistan. They also have boundary disputes with Pakistan which are a legacy left by the British Government. Every year a number of Pakhtoons go to Peshawar in Pakistan for jobs.

Their relations with India are good. If they have assistance from friendly countries without interference in internal affairs, they can develop their country.

JN: About 700 years ago at the time of Chengiz Khan, Afghanistan was a rich country with cities of more than a million inhabitants each, like Herat, etc. These places are now only villages.

Chou En-lai: What you say is confirmed by the historical records that we have, like the travel notes of Fa Hien and Huen Tsang who, when they came to India, also passed through Afghanistan. The Greek, Chinese and Indian civilisations met in Afghanistan.

1. This session was held at Rashtrapati Bhawan and began at 10.00 p.m.

JN: There was a great Buddhist university and school of medicine at Taxila near Peshawar.

Chou En-lai: One of the reasons for the present backwardness seems to be that some of their people have a nomadic history. If people remain nomads, agricultural production obviously cannot increase. In this connection, may I ask Your Excellency whether the desert in Western India was originally there?

JN: No. It has gradually grown due to sand drifts and imprudent cutting down of trees which reduced rainfall. Now we are planting trees.

The Bhakra-Nangal project which Your Excellency has seen will also enable reclamation of part of the land.

Chou En-lai: Your Excellency must have seen the joint statement issued after my visit to USSR. This dealt with the international situation in general outline. In our view there are three types of countries: (a) Socialist, (b) Capitalist-Imperialist, and (c) Nationalist Independent. Relations between (a) and (b) are antagonistic, but are capable of improvement.

Today, except for a handful, the overwhelming majority of people in any country do not want war. Socialist countries certainly do not, as they are engaged in internal reconstruction. Even imperialist countries do not want war. Britain and France do not and even in US, very few do. Thus, we feel that war is not inevitable and can be prevented. Here, the Nationalist-Independent countries can play an important role in trying to bring about a rapprochement between the antagonistic groups by relaxing tensions. Improvement in the relationship between Socialist and Capitalist countries will also benefit the Nationalist-Independent countries themselves.

The question is how to bring this about. In our joint statement it was pointed out that firstly, Socialist countries must improve relations among themselves and present to the world a united front. In the past, relationships between Socialist countries amongst themselves have not always been satisfactory. In this connection, I would draw Your Excellency's attention to the Russian statement of October 30[2] and the Chinese statement of November 1.[3]

---

2. The USSR statement issued on 31 October stated: "The Government of the Soviet Union emphatically condemns the acts of aggression against Egypt by the governments of Britain, France and Israel." And added that "this line of action is incompatible with the principles and purposes of the UN...."

3. The Chinese statement supported the Russian declaration condemning British, French and Israeli armed aggression against Egypt.

Imperialist countries thought they could take advantage of differences among Socialist countries. But such attempts are doomed to failure as will be clear from recent events in Hungary. Whatever the expectations of imperialist countries may have been, the result of the troubles in Hungary has only been to strengthen the unity among Socialist countries.

Both Socialist and the Nationalist Independent countries base their relationships on the Five Principles. They are, however, determined to repel aggression.

Our second point is that one of the best ways of improving relationship between Socialist and Capitalist countries is to press forward with disarmament. But US is actually enhancing its military budget – not only in terms of dollars, but in terms of the number of actual men under arms. Disarmament, however, will benefit the Imperialist countries themselves.

We also feel that it is possible to abolish the antagonistic military blocs and replace them by collective peace. The present period of truce can be used for internal reconstruction. We must, therefore, lose no time in pressing for disarmament.

Thirdly, as regards the Nationalist-Independent countries it is our view that their independence must be respected and in relationships with them the Ten Principles of Bandung must be observed. By extending economic assistance their political status can also be raised.

The Imperialist countries cannot repose any confidence in the Nationalist-Independent countries. In the Middle East, for example, the British and the French tried to hang on to their old privileges. When they committed aggression, it is true US opposed them. But since then US itself is trying to usurp their privileges in this area. Your Excellency has pointed out very aptly that if we are to believe that there is now a power vacuum in the Middle East countries, then these countries could not have been really independent. If there is a vacuum the countries themselves must fill it.

So far as China is concerned, we respect the independence of these countries, as our actions since the Bandung Conference fully prove. We do not try to pressurise them under any bloc. Our friendship with them does not exclude their friendship with others. We have no objection to their receiving aid from others provided no strings are attached. We fully recognise that they need aid to develop. But US aid is different. It is not limited to economic aid. Its object in the Middle East is precisely to take the place of Britain and France. US wishes to impose Eisenhower doctrine on these countries. US wants to make use of the Baghdad Pact and to enlarge its scope.

The recent Five-Power Declaration from Cairo clearly underlines the antagonism of these countries to the Eisenhower doctrine.

635

We feel the best course is to abolish military blocs. The next best is to make the blocs less effective. On the other hand, the purpose of the Eisenhower doctrine is to strengthen such blocs.

Eisenhower's statement that Communism wants to enter the Middle East is entirely contrary to facts. We certainly sympathise with these countries because we are against colonialism. Eisenhower, however, wishes to retain the privileges of the West in this region.

Up to a point, the West also wishes to relax tensions but at the same time it wishes to retain its privileges—an aim which by itself creates fresh tensions. Thus Western policy is wavering and full of contradictions. It confuses and misleads some of the Governments in this region.

As regards China, regardless of whether US recognises us or agrees to our admission to the UN, we shall continue our efforts to relax tensions. Only if a handful of Western adventurers risk a shooting war, shall we take recourse to arms to resist.

JN: Your Excellency has referred to many important aspects of the international situation for which I thank you. These questions are by no means simple. I shall only mention one or two things.

I agree that the majority of countries and peoples do not want war. I, however, doubt whether even a handful wants war, although they may feel that wars—at least local wars—are inevitable.

It is true that the tendency towards relaxation of tensions has been arrested and we are back again at the cold war phase. The problem is how to work back to relaxation of tensions. It seems to me that merely to point out the faults and errors of the other party will only increase tension.

I feel that the problem of disarmament is an integral part of the relaxation of tensions. The compulsion of events—I mean the development of nuclear weapons—has already induced a reconsideration of war as a policy. Even when we differ with a country, a peaceful approach helps in producing a better atmosphere and achieving a relaxation of tensions.

Once we rule out war, the only alternative is peaceful co-existence. There is no middle way. This involves a certain tolerance of those who differ from us. In other words, it means non-interference. We, therefore come back to the Five or Ten Principles.

Your Excellency was talking about refugees from Hungary. We have received certain figures of refugees coming out through Austria issued by the Inter-Governmental Committee for European Migration. Up to the end of last week the total number was 1,68,056. Of this number, 1,00,253 were sent to twenty-five other countries leaving 67,803 in Austria itself.

636

I am more interested in the future of Hungary than in what has happened in the past. I do hope that, as stated by Your Excellency, things will settle down. Kadar Government is anyhow the only government. We therefore recognise it and deal with it.

I also agree with Your Excellency when you say that the present situation in Hungary—both economic and political—is the result of (1) past mistakes; and (2) subversive activities. I have no doubt that there were subversive activities. But such subversive activities could be effective only if conditions were favourable for them to flourish. If such were the conditions after ten or fifteen years of socialism, I feel that something has gone wrong. I hope therefore that, in future, the socialist movement in any country will be more in line with the national aspirations of that country. Otherwise, internal conflicts are bound to continue.

Chou En-lai: There is much in common between our views on this question. I feel however that subversive activities can be very widespread and may go even so far as to affect the top leadership of a country as in Hungary—so that there is no remedy left to meet the situation but to call in Soviet troops.

As regards the past mistakes, the new leadership is trying to rectify these mistakes. It is true that socialism must be linked with the national situation in a country and with actualities. In the past, socialism has sometimes been divorced from realities. For example, too great an emphasis has been laid on industry to the detriment of agriculture. But, now, industries which have been started cannot be stopped for the sake of developing agriculture.

Another type of mistake in the past has been political persecution of some leaders. Kadar himself, for example, has been persecuted.

The US Government does not say outright that it refuses to recognise the Kadar Government, but the US Ambassador continues to refrain from presenting his credentials. Again the Americans continue to give protection to Cardinal Mindszenty,[4] a person whom even the Pope does not like.

In Hungary, in the past, on the one hand there has not been enough democracy—on the other there has not been enough of firm dictatorial action. The old leadership failed to give the correct lead. We have now made our suggestions and are trying to unite all political parties while at the same time eliminating classes.

4. Jozsef Mindszenty (1892-1975); Roman catholic clergyman; Primate of Hungary; 1945 and Cardinal, 1946; became internationally known in 1948 when he was charged with treason by the communist government; granted asylum in the US legation at Budapest, 1956-71; moved to Rome.

637

In fact, the recent incidents in Hungary is a lesson to all Socialist countries. The bourgeois revolutions of the 18th and 19th centuries had their setbacks and did not stabilise for a hundred years. It is no wonder, therefore, that Socialist revolutions which are much younger—should also have their setbacks. We consider the improvement of relations as between the Socialist countries themselves to be a very important point.

JN: In the history of the last one hundred years or so, we see many national revolts in Poland and Hungary. These countries are almost romantically nationalistic.

Chou En-lai: Last time also Your Excellency reminded me of this point about nationalism. I agree that in these countries national feeling is very strong. I also agree that socialism should take account of this fact instead of running away from it. Socialism, which we consider to be a better system, should be able to take cognisance of this and not permit reactionaries to make capital of this factor.

JN: I agree that Socialism is a better system. Socialism, however, has to join hands with the feeling and aspiration for national freedom. If in the public mind there is a conflict between the two, then both will suffer.

Chou En-lai: Quite true. If Socialism cannot join hands with nationalism, none can be working well and there must be something wrong.

JN: I must not keep Your Excellency up after midnight.
I would only like to mention that subsequent to my meeting Your Excellency earlier, in the evening, I learnt from Lady Mountbatten that Ella Maillart is already in Delhi.

(ii) Pakistan

1. The Threat from Pakistan[1]

I have read the memorandum of the Joint Intelligence Committee dated 17th November in regard to the threat of aggression from Pakistan. Although this matter is coming up before the Defence Committee, I am sending you this brief note.

2. I think that, on the whole, the Joint Intelligence Committee have taken too alarmist a view of the situation. It is true that Pakistan is facing internal troubles, both political and economic, and in fact is almost disintegrating slowly, and therefore there is always the risk of some wild adventure on its part. But I cannot conceive of even a wild adventure in the shape of actual war against India without some kind of approval or acquiescence by the United States of America. Pakistan has a large number of American trained personnel. Unless they get the approval of their own Government, they cannot directly or indirectly support a war. In fact they are likely to come in the way and actually obstruct any such development. I do not think it is at all likely that the United States can even give their tacit approval to any such move.

3. I therefore think it highly unlikely that Pakistan will think in terms of war against India in the foreseeable future.

4. The recent events in Egypt and Hungary, far from making such a war more likely, make it less likely.

5. The question of border troubles stands on a separate footing entirely and it is quite possible that we might have to face increased trouble on the ceasefire line and possibly elsewhere. It is possible that the old threat of pushing across a large number of refugees from Kashmir or tribesmen across the ceasefire line might take shape. We considered this matter a year or so ago with the Kashmir Government and devised some plan of action to meet this contingency,[2] which

---

1. Note to the Secretary General, Foreign Secretary and Commonwealth Secretary, MEA, 9 December 1956. JN Collection.
2. See *Selected Works* (second series), Vol. 30, pp. 338-340.

might well embarrass us. This, however, does not involve war in the usual sense. Therefore, the question of Pakistan's superiority in firepower and air force does not arise in this connection.

6. There is no chance whatever, as far as I can see, of UN forces coming to Kashmir. Certainly we will never agree to this. The question of oil is being kept in view. I am told that we have adequate supplies for the present at least and that there is no immediate danger of fresh supplies being lessened. However, we might even take some steps to restrict consumption.

7. So far as the supply of material and equipment are concerned, I am not in favour of our rushing round the world exploring alternative sources of supply. In effect this would mean going to the Soviet Union. It would be wholly undesirable for us to approach them at this stage.

8. In any event we should be alert and keep in readiness for any emergency, more especially of the border raid type.

2. To C.C. Desai[1]

New Delhi,
December 28, 1956

My dear C.C.,[2]

I have just returned from my tour abroad. Among the papers I have seen is your letter to M.J. Desai dated 18th December in which reference is made to certain complaints by Prime Minister Suhrawardy against D.N. Chatterjee[3] for his loose talk.

Whatever Pakistan may do or not do, it is up to us to observe normal proprieties. From your letter it would appear that D.N. Chatterjee did indulge in the type of talk referred to. In fact you refer to Alexander Symon[4] in this connection who might have informed the Pakistan Government of the talk, or Morrice James.[5] I think it was very unwise for you to ask Chatterjee to talk in this way to any member of the Diplomatic Corps and more especially to one from the UK High Commission. It is one thing to discuss subjects which are at issue with Pakistan and put our point of view. It is quite another to run down the Pakistan Government with another diplomat. I think we have been in the wrong in this matter. If I had a report of any diplomat in Delhi talking in this fashion about India, I would take strong exception.

You will remember that I wrote to you some time ago in which I asked you to be very cautious in dealings with the Pakistan Government and the Hindu

---

1. JN Collection.
2. India's High Commissioner to Pakistan.
3. Dwarka Nath Chatterjee (b. 1914); appointed to IFS as war service recruit, 1948; First Secretary, Paris, 1948-49; Principal Private Secretary to the Indian High Commissioner, London, 1949-54; Deputy Secretary, MEA, 1954-55; Deputy High Commissioner, Karachi, 1955-58; Consul General, Geneva, 1958-59; Minister, Washington, 1959-62; Ambassador, Leopoldville (Congo), 1962-64; High Commissioner, Australia, 1965-67; Acting High Commissioner, UK, 1967-68; Deputy High Commissioner, UK, 1968-69; Ambassador, France, 1969.
4. British High Commisioner in Pakistan, 1954-61.
5. John Morris Cairns James (1916-1989); joined the UK Dominion Office, 1939; member staff, UK High Commission, South Africa, 1946-47; with Commonwealth Relations Office, London, 1947-52; Deputy High Commissioner, Lahore, 1952-53; Karachi, 1955-56; Deputy High Commissioner, New Delhi, 1958-61; High Commissioner, Pakistan, 1961-65; Deputy Under-Secretary of State, CRO, London, 1966-68; High Commissioner to India, 1968.

Members of the Pakistan Assembly. This applies to foreign diplomats also. Even in trying to get what might be considered useful information, one has to be very cautious. One slip does us a lot of harm in all the information we might receive. I am anxious that great care should be exercised in these matters and I want you to warn all the members of our High Commission staff to be exceedingly careful in all these matters.

Yours sincerely,
Jawaharlal Nehru

3. Friendly Relations with Pakistan[1]

I met Mr Ataur Rahman,[2] Chief Minister, East Pakistan and Mr Abul Mansur,[3] Minister, East Pakistan, this morning. They spoke to me about their desire to increase friendly relations between Pakistan and India and, more especially, between East Pakistan and India. They wanted to consider trade relations apart from politics. East Pakistan had suffered greatly in the past because the Government in Karachi did not understand its problems. East Pakistan cannot

1. Note on talks with Ministers from East Pakistan, 18 January 1957. JN Collection.
2. Ataur Rahman Khan (1907-1991); East Pakistan politician; joined Dhaka district bar, 1937; secretary of the Dhaka district unit of the Krishak Praja Samiti, 1934-35; joined the Muslim League, 1944; played a role in formation of Awami Muslim League, 1949 and Vice-President of AML since its inception; joint secretary, United Front formed for launching 1954 elections; elected, member, Pakistan Constituent Assembly, 1955; leader of the opposition parliamentary party in the provincial assembly, 1955-56 and deputy leader of the opposition parliamentary party in the Constituent Assembly; Chief Minister, East Pakistan, 1956-58; elected president, Dhaka High Court Bar Association, 1969; member, Bar Council, 1970; floated the Jatiya League, 1969 and elected its president; arrested during India-Pakistan war 1971; elected as a member of Jatiya Sangsad, 1973 and 1979; joined the Cabinet of H.M. Ershad and was Prime Minister, Bangladesh, 1984-January 1985.
3. Abul Mansur Ahmed, Minister for Commerce and Industry, in the H.S. Suhrawardy Cabinet.

exist without a market in India. A trade pact[4] which they were discussing was really as regards East Pakistan. It did not affect the rest of the Pakistan much.

2. They said that they were very anxious to get some commodities from India. The talks with the Indian Delegation had been very friendly but, in regard to some of their major needs, they were told that India herself was in short supply and could not spare anything. They said that they realised this difficulty but, nevertheless, they hoped that India would be a little more generous to them in supplying these goods, at least to some extent. They could buy them elsewhere but they would much rather get them from India. Indeed, they wanted to concentrate on their trade with India rather than go to foreign countries. These trade relations would inevitably have wider effects in political relations also. They expected from India something more than a pure business deal.

3. I told them that our broad approach to this problem was to develop friendly relations with Pakistan on all fronts and certainly on the trade front. We were prepared to go as far as we possibly could but it was no easy matter for us to upset our own economy. I told them that I had suggested to our Delegation to view their requests as generously as possible and try to accommodate them.

4. They then referred to the report that India was getting out of the Barcelona Convention, and was likely to build the Ganga Barrage scheme. They said they were anxious that in any steps that we might take the economic interests of East Pakistan should be kept in mind. I told them that I did not know the exact developments but I could assure them that whatever we did we would keep in mind the economic interests of East Pakistan.

5. I further told them of our desire to cooperate with them in regard to the control of floods. It would not be feasible to have a joint board for this purpose. We had a board on our side. They could have their own Flood Control Board. The two boards could meet sometimes or their representatives could discuss matters.

6. They then referred to visas and said that they would very much like a relaxation. India had made some proposal which Pakistan had not ratified. Thereupon, India had withdrawn their proposal. This had created an impression that India was making the issue of visas more strict. They were very anxious that the ultimate objective aimed at should be to abolish visas and use only passports. For the time being we might have one kind of a visa only for a year and no police reporting.

7. They referred to the smuggling going on between East and West Bengal. Lately the price of paddy and rice has been much less in East Pakistan than in

4. A trade agreement between India and Pakistan was signed in New Delhi on 22 January 1957.

West Bengal. They had to do their utmost to stop this. East Pakistan could not continue if large-scale smuggling took place. They had, therefore, introduced a five-mile curfew belt from 6 p.m. to 6 a.m. This was a temporary affair. There was over two thousand miles of border between East Pakistan and India. It was impossible to cover this without full cooperation.

8. They referred to the imbalance of trade between Pakistan and India, which was unfavourable to India. They would like more imports to come from India. They mentioned various commodities, including oranges. They could supply as much jute as was required by India at fixed prices. In effect they wanted the same realistic trade relations with India.

9. This trade approach, though confined to trade matters only, was an experiment which might well have happy results in introducing a sane political outlook in Pakistan.

10. Copies of this note might be sent to the Minister of Commerce & Industry, CS and the leader of the delegation dealing with Pakistan delegation.

11. I do not know what the exact position is or what commodities are concerned, but I do think that every effort should be made to supply some articles which East Pakistan requires, even at some inconvenience to us. This is good for future trade relations and also in the political context of today it will be helpful. Even the fact of the East Pakistan Ministers coming here at this juncture has been severely criticised by the West Pakistan press.

(iii) Nepal

1. Talks with the Prime Minister of Nepal—I[1]

I had about an hour and a quarter's talk with the Prime Minister[2] of Nepal this evening. We discussed generally the international situation with special reference to Egypt and Hungary.

2. He said that he wished to remove any misapprehension in our minds about the Nepalese Government ignoring or bypassing Government of India. That was not their intention. But, naturally, he had to deal with the Chinese Government as well as with some Russian suggestions.[3] He had kept our Ambassador informed.

3. I told him that I had no objection at all to what he had done, but it seemed odd to me that information should come to me about his talks through Peking and Moscow, and not directly from him or from his Ambassador. I added that we had no wish to come in the way of Nepal Government, but in the nature of things, Nepal and India were closely connected, and we were deeply interested in what happened in Nepal. Our interest was in Nepal maintaining her independence and making progress.

4. There was some talk about consultations in regard to foreign affairs. I told him this was desirable, but it was obvious that we could not consult them about the hundred and one things that were constantly happening. We would gladly keep them informed about important matters. The more feasible course was for them to refer to us any matter that they were interested in, and we would send them our views.

5. He referred to our Military Mission and checkposts. I told him that we had sent our Military Mission and established checkposts at the invitation of the Nepal Government. If the Nepal Government wanted to put an end to this, we

---

1. Note to Subimal Dutt, the Foreign Secretary, T.N. Kaul and Bhagwan Sahay, India's Ambassador to Nepal, 3 December 1956. JN Collection.
2. Tanka Prasad Acharya visited India from 3 to 18 December 1956.
3. The Nepalese Government had not kept the Government of India informed about their moves to establish diplomatic and other relations with China and the USSR. See *Selected Works* (second series), Vol. 34, pp. 389-390, and Vol. 35, pp. 501-505.

shall withdraw our Mission and hand over the checkposts. They were there only temporarily to train the Nepalese people. We would be glad to withdraw them as they were a drain on our resources. He said that he did not want them to be withdrawn at this stage as they were doing useful work.

6. He then referred to the proposal to have elections in Nepal and especially asked me if it was better for a Constitution to be announced by the King or for a Constituent Assembly to be established. He attached importance to the continuance of the King. I agreed with him and said that we would continue this talk later.

2. Strengthening the Indo-Nepal Ties[1]

You all know that we have met here to welcome the Prime Minister of Nepal. Although he is a distinguished guest of ours, yet we do not feel that he is different from us. He is very near to us, just as Nepal is our neighbour. In reality, our two countries are tied by the silken bonds of geography, history and culture. Despite the historical and political changes that have taken place, the close relationship of culture is permanent. We therefore welcome tonight a close friend and neighbour.

A few years ago, we saw a revolution in Nepal and the Government which had existed for a hundred years was changed. There was a little trouble but what is surprising is that in spite of this everything was settled in a peaceful way. That was the first step but it was a big step to have changed the Government which had been in existence for a hundred years. After that the country progressed on peaceful lines. It is clear that we in India followed with interest what was happening in Nepal and the progress it made. Yesterday I was speaking to the Prime Minister when I told him that India was interested in two things—one, the independence of Nepal and second, its progress. To the extent that these exist in Nepal, it is of advantage to India also. We all know that during these years there were many difficulties. It was not easy to change the Government in Nepal. Other difficulties came in the way; there are still difficulties, but gradually

---

1. Speech at a banquet in honour of the Tanka Prasad Acharya, Prime Minister of Nepal, New Delhi, 4 December 1956. Press Information Bureau.

these were overcome and Nepal progressed. I am confident that we will be able to help Nepal in her progress and we will consult each other to our mutual benefit.

India is not unknown to you. Although you have come here for a few days you will see something of the country. During this tour of India, you will see those areas which you have not seen before, especially those where new projects are coming up and a new India is being made. We do not compete with other nations. Neither do we hope to do so nor is there any scope for this. We have our own methods following the footsteps of Mahatma Gandhi who was a unique personality of this age. We are ordinary mortals but his personality affected the hearts and minds of countless persons of this country. The path that we follow is to learn from other nations, and it is our endeavour to learn but at the same time we cannot forget the lessons which Mahatmaji taught and it is our endeavour to follow him. That is reflected in our relationship with foreign countries. It is epitomized in the word Panchsheel. People think that this is something new. This is hundreds of years old, rather thousands of years ago its foundation was laid in India. The word Panchsheel is 2,500 years old. It was current during Emperor Asoka's time and however much we might have strayed away, Mahatma Gandhi brought this message once again to us, and it guides our policy though occasionally, we might wander away. It is my belief that gradually the world will also get out of the turmoil and strife of today by following this path. That path leads us to friendship with other countries. But as I have already mentioned, it is not necessary to emphasise this in the case of Nepal, because history, geography, culture which bind our two nations are stronger than any temporary mistake which might be made. We are therefore very happy that you have come here as a representative of the Government of Nepal and as its Prime Minister. We will talk, discuss with each other and learn from each other and strengthen those ties.

I hope you will be able to see something of the new India which is now being fashioned. At the same time, we have not given up our past. We certainly would like to shed some of its evils but the essentials will remain. At the same time, we have to tread the new path. You will have a glimpse of this. We will try and learn something from your experience and advice. I hope that in your next trip, you will come for a longer period. Thus, we will be able to learn from each other what progress is being made.

3. Talks with the Prime Minister of Nepal—II[1]

I had further talks with the Prime Minister of Nepal yesterday for about an hour and a half.

2. He referred to the question of a Constitution for Nepal. I agreed with him that it would be preferable for the King to promulgate a Constitution rather than to have a Constituent Assembly elected for this purpose. Such an Assembly would probably discuss the question indefinitely without coming to a decision. It would consist of a number of small groups more interested in opposing than in getting anything through.

3. The Constitution promulgated by the King should be liberal and should, of course, allow for amendments by procedure laid down, such as two-thirds majority, etc. Further, it might state that the question of monarchy is not subject to amendment.

4. The Prime Minister then talked about the various parties in Nepal and said that no party had really any large popular backing. Anyone with little money could hire some people and give trouble. The government machinery also was bad and in fact there was not much machinery. He wanted to improve this machinery and for this he was in urgent need of money.

5. He said that he would like the Government of India to give a loan of rupees five crores which could be paid by us in the course of the next three years and would be repaid to us in the course of the next fifteen years. He was obviously very anxious to get this money.

6. I told him that apart from the normal difficulties in our way, the present moment was peculiarly unsuitable for us to make any considerable loan. We were facing difficult problems affecting our economy, and there was danger that if we did not take effective steps, a great deal of injury would be caused to the whole of our economic structure and to our Second Five Year Plan. We were doing something very unusual. On the eve of that Plan we were actually introducing new taxation measures because we were going to take no risk about our economic position. We were also restricting imports to save foreign exchange and taking other steps to prevent inflation. Altogether we were trying to save money as much as possible. In these circumstances, it seemed to me

---

1. Note to Secretary General, Foreign Secretary and Commonwealth Secretary, MEA, 6 December 1956. JN Collection.

extraordinarily difficult for us even to think of such a large loan, although we were anxious to help Nepal to the best of our ability.

7. I then discussed with him the condition of the Nepalese administration which did not appear to improve at all. Any money available would probably not be put to the best use and might even be wasted because of inefficiency or lack of integrity of the administration. Further, I pointed out that no attempt had been made to increase the internal resources in Nepal itself. Nepal's revenue apparently was three and a half crores per annum which was ridiculously small. The gap between the rich and the poor in Nepal was bigger than in any other country. No progress could be made unless these potential resources were tapped.

8. He agreed but said he could not do so because of lack of administrative machinery. Any attempt on his part to tax the rich heavily might result in trouble which he could not face. Also he had no apparatus even for collection. Therefore, he must build up that machinery first and, therefore, he must have money for that purpose.

9. I pointed out to him that this was a vicious circle and I rather doubted if lack of money was the chief drawback. It is the men that were required. Even a handful of men could make a difference.

10. I told him about this and other matters subsequently referred to in this note that if he put his requests on paper in the shape of an aide-memoire we could give them consideration. It was not enough to talk vaguely. It was not enough merely to talk without a proper written record. This kind of thing leads to misunderstanding. And so I asked him for a note. He did not seem to be particularly keen to give me an aide-memoire as requested, though he half consented to do so.

11. He referred to the foreign exchange position. I told him that we were perfectly willing to leave Nepal to manage its own foreign exchange. As it was, we were paying them much more than they were earning and it would be to our advantage that Nepal took it over. He was not quite prepared for the consequences of this, that is, he wanted to have his foreign exchange as well as help from us.

12. I asked him what help he was getting from China. He told me six crores of Indian rupees had been promised—two crores in cash and four crores in machinery or commodities. One crore in cash was likely to come soon. As for the commodities, he did not quite know what to get from China and he suggested that India might buy those goods or machinery from China and pay Nepal in cash for them. This would be set off against the Chinese aid. I pointed out that we were not in particular need of any commodities from China or machinery. What trade we had with China was on the basis of more or less barter or it was a purchase of rice. It would be difficult to make the arrangement he suggested.

13. He then told me that he proposed to use this one crore of rupees in cash from China to set up a cement factory and possibly a paper-making factory. He wanted to know if we could give him experts to set up these factories. I said that we would look into this matter. We would gladly help but I could not give him a definite reply without enquiry. Normally speaking, we would always try to give Nepal any technicians or trained personnel wanted, subject to our own requirements which were increasing.

14. He talked about the Kosi Project and said that it was not much of good to Nepal as Nepal could only get electric power which it could not utilize adequately. I said that if Nepal did not wish to associate itself with the Kosi Project, we were willing to drop it in so far as the Nepalese part was concerned, that is, the major part, and we would concentrate on the smaller measures on our side to prevent floods. He did not welcome this and said that he did not wish to come in the way of our project but he merely wanted to point out that it did not bring any relief to Nepal. He would much prefer our taking some project elsewhere in Nepal which would provide irrigation in some areas.

15. Later, at the banquet last night, the Prime Minister again pressed me to say something about the major loan he wanted. Shri Govind Ballabh Pant was also there. I again asked him for some kind of a definite proposal in writing which we could enquire into. It will have to be referred to our Planning Commission, to our Finance Ministry and to our Cabinet. Pantji said that any scheme for administrative reform should naturally be carefully worked out with priorities because everything could not be done at the same time. We would gladly help to the best of our ability, but there must be a carefully considered scheme.

(VI) OTHER COUNTRIES

(i) Ghana

1. To Kwame Nkrumah[1]

The Residency,
Indore,
January 4, 1957

My dear Kwame Nkrumah,[2]

Thank you for your letter[3] of the 18th December which has just reached me. I am at present in Indore in Central India attending the annual session of our Congress which is rather a big affair. As we are going to have our general elections all over India within two months' time, this session has assumed special importance.

I am happy to receive your letter. Few things have given us greater pleasure than the coming of independence to Ghana.[4] It is the one bright stop in Africa. Apart from its intrinsic importance, I earnestly trust that this independence will have a considerable influence on other parts of Africa. We are glad, of course, that it has been decided to integrate the Trust territory of Togoland with independent Ghana.[5]

All good wishes,

Yours sincerely,
Jawaharlal Nehru

1. JN Collection.
2. Prime Minister of Ghana.
3. Not available.
4. The Ghana Independence Bill, providing for the independence of the Gold Coast from 6 March 1957 within the Commonwealth, was enacted on 7 February 1957.
5. See *Selected Works* (second series), Vol. 34, p. 401.

2. To Kwame Nkrumah[1]

New Delhi,
January 22, 1957

My dear Prime Minister,

Thank you for your letter[2] of the 3rd January.

I am grateful to you for inviting our Government to send representatives to participate in the celebrations of the independence of the new State of Ghana. I would have been happy to participate in these celebrations myself. Indeed, even apart from these celebrations of a historic occasion, I have for some time past wanted to go to pay a visit to your country and to meet you and your colleagues. The occasion of these celebrations would have been particularly appropriate, and we would have rejoiced with you at the attainment of your goal of independence.

But the date of these celebrations[3] conflicts with our general elections. These general elections are held on a vast scale all over India. There are elections not only for our Parliament but also for our State legislatures. We have, as you perhaps know, a federal structure with a great deal of State autonomy, and each State has its own legislature dealing with subjects allotted to it. Normally, these general elections are held every five years, unless some constitutional crisis occurs when, of course, elections can be held at any time. We had our first general elections in the beginning of 1952, and now we are having our second general elections with an electorate of nearly two hundred millions. Practically every adult man and woman has a vote. The organisation of these elections is a terrific affair, and we have over a million polling booths, the idea being that every voter should have a polling booth within easy walking distance.

Not only every Minister of our Government but every other person also standing for election is busy in his own constituency as well as in an all-India sense. Just at this time it is not at all possible for me to leave the country or for me to ask any Minister to do so. I hope you will appreciate my difficulty.

Immediately after the elections, we shall have a new Government based on the majority party elected. Altogether there are, I believe, 3,700 candidates to be elected both for the central Parliament and the State legislatures.

---

1. JN Collection.
2. Not available.
3. From 5-7 March 1957.

I hope, therefore, that you will forgive me for not being able to accept your invitation for myself or on behalf of any of my colleagues in Government. We are anxious, however, that India should be associated with these celebrations and we shall endeavour to send you two representatives. One of these will represent our Ministry of External Affairs and the other our Ministry of Commerce and Industry.[4]

I send you all my good wishes on my own behalf and on behalf of my Government on this great occasion and trust that this will be the forerunner of progress and advancement of the people of Ghana.

Yours sincerely,
Jawaharlal Nehru

---

4. M.J. Desai, Commonwealth Secretary, MEA, led the Indian delegation to the Ghana independence celebrations in Accra.

3. To Kwame Nkrumah[1]

New Delhi,
January 22, 1957

My dear Prime Minister,
Thank you for your letter of the 3rd January in which you refer to various administrative arrangements which will come into effect on the coming of independence. We shall, of course, gladly help you in this matter to the best of our ability. The question of having a proper Code and Cypher Section is important. We are sending separately to our representative at Accra, a note on this subject, which describes in some detail how the Government of India dealt with this problem when India became independent in 1947. Our Acting Commissioner at Accra will explain the position to you. The matter can be further

---

1. JN Collection.

653

discussed with our delegation which will go to Accra to participate in the independence celebrations. If necessary, an official of your Government, who deals with matters connected with codes and cyphers, can come here to Delhi to look into our system himself. Obviously, the object of having a cypher is that it cannot be broken into by other governments.

I imagine that it will be more helpful if one of your officials comes here for this purpose rather than one of our cypher men to go to Accra. It is easier to understand and grasp a system which is working than for some theoretical information to be given about it.

In any event, this matter can be discussed when our representatives go to Accra for the celebrations.

Yours sincerely,
Jawaharlal Nehru

(ii) Algeria

1. To K.M. Panikkar[1]

New Delhi,
January 21, 1957

My dear Panikkar,[2]

Your letter[3] of January 18th.

I think that the French Government is gradually coming nearer to the realities of the situation in their colonial territories. But, I fear, the gap between reality and their thinking or their action is still a big one. Events have moved much faster than their minds. Their proposals in regard to Togoland were not satisfactory. We have taken up definite attitudes about these matters, both Togoland[4] and Algeria, and we can hardly go back on them. Any attempt to go back would not only be a reversal of our declared policies but also would create trouble with the Arab World.

About Algeria, the present policy of the French Government to which you refer, is almost exactly what Guy Mollet and Pineau told me in July last in Paris.[5] In fact, they went a little further in their talks with me, and I see no advance whatever.

The other day, I met the Director of the Agence France.[6] I told him that we had every sympathy for France and we quite realised her difficult position in Algeria because of the French settlers as well as the Sahara. Nevertheless, there was no possibility of settling this problem on any colonial basis and Algeria must have her freedom. If a proper approach was made on this basis, the interests of the French settlers could be safeguarded.

I see no alternative to a recognition of Algerian freedom. The Algerians and other Arabs have not an atom of faith left in the French Government's promises, and they would only accept facts and not assurances.

---

1. JN Collection.
2. India's Ambassador in Paris.
3. Not available.
4. See *Selected Works* (second series), Vol. 34, p. 401.
5. For Nehru's talks with the French leaders in Paris on 17 July 1956, see *Selected Works* (second series), Vol. 34, pp. 408-410.
6. Perhaps Nehru was referring to Jean Marin, Managing Director of AFP from 1954 to 1970.

Recent developments in Morocco and Tunisia indicate that if the situation is handled wisely, Algeria might well be friendly to the French. It is evident that the North African Arabs have a somewhat different approach from that of Egypt and the West Asian Arab countries. It is not for us to make any particular proposal. All we can say is that they should try their utmost to come to terms with the Algerian leaders. In this, they could well be helped by the Tunisian and the Moroccan leaders. Unfortunately, the French have lost credit so much all over this area that it will take some time and some definite steps to regain it.

You will remember the five points which I mentioned in Parliament in regard to Algeria.[7] Broadly speaking, those five points apply even now, with such variations as may be considered necessary.

Yours sincerely,
Jawaharlal Nehru

7. See *Selected Works* (second series), Vol. 33, pp. 481-483.

2. Message to V.K. Krishna Menon[1]

Your telegram No. 138, 6th February. Draft resolution on Algeria.[2] Prime Minister has instructed me to say we agree that in the circumstances you might refrain from co-sponsoring the resolution. In debate however we do not see how we could withhold our support and assume that it is your intention to vote for the resolution. As you say para 3 of the resolution might prove a bad precedent if applied to other situations. But we feel that in the Algerian context the proposal is one which we would not be justified in rejecting.

1. Cable from N.R. Pillai, Secretary General, MEA, New Delhi, 7 February 1957. V.K. Krishna Menon Papers, NMML.
2. Krishna Menon telegraphed from New York that some Asian countries including Pakistan had put in a draft resolution on Algeria and wanted India to co-sponsor it. He, added: "With the Kashmir issue pending it is embarrassing to co-sponsor resolution regarding self determination."

(iii) West Germany

1. To A.C.N. Nambiar[1]

New Delhi,
11th February 1957

My dear Nanu,[2]

I have just received three letters from you all dated 3rd February. You should have no hesitation in writing to me directly whenever you feel like it or want to draw my special attention to any matter.

Your first letter that I read was about Dr Goldmann's memorandum.[3] This memorandum struck me as very significant when I saw it first. I think that the approach he has made in it cannot be dismissed and it may well ultimately be the right solution. But I fear nothing of that kind can be considered at this stage. I gave a copy of that memorandum to Krishna Menon at the time.

Your second letter is about your meeting Dr Schacht.[4] There can be no doubt the Middle East has become the most dangerous and explosive part of the world. Oil may be the major reason. But there is something much more about it and, in the final analysis, this is associated with the whole East-West conflict. The situation is a bad one.

So far as the Soviet is concerned, I have no doubt at all that they want peace. Apart from other reasons, they have been shaken up by events in Hungary and

---

1. JN Collection.
2. India's Ambassssador in Bonn.
3. Nambiar's letter is not available. Perhaps the reference is to Nahum Goldmann (1895-1982), President of the World Jewish Congress, 1951-77.
4. Hjalmar Schacht (1877-1970); German financier; minister of economics, 1934-37; president of the German Federal Bank; dismissed in 1939 for disagreeing with Hitler over rearmament expenditure, and interned.

   Expressing his grave concern over the international situation, Schacht observed that, "the Soviet Union was not bent on war, but may be led to a dangerous path not excluding armed conflict, if the United States came to obtain a control over the Middle East with all its oil reserve."

in Eastern Europe. I believe they are going to make some fresh approach to this problem of the Middle East, though I doubt very much if it will produce any effect.

Anyhow, the joining together of oil and currency, as Dr Schacht suggests, and the creation of an oil pool is something about which we can do nothing.[5] It is the big powers that have to agree.

In connection with oil, I might tell you that the prospects of our increasing our oil output are bright. At any rate, we hope to have enough for our own purposes.

Now to your third letter of the 3rd February.[6] I do not quite understand what you mean by saying that the Government of India is not keen on receiving a delegation from Germany representing the German Ministry of Economy. I have been informed that the delegation is coming here in about a week's time, probably on the 17th or 18th, and in fact our Finance Minister and the Minister of Industries have both arranged to be here to meet them. Such a delegation would be welcome here. Our only difficulty at present was the elections when most Ministers are travelling about.

I hope you will be able to come here in the near future for consultations. It is not much good coming when we are mostly away touring for elections. Probably the best time will be about the middle of March.

Yours affectionately,
Jawaharlal

5. Schacht suggested "establishing a link between oil and currency to arrest inflationary trends." He also "stressed the importance of thinking in terms of an oil pool, not excluding China and without undue delay."
6. Referring to a communication which he had received from the Chancellor's office, Nambiar wrote: "The Ministry of Economy, it would appear, is under the belief based on information from India, that we do not consider it very opportune for a delegation to go over to India." Nambiar added: "Apparently behind this is also the desire to be apprised exactly of our reaction to the idea of a delegation from this country visiting India."

1. Cable to M.J. Desai[1]

Discussed Laos situation[2] with Canadian Government. I learned from them that agreement between Royal Laotian Government and Pathet Lao is for leader of Pathet Lao to be taken in as Deputy Premier. Canadians are anxious as we are that this agreement should be given effect. They have told me that they will press United States Government to this effect also.

2. You might inform our representative[3] in Laos of this. Also tell him that our advice is that Laotian Government should stick to this agreement and at the same time continue to press US for continuing the help they have been receiving. This is to say they should not break with the American Government in any way but make it clear that they have to adhere to this agreement as consequences otherwise would be bad in many ways.

3. I think that US will probably continue their help to Laotian Government but Laos must state its views clearly and firmly and at the same time in a friendly manner to them.

4. We are leaving for London this evening.

1. Camp: Ottawa, 23 December 1956. JN Collection.
2. Negotiations had been on in Vientiane since September 1956 between Prime Minister Souvanna Phouma and the Pathet Lao leader, Souphannou Vong, to decide whether a "Government of National Union" should be formed before or after the new elections for the National Assembly.
3. N.V. Raj Kumar.

2. Financial Help to Laos[1]

So far as any question of financial help is concerned, I am afraid it is almost completely beyond our capacity to give any such help now or in the foreseeable future. We are in a very difficult position in regard to foreign exchange and we are cutting down all our other expenses even to the extent of giving up or delaying many important activities under the Second Five Year Plan. It would be a little absurd for us to offer help to others involving foreign exchange when we find it difficult to meet our liabilities.

2. Apart from this, I am doubtful if it is proper for us to give help even in a small way. In a sense it would appear that we are competing with the US or, at any rate, trying to replace them to some extent in this matter. That may well have undesirable consequences. Our own ability to recommend help to Laos from the US will be affected. Also, it would be quite unreal and a little absurd for us to talk about receiving help from the US when we pretend to give help to others. The only possible help that I can conceive of is technical help, i.e. some technicians being sent. Also, perhaps some Indian products such as small scale machinery.

3. I am agreeable to a message being sent to the Government of Laos on our behalf. This might be on the following lines:

"The Government of India welcome the important step taken towards a political settlement in Laos announced in the joint communique issued by the Prime Minister of the Royal Laotian Government and the representative of the Pathet Lao forces on the 28th December, 1956.[2] The Government of India trust that this step will lead to other steps which will bring about a fuller settlement and will conduce to the independence and integrity of Laos so as to enable the Government of Laos to pursue a policy of peaceful and progressive development in order to increase the prosperity of the people of Laos. The Government of India are confident that all friendly countries will welcome this advance towards a political settlement in Laos and give it their support."

1. Note to M.J. Desai, Commonwealth Secretary, MEA, 17 January 1957. JN Collection.
2. The agreement provided for (a) the early formation of "Government of National Union"; (b) the return of the provinces of Phong Saly and Sam Neua to the royal administration; and (c) the "integration" of Pathet Lao rebels into the national community.

(v) West Asia

1. To Dwight D. Eisenhower[1]

New Delhi,
11 January 1957

My dear Mr President,

I am grateful to you for your message dated 7th January, which was delivered to me by your Charge d'Affaires[2] here the next day. I much appreciate your courtesy in sending me the full text of your message to the Congress[3] and in affording me the benefit of your personal comments[4] in elucidating the policy outlined in that message.

2. In the course of the personal talks that I was privileged to have with you, we discussed the situation in the Middle East[5] and I placed before you my own understanding of this situation and the forces at work is that area. During the past few years, and in particular in recent months, the countries and peoples of this area have been deeply stirred by events, which have come in the way of the natural historical process of change and consolidation. The most powerful urge of the peoples of the countries of the Middle East, as in countries under foreign domination, has been for national freedom. Another urge has been for social progress and higher living standards. Recent events have created apprehensions in their minds lest they might lose even the freedom they possess. A solution to those problems can only be found step by step and through patient effort. Before we can address ourselves to this task with any hope of success, the passions and

---

1. JN Collection.
2. Frederic P. Bartlett.
3. President Eisenhower asked the US Congress on 5 January for authority to use American military forces to protect the territorial integrity and political independence of any West Asian nation. He also proposed an economic aid programme for West Asia. The Congress passed the Eisenhower plan on 7 March 1957.
4. Eisenhower wrote: "The fact that we are seeking this authority (to use military forces) does not mean that we expect to have to use it. Indeed, it is our belief that a forthright statement of our policy with respect to aggression in the area should serve greatly to diminish the threat of aggression, and thus the possibility that force might have to be employed." He regretted "that our thinking in this matter had not, at the same time you were here, developed to the point where you and I could discuss it."
5. For Nehru's note on his talks with President Eisenhower in December 1956, see *ante*, pp. 539-543.

excitement roused by recent events must be allowed to cool down and existing tensions must be lowered.

3. I ventured to suggest to you that a military approach to these problems excited passions and created divisions among the Arab countries and thus added to the tension. It did not, in fact, give any assurance of security. It was for this reason that we had looked upon the Baghdad Pact as a disturbing factor in Western Asia.[6]

4. I do not think that, in existing circumstances, there is any danger of aggression in the Middle East from the Soviet Union. The Soviet Union is too much tied up with its difficulties in the East European countries. Even otherwise, nationalism is a far stronger force in the Middle East than any other.

5. It has been, and remains, my hope that the great prestige and influence of the United States will be directed towards the soothing of feelings and the removal of the sources of discord and friction, which alone can ensure the conditions in which an improvement can be sought for the good of the area and of the world as a whole.

With cordial personal regards,

Yours sincerely,
Jawaharlal Nehru

6. Eisenhower stated in his message: "As you know, we have been under great pressure to join the (Baghdad) Pact but decided against it because of the views of several of our friends, including yourself."

2. To Horace Alexander[1]

Raj Bhavan,
Calcutta,
January 16, 1957

My dear Horace,[2]

This is a very belated reply to your letter of the 7th December and it is going to be a very brief one. As a matter of fact, since you wrote to me, much has happened. I have been to the United States and had long talks with President Eisenhower. I think the talks were helpful, though I do not suppose they made any vital difference to the policy of either the United States or of India. It is good, however, to have this friendly approach.

You have made various proposals in your letter many of which are theoretically good. But, in existing circumstances, I doubt if any of them can be given effect to. It is difficult to take logic too far when national passions are involved. I suppose we can only go forward rather precariously, step by step. Now that the Suez Canal is likely to be cleared up during the course of some weeks, the next step that would appear would be the future of the Canal.

Meanwhile, the so-called Eisenhower Plan of the Middle East has not helped matters. I suppose that Eisenhower means well. But I am wholly unable to understand how a military approach of threats eases tension or helps in solving a problem. The whole Eisenhower-Dulles approach is based on an immediate danger from Communist aggression or infiltration in the Middle East. I see no such danger at present or, indeed, in the foreseeable future. It is quite possible, however, that this non-existent danger may appear on the scene if the policy of threats continues.

The countries of the Middle East are politically, economically and socially among the most backward. They are as far removed from Communism as any country can be. Indeed some of them are quite feudal. That, of course, does not mean that Russia cannot interfere. It does mean that Communism has no roots in any of these countries. The American policy is to support these feudal regimes in order to combat Communism. The result is that in the eyes of the people there the United States becomes partner with the feudal authorities. It is a pity that the great power and influence of the United States are not exercised more wisely.

All good wishes,

Yours sincerely,
Jawaharlal Nehru

1. JN Collection.
2. Associated with the Society of Friends' Peace Committee in London and author of *The Indian Firmament* and *India Since Cripps*.

3. Syria's Role in West Asia[1]

Many a formal speech has been made in the past in Delhi on the occasion of civic reception by foreign dignitaries. It is our good fortune that today we did not hear a formal speech from the President of Syria. Who is in a better position to throw light on the happenings in West Asia other than the President of Syria himself? Syria is in the heart of the region and, as the Syrian President said just now, many accusations have been flung at him because he and his country have not bowed down to external pressure.[2] Representatives of many countries, big and small, have come here. But as you know, the stature of a nation cannot be judged by the size of its population. India is a pretty large country with a huge population. But India's stature is considered high not because of her size or population but due to other factors. In that sense, Syria is not a very big country, either in size or its population. But it has a history stretching back to thousands of years and whenever I have the opportunity to visit that country or to overfly it, innumerable pictures of that ancient history float before my eyes.

Syria occupies a special place not only among the Arab countries but in the whole of Asia. It has a vital role to play in the historical processes that are going on in the region. So we are duty bound to give the President of this great country a hearty welcome. But apart from that, if you are familiar with his life, you will know that it has been one of great courage and sacrifice in the cause of his nation's struggle for freedom. Therefore we feel gratified by his visit.

We must consider it a great honour that he has come here at a time when his country is in the grip of extremely complex problems. We are very happy that he could come. But the things that he has mentioned about the relationship between Syria and India have made a profound impression upon me. What he has said has special importance in the context of happenings in West Asia and it

---

1. Speech at a civic reception to Shukri el-Kuwatli, the President of Syria, Red Fort, Delhi, 18 January 1957. AIR tapes, NMML, and *The Hindu*, 19 January 1957. Original in Hindi. The Syrian President visited India from 17 to 27 January 1957.
2. President Kuwatli, in his reply to the address of welcome presented to him on behalf of the citizens of Delhi, said that certain Western Powers alleged that Syria, by obtaining arms from the Soviet Union, had joined the Soviet camp. Denying these charges, he said that Syria had obtained arms from the Soviet Union for her self-defence and would join neither the American bloc nor the Soviet bloc, but would continue to follow a independent policy. Kuwatli also challenged the theory of a power vacuum existing in West Asia.

is bound to have its effect all over the world. The principles he has enunciated can be applied anywhere as fundamental principles.

As you know, the world has been in a state of flux during the last few years. In a sense, the First World War saw the dissolution of the Turkish Empire and the Arab countries became free. This story goes back to those days and even then, the great powers had jumped into the fray and tried to keep the newly independent nations under their shadow, whether they wanted it or not. They succeeded to some extent. There have been many other developments since then.

Then the Second World War broke out which shook the world to its foundations. Soon after that, about a year after the war ended, both our countries got Independence almost simultaneously. Other countries also became independent. But the interference of the great powers continued in many of them for various reasons, particularly in the oil-rich countries.

Well, it is said that the upheavals of the past few months have resulted in a vacuum there. Was it due to the influence of some foreign power? That is true to some extent. But if you think about it, what it really means is that other powers had continued to interfere till now in their internal affairs. This is the only inference. If people feel that there is a vacuum now, who filled it earlier? Normally a free and independent nation arranges its affairs according to its resources and stature, and with the help and cooperation of friendly countries. But earlier there was a great deal of pressure from the great powers which is why the people now feel that there is a vacuum. The same thing was said when British rule came to an end in India. Now the question arises: when there is a vacuum, who will fill it—an outside power or the people within the country?

This is very significant. There is once more talk of filling the vacuum and outside pressures are increasing. I can understand a friendly hand helping the underdeveloped nations to progress. Everyone accepts such cooperation. But the problem today with the great powers is that they often think in terms of the military approach in finding solutions.

I for one feel that even the history of the last few years has shown that nothing is solved by following this path. On the contrary it creates more complications. Apart from everything else, it is the spirit of nationalism and freedom which is dominant in Asia. The other aspiration which is equally significant is for progress, economic progress, and to get rid of poverty. But fundamentally, it is the desire to hold on to our hard won freedom which is very strong. It is strange that the great powers have not understood this even now. Those who try to scare us that unless we join them, communism will take over fail to understand that the thing which will protect us is our inner strength. We can be strong only by being truly independent, not by being the shadow of some great power. This is a fundamental issue.

665

You have heard some weighty words on an important issue in world affairs from our honoured guest and I hope you will remember them. It is the duty of one of the members of the municipal council to give the vote of thanks. But since I am here, I would like to thank our guest on behalf of all of us. As you know, apart from the President, there are several ministers of his government present here. I thank them for coming here as our guests and particularly for joining in this function.

4. India-Syria Joint Statement[1]

During his stay in Delhi, talks were held between the President of Syria and the Foreign Minister[2] of Syria and the Prime Minister of India.

These related to the international situation and, in particular, to the situation in the Middle East. The talks, which took place in a most cordial atmosphere, have shown a close similarity of views over a wide range of international problems.

It was agreed that among the most signal developments in recent times has been the emergence into freedom of a large number of countries of Asia and Africa. With freedom from colonial and imperialist domination has emerged a new thinking. This is embodied in the joint communique by Asian and African states in Bandung in April 1955. The desire of Syria and India for peace and friendship with all nations and to regulate their international relations on the basis of the Bandung principles were reaffirmed. These principles, particularly those of peaceful co-existence, non-aggression and non-intervention deserve to be commended to all nations. It is necessary that conditions should be created favourable for the development of international thinking on the lines of the Bandung declaration. The policy of non-alignment pursued by the two countries can best contribute to peace and harmony and to the realization of the Bandung principles.

The prime need of the hour is that the passions and conflicts which have recently convulsed the world and threatened world peace should be allowed to

1. Text of joint statement following talks with the President of Syria, 21 January 1957. From *The Hindustan Times*, 22 January 1957.
2. Salah Bitar.

666

subside. All nations should help in this process and nothing should be done which would aggravate the tensions and conflicts in the Middle East. Progressive forces working for freedom and stability and for the realization of the national aspirations of the people in this area should be encouraged so that they may help in healing divisions and conflicts. The UN with its recent increased authority can assist in this process. A big responsibility lies on the Big Powers in this regard.

In reviewing the recent grave events in the Middle East, satisfaction was expressed during the talks at the clear and unequivocal stand taken by the UN in regard to the aggression against Egypt. The several resolutions adopted by the UN in this regard represented a triumph of those principles upon which are founded the faith and hope of countries which have lately emerged into full independence. It is a matter of gratification that the common loyalty of the two countries to these principles had led to a widening area of cooperation between them.

In Egypt, it is a matter of concern that, while most foreign troops have been withdrawn, Israeli troops continue to occupy a part of Egyptian territory and the Gaza strip. Any further delay in the withdrawal of these troops is likely to create new dangers. It is hoped that the UN will ensure the complete withdrawal of all Israeli troops behind the Armistice lines.

The problems of the Middle East can only be solved if the countries in that are able, in complete freedom and without domination by any foreign power, to develop in accordance with their genius and traditions, more particularly in the economic and social fields, in order to raise the standards of living of their people. A military approach to the problems of this area will only serve to create further disharmony and instability besides contributing to the heightening of tension and endangering world peace. Intervention by the Big Powers in the form of military pacts and alliances is detrimental to peace and stability in the Middle East. The Baghdad Pact has caused bitter conflicts and divisions in the Arab world and has greatly increased international tensions.

The two countries have subscribed to the declaration at Bandung, that colonialism in all its manifestations is evil which should be brought to an end. They reaffirm their support of the cause of freedom and independence of all peoples under foreign domination which contribute a denial of fundamental human rights. In particular, they declare their strong support for the movement for national freedom in Algeria. They trust that the Algerian people will be enabled to exercise their right of self-determination and independence without further delay.

The President and the Prime Minister note with satisfaction the close and cordial relation existing between the Governments and peoples of Syria and

India. They reiterate the desire of the two countries to further strengthen their relations, and to this end they are resolved to bring about increasing cultural and economic cooperation between their countries.

5. The Soviet Proposal[1]

The Soviet Ambassador[2] has just been to see me and he handed to me a copy of a declaration which the Soviet Government propose to make, or rather it would be more correct to say that they are suggesting to the Governments of the USA, Britain and France to make a joint declaration with them on the lines suggested.[3]

2. I was told that this was, first of all, an unofficial translation. Secondly, that it was a confidential document and no publicity should be given to it at this stage. It is not even clear whether this document has been sent to the USA, Britain and France yet. The Ambassador did not know. But I take it that since it has been sent to us, it must have been sent not only to those three countries, but possibly to others also. I was told that the Soviet Government would probably give publicity to it themselves in the near future. For the present therefore, we must treat it as confidential.

3. The Soviet Ambassador added that the Soviet Government would welcome the expression of a positive opinion on behalf of India about this proposal.

4. I told him that we would naturally give it careful consideration. My broad reaction was that so far as India's policy was concerned, it fitted in with that.

1. Note to N.R. Pillai, Secretary General, MEA, 11 February 1957. JN Collection.
2. Mikhail A. Menshikov.
3. According to the proposed declaration, the Governments of the USSR, the USA, Britain, and France pledged to observe the following principles in their policy towards the countries of the Near and Middle East: (i) Maintenance of peace in the region by settling disputes through negotiations; (ii) Non-interference in the internal affairs of these countries and respect for their sovereignty and independence; (iii) Refusal from all kind of attempts to involve these countries into military blocs; (iv) Liquidation of foreign bases and withdrawal of foreign troops from the territories of these countries; (v) Refusal to supply arms to these countries; and (vi) Promotion of economic development of these countries.

But the proposal involved putting an end to military blocs and liquidation of foreign bases and withdrawal of foreign troops from Near and Middle East countries. This obviously raised basic questions and I rather doubted very much if the Western countries could, at this stage, agree to this. In particular, it involved the Baghdad Pact about which so much had been said recently.

5. I did not say this to him, but there was also the reference to the Bandung Conference.[4] One could hardly expect the Western countries to express approval of the declaration of the Bandung Conference.

4. The proposed declaration stated that the four powers "recognize and respect the high principles of the relations between the States, formulated at the Bandung Conference of the countries of Asia and Africa."

(VII) MISCELLANEOUS

1. To Earl Warren[1]

New Delhi,
6 December 1956

My dear Chief Justice,[2]

It was very good of you to write to me your letter of November 19 and I thank you for it.

We were very happy to welcome you and Mrs Warren in our country. Apart from the pleasure this visit gave, I am sure it has been helpful in promoting a better understanding between the United States and India which we, as well as you, so much desire. I entirely agree with you that in spite of many superficial differences, there is much that is common in the basic approach of our two countries. Unfortunately, not much is said about this and a great deal is said about the superficial differences.

I think that the time has come when we can look at each other in truer perspective and understand each other better. To the United States of America it is given to play a vital and leading part in world affairs. We in India are trying in our own way to fashion our destiny. We do not presume to interfere in the affairs of the rest of the world, nor have we the desire or capacity to do so. But, inevitably, no country can isolate itself from these currents and conflicts of the world, and so we have to play our part to some extent. I see no reason why that part should not lead us to an ever greater measure of cooperation with the United States.

I am greatly looking forward to my visit to the United States and only regret that it is going to be so brief. In particular, I look forward with pleasure to meeting you and Mrs Warren again.

With all good wishes,

Yours sincerely,
Jawaharlal Nehru

1. JN Collection.
2. (1891-1974); admitted to the California bar, 1914; practised in San Francisco and Oakland, 1914-17; served as deputy city attorney, chief deputy attorney and district attorney in various US States, 1919-39; Attorney-General, California, 1939-43; Governor, California, 1943-53; Chief Justice, United States Supreme Court, 1953-69.

2. To Vijayalakshmi Pandit[1]

.New Delhi,
6 December 1956

My dear Nan,

I have just received your letter of the 3rd December. Last night was the last function connected with foreign guests. It was a banquet by the Prime Minister of Nepal. Today, therefore, I could look after my own work to some extent. Unfortunately Dr Ambedkar[2] died this morning or in the course of the night. He appeared to be well last night and was working at his desk. He went to bed without any complaint whatever and did not wake up at all. That is the way one would like to die.

I have just a week now before we depart for the West. The American press has boosted up my visit to the United States so much as something in the nature of a world event that I am quite alarmed. If one expects so much from anything, one is bound to be disappointed. I think it is a very good thing that I shall meet President Eisenhower and have a fairly leisurely talk with him. But how we are going to change the world's course of history in a day or two is more than I can understand.

My stay in London on the 15th has been somewhat shortened by the insistence of the American pilot that we must leave at 6 p.m. at the latest on the 15th. This means that we shall have to spend quite a long time in a remote corner in Newfoundland. It also means that I shall have to leave for the airport at about 5:15. This gives very little time in London.

On my return, I do not quite know if there is possibility of any Minister there wanting to see me. I do not wish anything to be said on my part. But should they want to see me, naturally I shall have to do so. The only day is Christmas Day, which is not a good day.

Bijju Bhabi[3] has been very slowly recovering.

Yours affectionately,
Jawahar

1. JN Collection.
2. B.R. Ambedkar, one of the principal draftsmen of the Indian Constitution and Law Minister from 1947 to 1951.
3. Rameshwari Nehru, wife of Brijlal Nehru.

3. Cable to Subimal Dutt[1]

I am amazed at comments appearing in *Hindustan Times* and *Times of India* about Krishna Menon and my disagreements with him, especially referring to his not being present at my interviews with President Eisenhower. At any time such comments would have been undesirable and wrong, but at a time when I am here they can only be due to folly, malice or complete irresponsibility. I propose to take this matter up on my return but meanwhile please ask PRO to make it clear that there is no justification whatever for these comments. There has been no difference of opinion between Prime Minster and Krishna Menon and Prime Minister has repeatedly expressed his high appreciation of the work done by the Indian Delegation in the UN. At Prime Minister's talks with President no one else was present.

I am asking Krishna Menon to go to Cairo very soon to confer with Nasser.

Please inform Pantji that I am very angry with Durga Das.[2] No facilities should in future be given to him in the Ministry of External Affairs.

---

1. Camp: Ottawa, 22 December 1956. JN Collection. M.O. Mathai, Nehru's personal assistant, however, noted on a copy of this telegram: "After reconsideration this was not sent."
2. Correspondent of *The Hindustan Times*.

4. Irresponsible Newspaper Reporting[1]

I find on my return that some of our newspapers have been full of speculations about my talks in America and other countries. This is somewhat embarrassing for me and might embarrass others. It is difficult for me to go about contradicting what appears in the newspapers, even when this happens to be untrue.

2. What have distressed me even more are certain other references in the newspapers here. During my absence some Indian newspapers wrote in very unbecoming language about our colleague, Shri V.K. Krishna Menon, criticizing the part he took at the debates in the United Nations General Assembly. These remarks were telegraphed to the American papers and I read them there. The criticisms were entirely unjustified and had no real basis in fact. The timing of them was also most unfortunate. They gave a handle to many of our opponents in foreign countries who made much of them. They affected our position in the United Nations as the Leader of our Delegation was criticized and it was stated, quite wrongly, that his actions or speeches were not in consonance with our views. This, of course, was wholly incorrect as we have been in constant touch.

3. While I cannot object to any criticism of newspapers, what troubles me is that it is stated, or inference is allowed to be drawn, that the source of the news is from high Government circles.

4. Another matter which has distressed me is a discussion in the newspapers about the President of India. Again, it is quite open to the newspapers to discuss this subject and give their views. What I object to is dragging my name and other names into this discussion. In fact, it has been stated in the press that before I went to England, I, in common with other colleagues, came to a decision about the next President. As a matter of fact, there was no talk or even mention of this subject to me or by me and, so far as I am concerned, I had given no thought to the matter. It is very embarrassing for me, as it seems to me to some others, to have this kind of publicity to be given in regard to our highest office. I cannot go about writing to the press on this subject. But I have ventured to write to you so that any misapprehension that might have been created should be removed.

1. Note, 29 December 1956. JN Collection.

5. To Norodom Sihanouk[1]

The Residency,
Indore,
5 January 1957

My dear Norodom Sihanouk,

It has been a great pleasure to me to receive your friendly and generous letter of December 7th.[2] I hope you will forgive me for the delay in replying to it. It came when I had already left for the United States of America and it was only on my return that I received it. Since then I have been very fully occupied.

As I write this letter, I am in Indore in Central India attending the annual session of our National Congress. This annual Congress session is always a great event not only for our national organization, but for the country. As we are going to have our general elections beginning in about seven weeks' time, we have been busy with preparations for them and the selection of our candidates. We have also issued a long election manifesto.

This business of elections here is on a tremendous scale because we have adult suffrage and every man and woman above twenty-one is entitled to vote. We have now about two hundred million voters on our registers.

The organization of these elections is a highly complicated affair. In order to ensure that they are quite fair and impartial, we have an Election Commission which works independently of Government and organises these elections. This Commission is putting up over one million polling booths all over the country to facilitate voting and avoiding any voter having to go a long distance in order to vote.

All this is, you will observe, on a bigger scale of democratic elections than in any other country. Presently we shall start our election campaigns and I shall have to travel about India a good deal.

Your visit to Delhi made us all happy. My daughter Indira and I are both sorry that your daughter[3] could not come. I hope that she will be able to come here

---

1. JN Collection.
2. Norodom Sihanouk expressed his "profound and affectionate thanks for the very warm and comprehensive welcome", which he and the Cambodian delegation were given during their visit to India in connection with the Buddha Jayanti celebrations. He also conveyed his "respectful homage and thanks" to the President and "respectful salutations" to Indira Gandhi.
3. Sorya Roeungsi.

later. It was a pity that your visit was so short and that you could not yourself go to some other parts of India, both those of historic interest and those which demonstrate our new development schemes.

I am glad, however, that the distinguished members of your delegation to the Buddha Jayanti celebrations could tour about India a little and form some idea of our country and what we are doing here. They will be able to give you some account of this tour of theirs.

My visit to the United States of America was a short one, but I think it did much good because we could explain to each other our respective points of view. We found that although we differed about some matters of importance, we agreed in regard to many other matters. I am happy that this visit has brought our two countries somewhat nearer to each other, even though we may not agree in regard to some policies.

So far as we are concerned in India, we are firmly convinced that a policy of non-alignment to military blocs and alliances is not only the best for us but it also serves the cause of peace in the world. We want to be friends with all countries and to cooperate wherever possible. I feel that this is the only way to serve the cause of peace which is so essential.

I fear that the New Year is likely to be a difficult one. As we solve one problem in the world, others arise. We have to face these problems with courage and patience.

I send Your Royal Highness all my good wishes for this year and my hopes for the progress and prosperity of your country and people. My daughter Indira joins me in sending her regards to you.

Yours sincerely,
Jawaharlal Nehru

6. Press Comments on Krishna Menon[1]

You can certainly contradict (informally) the message from Sunder Kabadi. This message is wrong in every particular.[2]

(1) I have no intention of making any change in the work being done by Shri Krishna Menon in regard to international affairs.

(2) There is no question of Sir Anthony Eden refusing to see him in London as no request was made to him. Shri Krishna Menon met the Foreign Secretary, Mr Selwyn Lloyd, in London.

(3) Neither President Eisenhower nor Sir Anthony Eden said anything to me about Shri Krishna Menon. Also, there can be no question of either of them telling me that Shri Krishna Menon is persona non grata to them. He is not accredited either to the US Government or the UK Government, and it would be improper for any foreign Government to refer to our representatives elsewhere.

2. There has been in the United States and, to some extent, in England widespread propaganda against Shri Krishna Menon. For foreigners to indulge in this is one thing, but for our journalists either in foreign countries or in India to support this propaganda is highly improper. Shri Krishna Menon is far the ablest and the most outstanding figure in the United Nations. In carrying out India's policy, he comes into conflict with some policies of other countries and, because of his great ability, he creates an impression in the UN. This irritates others.

---

1. Note to A.R. Vyas, Deputy Press Information Officer, 9 January 1957. JN Collection.
2. In a dispatch from London published in the *Indian Express* of 9 January 1957, Sunder Kabadi stated that he understood "from the most reliable sources that following representations by British and American administrations," Prime Minister Nehru had decided to utilize the services of Krishna Menon at home in New Delhi instead of in international matters. He added that during Menon's recent visit to London, Eden had refused to see him. He further wrote that both Eisenhower and Eden had apparently informed the Indian Government that Menon was no longer persona grata with them.

7. To Apa B. Pant[1]

Circuit House,
Rajgir,
12 January 1957

My dear Apa,[2]

This evening at Nalanda, some time after you had gone, a number of Tibetans or perhaps Nepalese Tibetans came to me and told me that they wanted to make some presents to the Dalai Lama and the Panchen Lama. I told them that the two Lamas had gone. They did not seem to accept my word for this presumably because they had seen me with them.

Finally, they wanted to give me some money and scarves. I told them that there was no point in their giving these to me or, in the alternative, I asked them how they wanted me to use them. They insisted on giving the money and said that this should be handed over to the Dalai Lama and the Panchen Lama. Thereupon, I took this money and some scarves, etc. I am sending this to you in two envelopes. The one addressed to the Dalai Lama contains cash (notes) for Rs 207/- and four scarves; also some small stones. The other addressed to the Panchen Lama contains cash for Rs 140/6/-, one scarf and some small stones. Will you please give these to the Dalai Lama and the Panchen Lama respectively and tell them how I received the money on their behalf?

Yours sincerely,
Jawaharlal Nehru

1. JN Collection.
2. Political Officer in Sikkim.

8. To Ali Sastroamidjojo[1]

New Delhi,
19 January 1957

My dear Prime Minister,[2]

Your letter[3] of December 10 was handed to me yesterday by your Ambassador[4] in New Delhi. Together with this was a corrected version of the joint statement which the Prime Ministers of Burma, Ceylon, Indonesia and India had issued on the 14th November 1956.[5]

As you say, Prime Minister Suhrawardy holds a different opinion from that stated in our joint statement in regard to certain important matters. Indeed recent events have brought out this marked difference of opinion.[6]

But I do not quite understand how a joint statement which was issued by us to the public over two months ago can be subject to any change or variation. That statement is a matter of history. It cannot be changed. In the event of a meeting of the Prime Ministers of the Colombo countries taking place again, they can issue a fresh statement if they agree upon it. But the old statement must necessarily remain as it is.

1. JN Collection.
2. Of Indonesia.
3. Sastroamidjojo wrote that the written comments received by him from the Government of Pakistan on the joint statement issued by the Prime Ministers of India, Indonesia, Sri Lanka and Myanmar in New Delhi on 14 November 1956 corresponded with the conclusions he had drawn after his discussions in Karachi with Prime Minister Suhrawardy on 15 November 1956. Referring to the Egyptian crisis and the events in Hungary, Sastroamidjojo wrote that Suhrawardy "gave his active support in our stand on both these international problems, except minor alteration in the wordings", but he could not convince Suhrawardy that the paragraph in the joint statement about avoidance of military pacts was "not at all incompatible with the Bandung principles on this subject."
4. R.H. Abdul Kadir.
5. Sastroamidjojo, however, thought "it would be rather difficult to change our joint statement at this late hour", and added: "It would be satisfactory to me if the Prime Minister of Pakistan would be willing to subscribe to our joint statement with the reservations he has put forward in his letter."
6. Speaking at Lahore on 2 December 1956, Suhrawardy defended Pakistan's policy of military alliances. He said that in case Pakistan decided to remain neutral and weak, the immediate disadvantage to her would be that she would not be able to assert her rights. He stated: "We may have to give up our rights on Kashmir or canal waters and in our despair we may have to bow our heads to a superior and a more powerful neighbour."

It is open to Prime Minister Suhrawardy of course to state, if he so chooses, that he agrees to that statement subject to certain matters with which he does not agree.

As a matter of fact, all kinds of important developments have taken place during these past two months and that joint statement of ours is, to that extent, out of date.

With all good wishes to you,

Yours sincerely,
Jawaharlal Nehru

LETTERS TO CHIEF MINISTERS

1

New Delhi,
8 December, 1956

My dear Chief Minister,

My last letter was sent to you, I think, on the Vijaya Dashmi Day, October 14. I am exceedingly sorry for this big gap. The measure of my distress at this is to some extent the measure of the many activities that have rather overwhelmed me during this period. We have gone through, and indeed we are still going through, an international crisis of great magnitude which has demanded not only time but hard thinking. We have had the UNESCO Conference which attracted a very large number of eminent persons. We have also had the Buddha Jayanti celebrations which also attracted many distinguished visitors. Apart from the work done in these conferences, it became necessary to meet many of these guests of ours as well as to participate in numerous functions.

2. I do not propose to give you a list of our special visitors, but I would like to mention four of them: U Nu of Burma, Mr Chou En-lai, Premier of China, the Dalai Lama and the Panchen Lama.

3. I do not know how exactly to deal with this long period of seven weeks. There is much to write because event has succeeded event and sensation followed sensation. So fast has been the pace of these events that much that happened in October or November is already rather distant history and there is little point in my repeating here. I shall, however, say something about the international situation and some of the consequences of the events in Egypt and Hungary.[2]

4. What happened in Egypt and Hungary is of course of first importance for a variety of reasons and the world has been rather near a major war. I should, however, like to lay stress on two aspects particularly.

5. The first relates to Anglo-French action in Egypt. It is patent that this action has failed completely. It was aimed principally at bringing down the Nasser Government there and establishing a more pliable tool. This transformation was supposed to lead to a re-establishment of British influence over Western Asia and of French influence in Northern Africa and especially Algeria. In the result, it is President Nasser who has come out of it with greater strength and far greater

1. File Nos. 25(30)/56-57-PMS. These letters have also been printed in G. Pathasarathi (ed.), *Jawaharlal Nehru: Letters to Chief Ministers, 1947-1964*, Vol. 4, 1954-1957 (New Delhi, 1988), pp. 462-469 and 473-477.
2. See *ante*, pp. 544-554 and pp. 555-579. Also see *Selected Works* (second series) Vol. 35, pp. 334-351, for the situation in Egypt and Hungary; pp. 389-449, for the Suez Crisis; and pp. 450-484, for the developments of Hungary.

prestige, and both the UK and France have suffered tremendously in their prestige, apart from the great losses that they sustained.

6. This has demonstrated that it is very difficult now for an open reversion to colonialism. Even a strong power cannot do so at the expense of a weak country, because of world opinion, including of course Asian opinion, and the many other consequences that flow from this. Colonialism or foreign domination may well continue where it exists today for some time longer, but it is in retreat and has been dealt a hard blow. England and France, two great colonial powers, have not only suffered very greatly in prestige, but have also been shown up as really not strong enough to hold empires. In effect, this has changed the balance of power in the world.

7. The events in Hungary have demonstrated that militant communism, however powerful its backing, cannot be forcibly imposed for long over a country. Communism might possibly grow in a country if it is allied to nationalism and the country relies on its own strength. Hungary was for ten years under a Communist regime dominated over by the Soviet Union. During these ten years there was, no doubt, a great deal of propaganda and indoctrination. But, as events have proved, it could not stand up against the strong nationalist urge of the Hungarian people. Thus, Russia has not only suffered greatly in prestige by what it did in Hungary, but so-called international communism has also been shown to be much weaker than people imagined.

8. These two events are of world significance for the future and will, no doubt, gradually influence the policies of various countries.

9. Both in Egypt and Hungary the situation is still critical, though it would appear that the immediate danger of a major war has been avoided. At the same time, the cold war has come back and is likely to create a new crisis from time to time. It may be that we may get over this phase after some time and revert to the process of relaxation of tension, which was in evidence during the past year or more. I cannot say how long this may take.

10. During the past two weeks or so, I have spoken on several occasions in the Lok Sabha and the Rajya Sabha on international affairs[3] and, perhaps, you have read what I have said. It is important that we should have a clear idea of these happenings because the burden of shaping our own country's policy rests on us. We cannot adequately shoulder that burden by mere reactions to events, as most people do. The stakes are very heavy indeed and, by some fate or circumstance, India's responsibilities have grown. Reports come to us from many

3. For the text of Nehru's speeches in the Lok Sabha on 19 and 20 November 1956 on the international situation see *Selected Works* (second series), Vol. 35, pp. 351-388. Nehru also spoke on similar lines in the *Rajya Sabha* on 3, 4 and 7 December 1956.

of the West Asian countries that wherever an Indian flag is seen on the car of one of our representatives, crowds gather round to express their high appreciation of India and her policy, and expecting India to do something to help them. So also in Budapest. That is a terrible burden for us to carry. Our capacity to do anything is limited, and our good name has gone far beyond that capacity. This prospect rather frightens me.

11. It is easy enough to give expression to our views in brave language, condemning this country or that, but it is not easy to hold to the straight and narrow path which leads to peace. It is not easy to avoid extremes of expression when people are excited. The middle path is seldom approved of by those at either extreme.

12. What is the test we should apply? Certainly the test of principles, but the enunciation of principle is not enough and even a good principle shouted out at the wrong time may create dangers and lead to difficulties. If a great country, because of its own folly and mistakes, is driven into a position from which it cannot extricate itself without humiliation and abject surrender, then it is likely to prefer even war, whatever the consequences. We have seen England and France and Russia, no doubt because of their own mistakes, driven into a corner and trying desperately to find a way out without complete loss of dignity. If we prevent them from finding a way out, this might lead to desperation and even war. Therefore, it would seem that we should always try to have an honourable way of escape from a difficult position. I remember that Gandhiji always left a door open in this way, without ever sacrificing his principles. Gandhiji's wisdom and practical good sense justify themselves again and again.

13. England and France, losing the active help of the United States and having to face an angered public opinion, became too weak to carry on their rash adventure in Egypt and are trying to end it with such grace as they can. They are both in a very chastened mood, even though they may talk big to comfort themselves. The Soviet Union is not weak and relies on its own strength. Even so, it has bowed to world opinion to some extent. The danger is that it may be pushed too much in an attempt to humiliate it and then it may react wrongly. Both parties may dig their feet in, and when great powers do this, the consequences are likely to be very serious.

14. We have seen in Poland how far-reaching changes can be brought about if the situation is tackled wisely and peacefully.[4] The same background existed in

4. On 6 November, general amnesty was granted to all prisoners imprisoned for alleged fascist activities, the Church allowed more freedom and changes made in trade union leadership. On 13 November, changes were effected in Polish Government and Army Command and all cases against Poznan rioters were dropped. On 18 November, the ruling United Workers Party of Poland and the Soviet Union agreed that the Soviet Army would not interfere in Poland's internal affairs.

Hungary but with two major differences. Hungary did not have wise or effective leadership and the Egyptian crisis intervened. The Soviet Union was alarmed at what might well develop into a collapse of its authority in the East European countries and bring a hostile frontier right up to its own borders. There is nothing that Russia fears so much as a re-armed Germany. Twice in our lifetime German armies have invaded and brought havoc to Russia. Nobody in Eastern Europe ever forgets this fact. If the hostile frontier was brought to Russia's own border, and a re-armed Germany could go there with ease, then the fear of Russia would increase greatly and it may be thought that her own security was being endangered. It was probably for this reason that Russia acted in the way it did in Hungary and was faced by world disapproval.

15. How, then, are we to deal with this situation? I can offer no simple recipe. We may, however, lay down some broad considerations. The first one is that we should stand on our basic principles. That means that foreign forces should be withdrawn from Hungary, and Hungary should enjoy real independence with a political or economic structure of her people's choice. For this purpose, Soviet troops will have to withdraw. We should make it easy for the Soviet Union to do so. If we make it difficult then the process of withdrawal will be delayed, the crisis will continue and war may well result and come in the way of what we want to do.

16. It becomes ever more clearly evident to me that the system of pacts and alliances, whether it is NATO or the Warsaw Treaty or SEATO or the Baghdad Pact, weakens peace and maintains a constant dread of each other. If we ask the Russians to withdraw from East European countries, as we should logically, foreign bases in other foreign countries should also be liquidated. I am quite sure that if all these pacts and alliances are put an end to, there would be a great relief all over the world, the cold war will end and the return to normality would be hastened. This would also result in what is called the democratization of the East European countries. That process which started last year cannot be reversed now, though it may well be delayed.

17. As you perhaps know, I am going to the United States within a week to meet President Eisenhower. This visit of mine has been made much of by the American press, as if the future of the world depended on our talks. I am alarmed at this boosting, because it raises great expectations which are not likely to be fulfilled. This does not mean that I consider my visit to President Eisenhower of no value. Indeed, I think it is important and I hope it will yield good results. President Eisenhower has come back to his high office after a tremendous popular victory.[5] He represents a country which is the most powerful in the world. He is thus in a position to make a great difference to world events.

---

5. Eisenhower was re-elected US President for the second term on 6 November 1956.

686

18. While we seek and work for peace, Pakistan is again resounding with warlike cries and threats against India.[6] I am distressed about this, as it comes in the way of our normal relations and embitters them. There are all kinds of rumours of Pakistan indulging in trouble on the ceasefire line in Kashmir or the Indian border.

19. Parliament is continuing and is likely to last another two weeks or a little less. Among other measures which it is considering is the one containing new taxation proposals.[7] Such proposals could only be put forward on the eve of general elections if we felt their absolute necessity from the point of view of our economy and the Second Five Year Plan.

20. Meanwhile, we face increasing difficulties. Our foreign exchange resources have been reduced greatly during the past few months.[8] Prices have gone up[9] and certain inflationary trends are evident. We have to check these at all costs, and we have to increase our production as well as our exports. We have also to save wherever we can and avoid all unnecessary expenditure. You will be discussing these matters at the National Development Council[10] which is soon meeting and I shall therefore not say much about them except to put before you that the situation is a difficult one and requires all our efforts.

Yours sincerely,
Jawaharlal Nehru

6. For example, on 7 December, Pakistan's Foreign Minister charged that Nehru was himself an invader "of Hyderabad, Junagadh and Pondicherry". He said that India was spending Rs 300 crores on her armed forces "which I call a force of aggression."
7. On 30 November, a Supplementary Budget was introduced in Parliament levying excise duties on dividends, and on items such as wines, scooters, and watches. Tax on capital gains was also raised. These demands were discussed in Lok Sabha on 10 and 12 December and in Rajya Sabha on 15 December 1956.
8. Foreign exchange reserves had gone down to Rs 544 crores. After allowing for Rs 400 crores as minimum currency reserves and Rs 40 crores as minimum working balance, the Reserve Bank was left with Rs 100 crores only. Of these, Rs 91 crores had to be paid for import of machinery for Rourkela. Therefore, only Rs 10 crores were left.
9. Food prices had gone up by 6.4 per cent between September and November 1956.
10. The NDC met on 8 and 9 December 1956.
1. From 16 to 21 December 1956.

II

New Delhi,
23 January 1957

My dear Chief Minister,

After a long interval, I write to you again. During this period, since I wrote to you, I have been to the United States,[1] Canada[2] and England,[3] and met many leaders of these countries. On my way back, I also met Dr Adenauer,[4] Federal Chancellor of West Germany. In India, we have had important visitors. Premier Chou En-lai came again,[5] and the Dalai and the Panchen Lamas have also visited us. Recently, the President of Syria also came here.[6] He is still touring various parts of India.

2. A great many events have happened during these past six weeks, and now we are on the eve of our second general elections.[7] Most of you will be busy with these elections during the next six weeks or so.

3. Even as I write this letter, the Security Council of the UN must be discussing the Kashmir issue.[8] The air has been thick with rumours of Pakistan creating some trouble on the borders. The next few days will indicate what turn events are likely to take. We have a difficult task in the Security Council, because most of the members of that Council, for a variety of reasons, incline towards Pakistan. Many of them are in some kind of a military alliance with Pakistan. It is difficult to explain to them in a brief debate the long agony of these past nine years of the Kashmir story. I have no doubt that Shri Krishna Menon will present our case with force and ability. I have just heard that the US and the UK Governments are putting forward some kind of a resolution.[9] I have not seen this resolution yet. But I fear it is likely to be unsatisfactory from our point of view.

4. I do not wish to make this letter merely a record of the many events that have taken place during the past six weeks. You read about these happenings in

2. On 22 and 23 December 1956.
3. From 24 to 27 December 1956.
4. On 27 December 1956.
5. Visited India from 30 December 1956 to 1 January 1957.
6. Shukri el-Kuwatli visited India from 17 to 27 January 1957.
7. General elections took place from 24 February to 14 March 1957.
8. The Council discussed the issue from 16 January and was considering a draft resolution which was passed on 24 January 1957. Also see *ante*, pp. 337-351.
9. See *ante*, pp. 349-351.

the newspapers, and it would serve little purpose my repeating them. But I should like to draw your attention again to certain basic features of the present international situation.

5. After many years of the cold war, there appeared to be a relaxation of it. Gradually, the high tension and excitement lessened and the world appeared to be moving into a calmer and less militant atmosphere. We began to hope that this process would continue and lead to the progressive solution of our problems.

6. This was the broad outlook in the middle of 1956. Suddenly, the Suez Canal issue disturbed this relatively peaceful atmosphere, and then the Anglo-French invasion as well as the Israeli invasion of Egypt brought us near to war. In Central Europe, there was a national rising in Hungary. And now we are back to the old days of the cold war. The immediate crisis, that is the danger of war, has passed, but a deeper crisis continues and any kind of relief from tension is not in sight.

7. All these events have affected India in various ways and more particularly in regard to our Second Five Year Plan. Our difficulties have increased and are likely to endure. We can look forward to no early release from them. We cannot give up any part of our Plan and so we have to work all the harder.

8. President Eisenhower's recent messages containing what is called the "Eisenhower doctrine," have not brought any feeling of healing. Instead, they have intensified the conflicts in Western Asia and have made people think again largely in military terms. In the Soviet Union, there appears to be a going back from the process of "de-Stalinization" and a reversion to some extent to the rougher language and methods of past days. Hungary continues to suffer.

9. In Europe, we might distinguish between three major forces. The communist, that is essentially Soviet communism; the progressive communist, represented by Poland and with a considerable appeal in some other countries, and the non-communist or anti-communist. A feature of the past few months has been the coming into prominence of the so-called progressive communists who are largely influenced by the concept of national freedom as well as more individual freedom, within the socialist economy. This wave of change in the communist world is visible in the Soviet Union itself as well as, more especially, in Poland and the other East European countries. Someone has compared these movements to the Reformation in Europe, which resulted in the Protestant churches being formed. The comparison has some justification. Communism, as some kind of faith, has two aspects now: the orthodox one and the protestant one, but both are communism. Mostly, the communist parties in non-communist countries are very orthodox and, after some weeks of confusion, have lined up behind the

Soviet variety of communism, which means they support the Soviet Government. It is in the communist countries that we find this protestant variety of communism which threatens old style orthodoxy. After trying to come to terms with the protestants and partly doing so in Poland, orthodoxy has apparently got rather frightened at these developments and decided to put up a strong front to them. The People's Government of China also, sensing danger through these disruptionist movements, has lined up with the Soviet Union. Marshal Tito, the arch protestant, has been isolated.

10. I have no doubt that these protestant forces of reformation will continue and grow in strength because they represent both nationalism and the adaptation of the socialist creed to the peculiar circumstances of each country. But orthodoxy does not easily give in to reformism and we are seeing this bitter conflict in the countries of Eastern Europe. For the moment, only Poland has succeeded to some extent; the other countries of Eastern Europe have been brought to heel by the might of the Soviet Union supported by China. While these progressive and liberalizing tendencies will continue and will produce their effect, this may well take some time now. The immediate future is one of conflict. I had hoped that these bitter conflicts might be avoided so as to allow these progressive forces to function in a somewhat normal atmosphere. That hope has not been realized.

11. And yet, the very compulsion of events is leading to a more realistic approach to the vital question of disarmament. No one now can really think in terms of global war, and yet at the same time the big countries continue to prepare for it and to encourage military pacts and alliances, which give no security and only add to the tension and sense of conflict.

12. We have to live through this dangerous period and protect our own freedom as well as to continue with our Five Year Plans. To relax is to invite trouble and possibly disaster. The immediate future is not hopeful and we are likely to have hard times both in the national and the international spheres.

13. In two or three days we celebrate Republic Day and then we plunge into the elections, probably forgetting this ferment and turmoil of the world and our own major difficulties. But we cannot escape them and we shall have to keep in mind always that these elections will mean little if we weaken.

14. There is probably no country in the world, except some of the communist countries, which has not had repeated changes of governments during the past ten years. Only India is an exception to this and, because of this, we have been able to build up stability and put up a good record of progress. It seems to me important that during this critical period, our country should have this stability and sustained work. This is more important than any number of minor mistakes

that might be made. Rival groups and parties criticize and run down each other, but the basic enemies to be fought against are not rival parties but rather the basic weaknesses and difficulties that confront us, including our tendency to faction and disruption. The emotional integration of India still remains the most important need of our country.

15. I trust that in these difficult times we shall rise to the occasion and not lose ourselves in petty wrangles.

Yours sincerely,
Jawaharlal Nehru

10
MISCELLANEOUS

1. The Passing of B.R. Ambedkar[1]

Jawaharlal Nehru: Mr Speaker, Sir, I have to convey to the House the sad news of the death of Dr Ambedkar. Only two days ago, I believe, the day before yesterday, he was present in the other House of which he was a Member. The news, therefore, of his death today came as a shock to all of us who had no inkling of such a thing happening so soon.

Dr Ambedkar, as every Member of this House knows, played a very important part in the making of the Constitution of India, subsequently in the Legislative part of the Constituent Assembly and later in the Provisional Parliament. After that, he was not a Member of Parliament for some time. Then, he came back to the Rajya Sabha of which he was a sitting Member.

He is often spoken of as one of the architects of our Constitution. There is no doubt that no one took greater care and trouble over Constitution making than Dr Ambedkar. He will be remembered also for the great interest he took and the trouble he took over the question of Hindu Law reform. I am happy that he saw that reform in a very large measure carried out, perhaps not in the form of that monumental tome that he had himself drafted, but in separate bits. But, I imagine that the way he will be remembered most will be as a symbol of the revolt against all the oppressive features of Hindu society. He used language sometimes which hurt people. He sometimes said things which were perhaps not wholly justified. But, let us forget that. The main thing was that he rebelled against something against which all ought to rebel and we have, in fact, rebelled in various degrees. This Parliament itself represents in the legislation which it has framed, its repudiation of those customs or legacies from the past which kept down a large section of our people from enjoying their normal rights.

When I think of Dr Ambedkar, many things come to my mind, because he was a highly controversial figure. He was not a person of soft speech. But, behind all that was this powerful reaction and an act of rebellion against something that repressed our society for so long. Fortunately, that rebellion had the support, not perhaps in the exact way he wanted it, but in a large measure, the principle underlying that rebellion had the support of Parliament, and, I believe, every group and party represented here. Both in our public activities and in our legislative activities, we did our utmost to remove that stigma on

---

1. Statement in the Lok Sabha, 6 December 1956. *Lok Sabha Debates*, Vol. X, Part II, cols. 2059-2062. Extracts.

Hindu society. One cannot remove it completely by law, because custom is more deep-rooted and, I am afraid, it still continues in many parts of the country even though it may be considered illegal. That is true. But, I have no doubt that it is something that is in its last stages and may take a little time to vanish away. When both law and public opinion become more and more determined to put an end to state of affairs, it cannot last long. Anyhow, Dr Ambedkar, as I said, became prominent in his own way and a most prominent symbol of that rebellion. I have no doubt that, whether we agree with him or not in many matters, that perseverance, that persistence and that, if I may use the word, sometime, virulence of his opposition to all this did keep the people's mind awake and did not allow them to become complacent about matters which could not be forgotten, and helped in rousing up those groups in our country which had suffered for so long in the past. It is, therefore, sad that such a prominent champion of the oppressed and depressed in India and one who took such an important part in our activities, has passed away.

As the House knows, he was a Minister, a member of our Cabinet, for many years,[2] and I had the privilege of cooperating with him in our governmental work. I had heard of him and, of course, met him previously on various occasions. But, I had not come into any intimate contact with him. It was at the time of the Constituent Assembly that I got to know him a little better. I invited him to join the Government. Some people were surprised that I should do so, because, it was thought that his normal activities were of the opposition type rather than of the governmental type. Nevertheless, I felt at that time that he had played an important and very constructive role in the making of the Constitution and that he could continue to play a constructive role in governmental activities. Indeed, he did. In spite of some minor differences here and there, chiefly, if I may say so, not due to any matters of principle, but rather linguistic matters and language used, we cooperated in the Government for several years to our mutual advantage, I think. Anyhow, a very leading and prominent personality, who has left his mark in our public affairs and on the Indian scene, has passed away, a personality who was known to nearly all of us here, I suppose, and I feel sure that all of us feel very sad. We know him well. He had been unwell for a long time. Nevertheless, the passing of a person is painful. I am sure that you, Sir, and the House will convey our deep condolences and sympathy to his family....

2. Ambedkar was the Union Law Minister from 1947 to 1951.

2. Introducing the Hirakud Dam[1]

I think both of you once came with me to see the Hirakud Dam. I wonder if you remember it. This big dam has now been completed and today I came here to Hirakud to perform the opening ceremony.

This dam is a very big one, about three miles long. Then there are other dams roundabout. All these dams have stopped the flow of the Mahanadi river for the time being. The waters of the Mahanadi have therefore collected and have formed a very big lake.

The dam has got iron gates which can be moved up and down. By moving them, the water of the lake can be allowed to come through in any quantity desired. There are two ways of letting the water through. One is at the top spillway. It comes out in a sheet and rolls down the curved surface of the great dam. The other way is to open the smaller gates at the bottom called the sluices and the water rushes out.

When I pressed a button today, the water came out from the upper spillway. They were beautifully lighted in colours. The waters also came from the sluices in some places down below. Here they rushed out with great force and meeting the obstruction of a wall which had been erected as a barrier to stop the force of the waters, they rose up. In this way the waters rose up about 40 feet, breaking up into little bits and a cloud of drops rose higher still. This was very interesting to watch.

The dam and the big lake looked rather lovely. Of course the dam looks neat and clean now. Inside the dam, there is huge machinery. This machinery is worked from inside the dam and the water gates are opened from there.

Right inside the dam, far below the surface, there are two tunnels. One of these tunnels is a big and broad one and very long. The other is below the big tunnel and is a narrow one. These tunnels pass under the river. We went along these tunnels which were well lighted up by electricity.

You may remember that when we came to see this dam being made, there were huge machines at work. These machines are called earth-moving machines. They push the earth, level it or lift up large quantities of it in buckets and carry it elsewhere. There were also huge truck-like machines to press the earth down and make it solid. Then there are big cranes.

1. Note to Rajiv Gandhi and Sanjay Gandhi, Hirakud, Orissa, 13 January 1957. JN Collection.

When I was going along one road by the dam, I was surprised to see all these big machines lined up in two rows on either side of the road. They gave me welcome in their own way and it was a very odd way. They all started making noises as if they were working and belched out some smoke. The big buckets started opening and closing and moving up and down. Instead of earth, they threw some flowers. The other machines used for pushing or pressing earth went backwards and forwards a little as if they were performing some dance. All this looked very odd and amusing. It was the first time I had seen such a sight.

Out of the big lake that has been formed, canals go out long distances. Out of the big canals, small canals come out and so a very large area of land and fields gets the water from these canals and can grow food crops and other things. Thus, this water from the Mahanadi river which was being wasted and which sometimes rose in great floods and did much damage is now controlled and goes down these canals to give new life to the earth and plenty of foodgrains grow there to feed our people.

In addition to this, great and big hydroelectric works have been built to produce electricity. The water from the big lake is allowed to come down in a great rush and this makes big wheels and turbines go round. In this way electricity is produced. This electricity is carried by wires to far distances. It is then used for lighting and other purposes. It will also be used in factories to make the machines work.

So, you see, that this Mahanadi river will do a lot of good. Before this dam was made, it did a great deal of harm because of the floods. Now the floods have been largely stopped and controlled. Instead, the waters will irrigate the fields of thousands of farmers and produce food. They will also produce electricity for lighting and factories. The factories will produce many of the goods we require.

You will see what a lot of good this great dam is going to do to our people, not only now but for long years to come. Our poor people will get better food to eat and more goods to use and they will become prosperous.

In making this dam, thousands of persons have worked hard. There have been many engineers and foremen and mechanics and others. It is nearly nine years ago when I came here to lay the foundation stone of this great dam.[2] I was very happy today to be present here at Hirakud to see this completed dam and to press the button and see these waters flow out.

2. On 12 April 1948.

Just like this Hirakud Dam, there is the great dam that is being made at Bhakra where also a great lake will be created and electric power produced.

There are also many dams on the Damodar valley river which flows from Bihar to Bengal. In the south of India there is the Tungabhadra Dam. All over India these dams, big and small, are being made by our engineers and our workers. What a great deal of good will come out of these dams for our people.

I hope that both of you will be able to see some of these dams.

I am sending you a little book about this Hirakud Dam.

3. To G.P. Hutheesing[1]

New Delhi,
18 January 1957

My dear Raja,[2]

I have just received your letter of the 12th January.

It is rather odd for you to ask me for permission to stand for election to the Lok Sabha as an independent candidate. Associated as I am with the Congress, naturally, in so far as I am concerned, I would give my support to Congress candidates wherever they may stand. If a Congress candidate opposes you, as I presume someone will, naturally my support will go to him. This is not a personal matter, as you will realize, but the normal working in political affairs.

But if you ask me if I will have any personal objection to your standing, obviously I have none. You have every right to stand as anyone else has. There is absolutely no reason why your standing for election should affect any personal relations.

I have no recollection at all of what happened in 1952 when you say you stood on the PSP ticket. I could not have been much concerned about it, otherwise I would have remembered. I am afraid conclusions are drawn which have little justification. Krishna has sometimes written to me letters, not recently, which have surprised me because she imagined many things which did not exist.

1. JN Collection.
2. G.P. Hutheesing, husband of Krishna Hutheesing, Nehru's sister.

As for the two boys, I really do not understand what their present or future has got to do with this. They are fine young men and should do well in the future.

There is no question of disloyalty to me personally or to the family. There may be a question occasionally of something being done, politics quite apart, which distresses me. Krishna's article certainly distressed me and I considered it not only very immature but bad form.[3] There was no politics involved in it.

Yours affectionately,
Jawaharlal

3. For Nehru's comments on Krishna Hutheesing's article, see *Selected Works* (second series), Vol. 30, p. 540.

4. To Gurmukh Nihal Singh[1]

New Delhi,
23 January 1957

My dear Gurmukh Nihal Singhji,[2]

This evening, Farooq Abdullah, the son of Shaikh Abdullah, came to visit me. He is studying in the Medical College at Jaipur,[3] and I have taken some interest in his studies. Some time back, we also helped him to get a separate room to live in a hostel as he was unhappy to live with others.

Today, when he came he was naturally much exercised about the new developments in the Kashmir case, which is being heard in the Security Council. He was even more troubled by the excitement and bitterness which this had created, especially in Pakistan and to some extent in India. He told me that some students of the Medical College had even threatened him indirectly because he was the son of Shaikh Abdullah.

I do not like this kind of thing at all. Shaikh Abdullah may have acted wrongly according to our judgement. He has suffered for it and is still in detention. I do not think it is proper for any of us to say harsh things about Shaikh Abdullah. That would neither be decent, nor does it help. But, in any event, it is wholly wrong to blame his son, Farooq, for whatever his father may have done. I am anxious, therefore, that no untoward incident might happen.

I would suggest to you to send for the Principal[4] of the Medical College and tell him that we are interested in Farooq Abdullah and we would like him to be treated in a friendly way. The fact of the Kashmir dispute or his father's activities should not come in the way of our friendly treatment of Farooq. Also, that it would be very unfortunate from every point of view if any students or others behaved badly towards Farooq.

1. JN Collection.
2. (b. 1895); Professor of Economics and Political Science, later, Rama Verma Professor of Political Science, Banaras Hindu University, 1920-39; Dean, Faculty of Arts, BHU; Principal of H.L. College of Commerce, Ahmedabad, 1939-43; Principal, Ramjas College, Delhi, 1943-50; Sri Ram College of Commerce, Delhi, 1950-52; MLA, Delhi State (Congress), 1952 and Speaker, 1952-55; Leader of the Congress Party, Delhi State Legislature, and Chief Minister of Delhi, 1955-56; Governor of Rajasthan, 1956-62.
3. The Sawai Man Singh Medical College.
4. R.N. Kaslival.

I do not quite know what more we can do about this. But I think it is desirable that the Principal of the Medical College should be told what I have said above, so that he might keep this in mind.

Yours sincerely,
Jawaharlal Nehru

5. To Sudhir Ghosh[1]

Raj Bhavan,
Madras,
31 January 1957

My dear Sudhir,[2]

I have received your letter of the 30th January. There is no question of my disliking you.[3] It is true that some of the things you said and did seemed to me improper and I told you so. That had nothing personal about it. I am glad you are doing good work.[4]

Yours sincerely,
Jawaharlal Nehru

1. JN Collection.
2. An associate of Mahatma Gandhi who was PRO in the Indian High Commission, London in 1947. From 1960 to 1966 he was a Congress member of the Lok Sabha from West Bengal.
3. Ghosh wrote: "At five this morning on that spot in Birlaji's garden where Bapu died I saw you from a distance and I wondered if you still disliked me for my mistakes...I am not a bad man. On this day I ask you to believe it...You used to like me and I treasured the good opinion you had of me. I hope some day I can win it back."
4. Ghosh wrote that M.O. Mathai had "found me some work on the Steel Projects...They have offered to send me to Durgapur where I can work more with people than with paper. I would like to do that. I want nothing more; nor do I want to calculate what I will do next."

6. To Rukmini Devi Arundale[1]

Raj Bhavan,
Madras,
31 January 1957

My dear Rukmini Devi,[2]

Thank you for your letter of the 29th January. I hope that the sum of Rs 10,000/- which I sent you for the Kalakshetra will be of some help to you. I am sorry I could not send a bigger sum.

You know my interest in the Kalakshetra. I think that it is an institution deserving of all support. It is making a valuable contribution to the cultural life of our country. I attach considerable importance to our reviving the old cultural forms in the dance, music and drama and the Kalakshetra is doing this in a methodical way. I am glad that general education is included in the training and more especially knowledge of the Sanskrit language. Kalakshetra, though situated in Madras, receives students from all parts of India and I understand they arrive also from some foreign countries. Such an institution deserves full support and I hope you will get it.

Yours sincerely,
Jawaharlal Nehru

1. JN Collection.
2. President, Kalakshetra, Adyar, Chennai.

7. To Vijayalakshmi Pandit[1]

Anand Bhavan,
Allahabad,
6 February 1957

Nan dear,

I came to Allahabad this morning and have spent the day in various meetings in the district and in the city. The country is now fully in the grip of election fever. For the next five weeks most people will live in a state of excitement forgetting much of the world.

Yesterday we had a Cabinet meeting in Delhi and Ministers had to come from various parts of India to attend it. Keshava Deva Malaviya came and confessed that he was in a state of election intoxication and could hardly apply his mind to other matters.

Indu has been here and will continue to remain here except for tours to various parts of India. She is rather overdoing things, but in a psychological sense it is perhaps good for her. She is full of her work. Anand Bhawan is something like a *Shadikhana* with all kinds of odd people, working for the elections, staying in various parts of the house, and others coming in and out.

Tandonji has decided not to stand and so Lal Bahadur is standing from the city of Allahabad. You will be surprised to learn that Radhe Shyam Pathak[2] is opposing him on behalf of the PSP. Radhe appears to have lost all sense of balance or judgement.

I am going to Lucknow tomorrow and to Delhi the day after where I stay for a day or two and then go off again. Edwina is in Delhi, though I believe she is going to Jaipur tomorrow. She is returning to England, or, at any rate, leaving India on the 13th February. I believe she intends going to Cyprus. But whether she will go via London or direct I do not know. Probably she will go direct from Beirut.

I hope you have spoken to Ajit[3] in terms of what I said to you. He should be told that you have kept me informed of developments. I have not thus far spoken to his father or mother or to anyone else and I do not propose to do so unless

---

1. JN Collection.
2. Congressmen from Allahabad who later joined the Congress Socialist Party and then the Praja Socialist Party.
3. Son of G.P. Hutheesing and Krishna Hutheesing.

some further development takes place. It is my strong advice to Ajit to follow the advice and instructions he receives from the lawyers and to be completely frank with them. If he likes he can refer any matter to me through you. If he is not prepared to follow the lawyers' or our advice, then it is difficult for us to help him and his mother and father will probably have to be informed. I do not want to fall out with Betti[4] over this issue by keeping her in ignorance. At the same time I do not think she or Raja can help. They will merely get excited.

There is no point in your telling the Master or the Principal of his college anything. If the other party informs the Master, he will no doubt send for Ajit and speak to him. Ajit need not go into details with him, but just give him some indication and add that he had informed his aunt, i.e., you, who was dealing with the matter. If then the Master or Provost writes to you, you can suitably reply.

We must remember that this kind of thing is not very uncommon and normally people do not get excited over it. I am sure the Master will not, nor need all of us, feel unnerved. It is a relatively simple matter, though of course it may become a nuisance. There appears to be no need to worry. Much depends on Ajit and how he might behave. He has therefore to be treated gently and in a friendly way. At the same time, a little firmly also. Tell him that nothing very much can happen if he acts according to our advice. Otherwise, he might get into difficulties.

I received your telegram about your first interview with Macmillan in Delhi. In spite of what Macmillan says I do not accept that the British in the UN have behaved at all decently towards India. It is common knowledge not only in the UN but in the foreign missions in India that the British have taken the lead against India together with Iraq. The Swedish Ambassador[5] tells us so. So does the US Ambassador.[6] Selwyn Lloyd has been acting very improperly and has given us assurances which he has not kept. In fact, he has indulged in all kinds of prevarications.

My own information is that the British have briefed their press there to say that they do not recognize Kashmir as Indian territory and that they support the emergency force idea. Also that the Pakistan case has public support.

Therefore we cannot place too much reliance on Macmillan's statement to you. So far as we are concerned, we do not wish to fall out with the British and

---

4. Krishna Hutheesing was affectionately called by this name in the family.
5. Alva Myrdal.
6. Ellsworth Bunker.

we have tried to keep people's passion here down. We want to be friendly with the British, as indeed with other countries. But we cannot help reacting to what is happening in the UK.

Some of Macmillan's complaints against Krishna Menon are not justified by facts, such as his reference to disarmament discussion. It is true that inevitably we have to take a strong line, as we had to in the Egyptian matter, and in doing so one has to criticize the British attitude.

The attempt of the British Government or any other person to make out that Krishna Menon is playing a somewhat lone hand and is not fully supported by his Government must be sternly discouraged. We have been in constant contact with Krishna and the policy he has pursued has been in accordance with our own ideas. I have said so in public here on more than one occasion. Macmillan and others should therefore realize that they are dealing with the Government of India in this matter. It may be that Krishna lays greater emphasis in the way he says something. The whole point is that the UK Government should not get the idea that all of us are not fully pulling together. I cannot help some of the opposition press here. But broadly speaking there is amazing unanimity in India over this question of Kashmir and the UK's attitude to it. I know that almost the entire British press, except for Nye Bevan[7] and the *Tribune*, are attacking us. That has made me unhappy. But we cannot be bullied in this way and in any event feeling in India is so strong that we cannot possibly ignore it.

I am convinced that basically our attitude in the Kashmir matter is correct and we propose to adhere to it.

You will be sorry to learn that Amarnath Atal[8] died a few days ago in Jaipur. Also, that Hariharnath Muttoo[9] (Khema Didda's[10] husband) also died a short while ago at the age of 84. A third death more or less in the family has been that of Lachhmi Didda's husband. Lachhmi, you may remember, is the daughter of Mohanbhai's[11] sister.

I saw Mohanbhai this evening. He is gradually fading away and yet he was bright and cheerful. He was sitting on a chair as he finds it a little difficult to

---

7. Aneurin Bevan, British Labour MP.
8. Atal was Finance Minister of the erstwhile Jaipur State. He died on 2 February 1957.
9. (1872-1957); served in the Court of Wards, Bareilly, 1893-99; Deputy Collector, Bareilly, 1901-1921; Assistant Commissioner of Income Tax, 1921; Commissioner of Income Tax, Kanpur, 1921-27.
10. Khimvati Muttoo, was the daughter of Bansi Dhar Nehru.
11. Mohanlal Nehru, first cousin of Jawaharlal Nehru.

walk. He talked, but it was not very easy to understand all he said. He is now approaching his 82nd birthday.

Your loving brother,
Jawahar

8. To Pamela Mountbatten[1]

New Delhi,
10 February 1957

My dear Pamela,[2]

I have read the story of Neola. This was done on my way back by air today from Amritsar.

I warned you in my last letter[3] that I am no expert or trained critic. I have no idea what tests periodicals apply for publication or what their reading public might like. I can only, therefore, give you my own reactions to your story, and these are definitely positive.

I liked reading it, and I think that it is very well written. It flows on smoothly without any padding. The reader becomes more and more interested in Neola and to some extent, of course, in the girl and her reactions to Neola. Thus, it becomes a live story which leaves an impression and a memory after reading it.

Looked at from the point of view of an animal story, it is good, as it shows a great deal of intimate observation. I doubt if any expert zoologists have observed a *Neola* so carefully and noted its characteristics. Thus, your story has a certain scientific value.

1. JN Collection.
2. Younger daughter of the Mountbattens.
3. Replying to Pamela's letter of 14 January, Nehru wrote on 4 February (not printed): "Do not expect competent criticism. I have no experience of this kind." Nehru added that she had an "attractive style" and if she practised it "you will no doubt produce good stuff."

But the real thing about the story is the background of restrained emotion, which grows with the story. Because it is in the background and is restrained, it conveys a deeper impression to the reader than anything more obvious might have done. Writing about some event with which one is personally associated, is both easy and difficult. It is easy because one speaks from experience, it is difficult because one is apt to overdo it and give the wrong emphasis, making it too subjective. Your story is a balanced one, without any stresses and strains, simply told and gradually and imperceptibly making Neola something real for the reader.

So, these are my reactions. I have no doubt that it should be published. But I know nothing about English publishers. Talking about this to your mother this evening, she said that one difficulty would probably be about its length. It is something between a short story and a real long one, and publishers have certain fixed standards about the length of a story. Still, I think that it is so good that you are sure to find a periodical which will publish it. You must go ahead with this and you must also write some more.

Last night, we had the American singer, Eartha Kitt,[4] to dinner. I had never heard of her previously, but as the American Embassy were anxious that I should see her, I invited her. Later, I read in the newspapers that she was a very well known person and, indeed, she was described as the most exciting woman in the United States or the world. Naturally, I was interested in meeting such a person. As it happened, we were only three of us to dinner—your mother, Eartha Kitt and myself. Even Indira was away. I am afraid that I was not terribly impressed in any way by the lady. It is not fair for me to judge her because I have not seen her performing. But I did not see anything terribly attractive or exciting about her.

Yours sincerely,
Jawaharlal Nehru

---

4. Eartha Mae Kitt (b. 1928); American singer and actress; solo dancer for the Katherine Durham dance group in New York in 1948; a year later, she turned to nightclub singing; travelled to Europe where she performed in many cities and played leading stage role in Orson Welles's European production of *Faust*; returned to New York, 1952, and won acclaim for her appearance in the Broadway revue; starred in *Timbuktu*, 1978, an all-black version of the popular musical *kismet*; in the mid-1990s, toured in a one-woman show, across the USA, based on the life of the jazz singer Billie Holiday.

9. To Mahendra Pratap[1]

Raj Bhavan,
Patna,
February 15, 1957

Dear Shri Mahendra Pratap,[2]
I have your letter of today's date.

I agree with you entirely that students should not be exploited for political purposes, whether in elections or at any other time. At the same time, quite inevitably, they are bound to take interest in a general election which excites people so much. There are many public meetings. They can attend them if they so like.

In England, so far as I know, students as a group or in the shape of students organisations, do not participate in this type of politics, but individual students often canvass and otherwise take part in election campaigns. It is difficult to draw the line. One cannot prevent a grown-up student from taking interest in election campaign and even participating in it as an individual. Indeed, to some extent, this might even be approved in individual cases where the student seriously takes interest in such matters. What is wrong is the way in which students' organisations jump into the fray and indeed want to play an important part in the rough and ready of politics. Indeed they go further.

Most university students, I suppose, are voters. As such they may claim the right to participate in elections in various ways. All this is correct in theory, but what is wrong in practice is the exploitation of students as a group by any political party....

Yours sincerely,
Jawaharlal Nehru

---

1. File No. 16(11)/57-PMS. Extracts.
2. (b. 1915); Professor and Head, English Department, Bihar University and Principal, Sangat Singh College, Muzaffarpur since 1947; Professor English, Patna College and Gordon College, Rawalpindi, 1940-46; Dean, Faculty of Arts, Bihar University, 1960-62.

10. Talks with Cyrus L. Sulzberger[1]

...Later, lunched and talked for two and a half hours with Nehru under a peach tree whose pale pink blossoms drifted onto our plates. Afterward, we admired his pet panda. Black, white, and woolly, like an expensive toy, it is kept in a large net cage around a tree. We went in and he fed it dates and bamboo leaves and played with it. Its mate died a few weeks ago. Nehru clearly loves animals. Has a delightful golden retriever pup which he caressed fondly. The only people there were Marina[2] and myself,[3] his niece (Mme Pandit's daughter), and her husband.[4]

Nehru was wearing a white Gandhi cap which he later took off, exposing a sudden bald head much paler than his sunburned face. Also white, tight pants and a buttoned, homespun jacket. A rose was inserted in the second buttonhole.

Nehru just got back last night and goes off again on his electoral campaign. Elections here are very different from in the USA where radio and television have assumed great importance. Direct contact with the masses, public appearances, and speeches are the thing here. Nehru is astonished at the interest and patience of people who come out in the thousands, wait for hours in the hot sun, and then listen with great attention. I asked if he tried to discuss local issues, he said no; he didn't even know them. He left that to others. He talked about broad things: "Even international affairs, sometimes." The women are amazingly interested in politics. They have set a rule, to encourage them, to have 15 per cent of the candidates women.

I asked if he really had written (under a pseudonym) the analysis of Nehru published in a Calcutta review in 1937.[5] He said yes, he had written it for his own amusement then sent it to a woman friend. She passed it to someone else

1. Sulzberger's record of his talks with Nehru, New Delhi, 19 February 1956. From *The Last of the Giants* by C.L. Sulzberger, London, 1972, pp. 375-381. Extracts.
2. Wife of Sulzberger.
3. Cyrus Leo Sulzberger (1912-1993); columnist for *The New York Times*, 1954-1978; author of the column "Foreign Affairs"; authored 24 books, including biographies, memoirs, histories and novels.
4. Rita and Avtar Krishna Dar.
5. The article entitled 'The Rashtrapati' was published anonymously in *The Modern Review* (Calcutta), in November 1937. For the full text see *Selected Works* (first series), Vol. 8, pp. 520-523.

who had published it. Nobody guessed he had written it and Gandhi was even indignant, thinking some enemy was attacking Nehru.

I asked if he would stand by the self-analysis today; that the weaknesses of character he had attributed (tendency to dictatorship, etc.) had not come out in his political administration. He said that, after all, if a man could see such character weaknesses in himself and discuss them, that was proof in advance that he would never succumb to them. I asked if he found time to write anymore. He said no; not for ten years. Of course, occasionally, he wrote papers on such problems as tribal affairs. But this was part of his state work. He was not, after all, a professional writer. He wrote his first book when he was in prison and had little to do. Even so, it took him a year before he sat down to write. Then he thought about it for a month before he started.

He spoke of jail with a certain nostalgia. He was in a group of twelve and they shared the cooking chores. The only thing he ever learned to cook was "various preparations of eggs." Incidentally, he said he usually prepared the salad dressing at home, but today he allowed his niece—for the first time—to do so. Quite good.

Nehru thought Chou En-lai a brilliant man, one of the greatest he ever met. He gives the impression of being very open-minded; whether he is or not, that impression is most important. Of course he is obviously a sincere Communist ("I don't discuss this with him."), but he seems tolerant: "Perhaps, more conservative than the others." Nehru thought China showed more composure and confidence than Russia; that it had a greater cultural tradition and deeper internal roots. I asked if he saw any contest between Peking and Moscow for leadership in Asia. He said perhaps.

Nehru said the Russians could no longer treat their people in a Stalinist way. They were educated despite the fact they had spent forty years under the system. They didn't want a basic change; but more freedom (against secret police) and consumers goods. They had high enough wages and plenty of money; but nothing to buy. They were hungry for education. He was astonished at how much they read—"All heavy books; they have no light books."

He agreed that the Hungarian repression had been terrible. It was too bad it came at the time of Suez. Otherwise, he thought the Russians would have been forced to let go as they did with Poland. Nagy had made a mistake in openly appealing to the West. The Russians were convinced (wrongly of course) that the US had touched off the Hungarian revolt and approved the Anglo-French venture in Egypt. Tito was now on the spot.

I remarked that in his early days Nehru considered himself a Marxist-Socialist but his administrative record certainly did not confirm this. What was his dogma today? He said:

711

Marxism or Communism or Leninism—call it what you like—first impinged on my mind just after the Russian Revolution, when here in India we were in the thick of our own movement. Of course I was completely absorbed in Gandhi. We welcomed the Russian Revolution and thought it a good thing. Later on, however, I read Marx when I was in prison. I was much fascinated by his brilliant analysis of the changes wrought by the industrial revolution in England—although I never had much interest in his theory of surplus values.

But we were all so impressed by Gandhi; we thought he was following a more correct path than Marx and Lenin. Later on I said once that if I had to choose between communism and fascism I would choose the former. But that was a reaction to fascism, nothing more. Both communism and fascism have the same evil features; violence, cruelty, and oppression. But communism at least aims at something better. It is unfortunate, if inevitable, that communism has become so tied up with violence and suppression. As a pure economic theory it would have been more attractive. And we must remember that when Marx evolved his theory in the first half of the nineteenth century, there was no real democracy. He had to think of violent means of upsetting the controlling oligarchy.

I asked him, in the Indian revolution now, what were the relative roles of the individual and the state, of public and private enterprises and ownership. He replied:

In the modern world, everywhere, there is a conflict between an increasing centralization which makes for less individual liberty. It is hard to draw the line. But we would like to preserve individual liberty even at the risk of slower progress in the economic field. I refuse to accept any doctrinaire socialism. Our main objective is that all the people of India should have equal opportunities. And this they certainly don't have yet. It would be absurd to apply to India today the nineteenth century theories of Marx evolved with respect to England.

Ours is a pragmatic, not a dogmatic revolution. It aims at equal opportunity. Gandhi was not a Socialist in the real and generally accepted sense. But he always identified himself with the very poorest. He left with us the idea of identification with the poor and the suppressed. He used a fine phrase about himself once. He said: "I should like to wipe every tear from every eye."

I asked Nehru if he thought of any young man to succeed him in national and party leadership after he retires. He said:

None. I haven't tried to do this—although many people here have asked me the same question. It wouldn't lead to anything. People outside India are likely to take a one-sided view of me, of our organization and our government. It is true that I play an outstanding role, through force of circumstance. But this is not a question only of any ability I may have. Various circumstances have made me extraordinarily popular with the common people—not so much with the intellectuals and others. But I doubt if the same set of circumstances is ever likely to arise again. My popularity is connected with our pre-independence movement, not any actions since independence. And you can't recreate such circumstances.

I asked what, in his opinion, was holding India together; not politically—except during relatively brief periods of strong rule such as the Moghuls—but internally. The concept of India was always there and strong conquerors always thought to subdue India.

Culturally, we are remarkably united. In a sense, it is like the old idea of Christendom in Europe—but even more intense. Political divisions didn't upset the idea of a common culture here. Our chief places of pilgrimage are widely separated—south, east, and west; there were constant streams of pilgrims coming and going to them from all over India.

Another factor that was very important in the past is Sanskrit. This language has not been spoken since the days of Buddha—2,500 years ago. But it is still the language of the learned.

And then, the modern theme of unity was, strangely enough, brought about by Britain. The British enforced their unity. And our opposition to their rule was a unifying force. The Congress party started seventy-one years ago as a small movement, but it was always aimed at all India. Today we are politically and intellectually united. But we are not yet emotionally integrated. When something happens, passions break loose. India would be completely united against an external danger. But when we get complacent internally, then we fall out.

I asked what he envisioned as the long-range future for the subcontinent—some kind of federation for India, Pakistan, Burma, Ceylon? He answered:

If you had asked me that question fifteen or twenty years ago, I would have said that certainly we should have some kind of confederation, not federation, of independent states with common defence and economic policies. In theory, this should have been a normal development—something that would have come about this century, within the next thirty or forty years. Just at the beginning of the war I drafted the Congress resolution hinting at just this.[6] But the difficulty in our way now is if we talk about it, this upsets our neighbours because, of course, we are so much the bigger. Nevertheless this is, of course, the logical future path. There should be such a confederation with each member state maintaining its national independence intact.

How about the visit to Eisenhower? Was he impressed by him? Had it helped resolve misunderstandings between our two countries? He said:

I was greatly impressed by the President. He is a big man and very frank.

6. See *Selected Works* (second series), Vol. 10, pp. 122-138.

That is a great thing. But I don't understand—from a practical point of view—what your military policies can lead to. I am not suggesting that a country should be weak. But all this talk of strength and problems. Keeping a country strong is all right; but nevertheless one shouldn't speak of this strength too much. It is no secret that you are strong. And the Soviet Union is always talking about its strength also—even in a threatening way.

I mentioned all this to President Eisenhower—with some hesitation. I told him you were giving help to other nations, which was a very good thing. But so much of it was in the form of military aid; and that doesn't really help any country. Giving this aid to some countries merely helps strengthen the feudal and reactionary elements in them, and then you become associated with that in their public opinion. President Eisenhower admitted as much to me, and he said it was indeed a problem.

I noted that in one of our previous talks I had asked him on which side India would be in case of war. He had replied reluctantly that in the end it would be with the West because of a common political tradition and a dependence on maritime commerce.

Did I say that? Really? Well, most of our economic contacts are certainly with the West—our intellectual contacts also. And the mere fact of English being used and known here as a language and in our periodicals and books is important. Furthermore, of course, there is the bond of our governmental and parliamentary system.

But in the event of a war—I just don't know. We would certainly try and keep out of it. And what developments would lead into—I don't know. Geographically we are favourably situated. We are outside the normal way of war.

As he was getting restless, and as I saw my time was up, I then produced the hot one. Many Americans saw a contradiction between Nehru's advocacy of self-determination and his support of the UN—and his actions in Kashmir. How about it?

You must remember that soon after partition there were many things that had to be divided up between India and Pakistan. For example, we had jointly assumed the entire debt of the country and we owed each other a lot of money. We had given Pakistan some liquid cash. Our first fight came on this. We said we would give them a share of cash—about $25,000,000. Then we discussed what they would give us. There was no agreement and the discussions were postponed. Soon after this Pakistan invaded Kashmir; there was tension and anger in India. The question arose about our paying the $25,000,000. They were not only attacking Kashmir but fighting us. Our finance minister[7] saw no reason to pay

7. R.K. Shanmugham Chetty.

714

Pakistan when they were fighting us and there wasn't even full agreement on the rest of the arrangement. But, when Gandhi heard of this he was most upset. He said: "You have agreed to pay them $25,000,000. It doesn't matter what has happened subsequently. You must pay up." He was at that time having one of his fasts. He said: "You must keep your word." We paid. And the money was of extreme use to them in fighting us. They haven't paid us a *sou* of what they owe us aside from their interest on the external debt we assumed.

This is, of course, a most indirect argument. Nehru didn't look very proud of it himself. I asked if he thought the ultimate solution would not probably be de jure recognition of the present de facto dividing line in Kashmir as the frontier between India and Pakistan. He said: "As a dividing line it is a bad line—crossing through villages and that sort of thing. The proper line should have some sort of geographical features if possible—mountains, rivers, something."

While we were wandering and admiring the panda, he said suddenly: "Don't forget. In Russia they admire the United States very much for its techniques. The basic fear, however, is Germany."

715

11. To Mehr Chand Khanna[1]

Camp: Raj Bhavan,
Nagpur,
21 February 1957

My dear Mehr Chand,

Your letter of February 19[2] about the trust properties under Custodians.

I think that in regard to evacuee trust property of a non-religious character, the use made of them for schools, colleges and public institutions is good.

As for mosques, some as can be taken charge of by Muslim organizations should be handed over to them. But the problem still remains of others which cannot be looked after properly or taken charge of by various persons. I am glad you are sending a note on this to the Cabinet Committee. Before we make any decision, it would be desirable to consult some Muslim organizations like the Jamiat. Also because there is a joint committee of India and Pakistan in connection with shrines, etc., the matter should come up there. I should personally like these unused mosques to be used for such public purposes, chiefly schools, as may not be objected to by Muslims, but I would hesitate to take any step without full consultation with the people concerned.

Yours sincerely,
Jawaharlal Nehru

---

1. JN Collection.
2. Not available.

GLOSSARY

abhaya	fearlessness
abhinandan patra/manpatra	an address of welcome
acharya	a reverential term used for a teacher or guru
akhanda Bharat	undivided India
bhikku	a Buddhist mendicant
gram sevaks	voluntary village workers
Dravida desh	land of the Tamils
durries	floor mats
Hindu rashtra	Hindu nation
Jai Hind	victory to India
jagirdari	a system of landholding
ji/saheb/sahib	an affix denoting respect
mahanirvana	refers to the extinction of Buddha's worldly existence beyond the cycle of rebirth
neola	mongoose
panchsheel	five basic principles of international conduct
shadikhana	a wedding house
swaraj	self-rule
taluqdari	a system of landholding
tehsil	revenue sub-division
yagnya	religious sacrifice and oblation

ABBREVIATIONS

AFP	Agence France Press
AICC	All India Congress Committee
BHU	Banaras Hindu University
CSIR	Council of Scientific and Industrial Research
CWC	Congress Working Committee
HQ	Headquarters
IAS	Indian Administrative Service
ICAR	Indian Council of Agricultural Research
IPS	Indian Police Service
INA	Indian National Army
INTUC	Indian National Trade Union Congress
KMT	Kuomintang
LIC	Life Insurance Corporation
MEA	Ministry of External Affairs
MP	Member of Parliament
NATO	North Atlantic Treaty Organization
NCC	National Cadet Corps
NDC	National Development Council
NEFA	North East Frontier Agency
NMML	Nehru Memorial Museum & Library
NNRC	Neutral Nations Repatriation Commission
NR&SR	Natural Resources & Scientific Research, Ministry of
OSD	Officer on Special Duty
PA	Personal Assistant

719

PCART	Preparatory Committee for the Establishment of the Autonomous Region of Tibet
PEPSU	Patiala and East Punjab States Union
PRO	Public Relations Officer
PsOW	Prisoners of War
P&T	Posts and Telegraph
PTI	Press Trust of India
SEATO	South-East Asia Treaty Organization
SG	Secretary General, MEA
UK	United Kingdom
UN/UNO	United Nations Organization
UNCIP	United Nations Commission for India and Pakistan
UNEF	United Nations Emergency Force
UNESCO	United Nations Educational, Scientific, and Cultural Organization
UP	Uttar Pradesh
UPSC	Union Public Service Commission
US/USA	United States of America
WH&S	Works, Housing & Supply, Ministry of
USSR	Union of Soviet Socialist Republics

NAME INDEX

(Biographical footnotes in this volume and in volumes in the first series are italicized and those in the second series are given in block letters.)

Abdul Aziz ibn Saud (King of Saudi Arabia), 227
Abdul Kadir, R.H., 678 & fn
Abdullah, S.M., (*Vol. 7, p. 308*), 234 & fn, 343 & fn, 344 & fn, 345 & fn, 701
————; Farooq, 701
Abid Ali (*Vol. 15, Pt. II, p.118*), 305 & fn
Accra, 653 & fn, 654
Acharya, Tanka Prasad, (VOL. 17, P. 481), 439 & fn, 624, 625, 627, 628 & fn, 645 & fn, 646-648, 650, 671,
Acharya Tulsi, 179 & *fn*

Addis Ababa, 401 fn
Addu Atoll, 411 fn
Adenauer, Konrad, (VOL. 28, P. 570), 534 & fn, 536, 688
Afghanistan, 618, 633; Government of, 633
Africa, 30, 168, 200, 272, 373, 468 & fn, 522-523, 651, 666, 669 fn
Agence France (AFP), 655 & fn
Ahmed, Abul Mansur, 642 & fn
Ahmedabad, 114 & fn
Akola (Maharashtra), 401
Alexander, Horace, (*Vol. 6, p. 208*), 663 & fn
Algeria, 296, 299, 374, 655, 656, 667, 683
Ali, Mohammad, (VOL. 3, P. 316), 372
————, S. Fazl, (VOL. 3, P. 31), 238

fn, 239, 240, 241, 244, 248
Allahabad, 89 & fn, 90 & fn, 95, 96 & fn, 99, 100, 104, 113, 138-139, 141, 243, 331, 367, 401-402, 704 & fn
Allahabad Government House, 229
Allahabad Town Congress Committee, 94 fn
All India Agricultural Economics Conference, (28 December 1956, Cuttack), 164 & fn
All India Congress Committee, 94 & fn, 95, 210, 277, & fn, 294, 305, 312 & fn, 323 & fn, 324 & fn, 327, & fn
All Indian Economic Conference (26 December 1956, Cuttack), 164 & fn
All India Medical Council Bill, 201
Alva, Joachim, (VOL. 16, Pt. II, P. 587), 411 & fn
Alvares, Peter, (VOL. 27, P. 222), 309 & fn, 315
Ambedkar, B.R., (*Vol. 5, p. 299*), 671 & fn, 695, 696 & fn
America, 60, 168, 524
American Broadcasting Company, 501
American Revolution, 495, 516, 592
Amini, Ali, 551 & *fn*
Amritsar, 307 fn, 707
Anand Bhawan (Allahabad), 704
Andhra Pradesh, 137, 184 fn
Ansari, Hayatullah, (*Vol. 15, p. 581*), 294, 305 & fn
Anuvrat movement, 179 fn

265 fn, 262; Bankipore session (1912), 92 fn; Central Election Committee of, 52-53, 90, 92, 310-316, 319; Constitution of, 291 & fn; Indore session, (2-6 January, 1957), 5, 27, 59 fn, 260 fn; Lahore session (1930), 257 fn; Parliamentary Party, 209 fn, 260 fn; Subjects Committee of, 3, 31 fn; pledge, 274; Working Committee, 256 fn, 274, 305

Congress Election Manifesto, 31 fn, 95, 279, 282, 289, 291 fn, 300, 537 fn, 674

Constitution (India), 37, 60, 61, 63, 66, 68, 75, 87, 116, 236, 257, 261-264, 266, 336, 345-346, 423, 426, 460, 493, 671 fn, 695, 696; Preamble of, 285; Sixth Schedule of, 263 & fn

Constituent Assembly (India), 232 fn, 343 & fn, 390 fn, 423, 695, 696

Convention of Constantinople (1888), 496, 585 & fn

Cooper, John Sherman, (VOL. 28, P. 283), 357 & fn

Council of Scientific and Industrial Research, 218 & fn

Cousins, Norman, (VOL. 15, Pt. II, P. 36), 402 & fn, 468 & fn

Craig, May, 496

Cripps, Isabel, 578 fn
———, Judith, 578 & fn
———, Stafford, (Vol. 7, p. 471), 578 & fn

Cromwell, Oliver, 23 & fn

Cuttack, (Orissa), 12, 164, 390, 392

Cyprus, 374, 385, 478, 479 fn, 704

Czechoslovakia, 295, 430, 436 fn, 590, 633

Daily Mail, 381
Daily Telegraph, 381, 392
Dalai Lama, 185 & fn, 186, 227, 308,

595, 596 & fn, 597 & fn, 598-603, 609, 611-613, 615-616, 618-619, 623, 624 & fn, 677, 683, 688

Damodar (river), 699

Damodar Valley, 15, 33, 262

Dar, Avtar Krishna, 402 & fn, 710 & fn
———, Rita, 402 & fn, 710 & fn

Darhal, 346

Darjeeling, 624

Dasappa, H.C., 426 & fn

Davis, Spencer, 505

Debating Society (Trinity College, Cambridge University), 483

Delhi, 3, 5 fn, 10, 12, 14, 65, 78, 80, 83 fn, 110 fn, 142, 168, 175 fn, 178, 184 & fn, 185, 202, 219, 229, 238-240, 243, 246, 248, 280, 295, 308 fn, 311, 315, 330, 335 & fn, 354, 360, 362, 368, 375, 386, 390, 409 fn, 410, 439, 418, 468, 487, 490, 498, 518, 537, 581 fn, 586, 618-619, 624-625, 627-628, 638, 641 & fn, 664 & fn, 666, 674, 704-705; Municipality, 231 fn; Pradesh Congress Committee, 324 fn

Democratic Research Service, 255 & fn, 318

Dening, Maberly Esler, 628 & fn

De Rivera, Miguel Primo, 405 & fn

Desai, C.C., (VOL. 7, P.628), 83, 349, 641 & fn
———, Khandubhai, 323 fn
———, M.J., (VOL. 4, P. 155), 281 & fn, 335 fn, 641, 653 fn

Devi Lal, (VOL. 25, P. 205), 307 & fn

Dey, S.K., (Vol. 6, p. 96), 223 & fn

Dhaka, 83 fn, 380 fn, 642 fn

Dhar, D.P., (VOL.14, Pt. II, P. 153), 329 & fn

Dhebar, U.N., (VOL. 17, P. 406), 53 & fn, 91, 255 & fn, 274, 306-307, 311, 315 & fn, 316, 319, 538

fn, 600 & fn, 642 & fn, 678 & fn, 679

St Louis Post Dispatch, 495

Subbarayan, P., (*Vol.8, p. 359*), 344 fn

Sudan, 525 & fn, 570

Suez Canal, 30, 108, 165, 335 fn, 349 fn, 364 fn, 385, 391 fn, 430, 445 & fn, 453, 457 fn, 475, 480-481, 495-496, 530, 534, 541, 545 fn, 548 & fn, 550 fn, 551, 552, 553, & fn, 583, 585, & fn, 586, 587, 663, 689, 711

Sukhadia, Mohan Lal, 327 fn

Sundarlal, (*Vol. 4, p. 368*), 301 & fn

Sweden, 155, & fn, 365, 371,

Sydney Morning Herald, 501

Symons, Alexander, (VOL. 3, P. 314), 641 & fn

Syria, 429 & fn, 430, 551, 570 fn, 584, 664 & fn, 666, 667; Government of, 551

Tagore, Rabindranath, (*Vol. 11, p. 672*), 10, 189 & fn, 190 & fn, 191-192

Thacker, M.S., (VOL. 29, P. 141), 218 & fn

Taiwan, 481 fn, 500, 597-598, 605, 608; Government of, 218 & fn, 498

Tamil Nadu, 58

Tandon, P.D., (*Vol. 8, p. 231*), 89 & fn, 90, 704

Tan Yuan Shan, 186 & *fn*, 623

Tata, J.R.D., (*Vol. 11, p. 373*), 225 & fn

Tata Nagar, 32

Taxila (Pakistan), 205, 633

Thailand, 506, 570, & fn, 602,

Thimayya, K.S., (VOL, 4, P. 13), 236 & fn, 243, 246, 249

Thirty-eighth Parallel, 604

Thondhup, Gyalo, 597 & fn

Tibet, 235 & fn, 594, 595 & fn, 596-602, 605, 611, 614-615, 618, 620, 624, 625

Tilak, B.G. (*Vol. 1, p. 4*), 144, 256, 260

Time, 496

Times of India, The, 64 fn, 672

Tipu Sultan, 195 & fn, 196

Tito, Josip Broz, (VOL. 22, P. 414), 444, 555 & fn, 556 fn, 557 fn, 590, 690

Togoland, 651, 655

Tribune, 706

Tribhuvan, King, 627 & fn, 628 & fn

Trombay, 197 fn

Tuensang Frontier Division (Nagaland), 247, 248

Tungabhadra (river), 33, 262, 699

Tunisia, 373 fn, 374, 405 fn, 525 & fn, 570 & fn, 656; Government of, 373

Turkey, 56, & fn, 355, 430, 431, 465

Ujjain, 3

Union Public Service Commission, 210

United Kingdom, 29, 103, 108, 124, 139, 153, 155 & fn, 218 fn, 281, 287, 296, 339, 349 & fn, 352, 355 fn, 363, 365 & fn, 366, 368 fn, 370 & fn, 371 & fn, 373, 380 & fn, 381-383, 385, 388, & fn, 389 fn, 392, 393 & fn, 395 fn, 397-398, 402, 404-405, 409 fn, 411 fn, 412, 428-429, 438, 444, 447 fn, 449, 459-460, 468, 479 fn, 482, 489, 493, 502, 507, 532, 534, 537 fn, 542, 544 & fn, 545 fn, 546-547, 549 & fn, 550, 555, 577 fn, 583-584, 585 & fn, 586, 600, 621, 626, 628, 633, 634 & fn, 635, 641 fn, 668, 673, 676, 684-685, 688, 704, 706, 709, 712, 713; Government of, 30 fn, 82, 281, 362, 366, 367 & fn, 370-371, 382, 387 fn, 395 & fn, 397, 404, 418, 445, 478, 482, 668 fn, 676 fn, 706

United Nations Commission for India and Pakistan, 69-70, 88 & fn, 342, 349 fn, 351 fn, 356 fn, 364 fn, 368,

SUBJECT INDEX

Jawaharlal Nehru,
_____, addresses,
a public meeting in Indore, 3-11, in Kolkata, 25-43, in Chennai, 51-71, an election meeting: in Delhi, 72-89, in Allahabad, 89-105, in Lucknow, 106-120, in Jaipur, 123-137, in Karchana, 138-143, in Nagpur, 143-159, the Congress session in Indore, 282-289, 294-301, an informal meeting of delegates to the Congress session, Indore, 291-293, a banquet in honour of the Prime Minister of Nepal, New Delhi, 646-647, a civic reception in honour of the President of Syria, New Delhi, 664-666;
(in the USA) members of the Indian community, Washington, 472-477, a luncheon hosted by Richard M. Nixon, Washington, 483-485, a banquet hosted by John Foster Dulles, Washington, 486-490, addresses the people of the USA on television and radio, Washington, 490-493, a Press Conference, Washington, 494-505, the delegates of the UN General Assembly, New York, 506-514, a luncheon hosted by the Mayor of New York, 515-521, the Asian-African group at the UN, New York, 522-525, a conference of the Board of Directors of the Far East Council of Commerce and Industry, New York, 525-529, the Commonwealth group at the UN, New York, 529-530;
drafts, preamble to the Congress Election Manifesto, 256-260, the Congress Election Manifesto, 260-273, a

resolution on International Affairs, Congress session, Indore, 277-279, a resolution on the Conduct of the Election Campaign, Congress session, Indore, 279;
gives interview to Edgar McInnes, Ottawa, 530-532;
gives statements in the Rajya Sabha: on the international situation, 421-439, 440-456, on the relevance of Commonwealth membership, 456-466, on events in Hungary, 571-576;
gives a statement in the Lok Sabha on the death of B.R. Ambedkar, 695-696;
issues, a statement to the Press, 319-320, an appeal to the Press in support of Krishna Menon's candidature, 321-322, an appeal to the electorate of eastern Uttar Pradesh, 326, statements on Kashmir to the Press Trust of India, 397-398, 403-404, joint statement after talks with the President of Syria, 666-668;
sends messages to, the thirty-ninth session of the Indian Economic Conference and the seventeenth session of the All India Agricultural Economics Conference, 164, *Yojana*, a journal of the Planning Commission, 171, a souvenir of the Congress session, Indore, 290;
speaks at, the inauguration of the Hirakud dam, Cuttack, 11-20, Indian Science Congress, Kolkota, 20-25, the University of Madras, Chennai, 44-51, a gathering of students at Cuttack, 120-123, the inauguration of the Anuvrat week, New Delhi, 179-182, Visva-Bharati, Santiniketan, 189-192,

nation theory by people of, 70, relations between rest of India and, 387, stationing of UN forces in, 88, 362, 365, 388-389, 392, 404, 640

Kashmir issue, attitude of the people of Kashmir on, 42-43, 105, attitude of Security Council on, 67-71, 87-88, 105, 395, 397-398, 403-406, Colombian attitude on, 403-404, India's initial stand in UN on, 390, India's present stand in UN on, 64, 69, 110, 349, 354, 356, 364-365, 378, 382, 386, 403, 406, legalistic approach to, 337, 356, 360, 369, 378, Pakistan's approaches to USSR on, 361, 374-375, policy on 64-71, 83-88, 281, 335, 361, 378, 399-401, public opinion in India on, 366, 379, 706, S.M. Abdullah's so-called letter to Security Council on, 343-344, 348, Soviet attitude on, 350, 352-353, 357, 362, 375, 394, 403, Swedish attitude on, 363, 371-372, Tunisian attitude on, 373, UK attitude on, 349, 355, 363-366, 368-371, 381-383, 385-386, 393, 395, 402, 404, US attitude on, 347, 349, 380, 402

Kerala, proposal for an electoral arrangement with the Muslim League in, 310

labour, dignity of, 135, 266

Ladakh, education of Lama boys in, 235

Laos, technical help to, 660, US policy towards, 481, 435, 539, 593, 659

life, attitude of Indian people to, 484, balance in, 192, 198, moral and ethical approach to, 48, 265, pagan view of, 22, philosophical understanding of, 488

machine-building industry, 33, 263, 529, Soviet offer on, 176

Mahatma Gandhi, assassination of, 7,

G.K. Gokhale's comments on, 146, mission of, 124-127, the prophet of peace and non-violence, 50, 129, doctrine of the sword, 180, 510, training under, 50, 76, 127, 139, 144-146, 507-508, the wisdom and practical sense of, 685

Mandu, attractions of, 3, 182

Marxism, irrelevance of, 33-34, 59-60, 99, 502, 712

mathematics, an Indian prodigy in, 47, the importance of, 198

military alliances, system of, 70, 82, 298, 430, 462-463, 510, 513, 531, 575, 584

military bases, the setting up by foreign powers of, 464, 511, 513, in Maldives, 411

minorities, representation in elected bodies, 26, 91, 304, 316-317, safeguards for, 76, 91, concept of majority and minority, 100,

modern age, adaptability to, 3, 24, 74, 77, 100-101, 119, 290, 489, 523, form of worship in, 16, 48

Muslims, effect of Kashmir's accession on, 387, loss of touch with the mind of, 304, frustration among, 303-304

Nagas, policy towards, 236-237, 240-242, 244, 246-249, influence of women among, 240, education of, 240

National Anthem, singing of, 222

NEFA, Financial Adviser for, 238-239, entanglement of outsiders with women in, 238, slowing the pace of development in, 238, 248, tribals of, 240, 251-252, Verrier Elwin's book on, 251

Nepal, aid to, 648, 650, foreign policy of, 645, internal situation in, 648, recent history of, 626-629, relations with, 646, relations between China and, 625, 645, 649, relations between USSR and, 645